The Science of
The Art of Psychotherapy

The Norton Series on Interpersonal Neurobiology
Allan N. Schore, PhD, Series Editor
Daniel J. Siegel, MD, Founding Editor

The field of mental health is in a tremendously exciting period of growth and conceptual reorganization. Independent findings from a variety of scientific endeavors are converging in an interdisciplinary view of the mind and mental well-being. An interpersonal neurobiology of human development enables us to understand that the structure and function of the mind and brain are shaped by experiences, especially those involving emotional relationships.

The Norton Series on Interpersonal Neurobiology will provide cutting-edge, multidisciplinary views that further our understanding of the complex neurobiology of the human mind. By drawing on a wide range of traditionally independent fields of research—such as neurobiology, genetics, memory, attachment, complex systems, anthropology, and evolutionary psychology—these texts will offer mental health professionals a review and synthesis of scientific findings often inaccessible to clinicians. These books aim to advance our understanding of human experience by finding the unity of knowledge, or consilience, that emerges with the translation of findings from numerous domains of study into a common language and conceptual framework. The series will integrate the best of modern science with the healing art of psychotherapy.

A NORTON PROFESSIONAL BOOK

The Science of
The Art of Psychotherapy

ALLAN N. SCHORE

W. W. Norton & Company
New York • London

Library of Congress Cataloging-in-Publication Data

Schore, Allan N., 1943–
  The science of the art of psychotherapy / Allan N. Schore. — 1st ed.
    p. cm. — (Norton series on interpersonal neurobiology)
"A Norton professional book."
  Includes bibliographical references and index.
  ISBN 978-0-393-70664-2 (hardcover)
  1. Psychotherapy. I. Title.
  RC480.S255 2012
  616.89'14—dc23
                                                    2011050254

ISBN: 978-0-393-70664-2

W. W. Norton & Company, Inc., 500 Fifth Avenue, New York, N.Y. 10110
                              www.wwnorton.com
W. W. Norton & Company Ltd., Castle House, 75/76 Wells Street, London W1T 3QT

3 4 5 6 7 8 9 0

To Judy

I love you in a place
Where there's no space and time
I love you for my life
You are a friend of mine

May your hands always be busy
    May your feet always be swift
May you have a strong foundation
    When the winds of changes shift
May your heart always be joyful
    And may your song always be sung
May you stay forever young
    Forever young, forever young
May you stay forever young

—Bob Dylan, "Forever Young"

Contents

Acknowledgments

Over the last decade I have been heartened and deeply gratified by the reception of my work from so many sources. This substantial feedback about the impact of my ideas has taken various forms: large numbers of citations by other authors in a wide variety of clinical and scientific literatures, numerous stimulating dialogues with audiences around the world, direct expressions of interest and appreciation from my professional colleagues, and, via electronic communication, frequent contact from individuals in various walks of life whom I have not met, yet who felt compelled to express the personal meaning my work has had for them.

I would like to thank a number of people who have been fundamentally essential to this wide-reaching response to my writings. I am indebted to the translators of *Affect Regulation and the Repair of the Self* into Italian, French, and German: Roberto Speziale-Bagliacca, Giles de Lisle, and Eva Rass; and to Andre Sassenfeld's Spanish translation of my articles. It has been my pleasure to work with the following editors who have invited me to share my ideas in a number of clinical volumes and journals: Darcia Narvaez, Ruth Lanius, Barry Lester, Joshua Sparrow, Tessa Baradon, Diana Fosha, Paul Dell, John O'Neil, Jean Petrucelli, Jennifer McIntosh, Larry Nazarian, Carol Tossone, Susanne Bennett, Judy Nelson, Nancy VanDerHeide, William J. Coburn, Charles Carlini, Joe Palombo, Rick Leonhardt, Dan Siegel, and George Halasz. Over the last decade I have also been enriched by my research collaborators: Russell Meares, Dmitriy Melkonian, Ruth Lanius, and Gay Bradshaw.

I want to express my appreciation to a group of conference organizers who have sponsored a number of important national and international appearances: Marion Solomon, Jane Ryan, Joe Tucci, Bob Cassidy, and Dan Hill. Over the years I continue to benefit from my interactions with the clinicians in my Study Groups in Developmental Affective Neuroscience & Clinical Practice in Los Angeles, Berkeley, Portland, Seattle, Boulder, and Austin; and I extend thanks to the group leaders: Linda Chapman, Margaret Rossoff, David Willis, Sal Ziz, Sue Marriott, and Pat Ogden.

As editor of the Norton Series on Interpersonal Neurobiology, it has been a pleasure interacting with all the series authors, as well as with my colleague at

Norton, Deborah Malmud, who has been critical to its remarkable success. Thanks also to Vani Kannan, Ben Yarling, and especially Jean Blackburn for the work they have done in putting this book together.

On a more personal basis, I would like to thank Wolfgang Amadeus Mozart and Joseph Hayden for providing, on so many occasions, the background context that supports my creative musings. And I offer my gratitude to my children— David, for the numerous times I relied on his professional computer skills, and Beth, for her talents in computer graphics and the design for the cover of this book.

But most of all, to Judy. Wing to wing, oar to oar.

The Science of
The Art of Psychotherapy

Toward a New Paradigm
of Psychotherapy

In 1994, before the beginning of what was called "the decade of the brain," I wrote my first book, *Affect Regulation and the Origin of the Self: The Neurobiology of Emotional Development*. In that work, which was published at the end of the last century, I offered a description of the interpersonal neurobiological mechanisms by which the attachment relationship facilitates the development of the major self-regulatory structures in the infant's early maturing right brain. I also applied the developmental theory to generate models of the early etiology of a number of personality and psychiatric disorders that manifest fundamental deficits in affect regulation. Then, in expanding the regulation concept, I described the nonverbal affective mechanisms that lie at the heart of the psychotherapy process. In the course of the book I attempted to create an overarching interdisciplinary perspective that could more deeply explain some fundamental problems addressed by 20th-century developmental science, neurobiology, psychiatry, and psychoanalysis. At the time, the grounding of an entire volume in a transdisciplinary approach, as well as the proposal of an integrative overarching theory, was a radical prospect.

The book set out the major tenets of regulation theory, and everything I have written since then has elaborated on this interpersonal neurobiological model of the development, psychopathogenesis, and treatment of the implicit self. A fundamental principle of my work is that any developmental theory must integrate psychology and biology. For the last two decades, I have argued that no theory of human functioning can be restricted to only a description of psychological processes; it must also be consonant with what we now know about biological structural brain development. Three other themes that continue from literally the first paragraph of the first book are that the early stages of life are critical to the development of all later evolving structures and functions, that emotion is central to a deeper understanding of the human condition, and that unconscious processes lie at the core of the self, throughout the life span. The book thus also attempted to reintegrate psychoanalytic ideas of the unconscious mind into developmental science. *Affect Regulation and the Origin of the Self*—which is now in its 14th printing—was the first book to document not the cognitive development, but the social-emotional development of the infant.

The decade of the brain, which spanned from approximately 1995 to 2005, heralded the appearance of innovative neuroimaging technologies that allowed for studying the brain as it is processing external and internal information. The amount of neurobiological research on emotional and social processes increased exponentially over this period. In 2003 I followed up my 1994 book with two volumes that documented my ongoing work during that interval. In addition to presenting a large body of more recent studies, I continued to utilize the lens of regulation theory to demonstrate the clinical application of this new data. In *Affect Dysregulation and Disorders of the Self*, I expanded my interpersonal neurobiological models in chapters on affective neuroscience and developmental neuropsychiatry, and in *Affect Regulation and the Repair of the Self*, to developmentally oriented psychotherapy and developmental neuropsychoanalysis. These two volumes thus appeared at the end of the initial critical period that bridged 19th-century classical and 20th-century modern neuroscience's study of the brain, and classical and modern psychoanalysis' study of the mind. In the preface of the 2003 *Dysregulation* volume, I observed, "Over the course of what was known as 'the decade of the brain' neuroscience experienced *a remarkable growth spurt of new knowledge.*"

This book, *The Science of the Art of Psychotherapy*, offers a representative collection of essential expansions and elaborations of regulation theory since 2005. Following the format of the 2003 volumes, the chapters in Part I represent contributions to affect regulation therapy (ART) and clinical neuropsychoanalysis, and those in Part II to my ongoing work in developmental affective neuroscience and developmental neuropsychiatry. As in the last two books each chapter represents a further development of the theory at a particular point in time, and thus the collection in each section is presented in chronological order. Some of the earlier chapters have been reedited; the more recent ones contain a good deal of new material that has not been previously published.

Here, as in all my work of the last 20 years, I continue to use the term *regulation theory* in order to denote explicitly that what I am offering is a theory, a systematic exposition of the general principles of a science. Specifically, it is a formulation of an explanatory conception of the processes of development, which I have asserted is one of the fundamental objectives of science. As a basic theory it can be used for clinical purposes, and in a number of chapters I describe how neurobiologically informed "modern attachment theory" (Schore & Schore, 2008) has transformed classical attachment theory into a regulation theory, one that can serve as the scientific basis for ART. In addition regulation theory can be used as a fertile source of testable hypotheses for experimental research.

The reader will note that in a number of upcoming chapters written over this most recent period I refer to a *paradigm shift*. During this time what began as initial forays of the decade of the brain transformed into a torrent of 21st-century science's more complex (re-)explorations of the fundamental problems of brain/mind/body that are relevant to both researchers and clinicians. The *"remarkable growth spurt of new knowledge"* in neuroscience and development has generated a palpable change in paradigm not only in the life sciences but also in all the experimental and applied sciences and even the arts. Every chapter of this book describes, in some detail, how the paradigm shift is altering the entire field of mental health, including the practice of psychotherapy. In this Introduction I discuss how this book, like its three predecessors, actively contributes to the paradigm shift. And looking forward, I would like to offer some thoughts about how this transformation will impact the future directions of the mental health field.

In 2009 the American Psychological Association (APA) invited me to present a plenary address, "The Paradigm Shift: The Right Brain and the Relational Unconscious." In fact, that was the first time an APA plenary address was given by a member in private practice, and by a clinician who was also psychoanalytically informed. Essentially, what the APA wanted was something on the increasingly important role of affect in clinical and developmental psychology and neuroscience. In fact it suggested that I use the softer term *emotion revolution* instead of *paradigm shift*, but I declined the offer. And so I presented to the Convention interdisciplinary data indicating that both theory and research were changing focus from left brain conscious cognition to right brain unconscious affect. Furthermore, I argued that the paradigm shift was occurring not only within psychology but also across disciplines, and that psychology now needed to enter into a more intense dialogue with its neighboring biological sciences. In the address, I emphasized the relevance of developmental and affective neuroscience (more so than cognitive neuroscience) for clinical and abnormal psychology. I also suggested that the ongoing paradigm shift was not only integrating psychology and biology but also closing the gap between researchers and clinicians, which has always been a problem in psychology. As opposed to the previous decade, by this time the terms *interdisciplinarity* and *integration* had become accepted watchwords.

Recall that, in *The Structure of Scientific Revolutions*, Thomas Kuhn (1962) asserted that paradigms consist of sets of propositions or hypotheses that order an investigator's observations. When a paradigm is overthrown, a new one replaces it. As I look back over the last four decades, psychology (and also psychiatry) in the 1960s and 1970s were essentially utilizing a behavioral paradigm, and therefore it was a period of dominance of behavioral psychology. The brain, the body, and the unconscious were placed in an opaque "black box" that was not to be opened. In psychoanalysis, drives and motivational states were downgraded and relegated to the realm of metapsychology. And so were emotions, which Skinner said were beyond the pale of scientific investigation. Models of psychotherapeutic change revolved around changing the patient's maladaptive anxious *behaviors*.

In the 1970s and 1980s we moved into a period when science was observing not only external behavior but also internal cognitive processes (e.g., memory, attention, perception, representational schemas, consciousness, and language). And so we entered into a period of dominance of a cognitive paradigm and a directly related cognitive psychology, which also impacted models of psychopathology and psychotherapy. The fundamental principle in this paradigm was to change the patient's maladaptive conscious *cognitions*, and this was expressed in the creation of cognitive-behavioral therapy (CBT) models. We are now experiencing a period in which rapidly forming bodily based *emotions* and psychobiological states are dominant in both research and clinical models.

Reflecting this change in paradigm, in an article in the prestigious journal *Nature* (2009), Buchanan proclaimed,

> Behavioral science . . . ought to seek the simplest explanation for human behaviour first, looking to simple social signals, before constructing more complicated explanations based on language and conscious reasoning . . . language function presumably exists on top of a more archaic brain system for non-linguistic social signals. (p. 529)

At the same time my colleague in affective neuroscience, Jaak Panksepp, asserted, "The cognitive revolution, like radical neuro-behaviorism, intentionally sought to put emotions out of sight and out of mind. Now cognitive science must re-learn that ancient emotional systems have a power that is quite independent of neocortical cognitive processes" (2008, p. 51). Because the brain's emotional processing is extremely rapid and occurs beneath levels of conscious awareness, the focus of both clinical and research observations has shifted from explicit to implicit phenomena. In my own work I have offered a theoretical system that can model not only overt behaviors and conscious cognitions but also covert, unconscious affective states of brain/mind/body. The current paradigm shift has also served as an antidote to previous Cartesian divisions that have plagued psychiatry and psychology.

Furthermore, this *paradigm shift from behavior, to cognition, to bodily based emotion* has acted as an integrating force for forging stronger connections between the disciplines of psychology, social neuroscience, and psychiatry, all of which are now focusing on affective phenomena. Within behavioral biology it has generated a foundation for the emergence of a trans-species psychology (Bradshaw & Sapolsky, 2006; Northoff & Panksepp, 2008) that is centered in animal emotion (de Waal, 2011). Kuhn (1962) stated that a paradigm shift is by definition simultaneously expressed across scientific disciplines. Because of my experience as a reviewer of articles and being on the editorial staff of 35 journals across a number of scientific and clinical disciplines, I can offer some observations about this matter. Developmental psychological models, previously narrowly focused on cognitive development, are now actively exploring emotional and social development. Neuroscience is transitioning from studies of left brain language-based cognitive processes and voluntary motor functions to studies of the embodied functions of the right-lateralized emotion-processing limbic system and stress-regulating HPA axis. In addition to the shift from the left to the right brain, researchers are also moving down the neuraxis from cortical to subcortical systems and from the central nervous system (CNS) to the autonomic nervous system (ANS). This information is being rapidly incorporated into psychiatry. We are now seeing a surge of neuropsychiatric investigations on the dysregulation of the limbic and autonomic nervous systems in a wide array of psychiatric Axis I and Axis II disorders. Still to be resolved is the essential matter of whether the paradigm shift will influence and be incorporated into the upcoming fifth iteration of the American Psychiatric Association's *Diagnostic and Statistical Manual of Mental Disorders.*

Now it is true that the current surge of research is being fueled by advances in a variety of cutting-edge neuroimaging technologies that can observe and document ongoing brain structure–function relationships. The reader should note there is a major limitation to current *in vivo* imaging techniques—their limited temporal resolution does not allow them to capture the real-time dynamics of brain function. But even future advances in technology would not be enough. We also need an integrative psychoneurobiological theoretical model that can not only generate testable hypotheses but also conceptualize the vast amount of research and clinical data in a meaningful way. And we need an interpersonal neurobiological perspective that can account for brain-to-brain interactions. As editor of the Norton Series on Interpersonal Neurobiology, I see this quantitative leap and qualitative shift in emotion research as a powerful source of updated models of psychotherapeutic interventions that are grounded in developmental, affective, and social neuroscience. It is now clear that psychotherapeutic changes in conscious cognitions alone, without changes in emotion processing, are limited.

In fact, a clash of psychotherapy paradigms can currently be seen, especially in the treatment of more severe disorders that present with a history of relational trauma and thereby a deficit in affect regulation. In such cases emotion more than cognition is the focus of the change process, and so CBT is now being challenged by updated affectively focused psychodynamic models, including ART. In his most recent book my colleague Philip Bromberg (2011) also describes the paradigm shift in psychotherapy:

> Interpersonal and Relational writers largely have endorsed the idea that we are in fact confronted with a paradigm change and have conceptualized it as a transformation from a one-person to a two-person psychology. I feel that this formulation is accurate, and that three central clinical shifts are intrinsic to the conceptual shift: A shift from the primacy of content to the primacy of context, a shift from the pri-

macy of cognition to the primacy of affect, and a shift away from (but not yet an abandonment of) the concept of "technique." (p. 126)

In writings on the change mechanism from within the cognitive literature, Kazdin (2007) concludes, "Perhaps we can state more confidently now than before that whatever may be the basis of changes with cognitive therapy, it does not seem to be the cognitions as originally proposed" (p. 8). In his most recent overview of the current status of cognitive therapy, Beck, one of the founders of the field, describes the crucial importance of *context* and asserts, "The therapeutic relationship is a key ingredient of all psychotherapies, including cognitive therapy. . . . Many of the basic interpersonal variables common to other psychotherapies (e.g., warmth, accurate empathy, unconditional positive regard) serve as an important foundation for cognitive and symptomatic change" (Beck & Dozois, 2011, p. 401). The reader will note that a major tenet of the upcoming chapters prescribes that more so than the cognitive mechanisms of interpretation and insight, relational-affective processes between patient and therapist are at the core of the change mechanism. Indeed, a large body of basic research in clinical psychology on the therapeutic alliance is supporting a shift from a purely intrapsychic one-person psychology to a relational two-person psychology (e.g., Safran & Muran, 2000).

The current paradigm shift is also being driven by an upsurge in brain laterality research. The asymmetry of the brain was described at the onset of modern neurology in the 19th century. Even those outside of neuroscience are well aware that Broca and Wernicke located certain (but, importantly, not all) language functions in the left cerebral hemisphere. Less well known is the seminal work of Hughlings Jackson on the emotion-processing functions of the right hemisphere. Current technological advances have allowed for groundbreaking studies of the unique operations of each hemisphere, as a functional unit. Wide agreement now exists that brain asymmetry is an evolutionarily ancient mechanism of neural organization that occurs not only in humans but also in all mammalian and nonmammalian brains (Vallortigara & Rogers, 2005). In our species the specialization of the hemispheres is fundamentally involved in major psychological functions, including not only language, action, perception, and memory, but also emotion and stress regulation; and it is now thought of as a marker for the dysfunctions expressed in every form of psychopathology. In parallel to the ongoing "emotional revolution," modern neuroimaging techniques and the emergent fields of affective and social neuroscience are revitalizing science's interest in the essential and unique functions of the right brain.

In my 1994 book on affect regulation and emotional development, I deduced that the early maturing right brain hemisphere had to be centrally involved in the formation of attachment over the first 2 years. After all, many of the critical events in human infancy occur before the onset of left brain language centers. And so I integrated existing data (this was before the decade of the brain) to argue that infantile attachment experiences epigenetically induce the experience-dependent lateralization of specifically the early developing right brain. Furthermore, I offered extant data to argue that "the control system of attachment" described by John Bowlby, the creator of attachment theory, is centered in the orbitofrontal (ventromedial) cortex of the right brain. In 2001 I expanded the model to link up attachment pathology (early abuse and neglect) with alterations of the developmental trajectory of specifically the right brain. In the following chapters I cite a large body of ongoing research that confirms these hypotheses. A number of laboratories have documented the critical role of the orbitofrontal cortex in human attachment neurobiology (e.g., Barrett & Fleming, 2011; Minagawa-Kawai et al., 2009; Nitschke et al., 2004; Noriuchi, Kikuchi, & Senoo, 2008; Parsons, Young, Murray, Stein, & Kringelbach, 2010; Swain, Lorberbaum, Kose, & Strathearn, 2007). Indeed the development of the essential functions of the right brain over the life span is a central theme that runs throughout my work on development, psychopathogenesis, and psychotherapy.

In my APA plenary address I argued that the paradigm shift from cognition to emotion is paralleled by a shift from the left hemisphere to the right hemisphere. We can no longer think of "the brain" as two halves of a single entity. Rather, these two systems process different types of information in very different ways. Numerous studies now indicate that the right and left human brain hemispheres differ in macrostructure, ultrastructure, physiology, chemistry, and control of behavior. Indeed, the left hemisphere of the vertebrate brain is specialized for the control of well-established patterns of behavior under ordinary and familiar circumstances. In contrast, the right hemisphere is the primary seat of emotional arousal and the processing of novel information. Furthermore, there is now agreement that verbal, conscious, rational, and serial information processing takes place in the left hemisphere, whereas nonverbal, unconscious, holistic, and subjective emotional information processing takes place in the right. This book, like all my work, continues to incorporate ongoing studies of the right brain into my developmental and clinical models.

In 2003 I put forth the argument that the implicit, nonconscious survival functions of the right, and not the language functions of the left, are dominant in development and in psychotherapy. More recently I have described how the highest human functions—stress regulation, intersubjectivity, humor, empathy, compassion, morality, and creativity—are all right brain functions. I am also suggesting that an expanded capacity for right and not left brain processing lies at the core of clinical expertise. Much of the therapist's knowledge that accumulates with clinical experience is implicit, operates at rapid, unconscious levels beneath levels of awareness, and is spontaneously expressed as clinical intuition. On the other side of the right brain–to–right brain communications within the therapeutic alliance, I see the change mechanism of long-term psychotherapy as being located primarily in the connections between the patient's prefrontal, cortical, and subcortical areas of the right brain. With respect to the paradigm shift toward relationally oriented psychotherapy, clinical interpersonal neurobiological models of therapeutic change are now moving from left brain to right brain, from the mind to the body, and from the central to the autonomic nervous system.

This shift in paradigm into relational models of psychotherapy is being paralleled in social neuroscience studies of the essential role of the right brain in social interaction (e.g., Decety & Lamm, 2007; Semrud-Clikeman, Fine, & Zhu, 2011). Indeed, there is now a call to "move from a classical one-brain neuroscience toward a novel two-body approach" (Dumas, 2011, p. 349). A very recent dual-EEG study of spontaneous, reciprocal communication and social interaction documents an interbrain synchronization of the right temporoparietal regions in both interacting partners (Dumas, Nadel, Soussignan, Martinerie, & Garnero, 2010). A large body of research in affective neuroscience documents that this same right lateralized cortical system is dominant in social awareness related to the self (Keenan & Gorman, 2007; Schore, 2003a).

In a remarkable book published in 2009, *The Master and His Emissary*, psychiatrist Iain McGilchrist presents a comprehensive overview of brain laterality research and concludes that the difference between the two brain hemispheres is profound. The right and left hemispheres create coherent, utterly different, and often incompatible versions of the world with competing priorities and values. The left is detail oriented, prefers mechanisms to living things, and is inclined to self-interest, whereas the right has greater breadth, flexibility, and generosity. He states,

> I believe that the representation of the two hemispheres is not equal, and that while both contribute to our knowledge of the world, which therefore needs to be synthesized, one hemisphere, the right hemisphere, has precedence, in that it understands the knowledge that the other comes to have, and is alone able to synthesize what both know into a useable whole. (2009, p. 176)

McGilchrist's description of the "the primacy of the right hemisphere"—reflected in its unique contributions to the "primacy of affect," "the primacy of the unconscious will," and in the large body of evidence that indicates that "both thought and its expression originate in the right hemisphere"—mirrors my assertions of the paradigm shift from conscious cognition to unconscious affect, and that the right brain—the "emotional brain," the "social brain"—is dominant in psychotherapy. Indeed I have suggested that the emotional right hemisphere and not the linguistic left is dominant in the human experience, and that the most fundamental problems of human existence cannot be understood without addressing this primal realm. Over the last two decades a central theme of the body of my studies in developmental psychoanalysis and developmental affective neuroscience has been that the right hemisphere is not only dominant in infancy but over all stages of the life cycle.

Regarding early human development, it is now abundantly clear that the recent enormous expansion of knowledge in developmental neuroscience has been extraordinary. In a very recent editorial of an entire issue of the *Journal of Child Psychology and Psychiatry* entitled "Developmental Neuroscience Comes of Age," Leckman and March (2011) describe "the phenomenal progress of the past three decades of research." Alluding to the paradigm shift, they conclude,

> Over the past decade it has also become abundantly clear that in addition to the remarkable cascade of genetic, molecular and cellular events that ultimately lead to the formation of the billions of neurons that inhabit the human neocortex, the in utero and immediate postnatal environments and the dyadic relations between child and caregivers within the first years of life can have direct and enduring effects on the child's brain development and behavior. . . . [T]he *enduring impact of early maternal care and the role of epigenetic modifications of the genome during critical periods in early brain development in health and disease is likely to be one of the most important discoveries in all of science that have major implications for our field.* (p. 334)

Confirming the developmental hypotheses of my earlier books, there is now widespread agreement that during critical periods of infancy when the developing brain has heightened sensitivity to social environmental experiences, epigenetic programming by variations in maternal care imparts either a risk for or resilience to later psychopathology (Stevenson, Halliday, Marsden, & Mason, 2008). With respect to the latter, the principle that relational trauma in infancy alters the developmental trajectory of the brain in adolescence and adulthood is expressed in the principle, "The organized stepwise progression of neurodevelopment allows changes that interfere with a specific step earlier in life to modify functional output later in life" (Wei, David, Duman, Anisman, & Kaffman, 2010). Each year an estimated 3.7 million children are evaluated for childhood maltreatment (U.S. Department of Health and Human Services, 2009). A large body of research now reveals that severe alterations of the social environment, such as the maltreatment of abuse and neglect, imprint a brain developmental trajectory that is later susceptible to post-tramautic stress disorder, borderline personality disorder, schizophrenia, and major depression (Roth & Sweatt, 2011). It is important to note that this epigenetic mechanism is centrally involved in more than severe psychopathologies, even in creating individual differences in personality. Champagne asserts, *"even natural variations in the quality or quantity of maternal care can have a long-term impact on offspring brain and behavior"* (2011, p. 4, my italics).

We are now faced with the problem of how this rapidly expanding body of discoveries in development and neuroscience will be used in the mental health professions, not only in the delivery of service but also in the training of the next generation of psychotherapists. Older ideas about what is required for a basic knowledge base for all health care professions must now be updated and radically altered. In order to accomplish these goals, we must directly address that a major problem both clinicians and researchers are currently grappling with is not just the voluminous amount of new data but also the meaning of this data; that is, the way this interdisciplinary information is being conceptualized. Until recently there has been a bias against creating overarching "grand theories"; but I suggest we now have an urgent need for an overarching theoretical perspective that can integrate, synthesize, and make meaning out of the psychological-functional and biological-structural patterns embedded in the massive amount of data the mental health and life sciences are now generating.

Previously the Cartesian mind/body split has plagued not only psychology and psychiatry but also medicine in general, especially psychosomatic medicine, pediatrics, internal medicine, neurology, and dermatology. The current paradigm shift in research from cognition to emotion has been a major force in resolving the Cartesian problem and generating theoretical models that integrate biology and psychology, "nature and nurture." These models are being used to generate testable hypotheses about a number of clinical phenomena, including the mechanisms of psychotherapeutic change. In a recent article in *The Journal of the American Medical Association*, Glass (2008) concludes, "There is increasing evidence from studies of the 2-way relationship between brain structure and function on the one hand and emotion and behavior on the other indicating that such a notion of separate biological and psychological treatment effects is simplistic and inaccurate" (pp. 1588–1599).

The biopsychosocial perspective of regulation theory and its focus on adaptive and maladaptive bodily based emotional processes can serve as the basis for new integrative treatments of mind *and* body (Schore, 1994, 2003a). Toward that end in a presidential address to the American Psychosomatic Society, Richard Lane (2008) has stated, "The physiology of emotion is arguably the cornerstone of psychosomatic medicine . . . aversive emotional states are associated with adverse health outcomes" (p. 214). I see a deeper understanding of the interpersonal psychobiological origins and treatment of psychosomatic disorders as the next frontier. This work could also elucidate the adaptive and maladaptive developmental and characterological relational psychoneuroimmunological mechanisms by which different personalities cope with disease processes.

It is now becoming apparent that the idea that psychology (psychotherapy) changes the mind and that biology (pharmacology) changes the brain and the body is outmoded. In 2005 the Nobel Prize–winning psychiatrist Eric Kandel argued there is no longer any doubt that psychotherapy can result in detectable changes in the brain (Etkin, Pittenger, Polan, & Kandel, 2005). By 2008 Glass summarized the commonly accepted view: "Recent research in brain imaging, molecular biology, and neurogenetics has shown that psychotherapy changes brain function and structure. Such studies have shown that psychotherapy affects regional cerebral blood flow, neurotransmitter metabolism, gene expression, and persistent modifications in synaptic plasticity" (p. 1589). In a 2010 neuroimaging study published in *Psychotherapy Research*, Tschacher, Schildt, and Sander asserted, "psychotherapy research is no longer concerned with efficacy but rather with *how effective change occurs*" (p. 578, my italics).

These data challenge the current trend in psychiatry that focuses exclusively on psychopharmacology and devalues psychotherapy. This trend has been particularly alarming in child psychiatry. Psychiatry needs to reevaluate whether or not psychotherapy will be part of what it has to directly offer patients, rather than delegating it out to the other professions (Halasz, 2010). In addition, I suggest the paradigm shift from conscious cognition to unconscious affect and the ascendance of relational models of developmental and psychotherapeutic change also challenge "purely" psychological treatment models such as CBT, which is grounded in the assumption that "negative feelings are caused by 'irrational' thoughts and beliefs; therapy aims at changing beliefs" (Shedler, 2001, p. 56). Indeed in very recent research on patients with severe trauma, Foa reports, "explicitly addressing cognitions in therapy via cognitive restructuring is not necessary for ameliorating PTSD symptoms" (Moser, Cahill, & Foa, 2010, p. 74).

A large number of practicing clinicians now recognize that there are serious limitations of interventions that utilize mainly left brain conscious cognitive mechanisms to deal with the involuntary nonconscious affective and interpersonal deficits of the major psychiatric disorders. In upcoming chapters I will describe how paradigm-shifting forces are creating more complex developmental and clinical emotional models. This advance is allowing updated relational affectively focused psychotherapy such as ART to be used with populations heretofore seen as refractory to cognitive and behavioral psychotherapy. And so we are now seeing breakthroughs in the psychotherapeutic treatment of severe personality disorders, a group that was earlier thought to be refractory to "the talking cure."

The paradigm shift also includes a reevaluation of psychological assessment procedures with such patients before and during psychotherapy. In a creative contribution, Finn (2011), citing neuroimaging studies, contends that the Rorschach test and Adult Attachment Projective Picture System (AAP) are particularly sensitive to limbic functioning and right hemisphere disorganization and therefore to implicit deficits of early attachment trauma, whereas verbal self-report tests such as the Beck Depression Inventory and MMPI-2 tap more left hemisphere cortical functions and explicit models of self and other. I would add that the Adult Attachment Inventory (AAI) is also too heavily weighted to left hemispheric linguistic processes to be used to understand the deeper implicit mechanisms of the psychotherapy process.

Up until recently clinicians turned only to cognitive neuroscience to attempt to understand the deeper mechanisms of psychotherapeutic change. The limitations of this approach can be seen in the basically mechanistic conception that lies at the core of the discipline. In a very recent interview Michael Gazzaniga, "the father of the field," states, "In general, what we are trying to do in cognitive neuroscience is figure out how the human mind–brain *"machine"* works. Once this machine gets turned on, the question becomes, How does it work? just like one asks how any machine—biological or not—works" (2011, p. 4, my italics).

But psychotherapy involves changes not in the cognitions of the patient's human mind/brain machine but in the affective embodied experiences of his or her brain/mind/body. It thus is no surprise that currently all forms of psychological treatment are incorporating data from not so much cognitive but developmental, affective, and social neuroscience in order to expand more effective clinical models.

The advances in developmental neuroscience have implications for more than models of psychopathogenesis and treatment of adult disorders. Now that the traumatic attachment roots of psychopathology are being understood in terms of interpersonal neurobiology, I suggest that interventions, both preventive and therapeutic, need to take place in the critical earlier stages of life. Due to the significant breakthroughs in our understanding of attachment neurobiology, the gaps between theory, research, and clinical application are closing fast. Researchers studying the neurobiological and neuroendocrinological processes that underlie human mother–infant attachment now assert, "Understanding the motivational basis of healthy and at-risk parenting may open new theoretical vistas and clinical opportunities and may lead to the construction of more specific interventions that can target disruptions to maternal-infant bonding at an earlier stage and in a more accurate manner" (Atzil, Hendler, & Feldman, 2011, p. 11).

We need to focus psychotherapeutically, and not just psychopharmacologically, on the developmental precursors of Axis I and Axis II disorders in childhood, and not just on their adult manifestations. As opposed to the current overreliance on psychopharmacological interventions in children (Wong, Murray, Camilleri-Novak, & Stephens, 2004), recent interdisciplinary models integrating neuroscience and pediatrics are now focusing on reducing significant stress and adversity in the early periods of childhood (Shonkoff, Boyce, & McEwen, 2009). In a recent article in *Science*, "Protecting Brains, Not Simply Stimulating Minds," the pediatrician Jack Shonkoff boldly asserts,

> [A]ge 4 cannot be characterized as "early" with respect to brain development. For children in adverse environments, four years of inaction in the face of repeated threats to developing brain architecture are difficult to justify. . . . [a]dvances in neuroscience suggest that interventions that enhance the mental health, executive function skills, and self-regulation capacities of vulnerable mothers, beginning as early as pregnancy, suggest promising strategies to protect the developing brains of their children. (p. 983)

In order to deliver such services we must address the serious shortage of child psychotherapists and infant mental health workers.

Training programs in psychiatry, clinical psychology, psychoanalysis, clinical social work, and counseling must be updated from the educational models of the last century. These programs need to incorporate recent information not only about emotional development, the interpersonal neurobiology of attachment, the psychobiology of trauma, and the stress regulating effects of relational empathy but also about how these nonverbal bodily based affective dynamics are expressed in the therapeutic alliance between the clinician and infant, child, adolescent, and adult patients. This information about the primary role that regulated and dysregulated affects play out in relationships, especially unconscious affects, is also relevant to a more complex biopsychosocial understanding of not only psychopathogenesis but also the etiology of illness and disease. The communication and regulation of conscious and unconscious affects between the patient and the psychobiologically attuned empathic clinician are now being addressed not only in all mental health professions but also in medicine's interest in the nonverbal emotion communicating and regulating aspects of the patient–physician relationship (e.g., Adler, 2007).

Another central theme of the following chapters is that we are now seeing a resurgence of interest in subjective implicit, unconscious functions, and thereby in psychoanalysis, the science of unconscious processes. Modern psychoanalysis is being reenergized by advances in developmental psychoanalysis, which are describing the early intersubjective origins of the unconscious mind, and in neuropsychoanalysis, which are exploring how intersubjective communications impact internal psychic structure. For the past two decades I have provided clinical and research data indicating that the right brain is the biological substrate of the human unconscious. This conception is echoed in recent neuroscientific writings by Tucker and Moller (2007): "The right hemisphere's specialization for emotional communication through nonverbal channels seems to suggest a domain of the mind that is close to the motivationally charged psychoanalytic unconscious" (p. 91).

At the end of the 19th century Freud created the *Project for a Scientific Psychology* (1895/1966) "a psychology which shall be a natural science," and in so doing created the field of neuropsychoanalysis, the precursor of clinical psychoanalysis (Schore, 1997, 2010). By the beginning of the next century Freud had created the talking cure, a psychoanalytic technique centered in the clinical principle that the work of psychotherapy is always concerned with affect, thereby foreshadowing the current paradigm shift. By the end of the 20th century a number of authors returned to Freud's *Project* and, with the creation of modern neuropsychoanalysis, deepened our understanding of the right brain mechanisms that underlie nonverbal communication, transference, unconscious motivation, and the central role of affects. At present this attempt to use science, especially neuroscience, to understand more deeply the psychotherapeutic change process has expanded beyond the borders of psychoanalysis into all forms of the talking cure. Indeed, as a member of the editorial board of the *Journal of Unified Psychotherapy and Clinical Science*, I can attest to the fact that there is now a strong trend in psychology toward elucidating the basic mechanisms and common factors that underlie effective psychotherapy, and that psychodynamic concepts are being reincorporated into all clinical models. These models share the central construct that the therapeutic alliance conveys the major mechanisms of therapeutic action. In the hopefully near future, the reincorporation of updated relational neuropsychoanalytic models and advances in traumatology on the impact of attachment trauma on brain development could allow for the integration of the deep split between biological psychiatry and dynamic psychiatry.

In a recent meta-analysis of the growing body of research on the efficacy of psychodynamic psychotherapy, Shedler (2010) cites empirical evidence demonstrating that effect sizes of psychodynamic therapies are as large as those reported for other treatments that have been promoted as "evidence based." He offers data from a number of studies supporting the finding that the benefits of psychodynamic therapy are not just transitory, but endure and indeed increase with time. As opposed to cognitive therapies, "psychodynamic therapy sets in motion psychological processes that lead to ongoing change, even after therapy has ended" (p. 101). Shedler concludes that beyond symptom remission, "psychodynamic therapy may foster inner resources and capacities that allow richer, freer, and more fulfilling lives" (p. 107).

Other research on the effects of psychodynamic psychotherapy on patients with borderline personality disorder shows treatment benefits that equaled or exceeded those of another evidence-based treatment, dialectical behavior therapy (Clarkin, Levy, Lenzenweger, & Kernberg, 2007). Importantly, only borderline patients in psychodynamic treatment showed changes in underlying intrapsychic psychological mechanisms associated with symptom reduction, that is, changes in attachment organization and reflective function (Levy et al., 2006). Add to this another body of recent research that documents that long-term psychodynamic psychotherapy is effective in the treatment of patients with personality disorders, multiple mental disorders, and chronic mental disorders (Leichsenring & Rabung, 2008). In fact, my own developmental neuropsychoanalytic models are now being used both in research on Axis I borderline personality disorder (Meares, Schore, & Melkonian, 2011) and in the treatment of Axis II schizophrenic disorders (Hug & Lohne, 2009).

The current radical expansion of knowledge and paradigm shift has wider implications beyond the mental health professions to the cultural and political organization of societies. In my 2003 volumes I argued that the right hemisphere nonconscious implicit self, and not the left conscious explicit self, is dominant in human adaptive survival functions. Offering data at the neuropsychological, cultural, and historical levels, McGilchrist (2009) echoes this principle: "If what one means by consciousness is the part of the mind that brings the world into focus, makes it explicit, allows it to be formulated in language, and is aware of its own awareness, it is reasonable to link the conscious mind to activity almost all of which lies ultimately in the left hemisphere" (p. 188). He adds, however, "The world of the left hemisphere, dependent on denotative language and abstraction, yields clarity and power to manipulate things that are known, fixed, static, isolated, decontextualized, explicit, disembodied, general in nature, but ultimately lifeless" (p. 174). In contrast, "the right hemisphere . . . yields a world of individual, changing, evolving, interconnected, implicit, incarnate, living beings within the context of the lived world, but in the nature of things never fully graspable, always imperfectly known—and to this world it exists in a relationship of care" (p. 174). Indeed, the "emotional" right hemisphere "has the most sophisticated and extensive, and quite possibly most lately evolved, representation in the prefrontal cortex, the most highly evolved part of the brain" (p. 437).

An essential tenet of McGilchrist's volume (2009) is expressed in its title: *the right hemisphere is the master, and the left the emissary, which is willful, believes itself superior, and sometimes betrays the master, bringing harm to them both.* Offering interdisciplinary evidence that spans the sciences and the arts, he convincingly argues that the left hemisphere is increasingly taking precedence in the modern world, with potentially disastrous consequences. I agree that especially western cultures, even more so than in the past, are currently overemphasizing left brain functions. Our cultural conceptions of both mental and physical health, as well as the aims of all levels of education, continue to narrowly overstress rational, logical, analytic thinking over holistic, bodily based, relational right brain functions that are essential to homeostasis and survival. It is ironic that at a time when clinicians and researchers are making significant breakthroughs not only in right brain social-emotional models of optimal development but also in right brain models of the etiologies and treatment of a wide range of psychopathologies, strong economic and cultural inhibitory restraints and cutbacks are being felt by practitioners. How can we understand this? We are constantly told that the reason for this lies in objective economic factors. But the paradigm shift in psychology and neuroscience suggests subjective unconscious forces are at play here.

Listen to McGilchrist's (2009) description of what the world would look like if the left hemisphere were to become so far dominant that, at the phenomenological level, it managed more or less to suppress the right hemisphere's world altogether. He imagines that this left-brained world would lead to an increasing specialization and technicalizing of knowledge, as well as the following: increased bureaucratization, inability to see the big picture, focus on quantity and efficiency at the expense of quality, valuing technology over human interaction, lack of respect for judgment and skill acquired through experience, and devaluing of the unique, the personal, and the individual. Even more specifically,

> Knowledge that came through experience, and the practical acquisition of embodied skill, would become suspect, appearing either a threat or simply incomprehensible. . . . The concepts of skill and judgment, once considered the summit of human experience, but which come only slowly and silently with the business of living, would be discarded in favor of quantifiable and repeatable processes. . . . Skills themselves would be reduced to algorithmic procedures which could be drawn up, and even if necessary regulated, by administrators, since without that the mistrustful tendencies of the left hemisphere could not be certain that these nebulous "skills" were being evenly and "correctly" applied. . . . [F]ewer people would find themselves doing work involving contact with anything in the real, "lived" world, rather than with plans, strategies, paperwork, management and bureaucratic procedures. . . . Technology would flourish, as an expression of the left hemisphere's de-

sire to manipulate and control the world for its own pleasure, but it would be accompanied by a vast expansion of bureaucracy, systems of abstraction and control. (McGilchrist, 2009, p. 429)

Sound familiar? I suggest that this "imagined" left brain worldview now dominates not only our culture but also the current mental health field in the following forms: an overemphasis on psychopharmacology over psychotherapy, an undue influence of the insurance industry on defining "normative" and "acceptable" forms of treatment, an overidealization of "evidence-based practice," an underappreciation of the large body of studies on the effectiveness of the therapeutic alliance, a trend toward "manualization" of therapy, a training model that focuses on the learning of techniques rather than expanding relational skills, and a shift of psychotherapy from a profession to a business.

Can we reverse this current imbalance of the hemispheres? The paradigm shift has generated a quantum leap in our attempts to understand a number of fundamental questions of the human condition that can be elucidated by recent discoveries of the early developing right brain. A prime example is the surge of deeper explorations of our human origins by contemporary developmental science. In 2005 Insel and Fenton articulated this widely held principle: "Most mental illnesses . . . begin far earlier in life than was previously believed" (p. 590). More recently Leckman and March (2011) are asserting that "A scientific consensus is emerging that the origins of adult disease are often found among developmental and biological disruptions occurring during the early years of life" (p. 333). We need, *now*, to use recent knowledge in order to reflect more deeply and act more directly on what is required—at levels of the individual, family, and culture—to provide an optimal human context for both mental and physical health. In addition to culturally supporting the development of intellectual and cognitive abilities, we need to foster the individual's adaptive capacity to relate socially and emotionally to other human beings via the right brain functions of intersubjective communication, affect processing, empathy, and interactive stress regulation. The large body of studies on the critical survival functions of the right brain can be applied not only to individuals but also to cultures, including animal cultures (Bradshaw & Schore, 2007; Schore & Schore, 2008).

The upcoming chapters demonstrate that the new information that science is providing on attachment, trauma, affect regulation, and right brain development is directly relevant to the treatment of the social-emotional disturbances that lie at the core of a spectrum of psychiatric and personality disorders. But beyond that, this knowledge also has practical value in generating more complex models of human growth and development that specifically target optimization of brain plasticity and thereby human potential. This is especially true for brain development in the critical periods of the brain growth spurt in infancy. Other professions would also greatly profit from this knowledge. Judges and attorneys in the area of family law are now becoming extremely interested in using current neuroscience in order to make informed "Solomonian" decisions about "joint custodies" in the first year of life, the critical period of human attachment. They also need to be aware of what we now know about the enduring effects of relational attachment trauma in infancy (see Schore and McIntosh in *Family Court Review*, 2011).

We are currently seeing a continuous stream of information from neuroscience entering into education, the humanities, and the arts, which is also diffusing into the general public. This information can be used or misused. As a case in point, in 2005 *Time* magazine reported on the frontiers of brain research and the practical applications of the advances in neuroscience (McCarthy, 2005). In that article a number of interviewees described its relevance to neuroeconomics, and how brain centers involved in consumer habits and political decision making could be influenced by manipulations of unconscious processes. In contrast, in my portion of the article I spoke of developmental affective and social neuroscience as potential sources of a deeper understanding of the interpersonal neurobiological origins of empathy, trust, deception, emotional communication, and the regulation of violence—issues central to the human experience. As a member of the editorial advisory board of the *American Journal of Play*, I would now add that we need further research on the mechanisms of another basic motivational system of the human experience, play.

In one of the following chapters I offer sociological psychiatric data indicating clear signs that various aspects of the human condition are showing clinical signs of severe stress, and that this is expressed in an increase of emotional disorders in childhood and adolescence. One manifestation of the paradigm shift is a correction of previous developmental psychological cognitively focused models asserting that *all* children are "resilient." We now know this is imprecise, if not misleading. A large body of developmental neuroscience research clearly demonstrates that all children are not "resilient" but "malleable," for better or worse (Leckman & March, 2011). There is now compelling evidence that adverse developmental and biological disruptions occurring in the early years of life are rapidly increasing.

In 2003 I was a member of the Commission on Children at Risk that produced the report *Hardwired to Connect*. Citing extensive research, the Commission of 33 children's doctors, research scientists, and mental health professionals concluded: "The implications of this research are clear and profound: The declining mental health of many U.S. children is a pressing issue that plays a substantial role in many of today's emerging physical problems. Psychosomatic and psychosocial disorders have pronounced and long-lasting effects on both children's lives and society" (2003, p. 71). This disturbing trend continues. At present the American Academy of Childhood and Adolescent Psychiatry (AACAP) is describing a "crisis" in children's mental health needs: One in every five children has a diagnosable psychiatric disorder, and one in every ten suffers from a mental illness severe enough to impair everyday living (AACAP, n.d.). Most recently, a psychiatric epidemiological study of 10,000 adolescents documents a "high prevalence" of mental disorders in youth. These authors note, "Approximately one in every four to five youths in the U.S. meets the criteria for a mental disorder with severe impairment across their lifetime" (Merikangas et al., 2010, p. 980).

Here in the United States, how are we reacting to this crisis at the core of our culture? And if we are not responding, why not? In clinical models we speak of individuals having intrapsychic defenses against uncertainty, stress, and painful negative information. But defenses such as denial, repression, and even dissociation are collectively used by the culture to avoid more directly confronting the serious stressors that lie at its core. Forty years ago Jacob Bronowski offered the trenchant observation, "Think of the investment that evolution has made in the child's brain. . . . For most of history, civilizations have crudely ignored that enormous potential. In fact the longest childhood has been that of civilization, learning to understand that" (1973, p. 425).

In a current attempt to overcome that resistance and bring this problem closer to the forefront of cultural consciousness, my colleagues and I are producing two multiauthored volumes: *Evolution, Early Experience and Human Development: From Research to Practice and Policy* (Narvaez, Panksepp, Schore, & Gleason, in press), and *The Impact of Early Life Trauma on Health and Disease: The Hidden Epidemic* (Lanius, Vermetten, & Pain, 2010). Grounded in recent developmental neuroscience, psychiatry, and developmental psychology, these books cast light upon a number of serious psychological and social problems underlying our cultural blind spots. But more than that, contributing scholars from multiple disciplines offer practical thoughts about what types of early-life experiences are essential for optimal development of human brain and body systems—in order not only to generate greater understanding of scientific research and theory but also to promote informed public policy.

In the very first words of my 1994 volume I offered the controversial statement, "The understanding of early development is one of the fundamental objectives of science. The beginnings of living systems set the stage for every aspect of an organism's internal and external functioning throughout the lifespan." In 1996 I proposed, "the self-organization of the developing brain occurs in the context of a relationship with another self, another brain." This book, like its three predecessors, presents the reader with a continually expanding body of recent interdisciplinary data that indicates that these principles are now accepted in both the life sciences and the mental health field. In a recent overview of contemporary developmental neuroscience, Leckman and March (2011, p. 333) conclude, "our in utero and our early postnatal interpersonal worlds shape and mold the individuals (infants, children, adolescents, and adults and caregivers) we are to become." At this point in time there is converging evidence that we can maximize the short- and long-term effects of our interventions by concentrating on the period of the brain growth spurt—from the last trimester of pregnancy through the second year. Whether or not our governments will fund such sorely needed efforts remains to be seen.

In this volume, *The Science of the Art of Psychotherapy*, I offer expansions of regulation theory, including specific ideas about the direct implications of the paradigm shift for the clinical professions as well as the wider culture. As in previous writings, my intention as a clinician-scientist is directed toward informing psychotherapists about the latest relevant research findings, and scientists about very recent advances in clinical practice, thereby attempting to foster an enriched dialogue between these two domains of the mental health discipline. Toward that goal I continue to use the device of frequently citing verbatim the current voices of clinicians studying the mind and neuroscientists studying the brain in order to demonstrate their agreement on the centrality of bodily based affective phenomena, and to generate a common language that addresses the subjective emotional realm.

The first part of the book, Affect Regulation Therapy and Clinical Neuropsychoanalysis, contains chapters on the art of the craft of psychotherapy, offering interpersonal neurobiological models of the change mechanism in the treatment of all patients, but especially in patients with a history of early relational trauma. These chapters contain contributions on "modern attachment theory" and its focus on the essential nonverbal unconscious affective mechanisms that lie beneath the words of the patient and therapist, on clinical neuropsychoanalytic models of working with relational trauma and pathological dissociation, and on the use of affect regulation therapy in the emotionally stressful heightened affective moments of clinical enactments. Throughout the work the reader may semantically equate the terms *psychoanalytic* with *psychodynamic*, and *psychoanalyst* with *psychotherapist*.

Over the course of these chapters I present a model of brain/mind/body changes in not only the patient but also the therapist, addressing the development of therapeutic expertise and how clinical experience alters the therapist's right brain implicit functions. The trans-theoretical perspective of regulation theory can act as a lens that brings into focus the essential intra- and intersubjective aspects of any basic human adaptive or maladaptive self-function or behavior. It thus can be applied to any clinician's understanding of how his or her own subjectivity, acting at levels beneath conscious awareness, is accessed moment by moment in the psychotherapeutic process. Although many of the following clinical observations involve adult patients, the general therapeutic principles also apply to the change process of child and adolescent treatment.

The reader will note that my expositions of clinical problems take the same form as my earlier writings. As opposed to the customary strategy of presenting material from a specific case in order to elucidate general clinical principles, this approach attempts to model common fundamental mechanisms of unconscious intrapsychic and interpersonal phenomena and then apply them to the therapeutic context of a specific case. This perspective attempts to elucidate the science of the art of psychotherapy, and it parallels a current significant increase in scientific research on the psychotherapy process. In that expanding field Kazdin and Nock (2003) assert, "Study of mechanisms of treatment is probably the best short-term and long-term investment for improving clinical practice and patient care. . . . Understanding why treatment works can serve as a basis for maximizing treatment effects and ensuring that critical features are generalized to clinical practice" (p. 1117).

The chapters in the second part of the book, Developmental Affective Neuroscience and Developmental Neuropsychiatry, address the science that underlies regulation theory's clinical models of development and psychopathogenesis. The wide-ranging applications of the theory's overarching interpersonal neurobiological model of emotional and social development are expressed in the following contributions: the incorporation of developmental neuroscience into pediatric practice, ethological studies of wild elephants, theoretical expositions of pathological dissociation and relational trauma, experimental research on borderline personality disorder, an overview of current trends of cultural child rearing from the perspective of developmental affective neuroscience, the application of regulation theory to the clinical assessment of high-risk attachment relationships, and the contributions of modern attachment theory to family law. Although most mental health practitioners are actively involved in child, adolescent, and adult psychotherapeutic treatment, a major theme of the latter chapters is that the field now needs to more seriously attend to the problem of early assessment, intervention, and prevention.

REFERENCES

Adler, H. M. (2007). Toward a biopsychosocial understanding of the patient–physician relationship: An emerging dialogue. *Journal of General Internal Medicine, 22,* 280–285.

American Academy of Childhood and Adolescent Psychiatry (AACAP). (n.d.). *The campaign for America's kids.* Retrieved May 3, 2011, from http://www.campaignforameri caskids.org/

Atzil, S., Hendler, T., & Feldman, R. (2011). Specifying the neurobiological basis of human attachment: Brain, hormones, and behavior in synchronous and intrusive mothers. *Neuropsychopharmacology,* doi:10.1038/npp.2011.172.

Barrett, J., & Fleming, A. S. (2011). Annual research review: All mothers are not created equal: neural and psychobiological perspectives on mothering and the importance of individual differences. *Journal of Child Psychology and Psychiatry, 52,* 368–397.

Beck, A. T., & Dozois, D. J. A. (2011). Cognitive therapy: Current status and future directions. *Annual Review of Medicine, 62,* 397–409.

Bradshaw, G. A., & Sapolsky, R. M. (2006, November/December). Mirror, mirror. *American Scientist,* 487–489.

Bradshaw, G., & Schore, A. N. (2007). How elephants are opening doors: Developmental neuroethology, attachment, and social context. *Ethology, 113,* 426–436.

Bromberg, P. M. (2011). *The shadow of the tsunami and the growth of the relational mind.* New York: Routledge.

Bronowski, J. (1973). *The ascent of man.* New York: Little Brown.

Buchanan, M. (2009). Secret signals. *Nature, 457,* 528–530.

Champagne, F. A. (2011). Maternal imprints and the origins of variation. *Hormones and Behavior, 60,* 4–11.

Clarkin, J. F., Levy, K. N., Lenzenweger, M. F., & Kernberg, O. F. (2007). Evaluating three treatments for borderline personality disorder: A multiwave study. *American Journal of Psychiatry, 164,* 922–928.

Commission on Children at Risk. (2003). *Hardwired to connect. The new scientific case for authoritative communities.* New York: Institute for American Values.

Decety, J., & Lamm, C. (2007). The role of the right temporoparietal junction in social interaction: How low-level computational processes contribute to meta-cognition. *The Neuroscientist, 13,* 580–593.

de Waal, F. B. M. (2011). What is animal emotion? *Annals of the New York Academy of Sciences, 1224,* 191–206.

Dumas, G. (2011). Towards a two-body neuroscience. *Communicative and Integrative Biology, 4,* 349–352.

Dumas, G., Nadel, J., Soussignan, R., Martinerie, J., & Garnero, L. (2010). Inter-brain synchronization during social interaction. *PLoS ONE, 5,* e12166.

Etkin, A., Pittenger, C., Polan, H. J., & Kandel, E. R. (2005). Toward a neurobiology of psychotherapy: Basic science and clinical applications. *Journal of Neuropsychiatry and Clinical Neuroscience, 17,* 145–158.

Finn, S. E. (2011). Journeys through the valley of death: Multimethod psychological assessment and personality transformation in long-term psychotherapy. *Journal of Personality Assessment, 93,* 123–141.

Freud, S. (1966). Project for a scientific psychology. In J. Strachey (Ed. & Trans.), *The standard edition of the complete psychological works of Sigmund Freud* (Vol. 1, pp. 281–392). London: Hogarth Press. (Original work published 1895)

Gazzaniga, M. (2011). Interview with Michael Gazzaniga. *Annals of the New York Academy of Sciences, 1224,* 1–8.

Glass, R. M. (2008). Psychodynamic psychotherapy and research evidence. Bambi survives Godzilla? *The Journal of the American Medical Association, 300,* 1587–1589.

Halasz, G. (2010). In conversation with Allan Schore. *Australasian Psychiatry, 19,* 30–36.

Hug, E., & Lohne, P. (2009). A case study of the treatment of a patient with psychosis and drug dependence: Towards an integration of psychoanalytic and neuroscientific perspectives. *Psychosis, 1,* 82–92.

Insel, T. R., & Fenton, W. S. (2005). Psychiatric epidemiology. It's not just about counting anymore. *Archives of General Psychiatry, 62,* 590–592.

Kazdin, A. E. (2007). Mediators and mechanisms of change in psychotherapy research. *Annual Review of Clinical Psychology, 3,* 1–27.

Kazdin, A. E., & Nock, M. K. (2003). Delineating mechanisms of change in child and adolescent therapy: Methodological issues and research recommendations. *Journal of Child Psychology and Psychiatry, 44,* 1116–1129.

Keenan, J. P., & Gorman, S. (2007). The causal role of the right hemisphere in self-awareness: It is the brain that is selective. *Cortex, 43,* 1074–1082.

Kuhn, T. (1962). *The structure of scientific revolutions.* Chicago: University of Chicago Press.

Lane, R. D. (2008). Neural substrates of implicit and explicit emotional processes: A unifying framework for psychosomatic medicine. *Psychosomatic Medicine, 70,* 214–231.

Lanius, R. A., Vermetten, E., & Pain, C. (Eds.). (2010). *The impact of early life trauma on health and disease: The hidden epidemic.* Cambridge: Cambridge University Press.

Leckman, J. F., & March, J. S. (2011). Editorial: Developmental neuroscience comes of age. *Journal of Child Psychology and Psychiatry, 52,* 333–338.

Leichsenring, F., & Rabung, S. (2008). Effectiveness of long-term psychodynamic psycho-
    therapy: A meta-analysis. *The Journal of the American Medical Association, 300,* 1551–
    1565.
Levy, K. N., Meehan, K. B., Kelly, K. M., Reynoso, J. S., Weber, M., Clarkin, J. F., et al.
    (2006). Change in attachment patterns and reflective function in a randomized con-
    trol trial of transference focused psychotherapy for borderline personality disorder.
    Journal of Consulting and Clinical Psychology, 74, 1027–1040.
McCarthy, T. (2005, November 9). Getting inside your head. *Time.* Retrieved May 25,
    2011, from http://www.time.com/time/magazine/article/0,9171,1118381-2,00.html
McGilchrist, I. (2009). *The master and his emissary.* New Haven CT: Yale University
    Press.
Meares, R., Schore, A. N., & Melkonian, D. (2011). Is borderline personality a particu-
    larly right hemispheric disorder? A study of P3A using single trial analysis. *Australian
    and New Zealand Journal of Psychiatry, 45,* 131–139.
Merikangas, K. R., He, J. P., Burstein, M., Swanson, S. A., Avenevoli, S., Cui, L., et al.
    (2010). Lifetime prevalence of mental disorders in U.S. adolescents: Results from the
    National Comorbidity Survey Replication—Adolescent Supplement (NCS-A). *Jour-
    nal of the American Academy of Child & Adolescent Psychiatry, 49,* 980–989.
Minagawa-Kawai, U., Matsuoka, S., Dan, I., Naoi, N., Nakamura, K., & Kojima, S. (2009).
    Prefrontal activation associated with social attachment: Facial-emotion recognition in
    mothers and infants. *Cerebral Cortex, 19,* 284–292.
Moser, J. S., Cahill, S. P., & Foa, E. B. (2010). Evidence for poorer outcome in patients
    with severe negative trauma-related cognitions receiving prolonged exposure plus cog-
    nitive restructuring. *Journal of Nervous and Mental Disease, 198,* 72–75.
Narvaez, D. J., Panksepp, J., Schore, A. N., & Gleason, T. (Eds.). (in press). *Evolution,
    early experience and human development: From research to practice and policy.* New
    York: Oxford University Press.
Nitschke, J. B., Nelson, E. E., Rusch, B. D., Fox, A. S., Oakes, T. R., & Davidson, R. J.
    (2004). Orbitofrontal cortex tracks positive mood in mothers viewing pictures of their
    newborn infants. *NeuroImage, 21,* 583–592.
Noriuchi, M., Kikuchi, Y., & Senoo, A. (2008). The functional neuroanatomy of maternal
    love: Mother's response to infant's attachment behaviors. *Biological Psychiatry, 63,*
    415–423.
Northoff, G., & Panksepp, J. (2008). The trans-species concept of self and the subcortical-
    cortical midline system. *Trends in Cognitive Sciences, 12,* 259–264.
Panksepp, J. (2008). The power of the word may reside in the power of affect. *Integrative
    Psychological and Behavioral Science, 42,* 47–55.
Parsons, C. E., Young, K. S., Murray, L., Stein, A., & Kringelbach, M. L. (2010). The
    functional neuroanatomy of the evolving parent-infant relationship. *Progress in Neuro-
    biology, 91,* 220–241.
Roth, T. L., & Sweatt, J. D. (2011). Annual research review: Epigenetic mechanism and
    environmental shaping of the brain during sensitive periods of development. *Journal of
    Child Psychology and Psychiatry, 52,* 398–408.
Safran, J. D., & Muran, J. C. (2000). *Negotiating the therapeutic alliance: A relational
    treatment guide.* New York: Guilford Press.
Schore, A. N. (1994). *Affect regulation and the origin of the self.* Mahwah, NJ: Erlbaum.
Schore, A. N. (1996). The experience-dependent maturation of a regulatory system in the

orbital prefrontal cortex and the origin of developmental psychopathology. *Development and Psychopathology, 8,* 59–87.

Schore, A. N. (1997). A century after Freud's Project: Is a rapprochement between psychoanalysis and neurobiology at hand? *Journal of the American Psychoanalytic Association, 45,* 807–840.

Schore, A. N. (2001). The effects of relational trauma on right brain development, affect regulation, and infant mental health. *Infant Mental Health Journal, 22,* 201–269.

Schore, A. N. (2003a). *Affect regulation and the repair of the self.* New York: Norton.

Schore, A. N. (2003b). *Affect dysregulation and disorders of the self.* New York: Norton.

Schore, A. N. (2009, August 8). The paradigm shift: The right brain and the relational unconscious. Invited plenary address to the American Psychological Association 2009 Convention, Toronto, Canada. Retrieved September 16, 2009, from http://www.allan schore.com/pdf/SchoreAPAPlenaryFinal09.pdf

Schore, A. N. (2010). Allan Schore on Freud's work: It's all in "the right mind." Retrieved May 19, 2011, from http://simplycharly.com/freud/allan_schore_freud_interview.htm

Schore, A. N., & McIntosh, J. (2011). Family law and the neuroscience of attachment. *Family Court Review, 49,* 501–512.

Schore, J. R., & Schore, A. N. (2008). Modern attachment theory: The central role of affect regulation in development and treatment. *Clinical Social Work Journal, 36,* 9–20.

Semrud-Clikeman, M., Fine, J. G., & Zhu, D. C. (2011). The role of the right hemisphere for processing of social interactions in normal adults using functional magnetic resonance imaging. *Neuropsychobiology, 64,* 47–51.

Shedler, J. (2010). The efficacy of psychodynamic psychotherapy. *American Psychologist, 65,* 98–109.

Shonkoff, J. P. (2011). Protecting brains, not simply stimulating minds. *Science, 333,* 982–983.

Shonkoff, J. P., Boyce, W. T., & McEwen, B. S. (2009). Neuroscience, molecular biology, and the childhood roots of health disparities: Building a new framework for health promotion and disease prevention. *Journal of the American Medical Association, 301,* 2252–2259.

Stevenson, C. W., Halliday, D. M., Marsden, C. A., & Mason, R. (2008). Early life programming of hemispheric lateralization and synchronization in the adult medial prefrontal cortex. *Neuroscience, 155,* 852–863.

Swain, J. E., Lorberbaum, J. P., Kose, S., & Strathearn, L. (2007). Brain basis of early parent–infant interactions: Psychology, physiology, and *in vivo* functional neuroimaging studies. *Journal of Child Psychology and Psychiatry, 48,* 262–287.

Tschacher, W., Schildt, M., & Sander, K. (2010). Brain connectivity in listening to affective stimuli: A functional magnetic resonance imaging (fMRI) study and implications for psychotherapy. *Psychotherapy Research, 20,* 576–588.

Tucker, D. M., & Moller, L. (2007). The metamorphosis. Individuation of the adolescent brain. In D. Romer & E. F. Walker (Eds.), *Adolescent psychopathology and the developing brain. Integrating brain and prevention science* (pp. 85–102). Oxford, UK: Oxford University Press.

U.S. Department of Health and Human Services, Administration for Children and Families, Children's Bureau. Child maltreatment annual reports: national statistics on child abuse and neglect, 2009. Retrieved December 5, 2011 from http://www.acf.hhs.gov/ programs/cb/pubs/cm09/index.htm

Vallortigara, G., & Rogers, L. J. (2005). Survival with an asymmetrical brain: Advantages and disadvantages of cerebral lateralization. *Behavioral and Brain Sciences, 28,* 575–633.

Wei, L., David, A., Duman, R. S., Anisman, H., & Kaffman, A. (2010). Early life stress increases anxiety-like behavior in Balbc mice despite a compensatory increase in levels of postnatal maternal care. *Hormones and Behavior, 57,* 396–404.

Wong, I. C. K., Murray, M. L., Camilleri-Novak, D., & Stephens, P. (2004). Increased prescribing trends of paediatric psychotropic medications. *Archives of Disease in Childhood, 89,* 1131–1132.

PART I

AFFECT REGULATION THERAPY AND CLINICAL NEUROPSYCHOANALYSIS

CHAPTER 1

Modern Attachment Theory:
The Central Role of Affect Regulation
in Development and Treatment

With Judith R. Schore

Attachment theory, originally proposed by John Bowlby in 1969, has experienced a powerful resurgence over the last decade, not only in the mental health field but also in the biological sciences. Originating in an amalgam of psychoanalysis and behavioral biology, attachment theory is deceptively simple on the surface. It posits that the real relationships of the earliest stage of life indelibly shape us in basic ways, and, for the rest of the life span, attachment processes lie at the center of all human emotional and social functions. Bowlby's (1969) original descriptions occurred during a period of behaviorism and included an emphasis on the strange situation and secure base behaviors, which then gave way to the dominance of cognition and an emphasis on attachment narratives and reflective capacities. Despite these trends, we remind the reader of Ainsworth's (1969) characterization of Bowlby's seminal *Attachment* volume: "In effect what Bowlby has attempted is to update psychoanalytic theory in the light of recent advances in biology" (p. 998).

With the current incorporation of neurobiology into the theory, we now have a deeper understanding of how and why the early social environment influences all later adaptive functions. As a result of the recent integration of clinical data with developmental and neurobiological research, Bowlby's core ideas have been expanded into a therapeutically relevant model of human development. Indeed, in their recent overview of psychoanalytic developmental theories, Palombo, Bendicsen, and Koch (2009) conclude that current neuropsychological attachment theories are returning to the fundamental psychoanalytic questions posed by Freud's model of the human unconscious.

With its emphasis on human development, attachment theory shares with clinical social work a common biopsychosocial perspective. The field of social work has traditionally focused on two core issues—person-in-environment and relationship. This theoretical orientation encompasses not only psychological relational dynamics beginning in infancy but also individual biological and somatic factors and sociocultural influences that are both internalized and situational. This biopsychosocial perspective of social work is absolutely consonant with attachment theory's current explanation of the mechanisms that operate at the psychobiological core of the intersubjective context—the brain–mind–body–environment relational matrix out of which each individual emerges. We argue that individual development arises out of the relationship between the brain, mind, and body of both infant and caregiver held within a culture and environment that either supports, inhibits, or even threatens it. One of the key elements of a "culturally competent" social worker is an awareness of the clients' pertinent relational beginnings held by their particular culture. These relational origins are forged and expressed in nonverbal attachment communications in the first year and influenced by the cultural surroundings. They indelibly shape the individual's way of experiencing the world.

In addition, the fundamental biopsychosocial perspective of clinical social work, like attachment theory, highlights the critical importance of unconscious[1] forces that drive all human emotion, cognition, and behavior within a sociocultural matrix. Thus, clinical social work also has incorporated Freud's fundamental conception of the central role of the unconscious in everyday life. From its beginnings, attachment theory, grounded in psychoanalysis and behavioral biology, has focused on how real experiences, especially in childhood, directly impact the unconscious system. This is a core principle of psychodynamically oriented clinical social work. The links between psychoanalytic social work and other psychoanalytic disciplines have recently been strengthened by social work's rapid incorporation of recent advances in relational psychoanalysis, self psychology, and neuropsychoanalysis. Indeed the last decade has seen a resurgence and expansion of Freud's model. In the broader psychological literature, Bargh and Morsella (2008) now conclude, "Freud's model of the unconscious as the primary guiding influence over every day life, even today, is more specific and detailed than any to be found in contemporary cognitive or social psychology" (p. 73).

Over this same time period, classical attachment theory has also experienced a significant expansion. In 2000, A. Schore presented the Seventh Annual John Bowlby Memorial Lecture (2000b) and, returning to Bowlby's methodology of

---

1. In this chapter we equate "unconscious" with "nonconscious"; that is, implicit functions that occur beneath levels of awareness not because they are repressed but because they are too rapid to reach consciousness.

integrating biology and psychoanalysis, offered recent findings from "the decade of the brain" to argue that modern attachment theory is essentially a regulation theory. That same year he published an article in *Attachment & Human Development* identifying Bowlby's (1969) control system of attachment in the right brain. In an article in the 2001 issue of the *British Journal of Psychotherapy*, he then extrapolated his neuropsychoanalytic model of attachment to the clinical encounter, including psychobiological models of attachment in the therapeutic alliance, and right brain–to–right brain communications in the transference-countertransference relationship (Schore, 2001a).

The current transformation of modern attachment theory, informed by neuroscience, even more deeply elucidates the early experience–dependent development of the human unconscious system, which remains active over the course of the life span. Regulation theory is derived from interdisciplinary sources, and it has fostered a dialogue not only within but also among various fields (e.g., psychoanalysis, neuroscience, psychiatry, traumatology, developmental psychology, pediatrics), including clinical social work. In an excellent volume, *Neurobiology for Clinical Social Work*, Applegate and Shapiro (2005) apply attachment neurobiology specifically to social work practice, and they too maintain that this theory is highly compatible with the biopsychosocial emphasis of social work practice.

Another major force that has propelled the transformation in attachment theory is the ongoing intense interest in emotion and emotion regulation. In fact, a number of clinical and scientific disciplines are now experiencing a paradigm shift from cognition to the primacy of affect, and this transition is expressed in a shift from cognitive to emotional theories of development. In a recent contribution to regulation theory, we argued that any theory of development and its corresponding theory of therapy must include psychobiological findings regarding precisely how early emotional transactions with the primary object impact the development of psychic structure; that is, how affective attachment communications facilitate the maturation of brain systems involved in affect arousal and self-regulation (Schore & Schore, 2008). The rich intricacy of an integrative theory of neurobiology and attachment links brain, mind, and body and encompasses the essential elements that allow us to comprehend and treat attachment-related disorders of self and affect regulation more effectively. There is currently both an experimental and a clinical focus on how affective bodily based attachment processes are aroused, communicated, and regulated within the mother–infant[2] dyad. There also is an emphasis on how psychobiological attunement and relational stress impact, both positively and negatively, the experience-dependent maturation of early developing brain regulatory systems.

Fifteen years ago, A. Schore outlined the essential role of attachment in the

---

2. Throughout this chapter, we refer to "mother" interchangeably with "primary caregiver(s)." We are referring to the primary attachment figure, although we recognize that the infant's primary attachment figure may not be the mother.

regulation of affect and emotional development. In his seminal 1994 volume, he integrated a large amount of existing interdisciplinary data and proposed that attachment transactions are critical to the development of structural right brain systems involved in the nonconscious processing of emotion, modulation of stress, self-regulation, and thereby the functional origins of the bodily based affective core of the implicit self that operates automatically and rapidly, beneath levels of awareness. In 2000, within an introduction to a reissue of Bowlby's (1969) classic volume, *Attachment*, A. Schore proposed, "In essence, a central goal of Bowlby's first book is to demonstrate that a mutually enriching dialogue can be organized between the biological and psychological realms" (p. 24), and argued that attachment theory stresses the primacy of affect and is fundamentally a regulation theory. This linkage of the theory with affective dynamics was mirrored in Fonagy, Gergely, Jurist, and Target's (2002) *Affect Regulation, Mentalization, and the Development of the Self*. Indeed, Fonagy and Target (2002) concluded "the whole of child development to be the enhancement of self-regulation." In parallel work on attachment from the social psychology perspective, Mikulincer, Shaver, and Pereg (2003) have offered extensive work on "attachment theory and affect regulation."

The current shift of attachment theory from its earlier focus on behavior and cognition into affect and affect regulation reflects the broader trend in the psychological sciences. In a recent editorial of the journal *Motivation and Emotion*, Ryan (2007) asserts:

> After three decades of the dominance of cognitive approaches, motivational and emotional processes have roared back into the limelight. Both researchers and practitioners have come to appreciate the limits of exclusively cognitive approaches for understanding the initiation and regulation of human behavior. (p. 1)

This renewed emphasis on the emotional and social aspects of early development has allowed for a transformation of attachment theory into a pragmatic framework for models of both psychopathogenesis and the change process in psychotherapy. In our work, we have suggested that regulation theory can generate complex models of psychopathogenesis by linking early attachment stressors to the neurobiology of impaired emotional development, enduring deficits in affect dysregulation, and the genesis of personality disorders. The application of attachment principles to psychotherapy models also has been elucidated by focusing the treatment upon the affective dynamics of right brain internal working models encoding coping strategies of affect regulation that are activated within the therapeutic alliance (Schore, 1994, 2001b, 2002, 2003a). In other words, the therapeutic relationship and the clinical social worker's use of self are central to interventions ranging from casework management to foster home placement, adoption, and short- and long-term psychotherapy.

Without the psychobiological component, earlier classical models of attachment did not directly address clinical phenomena that are essential to both developmental assessment and psychotherapy. A fundamental question of models of the change process of psychotherapy is, how do relational experiences positively impact psychic structure? By integrating developmental and biological data, the fundamental links between attachment functions and their enduring effect on developing psychic structure throughout the life span are expressed in the developmental neuropsychology of, specifically, the early maturing right brain. This right-lateralized emotional brain is deeply connected into the body and the autonomic nervous system (ANS), and it has a different anatomy, physiology, and biochemistry than the later-forming left hemisphere. The right hemisphere processes not only emotion but, more precisely, unconscious emotion and is the locus of an implicit procedural memory system.

A central principle of our work thus dictates that attachment experiences shape the early organization of the right brain, the neurobiological core of the human unconscious (Schore, 2003b). Indeed, therapeutic interventions are rooted in these same implicit dynamic relational processes. In treatment, these right brain affectively charged attachment experiences are communicated and regulated within the therapeutic alliance. The co-creation of an attachment relationship between the empathic social worker and the client has been seen as the *sine qua non* of clinical practice, and respect for the individual is, and always has been, paramount. The current expansion of neurobiologically supported attachment principles of interactive affect communication and regulation that occur beneath levels of awareness both explains and justifies this approach. The mechanisms of developmental change thus include modifications in both psychic function and structure, not only in the earliest stage but also in all subsequent stages of development. We argue that modern attachment/regulation theory is consonant with the recent relational intersubjective trend in the psychodynamic literature; and it can be readily incorporated into the core of social work education, theory, research, and practice.

Toward that end, in this chapter we outline the general precepts of modern attachment theory and its relevance to the practice of clinical social work. We begin with an overview of the central role of unconscious interactive regulation in establishing attachment relationships and the lifelong impact this has on the development of the right brain and the implicit self. We then present the clinical applications of regulation theory in a section on interpersonal neurobiology of implicit nonverbal communications within the therapeutic alliance, followed by a discussion of affective bodily based transference-countertransference transactions. Finally, we offer some further thoughts on the implications of neurobiological models of attachment for clinical social work. In doing so, we assume some familiarity with the basic concepts of classical attachment theory, object relations, self and relational psychology, and focus on integrating these models with their neurobiological underpinnings in order to offer an interpenetrating and overarching theory that is consonant with the biopsychosocial foundations of clinical social work.

INTRODUCTION: THE PSYCHOBIOLOGICAL CORE OF DEVELOPMENTAL ATTACHMENT COMMUNICATIONS—INTERACTIVE REGULATION

The essential task of the first year of human life is the creation of a secure attachment bond of emotional communication between the infant and the primary caregiver. In order to enter into this communication, the mother must be psychobiologically attuned to the dynamic shifts in the infant's bodily based internal states of central and autonomic arousal. During the affective communications embedded in mutual gaze episodes, the psychobiologically attuned, sensitive caregiver appraises nonverbal expressions of the infant's arousal and then regulates these affective states, both positive and negative. The attachment relationship mediates the dyadic regulation of emotion, wherein the mother (primary caregiver) co-regulates the infant's postnatally developing central (CNS) and autonomic (ANS) nervous systems.

In this dialogic process, the more the mother contingently tunes her activity level to the infant during periods of social engagement, the more she allows him to recover quietly in periods of disengagement; and the more she attends to his reinitiating cues for reengagement, the more synchronized their interaction. In play episodes of affect synchrony, the pair are in affective resonance, and in such, an amplification of vitality affects and a positive state occurs. In moments of interactive repair, the "good-enough" caregiver who has mis-attuned can regulate the infant's negative state by accurately re-attuning in a timely manner. The regulatory processes of affect synchrony, which creates states of positive arousal, and interactive repair, which modulates states of negative arousal, are the fundamental building blocks of attachment and its associated emotions; and resilience in the face of stress and novelty is an ultimate indicator of attachment security. Through sequences of attunement, mis-attunement, and re-attunement, an infant becomes a person, achieving a "psychological birth" (Mahler, Pine, & Bergman, 1975). This preverbal matrix forms the core of the incipient self.

Thus, emotion is initially regulated by others, but over the course of infancy it becomes increasingly self-regulated as a result of neurophysiological development. These adaptive capacities are central to self-regulation, the ability to flexibly regulate psychobiological states of emotions through interactions with other humans, interactive regulation in interconnected contexts, and without other humans, autoregulation in autonomous contexts. Attachment—the outcome of the child's genetically encoded biological (temperamental) predisposition *and* the particular caregiver environment—thus represents the regulation of biological synchronicity between and within organisms.

The fundamental role of nonconscious attachment dynamics is therefore interactive psychobiological regulation. According to Pipp and Harmon (1987), "It may be that . . . we are biologically connected to those with whom we have close relationships. . . . Homeostatic regulation between members of a dyad is a stable aspect of all intimate relationships throughout the lifespan" (p. 650). At the most fundamental level, attachment represents the evolutionary mechanism by which we are sociophysiologically connected to others (Adler, 2002); and nonconscious implicit interactive regulation is the central mechanism that underlies all essential survival functions of the human self-system (Schore, 2003a, 2003b).

This principle is echoed in current developmental brain research, wherein Ovtscharoff and Braun (2001, p. 33) report that "The dyadic interaction between the newborn and the mother . . . serves as a regulator of the developing individual's internal homeostasis." Notice the similarity to Kohut's (1971) proposal that the infant's dyadic regulatory transactions with the maternal self-object allow for maintenance of his or her homeostatic equilibrium. Furthermore, attachment regulatory transactions impact the development of psychic structure; that is, they generate brain development (Schore, 1994). In very recent writings, Fonagy and Target (2005, p. 334) conclude,

> If the attachment relationship is indeed a major organizer of brain development, as many have accepted and suggested (e.g., Schore, 1997, 2003a), then the determinants of attachment relationships are important far beyond the provision of a fundamental sense of safety or security (Bowlby, 1988).

Even more specifically, the regulatory function of the mother–infant interaction acts as an essential promoter of the development and maintenance of synaptic connections during the establishment of functional circuits of the right brain (Cozolino, 2002; Henry, 1993; Schore, 1994; Siegel, 1999; Sullivan & Gratton, 2002). A growing number of studies now support the observation that right-lateralized limbic areas responsible for the regulation of autonomic functions and higher cognitive processes are involved in the "formation of social bonds," are "part of the circuitry supporting human social networks," and that the "the strong and consistent predominance for the right hemisphere emerges postnatally" (Allman, Watson, Tetreault, & Hakeem, 2005, p. 367).

Confirming this, in a recent near-infrared spectroscopy study of infant–mother attachment at 12 months, the researchers conclude: "Our results are in agreement with that of Schore (2000) who addressed the importance of the right hemisphere in the attachment system" (Minagawa-Kawai et al., 2009, p. 289). Neuroscientists studying the human social brain now contend that throughout the life span, "The neural substrates of the perception of voices, faces, gestures, smells and pheromones, as evidenced by modern neuroimaging techniques, are characterized by a general pattern of right-hemispheric functional asymmetry" (Brancucci, Lucci, Mazzatenta, & Tommasi, 2009, p. 895).

Because implicit attachment regulatory functions mature so very early in development, before later-forming verbal explicit systems, A. Schore (1994, 2003a, 2003b) has focused upon the unique operations of the earlier maturing (Chiron et al., 1997) right hemisphere. From infancy throughout all later stages of the life span, this early evolving right-lateralized system is centrally involved in implicit processes and in the control of vital functions supporting survival and enabling the organism to cope with stresses and challenges. He has therefore suggested that the implicit self-system of the right brain that evolves in preverbal stages of development represents the biological substrate of the dynamic unconscious (Schore, 2002a). In accord with this model, Keenan, Gallup, and Falk (2003) conclude,

> By casting the right hemisphere in terms of self, we have a revolutionary way of thinking about the brain. A new model of the brain, therefore, must take into account the primary importance of the right hemisphere in establishing and maintaining our sense of awareness of ourselves and others. (p. 252)

Studies in neuroscience now report that this early maturing right hemisphere is centrally involved in "maintaining a coherent, continuous and unified sense of self" (Devinsky, 2000), and that a right frontal lobe process, one that connects "the individual to emotionally salient experiences and memories underlying self-schemas, is the glue holding together a sense of self" (Miller et al., 2001, p. 821). Using functional magnetic resonance imaging, Buchheim et al. (2006) report that the Adult Attachment Projective Picture System activates the right inferior frontal cortex, an area involved in "the control processes involved in emotion regulation."

RIGHT BRAIN NONVERBAL ATTACHMENT COMMUNICATION: THE INTERSUBJECTIVE ORIGINS OF THE IMPLICIT SELF

A. Schore has described how the emotion-processing limbic circuits of the infant's developing right brain, which are dominant for the emotional sense of self, are influenced by implicit intersubjective affective transactions embedded in the attachment relationship with the mother (Schore, 1994, 2005). Implicit processing underlies the quick and automatic handling of nonverbal affective cues in infancy, and "is repetitive, automatic, provides quick categorization and decision-making, and operates outside the realm of focal attention and verbalized experience" (Lyons-Ruth 1999, p. 576). Trevarthen (1990) described how prosodic vocalizations, coordinated visual eye-to-eye messages, and tactile and body gestures, serve as channels of communicative signals in the proto dialogues between infant and mother, which induce instant emotional effects. Bowlby (1969) also described "facial expression, posture, and tone of voice" as the essential vehicles of attachment communications between the emerging self and the primary object (Schore, 2001a). The dyadic implicit processing of these nonverbal attachment communications are the product of the operations of the infant's right hemisphere interacting with the mother's right hemisphere. Attachment experiences are thus imprinted in an internal working model that encodes strategies of affect regulation acting at implicit nonconscious levels.

Neuroscientists have documented that visual input to the right (and not left) hemisphere during infancy is essential for the development of the capacity to efficiently process information from faces (Le Grand, Lucci, Mazzatenta, & Tommasi, 2003). These findings support earlier speculations in the psychoanalytic literature that "The most significant relevant basic interactions between mother and child usually lie in the visual area: the child's bodily display is responded to by the gleam in the mother's eye" (Kohut, 1971, p. 117); that early mental representations are specifically visually oriented (Giovacchini, 1981); and that historical visual imagery is derivative of events of early phases of development (Anthi, 1983).

With respect to the infant's ability to process the emotional tone of the voice, prosody, it is now thought that:

> The right hemisphere of the neonate is actively involved in the perception of speech melody and the intonations of the voices of mother and surrounding people. The pre-speech stage of child development is characterized by interactions of the descriptive and emotional components due mainly to mechanisms operating within the hemispheres on the principle of non-verbal communication. (Bogolepova & Malofeeva, 2001, p. 353)

And on the other side of the right brain–to–right brain communication system within the attachment dyad, researchers describe the mother's processing capacities: "A number of functions located within the right hemisphere work together to aid monitoring of a baby. As well as emotion and face processing the right hemisphere is also specialized in auditory perception, the perception of intonation, attention, and tactile information" (Bourne & Todd, 2004, pp. 22–23).

It is important to note that these early experiences may be regulated or dysregulated, imprinting either secure or insecure attachments. Watt (2003, p. 109) observes, "If children grow up with dominant experiences of separation, distress, fear and rage, then they will go down a bad pathogenic developmental pathway, and it's not just a bad psychological pathway but a bad neurological pathway." This is due to the fact that during early critical periods organized and disorganized insecure attachment histories are "affectively burnt in" the infant's rapidly developing right brain (Schore, 2001a, 2003a). These stressful relational experiences are encoded in unconscious internal working models in the right, and not left, brain. In a study of hemispheric lateralization of avoidant attachment, Cohen and Shaver (2004) conclude, "Emotional negativity and withdrawal motivation have been connected in psychophysiological studies with the right frontal lobe of the brain" (p. 801), and that avoidant individuals show "a right hemisphere advantage for processing negative emotion and attachment-related words" (p. 807).

Summarizing a large body of neuropsychological data, Feinberg and Keenan (2005) conclude:

> The right hemisphere, particularly the right frontal region, under normal circum-
> stances plays a crucial role in establishing the appropriate relationship between the
> self and the world . . . dysfunction results in a two-way disturbance of personal relat-
> edness between the self and the environment that can lead to disorders of both
> under and over relatedness between the self and the world. (p. 15)

In relationally oriented therapeutic contexts that optimize intersubjective communication and interactive regulation, deficits in internal working models of the
self and the world are gradually repaired. Recal that Bowlby (1988) asserted that
the restoring into consciousness and reassessment of internal working models is
the essential task of psychotherapy.

Decety and Chaminade's (2003) characterization of higher right brain functions is directly applicable to psychotherapy of disorders of the self:

> Mental states that are in essence private to the self may be shared between indi-
> viduals. . . . Thus it makes sense that self-awareness, empathy, identification with
> others, and more generally intersubjective processes, are largely dependent upon
> the right hemisphere resources, which are the first to develop. (p. 591)

These particular implicit right brain operations are essential for adaptive interpersonal functioning and are specifically activated in the therapeutic alliance.
Right brain increases in "implicit relational knowledge" stored in the nonverbal
domain (Stern et al., 1998) thus lie at the core of the psychotherapeutic change
process.

As the right hemisphere is also dominant for the broader aspects of communication and for subjective emotional experiences, the implicit communication of
affective states between the right brains of the members of the infant–mother
and patient–therapist dyads is thus best described as "intersubjectivity." The neurobiological correlate of this intersubjectivity principle is expressed in the dictum, "the self-organization of the developing brain occurs in the context of a
relationship with another self, another brain" (Schore, 1996, p. 60). This is true
in both the developmental and the therapeutic growth-facilitating contexts. The
interpersonal neurobiology of modern attachment theory has thus been a rich
source of information about the essential role of nonconscious nonverbal right
communications in the psychotherapy relationship.

RIGHT BRAIN NONVERBAL ATTACHMENT
COMMUNICATION: IMPLICIT COMMUNICATIONS
WITHIN THE THERAPEUTIC ALLIANCE

It is now accepted that the "non-verbal, prerational stream of expression that
binds the infant to its parent continues throughout life to be a primary medium
of intuitively felt affective-relational communication between persons" (Orlinsky
& Howard, 1986, p. 343). Right brain transactions also mediate the relational

unconscious as it is expressed in the psychoanalytic encounter, and Lyons-Ruth's (2000) description of affective exchanges of implicit relational knowledge within the therapeutic alliance:

> Most relational transactions rely heavily on a substrate of affective cues that give an evaluative valence or direction to each relational communication. These occur at an implicit level of rapid cueing and response that occurs too rapidly for simultaneous verbal transaction and conscious reflection. (pp. 91–92)

Scaer (2005) describes essential implicit communications embedded within the therapist–client relationship:

> Many features of social interaction are nonverbal, consisting of subtle variations of facial expression that set the tone for the content of the interaction. Body postures and movement patterns of the therapist . . . also may reflect emotions such as disapproval, support, humor, and fear. Tone and volume of voice, patterns and speed of verbal communication, and eye contact also contain elements of subliminal communication and contribute to the unconscious establishment of a safe, healing environment. (pp. 167–168)

These right brain communications convey expressions of "the personality of the therapist" more so than do conscious verbalizations.

These developmental studies have direct relevance to the psychotherapeutic process based on the commonality of implicit intersubjective right brain–to–right brain emotion-transacting and -regulating mechanisms in the caregiver–infant relationship and the therapist–patient relationship. A. Schore describes the nature of implicit and explicit processes in the psychotherapeutic context:

> During the treatment, the empathic therapist is consciously, explicitly attending to the patient's verbalizations in order to objectively diagnose and rationalize the patient's dysregulating symptomatology. But she is also listening and interacting at another level, an experience-near subjective level, one that implicitly processes moment-to-moment socioemotional information at levels beneath awareness. (Schore, 2003b, p. 52)

A fundamental question of treatment is how we work with what is being communicated but not symbolized with words. In discussing subsymbolic processing, Bucci (2002) observes, "We recognize changes in emotional states of others based on perception of subtle shifts in their facial expression or posture, and recognize changes in our own states based on somatic or kinesthetic experience" (p. 194). These implicit communications are expressed within the therapeutic alliance between the client's and therapist's right brain systems.

> Human beings rely extensively on nonverbal channels of communication in their day-to-day emotional as well as interpersonal exchanges. The verbal channel, lan-

guage, is a relatively poor medium for expressing the quality, intensity and nuanc-
ing of emotion and affect in different social situations . . . the face is thought to
have primacy in signaling affective information. (Mandal & Ambady, 2004, p. 23)

In the developmental attachment context, right brain–to–right brain auditory
prosodic communications also act as an essential vehicle of implicit communications within the therapeutic relationship. The right hemisphere is important in
the processing of the "music" behind our words. When listening to speech, we
rely upon a range of cues on which to base our inference as to the communicative intent of others. To interpret the meaning of speech, how something is said
is as important as what is actually said. Prosody conveys different shades of meaning by means of variations in stress and pitch—irrespective of the words and
grammatical construction (Mitchell, Elliott, Barry, Crittenden, & Woodruff,
2003). These data support suggestions that the preverbal elements of language—
intonation, tone, force, and rhythm—stir up reactions derived from the early
mother–child relationships (Greenson, 1978). In the recent literature on the psychotherapeutic context, Andrade concludes, "It is the affective content of the
analyst's voice—and not the semantic content—that has an impact on the patient's store of implicit memories" (2005, p. 683).

During heightened affective moments, these right brain dialogues between
the relational unconscious of both the patient and the therapist (like the attachment communications of the infant and mother) are examples of "primary process communication" (Dorpat, 2001). According to this author, "The primary
process system analyzes, regulates, and communicates an individual's relations
with the environment":

[A]ffective and object-relational information is transmitted predominantly by primary process communication. Nonverbal communication includes body movements (kinesics), posture, gesture, facial expression, voice inflection, and the
sequence, rhythm, and pitch of the spoken words. (Dorpat, 2001, p. 451)

Interestingly, in addition to psychoanalytic authors who have implicated the
right brain in primary process functions (see Schore, 1994), neuroscience
researchers now contend that "the right hemisphere operates in a more free-
associative, primary process manner, typically observed in states such as dreaming or reverie" (Grabner, Fink, & Neubauer, 2007, p. 228).

It is important to stress that all of these implicit nonconscious right brain–
mind–body nonverbal communications are bidirectional and thereby intersubjective (see Schore 2003b for a right hemisphere–to–right hemisphere model of
projective identification, a fundamental process of implicit communication
within the therapeutic alliance). Meares (2005) describes,

Not only is the therapist being unconsciously influenced by a series of slight and, in
some cases, subliminal signals, so also is the patient. Details of the therapist's pos-

ture, gaze, tone of voice, even respiration, are recorded and processed. A sophisticated therapist may use this processing in a beneficial way, potentiating a change in the patient's state without, or in addition to, the use of words. (p. 124)

Implicit right brain–to–right brain intersubjective transactions lie at the core of the therapeutic relationship. They mediate what Sander (1992) calls "moments of meeting" between patient and therapist. Current neurobiological data suggest that "While the left hemisphere mediates most linguistic behaviors, the right hemisphere is important for broader aspects of communication" (van Lancker & Cummings, 1999). In light of this, A. Schore (2003b) has proposed that just as the left brain communicates its states to other left brains via conscious linguistic behaviors, so the right brain nonverbally communicates its unconscious states to other right brains that are tuned to receive these communications. Regulation theory thus describes how implicit systems of the therapist interact with implicit systems of the patient; psychotherapy is not the "talking" but the "communicating" cure.

TRANSFERENCE-COUNTERTRANSFERENCE: IMPLICIT RIGHT BRAIN–MIND–BODY TRANSACTIONS

Advances in neuroscience now clearly suggest that the capacity to receive and express communications within the implicit realm is optimized when the clinician is in a state of right brain receptivity. Marcus (1997) observes, "The analyst, by means of reverie and intuition, listens with the right brain directly to the analysand's right brain" (p. 238). The neuroscience literature holds that "The left hemisphere is more involved in the foreground-analytic (conscious) processing of information, whereas the right hemisphere is more involved in the background-holistic (subconscious) processing of information" (Prodan, Orbelo, Testa, & Ross, 2001, p. 211).

Indeed, the right hemisphere uses an expansive attention mechanism that focuses on global features, whereas the left uses a restricted mode that focuses on local detail (Derryberry & Tucker, 1994). In contrast to the left hemisphere's activation of "narrow semantic fields," the right hemisphere's "coarse semantic coding is useful for noting and integrating distantly related semantic information" (Beeman, 1998), a function that allows for the process of free association. Bucci (1993) has described free association as following the tracks of nonverbal schemata by loosening the hold of the verbal system on the associative process and giving the nonverbal mode the chance to drive the representational and expressive systems, that is, by shifting dominance from a left to a right hemispheric state.

These nonverbal affective and thereby mind–body communications are expressions of the right brain, which is centrally involved in the analysis of direct kinesthetic information received by the subject from his own body, an essential implicit process. This hemisphere, and not the linguistic, analytic left, contains the most comprehensive and integrated map of the body state available to the brain (Damasio, 1994). The therapist's right hemisphere allows him or her to know the patient "from the inside out" (Bromberg, 1991, p. 399). To do this the clinician must access his or her own bodily based intuitive responses to the patient's communications. In an elegant description, Mathew (1998) evocatively portrays this omnipresent implicit process of bodily communications:

> The body is clearly an instrument of physical processes, an instrument that can hear, see, touch and smell the world around us. This sensitive instrument also has the ability to tune in to the psyche: to listen to its subtle voice, hear its silent music and search into its darkness for meaning. (p. 17)

Intersubjectivity is thus more than a match or communication of explicit cognitions. The intersubjective field co-constructed by two individuals includes not just two minds but two bodies (Schore, 1994, 2003a, 2003b). At the psychobiological core of the intersubjective field is the attachment bond of emotional communication and interactive regulation. Recall Pipp and Harmon's (1987) assertion that the fundamental role of nonconscious attachment dynamics is interactive regulation. Implicit unconscious intersubjective communications are interactively communicated and regulated and dysregulated *psychobiological somatic processes* that mediate shared conscious and unconscious emotional states, not just mental contents. The essential biological purpose of intersubjective communications in all human interactions, including those embedded in the psychobiological core of the therapeutic alliance, is the regulation of right brain–mind–body states. These ideas resonate with Shaw's (2004) conclusion:

> Psychotherapy is an inherently embodied process. If psychotherapy is an investigation into the intersubjective space between client and therapist, then as a profession we need to take our bodily reactions much more seriously than we have so far because . . . the body is "the very basis of human subjectivity." (p. 271)

There is now a growing consensus that despite the existence of a number of distinct theoretical perspectives in clinical work, the concepts of transference and countertransference represent a common ground. Recent psychoanalytic models of transference now contend that "no appreciation of transference can do without emotion" (Pincus, Freeman, & Modell, 2007, p. 634), and that "transference is distinctive in that it depends on early patterns of emotional attachment with caregivers" (p. 636). Clinical theoreticians describe transference as "an established pattern of relating and emotional responding that is cued by something in the present, but oftentimes calls up both an affective state and thoughts that may have more to do with past experience than present ones" (Maroda, 2005, p. 134). This conception is echoed in neuroscience, wherein Shuren and Grafman (2002) assert,

> The right hemisphere holds representations of the emotional states associated with events experienced by the individual. When that individual encounters a familiar scenario, representations of past emotional experiences are retrieved by the right hemisphere and are incorporated into the reasoning process. (p. 918)

Other researchers report that the right hemisphere is fundamentally involved in the unconscious processing of emotional stimuli (Mlot, 1998) and in autobiographical memory (Markowitsch, Reinkemeier, Kessler, Koyuncu, & Heiss, 2000).

According to Gainotti (2006), "the right hemisphere may be crucially involved in those emotional memories which must be reactivated and reworked during the psychoanalytical treatment" (p. 167). In discussing the role of the right hemisphere as "the seat of implicit memory," Mancia (2006) notes: "The discovery of the implicit memory has extended the concept of the unconscious and supports the hypothesis that this is where the emotional and affective—sometimes traumatic—presymbolic and preverbal experiences of the primary mother–infant relations are stored" (p. 83). These implicit procedural memories are expressed in transferential right brain–to–right brain nonverbal communications of fast acting, automatic, regulated, and especially dysregulated bodily based stressful emotional states. Transference has been described as "an expression of the patient's implicit perceptions and implicit memories" (Bornstein, 1999, p. 170).

Transference-countertransference transactions thus represent nonconscious nonverbal right brain–mind–body communications. Facial indicators of transference are expressed in visual and auditory affective cues quickly appraised from the therapist's face. Countertransference is similarly currently defined in nonverbal implicit terms as the therapist's "autonomic responses that are reactions on an unconscious level to nonverbal messages" (Jacobs, 1994). In monitoring somatic countertransferential responses, the empathic clinician's psychobiologically attuned right brain tracks at a preconscious level, not only the arousal rhythms and flows of the patient's affective states but also her own somatic countertransferential, interoceptive, bodily based affective responses to the patient's implicit facial, prosodic, and gestural communications. In this manner, "The right hemisphere, in fact, truly interprets the mental state not only of its own brain, but the brains (and minds) of others" (Keenan, Rubio, Racioppi, Johnson, & Barnacz, 2005, p. 702).

It is certainly true that the clinician's left brain conscious mind is an important contributor to the treatment process. But perhaps more so than other treatment modalities, psychodynamic psychotherapeutic models have focused upon the critical functions of the therapist's "unconscious right mind." The right hemisphere plays a dominant role in the processing of self-relevant information (Molnar-Szakacs, Uddin, & Iacoboni, 2005), affective theory of mind (Schore, 2003b), empathy (Schore, 1994; Shamay-Tsoory, Tomer, Berger, & Aharon-Peretz, 2003), as well as in mentalizing (Ohnishi et al., 2004). A neuropsychoanalytic right brain perspective of the treatment process allows for a deeper understanding of the critical factors that operate at implicit levels of the therapeutic alliance, beneath the exchanges of language and explicit cognitions.

In this intersubjective dialogue, the psychobiologically attuned, intuitive clinician, from the first point of contact, is learning the nonverbal moment-to-moment rhythmic structures of the client's internal states, and is relatively flexibly and fluidly modifying his or her own behavior to synchronize with that structure, thereby co-creating with the client a growth-facilitating context for the organization of the therapeutic alliance. The attachment between therapist and client is established over time, allowing for the expression of experiences that resonate with the original infant–mother intersubjective history of the first 2 years. If that was an insecure attachment to begin with, co-creating a new, secure interaction will take even longer.

Over the ensuing stages of the treatment, the sensitive, empathic clinician's monitoring of unconscious process rather than content calls for right brain attention to his or her matching the patient's implicit affective-arousal states. The empathic therapist also resonates with the client's simultaneous implicit expressions of engagement and disengagement within the co-constructed intersubjective field. This in turn allows the clinician to act as an interactive regulator of the patient's psychobiological states. Ultimately, effective psychotherapeutic treatment of early evolving self-pathologies (severe personality disorders) facilitates changes in complexity of the right hemispheric unconscious system.

FURTHER IMPLICATIONS OF REGULATION THEORY FOR CLINICAL SOCIAL WORK: MODELS OF CLINICAL EXPERTISE

We suggest that clinical expertise, especially with severely disturbed patients, relies more on nonconscious nonverbal right brain than conscious verbal left brain functions. Clinical efficacy is more than explicit left hemispheric technical skill in interpretation. Rather, increasing levels of clinical effectiveness with a broader spectrum of patients fundamentally involves more complex learning of a number of nonconscious functions of the therapist's right brain that are expressed in the therapeutic alliance. All technique sits atop these right brain implicit skills, which deepen and expand with clinical experience: the ability to receive and express nonverbal affective communications; clinical sensitivity; use of subjectivity/intersubjectivity; empathy; and affect regulation. Neuroscience now indicates that intuition (Allman et al., 2005), creativity (Grabner et al., 2007), and indeed insight (Jung-Beeman et al., 2004), are all right, and not left, brain functions.

A Presidential Task Force on Evidence-Based Practice prepared by the American Psychological Association (2006) now suggests,

> Central to clinical expertise is interpersonal skill, which is manifested in forming a therapeutic relationship, encoding and decoding verbal and nonverbal responses,

creating realistic but positive expectations, and responding empathically to the patient's explicit and implicit experiences and concerns. (p. 277)

The task force further notes, "Research suggests that sensitivity and flexibility in the administration of therapeutic interventions produces better outcomes than rigid application of . . . principles" (p. 278).

Sensitivity has, of course, been well studied in the developmental attachment literature, wherein researchers observe that maternal sensitivity cultivates synchronous, reciprocal, and jointly satisfying mother–infant interactions, which in turn foster the development of a secure attachment relationship. In adult attachment studies, Schachner, Shaver, and Mikulincer (2005) argue, "nonverbal behavior and sensitivity to a relationship partner's nonverbal behavior importantly influence the quality of interpersonal interactions and relationships, including attachment relationships" (p. 141). We suggest that this attachment principle applies to the therapeutic relationship as well.

The dictionary definition of sensitivity is "susceptible to the attitudes, feelings, or circumstances of others; *registering very slight differences or changes of emotion*" (*American Heritage Dictionary*). In previous writings A. Schore (2003b) describes the operations of the therapist's right brain by which the sensitive clinician's oscillating attentiveness is focused on barely perceptible cues that signal a change in state and on nonverbal behaviors and shifts in affects. In discussing "the art of psychotherapy," Bugental (1987) stresses the importance of the sensitive clinician's ability to "learn to experience finer and finer distinctions or nuances." He states, "The primary instrument brought to the support of the client's therapeutic efforts is the therapist's trained, practiced, and disciplined sensitivity. In many ways, this sensitivity is akin to a musical instrument which must be carefully prepared, maintained, tuned, and protected" (p. 222). The clinician's capacity for intersubjective communication depends upon her "being open to intuitive sensing of what is happening in the back of the patient's words and, often, back of his conscious awareness" (p. 11).

This clinical sensitivity to even low levels of nonverbal attachment communications allows for the clinician's involvement in a wider array of co-created, affectively charged intersubjective fields. These collaborations of the client's and therapist's subjectivities mediate right brain communications of dysregulated affective states. The importance of this connection is stressed by Whitehead (2006):

[E]very time we make therapeutic contact with our patients we are engaging profound processes that tap into essential life forces in our selves and in those we work with. . . . *Emotions are deepened in intensity and sustained in time when they are intersubjectively shared. This occurs at moments of deep contact.* (p. 624, italics added)

It is important to note that in addition to clinical sensitivity to the patient's emotional communications, the therapist's ability to interactively regulate the patient's affective states is critical to the therapeutic process. Ogden (2005) and her colleagues conclude,

> Interactive psychobiological regulation . . . provides the relational context under which the client can safely contact, describe and eventually regulate inner experience. . . . It is the patient's experience of empowering action in the context of safety provided by a background of the empathic clinician's psychobiologically attuned interactive affect regulation that helps effect . . . change. (p. 22)

These clinical principles apply especially to working in enactments with patients with a history of relational attachment trauma and pathological dissociation (Ginot, 2009; Schore, 2007). Such work implies a profound commitment by both participants in the therapeutic dyad and a deep emotional involvement on the part of the therapist (Tutte, 2004).

An attachment-based clinical approach highlights the unconscious nonverbal affective factors more than the conscious verbal cognitive factors as the essential change process of psychotherapy. Thus, at the most essential level, the intersubjective work of psychotherapy is not defined by what the therapist does for the patient, or says to the patient (left brain focus). Rather, the key mechanism is how to be with the patient, especially during affectively stressful moments (right brain focus).

Bowlby stated that attachment behavior was based on the need for safety and a secure base. We have demonstrated that attachment is more than this; it is the essential matrix for creating a right brain self that can regulate its own internal states and external relationships. Attachment intersubjectivity allows psychic structure to be built and shaped into a unique human being. Our task as therapists is to understand and facilitate this developmental process with our clients. The discipline of clinical social work dictates that we do this in the wider context of the culture and society. Regulation theory enhances and deepens the field's bio-psycho-social-cultural perspective.

CONCLUSION: MODERN REGULATION THEORY

An explosion of developmental and neurobiological research has added substantially to the theoretical understanding of the 110 years since Freud (1895/1966) first published his *Project for a Scientific Psychology* (Schore, 1997). Having been grounded in drive, ego, object relations, self psychology, and relational psychology through the 1980s, the addition of attachment theory has moved psychodynamic clinicians' sensibilities into an awareness of real experience and a keen focus on early development as the root of all. Then, beginning in the 1990s, the advances in neuroscience, added to the temperament research, the biological component in our biopsychosocial frame, have provided a remarkable underpinning and expansion of all the pertinent developmental psychoanalytic theoretical concepts that came before. Using this knowledge on a daily basis, finding new understandings in clinical assessments, shaping therapeutic interventions from relevant theory, and providing a unique awareness of the adaptive nonconscious functions of the implicit self are some of the profound results of this theoretical integration.

Thus, we are proposing the concept of modern attachment/regulation theory as an amalgam of Bowlby's attachment theory, updated internal object relations theories, self psychology, and contemporary relational theory—all informed by neuroscience and infant research. This is a profoundly developmental approach. The developmental understanding that arises from this theory leads to a corresponding modern attachment/regulation theory of therapy. This therapeutic approach is rooted in a consciousness of early dyadic regulation, a thorough knowledge of right hemispheric emotional development, and a deep understanding of the dynamics of implicit procedural memory. Awareness of the right brain mechanisms that underlie bodily based nonverbal communication is essential in this approach. A keen apperception of one's own somatic countertransference is a key element in the intersubjectivity between therapist and client. We know the effects of stressors on the self-system, from mild and "ordinary" peculiarities that create and shape individuality, to severe trauma and neglect that interfere with and derail normal development and that require long-term therapeutic involvement for the client to get back on track (Schore, 2002).

Modern attachment/regulation theory explains how these "external" developmental and therapeutic attachment experiences are transformed into "internal" regulatory capacities. And we know from research that this intensive therapeutic relationship can repair damage and create a new structure that is more able to cope with the demands of life. The intersubjective process of developing a true self that can enter into meaningful relationships shows us how the internal world is structured on a psychophysiological base, which takes into account the unique genetic endowment of the particular infant in interaction with his or her relational environment. The psychotherapeutic process is based on this dynamic and can act as a growth-facilitating social environment to promote not only the development of an "earned secure" attachment (Phelkos, Belsky, & Crnic, 1998) but also the expansion of the right brain human unconscious. In a recent overview, Glass (2008) concludes, "Recent research in brain imaging, molecular biology, and neurogenetics has shown that psychotherapy changes brain function and structure. Such studies have shown that psychotherapy affects regional cerebral blood flow, neurotransmitter metabolism, gene expression, and persistent modifications in synaptic plasticity" (p. 1589).

A regulation model of attachment deepens the bio-psycho-social-cultural perspective of clinical social work. Furthermore, the developmental model of modern attachment theory has implications not only for the social work profession's involvement in the psychotherapeutic treatment of individuals but also for the culture, an area of prime interest to social work. Tucker (1992) observes, "the baby brain must begin participating effectively in the process of social information transmission that offers entry into the culture" (p. 79). He asserts that social interaction that promotes brain differentiation is the mechanism for teaching "the epigenetic patterns of culture" (p. 122), and that successful social development requires a high degree of skill in negotiating emotional communication, "much of which is nonverbal" (p. 80). Tucker concludes that such emotional information engages "specialized neural networks in humans, within the right hemisphere" (p. 80). This conceptualization clearly suggests an important and unique role for clinical social work in infant mental health and optimal right brain development, particularly for attachment programs aimed at prevention and early intervention.

This chapter outlines and highlights a large and important body of knowledge that requires careful study. It is outside the usual social work "comfort zone" and thus often omitted in current master's and doctoral education. We cannot afford to continue overlooking the valuable insights available by applying neuroscientific knowledge to social work and psychotherapeutic principles. The expanding knowledge of these disciplines needs to be incorporated in our professional curriculum to promote not only a more profound understanding of the impact of diversity but also more effective relational and therapeutic skills.

REFERENCES

Adler, H. M. (2002). The sociophysiology of caring in the doctor–patient relationship. *Journal of General Internal Medicine, 17*, 883–890.

Ainsworth, M. D. S. (1969). Object relations, dependency and attachment: A theoretical review of the infant–mother relationship. *Child Development, 40*, 969–1025.

Allman, J. M., Watson, K. K., Tetreault, N. A., & Hakeem, A. Y. (2005). Intuition and autism: A possible role for Von Economo neurons. *Trends in Cognitive Sciences, 9*, 367–373.

Andrade, V. M. (2005). Affect and the therapeutic action in psychoanalysis. *International Journal of Psychoanalysis, 86*, 677–697.

Anthi, P. R. (1983). Reconstruction of preverbal experience. *Journal of the American Psychoanalytic Association, 31*, 33–58.

APA Presidential Task Force on Evidence-Based Practice. (2006). Evidence-based practice in psychology. *American Psychologist, 61*, 271–285.

Applegate, J. S., & Shapiro, J. R. (2005). *Neurobiology for clinical social work: Theory and practice.* New York: Norton.

Bargh, J. A., & Morsella, E. (2008). The unconscious mind. *Perspectives on Psychological Science, 3*, 73–79.

Beeman, M. (1998). Coarse semantic coding and discourse comprehension. In M. Beeman & C. Chiarello (Eds.), *Right hemisphere language comprehension.* Mahwah, NJ: Erlbaum.

Bogolepova, I. N., & Malofeeva, L. I. (2001). Characteristics of the development of speech motor areas 44 and 45 in the left and right hemispheres of the human brain in early post-natal ontogenesis. *Neuroscience and Behavioral Physiology, 31*, 13–18.

Bornstein, R. F. (1999). Source amnesia, misattribution, and the power of unconscious perceptions and memories. *Psychoanalytic Psychology, 16*, 155–178

Bourne, V. J., & Todd, B. K. (2004). When left means right: An explanation of the left cradling bias in terms of right hemisphere specializations. *Developmental Science, 7,* 19–24.

Bowlby, J. (1969). *Attachment and loss: Vol. 1. Attachment.* New York: Basic Books.

Bowlby, J. (1988). *A secure base* (2nd ed). New York: Basic Books.

Brancucci, A., Lucci, G., Mazzatenta, A., & Tommasi, L. (2009). Asymmetries of the human social brain in the visual, auditory and chemical modalities. *Philosophical Transactions of the Royal Society of London Biological Sciences, 364,* 895–914.

Bromberg, P. M. (1991). On knowing one's patient inside out: The aesthetics of unconscious communication. *Psychoanalytic Dialogues, 1,* 399–422.

Bucci, W. (1993). The development of emotional meaning in free association: A multiple code theory. In A. Wilson & J. E. Gedo (Eds.), *Hierarchical concepts in psychoanalysis.* New York: Guilford Press.

Bucci, W. (2002). The referential process, consciousness, and the sense of self. *Psychoanalytic Inquiry, 5,* 766–793.

Buchheim, A., Erk, S., George, C., Kachele, H., Ruchsow, M., Spitzer, M., et al. (2006). Measuring attachment representation in an fMRI environment: A pilot study. *Psychopathology, 39,* 144–152.

Bugental, J. F. (1987). *The art of the psychotherapist.* New York: Norton.

Chiron, C., Jambaque, I., Nabbout, R., Lounes, R., Syrota, A., & Dulac, O. (1997). The right brain hemisphere is dominant in human infants. *Brain, 120,* 1057–1065.

Cohen, M. X., & Shaver, P. R. (2004). Avoidant attachment and hemispheric lateralization of the processing of attachment- and emotion-related words. *Cognition and Emotion, 18,* 799–814.

Cozolino, L. (2002). *The neuroscience of psychotherapy.* New York: Norton.

Damasio, A. R. (1994). *Descartes' error.* New York: Grosset/Putnam.

Decety, J., & Chaminade, T. (2003). When the self represents the other: A new cognitive neuroscience view on psychological identification. *Consciousness and Cognition, 12,* 577–596.

Derryberry, D., & Tucker, D. M. (1994), Motivating the focus of attention. In P. M. Niedentahl & S. Kiyayama (Eds.), *The heart's eye: emotional influences in perception and attention.* San Diego: Academic Press.

Devinsky, O. (2000). Right cerebral hemispheric dominance for a sense of corporeal and emotional self. *Epilepsy & Behavior, 1,* 60–73.

Dorpat, T. L. (2001). Primary process communication. *Psychoanalytic Inquiry, 3,* 448–463.

Feinberg, T. E., & Keenan, J. P. (2005). Where in the brain is the self? *Consciousness and Cognition, 14,* 661–678.

Fonagy, P., Gergely, G., Jurist, E. L., & Target, M. (2002). *Affect regulation, mentalization and the development of the self.* New York: Other Press.

Fonagy P., & Target, M. (2002). Early intervention and the development of self-regulation. *Psychoanalytic Inquiry, 22,* 307–335.

Fonagy, P., & Target, M. (2005). Bridging the transmission gap: An end to an important mystery of attachment research? *Attachment & Human Development, 7,* 333–343.

Freud, S. (1966). Project for a scientific psychology. In J. Strachey (Ed. & Trans.), *The standard edition of the complete psychological works of Sigmund Freud* (Vol. I, pp. 295–397). London: Hogarth Press. (Original work published 1895)

Gainotti, G. (2006). Unconscious emotional memories and the right hemisphere. In M.

Mancia (Ed.), *Psychoanalysis and neuroscience* (pp. 151–173). Milan, Italy: Springer Milan.

Giovacchini, P. I. (1981). Object relations, deficiency states, and the acquisition of psychic structure. In S. Tutman, C. Kaye, & M. Zimmerman (Eds.), *Object and self: A developmental approach* (pp. 397–427). New York: International Universities Press.

Ginot, E. (2009). The empathic power of enactments. The link between neuropsychological processes and an expanded definition of empathy. *Psychoanalytic Psychology, 26*, 290–309.

Glass, R. M. (2008). Psychodynamic psychotherapy and research evidence. Bambi survives Godzilla? *The Journal of the American Medical Association, 300*, 1587–1589.

Grabner, R. H., Fink, A., & Neubauer, A. C. (2007). Brain correlates of self-related originality of ideas: Evidence from event-related power and phase-locking changes in the EEG. *Behavioral Neuroscience, 121*, 224–230.

Greenson, R. (1978). *Explorations in psychoanalysis.* New York: International Universities Press.

Henry, J. P. (1993). Psychological and physiological responses to stress: The right hemisphere and the hypothalamo-pituitary-adrenal axis, an inquiry into problems of human bonding. *Integrative Physiological and Behavioral Science, 28*, 369–387.

Jacobs, T. J. (1994). Nonverbal communications: Some reflections on their role in the psychoanalytic process and psychoanalytic education. *Journal of the American Psychoanalytic Association, 42*, 741–762.

Jung-Beeman, M., Bowden, E. M., Haberman, J., Frymiare, J. L., Arambel-Liu, S., Greenblatt, R., et al. (2004). Neural activity when people solve verbal problems with insight. *PLoS Biology, 2*, 0500–0510.

Keenan, J. P., Gallup, G. G., & Falk, D. (2003). *The face in the mirror: The search for the origins of consciousness.* New York: HarperCollins.

Keenan, J. P., Rubio, J., Racioppi, C., Johnson, A., & Barnacz, A. (2005). The right hemisphere and the dark side of consciousness. *Cortex, 41*, 695–704.

Kohut, H. (1971). *The analysis of the self.* New York: International University Press.

Le Grand, R., Mondloch, C., Maurer, D., & Brent, H. P. (2003). Expert face processing requires visual input to the right hemisphere during infancy. *Nature Neuroscience, 6*, 1108–1112.

Lyons-Ruth, K. (1999). The two-person unconscious: Intersubjective dialogue, enactive relational representation, and the emergence of new forms of relational organization. *Psychoanalytic Inquiry, 19*, 576–617.

Lyons-Ruth, K. (2000). "I sense that you sense that I sense . . .": Sander's recognition process and the specificity of relational moves in the psychotherapeutic setting. *Infant Mental Health Journal, 21*, 85–98.

Mahler, M., Pine, F., & Bergman, A. (1975). *The psychological birth of the human infant.* New York: Basic Books

Mancia, M. (2006). Implicit memory and early unrepressed unconscious: Their role in the therapeutic process (How the neurosciences can contribute to psychoanalysis). *International Journal of Psychoanalysis, 87*, 83–103.

Mandal, M. K., & Ambady, N. (2004). Laterality of facial expressions of emotion: Universal and culture-specific influences. *Behavioral Neurology, 15*, 23–34.

Marcus, D. M. (1997). On knowing what one knows. *Psychoanalytic Quarterly, 66*, 219–241.

Markowitsch, H. J., Reinkemeier, A., Kessler, J., Koyuncu, A., & Heiss, W. D. (2000).

Right amygdalar and temperofrontal activation during autobiographical, but not fictitious memory retrieval. *Behavioral Neurology, 12,* 181–190.

Maroda, K. J. (2005). Show some emotion: Completing the cycle of affective communication. In L. Aron & A. Harris (Eds.), *Revolutionary connections. Relational psychoanalysis: Vol. II. Innovation and expansion* (pp. 121–142). Hillsdale, NJ: Analytic Press.

Mathew, M. (1998). The body as instrument. *Journal of the British Association of Psychotherapists, 35,* 17–36.

Meares, R. (2005). *The metaphor of play. Origin and breakdown of personal being* (3rd ed.). London: Routledge.

Mikulincer, M., Shaver, P. R., & Pereg, D. (2003). Attachment theory and affect regulation: The dynamics, development, and cognitive consequences of attachment-related strategies. *Motivation and Emotion, 27,* 77–102.

Miller, B. L., Seeley, W. W., Mychack, P., Rosen, H. J., Mena, I., & Boone, K. (2001). Neuroanatomy of the self. Evidence from patients with frontotemporal dementia. *Neurology, 57,* 817–821.

Minagawa-Kawai, Y., Matsuoka, S., Dan, I., Naoi, N., Nakamura, K., & Kojima, S. (2009). Prefrontal activation associated with social attachment: Facial-emotion recognition in mothers and infants. *Cerebral Cortex, 19,* 284–292.

Mitchell, R. L. C., Elliott, R., Barry, M., Crittenden, A., & Woodruff, P. W. R. (2003). The neural response to emotional prosody, as revealed by functional magnetic resonance imaging. *Neuropsychologia, 41,* 1410–1421.

Mlot, C. (1998). Probing the biology of emotion. *Science, 280,* 1005–1007.

Molnar-Szakacs, I., Uddin, L. Q., & Iacoboni, M. (2005). Right-hemisphere motor facilitation by self-descriptive personality-trait words. *European Journal of Neuroscience, 21,* 2000–2006.

Ogden, P., Pain, C., Minton, K., & Fisher, J. (2005). Including the body in mainstream psychotherapy for traumatized individuals. *Psychologist-Psychoanalyst, 25,* 19–24.

Ohnishi, T., Moriguchi, Y., Matsuda, H., Mori, T., Hirakata, M., Imabayashi, E., et al. (2004). The neural network for the mirror system and mentalizing in normally developed children: An fMRI study. *NeuroReport, 15,* 1483–1487.

Orlinsky, D. E., & Howard, K. I. (1986). Process and outcome in psychotherapy. In S. L. Garfield & A. E. Bergin (Eds.), *Handbook of psychotherapy and behavior change* (3rd ed.). New York: Wiley.

Ovtscharoff, W., Jr., & Braun, K. (2001). Maternal separation and social isolation modulate the postnatal development of synaptic composition in the infralimbic cortex of *octodon degus. Neuroscience, 104,* 33–40.

Palombo, J., Bendicsen, H. K., & Koch, B. J. (2009). *Guide to psychoanalytic developmental theories.* New York: Springer.

Phelkos, J. L., Belsky, J., & Crnic, K. (1998). Earned security, daily stress, and parenting: A comparison of five alternative models. *Development and Psychopathology, 10,* 21–38.

Pincus, D., Freeman, W., & Modell, A. (2007). A neurobiological model of perception: Considerations for transference. *Psychoanalytic Psychology, 24,* 623–640.

Pipp, S., & Harmon, R. J. (1987). Attachment as regulation: A commentary. *Child Development, 58,* 648–652.

Prodan, C. I., Orbelo, D. M., Testa, J. A., & Ross, E. D. (2001). Hemispheric differences in recognizing upper and lower facial displays of emotion. *Neuropsychiatry, Neuropsychology and Behavioral Neurology, 14,* 206–212.

Ryan, R. (2007). Motivation and emotion: A new look and approach for two reemerging fields. *Motivation and Emotion, 31,* 1–3.

Sander, L. (1992). Letter to the editor. *International Journal of Psychoanalysis, 73,* 582–584.

Scaer, R. (2005). *The trauma spectrum: Hidden wounds and human resiliency.* New York: Norton.

Schachner, D. A., Shaver, P. R., & Mikulincer, M. (2005). Patterns of nonverbal behavior and sensitivity in the context of attachment relationships. *Journal of Nonverbal Behavior, 29,* 141–169.

Schore, A. N. (1994). *Affect regulation and the origin of the self.* Mahwah, NJ: Erlbaum.

Schore, A. N. (1996). The experience-dependent maturation of a regulatory system in the orbital prefrontal cortex and the origin of developmental psychopathology. *Development and Psychopathology, 8,* 59–87.

Schore, A. N. (1997). A century after Freud's *Project*: Is a rapprochement between psychoanalysis and neurobiology at hand? *Journal of the American Psychoanalytic Association, 45,* 807–840.

Schore, A. N. (2000). Attachment and the regulation of the right brain. *Attachment & Human Development, 2,* 23–47.

Schore, A. N. (2001a). The effects of a secure attachment relationship on right brain development, affect regulation, and infant mental health. *Infant Mental Health Journal, 22,* 7–66.

Schore, A. N. (2001b). The Seventh Annual John Bowlby Memorial Lecture. Minds in the making: Attachment, the self-organizing brain, and developmentally-oriented psychoanalytic psychotherapy. *British Journal of Psychotherapy, 17,* 299–328.

Schore, A. N. (2002). Advances in neuropsychoanalysis, attachment theory, and trauma research: Implications for self psychology. *Psychoanalytic Inquiry, 22,* 433–484.

Schore, A. N. (2003a). *Affect dysregulation and disorders of the self.* New York: Norton.

Schore, A. N. (2003b). *Affect regulation and the repair of the self.* New York: Norton.

Schore, A. N. (2005). Attachment, affect regulation, and the developing right brain: Linking developmental neuroscience to pediatrics. *Pediatrics in Review, 26,* 204–211.

Schore, A. N. (2007). Review of *Awakening the dreamer: Clinical journeys* by Philip M. Bromberg. *Psychoanalytic Dialogues, 17,* 753–767.

Schore, J. R., & Schore, A. N. (2008). Modern attachment theory: The central role of affect regulation in development and treatment. *Clinical Social Work Journal, 36,* 9–20.

Shamay-Tsoory, S. G., Tomer, R., Berger, B. D., & Aharon-Peretz, J. (2003). Characterization of empathy deficits following prefrontal brain damage: The role of the right ventromedial prefrontal cortex. *Journal of Cognitive Neuroscience, 15,* 324–337.

Shaw, R. (2004). The embodied psychotherapist: An exploration of the therapists' somatic phenomena within the therapeutic encounter. *Psychotherapy Research, 14,* 271–288.

Shuren, J. E., & Grafman, J. (2002). The neurology of reasoning. *Archives of Neurology, 59,* 916–919.

Siegel, D. J. (1999). *Developing mind: Toward a neurobiology of interpersonal experience.* New York: Norton.

Simpson, G., Williams, J., & Segall, A. (2007). Social work education and clinical learning. *Clinical Social Work Journal, 35,* 3–14.

Stern, D. N., Bruschweiler-Stern, N., Harrison, A. M., Lyons-Ruth, K., Morgan, A. C., Nahum, J. P., et al. (1998). The process of therapeutic change involving implicit knowledge: Some implications of developmental observations for adult psychotherapy. *Infant Mental Health Journal, 19,* 300–308.

Sullivan, R. M., & Gratton, A. (2002). Prefrontal cortical regulation of hypothalamic-pituitary-adrenal function in the rat and implications for psychopathology: Side matters. *Psychoneuroendocrinology, 27,* 99–114.

Trevarthen, C. (1990). Growth and education of the hemispheres. In C. Trevarthen (Ed.), *Brain circuits and functions of the mind* (pp. 334–363). Cambridge, UK: Cambridge University Press.

Tucker, D. M. (1992). Developing emotions and cortical networks. In M. R. Gunnar & C. A. Nelson (Eds.), *Minnesota symposium on child psychology: Vol. 24. Developmental behavioral neuroscience* (pp. 75–128). Hillsdale, NJ: Erlbaum.

Tutte, J. C. (2004). The concept of psychical trauma: A bridge in interdisciplinary space. *International Journal of Psychoanalysis, 85,* 897–921.

van Lancker, D., & Cummings, J. L. (1999). Expletives: Neurolinguistic and neurobehavioral perspectives on swearing. *Brain Research Reviews, 31,* 83–104.

Watt, D. F. (2003). Psychotherapy in an age of neuroscience: Bridges to affective neuroscience. In J. Corrigall & H. Wilkinson (Eds.), *Revolutionary connections. Psychotherapy and neuroscience* (pp. 79–115). London: Karnac.

Whitehead, C .C. (2006). Neo-psychoanalysis: A paradigm for the 21st century. *Journal of the Academy of Psychoanalysis and Dynamic Psychiatry, 34,* 603–627.

CHAPTER 2

Relational Trauma and the Developing Right Brain: An Interface of Psychoanalytic Self Psychology and Neuroscience

At the present time a number of scientific and clinical disciplines are simultaneously experiencing a rapid expansion of relevant data and even a reorganization of their underlying theoretical concepts. Indeed the term *paradigm shift* is appearing in a number of literatures. Although current significant advances in various technologies and the computer sciences have catalyzed this growth spurt, an important contributor has been the rapid communication of information not only within but also between disciplines. In this period of accelerated growth of essential information about the human condition and the natural world, the transfer of knowledge across disciplinary boundaries is occurring at a faster rate. This trend is reflected in an increasing interest in interdisciplinary studies, and in integrated models that synthesize data generated at the interface of different scientific and clinical fields.

Within this context there exists a potential for new and fresh solutions to certain fundamental problems, especially those concerning the essential mechanisms that lie at the core of adaptive and maladaptive human functions. Until very recently these problems have been studied from the unique vantage points of various scientific perspectives that span the sociological, psychological, biological, and chemical domains. The overemphasis on specialization within each of these disciplines has also fostered their isolation from one another, which has in turn inadvertently increased an artificial dichotomous separation between, for example, psychology and biology, brain and mind, mind and body, cognition and emotion. Earlier impermeable boundaries of knowledge between disciplines also intensified a tension and indeed a conflict between those studying uncon-

scious involuntary processes and those studying conscious voluntary processes;
that is, between psychoanalysis, the science of unconscious process, and psychology, the study of behavior.

This ambivalent relationship between psychoanalysis and the other sciences
has existed since its creation by Sigmund Freud. And yet it is often forgotten
that Freud's early career was in neurology, and that in 1895 he wrote *Project for
a Scientific Psychology*, an attempt to create "a psychology which shall be a
natural science" (Schore, 1997a). In this remarkable document Freud utilized
what was then known about neurophysiology and biology to begin to construct
a set of regulatory principles for psychological processes and a neuropsychological model of brain function. Freud did not publish the *Project* in his lifetime
and over the course of his career never returned to the problem of creating a
model that could integrate the biological and psychological realms. And yet he
predicted that at some point in the future "we shall have to find a point of contact with biology" (Freud, 1913/1955). Freud thus saw neurobiology as a discipline that could bridge the gap between biology and psychoanalysis, especially
in the study of the unconscious and its fundamental impact on all aspects of the
human experience.

Over the course of the last century a number of significant transformations
have occurred in Freud's theory, although much of this work has not transferred
outside of the field. The theoretical core of psychoanalysis, almost unchanged
for most of its first century, is now undergoing a substantial reformulation from
an intrapsychic unconscious to a relational unconscious, whereby the unconscious mind of one communicates with the unconscious mind of another. The
scaffolding of clinical psychoanalysis is supported by conceptions of psychic development and structure, and it is these basic concepts that are now being refor-
mulated. Self psychology, emergent from the seminal work of Heinz Kohut,
represents perhaps the most significant updating of classical psychoanalysis since
its inception. In 1971, Kohut, trained in neurology and then psychoanalysis,
published his classic volume *The Analysis of the Self*, a detailed exposition of the
central role of the self in human existence. He subsequently expanded the theoretical framework of self psychology in a second volume, *The Restoration of the
Self* (1977), and finally in *How Does Analysis Cure?* (1984).

In all his clinical work and writings, Kohut attempted to explore the four basic
problems of psychoanalysis he initially addressed in his seminal volume: How do
early relational affective transactions with the social environment facilitate the
emergence of self? (*development of the self*) How are these experiences internalized into maturing self-regulating structures? (*structuralization of the self*) How
do early deficits of self-structure lead to later self-pathologies? (*psychopathogenesis*) and How can a therapeutic relationship lead to a restoration of self? (*mechanism of psychotherapeutic change*)

Despite the fact that he was originally trained as a neurologist, Kohut was
highly ambivalent about the incorporation of scientific data into the core of psychoanalytic self psychology. Indeed, like Freud before him, he eschewed his ear-

lier neurological knowledge and attempted to create a purely psychological model of the unconscious systems that underlie all human functioning. However, in the last 10 years, over the course of and since the "decade of the brain," an interdisciplinary perspective has emerged within both psychoanalysis and the disciplines that border it. Due to a common interest in the essential rapid bodily based affective processes that lie beneath conscious awareness, a productive dialogue is now occurring between psychoanalysis and neuroscience. This convergence has facilitated the emergence of a new discipline, neuropsychoanalysis, and a subspecialization, developmental psychoanalysis (Schore, 1997a). This discipline returns to Freud's attempt to create "a psychology which shall be a natural science" by specifically focusing on the essential psychobiological role of the unconscious in all human affect, cognition, and behavior.

In a number of works I have suggested that the time is right for a rapprochement between psychoanalysis and the biological sciences (Schore, 1994, 1997a, 2002a, 2002b, 2003a, 2005a). In this period when neuroscience is "rediscovering the unconscious," neuropsychoanalysis is identifying the "intrapsychic" brain systems involved in a redefined dynamic unconscious, and developmental psychoanalysis is generating a complex model of the social-emotional origins of the self and the early ontogeny of the biological substrate of the human unconscious. It is now clear that Freud was correct in positing the unconscious mind develops before the conscious, and that the early development of the unconscious is equivalent to the genesis of a self-system that operates beneath conscious verbal levels for the rest of the life span. I believe a deeper understanding of early human development can never be attained by narrowly focusing infant studies on the precursors of language, conscious thought, and voluntary behavior.

A complete model of human development (and psychoanalysis) can only be psychobiological, not merely psychological. A deeper understanding of one of the fundamental questions of science, why early developmental processes are essential to the short- and long-term survival of the organism, will not come from single or even multiple discoveries within any one discipline (Schore, 1994). Rather, an integration of related fields is essential to the creation of a heuristic model of both developmental structures and functions that can accommodate and interpret the data of various biological and psychological disciplines, and can freely shift back and forth between their different levels of analysis.

In this chapter on the integration of self psychology and neuroscience, I outline my neuropsychoanalytic work on the interpersonal neurobiological origins of the self. I first present a brief overview of Kohut's concepts that represent the core of self psychology. Subsequently I integrate interdisciplinary data in order to construct a neuropsychoanalytic conception of the *development* and *structuralization* of the self, focusing on the experience-dependent maturation of the early developing right brain. Then, in a major focus of this work, I apply this developmental neuropsychoanalytic perspective to the *psychopathogenesis* of severe deficits in the self-system. Citing my work in this area, I articulate a model of the self psychology and neurobiology of early relational trauma and the etiology of pathological dissociation, an early forming defense that is a cardinal feature of a number of early forming psychopathologies. I end with some thoughts on *psychotherapeutic change* and argue that the time is right for a rapprochement between psychoanalysis and neuroscience. Throughout I suggest that the "point of contact with biology" that Freud referred to is specifically the central role of right brain psychobiological processes in the unconscious regulation of affect, motivation, and cognition, areas of intense interest to both contemporary self psychology and neuroscience.

SELF PSYCHOLOGICAL DEVELOPMENTAL MODELS: PSYCHOBIOLOGY OF ATTACHMENT

Perhaps Kohut's most original and outstanding intellectual contribution was his developmental construct of selfobject. Indeed, self psychology is built upon a fundamental developmental principle—that parents with mature psychological organizations serve as selfobjects that perform critical regulatory functions for the infant who possesses an immature, incomplete psychological organization. The child is thus provided, at nonverbal levels beneath conscious awareness, with selfobject experiences that directly affect the vitalization and structural cohesion of the self. The selfobject construct contains two important theoretical components. First, the concept of the mother–infant pair as a self–selfobject unit emphasizes that early development is essentially interdependence between self and objects in a system. This core concept was a major intellectual impetus for the expansion of the intersubjective perspective in psychoanalysis. Indeed, Kohut's emphasis on the dyadic aspects of unconscious communications shifted psychoanalysis from a solely intrapsychic to a more balanced relational perspective. This challenged psychoanalysis to integrate the realms of a one-person psychology and a two-person psychology.

The second component of the selfobject construct is the concept of regulation. In his developmental speculations, Kohut (1971, 1977) stated that the infant's dyadic reciprocal regulatory transactions with selfobjects allow for the maintenance of his or her internal homeostatic equilibrium. These regulating self–selfobject experiences provide the particular intersubjective affective experiences that evoke the emergence and maintenance of the self (Kohut, 1984). Siegel observes, "Kohut makes major contributions to the understanding of emotional life, and his conceptualizations have far-reaching implications for the understanding and treatment of emotional states" (1996). Kohut's idea that regulatory systems are fundamentally involved with affect is supported in current interdisciplinary studies, which are highlighting not only the centrality of affect but also affect regulation.

Despite his intense interest in the early ontogeny of the self, over the course of his career Kohut neither spelled out the precise developmental details of his model, nor did he attend to the significant advances in developmental psychology and psychoanalysis that were occurring simultaneously to his own theorizing. There is now agreement that current psychoanalysis is "anchored in its scientific base in developmental psychology and in the biology of attachment and affects" (Cooper, 1987). At this point in time, self psychology is incorporating a broad range of current developmental research into its theoretical model. In my own contributions to this effort, I have integrated recent advances in attachment theory into the field (Schore, 2002b, 2003a, 2005b).

Overviewing and integrating these data, it is now established that the essential task of the first year of human life is the creation of a secure attachment bond of emotional communication between the infant and the primary caregiver. Research now suggests "learning how to communicate represents perhaps the most important developmental process to take place during infancy" (Papousek & Papousek, 1995). Through visual-facial, auditory-prosodic, and tactile-gestural communications, caregiver and infant learn the rhythmic structure of the other and modify their behavior to fit that structure, thereby co-creating a specifically fitted interaction.

Kohut described critical episodes of "empathic mirroring," in which "The most significant relevant basic interactions between mother and child usually lie in the visual area: The child's bodily display is responded to by the gleam in the mother's eye" (Kohut, 1971). During bodily based affective communications embedded in mutual gaze transactions, the psychobiologically attuned mother synchronizes the spatiotemporal patterning of her exogenous sensory stimulation with the spontaneous overt manifestations of the infant's organismic rhythms. By way of this contingent responsivity, the mother appraises the nonverbal expressions of her infant's internal arousal and affective states, regulates them, and communicates them back to the infant. To accomplish this, the primary caregiver must successfully modulate nonoptimal high or low levels of stimulation that would induce supra-heightened or extremely low levels of arousal in the child. Secure attachment depends upon the mother's sensitive psychobiological attunement to the infant's internal states of arousal.

Importantly, research now clearly demonstrates that the primary caregiver is not always attuned and optimally mirroring, that there are frequent moments of mis-attunement in the dyad, ruptures of the attachment bond. The disruption of attachment bonds leads to a regulatory failure and an impaired autonomic homeostasis. Studies of "interactive repair" following dyadic mis-attunement (Tronick, 1989) support Kohut's (1977) assertion that the parental selfobject acts to "remedy the child's homeostatic imbalance." In this pattern of "disruption and repair" (Beebe & Lachmann, 1994), the "good enough" caregiver who induces a stress response through mis-attunement re-invokes a re-attunement, a regulation of the infant's negatively charged arousal, in a timely fashion.

In current psychobiological models, attachment is defined as the interactive regulation of states of biological synchronicity between and within organisms (Schore, 2000, 2003a, 2005b). The dual regulatory processes of affect synchrony, which creates states of positive arousal, and interactive repair, which modulates states of negative arousal, are the fundamental building blocks of attachment and its associated emotions. These interactive regulatory mechanisms optimize the communication of emotional states within an intimate dyad and represent the psychobiological underpinning of empathy, a phenomenon of intense interest to self psychology. Kohut (1977) deduced that as a result of the empathic merger of the child's rudimentary psyche with the maternal selfobject's highly developed psychic organization, the child experiences the feeling states of the selfobject as if they were his or her own. Selfobjects are thus external psychobiological regulators that facilitate the regulation of affective experiences, and they act at nonverbal levels beneath conscious awareness in the regulation of self-esteem and the maintenance of self-cohesiveness (Schore, 1994, 2002b).

SELF PSYCHOLOGICAL MODELS OF STRUCTURALIZATION: LINKS TO INTERPERSONAL NEUROBIOLOGY

A cardinal principle of self psychology dictates that, as a result of optimal self–selfobject relational experiences, the infant becomes able to perform the drive-regulating, -adaptive, and -integrating functions that had previously been performed by the external object. Kohut specifically posited that phase-appropriate maternal optimal frustrations of the infant elicit "transmuting internalization," the developmental process by which selfobject function is internalized by the infant and psychological regulatory structures are formed. Developmental data are consonant with this, although interdisciplinary data emphasize that not only optimal stressful frustration but also interactive repair is essential to the formation of a structural system that can regulate stressful affect. The formative experiences of the self are built out of internalized selfobject functions, which facilitate the emergence of more complex regulatory structures.

Recent research also supports Kohut's speculation that the infant's regulatory transactions with the maternal selfobject allow for maintenance of the infant's homeostatic equilibrium. According to Ovtscharoff and Braun (2001), "The dyadic interaction between the newborn and the mother . . . serves as a regulator of the developing individual's internal homeostasis. The regulatory function of the newborn–mother interaction may be an essential promoter to ensure the normal development and maintenance of synaptic connections during the establishment of functional brain circuits" (p. 33). These researchers conclude that subtle emotion-regulating attachment interactions permanently alter the brain by establishing and maintaining developing limbic circuits (Ziabreva, Poeggel, Schnabel, & Braun, 2003).

A large body of studies now clarifies the developmental neurobiology of the selfobject mechanism. In my own work I have suggested that the self-organization of the developing brain occurs in the context of a relationship with another self, another brain. More specifically, the self–selfobject relationship is embedded in infant–caregiver right-hemisphere–to–right-hemisphere affective attachment communications (Schore, 1994, 2000, 2003a, 2005a). In light of the observations that the emotion-processing human limbic system myelinates in the first year and a half (Kinney, Brody, Kloman, & Gilles, 1988), and that the early maturing right hemisphere (Allman, Watson, Tetreault, & Hakeem, 2005; Bogolepova & Malofeeva, 2001; Chiron et al., 1997; Gupta et al., 2005; Sun et al., 2005)—which is deeply connected into the limbic system—is undergoing a growth spurt at this time, attachment experiences specifically impact limbic and cortical areas of the developing right cerebral hemisphere (Cozolino, 2002; Henry, 1993; Schore, 1994; Siegel, 1999).

In very recent work on mother–infant emotional communication, Lenzi et al. (2009) offer data from a functional magnetic resonance imaging study "supporting the theory that the right hemisphere is more involved than the left hemisphere in emotional processing and thus, mothering" (p. 1131). Also confirming this model, Minagawa-Kawai et al. (2009) report a near-infrared spectroscopy study of infant–mother attachment at 12 months and conclude, "our results are in agreement with that of Schore (2000) who addressed the importance of the right hemisphere in the attachment system." (p. 289). Supporting Kohut's speculations on empathic mirroring, neuroscience researchers now conclude that developing children rely upon a "right hemisphere–mirroring mechanism—interfacing with the limbic system that processes the meaning of observed or imitated emotion" (Dapretto et al., 2006, p. 30).

Ongoing neurobiological research on the mother–infant intersubjective dialogue indicates, "A number of functions located within the right hemisphere work together to aid monitoring of a baby. As well as emotion and face processing the right hemisphere is also specialized in auditory perception, the perception of intonation, attention, and tactile information" (Bourne & Todd, 2004, pp. 22–23). Social experiences thus facilitate the experience-dependent critical period maturation of right brain systems that process visual-facial, auditory-prosodic, and tactile-gestural affective communications. From infancy through all later stages of the life span, the right hemisphere is dominant for the nonconscious reception, expression, and communication of emotion, as well as the cognitive and physiological components of emotional processing (Schore, 2003a, 2003b). With respect to empathy, a core process of self psychology, it is now thought that "self-awareness, empathy, identification with others, and more generally intersubjective processes, are largely dependent upon . . . right hemisphere resources, which are the first to develop" (Decety & Chaminade, 2003, p. 591).

Furthermore, the "complex psychological regulatory structures" described by self psychology can now be located in "the right hemispheric specialization in regulating stress- and emotion-related processes" (Sullivan & Dufresne, 2006). Indeed, the brain's major self-regulatory systems are located in the orbital prefrontal areas of the right hemisphere that undergo an anatomical maturation in postnatal periods of mammalian development (Bradshaw & Schore, 2007). The experience-dependent maturation of this affect regulatory system is thus directly related to the origin of the self (Schore, 1994). Earlier research documented that the development of the self and self-awareness is reflected in the ability of 2-year-olds to recognize their own visual image in a mirror (Amsterdam, 1972). Functional magnetic resonance neuroimaging studies show that when subjects look at an image of their own face, activation is seen in the occipito-temporo-parietal junction and the right frontal operculum (Sugiura et al., 2005), and that self-face recognition activates a frontoparietal "mirror" network in the right hemisphere (Uddin, Kaplan, Molnar-Szakacs, Zaidel, & Iacoboni, 2005).

Indeed, a substantial amount of research indicates that the right hemisphere is specialized for generating self-awareness and self-recognition, and for the processing of "self-related material" (Decety & Chaminade, 2003; Feinberg & Keenan, 2005; Fossati et al., 2004; Miller et al., 2001; Perrin et al., 2005; Platek, Keenan, Gallup, & Mohamed, 2004). Neuroscientists now suggest that the essential function of the right lateralized system is to "maintain a coherent, continuous, and unified sense of self" (Devinsky, 2000). Summarizing this knowledge, Molnar-Szakacs, Uddin, and Iacoboni (2005) assert, "Studies have demonstrated a special contribution of the right hemisphere (RH) in self-related cognition, own-body perception, self-awareness, autobiographical memory and theory of mind. Many studies of self-face recognition have also found an RH advantage, suggesting a special role for the RH in processing material related to the self" (p. 2000). These data clearly indicate that self psychology is in essence a psychology of the unique functions of the right brain.

SELF PSYCHOLOGICAL MODELS OF PSYCHOPATHOGENESIS: NEGATIVE IMPACT OF ATTACHMENT TRAUMA ON THE RIGHT BRAIN

At the core of Kohut's model of psychopathogenesis is the central hypothesis that the mother's traumatic failures in empathic mirroring lead to enduring defects in the infant's emerging self. Self psychology thus proposes that disturbed physiological regulation results from primary disturbances in selfobject experiences, and that a defective self and an impaired regulatory structure lie at the foundation of early forming psychopathologies. Kohut (1971) highlighted the importance of "the role of specific environmental factors (the personality of the parents, for example; certain *traumatic* external events) in the genesis of the developmental arrest" (p. 11), especially when "the mother's responses are grossly unempathetic and unreliable . . . no transmuting internalization can take place, and the psyche . . . does not develop the various internal functions which re-establish narcissistic equilibrium" (p. 65).

Although there is a long history of controversy within psychoanalysis, the field is now very interested in the problem of trauma and in the unique survival defenses for dealing with early relational trauma. Laub and Auerhahn (1993) propose that the essential experience of trauma is a disruption of the link between the "self" and the mothering "empathic other," and therefore the maternal introject, or mothering (selfobject regulatory) function, is deficient or "damaged." They further contend, "It is the nature of trauma to elude our knowledge because of both defense and deficit . . . To protect ourselves from affect, we must, at times, avoid knowledge. We defend against feelings of rage, cynicism, shame, and fear by not knowing them consciously. Trauma also overwhelms and defeats our capacity to organize it" (p. 288). In line with these self psychological principles, current neuropsychoanalytic models now posit that under the impact of developmental trauma, specific defensive and defective regulatory structures develop that lie at the core of the patient's psychopathology (Schore, 2002b).

Psychoanalysis, psychiatry, and developmental traumatology are all now converging on dissociation, the bottom-line *survival defense* against overwhelming, unbearable emotional experiences. Longitudinal attachment research demonstrates an association between traumatic childhood events and proneness to dissociation, described as "detachment from an unbearable situation," "the escape when there is no escape," and "a last resort defensive strategy" (Schore, 2003b, 2009). Although Kohut never used the term *dissociation*, in his last book (1984) he characterized an early interaction in which the traumatized child "walls himself off" from traumatizing experiences:

> If the mother's empathic ability has remained infantile, that is, if she tends to respond with panic to the baby's anxiety, then a deleterious chain will be set into motion. She may chronically wall herself off from the baby, thus depriving him of the beneficial effect of merging with her as she returns from experiencing mild anxiety to calmness. Alternatively, she may continue to respond with panic, in which case two negative consequences may ensue: the mother may lay the groundwork in the child for a lifelong propensity toward the uncurbed spreading of anxiety or other emotions, or by forcing the child to wall himself off from such an overly intense and thus traumatizing [experience, she] may foster in the child an impoverished psychic organization, the psychic organization of a person who will later be unable to be empathic himself, to experience human experiences, in essence, to be fully human. (p. 83)

What can ongoing studies in developmental psychology, affective neuroscience, and neuropsychoanalysis tell us about the neurobiology and neuropsychology of attachment-relational trauma, and about dissociation, the mechanism by which humans "wall themselves off" from overwhelming emotional trauma? In this last section I discuss interdisciplinary studies indicating that experiences with a traumatizing caregiver negatively impact the child's attachment security, right brain maturation, and sense of self, and thereby lay the groundwork for the use of pathological dissociation in various self-pathologies.

Developmental Psychobiology of Relational Trauma

During the brain growth spurt, relational trauma–induced arousal dysregulation precludes the aforementioned visual-facial, auditory-prosodic, and tactile-gestural attachment communications and alters the development of essential right brain functions. In contrast to an optimal attachment scenario, in a growth-inhibiting relational environment, the primary caregiver induces traumatic states of enduring negative affective arousal in the child. This caregiver is inaccessible, reacts to her infant's expressions of emotions and stress inappropriately and/or rejectingly, and therefore shows minimal or unpredictable participation in the various types of arousal-regulating processes. Instead of modulating she induces extreme levels of stimulation and arousal, very high in abuse and/or very low in neglect. Because the caregiver provides no interactive repair, the infant's intense negative affective states last for long periods of time.

Studies in developmental traumatology reveal that the infant's psychobiological reaction to trauma is comprised of two separate response patterns: hyperarousal and dissociation (Schore, 2001, 2002c). In the initial hyperarousal stage, the maternal haven of safety suddenly becomes a source of threat, triggering a startle reaction in the infant's right hemisphere, the locus of both the attachment and the fear motivational systems. The maternal stressor activates the hypothalamic-pituitary-adrenal (HPA) stress axis, eliciting a sudden increase of the energy-expending sympathetic component of the infant's autonomic nervous system (ANS). This results in significantly elevated heart rate, blood pressure, and respiration, the somatic expressions of a dysregulated psychobiological state of fear-terror. This active state of sympathetic hyperarousal is expressed in increased secretion of corticotropin releasing factor (CRF)—the brain's major stress hormone. CRF regulates sympathetic catecholamine activity, creating a hypermetabolic state in the developing brain.

But a second, later forming reaction to relational trauma is dissociation, in which the child disengages from stimuli in the external world—traumatized infants are observed to be "staring off into space with a glazed look." This parasympathetic dominant state of conservation-withdrawal occurs in helpless and hopeless stressful situations in which the individual becomes inhibited and strives to avoid attention in order to become "unseen." The dissociative metabolic shutdown state is a primary regulatory process by which the stressed individual passively disengages in order to conserve energies, foster survival by the risky posture of feigning death, and allow restitution of depleted resources by immobility. In this hypometabolic state heart rate, blood pressure, and respiration are decreased, while pain numbing and blunting endogenous opiates are elevated. This energy-conserving parasympathetic (vagal) mechanism mediates the "profound detachment" of dissociation.

In fact there are two parasympathetic vagal systems in the brain stem medulla (Porges, 1997). The ventral vagal complex rapidly regulates cardiac output to foster fluid engagement and disengagement with the social environment, aspects of a secure attachment bond of emotional communication. On the other hand, activity of the dorsal vagal complex—associated with intense emotional states and immobilization—is responsible for the severe metabolic depression, hypoarousal, and pain blunting of dissociation. The traumatized infant's sudden state switch from sympathetic hyperarousal into parasympathetic dissociation is described by Porges (1997) as "the sudden and rapid transition from an unsuccessful strategy of struggling requiring massive sympathetic activation to the metabolically conservative immobilized state mimicking death associated with the dorsal vagal complex" (p. 75). Whereas the ventral vagal complex exhibits rapid and transitory activations, the dorsal vagal nucleus exhibits an involuntary and prolonged pattern of vagal outflow, creating lengthy "void" states associated with pathological dissociative detachment.

How are the dual traumatic contexts of hyperarousal and dissociative hypoarousal expressed behaviorally within the mother–infant dyad? Observational research demonstrates a link between frightening maternal behavior, dissociation, and disorganized infant attachment (Schuengel, Bakermans-Kranenburg, & Van IJzendoorn, 1999). Hesse and Main (1999) observe the mother's frightening behavior: "in non-play contexts, stiff-legged 'stalking' of infant on all fours in a hunting posture; exposure of canine tooth accompanied by hissing; deep growls directed at infant" (p. 511). In recent work, Hesse and Main (2006) document a fear alarm is triggered in the infant when the mother enters a dissociative freeze state: "Here the parent appears to have become completely unresponsive to, or even aware of, the external surround, including the physical and verbal behavior of their infant. . . . [W]e observed one mother who remained seated in an immobilized and uncomfortable position with her hand in the air, blankly staring into space for 50 sec" (p. 321). Note the intergenerational transmission of not only relational trauma but also the bottom-line defense against traumatic emotional experiences, dissociation.

Right Brain Pathological Dissociation and Self Psychological Deficits

Workers in the field of developmental traumatology now assert that the overwhelming stress of maltreatment in childhood is associated with adverse influences on more than just behavior, but also on brain development (De Bellis et al., 1999). During the intergenerational transmission of attachment trauma, the infant is matching the rhythmic structures of the mother's dysregulated arousal states. This synchronization is registered in the firing patterns of the stress-sensitive corticolimbic regions of the right brain, dominant for coping with negative affects (Davidson, Ekman, Saron, Senulis, & Friesen, 1990). Describing the essential survival functions of this lateralized system, Schutz (2005) notes, "The right hemisphere operates a distributed network for rapid responding to danger and other urgent problems. It preferentially processes environmental challenge, stress and pain and manages self-protective responses such as avoidance and escape" (p. 15). The right brain is fundamentally involved in an avoidant-defensive mechanism for coping with emotional stress, including the passive survival strategy of dissociation.

Current neurobiological data can be utilized to create models of the mechanism by which attachment trauma negatively impacts the right brain. Adamec, Blundell, & Burton (2003) report experimental data that "implicate neuroplasticity in right hemispheric limbic circuitry in mediating long-lasting changes in negative affect following brief but severe stress" (p. 1264). According to Gadea, Gomez, Gonzalez-Bono, and Salvador (2005), mild to moderate negative affective experiences activate the right hemisphere, but an intense experience "might interfere with right hemisphere processing, with eventual damage if some critical point is reached" (p. 136). This damage is specifically hyperarousal-induced apoptotic cell death in the hypermetabolic right brain. Thus, via a switch into a hypoarousal, a hypometabolic state allows for cell survival at times of intense excitotoxic oxidative stress (Schore, 1997b, 2001, 2002c, 2003b).

Recall that right cortical areas and their connections with right subcortical structures are in a critical period of growth during early human development. The massive psychobiological stress associated with attachment trauma sets the stage for the characterological use of right brain pathological dissociation when encountering later stressors. Converging evidence indicates that early abuse negatively impacts limbic system maturation, producing enduring neurobiological alterations that underlie affective instability, inefficient stress tolerance, memory impairment, and dissociative disturbances. In this manner, traumatic stress in childhood leads to self-modulation of painful affect by directing attention away from internal emotional states (Lane, Ahern, Schwartz, & Kaszniak, 1997). The right brain, dominant for attention (Raz, 2004) and pain processing (Symonds, Gordon, Bixby, & Mande, 2006), thus generates dissociation, a defense by which intense negative affects associated with emotional pain are blocked from consciousness.

Congruent with developmental and clinical models, Spitzer, Wilert, Grabe, Rizos, and Freyberger (2004) report a transcranial magnetic stimulation study of adults and conclude, "In dissociation-prone individuals, a trauma that is perceived and processed by the right hemisphere will lead to a 'disruption in the usually integrated functions of consciousness" (p. 168). In functional magnetic resonance imaging research, Lanius et al. (2005) show predominantly right hemispheric activation in psychiatric patients while they are dissociating. They conclude that dissociation, an escape from the overwhelming emotions associated with the traumatic memory, can be interpreted as representing a nonverbal response to the traumatic memory.

These studies are exploring the evolution of a developmentally impaired regulatory system and provide evidence that prefrontal cortical and limbic areas of the right hemisphere are centrally involved in the deficits in mind and body associated with a pathological dissociative response (Schore, 2002c, 2009). This hemisphere, more so than the left, is densely reciprocally interconnected with emotion-processing limbic regions, as well as with subcortical areas that generate both the arousal and autonomic bodily based aspect of emotions. Sympathetic nervous system activity is manifest in tight engagement with the external environment and high level of energy mobilization, whereas the parasympathetic component drives disengagement from the external environment and utilizes low levels of internal energy (Recordati, 2003). These ANS components are uncoupled in relational trauma.

In a recent psychoanalytic formulation that echoes Kohut's "uncurbed spreading of anxiety or other emotions," Bromberg (2006) links right brain trauma to autonomic hyperarousal, "a chaotic and terrifying flooding of affect that can threaten to overwhelm sanity and imperil psychological survival" (p. 33). Dissociation is then automatically and immediately triggered as the fundamental defense to the arousal dysregulation of overwhelming affective states. And in the psychiatric literature, Nijenhuis (2000) asserts that "somatoform dissociation" is an outcome of early onset traumatization expressed as a lack of integration of sensorimotor experiences, reactions, and functions of the individual's self-representation. Dissociatively detached individuals are not only detached from the environment but also from the self—their body, their actions, and their sense of identity (Allen, Console, & Lewis, 1999). Crucian et al. (2000) describe "a dissociation between the emotional evaluation of an event and the physiological reaction to that event, with the process being dependent on intact right hemisphere function" (p. 643).

Pathological dissociation thus reflects the chronic disintegration of a right brain system and a resultant adaptive failure of its capacity to rapidly and nonconsciously detect, process, and cope with unbearable emotional information and overwhelming survival threat. A poorly developed right cortical-subcortical implicit self-system is inefficient at recognizing and processing external stimuli (exteroceptive information coming from the relational environment) and on a moment-to-moment basis integrating them with internal stimuli (interoceptive information from the body). This too frequent failure of integration of the higher right hemisphere with the lower right brain induces an instant collapse of both subjectivity and intersubjectivity, even at lower levels of interpersonal stress.

In summary, the developing brain imprints not only the overwhelming affective states that are at the core of attachment trauma but also the primitive defense used against these affects—the regulatory strategy of dissociation. It is now established that maternal care influences both the infant's reactivity (Menard, Champagne, & Meaney, 2004), and the transmission of individual differences in defensive responses (Parent et al., 2005). A large body of psychiatric, psychological, and neurological studies supports the link between childhood trauma and pathological dissociation (e.g., Dikel, Fennell, & Gilmore, 2003; Draijer & Langeland, 1999; Liotti, 2004; Macfie, Cicchetti, & Toth, 2001; Merckelbach & Muris, 2001).

CONCLUSION: RAPPROCHEMENT BETWEEN PSYCHOANALYSIS AND NEUROSCIENCE

Researchers now conclude that, due to dissociation, elements of a trauma are not integrated into a unitary whole or an integrated sense of self (van der Kolk et al., 1996). The symptomatology of pathological dissociation, or what Kohut described as "walling oneself off" from intense, traumatizing experience, thus represents a structural impairment and deficiency of the right brain, the locus of a "corporeal image of self" (Devinsky, 2000), affective empathy (Decety & Chaminade, 2003; Schore, 1994), and a "sense of humanness" (Mendez & Lim, 2004).

Recall Kohut's speculation that early trauma acts as a growth-inhibiting environment for the developing self, one which generates "an impoverished psychic organization," a deficit in being empathic, and an inability "to be fully human." The self-depleting, structure-altering cost of characterological dissociation is thus a central psychopathogenetic concept of both self psychology and neuroscience.

A central tenet of Kohut's model of psychopathogenesis is that the long-term effects of chronic maternal failure to provide growth-facilitating selfobject regulatory functions is the genesis of a "developmental arrest." Recall the self psychological proposal that due to early trauma the developing selfobject regulatory function is deficient or "damaged." This developmental impairment can now be identified as a maturational failure of the right brain affect regulatory system. A large body of clinical observations and psychiatric research strongly suggests that the most significant consequence of early relational trauma is the child's failure to develop the capacity to self-regulate the intensity and duration of emotional states. The principle that maltreatment in childhood is associated with adverse influences on brain development specifically refers to an impairment of a higher circuit of emotion regulation on the right side of the brain.

At the beginning of this chapter I stated that a central area of inquiry of Kohut's psychoanalytic theory was the problem of how the therapeutic relationship scaffolds the "restoration of self." Early relational trauma and the characterological use of the right brain strategy of pathological dissociation are common elements of the histories of severe self-pathologies of personality disorders, a clinical population of increasing interest to self psychology and psychotherapists in general. A large multicenter study of adult patients with a history of early childhood trauma reports that psychotherapy is an essential element of the treatment of such cases, and indeed is superior to pharmacotherapy as an effective intervention (Nemeroff et al., 2003).

Any psychotherapeutic intervention with these patients must treat not only traumatic symptoms but also the dissociative defense (Bromberg, 2006). Spitzer, Barnow, Freyberger, and Grabe's (2007) research shows that higher levels of dissociation predict poorer outcome in patients in psychodynamic psychotherapy. These authors conclude dissociative patients have an insecure attachment pattern negatively affecting the therapeutic relationship, and that they dissociate as a response to negative emotions arising in psychotherapy. Clinical authors now suggest that the treatment of traumatic dissociation is essential to effective psychotherapy with these patients (Schore, 2007; Spiegel, 2006).

The self psychological focus on selfobject regulation clearly suggests that deficits and defenses of affect and affect regulation are a primary focus of the treatment of these early forming psychopathologies. With respect to the mechanism of change, Kohut (1984) postulated "psychoanalysis cures by the laying down of psychological structure." This structure is essentially in the right brain and its limbic emotion-regulating circuits. Studies indicate that emotional self-regulatory processes constitute the core of psychotherapeutic approaches (Beauregard, Levesque, & Bourgouin, 2001); that the development of self-regulation is open to change in adult life, providing a basis for what is attempted in therapy (Posner & Rothbart, 1998); and that psychotherapy affects clinical recovery by modulating limbic and cortical regions (Goldapple et al., 2004).

In addition to a more complex understanding of the psychotherapy change process, an integration of neuroscience and self psychology has another important potential benefit. Psychoanalysis, neuroscience, and child psychiatry all share the well-established psychopathogenetic principle that maltreatment in childhood is associated with adverse influences on the infant's brain–mind–body and thereby alters the developmental trajectory of the self over the ensuing life span. Interdisciplinary research that incorporates psychoanalytic self psychology with the developmental and biological sciences can deepen our understanding of the underlying psychoneurobiological mechanisms by which early relational trauma mediates the unconscious intergenerational transmission of the deficits in affect regulation of early forming self-psychopathologies. This information may in turn generate more effective models of early intervention during the brain growth spurt and thereby for the prevention of a broad range of psychiatric disorders.

REFERENCES

Adamec, R. E., Blundell, J., & Burton, P. (2003). Phosphorylated cyclic AMP response element bonding protein expression induced in the periaqueductal gray by predator stress; its relationship to the stress experience, behavior, and limbic neural plasticity. *Progress in Neuro-Psychopharmacology & Biological Psychiatry, 27*, 1243–1267.

Allen, J. G., Console, D. A., & Lewis, L. (1999). Dissociative detachment and memory impairment: Reversible amnesia or encoding failure? *Comprehensive Psychiatry, 40*, 160–171.

Allman, J. M., Watson, K. K., Tetreault, N. A., & Hakeem, A. Y. (2005). Intuition and autism: A possible role for Von Economo neurons. *Trends in Cognitive Sciences, 9*, 367–373.

Amsterdam, B. (1972). Mirror self-image reactions before age two. *Developmental Psychobiology, 5*, 297–305.

Beauregard, M., Levesque, J., & Bourgouin, P. (2001). Neural correlates of conscious self-regulation of emotion. *Journal of Neuroscience, 21*, RC165.

Beebe, B., & Lachmann, F. M. (1994). Representations and internalization in infancy: Three principles of salience. *Psychoanalytic Psychology, 11*, 127–165.

Bogolepova, I. N., & Malofeeva, L. I. (2001). Characteristics of the development of speech motor areas 44 and 45 in the left and right hemispheres of the human brain in early post-natal ontogenesis. *Neuroscience and Behavioral Physiology, 31*, 13–18.

Bourne, V. J., & Todd, B. K. (2004). When left means right: An explanation of the left cradling bias in terms of right hemisphere specializations. *Developmental Science, 7*, 19–24.

Bradshaw, G. A., & Schore, A. N. (2007). How elephants are opening doors: Developmental neuroethology, attachment and social context. *Ethology, 113*, 426–436.

Bromberg, P. M. (2006). *Awakening the dreamer: Clinical journeys.* Mahwah, NJ: Analytic Press.

Chiron, C., Jambaque, I., Nabbout, R., Lounes, R., Syrota, A., & Dulac, O. (1997). The right brain hemisphere is dominant in human infants. *Brain, 120*, 1057–1065.

Cooper, A. M. (1987). Changes in psychoanalytic ideas: Transference interpretation. *Journal of the American Psychoanalytic Association, 35*, 77–98.

Cozolino, L. (2002). *The neuroscience of psychotherapy*. New York: Norton.

Crucian, G. P., Hughes, J. D., Barrett, A. M., Williamson, D. J. G., Bauer, R. M., Bowres, D., et al. (2000). Emotional and physiological responses to false feedback. *Cortex, 36*, 623–647.

Dapretto, M., Davies, M. S., Pfeifer, J. H., Scott, A. A., Sigman, M., Bookheimer, S. Y., et al. (2006). Understanding emotions in others: Mirror neuron dysfunction in children with autism spectrum disorders. *Nature Neuroscience, 9*, 28–31.

Davidson, R. J., Ekman, P., Saron, C., Senulis, J., & Friesen, W. V. (1990). Approach/withdrawal and cerebral asymmetry: 1. Emotional expression and brain physiology. *Journal of Personality and Social Psychology, 58*, 330–341.

De Bellis, M. D., Baum, A. S., Birmaher, B., Keshavan, M. S., Eccard, C. H., Boring, A. M., et al. (1999). Developmental traumatology: Part I. Biological stress systems. *Biological Psychiatry, 45*, 1259–1270.

Decety, J., & Chaminade, T. (2003). When the self represents the other: A new cognitive neuroscience view on psychological identification. *Consciousness and Cognition, 12*, 577–596.

Devinsky, O. (2000). Right cerebral hemisphere dominance for a sense of corporeal and emotional self. *Epilepsy & Behavior, 1*, 60–73.

Dikel, T. N., Fennell, E. B., & Gilmore, R. L. (2003). Posttraumatic stress disorder, dissociation, and sexual abuse history in epileptic and nonepileptic seizure patients. *Epilepsy & Behavior, 4*, 644–650.

Draijer, N., & Langeland, W. (1999). Childhood trauma and perceived parental dysfunction in the etiology of dissociative symptoms in psychiatric inpatients. *American Journal of Psychiatry, 156*, 379–385.

Feinberg, T., & Keenan, J. P. (2005). Where in the brain is the self? *Consciousness and Cognition, 14*, 661–678.

Fossati, P., Hevenor, S. J., Lepage, M., Graham, S. J., Grady, C., Keightley, M. L., et al. (2004). Distributed self in episodic memory: Neural correlates of successful retrieval of self-encoded positive and negative personality traits. *NeuroImage, 22*, 1596–1604.

Freud, S. (1955). The claims of psycho-analysis to scientific interest. In J. Strachey (Ed. & Trans.), *The standard edition of the complete psychological works of Sigmund Freud* (Vol. 13, pp. 165–190). London: Hogarth Press. (Original work published 1913)

Gadea, M., Gomez, C., Gonzalez-Bono, R. E., & Salvador, A. (2005). Increased cortisol and decreased right ear advantage (REA) in dichotic listening following a negative mood induction. *Psychoneuroendocrinology, 30*, 129–138.

Goldapple, K., Segal, Z., Garson, C., Lau, M., Bieling, P., Kennedy, S., et al. (2004). Modulation of cortical-limbic pathways in major depression. *Archives of General Psychiatry, 61*, 34–41.

Gupta, R. K., Hasas, K. M., Trivedi, R., Pradhan, M., Daqs, V., Parikh, N. A., et al. (2005). Diffusion tensor imaging of the developing human cerebrum. *Journal of Neuroscience Research, 81*, 172–178.

Henry, J. P. (1993). Psychological and physiological responses to stress: The right hemisphere and the hypothalamo-pituitary-adrenal axis, an inquiry into problems of human bonding. *Integrative Physiological & Behavioral Science, 28*, 369–387.

Hesse, E., & Main, M. M. (1999). Second-generation effects of unresolved trauma in nonmaltreating parents: Dissociated, frightened, and threatening parental behavior. *Psychoanalytic Inquiry, 19*, 481–540.

Hesse, E., & Main, M. M. (2006). Frightened, threatening, and dissociative parental behavior in low-risk samples: Description, discussion, and interpretations. *Development and Psychopathology, 18*, 309–343.

Kinney, H. C., Brody, B. A., Kloman, A. S., & Gilles, F. H. (1988). Sequence of central nervous system myelination in human infancy: II. Patterns of myelination in autopsied infants. *Journal of Neuropathology and Experimental Neurology, 47*, 217–234.

Kohut, H. (1971). *The analysis of the self*. New York: International Universities Press.

Kohut, H. (1977). *The restoration of the self*. New York: International Universities Press.

Kohut, H. (1984). *How does analysis cure?* Chicago: University of Chicago Press.

Lane, R. D., Ahern, G. L., Schwartz, G. E., & Kaszniak, A. W. (1997). Is alexithymia the emotional equivalent of blindsight? *Biological Psychiatry, 42*, 834–844.

Lanius, R. A., Williamson, P. C., Bluhm, R. L., Densmore, M., Boksman, K., Neufeld, R. W. J., et al. (2005). Functional connectivity of dissociative responses in posttraumatic stress disorder: A functional magnetic resonance imaging investigation. *Biological Psychiatry, 57*, 873–884.

Laub, D., & Auerhahn, N. (1993). Knowing and not knowing massive psychic trauma: Forms of traumatic memory. *International Journal of Psychoanalysis, 74*, 287–302.

Lenzi, D., Trentini, C., Pantano, P., Macaluso, E., Iacoboni, M., Lenzi, G. I., et al. (2009). Neural basis of maternal communication and emotional expression processing during infant preverbal stage. *Cerebral Cortex, 19*, 1124–1133.

Liotti, G. (2004). Trauma, dissociation, and disorganized attachment: Three strands of a single braid. *Psychotherapy: Theory, Research, Training, 41*, 472–486.

Macfie, J., Cicchetti, D., & Toth, S. L. (2001). Dissociation in maltreated versus nonmaltreated preschool-age children. *Child Abuse & Neglect, 25*, 1253–1267.

Menard, J. L., Champagne, D. L., & Meaney, M. J. P. (2004). Variations in maternal care differentially influence "fear" reactivity and regional patterns of cFos immunoreactivity in response to the shock-probe burying test. *Neuroscience, 129*, 297–308.

Mendez, M. F., & Lim, G. T. H. (2004). Alterations of the sense of "humanness" in right hemisphere predominant frontotemporal dementia patients. *Cognitive and Behavioral Neurology, 17*, 133–138.

Merckelbach, H., & Muris, P. (2001). The causal link between self-reported trauma and dissociation: A critical review. *Behavior Research and Therapy, 39*, 245–254.

Miller, B. L., Seeley, W. W., Mychack, P., Rosen, H. J., Mena, I., & Boone, K. (2001). Neuroanatomy of the self. Evidence from patients with frontotemporal dementia. *Neurology, 57*, 817–821.

Minagawa-Kawai, Y., Matsuoka, S., Dan, I., Naoi, N., Nakamura, K., & Kojima, S. (2009). Prefrontal activation associated with social attachment: Facial-emotion recognition in mothers and infants. *Cerebral Cortex, 19*, 284–292.

Molnar-Szakacs, I., Uddin, L. Q., & Iacoboni, M. (2005). Right-hemisphere motor facilitation by self-descriptive personality-trait words. *European Journal of Neuroscience, 21*, 2000–2006.

Nemeroff, C. B., Heim, C., Thase, M. E., Klein, D. N., Rush, A. J., Schatzberg, A. F., et al. (2003). Differential responses to psychotherapy versus pharmacology in patients with chronic forms of major depression and childhood trauma. *Proceedings of the National Academy of Sciences of the United States of America, 100*, 14293–14296.

Nijenhuis, E. R. S. (2000). Somatoform dissociation: Major symptoms of dissociative disorders. *Journal of Trauma & Dissociation, 1*, 7–32.

Ovtscharoff, W., Jr., & Braun, K. (2001). Maternal separation and social isolation modulates the postnatal development of synaptic composition in the infralimbic cortex of *Octodon degus*. *Neuroscience, 104*, 33–40.

Papousek, H., & Papousek, M. (1995). Intuitive parenting. In M. H. Bornstein (Ed.), *Handbook of parenting: Vol. II. Ecology and biology of parenting* (pp. 117–136). Hillsdale, NJ: Erlbaum.

Parent, C., Zhang, T-Y., Caldji, C., Bagot, R., Champagne, F. A., Pruessner, J., et al. (2005). Maternal care and individual differences in defensive responses. *Current Directions in Psychological Science, 12*, 229–233.

Perrin, F., Maquet, P., Peigneux, P., Ruby, P., Degueldre, C., Balteau, E., et al. (2005). Neural mechanisms involved in the detection of our first name: A combined ERPs and PET study. *Neuropsychologia, 43*, 12–19.

Platek, S. M., Keenan, J. P., Gallup, G. G., & Mohamed, F. B. (2004). Where am I? The neurological correlates of self and other. *Cognitive Brain Research, 19*, 114–122.

Porges, S. W. (1997). Emotion: An evolutionary by-product of the neural regulation of the autonomic nervous system. *Annals of the New York Academy of Science, 807*, 62–77.

Posner, M. I., & Rothbart, M. K. (1998). Attention, self-regulation, and consciousness. *Philosophical Transactions of the Royal Society of London B, 353*, 1915–1927.

Raz, A. (2004). Anatomy of attentional networks. *Anatomical Record, 281B*, 21–36.

Recordati, G. (2003). A thermodynamic model of the sympathetic and parasympathetic nervous systems. *Autonomic Neuroscience: Basic and Clinical, 103*, 1–12.

Schore, A. N. (1994). *Affect regulation and the origin of the self*. Mahwah, NJ: Erlbaum.

Schore, A. N. (1997a). A century after Freud's *Project*: Is a rapprochement between psychoanalysis and neurobiology at hand? *Journal of the American Psychoanalytic Association, 45*, 807–840.

Schore, A. N. (1997b). Early organization of the nonlinear right brain and development of a predisposition to psychiatric disorders. *Development and Psychopathology, 9*, 595–631.

Schore, A. N. (2000). Attachment and the regulation of the right brain. *Attachment & Human Development, 2*, 22–41.

Schore, A. N. (2001). The effects of relational trauma on right brain development, affect regulation, and infant mental health. *Infant Mental Health Journal, 22*, 201–269.

Schore, A. N. (2002a). The right brain as the neurobiological substratum of Freud's dynamic unconscious. In D. Scharff (Ed.), *The psychoanalytic century: Freud's legacy for the future* (pp. 61–88). New York: Other Press.

Schore, A. N. (2002b). Advances in neuropsychoanalysis, attachment theory, and trauma research: Implications for self psychology. *Psychoanalytic Inquiry, 22*, 433–484.

Schore, A. N. (2002c). Dysregulation of the right brain: A fundamental mechanism of traumatic attachment and the psychopathogenesis of posttraumatic stress disorder. *Australian & New Zealand Journal of Psychiatry, 36*, 9–30.

Schore, A. N. (2003a). *Affect regulation and the repair of the self*. New York: Norton.

Schore, A. N. (2003b). *Affect dysregulation and the disorders of the self*. New York: Norton.

Schore, A. N. (2005a). A neuropsychoanalytic viewpoint. Commentary on paper by Steven H. Knoblauch. *Psychoanalytic Dialogues, 15*, 829–853.

Schore, A. N. (2005b). Attachment, affect regulation, and the developing right brain: Linking developmental neuroscience to pediatrics. *Pediatrics in Review, 26*, 204–212.

Schore, A. N. (2007). Review of *Awakening the dreamer: Clinical journeys* by Philip M. Bromberg. *Psychoanalytic Dialogues, 17*, 753–767.

Schore, A. N. (2009). Attachment trauma and the developing right brain: Origins of pathological dissociation. In P. F. Dell & J. A. O'Neil (Eds.), *Dissociation and the dissociative disorders: DSM-V and beyond* (pp. 107–141). New York: Routledge.

Schuengel, C., Bakermans-Kranenburg, M. J., & Van IJzendoorn, M. H. (1999). Frightening maternal behavior linking unresolved loss and disorganized infant attachment. *Journal of Consulting and Clinical Psychology, 67*, 54–63.

Schutz, L. E. (2005). Broad-perspective perceptual disorder of the right hemisphere. *Neuropsychology Review, 15*, 11–27.

Siegel, A. M. (1996). *Heinz Kohut and the psychology of the self*. London and New York: Routledge.

Siegel, D. J. (1999). *Developing mind: Toward a neurobiology of interpersonal experience*. New York: Guilford Press.

Spiegel, D. (2006). Recognizing traumatic dissociation. *American Journal of Psychiatry, 163*, 566–568.

Spitzer, C., Barnow, S., Freyberger, H. J., & Grabe, H. J. (2007). Dissociation predicts symptom-related treatment outcome in short-term inpatient psychotherapy. *Australian and New Zealand Journey of Psychiatry, 41*, 682–687.

Spitzer, C., Wilert, C., Grabe, H.-J., Rizos, T., & Freyberger, H. J. (2004). Dissociation, hemispheric asymmetry, and dysfunction of hemispheric interaction: A transcranial magnetic approach. *Journal of Neuropsychiatry and Clinical Neuroscience, 16*, 163–169.

Sugiura M., Watanabe, J., Maeda, Y., Matsue, Y., Fukuda, H., & Kawashima, R. (2005). Cortical mechanisms of visual self-recognition. *NeuroImage, 24*, 143–189.

Sullivan, R. M., & Dufresne, M. M. (2006). Mesocortical dopamine and HPA axis regulation: Role of laterality and early environment. *Brain Research, 1076*, 49–59.

Sun, T., Patoine, C., Abu-Khalil, A., Visader, J., Sum, E., Cherry, T. J., et al. (2005). Early asymmetry of gene transcription in embryonic human left and right cerebral cortex. *Science, 308*, 1794–1798.

Symonds, L. L., Gordon, N. S., Bixby, J. C., & Mande, M. M. (2006). Right-lateralized pain processing in the human cortex: An fMRI study. *Journal of Neurophysiology, 95*, 3823–3830.

Tronick, E. Z. (1989). Emotions and emotional communication in infants. *American Psychologist, 44*, 112–119.

Uddin, L. Q., Kaplan, J. T., Molnar-Szakacs, I., Zaidel, E., & Iacoboni, M. (2005). Self-face recognition activates a frontoparietal "mirror" network in the right hemisphere: An event-related fMRI study. *NeuroImage, 25*, 926–935.

van der Kolk, B. A., Pelcovitz, D., Roth, S., Mandel, F. S., McFarlane, A., & Herman, J. L. (1996). Dissociation, somatization, and affect dysregulation: The complexity of adaptation to trauma. *American Journal of Psychiatry, 153*, 83–93.

Ziabreva, I., Poeggel, G., Schnabel, R., & Braun, K. (2003). Separation-induced receptor changes in the hippocampus and amygdala of *Octodon degus*: Influence of maternal vocalizations. *Journal of Neuroscience, 23*, 5329–5336.

CHAPTER 3

Right Brain Affect Regulation: An Essential Mechanism of Development, Trauma, Dissociation, and Psychotherapy

There is currently an increasing awareness, indeed a palpable sense, that a number of clinical disciplines are undergoing a significant transformation, a paradigm shift. A powerful engine for the increased energy and growth in the mental health field is the ongoing dialogue it is having with neighboring disciplines, especially developmental science, biology, and neuroscience. This mutually enriching communication is centered on a common interest in the primacy of affect in the human condition. In the present interdisciplinary environment, psychological studies on the critical role of emotional contact between humans are now being integrated with biological studies on the impact of these relational interactions on brain systems that regulate emotional bodily based survival functions.

By definition, a paradigm shift occurs simultaneously across a number of different fields, and it induces an increased dialogue between the clinical and applied sciences. This transdisciplinary shift is articulated by Richard Ryan in a recent editorial of the journal *Motivation and Emotion*:

> After three decades of the dominance of cognitive approaches, motivational and emotional processes have roared back into the limelight. . . . More practically, cognitive interventions that do not address motivation and emotion are increasingly proving to be short-lived in their efficacy, and limited in the problems to which they can be applied. (2007, p. 1)

Echoing this, the neuroscientist Jaak Panksepp now boldly asserts,

The cognitive revolution, like radical neuro-behaviorism, intentionally sought to put emotions out of sight and out of mind. Now cognitive science must re-learn that ancient emotional systems have a power that is quite independent of neocortical cognitive processes. . . . These emotional substrates promote cognitive-object relations, optimally through rich emotional experiences. (2008, p. 51)

And in the psychotherapy literature, Karen Maroda sets forth this challenge:

From my experience there are more therapists who have painfully sat on their emotions, erroneously believing that they were doing the right thing. For these therapists, the prospect of using their emotional responses constructively for the patient is a potentially rewarding and mutually healthy experience . . . perhaps we can explore the therapeutic nature of affect, freeing both our patients and ourselves. (2005, p. 140)

In contrast to the prevailing privileged status of verbal, conscious cognition, in my first book on regulation theory I suggested that emotional communications between therapist and patient lie at the psychobiological core of the therapeutic alliance, and that right brain–to–right brain emotional processes are essential to development, psychopathology, and psychotherapy (Schore, 1994). Indeed, very recent clinical research reports that the more therapists facilitate the affective experience/expression of patients in psychotherapy, the more patients exhibit positive changes, and that therapist affect facilitation is a powerful predictor of treatment success (Diener, Hilsenroth, & Weinberger, 2007).

In this chapter, after a brief introduction, I will discuss updates of my work on the essential right brain process of nonconscious affect regulation in development, in psychopathogenesis and trauma dissociation, and finally in the interpersonal neurobiology of a number of essential right brain processes that lie at the core of the change process of psychotherapy. Reflecting the ongoing interdisciplinary dialogue, I will frequently cite the verbatim observations of both scientists studying the brain and clinicians studying the mind.

INTRODUCTION: REGULATION THEORY AND THE PRIMACY OF AFFECTIVE STRUCTURES AND FUNCTIONS

A central theme running throughout all my work is the exploration of the primacy of affective processes in various critical aspects of the human experience. Lane, Ahern, Schwartz, and Kaszniak stress the evolutionary functions of both implicit and explicit affects:

Primary emotional responses have been preserved through phylogenesis because they are adaptive. They provide an immediate assessment of the extent to which goals or needs are being met in interaction with the environment, and they reset the organism behaviorally, physiologically, cognitively, and experientially to adjust to these changing circumstances. (2008, p. 225)

My studies in affective and developmental neuroscience have suggested that the adaptive survival functions of the right hemisphere, the "locus of emotional brain," are dominant in relational contexts at all stages of the life span, including the intimate context of psychotherapy.

In ongoing contributions I have integrated a large body of clinical and neuro-biological data to argue that the right brain implicit self represents the biological substrate of the human unconscious mind and is intimately involved in the processing of bodily based affective information associated with various motivational states. Lichtenberg observes a central focus of the psychotherapeutic encounter:

> To appreciate the patient's motivation, we need to . . . discern the emotional experience he or she seeks. At times, the goal sought will be self-evident to patient and [therapist]. At other times, the goal will lie *out of awareness* and will be difficult to ascertain. . . . The golden thread in assessing motivation lies in discovering the affect being sought in conjunction with the behavior being investigated. (2001, p. 440, my italics)

Relevant to the renewed interest in emotion in models of the change process in both development and psychotherapy, there is now a growing body of evidence indicating that "In most people, the verbal, conscious and serial information processing takes place in the left hemisphere, while the unconscious, nonverbal and emotional information processing mainly takes place in the right hemisphere" (Larsen, Brand, Bermond, & Hijman, 2003, p. 534). The right hemisphere is dominant for the recognition of emotions, the expression of spontaneous and intense emotions, and the nonverbal communication of emotions (see Schore, 2003a, 2003b for references). The central role of this hemisphere in survival functions is outlined by Schutz:

> The right hemisphere operates a distributed network for rapid responding to danger and other urgent problems. It preferentially processes environmental challenge, stress and pain and manages self-protective responses such as avoidance and escape. . . . Emotionality is thus the right brain's "red phone," compelling the mind to handle urgent matters without delay. (2005, p. 15)

Furthermore, an important ongoing trend in interdisciplinary studies is on not just emotion but unconscious, implicit emotion. At the beginning of the last century, Freud speculated, "Unconscious ideas continue to exist after repression as actual structures in the system *Ucs*, whereas all that corresponds in that system to unconscious affects is a potential beginning which is prevented from developing" (1915/1957b, p. 178). In my own work on unconscious (implicit) affect, I have suggested that bodily based affects are "the center of empathic communication," and that "the regulation of *conscious and unconscious feelings* is placed in the center of the clinical stage" (Schore, 1994). Mitrani (2007) asserts, "I propose that the act of introjecting the patient may be the most difficult aspect of our work, as it is not a matter of good will or good training, but an unconscious act governed by unconscious factors" (p. 834). Maroda (2005) challenges therapists to ponder an essential clinical problem: "How do you relate empathically to an unexpressed emotion?" (p. 136). I will argue that unconscious affects can be best understood as not repressed but dissociated affects, and that later-forming repression is associated with left hemispheric inhibition of affects generated by the right brain, whereas early forming dissociation reflects a dysregulation of affects resulting from the dis-integration of the right brain itself.

Although this topic has been controversial, neuroscience now demonstrates a "right hemispheric dominance in processing of *unconscious negative emotion*" (Sato & Aoki, 2006). Other studies now document a "cortical response to *subjectively unconscious danger*" (Carretie, Hinojosa, Mercado, & Tapia, 2005). For example, basic research on the neurobiology of survival mechanisms clearly shows that the emotion of fear "is not necessarily conscious; a fearful response may be evoked even when one is not fully aware of being 'afraid.'. . . As with emotion itself, the enhanced memory for emotional experiences may proceed at a relatively subconscious level, without clear awareness" (Price, 2005, p. 135).

Neurobiological studies also demonstrate that the right cortical hemisphere is centrally involved in "the processing of self-images, at least when self-images are not consciously perceived" (Theoret et al., 2004, p. 57). Deep psychotherapeutic changes alter not only conscious but also unconscious self-image associated with nonconscious internal working models of attachment. Both unconscious negative emotions and unconscious self-images are important elements of the psychotherapy process, especially with the more severe self-pathologies.

Thus, the essential roles of the right brain in the "unconscious processing of emotional stimuli" and in "emotional communication" are directly relevant to recent clinical models of an "affective unconscious" and a "relational unconscious," whereby "one unconscious mind communicates with another unconscious mind" (Schore, 2003a). In a number of writings I have described in some detail the fundamental role of right brain–to–right brain communications across an intersubjective field embedded within the therapeutic alliance (Schore, 1994, 2002a, 2005a, 2007). This dialogue of ultrarapid bodily based affective communications in patient–therapist (and infant–mother) attachment transactions occurs beneath levels of conscious awareness of both members of the dyad.

Another area of common, intense interdisciplinary interest is the self-regulation of emotion. Affect regulation is usually defined as the set of control processes by which we influence, consciously and voluntarily, the emotions we have, and how we experience and behaviorally express them. However, "Most of moment to moment psychological life occurs through nonconscious means . . . various nonconscious mental systems perform the lion's share of the self-regulating burden, beneficently keeping the individual grounded in his or her environment" (Bargh & Chartrand, 1999, p. 462). Greenberg now asserts, "The field has yet to pay adequate attention to implicit and relational processes of regulation" (2008, p. 414). Applying this principle to psychotherapy, Ryan notes, "Both researchers and practitioners have come to appreciate the limits of exclusively cognitive approaches for understanding the initiation and regulation of human behavior" (2007, p. 1).

Indeed a large body of data suggests unconscious affect regulation is more essential than conscious emotion regulation in human survival functions (Schore, 1994, 2003a, 2003b, 2007). There is agreement among both scientists and clinicians that this essential adaptive capacity evolves in early attachment experiences:

> The developmental achievement of a sense of self that is simultaneously fluid and robust depends on how well the capacity for affect regulation and affective competency has been achieved. . . . When these early patterns of interpersonal interaction are relatively successful, they create a stable foundation for relational affect regulation that is internalized as nonverbal and unconscious. Thus, further successful negotiation of interpersonal transactions at increasingly higher levels of self-development and interpersonal maturity is made possible. (Bromberg, 2006, p. 32)

RIGHT BRAIN PROCESSES IN DEVELOPMENT: THE INTERPERSONAL NEUROBIOLOGY OF SECURE ATTACHMENT

As summarized in a recent contribution on modern attachment theory (Schore & Schore, 2008), the essential task of the first year of human life is the creation of a secure attachment bond between the infant and his or her primary caregiver. Secure attachment depends upon the mother's sensitive psychobiological attunement to the infant's dynamically shifting internal states of arousal. Through visual-facial, auditory-prosodic, and tactile-gestural communication, caregiver and infant learn the rhythmic structure of the other and modify their behavior to fit that structure, thereby co-creating a "specifically fitted interaction." Congruent with the models of nonconscious communication discussed above, developmental researchers now describe this nonverbal intersubjective communication:

> Preverbal communication . . . is the realm of non-consciously regulated intuitive behavior and implicit relational knowledge. Whether information is transferred or shared, which information gets across, and on which level it is "understood," does not necessarily depend on the sender's intention or conscious awareness. (Papousek, 2007, p. 258)

During these bodily based affective communications, the attuned mother synchronizes the spatiotemporal patterning of her exogenous sensory stimulation with the infant's spontaneous expressions of his endogenous organismic rhythms. Via this contingent responsivity, the mother appraises the nonverbal expressions of her infant's internal arousal and affective states, regulates them, and communicates them back to the infant. To accomplish this, the mother must successfully modulate nonoptimal high *or* nonoptimal low levels of stimulation, which would induce supra-heightened or extremely low levels of arousal in the infant.

In play episodes of affect synchrony, the pair are in affective resonance, and in such, an amplification of vitality affects and a positive state occurs. In moments of interactive repair the "good-enough" caregiver who has mis-attuned can regulate the infant's negative state by accurately re-attuning in a timely manner. The regulatory processes of affect synchrony, which creates states of positive arousal and interactive repair that modulate states of negative arousal, are the fundamental building blocks of attachment and its associated emotions, and resilience in the face of stress and novelty is an ultimate indicator of attachment security (Schore, 2005b).

These adaptive capacities are central to the dual processes of self-regulation: *interactive regulation*, the ability to flexibly regulate psychobiological states of emotions with other humans in interconnected contexts, and *autoregulation*, which occurs apart from other humans in autonomous contexts. According to Pipp and Harmon, "It may be that . . . we are biologically connected to those with whom we have close relationships. . . . Homeostatic regulation between members of a dyad is a stable aspect of all intimate relationships throughout the lifespan" (1987, p. 651). The evolutionary mechanism of attachment, the interactive regulation of emotion, thus represents the regulation of biological synchronicity between and within organisms (Bradshaw & Schore, 2007).

In line with earlier proposals that emotional attachment experiences during early critical periods of development facilitate the experience-dependent maturation of emotion-regulatory brain circuits (Schore, 1994), neuroscientists now assert:

> [T]he mother functions as a regulator of the socio-emotional environment during early stages of postnatal development . . . subtle emotional regulatory interactions, which obviously can transiently or permanently alter brain activity levels . . . may play a critical role during the establishment and maintenance of limbic system circuits. (Ziabreva, Poeggel, Schnabel, & Braun, 2003, p. 5334)

It is well established that the human central nervous system (CNS) limbic system extensively myelinates in the first year and a half and that the early maturing right hemisphere—which is deeply connected into the limbic system—undergoes a growth spurt at this time (Bogolepova and Malofeeva, 2001; Chiron et al., 1997; Geschwind & Galaburda, 1987; Gupta et al., 2005; Howard and Reggia, 2007; Moskal, Kroes, Otto, Rahimi, & Claiborne, 2006; Sun et al., 2005; Trevarthen, 1996).

The right hemisphere also has tight connections with the involuntary autonomic nervous system (ANS), which controls visceral organs, effectors in the skin, and the cardiovascular system. Also known as the vegetative nervous system, from the Latin, *vegetare* (to animate or bring to life), it is responsible for the generation of what Stern (1985) calls "vitality affects." Via a right-lateralized vagal circuit of emotion regulation, "the right hemisphere—including the right cortical and subcortical structures—would promote the efficient regulation of autonomic function via the source nuclei of the brain stem" (Porges, Doussard-Roosevelt, & Maiti, 1994, p. 175). Affect-regulating attachment experiences specifically impact cortical and limbic-autonomic circuits of the developing right cerebral hemisphere (Cozolino, 2002; Henry, 1993; Schore, 1994, 2005b; Siegel, 1999). For the rest of the life span, internal working models of the attachment relationship with the primary caregiver, stored in the right brain, encode strategies of affect regulation that nonconsciously guide the individual through interpersonal contexts.

Earlier speculations (Schore, 1994) are now supported by current studies, which observe that right-lateralized limbic areas responsible for the regulation of autonomic functions and higher cognitive processes are involved in the "formation of social bonds," are "part of the circuitry supporting human social networks," and that the "the strong and consistent predominance for the right hemisphere emerges postnatally" (Allman, Watson, Tetreault, & Hakeem, 2005, p. 367). In very recent work on mother–infant emotional communication, Lenzi et al. (2009) offer data from a functional magnetic resonance imaging study "supporting the theory that the right hemisphere is more involved than the left hemisphere in emotional processing and thus, mothering" (p. 1131). Also confirming this model, Minagawa-Kawai et al. (2009) report a near-infrared spectroscopy study of infant–mother attachment at 12 months and conclude, "our results are in agreement with that of Schore (2000) who addressed the importance of the right hemisphere in the attachment system" (p. 289). Summarizing these data, Rotenberg concludes,

> The main functions of the right hemisphere . . . the ability to grasp the reality as a whole; the emotional attachment to the mother (Schore, 2003a); the regulation of withdrawal behavior in the appropriate conditions (Davidson & Cacioppo, 1992); the integration of affect, behavior and autonomic activity (Schore, 2003a) are the basic functions of survival (Saugstad, 1998) and for this reason are the first to appear. (2004, p. 864)

RIGHT BRAIN PROCESSES IN DEVELOPMENT: THE INTERPERSONAL NEUROBIOLOGY OF ATTACHMENT TRAUMA

During the brain growth spurt (last trimester pregnancy through second year), relational trauma–induced arousal dysregulation precludes the aforementioned facial-visual, auditory-prosodic, and tactile-gestural attachment communications and alters the development of essential right brain functions. In contrast to an optimal attachment scenario, in a relational growth-inhibiting early environment, the primary caregiver induces traumatic states of enduring negative affect in the child. This caregiver is inaccessible and reacts to her infant's expressions of emotions and stress inappropriately and/or rejectingly, and therefore shows minimal or unpredictable participation in the various types of arousal-regulating processes. Instead of modulating she induces extreme levels of stimulation and arousal, very high in abuse and/or very low in neglect. Because she provides no interactive repair, the infant's intense negative affective states last for long periods of time. These deficits in maternal function outwardly reflect her own internal stressful states of dysregulated arousal.

Psychophysiological studies of human maternal behavior directed toward infants clearly indicate that

> Stress is an important factor that may affect social interactions, especially the mother–child interaction. Mothers during stressful life episodes were less sensitive, more irritable, critical and punitive. . . . Moreover, stressed mothers showed less warmth and flexibility in interactions with their children. . . . Overall, stress seems to be a factor that has the power to disrupt parenting practices seriously and results in a lower quality of the mother–child interaction. (Suter, Huggenberger, & Schachinger, 2007, p. 46)

These authors demonstrate that this impacts the female's autonomic nervous system and specifically disrupts her right hemisphere.

On the other side of the mother–infant dyad, interdisciplinary evidence indicates that the infant's psychobiological reaction to traumatic stress is comprised of two separate response patterns: hyperarousal and dissociation. In the initial hyperarousal stage, the maternal haven of safety suddenly becomes a source of threat, triggering an alarm or startle reaction in the infant's right hemisphere, the locus of both the attachment system and the fear motivational system. This maternal stressor activates the infant's hypothalamic-pituitary-adrenal (HPA) stress axis, thereby eliciting a sudden increase of the energy-expending sympathetic component of the infant's ANS, resulting in significantly elevated heart rate, blood pressure, and respiration—the somatic expressions of a dysregulated hypermetabolic psychobiological state of fear-terror.

But a second, later forming reaction to relational trauma is dissociation, in which the child disengages from stimuli in the external world—traumatized infants are observed to be "staring off into space with a glazed look." This parasympathetic dominant state of conservation-withdrawal occurs in helpless and hopeless stressful situations in which the individual becomes inhibited and strives to avoid attention in order to become "unseen" (Schore, 1994, 2001). The dissociative metabolic shutdown state is a primary regulatory process, used throughout the life span, in which the stressed individual passively disengages in order to conserve energies, foster survival by the risky posture of feigning death, and allow restitution of depleted resources by immobility. In this passive hypometabolic state, heart rate, blood pressure, and respiration are decreased, while pain-numbing and -blunting endogenous opiates are elevated. It is this energy-conserving parasympathetic (vagal) mechanism that mediates the "profound detachment" of dissociation, a metabolic strategy for coping with what Porges (1997) terms "life threat."

In fact there are two parasympathetic vagal systems in the brain stem medulla. The ventral vagal complex rapidly regulates cardiac output to foster fluid engagement and disengagement with the social environment, and exhibits rapid and transitory patterns associated with perceptive pain and unpleasantness, all aspects of a secure attachment bond of emotional communication. On the other hand, activity of the dorsal vagal complex is associated with intense emotional states and immobilization, and is responsible for the severe hypoarousal and pain blunting of dissociation (see Figure 3.1). The traumatized infant's sudden state switch from sympathetic hyperarousal to parasympathetic dissociation is described by Porges as

> the sudden and rapid transition from an unsuccessful strategy of struggling requiring massive sympathetic activation to the metabolically conservative immobilized state mimicking death associated with the dorsal vagal complex. (1997, p. 75)

Porges (1997) describes the involuntary and often prolonged characteristic pattern of vagal outflow from the dorsal vagal nucleus. This long-lasting state of dorsal vagal parasympathetic activation accounts for the extensive duration of "void" states associated with pathological dissociative detachment (Allen, Console, & Lewis, 1999), and for what Bromberg (2006) calls dissociative "gaps" in subjective reality, "spaces" that surround self-states and thereby disrupt coherence among highly affectively charged states. These "gaps" are also discussed in the developmental psychoanalytic literature. Winnicott (1958) notes that a particular failure of the maternal holding environment causes a discontinuity in the baby's need for "going-on-being"; and Kestenberg (1985) refers to this as "dead

FIGURE 3.1. Dynamic patterns of regulated and dysregulated autonomic arousal. From Wheatley-Crosbie, 2006; adapted from Levine, 1997, Porges, 2006, and Ogden, 2006.

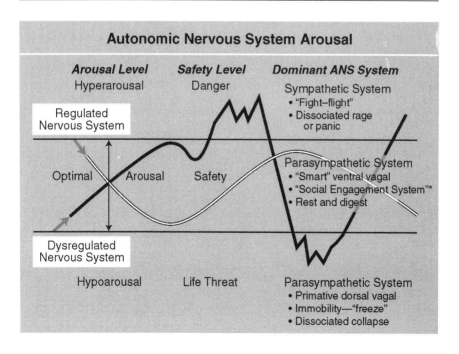

spots" in the infant's subjective experience, an operational definition of the restriction of consciousness of dissociation. At all points of the life span, dissociation is conceptualized as "a basic part of the psychobiology of the human trauma
response: a protective activation of altered states of consciousness in reaction to
overwhelming psychological trauma" (Loewenstein, 1996, p. 312).

Dissociation in infants has been studied with the still-face procedure, an experimental paradigm of traumatic neglect. In the still-face, the infant is exposed
to a severe relational stressor: The mother maintains eye contact with the infant,
but she suddenly totally inhibits all vocalization and suspends all emotionally
expressive facial expressions and gestures. This intense relational stressor triggers
an initial increase of interactive behavior and arousal in the infant. According to
Tronick (2004), the infant's confusion and fearfulness at the break in connection
is accompanied by the cognition that "this is threatening." This stress response is
then followed by sad facial expression, gaze aversion, withdrawal, self-comforting
behavior, loss of postural control, and ultimately bodily collapse.

Most interestingly, this behavior is accompanied by a "dissipation of the infant's state of consciousness" and a diminishment of self-organizing abilities that
reflect "disorganization of many of the lower level psychobiological states, such
as metabolic systems." Tronick (2004) suggests that infants who have a history of
chronic breaks of connections exhibit an "extremely pathological state" of emotional apathy. He equates this state with Spitz's cases of hospitalism, Harlow's
isolated monkeys, Bowlby's withdrawn children, and Romanian orphans who fail
to grow and develop. Such infants ultimately adopt a communication style of
"stay away; don't connect." This defensive stance is a very early forming, yet already chronic, pathological dissociation that is associated with loss of ventral vagal activation and dominance of dorsal vagal parasympathetic states.

In parallel to still-face studies, ongoing attachment research underscores a
link between frightening maternal behavior, dissociation, and disorganized infant attachment (Schuengel, Bakermans-Kranenburg, & Van IJzendoorn, 1999).
Hesse and Main (1999) point out that the disorganization and disorientation of
type "D" attachment associated with abuse and neglect phenotypically resembles dissociative states. In more recent work, Hesse and Main observe that when
the mother enters a dissociative state, a fear alarm state is triggered in the infant.
The caregiver's entrance into the dissociative state is expressed as "parent suddenly completely 'freezes' with eyes unmoving, half-lidded, despite nearby
movement; parent addresses infant in an 'altered' tone with simultaneous voicing and devoicing" (2006, p. 320). In describing the mother as she submits to the
freeze state, they note:

> Here the parent appears to have become completely unresponsive to, or even aware
> of, the external surround, including the physical and verbal behavior of their in-
> fant. . . . [W]e observed one mother who remained seated in an immobilized and
> uncomfortable position with her hand in the air, blankly staring into space for 50
> sec. (p. 321)

In an EEG study of 5-month-old infants looking at a "blank face," Bazhenova et al. report increases in vagal activity "over the right posterior temporal scalp area and over anterior scalp areas. . . . This observation suggests greater right hemisphere involvement in face processing during blank face" (2007, p. 73).

During these episodes of the intergenerational transmission of attachment trauma, the infant is matching the rhythmic structures of the mother's dysregulated arousal states. This synchronization is registered in the firing patterns of the stress-sensitive corticolimbic regions of the right brain, dominant for survival and the human stress response (Schore, 1994; Wittling, 1995). Adamec, Blundell, and Burton (2003) report findings that "implicate neuroplasticity in right hemispheric limbic circuitry in mediating long-lasting changes in negative affect following brief but severe stress" (p. 1264). Gadea, Gomez, Gonzalez-Bono, Espert, and Salvador (2005) conclude that an intense experience "might interfere with right hemisphere processing, with eventual damage if some critical point is reached" (p. 136). Recall that right cortical areas and their connections with right subcortical structures are in a critical period of growth during the early stages of human development. The massive ongoing psychobiological stress associated with dysregulated attachment trauma sets the stage for the characterological use of right brain unconscious pathological dissociation over all subsequent periods of human development.

RIGHT BRAIN PROCESSES IN PSYCHOPATHOGENESIS: THE NEUROBIOLOGY OF PATHOLOGICAL DISSOCIATION

In the neuropsychoanalytic literature, Watt contends, "If children grow up with dominant experiences of separation, distress, fear and rage, then they will go down a bad pathogenic developmental pathway, and it's not just a bad psychological pathway but a bad neurological pathway" (2003, p. 109). Neurobiological research on patients with a history of relational trauma also demonstrates continuity over the course of the life span of the expression of this primitive autoregulation defense. It is now accepted that early childhood abuse specifically alters limbic system maturation, producing neurobiological alterations that act as a biological substrate for a variety of psychiatric consequences. These include affective instability, inefficient stress tolerance, memory impairment, psychosomatic disorders, and dissociative disturbances (Schore, 2001, 2002b).

In a transcranial magnetic stimulation study of adults, Spitzer et al. report, "In dissociation-prone individuals, a trauma that is perceived and processed by the right hemisphere will lead to a 'disruption in the usually integrated functions of consciousness'" (2004, p. 168). In functional magnetic resonance imaging research, Lanius et al. (2005) show predominantly right hemispheric activation in post-traumatic stress disorder (PTSD) patients while they are dissociating. They conclude that patients dissociate in order to escape from the overwhelming emo-

tions associated with the traumatic memory, and that dissociation can be interpreted as representing a nonverbal response to the traumatic memory.

These and other studies are presently exploring the evolution of a developmentally impaired regulatory system over all stages of life. They provide evidence
that orbitofrontal (ventromedial) cortical and limbic areas (anterior cingulate,
insula, periaqueductal gray, amygdala) of particularly the right hemisphere are
centrally involved in the deficits in mind and body associated with a pathological
dissociative response (Schore, 2003a, 2000b, 2009). This hemisphere, more so
than the left, is densely reciprocally interconnected with emotion-processing limbic regions, as well as with subcortical areas that generate both the arousal and
the autonomic (sympathetic and parasympathetic) bodily based aspect of emotions (see Figure 3.2). Sympathetic nervous system activity is manifested in tight

FIGURE 3.2.   Vertical axis of right brain cortical-subcortical limbic-autonomic circuits
and subsequent connections into the left brain.

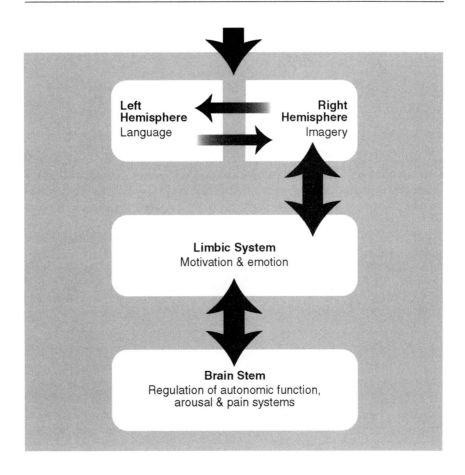

engagement with the external environment and a high level of energy mobilization and utilization, whereas the parasympathetic component drives disengagement from the external environment and utilizes low levels of internal energy (Recordati, 2003). These components of the ANS are uncoupled in traumatic states of pathological dissociation.

In line with the current shift from "cold cognition" to the primacy of bodily based "hot affects," clinical research on dissociation is focusing on "somatoform dissociation," an outcome of early onset traumatization. This is expressed as a lack of integration of sensorimotor experiences, reactions, and functions of the individual and his or her self-representation (Nijenhuis, 2000). Thus, "dissociatively detached individuals are not only detached from the environment, but also from the self—their body, their own actions, and their sense of identity" (Allen et al., 1999, p. 165). The right anterior insula, which integrates somatosensory and autonomic functions in order to generate visceral awareness of subjective emotional states (Craig, 2004; Critchley et al., 2004), is deactivated in dissociation (Lanius et al., 2010). These data indicate impaired functions of the right cerebral hemisphere, the locus of the "emotional" or "corporeal self" (Devinsky, 2000). Crucian et al. (2000) describe "a dissociation between the emotional evaluation of an event and the physiological reaction to that event, with the process being dependent on intact right hemisphere function" (p. 643). McGilchrist (2009) asserts that dissociation, "a relative hypofunction of the right hemisphere," manifests as "a sense of being cut off—and often a craving to be cut off—from one's feelings, and from embodied existence, a loss of depth of emotion and capacity of empathy, a fragmentation of the sense of self" (p. 406).

I have offered interdisciplinary evidence indicating that the implicit self, the human unconscious mind, is located in the right brain (Schore, 1994, 2003b, 2005a). The lower subcortical levels of the right brain (the deep unconscious) contain all the major motivational systems (including attachment, fear, sexuality, aggression, disgust, etc.) and generate the somatic autonomic expressions and arousal intensities of all emotional states. When optimally functioning, higher orbitofrontal-limbic levels of the right hemisphere generate a conscious emotional state that expresses the affective output of these motivational systems (Schore, 1994). This right lateralized hierarchical prefrontal system performs an essential adaptive motivational function—the relatively fluid switching of internal bodily based states in response to changes in the external environment that are nonconsciously appraised to be personally meaningful (Schore, 1994).

On the other hand, pathological dissociation—an enduring outcome of early relational trauma—is manifest in a maladaptive, highly defensive, rigid, and closed system, one that responds to even low levels of intersubjective stress with parasympathetic dorsal vagal hypoarousal and heart rate deceleration. This fragile unconscious system is susceptible to mind–body metabolic collapse and thereby a loss of energy-dependent synaptic connectivity within the right brain, expressed in a sudden implosion of the implicit self and a rupture of self-continuity. This dis-integration of the right brain and collapse of the implicit self are signaled by the amplification of the parasympathetic affects of shame and disgust, and by the cognitions of hopelessness and helplessness. Because the right hemisphere mediates the communication and regulation of emotional states, the rupture of intersubjectivity is accompanied by an instant dissipation of safety and trust.

Dissociation thus reflects the inability of the vertical axis of the right brain cortical-subcortical implicit self-system (see right side of Figure 3.2) to recognize and process external stimuli (exteroceptive information coming from the relational environment) and, on a moment-to-moment basis, to integrate them with internal stimuli (interoceptive information from the body, somatic markers, the "felt experience"). This failure of integration of the higher right hemisphere with the lower right brain induces an instant collapse of both subjectivity and intersubjectivity. Stressful and painful emotional states associated with intensely high or low levels of arousal are not experienced in consciousness, but remain in implicit memory as dysregulated, dissociated unconscious affects (Schore, 2009).

This developmental model of relational trauma describes the psychoneurobiological mechanisms that underlie Janet's conceptualization of dissociation. As described by van der Kolk, Weisaeth, and van der Hart:

> Janet proposed that when people experience *"vehement emotions,"* their minds may become incapable of matching their *frightening experiences* with existing cognitive schemes. As a result the memories of the experience cannot be integrated into personal awareness; instead, they are split off [dissociated] from consciousness and voluntary control . . . extreme *emotional arousal* results in failure to *integrate* traumatic memories. . . . The memory traces of the trauma linger as unconscious "fixed ideas" that cannot be "liquidated" . . . they continue to intrude as terrifying perceptions, obsessional preoccupations, and *somatic reexperiences.* (1996, p. 52, my italics)

In clinical studies Kalsched (2005, p. 174) describes operations of defensive dissociative processes used by the child during traumatic experience by which "Affect in the body is severed from its corresponding images in the mind and thereby an unbearably painful meaning is obliterated." There is now agreement that "traumatic stress in childhood could lead to self-modulation of painful affect by directing attention away from internal emotional states" (Lane, Ahern, Schwartz, & Kaszniak, 1997, p. 840). The right hemisphere is dominant not only for regulating affects but also for attention (Raz, 2004), negative affect (Davidson & Cacioppo, 1992), and pain processing (Symonds, Gordon, Bixby, & Mande, 2006). And so the right brain strategy of dissociation represents the ultimate defense for blocking conscious awareness of emotional pain. If early trauma is experienced as "psychic catastrophe," the autoregulatory strategy of dissociation is expressed as "detachment from an unbearable situation," "a submission and resignation to the inevitability of overwhelming, even psychically deadening danger," and "a last resort defensive strategy" (Schore, 2009).

RIGHT BRAIN PROCESSES IN PSYCHOTHERAPY: UNCONSCIOUS AFFECT, TRANSFERENCE, AND PRIMARY PROCESS

At the beginning of this chapter I suggested that the regulation of not only conscious but also unconscious affects is an essential mechanism of the psychotherapeutic change process. All forms of therapy currently view affect dysregulation as a fundamental condition of every psychiatric disorder (Taylor, Bagby, & Parker, 1997), including personality disorders (Sarkar & Adshead, 2006), and therefore share a common goal of improving the effectiveness of emotional self-regulatory processes (Beauregard, Levesque, & Bourgouin, 2001). In terms of regulation theory, defense mechanisms are forms of emotional regulation strategies for avoiding, minimizing, or converting affects that are too difficult to tolerate. Treatment, especially of early forming severe psychopathologies, must attend not only to conscious dysregulated affects but also to the early forming survival defense that protects patients from consciously experiencing overwhelming painful negative affects—dissociation. This bottom-line defense thus represents the major counterforce to the emotional-motivational aspects of the change process in psychotherapy (Schore, 2007). This clinical principle is supported by research showing that insecurely attached dissociative patients dissociate as a response to negative emotions arising in psychodynamic psychotherapy, leading to a less favorable treatment outcome (Spitzer, Barnow, Freyberger, & Grabe, 2007).

Basic research suggests, "While the left hemisphere mediates most linguistic behaviors, the right hemisphere is important for broader aspects of communication" (Van Lancker & Cummings, 1999, p. 95). Incorporating these data into regulation theory's model of the psychotherapeutic process, I have delineated the central role of implicit right brain–to–right brain nonverbal communications (facial expression, prosody, gesture) in unconscious transference-countertransference affective transactions, an essential element of treatment of severe psychopathologies and a common mechanism of all forms of psychotherapy. Interdisciplinary data and updated clinical models lead me to conclude that the right hemisphere is dominant in treatment, and that psychotherapy is not the "talking cure" but the affect communicating and regulating cure (Schore, 2005a).

Clinical workers now describe transference as "an established pattern of relating and emotional responding that is cued by something in the present, but oftentimes calls up both an affective state and thoughts that may have more to do with past experience than present ones" (Maroda, 2005, p. 134). In a parallel formulation, neuroscience now documents that the right hemisphere is fundamentally involved in the unconscious processing of emotional stimuli (Mlot, 1998), and that

> The right hemisphere holds representations of the emotional states associated with events experienced by the individual. When that individual encounters a familiar scenario, representations of past emotional experiences are retrieved by the right

hemisphere and are incorporated into the reasoning process. (Shuren & Grafman, 2002, p. 918)

With direct relevance to transference-countertransference communications, Howard and Reggia assert, "The right hemisphere develops a specialization for cognitive functions of a more ancient origin and the left for a specialization for functions of more modern origin" (2007, p. 121).

An outstanding example of an ancient cognitive function is the primary process cognition system that emerges in human infancy, before secondary process. In recent psychological studies, Russ (2000–2001) concludes, "primary-process is a subtype of affect in cognition that consists of content around which the child had experienced early intense feeling states . . . current primary-process expressions could reflect these early encodings of fused affect and cognition" (p. 31). In line with current developmental and relational models, I have argued that right brain–to–right brain communications represent interactions of the patient's unconscious primary process system and the therapist's primary process system (Schore, 1994), and that primary process cognition is the major communicative mechanism of the relational unconscious.

In a significant advance in our understanding of the dynamic processes of the relational unconscious, Dorpat (2001) describes the process of "primary process communication." In a striking similarity to attachment communications, Dorpat asserts the following: that the primary process system is immediately and directly involved with perception; that it analyzes, regulates, and communicates an individual's relations with the environment; that this nonverbal communication includes both body movements, posture, gesture, facial expression, voice inflection, and the sequence, rhythm, and pitch of the spoken words; and that its major function is to make unconscious, automatic, and rapid evaluations of current events involving self and others. He notes, "Both primary process communication and secondary process communication are present in ordinary conversation where objective, factual (secondary process) information is transmitted by the meaning of uttered words and where affective and object-relational information is transmitted predominantly by primary process communication" (p. 451).

In direct relevance to the psychotherapy process, neuroscience authors contend, "The right hemisphere operates in a more free-associative, primary process manner, typically observed in states such as dreaming or reverie" (Grabner, Fink, & Neubauer, 2007, p. 228). Split brain neurobiological studies by Galin (1974) and Hoppe (1977) established that the right hemisphere generates primary process cognition whereas the left generates secondary process cognition. Pioneering psychological studies of these two processing modes by Martindale and Hasenfus (1978) demonstrate that logical, analytical secondary process cognition accompanies medium levels of cortical arousal, whereas primary process accompanies either high or low levels of cortical arousal (see Figure 3.3).

FIGURE 3.3.   Relationship between primary and secondary process and arousal.

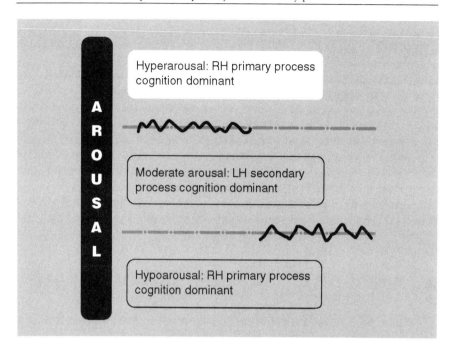

RIGHT BRAIN PROCESSES IN PSYCHOTHERAPY:
ENACTMENTS, AUTONOMIC AROUSAL
DYSREGULATION, AND DISSOCIATION

With an eye to the therapy process, Dorpat (2001) conceptualizes primary and secondary process as parallel and relatively independent systems for the reception, analysis, processing, storing, and communication of information, and that in different contexts one or the other may predominate. Primary process functions specifically prevail "in the activation and deactivation of certain schema; in the arousal and regulation of specific affects; in the initiation of defensive and adaptive activities designed to cope with the event being processed; and in nonverbal communication. The subject may or may not be aware of this unconscious process" (p. 450).

Right brain primary process–to–right brain primary process transference-countertransference nonverbal communications especially predominate in stressful contexts of clinical enactments. In a major contribution integrating clinical models and neurobiological data, Ginot (2007, p. 317) convincingly argues, "Increasingly, enactments are understood as powerful manifestations of the intersubjective process and as inevitable expressions of complex, though largely *unconscious self-states and relational patterns*" (my italics).

In line with earlier neuropsychoanalytic speculations (Schore, 1997) and in support of the central thesis of this chapter, Ginot observes,

> This focus on enactments as communicators of affective building blocks also reflects a growing realization that explicit content, verbal interpretations, and the mere act of uncovering memories are insufficient venues for curative shifts. . . . As intense manifestations of transference-countertransference entanglements, enactments seem to generate interpersonal as well as internal processes eventually capable of promoting integration and growth. (2007, pp. 317–318)

She concludes that these "unconscious affective interactions" "bring to life and consequently alter implicit memories and attachment styles." Recall the hypothesis of Stern et al. (1998) that "implicit relational knowledge" stored in the nonverbal domain is at the core of therapeutic change.

In previous neuropsychoanalytic work, I offered interdisciplinary evidence showing that the right hemisphere is the locus of implicit memory (Schore, 1999). In discussing the role of the right hemisphere as "the seat of implicit memory," Mancia 2006) notes, "The discovery of the implicit memory has extended the concept of the unconscious and supports the hypothesis that this is where the emotional and affective—sometimes traumatic—presymbolic and preverbal experiences of the primary mother–infant relations are stored" (p. 83). I further suggest that these implicit memories are encoded in high (hyperarousal) and low (hypoarousal) arousal states. These are marked by, respectively, bodily state-dependent memories of dysregulated sympathetic dominant energy-expending extreme increases of autonomic arousal (heart rate acceleration) as well as parasympathetic dominant energy-conserving extreme decreases of arousal (heart rate deceleration). The principle of state-dependent recall of implicit memories thus applies to each of these two domains: achieving a particular bodily state is necessary to access certain affects, behaviors, and cognitions.

It is often overlooked that affects reflect an individual's internal state and have a hedonic (valenced) dimension and *an arousal (intensity-energetic) dimension* (Schore, 1994). A body of studies now demonstrates that the right hemisphere is generally more important than the left in activating arousal systems (Heilman, 1997; Meadows & Kaplan, 1994), yet more capable of operating at reduced arousal levels (Casagrande & Bertini, 2008). The right brain is superior in processing emotional arousal and in the automatic response to emotional stimuli (Gainotti, Caltarirone, & Zoccolotti, 1993), and predominantly affected by feedback of bodily stress-induced arousal (Critchley et al., 2004). As opposed to left brain "anxious apprehension" expressed in cognitive anxiety, worry, verbal rumination, and muscle tension, right brain "anxious arousal" is associated with panic states and somatic symptoms including shortness of breath, pounding heart, dizziness, sweating, and feelings of choking. In this latter state the right side of the brain continuously monitors the external environment for threat and "exerts hierarchical control over the autonomic and somatic functions for responding to threat" (Nitschke, Heller, Palmieri, & Miller, 1999, p. 635).

In states of right hemispheric hyperarousal that generate a massive density of intense sympathetic dominant, energy-expending, high-arousal negative affect, arousal levels are so extremely elevated that they interfere with the individual's capacity to adaptively engage with the social (object relational, intersubjective) environment. Bromberg (2006) links trauma, at any point in the life span, to autonomic hyperarousal, "a chaotic and terrifying flooding of affect that can threaten to overwhelm sanity and imperil psychological survival" (p. 33).

In contrast, states of right hemispheric parasympathetic dominant, energy-conserving hypoarousal generate a massive density of intense low-arousal negative affect. In these latter affective states, arousal levels are so extremely reduced that they interfere with an individual's capacity to adaptively disengage from the social environment. Thus, early relational trauma, reactivated in transference-countertransference enactments, manifests in dysregulated autonomic hyperarousal associated with sympathetic-dominant affects (panic-terror, rage, and pain) and heart rate acceleration (tachycardia), as well as in dysregulated autonomic hypoarousal and parasympathetic-dominant affects (shame, disgust, and hopeless despair) and heart rate deceleration (bradycardia).

Visualizing this conception, in Figure 3.4 the central zone reflects operations of both the left and right hemispheres in states of moderate arousal. Left hemi-

FIGURE 3.4. Affect associated with right brain sympathetic hyperarousal and parasympathetic hypoarousal.

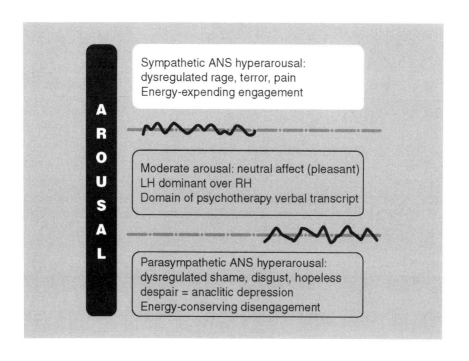

A
R
O
U
S
A
L

Sympathetic ANS hyperarousal:
dysregulated rage, terror, pain
Energy-expending engagement

Moderate arousal: neutral affect (pleasant)
LH dominant over RH
Domain of psychotherapy verbal transcript

Parasympathetic ANS hyperarousal:
dysregulated shame, disgust, hopeless
despair = anaclitic depression
Energy-conserving disengagement

spheric secondary process is dominant in states of neutral affect and autonomic balance. This middle band of neutral (pleasant) affect is bounded by (1) an upper band of right brain sympathetic dominant, energy-expending, high-arousal affects associated with tight engagement with the environment and (2) a lower band of right brain parasympathetic dominant, energy-conserving, low-arousal affects and disengagement from the external environment (Recordati, 2003).

In terms of Porges' (1997) polyvagal model (see Figure 3.5), the sympathetic hyperarousal zone processes states of danger (fight–flight), whereas the dorsal vagal hypoarousal system is dominant in states of life survival–threat (see Schore, 2009). Recall that the early development of these two stress-responsive psychobiological domains is directly impacted by dysregulated attachment experiences (abuse and neglect). These right brain imprinted implicit memories of the hyperarousal and dissociative-hypoarousal responses to early relational trauma are reactivated in the transference-countertransference.

Clinical work in these dyadic enactments implies both a profound commitment of therapeutic participants and a deep emotional involvement on the thera-

FIGURE 3.5.   Porges' polyvagal model. From Wheatley-Crosbie (2006), adapted from Porges, 2006.

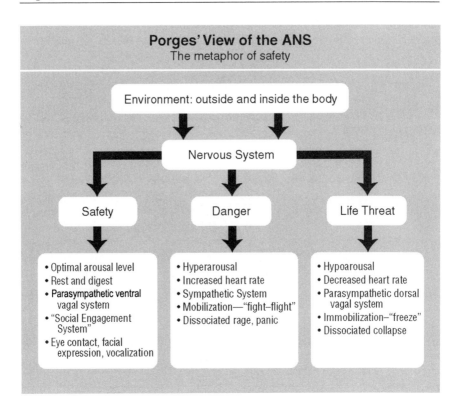

pist's part (Tutte, 2004). In these highly stressful contexts the therapist's affect tolerance is a critical factor determining the range, types, and intensities of emotions that are explored or disavowed in the transference-countertransference relationship and the therapeutic alliance (Schore, 2003b).

A general principle of this work is that the sensitive empathic therapist allows the patient to reexperience dysregulating affects in *affectively tolerable doses in the context of a safe environment, so that overwhelming traumatic feelings can be regulated and integrated into the patient's emotional life.* In agreement with Ogden et al. (2005), Bromberg (2006) also points out that the therapeutic relationship must "feel safe but not perfectly safe. If it were even possible for the relationship to be perfectly safe, which it is not, there would be no potential for safe surprises . . ." (p. 95). This affect-focused work occurs of at *the edges of the regulatory boundaries of the windows of affect tolerance* (Figure 3.6), or what Lyons-Ruth describes as the "fault lines" of self-experience where "interactive negotiations have failed, goals remain aborted, negative affects are unresolved, and conflict is experienced" (2005, p. 21).

In Figure 3.6, note the term *"windows* of affect tolerance." This differs from the usual concept of "window of tolerance," which describes the range of opti-

FIGURE 3.6.   Regulatory boundaries at the edges of windows of affect tolerance. Adapted from Ogden, Minton, & Pain, 2006.

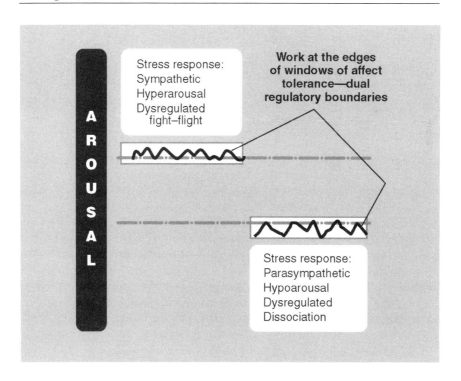

mal level of arousal to sustain secondary process cognition (conscious, verbal, explicit) and striatal motor activities (voluntary action; controlled overt behavior). These "cognitive and behavioral" functions are dependent upon a moderate rather than a high- or low-arousal range, represented by a classical "inverted U." At very low or very high arousal levels (the tails of the inverted U), left brain functions such as verbal cognition and analytical processing disorganize and fall off in efficiency. This window of optimal verbal processing and overt behavioral expression reflects moderate arousal levels that sustain left hemispheric functions. Current cognitive-behavioral insight-driven clinical models and psychological counseling operate in this arousal range and focus on these left hemispheric functions.

On the other hand, the right brain has a different and a wider range of arousal tolerance to sustain its unique nonconscious psychobiological functions. Because this system can operate at very high or very low arousal levels, it can therefore sustain a broad spectrum of adaptive survival and communication functions at very high or very low levels of metabolic energy. At these stressful extremes, although left brain functions of the conscious mind decrease in efficiency (either tail of the inverted U), right brain functions become more organized and efficient, and therefore become dominant over the left brain functions. Right brain "windows of affect tolerance" thus refer to an optimal range of arousal for different positive and negative affects and motivational states, which vary in arousal intensity, from extremely high to extremely low. This range of affect tolerance is severely restricted in the emotionally deadening defense of pathological dissociation. An expansion of both negative and positive affect tolerance is a goal of the affectively focused psychotherapy described in this chapter.

An essential clinical principle in working at the edges of right brain windows of affect tolerance dictates that at some point the threatening dissociated affect must be activated, but in trace form, and regulated sufficiently so as not to trigger new avoidance. "The questions of how much and when to activate or to permit this activation, so as to repair the dissociation rather than reinforce it, must be addressed specifically for each patient" (Bucci, 2002, p. 787). According to Bromberg, "Clinically, the phenomenon of dissociation as a defense against self-destabilization . . . has its greatest relevance during enactments, a mode of clinical engagement that requires a [therapist's] closest attunement to the unacknowledged affective shifts in his own and the patient's self-states" (2006, p. 5). This self-destabilization of the emotional right brain in clinical enactments can take one of two forms: high-arousal explosive fragmentation or low-arousal implosion of the implicit self (see Figure 3.7).

RIGHT BRAIN PROCESSES IN PSYCHOTHERAPY: CO-CONSTRUCTION OF INTERSUBJECTIVE FIELDS

In Figure 3.7, visualize two planes of one window of affect tolerance in parallel to another window: One represents the patient's window of affect tolerance, and the other the therapist's window of affect tolerance. At the edges of the windows,

FIGURE 3.7.   Psychobiology of high- and low-arousal enactments.

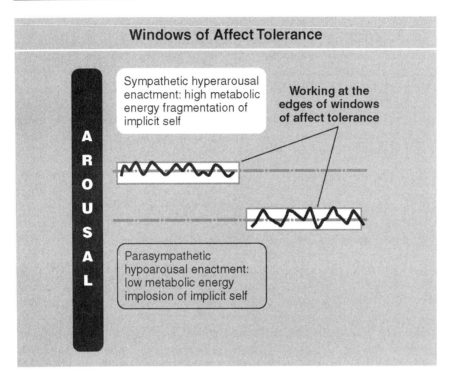

which are the regulatory boundaries, the psychobiologically attuned empathic therapist, on a moment-to-moment basis, implicitly tracks and matches the patterns of rhythmic crescendos/decrescendos of the patient's regulated and dysregulated ANS with his or her own ANS crescendos/decrescendos. When the patterns of synchronized rhythms (represented as oscillating dynamic changes within the windows) are in interpersonal resonance, this right brain–to–right brain "specifically fitted interaction" generates amplified energetic processes of arousal, and this interactive affect regulation in turn co-creates an intersubjective field between the surfaces of two parallel planes.

The dynamic intersubjective field is described by Stern (2004) as "the domain of feelings, thoughts, and knowledge that two (or more) people share about the nature of their current relationship. . . . *This field can be reshaped. It can be entered or exited, enlarged or diminished, made clearer or less clear*" (p. 243, my italics). In my work on the interpersonal neurobiology of intersubjectivity, I have asserted that the right hemisphere is dominant for "subjective emotional experiences," and that the interactive "transfer of affect" between the right brains of the members of therapeutic dyad is therefore best described as "intersubjectivity" (Schore, 1999). *An intersubjective field is more than just an interaction of two minds, but also that of two bodies*, which—when in affective resonance—elicit an amplification and integration of both CNS and ANS arousal (see chapter 3 of

Schore, 2003b, on the communication of affects in an intersubjective field via projective identification).

At present there is an intense interest in incorporating the body into psychotherapeutic treatment. The solution to this problem is to integrate into clinical models information about the autonomic nervous system, "the physiological bottom of the mind" (Jackson, 1931). This system generates vitality affects and controls the cardiovascular system, effectors on the skin, and visceral organs. Stress-induced alterations in these dynamic psychobiological parameters mediate the therapist's somatic countertransference to the patient's nonverbal communications within a co-constructed intersubjective field. In previous writings on the psychophysiology of countertransference, I stated:

> Countertransferential processes are currently understood to be manifest in the capacity to recognize and utilize the sensory (visual, auditory, tactile, kinesthetic, and olfactory) and affective qualities of imagery which the patient generates in the psychotherapist (Suler, 1989). Similarly, Loewald (1986) points out that countertransference dynamics are appraised by the therapist's observations of his own visceral reactions to the patient's material. (Schore, 1994, p. 451)

Recall that the ANS contains dissociable sympathetic energy-expending and parasympathetic energy-conserving components. Extending this intraorganismic concept to the interpersonal domain, two dissociable intersubjective fields may be co-created: (1) A sympathetic dominant, high-energy intersubjective field processes state-dependent implicit memories of object relational-attachment transactions in high-arousal states (Table 3.1); and (2) a parasympathetic dominant, low-energy intersubjective field processes state-dependent implicit memories of object relational-attachment transactions in low-arousal states (Table 3.2).

Note the contrast of somatic transference-countertransferences in the dual intersubjective fields. Also, the form of primary process expressions in affect, cognition, and behavior differ in ultra-high and low-arousal altered states of consciousness. Thus high- and low-arousal states associated with terror and shame, respectively, will show qualitatively distinct patterns of primary process nonverbal communication of "body movements (kinesics), posture, gesture, facial expression, voice inflection, and the sequence, rhythm, and pitch of the spoken

---

TABLE 3.1   High Energy Charge Intersubjective Field

Hyperarousal = hypermetabolic CNS-ANS limbic-autonomic circuits = stressful sympathetic dominant, energy-expending psychobiological states.

High-energy explosive dyadic enactments; fragmenting implicit self.

Sympathetic dominant intersubjectivity; over-engagement with social environment.

Somatic countertransference to communicated high-arousal affects expressed in heart rate acceleration. Focus on exteroceptive sensory information.

Regulation/dysregulation of hyperaroused affective states (aggression-rage, panic-terror, sexual arousal, excitement-joy).

TABLE 3.2   Low Energy Charge Intersubjective Field

Low arousal = hypometabolic CNS-ANS circuits = stressful parasympathetic dominant, energy-conserving psychobiological states.

Low-energy implosive dyadic enactments; collapsing implicit self.

Parasympathetic-dominant intersubjectivity; dissociation/disengagement from social environment.

Somatic countertransference to communicated low-arousal affects expressed in heart rate deceleration. Focus on interoceptive information.

Regulation/dysregulation of hyporaroused affective states (shame, disgust, abandonment, hopeless despair).

words" (Dorpat, 2001, p. 451). Recall that sympathetic nervous system activity is manifest in tight engagement with the external environment and a high level of energy mobilization and utilization, whereas the parasympathetic component drives disengagement from the external environment and utilizes low levels of internal energy. This principle applies not only to overt interpersonal behavior but also to covert intersubjective engagement-disengagement with the social environment, the coupling and decoupling of mind–bodies and internal worlds.

Recent models of the ANS indicate that although reciprocal activation usually occurs between the sympathetic and parasympathetic systems, they are also able to uncouple and act unilaterally (Schore, 1994). Thus the sympathetic hyperarousal zone and parasympathetic hypoarousal zone represent two discrete intersubjective fields of psychobiological attunement, rupture, and interactive repair of what Bromberg (2006) terms "collisions of subjectivities" (Figure 3.8).

RIGHT BRAIN PROCESSES IN PSYCHOTHERAPY: CLINICAL WORK IN THE LOW-ENERGY INTERSUBJECTIVE FIELD

It should be noted that just as emotion researchers have overemphasized sympathetic dominant affects and motivations (flight–fight), so have clinicians overly focused on the reduction of anxiety-fear or aggression-rage states. An outstanding example of this continuing bias is the devaluation of the critical role of dysregulated parasympathetic shame and disgust states in almost all psychotherapeutic models. Similarly, psychodynamic affective approaches have highlighted the roles of rage and fear-terror in high-arousal enactments, and subsequent explosive fragmentation of the high-energy intersubjective field and the implicit self. As a result there has been an underemphasis on the low-energy, parasympathetic dominant intersubjective field. This is problematic, because clinical work with parasympathetic dissociation, "detachment from an unbearable situation," is always associated with parasympathetic shame and disgust dynamics. Indeed two of the most prominent shame theoreticians, Gershon Kaufman (1989) and Michael Lewis (1992), have hypothesized that dissociative disorders represent a pa-

FIGURE 3.8.   High- and low-energy intersubjective fields.

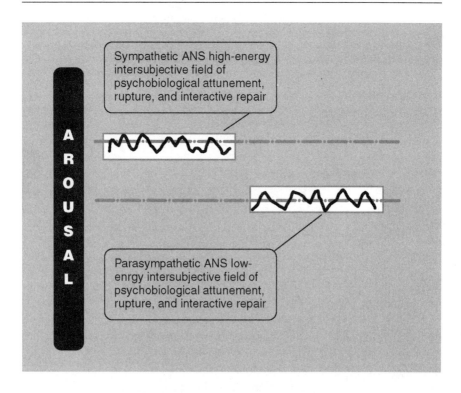

thology of the self based fundamentally on unacknowledged (implicit) shame. I would like to offer some thoughts about these two potent negative affects that appear in the low-arousal intersubjective field.

In my very first work I proposed that the parasympathetic state of shame, a highly visual affect subjectively experienced as a "spiraling downward," represents a sudden shift from sympathetic energy-expending hyperarousal to parasympathetic (dorsal vagal) energy-conserving hypoarousal (Schore, 1991). I expanded this model in my 1994 book, in which I offered a developmental model of the interpersonal attachment origins of the primary social emotion of shame in socialization dynamics that onset in the second year. At about 14 months,

> [T]he toddler, in an activated, hyperstimulated, high arousal state of stage-typical ascendant excitement and elation, exhibits itself during a reunion with the caregiver. Despite an excited expectation of a psychobiologically attuned shared positive affect state with the mother and a dyadic amplification of the positive affects of excitement and joy, the infant unexpectedly encounters a facially expressed affective misattunement, thereby triggering a sudden shock-induced deflation of narcissistic affect. The infant is thus propelled into an intensified low arousal state which

he cannot yet autoregulate. Shame represents this rapid transition from a preexisiting high arousal positive hedonic state to a low arousal negative hedonic state. (1994, p. 203)

In the same work I integrated various observations of shame researchers and clinicians in order to describe the prototypical painful autonomic concomitants of the nonverbal, highly visual emotion of shame, including its rapid (re)expression in the intersubjective field during a stressful mis-attunement-triggered rupture of right brain–to–right brain therapist–patient attachment communications. At all stages of the life span, the mis-attuned relational transactions of shame trigger gaze aversion (Tomkins, 1963), a response of hiding the face "to escape from this being seen or from the one who sees" (Wright, 1991, p. 30) and a state of withdrawal (Lichtenberg, 1989). Under the lens of a "shame microscope" which amplifies and expands this negative affect (Malatesta-Magai, 1991), visible defects, narcissistically charged undesirable aspects of the self, are exposed (Jacobson, 1964). "It is as though something we were hiding from everyone is suddenly under a burning light in public view" (Izard, 1991, p. 332). Shame throws a "flooding light" upon the individual (Lynd, 1958), who then experiences "a sense of displeasure plus the compelling desire to disappear from view" (Frijda, 1988, p. 351), and "an impulse to bury one's face, or to sink, right then and there, into the ground" (Erikson, 1950, p. 223). This impels him or her to "crawl through a hole" and culminates in feeling as if he or she "could die" (Lewis, 1971, p. 198).

The sudden shock-induced deflation of positive affect that supports grandiose omnipotence has been phenomenologically characterized as a whirlpool—a visual representation of a spiral (Potter-Effron, 1989)—and as a "flowing off" or "leakage" through a drain hole in the middle of one's being (Sartre, 1957, p. 256). The individual's subjective conscious experience of this affect is thus a sudden, unexpected, and rapid transition from what Freud (1957a) called "primary narcissism"—a sense of being "the center and core of the universe"—to what Sartre (1957) described as a shame-triggered "crack in my universe" (Schore, 1994, p. 208). Note the right brain perceptual and painful bodily based alterations that herald an implosion of the implicit self and a state of passive disengagement.

Sylvan Tomkins (1963), a pioneer in affective science, contrasted the pain associated with the sympathetic terror state with that of the parasympathetic shame state:

Though terror speaks of life and death and distress makes of the world a vale of tears, yet shame strikes deepest into the heart of man. While terror and distress hurt, they are wounds inflicted from outside which penetrate the smooth surface of the ego; but shame is felt as an inner torment, a sickness of the soul. It does not matter whether the humiliated one has been shamed by derisive laughter or whether he mocks himself. In either event he feels himself naked, defeated, alienated, lacking in dignity or worth. (p. 118)

Thus, the chronic dysregulation of the low-arousal intersubjective field may be even more painful than that of that of the high-arousal intersubjective field. Ulanov (2001) describes the reemergence in the therapeutic relationship of traumatic maternal–infant experiences that produce an "absence of self":

> Failure of environmental support at this level of being results in maiming. Clinically, I have found that communication from this level of hurt takes a long time to arrive and then announces itself as unspeakable. The transference-countertransference field carries the agony that words cannot capture because injury occurred before words did. A sense of desolation fills the space between analyst and analysand; despair clouds the atmosphere, eclipsing any bright hope for recovery. The analytic couple dwells in a blighted landscape. Both feel the hopelessness that anything might grow here. (p. 69)

Recall that the collapse of the implicit self and subsequent disengagement are not expressed actively but passively, and may be overtly subtle. In an intersubjective resonant context the implosion is signaled in several ways: affectively by an amplification of the parasympathetic affects of shame and disgust, behaviorally by an entrance into a state of conservation-withdrawal and an attempt to avoid attention in order to become "unseen," and cognitively by a sense of hopelessness and helplessness. These are all common accompaniments of relational traumatic experiences from infancy onward. The low-energy intersubjective field can be the most difficult countertransference for the clinician to consciously recognize and tolerate, and it is thus a potent context to potentially trigger a dissociative defense.

Noting that shame dynamics are hidden in both members of the therapeutic dyad, Kilborne (2003) concludes, "We hide our shame . . . from others because we want others to be blind to what we cannot tolerate seeing" (p. 286). Mann (2010) writes that visual shame affect stemming from unconscious early traumatic experiences reemerges in the clinical setting, along with the defenses that disguise the searing painful affect. Because the anticipatory dread of scornful gaze can cause mortification, it is accompanied by gaze aversion. Mann concludes that transference-countertransference exchanges of enactments, though susceptible to mutual projective identifications that set off reciprocal shaming in order to turn the tables on the shamer, are essential to working through traumatic shame dynamics.

Working deep in the low-arousal intersubjective field, Bromberg (2006) observes that shame is present in those patients who "disappear" when what is being discussed touches upon unprocessed early trauma, and that shame is the most powerful affect a person is unable to modulate. Utilizing a relational perspective to look at both sides of the therapeutic dyad, he concludes,

> The task that is most important, and simultaneously most difficult for the [therapist], is to watch for signs of dissociated shame both in himself and in his patient—

shame that is being evoked by the therapeutic process itself in ways that the [thera-
pist] would just as soon not have to face. . . . The reason that seemingly repeated
enactments are struggled with over and over again in the therapy is that the [thera-
pist] is over and over pulled into the same enactment to the degree he is not attending to the arousal of shame. (2006, p. 80)

Broucek (1991) points out that the therapist's avoidance of self-exposure is an
avoidance of shame experience and at the same time a source of shame for the
patient.

Perhaps the most pointed observation is made by Nathanson:

The entire system of psychotherapy, as we had been taught it, worked only if we
overlooked the shame that we produced day in and day out in our therapeutic work.
. . . It became clear that post-Freudian society had been treated for almost everything
but shame, and that the degree and severity of undiagnosed and untreated shame
problems far exceeded anything we had ever imagined. (1996, p. 3, my italics)

This observation is perhaps even more true today than it was 15 years ago. It also
implies that in our present culture shame has gone even more "underground";
that is, more patients are presenting with unconscious, dissociated shame (a
common feature of narcissistic disorders, wherein shame and not anxiety is the
keystone affect).

   This clinical principle is echoed in recent psychiatric research on patients
with a trauma history (borderline personality disorder). Alluding to dissociated
shame, Rusch et al. (2007) document that these patients manifest "high implicit
or unconscious shame-proneness" and are therefore "likely to be particularly
emotionally vulnerable or dysregulated" (p. 501). They conclude that treatment
must address not only the explicit but also the implicit aspects of shame, and that
"The failure to recognize shame within the patient–therapist relationship and
the central role of shame in the patient's inner experience jeopardizes the success of any psychotherapy" (p. 506).

   In my 1994 book I also discussed the developmental origins of another parasympathetic affect that is perhaps even more overlooked than shame: disgust, an
affect associated with olfactory processing. Disgust, a basic emotion (Darwin,
1872/1965), is expressed early in infants as distaste (Rozin & Fallon, 1987), and
in rejection and avoidance behaviors (Izard, 1991). Kaufman (1989) offers the
observation, "The face pulls away in dissmell from the offending, 'bad-smelling'
other, and in disgust the face spits out the 'bad-tasting' other . . . the parent similarly rejects the child as if it, too, were bad-smelling or bad-tasting, pulling away
in dissmell or spitting out in disgust" (p. 40). At later points in the life span, disgust is a central threat emotion associated with distress and avoidance behavior in
reaction to psychological contamination and violation. It is triggered by body
odors and rotting, death, offensive and contaminating body products, inappropriate sexual behaviors, and body envelope violations (e.g., blood, injuries, gore,

mutilations). Note these stimuli are associated with relational trauma and are common components of traumatic olfactory-imprinted images. Studying various disgust elicitors, Sarlo, Buodo, Poli, and Palomba, (2005) report specific activation of right posterior regions.

With direct bearing on the preceding proposal of distinct sympathetic energy-expending and parasympathetic energy-conserving intersubjective fields, Krusemark and Li (2011) assert that parasympathetic disgust states, like sympathetic fear states, are associated with threats to survival, yet they incite divergent autonomic mechanisms in the human defense system. Their research demonstrates that disgust at the autonomic physiological level increases parasympathetic responses, reducing heart rate (bradycardia), respiration and blood pressure, thus suppressing activity and initiating a state of inhibition and passive coping. On the other hand, sympathetic fear states swing these systems in the opposite direction, prompting a state of excitation, active coping, and flight or fight. At the cognitive level, fear elicits an instant response to orient attention (hypervigilance) and augment sensory acquisition, whereas disgust provokes immediate suppression of visual attention and sensory rejection. Krusemark and Li conclude that the "universal facial expressions of fear and disgust comprise opposite biomechanical properties modulating visual and olfactory sensors with widened versus narrow eyes and nostrils, increasing sensory intake in fear and dampening it in disgust" (p. 3434). Using visual event–related potential indexes, they show a rapid discrimination between fear and disgust as early as 96 milliseconds after presentation of a threat stimulus. These data bear directly upon the differential interoceptive and exteroceptive aspects of fear versus disgust in transference-countertransference communications of various forms of relational trauma.

In parallel recent clinical research, Rusch et al. (2010) note that pathological (dysregulated) disgust is associated with eating disorders, phobic and obsessive disorders, schizophrenia, sexually traumatized individuals, post-traumatic stress disorder (PTSD), and borderline personality disorder (BPD). Note that most of these have their origins in developmental psychopathology and histories of relational trauma. These authors cite other research showing that women with BPD expressed increased facial expressions of disgust during an attachment interview. On the basis of this previous work, their study reports women with BPD and/or PTSD exhibit heightened disgust sensitivity, and more disgust-prone *implicit* self-concept. Their finding that "disgust appears to be elevated at implicit and explicit levels in trauma related disorders" supports the importance of dissociated disgust in the treatment of attachment pathologies. In fact, Rusch et al. conclude, "In these patients with traumatic experiences, disgust may play an important role beside shame, anxiety or anger, and psychotherapists should try to address pathological disgust that may operate outside conscious awareness or control." This clinical work with unconscious (implicit) dysregulated affect takes place in the low-energy intersubjective field of psychobiological attunement, rupture, and interactive repair.

RIGHT BRAIN PROCESSES IN PSYCHOTHERAPY: INTERACTIVE AFFECT REGULATION AS A CENTRAL MECHANISM OF THE CHANGE PROCESS

Various authors have characterized the subtle psychological activities of the sensitive clinician who scaffolds the co-creation of an intersubjective field with the patient. Bromberg (2006) describes the left brain state that the clinician must exit from in order to co-participate in this field:

> When [a therapist] gives up his attempts to "understand" his patient and allows himself to know his patient through the ongoing intersubjective field they are sharing at that moment, an act of recognition (not understanding) takes place in which words and thoughts come to symbolize experience instead of substitute for it. (p. 2006, 11)

This moment of contact and thereby communication between two subjectivities has been termed a "moment of meeting" (Stern, 2004). The level and quality of this intersubjective contact is intimate, direct, and intense, and is best described as "relational depth," defined as

> A state of profound contact and engagement between two people, in which each person is fully real with the Other, and able to understand and value the other's experiences at a high level. (Mearns & Cooper, 2005, p. 63)

In order to optimize this deep intersubjective connection, the clinician must go to the limit of his subjective possibilities; otherwise, the patient will be unable to follow suit (Jung, 1946). Lichtenberg (2001) notes that staying with the patient's immediate subjective communication longer and more intensely usually gains more understanding than that achieved by either a defense focus or a genetic focus on what is not said. Whitehead describes the affect-amplifying effects encountered in the deep strata of the unconscious:

> Every time we make therapeutic contact with our patients we are engaging profound processes that tap into essential life forces in our selves and in those we work with. . . . *Emotions are deepened in intensity and sustained in time when they are intersubjectively shared.* This occurs at moments of *deep contact.* (2006, p. 624, my italics)

As previously discussed, a central tenet of regulation theory dictates that the interpersonal resonance within an intersubjective field triggers an amplification of state. The resultant co-created increased arousal (metabolic energy) allows for hypoaroused. dissociated unconscious affects to be intensified and thereby experienced in consciousness as a subjective emotional state. This bottom-up interactive regulation enables affect beneath conscious awareness to be intensified and sensed in both. Thus the "potential beginning" of an unconscious affect (Freud, 1915/1957b) is intersubjectively energized into emergence. According to Fosha (2005), the initiating mechanism of the change process is the alteration of "defense-dominated functioning" and "the state transformation leading to the visceral experience of core affective phenomena within an emotionally engaged therapeutic dyad" (p. 519).

As in all attachment dynamics, a dyadic amplification of arousal-affect *intensity* generated in a resonant transference-countertransference context facilitates the intensification of the felt sense in both therapist and patient. This same interpersonal psychobiological mechanism *sustains* the affect in time; that is, the affect is "held" within the intersubjective field long enough for it to reach conscious awareness in both members of a psychobiologically attuned therapeutic dyad. It should be noted that this affect charging-amplifying regulatory process includes an intensification of both negative and positive affect in an intersubjective field.

But more than empathic affect, attunement and deep contact are required for further therapeutic progression: At the psychobiological core of the intersubjective field is the attachment bond of emotional communication *and* affect regulation. The clinician's psychobiological interactive regulation/repair of dysregulated, especially unconscious (dissociated), bodily based affective states is an essential therapeutic mechanism. Recall Bucci's (2002) proscription that the threatening dissociated affect must be sufficiently regulated. Sands (1994) notes that "Dissociative defenses serve to regulate relatedness to others. . . . The dissociative patient is attempting to stay enough in a relationship with the human environment to survive the present while, at the same time, keeping the needs for more intimate relatedness sequestered but alive" (p. 149).

Due to early learning experiences of severe attachment failures, the patient accesses pathological dissociation in order to anticipate and cope with potential dysregulation of affect by anticipating trauma before it arrives. In characterological dissociation an autoregulatory strategy of involuntary autonomic disengagement is initiated and maintained to prevent potentially dysregulating intersubjective contact with others. But as the patient continues through the change process, he or she becomes more able to forgo autoregulation for interactive regulation when under interpersonal stress. Fosha (2005, p. 527) stresses this important principle: "dyadic affect regulation is a process that is central, not only in infancy, but from the cradle to the grave, *a fortiori* when we are faced with (categorical) emotions of such intensity that they overwhelm us, in the moment seeming beyond the capacity of our available resources to handle (i.e., that being the definition of trauma)."

Similarly, Ogden and her colleagues conclude,

> Interactive psychobiological regulation (Schore, 1994) provides the relational context under which the client can safely contact, describe and eventually regulate inner experience. . . . It is the patient's experience of empowering action in the con-

text of safety provided by a background of the empathic clinician's psychobiologically attuned interactive affect regulation that helps effect . . . change. (2005, p. 22)

This interactive affect regulation occurs at the edge of the regulatory boundaries of both high- and low-arousal intersubjective fields.

In this work Bromberg warns, "An interpretative stance . . . not only is thereby useless during an enactment, but also escalates the enactment and rigidifies the dissociation" (2006, p. 8). Maroda offers the caveat, "Interpretations given when affect is needed amounts to anti-communication, resulting in the patient getting worse" (2005, p. 138). A therapeutic focus on regulating not only conscious but also unconscious (dissociated) affect highlights the conclusion that the implicit nonverbal affective factors, more than the explicit verbal cognitive (insight) factors, lie at the core of the change process in the treatment of more severely disturbed patients. At the most fundamental level, the intersubjective work of psychotherapy is not defined by what the clinician does for the patient or says to the patient (left brain focus). Rather, the key mechanism is *how to be with the patient*, especially during affectively stressful moments when the patient's implicit core self is dis-integrating in real time (right brain focus).

Note the similarity of working at the right brain regulatory boundaries in the heightened affective moment of enactments to Lichtenberg's "disciplined spontaneous engagements" that occur within "an ambience of safety":

Spontaneous refers to the [therapist's] often unexpected comments, gestures, facial expressions, and actions that occur as a result of an unsuppressed emotional upsurge. These communications seem more to pop out than to have been planned or edited. The [therapist] may be as surprised as the patient. By engagement, we refer to communications and disclosures that are more enactments than thought-out responses. (2001, p. 445)

Tronick's "moments of meeting," a novel form of engagement of the therapeutic dyad, also occur at the regulatory boundaries:

The [therapist] must respond with something that is experienced as specific to the relationship with the patient and that is expressive of her own experience and personhood, and carries her signature. . . . It is dealing with "what is happening here and now between us." The strongest emphasis is on the now because of the affective immediacy. . . . It requires spontaneous responses and . . . need never be verbally explicated, but can be, after the fact. (2007, p. 436)

According to Greenberg and Pavio (1997), re-experiencing the traumatic experience in therapy within the safety and security of an empathic, supportive therapist provides the person with a new experience. This new experience is specifically the clinician's interactive regulation of the patient's communicated dysregulated right brain hyperaroused and hypoaroused affective states. In support of this model, current experimental researchers report "as suggested in clinical practice, it is necessary to 'revisit' an emotionally distressing memory before it can be controlled" (Depue, Curran, & Banich, 2007, p. 218).

Adler describes this dyadic psychobiological mechanism of the psychotherapeutic change process:

> Because people in a caring, i.e., empathic relationship convey emotional experiences to each other, they also convey physiological experiences to each other, and this sociophysiologic linkage is relevant to understanding the direct physiologic consequences of caring in the doctor–patient relationship—*for both parties*. (2002, p. 885, my italics)

He further argues that the therapeutic relationship—the interaction between the patient's emotional vulnerability and the doctor's emotional availability—represents a prime example of how individuals in an empathic relationship co-regulate each other's autonomic activity. More specifically, the therapeutic relationship can act as "the antithesis of the fight–flight response" and "the experience of feeling cared about in a relationship reduces the secretion of stress hormones and shifts the neuroendocrine system toward homeostasis" (2002, p. 883). Adler argues that in this way social bonds of attachment embedded in the therapeutic relationship reduce stress-induced arousal.

Ongoing episodes of therapeutic interactive regulation of affective arousal impact the patient's threshold of activation of a right brain stress response to a social stressor. Bromberg observes that "the processing to be safer and safer so that the person's tolerance for potential flooding of affect goes up" (2006, p. 79). Resultantly,

> The patient's threshold for "triggering" increase, allowing her increasingly to hold on to the ongoing relational experience (the full complexity of the here and now with the therapist) as it is happening, with less and less need to dissociate; as the processing of the here and now becomes more and more immediate, it becomes more and more experientially connectable to her past. (p. 69)

Effective work at the regulatory boundaries of right brain low- and high-arousal states ultimately broadens the windows of affect tolerance, thereby allowing for a wider variety of more intense and enduring affects that accompany each motivational state in future intersubjective contexts (see Figure 3.9).

LeDoux (2002) offers an elegant description of this advance of emotional development:

> Because emotion systems coordinate learning, the broader the range of emotions that [an individual] experiences the broader will be the emotional range of the self that develops. . . . And because more brain systems are typically active during emotional than during nonemotional states, and the intensity of arousal is greater, the opportunity for coordinated learning across brain systems is greater during emotional states. By coordinating parallel plasticity throughout the brain, emotional states promote the development and unification of the self. (p. 322)

FIGURE 3.9.   Psychotherapy expands windows of affect tolerance.

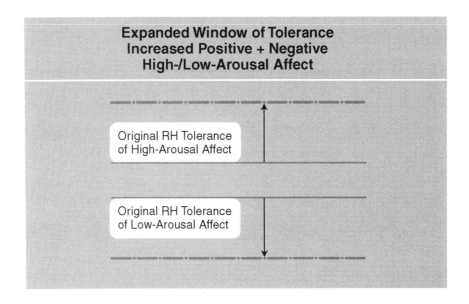

Growth-facilitating experiences co-created at the regulatory boundaries thus promote the "affective building blocks of enactments" (Ginot, 2007). The patient's increased ability to consciously experience and communicate a wider range of positive and negative affects is due to a developmental advance in the capacity to regulate affect. This further maturation of adaptive self-regulation is in turn reflected in the appearance of more complex emotions that result from the simultaneous blending of different affects, and in an expansion in the "affect array."

RIGHT BRAIN PROCESSES IN PSYCHOTHERAPY: NEUROBIOLOGY OF INCREASED COMPLEXITY OF THE RIGHT BRAIN IMPLICIT SELF

Psychotherapy of attachment pathologies and severe personality disorders must focus on unconscious affect and the survival defense of pathological dissociation, "a structured separation of mental processes (e.g., thoughts, emotions, conation, memory, and identity) that are ordinarily *integrated*" (Spiegel & Cardeña, 1991, p. 367). Overwhelming traumatic feelings that are not regulated cannot be adaptively integrated into the patient's emotional life. This dissociative deficit specifically results from a lack of integration of the right hemisphere, the emotional brain. But effective therapy can positively alter the developmental trajectory of the deep right brain and facilitate the *integration* between cortical and subcortical right brain systems. This enhanced interconnectivity allows for an increased complexity of defenses of the emotional right brain, coping strategies for regulating stressful affect that are more flexible and adaptive than pathological dissociation. This in turn enhances the further maturation of the right hemisphere core of the self and its central involvement in "patterns of affect regulation that *integrate* a sense of self across state transitions, thereby allowing for a continuity of inner experience" (Schore, 1994, p. 33).

Concordant with this model of the change mechanism of psychotherapy, Fosha (2005) describes, "A state in which affective and cognitive processes are seamlessly *integrated*, the core state that follows the experience of core affect is optimally suited for the therapeutic integration and consolidation that translate deep in-session changes into lasting therapeutic results" (p. 523). In this state transformation "our view opens up: the entirety of the emotional landscape is visible, and it is evenly illuminated"; and adaptive resources, resilience, and mindful understanding are available to the individual. Fosha speculates this "wide angle lens" is "a capacity centrally mediated by the prefrontal cortex and the orbitofrontal cortex, the ultimate neuro-integrators of the meaning of personal experience (Schore, 2003b; Siegel, 2003)," and it generates "a cohesive and coherent autobiographical narrative" (p. 523). The latter is "primarily mediated by the right hemisphere's prefrontal cortex."

The increased resilience of unconscious strategies of stress regulation that results from an optimal psychotherapeutic experience represents an experience-dependent maturation of "the right hemispheric specialization in regulating stress—and emotion-related processes" (Sullivan & Dufresne, 2006). Studies now indicate that the right hemisphere, which is dominant for autobiographical memory (Markowitsch, Reinkemeier, Kessler, Koyuncu, & Heiss, 2000), provides access to a triggering mechanism that initiates autonomic sympathetic and parasympathetic reactions to socioemotional signals (Spence, Shapiro, & Zaidel, 1996). The regulation of emotional stress is essentially mediated by higher right cortical regulation of lower autonomic structures and peripheral organs. Indeed, anterior areas of the right hemisphere are involved in the control of autonomic activation (Aftanas, Savotina, Makhnev, & Reva, 2005), and right orbitofrontal (ventromedial) cortical activity acts to regulate the sympathetic nervous system (Critchley, Elliott, Mathias, & Dolan, 2000; Hilz et al., 2006).

In a neuroanatomical description that echoes Fosha's (2005) description of the "wide angle lens" of the orbitofrontal core state, current studies conclude, "the rich connections of orbitofrontal cortex endow it with a panoramic view of the entire external environment, as well as the internal environment associated with motivational factors" (Barbas, 2007, p. 239). According to this author, "medial and orbitofrontal cortices, which are associated with appreciation of emotions, project to hypothalamic autonomic centers, which innervate brainstem and spinal autonomic autonomic structures. The latter, in turn, innervate peripheral organs whose activity is markedly increased in emotional arousal" (Barbas, Saha, Rempel-Clower, & Ghashghaei, 2003). It is now established that "The peripheral physiological arousal and action tendencies associated with emotion are implicit in the sense that they occur automatically and *do not require conscious processing to be executed efficiently*" (Lane et al., 2008, p. 217, my italics). Note that the left brain explicit verbal system that analytically processes interpretations is never directly involved in regulating sympathetic nervous system activity. Both secure attachment experiences and effective psychotherapy increase the complexity of the right brain affect-regulating system.

The right hemisphere continues its growth spurts over the stages of the life span, thereby allowing for therapy-induced plasticity in the system. The structural changes that occur from effective psychotherapy take place in descending right cortical top-down pathways from orbitofrontal and ventral medial prefrontal cortices to the amygdala and hypothalamus. They thereby provide a more effective mechanism of prefrontal control of the autonomic nervous system and thus in processes underlying the recognition and expression of emotions. Psychotherapy of patients with attachment pathologies who all too frequently experience traumatic fearful states of arousal, directly impacts and potentially alters right-lateralized dysregulations of the fear-terror system, driven by the subcortical right amygdala, which specializes in fear conditioning (Baker & Kim, 2004) and "unseen fear" (Morris, Ohman, & Dolan, 1999). Importantly, prefrontal areas that inhibit emotional memories and suppress emotional reactivity are lateralized predominantly to the right hemisphere (Depue et al., 2007, p. 218). The observations of Phelps, Delgado, Nearing, and LeDoux (2004) directly relate to the learning process of the psychotherapy context:

> Understanding how fears are acquired is an important step in our ability to translate basic research to the treatment of fear-related behaviors. Understanding how learned fears are diminished may be even more valuable . . . the amygdala may play an important role in extinction learning as well as acquisition and that ventromedial prefrontal cortex may be particularly involved in the retention of extinction learning. (p. 903)

Efficient functions of the right brain implicit self are essential for the following: the reception, expression, and communication of socioaffective information; the unconscious regulation of physiological, endocrinological, neuroendocrine, cardiovascular, and immune functions. Hartikainen, Ogawa, Soltani, and Knight summarize the critical role of nonconscious emotion processing for human survival:

> In unpredictable environments, emotions provide rapid modulation of behavior. From an evolutionary perspective, emotions provide a modulatory control system that facilitates survival and reproduction. Reflex-like reactions to emotional events can occur before attention is paid to them. . . . Neuropsychological evidence supports a right hemispheric bias for emotional and attentional processing in humans. (2007, p. 1929)

At the outset of this chapter I asserted that the emerging paradigm shift is highlighting the primacy of affect in human development, psychopathogenesis, and treatment. A large body of research in the neuroscience literature suggests a special role of the right hemisphere in empathy, identification with others, trust, intersubjective processes, autobiographical memories, own body perception, self-awareness, self-related cognition, affective theory of mind, as well as self-images that are not consciously perceived—all essential components of the therapeutic process (see Schore & Schore, 2008, for references).

A fundamental theme of this work is that bodily based right brain affect, including specifically unconscious affect, needs to be addressed in updated psychotherapeutic interventions. Studies confirm that "The left hemisphere is more involved in the foreground-analytic (conscious) processing of information, whereas the right hemisphere is more involved in the background-holistic (sub-conscious) processing of information" (Prodan, Orbelo, Testa, & Ross, 2001, p. 211); and that "The left side is involved with conscious response and the right with the unconscious mind" (Mlot, 1998, p. 1006). Due to its unique neuroanatomical and neurobiological properties,

> [T]he more "diffuse" organization of the right hemisphere has the effect that it responds to any stimulus, even speech stimuli, more quickly and, thus, earlier. The left hemisphere is activated after this and performs the slower semantic analysis and synthesis . . . the arrival of an individual signal initially in the right hemisphere and then in the left is more "physiological." (Buklina, 2005, p. 479)

Even more than the patient's late-acting rational, analytical, and verbal left mind, the growth-facilitating psychotherapeutic relationship needs to directly access the regulatory boundaries and deeper psychobiological strata of both the patient's and the clinician's right minds. Alvarez asserts, "Schore points out that at the more severe levels of psychopathology, it is not a question of making the unconscious conscious: rather it is a question of restructuring the unconscious itself" (2006, p. 171).

Earlier I suggested that the right hemisphere is dominant in the change process of psychotherapy. Neuroscience authors now conclude that although the left hemisphere is specialized for coping with predictable representations and strategies, the right predominates not only for organizing the human stress response (Wittling, 1995) but also for coping with and assimilating novel situations (Podell, Lovell, & Goldberg, 2001) and ensuring the formation of a new program of interaction with a new environment (Ezhov & Krivoschchekov, 2004). Indeed,

> The right brain possesses special capabilities for processing novel stimuli. . . . Right-brain problem solving generates a matrix of alternative solutions, as contrasted with the left brain's single solution of best fit. This answer matrix remains active while alternative solutions are explored, a method suitable for the open-ended possibilities inherent in a novel situation. (Schutz, 2005, p. 13)

Recall that resilience in the face of stress and novelty is an indicator of attachment security, and so therapeutic changes in the patient's internal working model, which is encoding strategies of affect regulation, reflect structural alterations within the right brain.

The functions of the emotional right brain are essential to the self-exploration process of psychotherapy, especially of unconscious affects that can be integrated into a more complex implicit sense of self. Both optimal development and effective psychotherapy promote more than cognitive changes of the conscious mind, but an expansion of the right brain implicit self, the biological substrate of the human unconscious.

REFERENCES

Adamec, R. E., Blundell, J., & Burton, P. (2003). Phosphorylated cyclic AMP response element bonding protein expression induced in the periaqueductal gray by predator stress; its relationship to the stress experience, behavior, and limbic neural plasticity. *Progress in Neuro-Psychopharmacology & Biological Psychiatry, 27*, 1243–1267.

Adler, H. M. (2002). The sociophysiology of caring in the doctor–patient relationship. *Journal of General Internal Medicine, 17*, 883–890.

Aftanas, L. I., Savotina, L. N., Makhnev, V. P., & Reva, N. V. (2005). Analysis of evoked EEG synchronization and desynchronization during perception of emotogenic stimuli: Association with autonomic activation processes. *Neuroscience and Behavioral Physiology, 35*, 951–957.

Allen, J. G., Console, D. A., & Lewis, L. (1999). Dissociative detachment and memory impairment: Reversible amnesia or encoding failure? *Comprehensive Psychiatry, 40*, 160–171.

Allman, J. M., Watson, K. K., Tetreault, N. A., & Hakeem, A. Y. (2005). Intuition and autism: A possible role for Von Economo neurons. *Trends in Cognitive Sciences, 9*, 367–373.

Alvarez, A. (2006). Some questions concerning states of fragmentation: Unintegration, under-integration, disintegration, and the nature of early integrations. *Journal of Child Psychotherapy, 32*, 158–180.

Baker, K. B., & Kim, J. J. (2004). Amygdalar lateralization in fear conditioning: Evidence for greater involvement of the right amygdala. *Behavioral Neuroscience, 118*, 15–23.

Barbas, H. (2007). Flow of information for emotions through temporal and orbitofrontal pathways. *Journal of Anatomy, 211*, 237–249.

Barbas, H., Saha, S., Rempel-Clower, N., & Ghashghaei, T. (2003). Serial pathways from primate prefrontal cortex to autonomic areas may influence emotional expression. *BMC Neuroscience, 4*, 25.

Bargh, J. A., & Chartrand, T. L. (1999). The unbearable automaticity of being. *American Psychologist, 54*, 462–479.

Bazhenova, O. V., Stroganova, T. A., Doussard-Roosevelt, J. A., Posikera, I. A., & Porges, S. W. (2007). Physiological responses of 5-month-old infants to smiling and blank faces. *International Journal of Psychophysiology, 63*, 64–76.

Beauregard, M., Levesque, J., & Bourgouin, P. (2001). Neural correlates of conscious self-regulation of emotion. *Journal of Neuroscience, 21*, RC165.

Bogolepova, I. N., & Malofeeva, L. I. (2001). Characteristics of the development of speech motor areas 44 and 45 in the left and right hemispheres of the human brain in early post-natal ontogenesis. *Neuroscience and Behavioral Physiology, 31*, 13–18.

Bradshaw, G. A., & Schore, A. N. (2007). How elephants are opening doors: Developmental neuroethology, attachment and social context. *Ethology, 113*, 426–436.

Bromberg, P. M. (2006). *Awakening the dreamer: Clinical journeys.* Mahwah, NJ: Analytic Press.

Broucek, F. J. (1991). *Shame and the self.* New York: Guilford Press.

Bucci, W. (2002). The referential process, consciousness, and sense of self. *Psychoanalytic Inquiry, 22*, 766–793.

Buklina, S. B. (2005). The corpus callosum, interhemispheric interactions, and the function of the right hemisphere of the brain. *Neuroscience and Behavioral Physiology, 35*, 473–480.

Carretie, L., Hinojosa, J. A., Mercado, F., & Tapia, M. (2005). Cortical response to subjectively unconscious danger. *NeuroImage, 24*, 615–623.

Casagrande, M., & Bertini, M. (2008). Night-time right hemisphere superiority and daytime left hemisphere superiority: A repatterning of laterality across wake-sleep-wake states. *Biological Psychology, 77*, 337–342.

Chiron, C., Jambaque, I., Nabbout, R., Lounes, R., Syrota, A., & Dulac, O. (1997). The right brain hemisphere is dominant in human infants. *Brain, 120*, 1057–1065.

Cozolino, L. (2002). *The neuroscience of psychotherapy.* New York: Norton.

Craig, A. D. (2004). Human feelings: Why are some more aware than others? *Nature Neuroscience, 7*, 239–241.

Critchley, H. D., Elliott, R., Mathias, C. J., & Dolan, R. J. (2000). Neural activity relating to generation and representation of galvanic skin conductance responses: A functional magnetic resonance imaging study. *Journal of Neuroscience, 20*, 3033–3040.

Critchley, H. D., Wiens, S., Rothstein, P., Ohman, A., & Dolan, R. J. (2004). Neural systems supporting interoceptive awareness. *Nature Neuroscience, 7*, 189–195.

Crucian, G. P., Hughes, J. D., Barrett, A. M., Williamson, D. J. G., Bauer, R. M., Bowres, D., et al. (2000). Emotional and physiological responses to false feedback. *Cortex, 36*, 623–647.

Darwin, C. (1965). *The expression of emotion in man and animals.* Chicago: University of Chicago Press, 1965. (Original work published 1872)

Davidson, R. J., & Cacioppo, J. T. (1992). New developments in the scientific study of emotion: An introduction to the special section. *Psychological Science, 3*, 21–22.

Depue, B. E., Curran, T., & Banich, M. T. (2007). Prefrontal regions orchestrate suppression of emotional memories via a two-phase process. *Science, 317*, 215–219.

Devinsky, O. (2000). Right cerebral hemisphere dominance for a sense of corporeal and emotional self. *Epilepsy & Behavior, 1*, 60–73.

Diener, M. J., Hilsenroth, M. J., & Weinberger, J. (2007). Therapist affect focus and patient outcomes in psychodynamic psychotherapy: A meta-analysis. *American Journal of Psychiatry, 164*, 936–941.

Dorpat, T. L. (2001). Primary process communication. *Psychoanalytic Inquiry, 3*, 448–463.

Erikson, E. (1950). *Childhood and society.* New York: Norton.

Ezhov, S. N., & Krivoschekov, S. G. (2004). Features of psychomotor responses and interhemispheric relationships at various stages of adaptation to a new time zone. *Human Physiology, 30*, 172–175.

Fosha, D. (2005). Emotion, true self, true other, core state: Toward a clinical theory of affective change process. *Psychoanalytic Review, 92*, 513–551.

Freud, S. (1957a). On narcissism: An introduction. In J. Strachey (Ed. & Trans.), *The standard edition of the complete psychological works of Sigmund Freud* (Vol. 14, pp. 67–102). London: Hogarth Press. (Original work published 1915)

Freud, S. (1957b). The unconscious. In J. Strachey (Ed. & Trans.), *The standard edition of the complete psychological works of Sigmund Freud* (Vol. 14, pp. 159–205). London: Hogarth Press. (Original work published 1915)

Freud, S. (1961). New introductory lectures on psycho-analysis. In J. Strachey (Ed. & Trans.), *The standard edition of the complete psychological works of Sigmund Freud* (Vol. 22, pp. 1–183). London: Hogarth Press. (Original work published 1933)

Frijda, N. H. (1988). The laws of emotion. *American Psychologist, 43*, 349–358.

Gadea, M., Gomez, C., Gonzalez-Bono, E., Espert, R., & Salvador, A. (2005). Increased cortisol and decreased right ear advantage (REA) in dichotic listening following a negative mood induction. *Psychoneuroendocrinology, 30*, 129–138.

Gainotti, G., Caltarirone, C., & Zoccolotti, P. (1993). Left/right and cortical/subcortical dichotomies in the neuropsychological study of human emotions. *Cognition and Emotion, 7*, 71–93.

Galin, D. (1974). Implications for psychiatry of left and right cerebral specialization: A neuropsychological context for unconscious processes. *Archives of General Psychiatry, 31*, 572–583.

Geschwind, N., & Galaburda, A. M. (1987). *Cerebral lateralization: Biological mechanisms, associations, and pathology*. Boston: MIT Press.

Ginot, E. (2007). Intersubjectivity and neuroscience. Understanding enactments and their therapeutic significance within emerging paradigms. *Psychoanalytic Psychology, 24*, 317–332.

Grabner, R. H., Fink, A., & Neubauer, A. C. (2007). Brain correlates of self-related originality of ideas: Evidence from event-related power and phase-locking changes in the EEG. *Behavioral Neuroscience, 121*, 224–230.

Greenberg, L. S. (2008). Emotion coming of age. *Clinical Psychology: Science and Practice, 14*, 414–421.

Greenberg, L. S., & Pavio, S. C. (1997). *Working with emotions in psychotherapy*. New York: Guilford Press.

Gupta, R. K., Hasan, K. M., Trivedi, R., Pradhan, M., Das, V., Parikh, N. A., et al. (2005). Diffusion tensor imaging of the developing human cerebrum. *Journal of Neuroscience Research, 81*, 172–178.

Hartikainen, K. M., Ogawa, K. H., Soltani, M., & Knight, R. T. (2007). Emotionally arousing stimuli compete for attention with left hemispace. *NeuroReport, 18*, 1929–1933.

Heilman, K. M. (1997). The neurobiology of emotional experience. *Journal of Neuropsychiatry & Clinical Neurosciences, 9*, 439–448.

Henry, J. P. (1993). Psychological and physiological responses to stress: The right hemisphere and the hypothalamo-pituitary-adrenal axis, an inquiry into problems of human bonding. *Integrative Physiological and Behavioral Science, 28*, 369–387.

Hesse, E., & Main, M. M. (1999). Second-generation effects of unresolved trauma in nonmaltreating parents: Dissociated, frightened, and threatening parental behavior. *Psychoanalytic Inquiry, 19*, 481–540.

Hesse, E., & Main, M. M. (2006). Frightened, threatening, and dissociative parental behavior in low-risk samples: Description, discussion, and interpretations. *Development and Psychopathology, 18*, 309–343.

Hilz, M. J., Devinsky, O., Szcepanska, H., Borod, J. C., Marthol, H., & Tutaj, M. (2006).

Right ventromedial prefrontal lesions result in paradoxical cardiovascular activation with emotional stimuli. *Brain, 129,* 3343–3355.

Hoppe, K. D. (1977). Split brains and psychoanalysis. *Psychoanalytic Quarterly, 46,* 220–244.

Howard, M. F., & Reggia, J. A. (2007). A theory of the visual system biology underlying development of spatial frequency lateralization. *Brain and Cognition, 64,* 111–123.

Izard, C. E. (1991). *The psychology of emotions.* New York: Plenum Press.

Jackson, J. H. (1931). *Selected writings of J. H. Jackson: Vol. I.* London: Hodder and Soughton.

Jacobson, E. (1964). *The self and the object world.* New York: International Universities Press.

Jung, C. G. (1946). The psychology of the transference (R. F. C. Hull, trans.). Ark Edition. London: Routledge & Kegan Paul.

Kalsched, D. (2005). Hope versus hopelessness in the psychoanalytic situation and Dante's *Divine Comedy, 72,* 167–187.

Kaufman, G. (1989). *The psychology of shame. Theory and treatment of shame-based syndromes.* New York: Springer.

Kestenberg, J. (1985). The flow of empathy and trust between mother and child. In E. J. Anthony & G. H. Pollack (Eds.), *Parental influences in health and disease* (pp. 137–163). Boston: Little Brown.

Kilborne, B. (2003). Shame and shame dynamics. Special issue. *American Journal of Psychoanalysis, 63,* 285–287.

Krusemark, E. A., & Li, W. (2011). Do all threats work the same way? Divergent effects of fear and disgust on sensory perception and attention. *Journal of Neuroscience, 31,* 3429–3434.

Lane, R. D., Ahern, G. L., Schwartz, G. E., & Kaszniak, A. W. (1997). Is alexithymia the emotional equivalent of blindsight? *Biological Psychiatry, 42,* 834–844.

Lane, R. D., Ahern, G. L., Schwartz, G. E., & Kaszniak, A. W. (2008). Neural substrates of implicit and explicit emotional processes: A unifying framework for psychosomatic medicine. *Psychosomatic Medicine, 70,* 214–231.

Lanius, R. A., Vermetten, E., Loewenstein, R. J., Brand, B., Schmahl, C., Bremner, J. D., et al. (2010). Emotion modulation in PTSD: Clinical and neurobiological evidence for a dissociative subtype. *American Journal of Psychiatry, 167,* 640–647.

Lanius, R. A., Williamson, P. C., Bluhm, R. L., Densmore, M., Boksman, K., Neufeld, R. W. J., et al. (2005). Functional connectivity of dissociative responses in posttraumatic stress disorder: A functional magnetic resonance imaging investigation. *Biological Psychiatry, 57,* 873–884.

Larsen, J. K., Brand, N., Bermond, B., & Hijman, R. (2003). Cognitive and emotional characteristics of alexithymia. A review of neurobiological studies. *Journal of Psychosomatic Research, 54,* 533–541.

LeDoux, J. (2002). *Synaptic self: How our brains become who we are.* New York: Viking.

Lenzi, D., Trentini, C., Pantano, P., Macaluso, E., Iacaboni, M., Lenzi, G. I., et al. (2009). Neural basis of maternal communication and emotional expression processing during infant preverbal stage. *Cerebral Cortex, 19,* 1124–1133.

Levine, P. (1997). Waking the tiger: Healing trauma—the innate capacity to transform overwhelming experiences. Berkeley: North Atlantic Books.

Lewis, H. B. (1971). *Shame and guilt in neurosis.* New York: International Universities Press.

Lewis, M. (1992). *Shame: The exposed self.* New York: Free Press.

Lichtenberg, J. D. (1989). *Psychoanalysis and motivation.* Hillsdale, NJ: Analytic Press.

Lichtenberg, J. (2001). Motivational systems and model scenes with special reference to bodily experience. *Psychoanalytic Inquiry, 21,* 430–447.

Loewald, H. (1986). Transference–countertransference. *Journal of the American Psychoanalytic Association, 34,* 275–285.

Loewenstein, R. J. (1996). Dissociative amnesia and dissociative fugue. In L. K. Michaelson & W. J. Ray (Eds.), *Handbook of dissociation: Theoretical, empirical, and clinical perspectives* (pp. 307–336). New York: Plenum.

Lynd, H. M. (1958). *On shame and the search for identity.* New York: Harcourt Brace.

Lyons-Ruth, K. (2005). The two-person unconscious: Intersubjective dialogue, enactive representation, and the emergence of new forms of relational organization. In L. Aron & A. Harris (Eds.), *Relational psychoanalysis* (Vol. II, pp. 2–45). Hillsdale, NJ: Analytic Press.

Malatesta-Magai, C. (1991). Emotional socialization: Its role in personality and developmental psychopathology. In D. Cicchetti & S. L. Toth (Eds.), *Internalizing and externalizing expressions of dysfunction: Rochester symposium on developmental psychopathology* (Vol. 2, pp. 203–224). Hillsdale, NJ: Erlbaum.

Mancia, M. (2006). Implicit memory and early unrepressed unconscious: Their role in the therapeutic process (How the neurosciences can contribute to psychoanalysis). *International Journal of Psychoanalysis, 87,* 83–103.

Mann, M. (2010). Shame veiled and unveiled: The shame affect and its re-emergence in the clinical setting. *American Journal of Psychoanalysis, 70,* 270–281.

Markowitsch, H. J., Reinkemeier, A., Kessler, J., Koyuncu, A., & Heiss, W.-D. (2000). Right amygdalar and temperofrontal activation during autobiographical, but not fictitious memory retrieval. *Behavioral Neurology, 12,* 181–190.

Maroda, K. J. (2005). Show some emotion: Completing the cycle of affective communication. In L. Aron & A. Harris (Eds.), *Revolutionary connections. Relational psychoanalysis: Vol. II. Innovation and expansion* (pp. 121–142). Hillsdale, NJ: Analytic Press.

Martindale, C., & Hasenfus, N. (1978). EEG differences as a function of creativity, stage of the creative process, and effort to be original. *Biological Psychology, 6,* 157–167.

McGilchrist, I. (2009). *The master and his emissary.* New Haven CT: Yale University Press.

Meadows, M., & Kaplan, R. F. (1994). Dissociation of autonomic and subjective responses to emotional slides in right hemisphere damaged patients. *Neuropsycholgia, 32,* 847–856.

Mearns, D., & Cooper, M. (2005). *Working at relational depth in counseling and psychotherapy.* London: Sage.

Minagawa-Kawai, Y., Matsuoka, S., Dan, I., Naoi, N., Nakamura, K., & Kojima, S. (2009). Prefrontal activation associated with social attachment: Facial-emotion recognition in mothers and infants. *Cerebral Cortex, 19,* 284–292.

Mitrani, J. (2007). Some technical implications of Klein's concept of "premature ego development." *International Journal of Psychoanalysis, 88,* 825–842.

Mlot, C. (1998). Probing the biology of emotion. *Science, 280,* 1005–1007.

Morris, J. S., Ohman, A., & Dolan, R. J. (1999). A subcortical pathway to the right amygdala mediating "unseen" fear. *Proceedings of the National Academy of Sciences of the United States of America, 96,* 1680–1685.

Moskal, J. R., Kroes, R. A., Otto, N. J., Rahimi, O., & Claiborne, B. J. (2006). Distinct patterns of gene expression in the left and right hippocampal formation of developing rats. *Hippocampus, 16,* 629–634.

Nathanson, D. L. (1996). A conversation with Donald Nathanson. *Nathanson Biosketch\ Behavior OnLine Home Page\Behavior Online Forums*. Retrieved May 25, 2010, from www.behavior.net/column/nathanson

Nijenhuis, E. R. S. (2000). Somatoform dissociation: Major symptoms of dissociative disorders. *Journal of Trauma & Dissociation, 1*, 7–32.

Nitschke, J. B., Heller, W., Palmieri, P. A., & Miller, G. A. (1999). Contrasting patterns of brain activity in anxious apprehension and anxious arousal. *Psychophysiology, 36*, 628–637.

Ogden, P. (2006). *Empowering the body in the treatment of trauma: The role of sensorimotor processing in trauma*. Paper presented at the UCLA Lifespan Learning Institute Conference, Los Angeles, CA.

Ogden, P., Minton, K., & Pain, C. (2006). *Trauma and the body: A sensorimotor approach to psychotherapy*. New York: Norton.

Ogden, P., Pain, C., Minton, K., & Fisher, J. (2005). Including the body in mainstream psychotherapy for traumatized individuals. *Psychologist-Psychoanalyst, XXV*, 19–24.

Panksepp, J. (2008). The power of the word may reside in the power of affect. *Integrative Psychological & Behavioral Science, 42*, 47–55.

Papousek, M. P. (2007). Communication in infancy: An arena of intersubjective learning. *Infant Behavior & Development, 30*, 258–266.

Phelps, E. A., Delgado, M. R., Nearing, K. I., & LeDoux, J. E. (2004). Extinction learning in humans: Role of the amygdala and vmPFC. *Neuron, 43*, 897–905.

Pincus, D., Freeman, W., & Modell, A. (2007). A neurobiological model of perception. Considerations for transference. *Psychoanalytic Psychology, 24*, 623–640.

Pipp, S., & Harmon, R. J. (1987). Attachment as regulation: A commentary. *Child Development, 58*, 648–652.

Podell, K., Lovell, M., & Goldberg, E. (2001). Lateralization of frontal lobe functions. In S. P. Salloway, P. F. Malloy, and J. D. Duffy (Eds.), *The frontal lobes and neuropsychiatric illness* (pp. 83–89). London: American Psychiatric Publishing.

Porges, S. W. (1997). Emotion: An evolutionary by-product of the neural regulation of the autonomic nervous system. *Annals of the New York Academy of Sciences, 807*, 62–77.

Porges, S. W. (2006). *Love or trauma: How neural mechanisms mediate bodily responses to proximity and touch*. Paper presented at the UCLA Lifespan Learning Institute Conference, Los Angeles, CA.

Porges, S. W., Doussard-Roosevelt, J. A., & Maiti, A. K. (1994). Vagal tone and the physiological regulation of emotion. *Monograph of the Society for Research in Child Development, 59*, 167–186.

Potter-Effron, R. T. (1989). *Shame, guilt and alcoholism: Treatment issues in clinical practice*. New York: Haworth Press.

Price, J. L. (2005). Free will versus survival: Brain systems that underlie intrinsic constraints on behavior. *Journal of Comparative Neurology, 493*, 132–139.

Prodan, C. I., Orbelo, D. M., Testa, J. A., & Ross, E. D. (2001). Hemispheric differences in recognizing upper and lower facial displays of emotion. *Neuropsychiatry, Neuropsychology, and Behavioral Neurology, 14*, 206–212.

Raz, A. (2004). Anatomy of attentional networks. *Anatomical Records, 281B*, 21–36.

Recordati, G. (2003). A thermodynamic model of the sympathetic and parasympathetic nervous systems. *Autonomic Neuroscience: Basic and Clinical, 103*, 1–12.

Rotenberg, V. S. (2004). The ontogeny and asymmetry of the highest brain skills and the pathogenesis of schizophrenia. *Behavioral and Brain Sciences, 27*, 864–865.

Rozin, P., & Fallon, A. E. (1987). A perspective on disgust. *Psychological Review, 94*, 23–41.

Rusch, N., Lieb, K., Gottler, I., Hermann, C., Schramm, E., Richter, H., et al. (2007). Shame and implicit self-concept in women with borderline personality disorder. *American Journal of Psychiatry, 164*, 500–508.

Rusch, N., Schulz, D., Valerius, G., Steil, R., Bohus, M., & Schmahl, C. (2010, December 5). Disgust and implicit self-concept in women with borderline personality disorder and posttraumatic stress disorder. *European Archives of Psychiatry and Clinical Neuroscience.* Retrieved July 14, 2011, from http://www.ncbi.nlm.nih.gov/pubmed/21132504

Russ, S. W. (2000–2001). Primary-process thinking and creativity: Affect and cognition. *Creativity Research Journal, 13*, 27–35.

Ryan, R. (2007). *Motivation and emotion*: A new look and approach for two reemerging fields. *Motivation and Emotion, 31*, 1–3.

Sands, S. H. (1994). What is dissociated? *Dissociation, 7*, 145–152.

Sarkar, J., & Adshead, G. (2006). Personality disorders as disorganization of attachment and affect regulation. *Advances in Psychiatric Treatment, 12*, 297–305.

Sarlo, M., Buodo, G., Poli, S., & Palomba, D. (2005). Changes in EEG alpha power to different disgust elicitors: The specificity of mutilations. *Neuroscience Letters, 382*, 291–296.

Sartre, J-P. (1957). *Being and nothingness.* London: Methuen.

Sato, W., & Aoki, S. (2006). Right hemisphere dominance in processing unconscious emotion. *Brain and Cognition, 62*, 261–266.

Saugstad, L. F. (1998). Cerebral lateralization and rate of maturation. *International Journal of Psychophysiology, 28*, 37–62.

Schore, A. N. (1991). Early superego development: The emergence of shame and narcissistic affect regulation in the practicing period. *Psychoanalysis and Contemporary Thought, 14*, 187–250.

Schore, A. N. (1994). *Affect regulation and the origin of the self.* Mahwah, NJ: Erlbaum.

Schore, A. N. (1997). Interdisciplinary developmental research as a source of clinical models. In M. Moskowitz, C. Monk, C. Kaye, & S. Ellman (Eds.), *The neurobiological and developmental basis for psychotherapeutic intervention* (pp. 1–71). Northvale, NJ: Jason Aronson.

Schore, A. N. (1999). Commentary on emotions: Neuro-psychoanalytic views. *Neuro-Psychoanalysis, 1*, 49–55.

Schore, A. N. (2000). Attachment and the regulation of the right brain. *Attachment & Human Development, 2*, 22–41.

Schore, A. N. (2001). The effects of relational trauma on right brain development, affect regulation, and infant mental health. *Infant Mental Health Journal, 22*, 201–269.

Schore, A. N. (2002a). Advances in neuropsychoanalysis, attachment theory, and trauma research: Implications for self psychology. *Psychoanalytic Inquiry, 22*, 433–484.

Schore, A. N. (2002b). Dysregulation of the right brain: A fundamental mechanism of traumatic attachment and the psychopathogenesis of posttraumatic stress disorder. *Australian & New Zealand Journal of Psychiatry, 36*, 9–30.

Schore, A. N. (2003a). *Affect dysregulation and disorders of the self.* New York: Norton.

Schore, A. N. (2003b). *Affect regulation and the repair of the self.* New York: Norton.

Schore, A. N. (2003c). Early relationship trauma, disorganized attachment, and the development of a predisposition to violence. In M. F. Solomon & D. J. Siegel, (Eds.), *Heal-

ing trauma: Attachment, trauma, the brain and the mind (pp. 107–167). New York: Norton.

Schore, A. N. (2005a). A neuropsychoanalytic viewpoint. Commentary on paper by Steven H. Knoblauch. *Psychoanalytic Dialogues, 15,* 829–853.

Schore, A. N. (2005b). Attachment, affect regulation, and the developing right brain: Linking developmental neuroscience to pediatrics. *Pediatrics in Review, 26,* 204–211.

Schore, A. N. (2007). Review of *Awakening the dreamer: Clinical journeys* by Philip M. Bromberg. *Psychoanalytic Dialogues, 17,* 753–767.

Schore, A. N. (2009). Attachment trauma and the developing right brain: Origins of pathological dissociation. In P. F. Dell & J. A. O'Neil (Eds.), *Dissociation and the dissociative disorders: DSM-V and beyond* (pp. 107–141). New York: Routledge.

Schore, J. R., & Schore, A. N. (2008). Modern attachment theory: The central role of affect regulation in development and treatment. *Clinical Social Work Journal, 36,* 9–20.

Schuengel, C., Bakermans-Kranenburg, M. J., & Van IJzendoorn, M. H. (1999). Frightening maternal behavior linking unresolved loss and disorganized infant attachment. *Journal of Consulting and Clinical Psychology, 67,* 54–63.

Schutz, L. E. (2005). Broad-perspective perceptual disorder of the right hemisphere. *Neuropsychology Review, 15,* 11–27.

Shuren, J. E., & Grafman, J. (2002). The neurology of reasoning. *Archives of Neurology, 59,* 916–919.

Siegel, D. J. (1999). *The developing mind: Toward a neurobiology of interpersonal experience.* New York: Guilford Press.

Siegal, D. J. (2003). An interpersonal neurobiology of psychotherapy: The developing mind and the resolution of trauma. In M. F. Solomon & D. J. Siegel (Eds.), *Healing trauma: Attachment, trauma, the brain and the mind* (pp. 1–54). New York: Norton.

Spence, S., Shapiro, D., & Zaidel, E. (1996). The role of the right hemisphere in the physiological and cognitive components of emotional processing. *Psychophysiology, 13,* 112–122.

Spiegel, D., & Cardeña, E. (1991). Disintegrated experience: The dissociative disorders revisited. *Journal of Abnormal Psychology, 100,* 366–378.

Spitzer, C., Barnow, S., Freyberger, H. J., & Grabe, H. J. (2007). Dissociation predicts symptom-related treatment outcome in short-term inpatient psychotherapy. *Australian and New Zealand Journal of Psychiatry, 41,* 682–687.

Spitzer, C., Wilert, C., Grabe, H-J., Rizos, T., & Freyberger, H. J. (2004). Dissociation, hemispheric asymmetry, and dysfunction of hemispheric interaction: A transcranial magnetic approach. *Journal of Neuropsychiatry and Clinical Neurosciences, 16,* 163–169.

Stern, D. N. (2004). *The present moment in psychotherapy and everyday life.* New York: Norton.

Stern, D. N., Sander, L., Nahum, J. P., Harrison, A. M., Lyons-Ruth, K., Morgan, A. C., et al. (1998). Non-interpretive mechanisms in psychoanalytic therapy. *International Journal of Psychoanalysis, 79,* 903–921.

Suler, J. R. (1989). Mental imagery in psychoanalytic treatment. *Psychoanalytic Psychology, 6,* 343–366.

Sullivan, R. M., & Dufresne, M. M. (2006). Mesocortical dopamine and HPA axis regulation: Role of laterality and early environment. *Brain Research, 1076,* 49–59.

Sun, T., Patoine, C., Abu-Khalil, A., Visvader, J., Sum, E., Cherry, T. J., et al. (2005). Early asymmetry of gene transcription in embryonic human left and right cerebral cortex. *Science, 308,* 1794–1798.

Suter, S. E., Huggenberger, H. J., & Schachinger, H. (2007). Cold pressor stress reduces left cradling preference in nulliparous human females. *Stress, 10*, 45–51.

Symonds, L. L., Gordon, N. S., Bixby, J. C., & Mande, M. M. (2006). Right-lateralized pain processing in the human cortex: An fMRI study. *Journal of Neurophysiology, 95*, 3823–3830.

Taylor, G. J., Bagby, R. M., & Parker, J. D. A. (1997). *Disorders of affect regulation: Alexithymia in medical and psychiatric illness.* Cambridge, UK: Cambridge University Press.

Theoret, H., Kobayashi, M., Merabet, L., Wagner, T., Tormos, J. M., & Pascual-Leone, A. (2004). Modulation of right motor cortex excitability without awareness following presentation of masked self-images. *Cognitive Brain Research, 20*, 54–57.

Tomkins, S. (1963). *Affect/imagery/consciousness: Vol. 2. The negative affects.* New York: Springer.

Trevarthen, C. (1996). Lateral asymmetries in infancy: Implications for the development of the hemispheres. *Neuroscience and Biobehavioral Reviews, 20*, 571–586.

Tronick, E. Z. (2004). Why is connection with others so critical? Dyadic meaning making, messiness and complexity governed selective processes which co-create and expand individuals' states of consciousness. In J. Nadel & D. Muir (Eds.), *Emotional development.* New York: Oxford University Press.

Tronick, E. Z. (2007). *The neurobehavioral and social-emotional development of infants and children.* New York: Norton.

Tutte, J. C. (2004). The concept of psychical trauma: A bridge in interdisciplinary space. *International Journal of Psychoanalysis, 85*, 897–921.

Ulanov, A. B. (2001). *Finding space. Winnicott, God, and psychic reality.* Louisville, KY: Westminster John Knox Press.

van der Kolk, B. A., Weisaeth, L., & van der Hart, O. (1996). History of trauma in psychiatry. In B. A. van der Kolk, A. C. McFarlane, & L. Weisaeth (Eds.), *Traumatic stress: The effects of overwhelming experience on mind, body, and society* (pp. 47–74). New York: Guilford Press.

Van Lancker, D., & Cummings, J. L. (1999). Expletives: Neurolinguistic and neurobehavioral perspectives on swearing. *Brain Research Reviews, 31*, 83–104.

Watt, D. F. (2003). Psychotherapy in an age of neuroscience: Bridges to affective neuroscience. In J. Corrigall & H. Wilkinson (Eds.), *Revolutionary connections. Psychotherapy and neuroscience* (pp. 79–115). London: Karnac.

Wheatley-Crosbie, J. R. (2006). Healing traumatic reenactment: Psyche's return from soma's underworld. *USA Body Psychotherapy Journal, 5*, 10–28.

Whitehead, C. C. (2006). Neo-psychoanalysis: A paradigm for the 21st century. *Journal of the Academy of Psychoanalysis and Dynamic Psychiatry, 34*, 603–627.

Winnicott, D. W. (1958). The capacity to be alone. *International Journal of Psycho-Analysis, 39*, 416–420.

Wittling, W. (1995). The right hemisphere and the human stress response. *Acta Physiologica Scandinavica, 161* (Supplement 640), 55–59.

Wright, K. (1991). *Vision and separation: Between mother and baby.* Northvale NJ: Jason Aronson.

Ziabreva, I., Poeggel, G., Schnabel, R., & Braun, K. (2003). Separation-induced receptor changes in the hippocampus and amygdala of *Octodon degus*: Influence of maternal vocalizations. *Journal of Neuroscience, 23*, 5329–5336.

CHAPTER 4

The Right Brain Implicit Self Lies at the Core of Psychoanalysis

For the last two decades my work on regulation theory has focused on the origin, psychopathogenesis, and psychotherapeutic treatment of the early forming subjective implicit self. These neuropsychoanalytic studies of the evolution of psychic structure attempt to understand more deeply the essential psychological processes and biological mechanisms that underlie the psychobiological substrate of the human unconscious described by Freud. Over this same time period the study of implicit unconscious phenomena has finally become a legitimate area of not only psychoanalytic but also scientific inquiry. In 2002 the neuroscientist Joseph LeDoux wrote in the journal *Science*, "That explicit and implicit aspects of the self exist is not a particularly novel idea. It is closely related to Freud's partition of the mind into conscious, preconscious (accessible but not currently accessed), and unconscious (inaccessible) levels" (p. 28). Over the course of my writings I have provided a substantial amount of interdisciplinary evidence supporting the proposition that the early developing right brain generates the implicit self, the structural system of the human unconscious (Schore, 1994, 2003a, 2005, 2007). This conception is echoed in recent neuroscientific writings by Tucker and Moller (2007), who state, "The right hemisphere's specialization for emotional communication through nonverbal channels seems to suggest a domain of the mind that is close to the motivationally charged psychoanalytic unconscious" (p. 91).

One of the major trends in current neuroscience that is directly relevant to all psychotherapists (but especially psychoanalytically informed clinicians) is the upsurge in brain laterality research. Authors are now concluding, "The right hemisphere has been linked to implicit information processing, as opposed to the more explicit and more conscious processing tied to the left hemisphere" (Happaney, Zelazo, & Stuss, 2004, p. 7). With respect to hemispheric information-processing strategies, psychophysiological researchers are reporting, "in most people the analytical . . . verbal component being associated with left-hemispheric structures, while the nonverbal, symbolic, and unconscious components are associated with activity in structures of the right hemisphere" (Aftanas & Varlamov, 2007, p. 71). Perhaps the clearest description of the fundamental differences between the hemispheres is offered by McGilchrist (2009):

> If what one means by consciousness is the part of the mind that brings the world into focus, makes it explicit, allows it to be formulated in language, and is aware of its own awareness, it is reasonable to link the conscious mind to activity almost all of which lies ultimately in the left hemisphere (p. 188). . . . The right hemisphere, by contrast, yields a world of individual, changing, evolving, interconnected, implicit, incarnate, living beings within the context of the lived world, but in the nature of things never fully graspable, always imperfectly known—and to this world it exists in a relationship of care. (p. 174).

Furthermore, temporal differences exist between right implicit and left explicit processing. Mirroring Freud's idea that early unconscious processes precede later conscious processes, neuroimaging research on affective processing in psychotherapy reports "activation of structures in the right hemisphere (the 'emotional' hemisphere) preceded activation of left-hemispheric structures. These findings are in accordance with a leading role of right-hemispheric structures in the processing of affective stimuli" (Tschacher, Schildt, & Sander, 2010, p. 584). Buklina (2005) describes the general dynamic principle:

> [T]he more "diffuse" organization of the right hemisphere has the effect that it responds to any stimulus, even speech stimuli, more quickly and, thus, earlier. The left hemisphere is activated after this and performs the slower semantic analysis . . . the arrival of an individual signal initially in the right hemisphere and then in the left is more "physiological." (p. 479; see Figure 4.1)

An essential theme of this contribution of regulation theory is that current clinical and experimental studies of the rapid acting unconscious, right brain "physiological" implicit system can do more than support a clinical psychoanalytic model of treatment, but rather this interdisciplinary information can elucidate the mechanisms that lie at the core of psychoanalysis. The body of my work strongly suggests the following organizing principles. The concept of a single unitary "self" is as misleading as the idea of a single unitary "brain." The left and right hemispheres process information in their own unique fashion and represent a conscious left brain self-system and an unconscious right brain self-system. Despite the designation of the verbal left hemisphere as "dominant" due to its capacities for explicitly processing language functions, it is the emotion-processing right hemisphere and its implicit homeostatic-survival and communication functions that are truly dominant in human existence (Schore, 2003a). The early forming implicit self continues to develop, and it operates in qualitatively differ-

Figure 4.1.   Implicit processing of right brain and subsequent connections into left brain explicit system. Note the vertical axis of right brain on the right side of the figure.

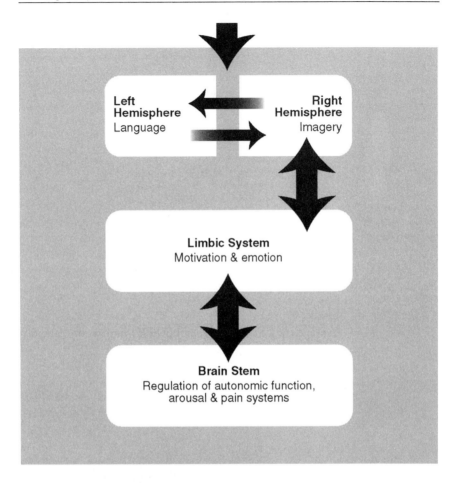

ent ways from the later-forming conscious explicit self. Recall Freud's (1916–1917/1961 & 1963) assertion that the unconscious is "a special realm, with its own desires and modes of expression and peculiar mental mechanisms not elsewhere operative." In essence, my work is an exploration of this "special realm."

This neuropsychoanalytic perspective echoes Freud's fundamental assertion that the central questions of the human condition, which psychoanalysis directly addresses, can never be found in knowledge of how the conscious mind of the explicit self-system works, but rather in a deeper understanding of the implicit psychobiological mechanisms of the unconscious mind. Other fields of study are now appreciating the importance of this unconscious realm in all levels of human existence. In the broader psychological literature, Bargh and Morsella (2008, p. 73) conclude, "Freud's model of the unconscious as the primary guiding influence over every day life, even today, is more specific and detailed than any to be found in contemporary cognitive or social psychology." Thus, not only psychoanalysis but also a large number of disciplines in both the sciences and the arts are now experiencing a paradigm shift from explicit conscious cognition to implicit unconscious affect (Schore, 2009a). In a recent editorial of the journal *Motivation and Emotion*, Richard Ryan asserts, "After three decades of the dominance of cognitive approaches, motivational and emotional processes have roared back into the limelight" (2007, p. 1). A large number of interdisciplinary studies are now converging upon the centrality of these implicit right brain motivational and emotional processes that are essential to adaptive functioning.

ROLE OF IMPLICIT LEARNING IN CONTEMPORARY PSYCHOANALYSIS

In this work I differentiate a surface, verbal, conscious, analytic explicit self versus a deeper nonverbal, nonconscious, holistic, emotional, corporeal implicit self. These two lateralized systems contain qualitatively different forms of cognition and therefore unique ways of "knowing," as well as different memory systems and states of consciousness. Neuroscientists contend, "Because the right and left hemispheres store different forms of knowledge and mediate different forms of cognitive activity, different neuronal architectures probably exist within the association cortices of the hemispheres" (Heilman, Nadeau, & Beversdorf, 2003, p. 374). Cognitive scientists now assert that when an individual generates thoughts, "conscious thought stays firmly under the searchlight, [whereas] unconscious thought ventures out to the dark and dusty nooks and crannies of the mind" (Dijksterhuis & Meurs, 2006, p. 138). This latter implicit process is, of course, essential to all psychodynamic clinical approaches.

But I will argue that implicit (nonconscious) functions are much more than just the thinking, learning, memory, and attention processes highlighted by cognitive psychology. A psychological theory of cognition, even unconscious cognition, cannot penetrate the fundamental questions of development, psychopathology, and the change process of psychotherapy. In addition to *implicit cognition* (right brain unconscious processing of exteroceptive information from the outer world and interoceptive information from the inner world), the implicit concept also includes *implicit affect, implicit communication, and implicit self-regulation*. The ongoing paradigm shift from the explicit cognitive to the implicit affective realm is driven by both new experimental data on emotional processes and updated clinical models for working with affective systems.

Freud (1915/1957) stressed that the work of psychotherapy is always concerned with affect states. In my first book I expanded upon this therapeutic principle, asserting that affects are "the center of empathic communication" and that "the regulation of conscious and *unconscious feelings* is placed in the center of the clinical stage" (Schore, 1994). Consonant with these ideas, the essential clinical role of *implicit affect* is underscored in current neuroscience research reporting unconscious processing of emotional stimuli is specifically associated with activation of the right and not the left hemisphere (Morris, Ohman, & Dolan,

1998), and documenting a "right hemispheric dominance in processing of unconscious negative emotion" (Sato & Aoki, 2006) and a "cortical response to subjectively unconscious danger" (Carretie, Hinojosa, Mercado, & Tapia, 2005). This work establishes the validity of the concept of unconscious (and also dissociated) affect, a common focus of the treatment of pathological defenses.

In this same volume I offered a model of *implicit communications* within the therapeutic relationship, whereby right brain–to–right brain transference-countertransference communications represent interactions of the patient's and therapist's unconscious primary process systems (Schore, 1994). A body of studies indicates that although the left hemisphere mediates most linguistic behaviors, the right hemisphere is important for the broader aspects of communication, mediated by a "relational unconscious" (Schore, 2009a). This research also indicates that "The right hemisphere operates in a more free-associative, primary process manner, typically observed in states such as dreaming or reverie" (Grabner, Fink, & Neubauer, 2007, p. 228).

Congruent with this model, Dorpat (2001) describes the implicit process of "primary process communication" expressed in "both body movements (kinesics), posture, gesture, facial expression, voice inflection, and the sequence, rhythm, and pitch of the spoken words" (p. 451). He suggests affective and object-relational information are transmitted predominantly by primary process communication, whereas secondary process communication has a highly complex and powerful logical syntax but lacks adequate semantics in the field of relationships. Stern (2004) argues that the "comfortable, rich, implicit pre-verbal world is fractured into unrecognizable pieces by attaching language to his implicit experiences. . . . The loss is of wholeness, felt truth, richness, and honesty" (p. 144). In light of the fact that the left hemisphere is dominant for certain aspects of language and the right is for emotional communication, I have proposed the psychotherapy process is best described not as "the talking cure" but as "the communicating cure" (Schore, 2005). Chused (2007) now asserts, "I suspect our field has not yet fully appreciated the importance of this implicit communication" (p. 879).

With regard to *implicit cognition*, I have recently suggested that primary process cognition underlies clinical intuition, a major factor in therapeutic effectiveness (Schore & Schore, 2008). Indeed, the definition of *intuition*, "the ability to understand or know something immediately, without conscious reasoning" (*Compact Oxford English Dictionary of Current English*, 2005), clearly implies right and not left brain processing. Psychological theoreticians now assert that intuition depends on accessing large banks of implicit knowledge formed from unarticulated person–environment exchanges that occur between environmental input and the individual's phenomenological experience (Narvaez, 2010). It operates on a nonverbal level, with little effort, deliberation, or conscious awareness, and is thus characterized as "phenomenally unconscious" (Buchner & Wippich, 1998).

Bohart (1999) contends that in the psychotherapy context, "what I extract perceptually and intuitively from lived experience is far more compelling than thought information" (p. 294). In an important article on this theme, Welling concludes,

> The psychotherapist who considers his methods and decisions exclusively the result of conscious reasoning is most likely mistaken. No therapist can reasonably deny following hunches, experiencing sudden insights, choosing directions without really knowing why, or having uncanny feelings that turn out to be of great importance for therapy. All these phenomena are occurrences of intuitive modes of functioning. (2005, p. 19)

Last, the central theme in all of my writings is *implicit affect regulation* in the organization of the self. An inability to implicitly regulate the intensity of emotions is a major outcome of early relational trauma, and this deficit is a central focus of the psychotherapy of a large number of psychiatric disorders. Citing my work, Greenberg now proposes,

> An issue of major clinical significance then is generating theory and research to help understand to what extent automatic emotion processes can be changed through deliberate processes and to what extent only through more implicit processes based on new emotional and/or relational experiences. Stated in another way the question becomes how much emotional change requires *implicit experiential learning vs. explicit conceptual learning*. (2007, p. 416, my italics)

In agreement with current trends in modern relational psychoanalysis, Greenberg concludes, "The field has yet to pay adequate attention to implicit and relational processes of regulation" (p. 414).

In the following I discuss and update my work on the right brain implicit self. After a brief discussion of implicit processes in early development, psychopathogenesis, and dissociation, I describe the essential role of implicit unconscious affect in psychotherapeutic change processes. The bulk of this work represents a clinical expansion of regulation theory, wherein I focus on the expression of right brain unconscious mechanisms in affect-laden enactments, and in the therapist's moment-to-moment navigation through these heightened affective moments not by explicit secondary process cognition, but by implicit primary process clinical intuition. Direct access to implicit affective processes will be shown to be essential to the co-creation of corrective emotional experiences and, indeed, to effective treatment.

IMPLICIT PROCESSES IN EARLY DEVELOPMENT AND PSYCHOPATHOGENESIS

The concept of the unconscious, once uniquely studied by psychoanalysis, is crossing interdisciplinary boundaries. Infant researchers now assert, "Preverbal communication . . . is the realm of non-consciously regulated intuitive behavior and implicit relational knowledge. Whether information is transferred or shared, which information gets across, and on which level it is 'understood,' does not necessarily depend on the sender's intention or conscious awareness" (Papousek, 2007, p. 258). This relational information is transmitted in psychobiological exchanges embedded in the co-created attachment bond. During spontaneous right brain–to–right brain visual-facial, auditory-prosodic, and tactile-proprioceptive emotionally charged attachment communications, the sensitive, psychobiologically attuned caregiver regulates, at an implicit level, the infant's states of arousal (Schore, 1994). Note that implicit relational knowledge is not purely psychological, but essentially psychobiological, mind *and* body.

These nonverbal interactions with the social environment are occurring during a critical period of growth of the early developing right hemisphere (Chiron et al., 1997). A large body of experimental data now supports the developmental principle that implicit affective interactions directly impact the experience-dependent maturation of the right hemisphere (Ammaniti & Trentini, 2009; Schore 1994, 2003a, 2003b, 2009b, 2009c; Siegel, 1999). The highest centers of this hemisphere, especially the orbitofrontal cortex, the locus of Bowlby's attachment system, act as the brain's most complex affect and stress regulatory system (Cerqueira, Almeida, & Sousa, 2008; Schore, 1994, 2000). Confirming this interpersonal neurobiological model, a near-infrared spectroscopy study of infant–mother attachment at 12 months concludes, "our results are in agreement with that of Schore (2000) who addressed the importance of the right hemisphere in the attachment system" (Minagawa-Kawai et al., 2009, p. 289). Similarly, using magnetoencephalography, Kringelbach et al. (2008) show that the orbitofrontal cortex and right fusiform gyrus act as "a specific neural signature for parental instinct," responding to the face of an infant in 130 milliseconds. Neuroscientists now contend that throughout the life span, "The neural substrates of the perception of voices, faces, gestures, smells and pheromones, as evidenced by modern neuroimaging techniques, are characterized by a general pattern of right-hemispheric functional asymmetry" (Brancucci, Lucci, Mazzatenta, & Tommasi, 2009, p. 895).

But the right brain imprints not only regulated but also dysregulated attachment experiences, and therefore relational trauma (Schore, 2001, 2009b). During critical periods of early socialization, trauma-induced arousal dysregulation precludes the forementioned facial-visual, auditory-prosodic, and tactile-proprioceptive attachment communications and thereby alters the development of essential right brain functions. In contrast to an optimal attachment scenario, in a relational growth-inhibiting early environment the primary caregiver of an insecure, disorganized, disoriented infant induces traumatic states of enduring negative affect in the child. This inaccessible caregiver reacts to her infant's expressions of emotions and stress inappropriately and/or rejectingly, and therefore shows minimal or unpredictable participation in the various types of arousal regulating processes. Instead of modulating, she induces extreme levels of stressful stimulation and arousal that are very high in abuse and/or very low in neglect.

Because she provides no interactive repair, the infant's intense negative affective states last for long periods of time.

Beebe and her colleagues (2010) now describes research on four-month-old infants who later show disorganized attachment. Specifically what predicted disorganized attachment was "*not being sensed and known* by the mother, and *confusion in sensing and knowing himself* (p. 199, emphasis in original). Furthermore, all communication modalities were affected such as "attention, touch . . . spatial orientation as well as facial and vocal affect, and facial-visual engagement" (p. 119). On the other side of the dyad they observe that the mothers of these infants are overwhelmed with their own unresolved abuse or trauma, and therefore cannot bear to intersubjectively engage with their infants' distress. Thus, because these mothers are unable to regulate their own distress, they cannot regulate their infant's distress. These caregivers are unable to allow themselves to be emotionally affected by their infant's dysregulated state, thus they "*shut down*" emotionally, closing their faces, looking away from the infant's face, and thereby failing to coordinate with the infant's emotional state. Beebe interprets this fearful maternal behavior as a *defensive dissociation*, a strategy that protects the mother from the facial and visual intimacy that would come from "joining" the infant's distressed moments. This type of mother thus shows disrupted and contradictory forms of affective communication, especially around the infant's need for comfort when distressed (Beebe et al., 2010).

During these episodes of the intergenerational transmission of attachment trauma, the infant is matching the rhythmic structures of the mother's dysregulated states of both hyperarousal and dissociative hypoarousal (see Schore 2002, 2007, 2009b, 2009c). In a recent prospective study, Dutra et al. (2009) observe that maternal disrupted affective communications and lack of involvement in the regulation of stressful arousal are associated with the child's use of dissociation, "one of the few available means for achieving a modicum of relief from fearful arousal." This in turn leads the child "not to acknowledge pain and distress within a set of caregiving relationships that are vital for survival" (p. 388). The massive psychobiological stress associated with disorganized-disoriented attachment trauma sets the stage for the characterological use of right brain pathological dissociation over all subsequent periods of human development (Schore, 2002, 2009b, 2009c). In this manner, "traumatic stress in childhood could lead to self-modulation of painful affect by directing attention away from internal emotional states" (Lane, Ahern, Schwartz, & Kaszniak, 1997, p. 840).

At all points of the life span, pathological dissociation is expressed as the inability of the right brain cortical-subcortical implicit self-system to recognize and process external stimuli (exteroceptive information coming from the relational environment) and on a moment-to-moment basis integrate them with internal stimuli (interoceptive information from the body, somatic markers, the "felt experience") (Schore, 2003b, 2007). It thus interrupts the right brain's capacity to generate a conscious affect. Recall Freud's speculation, "Unconscious ideas continue to exist after repression as actual structures in the system *Ucs*, whereas all that corresponds in that system to unconscious affects is a potential beginning which is prevented from developing" (1915/1957, p. 178). These data clearly suggest a paradigm shift in psychoanalytic models of psychopathogenesis, from Oedipal repression to pre-Oedipal dissociation, the "bottom-line defense."

Neuroscientists contend that the right hemisphere is centrally involved in "maintaining a coherent, continuous and unified sense of self" (Devinsky, 2000). The survival strategy of pathological dissociation is expressed as a dis-integration of the right brain emotional-corporeal implicit self, the biological substrate of the human unconscious. Individuals with an attachment history of what Kestenberg (1985) referred to as "dead spots" in the infant's subjective experience subsequently access pathological dissociation ("feigned death") in moments of relational stress, and characterologically experience episodes of "psychic death" and an inability to sustain an inner sense of "aliveness" (Bach, 2008). Thus there is a deficit in implicitly generating and integrating what Stern (2004) calls "a present moment," the basic fabric of lived experience created in continuous small packages of interactions with others. Stern further postulates that present moments are infused with vitality affects, that they are the smallest molar unit of psychologically meaningful relational experience that exhibit temporal and rhythmic patterning, and that they operate at an implicit/procedural "core" level of consciousness. Dissociation, a dis-integrator of the conscious subjective experience of a present moment ("an uninterrupted now"; Stern, 2004), is "a basic part of the psychobiology of the human trauma response: a protective activation of altered states of consciousness in reaction to overwhelming psychological trauma" (Loewenstein, 1996, p. 312).

The fragile unconscious system of such personalities is susceptible to mind–body metabolic collapse and thereby a loss of energy-dependent synaptic connectivity within the right brain and an inability to generate vitality affects. This is expressed in a sudden implosion of the implicit self, a rupture of self-continuity, and a loss of an ability to experience a conscious affect. This collapse of the implicit self is signaled by the amplification of the affects of shame and disgust, and by the cognitions of hopelessness and helplessness. Because the right hemisphere mediates the communication and regulation of emotional states, the rupture of intersubjectivity is accompanied by an instant dissipation of safety and trust, a common occurrence in the treatment of the right brain deficits of severe personality disorders (Schore, 2007, 2009b).

Clinical research on dissociation is directly relevant to the treatment of such patients. In a transcranial magnetic stimulation study of adults, Spitzer et al. (2004) report, "In dissociation-prone individuals, a trauma that is perceived and processed by the right hemisphere will lead to a 'disruption in the usually integrated functions of consciousness'" (p. 168). In functional magnetic resonance imaging research, Lanius et al. (2005) show predominantly right hemispheric activation in post-traumatic stress disorder (PTSD) patients while they are dissociating. They conclude that patients dissociate in order to escape from the overwhelming emotions associated with the traumatic memory, and that dissociation can be interpreted as representing a nonverbal response to the traumatic memory. This bottom-line defense represents the major counterforce to the emotional-motivational aspects of the change process in psychotherapy (Schore, 2007). Research shows that insecurely attached dissociative patients dissociate as a response to negative emotions arising in psychodynamic psychotherapy, leading to a less favorable treatment outcome (Spitzer, Barnow, Freyberger, & Grabe, 2007).

IMPLICIT PROCESSES IN PSYCHOTHERAPY

A major tenet of my work dictates that the relevance of developmental attachment studies to the treatment process lies in the commonality of implicit right brain–to–right brain affect communicating and regulating mechanisms in the caregiver–infant and the therapist–patient relationship (the therapeutic alliance). Not only psychoanalytic-based treatment models, but also all forms of psychotherapy are now articulating the centrality of the therapeutic alliance and turning to attachment theory as the prime theoretical model (Schore, 2000). Within the therapeutic dyad, not left brain verbal explicit patient–therapist discourse but right brain implicit nonverbal affect-laden communication directly represents the attachment dynamic. Just as the left brain communicates its states to other left brains via conscious linguistic behaviors, so the right brain nonverbally communicates its unconscious states to other right brains that are tuned to receive these communications. On this matter Stern suggests,

> Without the nonverbal it would be hard to achieve the empathic, participatory, and resonating aspects of intersubjectivity. One would only be left with a kind of pared down, neutral "understanding" of the other's subjective experience. One reason that this distinction is drawn is that in many cases the analyst is consciously aware of the content or speech while processing the nonverbal aspects out of awareness. With an intersubjectivist perspective, a more conscious processing by the analyst of the nonverbal is necessary. (2005, p. 80)

Studies show that 60% of human communication is nonverbal (Burgoon, 1985).

Writing on therapeutic "nonverbal implicit communications," Chused (2007) asserts, "It is not that the information they contain cannot be verbalized, only that sometimes only a nonverbal approach can deliver the information in a way it can be used, particularly when there is no conscious awareness of the underlying concerns involved" (p. 879). These ideas are echoed by Hutterer and Liss (2006), who state that nonverbal variables such as tone, tempo, rhythm, timbre, prosody, and amplitude of speech, as well as body language signals, may need to be reexamined as essential aspects of therapeutic technique. It is now well established that the right hemisphere is dominant for nonverbal (Benowitz et al., 1983) and emotional (Blonder, Bowers, & Heilman, 1991) communication.

Recent neuroscientific information about the emotion-processing right brain is also directly applicable to models of the psychotherapy change process. Decety and Chaminade describe right brain operations essential for adaptive interpersonal functioning, ones specifically activated in the therapeutic alliance: "Mental states that are in essence private to the self may be shared between individuals . . . self-awareness, empathy, identification with others, and more generally inter-subjective processes, are largely dependent upon . . . right hemisphere resources, which are the first to develop" (2003, p. 591). Referring to other fundamental processes explored in psychotherapy, Uddin et al. conclude, "The emerging picture from the current literature seems to suggest a special role of the right hemisphere in self-related cognition, own body perception, self-awareness and autobiographical memories" (2006, p. 65). And with respect to the relational mechanism within the therapeutic alliance, Keenan and his colleagues assert, "The right hemisphere, in fact, truly interprets the mental state not only of its own brain, but the brains (and minds) of others" (2005, p. 702).

This hemisphere is centrally involved in "implicit learning" (Hugdahl, 1995), and "implicit relational knowledge" stored in the nonverbal domain is now proposed to be at the core of therapeutic change (Stern et al., 1998). Describing the right hemisphere as "the seat of implicit memory," Mancia (2006) observes, "The discovery of the implicit memory has extended the concept of the unconscious and supports the hypothesis that this is where the emotional and affective— sometimes traumatic—presymbolic and preverbal experiences of the primary mother–infant relations are stored" (p. 83). Right brain autobiographical memory (Markowitsch, Reinkemeier, Kessler, Koyuncu, & Heiss, 2000), which stores insecure attachment histories, is activated in the therapeutic alliance, especially under relational stress. Cortina and Liotti (2007) point out that "experience encoded and stored in the implicit system is still alive and carried forward as negative expectations in regard to the availability and responsiveness of others, although this knowledge is unavailable for conscious recall" (p. 207). These expectations are in turn expressed in the alliance. Such affective communications "occur at an implicit level of rapid cueing and response that occurs too rapidly for simultaneous verbal transaction and conscious reflection" (Lyons-Ruth, 2000, pp. 91–92).

More specifically, spontaneous nonverbal transference-countertransference interactions at preconscious-unconscious levels represent implicit right brain–to–right brain nonverbal communications of fast-acting, automatic, regulated, and especially dysregulated bodily based stressful emotional states between patient and therapist (Schore, 1994). Transference is therefore an activation of right brain autobiographical memory, as autobiographical negatively valenced, high-intensity emotions are retrieved from specifically the right (and not left) medial temporal lobe (Buchanan, Tranel, & Adolphs, 2006). Neuropsychoanalytic models of transference (Pincus, Freeman, & Modell, 2007) now contend that "no appreciation of transference can do without emotion" (p. 634), and that "transference is distinctive in that it depends on early patterns of emotional attachment with caregivers" (p. 636).

Transference can be described as "an established pattern of relating and emotional responding that is cued by something in the present, but it oftentimes calls up both an affective state and thoughts that may have more to do with past experience than present ones" (Maroda, 2005, p. 134). Writing about unconscious emotional memories, Gainotti asserts, "the right hemisphere may be crucially involved in those emotional memories which must be reactivated and reworked during the psychoanalytical treatment" (2006, p. 167). These right brain communications are in turn processed by the psychobiologically attuned empathic clinician. Rizzuto observes, "I suggest that the analyst listens with his or her entire unconscious memory as a tool, that is, an affective, relational, and representational memory to be able to hear the whole patient" (2008, p. 744). Interestingly, these emotional communications are more efficiently processed in the clinician's left ear (right hemisphere; Sim & Martinez, 2005).

IMPLICIT PROCESSES IN CLINICAL ENACTMENTS

The quintessential clinical context for a right brain transferential-countertransferential implicit communication of a dysregulated emotional state is the heightened affective moment of a clinical enactment. There is now agreement that enactments, "events occurring within the dyad that both parties experience as being the consequence of behavior in the other" (McLaughlin, 1991), are fundamentally mediated by nonverbal unconscious relational behaviors within the therapeutic alliance (Ginot, 2007; Schore, 2003a). These are transacted in moment-to-moment right brain–to–right brain visual-facial, auditory-prosodic, and tactile-proprioceptive emotionally charged attachment communications, as well as in gestures and body language, rapidly expressed behaviors that play a critical role in the unconscious communications embedded within the enactment. These rapid implicit transactions occur in milliseconds, in the temporal domain of Stern's (2004) "present moment," an event that lasts 4 seconds or less.

Intersubjective communications impact not only mental but also psychobiological systems in both patient and therapist. Aron observes, "patient and analyst mutually regulate each other's behaviors, enactments, and states of consciousness such that each gets under the other's skin, each reaches into the other's guts, each is breathed in and absorbed by the other. . . . [T]he analyst must be attuned to the nonverbal, the affective . . . to his or her bodily responses (1998, p. 26). This dyadic psychobiological mechanism allows for the detection of unconscious affects and underlies the premise that "an enactment, by patient or analyst, could be evidence of something which has not yet been 'felt' by them" (Zanocco et al., 2006, p. 153).

In *Affect Regulation and the Repair of the Self*, I offered a chapter, "Clinical Implications of a Psychoneurobiological Model of Projective Identification" (Schore, 2003a). The entire chapter on moment-to-moment implicit nonverbal communications within an enactment focuses on phenomena that take place in "a moment," literally a split second. In it I offer a slow motion analysis of the rapid dyadic psychobiological events that occur in a clinical heightened affective moment. Freud's dictum, "It is a very remarkable thing that the *Ucs* of one human being can react upon that of another, *without passing through the Cs*" (1915/1957, p. 194, my italics), is thus neuropsychoanalytically understood as a right brain–to–right brain communication from one relational unconscious to another. Freud's concept of the state of receptive readiness as "evenly suspended attention" can also be identified as a function of the right hemisphere, which uses an expansive broad attention mechanism that focuses on global features (as opposed to the left hemisphere, which narrowly focuses on local detail; Derryberry & Tucker, 1994).

That chapter also discusses how a spontaneous enactment can either blindly repeat a pathological object relation through the therapist's deflection of projected negative states and intensification of interactive dysregulation and defensiveness, or creatively provide a novel relational experience via the therapist's autoregulation of projected negative states and co-participation in interactive repair. Although these are the most stressful moments of the treatment, in an optimal context the empathic therapist can potentially act as an implicit regulator of the patient's conscious and dissociated unconscious affective states. This dyadic psychobiological corrective emotional experience can lead to the emergence of a more complex psychic structure by increasing the connectivity of right brain limbic-autonomic circuits.

Consonant with this conception of implicit communication (and citing my right brain neurobiological model), Ginot asserts,

> By allowing implicit relational and emotional patterns to be fully experienced within the analytic process, enactment enables both participants, and especially the analyst, to attain an unmediated connection with what cannot yet be verbalized, a connection that essentially construes an empathic resonance. (2009, p. 290)

As opposed to earlier left brain cognitive models that viewed enactments as the clinician's technical mistakes or the patient's acting out, Ginot proposes, "the analyst's sensitivity, or her right brain readiness to be fully attuned to nonverbal communication, is a necessary therapeutic skill. Becoming entangled in an enactment, although at first out of awareness, is a surprising facet of such sensitivity" (2009, p. 297). In earlier work she argued, "Increasingly, enactments are understood as powerful manifestations of the intersubjective process and as inevitable expressions of complex, though largely unconscious self-states and relational patterns" (Ginot, 2007, p. 317). These unconscious affective interactions "bring to life and consequently alter implicit memories and attachment styles" (p. 317). Ginot further states that such intense manifestations of transference-countertransference entanglements "generate interpersonal as well as internal processes eventually capable of promoting integration and growth" (pp. 317–318).

In parallel work Zanocco et al. (2006) characterize the critical function of empathic physical sensations in the enactment and their central role in "the foundation of developing psychic structure of a human being" (p. 145). Enactments reflect "processes and dynamics originating in the primitive functioning of the mind," and they allow the analyst to access a way of interacting with those patients who are not able to give representation to their instinctual impulses. These early "primary" activities are expressed in "an unconscious mental activity which does not follow the rules of conscious activity. There is no verbal language involved. Instead, there is a production of images that do not seem to follow any order, and, even less, any system of logic" (p. 145). Note the allusions of imagery to implicit primary process cognition and right brain representations (see top of Figure 4.1). A large body of research demonstrates that "whenever an image is either fleetingly presented, or presented in a degraded form, so that only partial information is available, a right-hemisphere superiority emerges" (McGilchrist, 2010, p. 509).

That said, it is important to repeat that this relational mechanism is especially prominent during stressful ruptures of the therapeutic alliance. Ginot observes,

> As these interactions might give expression to dissociated painful, angry, and defensive self-states, the empathic aspects in enactments do not depend on the analyst's ability to experience empathy for the patient's difficulties. The empathic component is found in the analyst's readiness and ability to resonate with what is not verbalized but nonconsciously transmitted nonetheless. (2009, p. 300)

Enactments occur at the edges of the regulatory boundaries of affect tolerance (Schore, 2009d), or what Lyons-Ruth describes as the "fault lines" of self-experience where "interactive negotiations have failed, goals remain aborted, negative affects are unresolved, and conflict is experienced" (2005, p. 21). In light of the principle that an enactment can be a turning point in an analysis in which the relationship is characterized by a mode of resistance/counterresistance (Zanocco et al., 2006), these moments call for the therapist's most complex clinical skills.

This is due to the fact that such heightened affective moments induce the most stressful countertransference responses, including the clinician's implicit coping strategies that are formed in his or her own attachment history. These right brain systems regulate intense states of object relational–induced negative affect. Recall the "right hemispheric dominance in processing of unconscious negative emotion" (Sato & Aoki, 2006). Davies (2004) documents, "It seems to me intrinsic to relational thinking that these 'bad object relationships' not only will but must be reenacted in the transference-countertransference experience, that indeed such reenacted aggression, rage, and envy are endemic to psychoanalytic change within the relational perspective" (p. 714). Looking at the defensive aspect, Bromberg (2006) reports, "Clinically, the phenomenon of dissociation as a defense against self-destabilization . . . has its greatest relevance during enactments, a mode of clinical engagement that requires an analyst's closest attunement to the unacknowledged affective shifts in his own and the patient's self-states" (p. 5).

On the other hand, Plakun (1999) observes that the therapist's "refusal of the transference," particularly the negative transference, is an early manifestation of an enactment. The therapist's "refusal" is expressed implicitly and spontaneously in nonverbal communications, not explicitly in the verbal narrative. Russell (1998) contends that "The most important source of resistance in the treatment process is the therapist's resistance to what the patient feels" (p. 19). Bromberg offers the principle,

> A therapeutic posture that systematically tries to avoid collisions between the patient's and analyst's subjectivities is eventually experienced as disconfirming the *vitality* of the patient's dissociated self-states that are trying to find relational existence. If the analyst is not responding *affectively* and *personally* to these parts, they are robbed of a human context in which to be recognized and come alive. (2009, p. 358, my italics)

A relational perspective from dynamic system theory clearly applies to the synergistic effects of the therapist's transient or enduring countertransferential affective "mindblindness" and the patient's negatively biased transferential expectation in the co-creation of an enactment. This dyadic attunement of defensive states is described by Bromberg (2011), who observes that if the therapist is "too long listening to the 'material' without being alive to his own internal experience of the relationship itself, a dissociative process often begins to develop in the therapist that may have started in the patient but quickly becomes a cocoon that envelops both patient and therapist" (p. 39). Note my use of the term *attunement* as a dyadic co-created matching of dissociative defensive states.

Making this work even more emotionally challenging, Renik (1993) offers the important observation that countertransference enactments cannot be recognized until one is already in them. Rather spontaneous activity is expressed by the clinician's right brain, described by Lichtenberg, Lachmann, and Fosshage (1996, pp. 213–214) as a "disciplined spontaneous engagement." These authors observe that such events occur "at a critical juncture in analysis," and they are usually prompted by some breach or miscommunication that requires "a human response." Although there is a danger of "exchanges degenerating into mutually traumatizing disruptions" that "recreate pathogenic expectations," the clinician's communications signal a readiness to participate authentically in the immediacy of an enactment. This is spontaneously expressed in the clinician's facial expressions, gestures, and unexpected comments that result from an "unsuppressed emotional upsurge." These communications seem more to pop out than to have been planned or edited, and they provide "intense moments that opened the way for examination of the role enactments into which the analyst had fallen unconsciously."

These "communications" are right brain, emotional primary process communications and not left brain, rational, logical secondary process communications. Thus explicit, conscious, verbal voluntary responses are inadequate to prevent, facilitate, or metabolize implicit emotional enactments. Bromberg (2006) refers to this in his assertion, "An interpretative stance . . . not only is thereby useless during an enactment, but also escalates the enactment and rigidifies the dissociation" (p. 8). Andrade concludes,

> As a primary factor in psychic change, interpretation is limited in effectiveness in pathologies arising from the verbal phase, related to explicit memories, with no effect in the pre-verbal phase where implicit memories are to be found. Interpretation—the method used to the exclusion of all others for a century—is only partial; when used in isolation it does not meet the demands of modern broad-based-spectrum psychoanalysis. (2005, p. 677)

But if not an explicit verbal response and analytic reasoning, then what type of implicit cognition would the therapist use in order to guide him or her through stressful negative affective states, such as terror, rage, shame, disgust, and so on? What implicit right brain coping strategy could not only autoregulate the intense affect but also at the same time allow the clinician to maintain "an attunement to the unacknowledged affective shifts in his own and the patient's self-states"?

IMPLICIT PROCESSES AND CLINICAL INTUITION

In my introduction I proposed that the therapist's moment-to-moment navigation through these problematic heightened affective moments occurs not by explicit, verbal secondary process cognition, but by implicit, nonverbal primary process clinical intuition. Writing in the psychological literature, Dijksterhuis and Nordgren (2006) describe intuitions that are the result of "thorough unconscious thought" and report, "immediate intuitions that were good were made by experts (perhaps they have so much knowledge that they can think unconsciously very quickly)" (p. 106). Narvaez (2010) notes that individuals who access "experience-based, postreflective, well-educated intuition" behave differently; that is, "they know what action would be effective and how to carry it out. Moreover, they have 'negative expertise'—they know what actions not to take in solving a problem and pay attention to intuitions that signal uncertainty" (p. 171). Citing a large body of research, she concludes that whereas novices use conscious, effortful methods to solve problems, the well-educated intuition of experts incorporates "far more sophisticated unconscious deep and automatic knowledge that may have been painfully learned . . ." (p. 171).

Neuroscientists now define the creative process of intuition as "difficult to articulate, affect-laden recognition or judgments, which are based on prior learning and experience, that are arrived at through holistic associations" (Volz, Rubsamen, & von Cramon, 2008, p. 319). Current brain research on human decision making articulates dual-process theories that clearly differentiate reasoning,—which is slow, controlled, and effortful—from intuition—which is fast, emotional, effortless, and creative (Kuo, Sjostrom, Chen, Wang, & Huang, 2009). From a social neuroscience perspective, intuition is now being defined as "the subjective experience associated with the use of knowledge gained through implicit learning" (Lieberman, 2000, p. 109). The description of intuition as "direct knowing that seeps into conscious awareness without the conscious mediation of logic or rational process" (Boucouvalas, 1997, p. 7) describes a right and not a left brain function. Bugental (1987) refers to the therapist's "intuitive sensing of what is happening in the patient back of his words and, often, back of his conscious awareness" (p. 11). In his last work Bowlby (1991) speculated, "Clearly the best therapy is done by the therapist who is naturally intuitive and also guided by the appropriate theory" (p. 16).

In a groundbreaking article, Welling (2005) notes that intuition is associated with preverbal character, affect, sense of relationship, spontaneity, immediacy, gestalt nature, and global view (all functions of the holistic right brain). He further points out that "There is no cognitive theory about intuition" (p. 20), and therefore "What is needed is a model that can describe the underlying formal process that produces intuition phenomena" (pp. 23–24). Developmental psychoanalysis and neuropsychoanalysis can make important contributions to our understanding of the sources and mechanism of not only maternal but also clinical intuition. In line with the previously cited conclusion of Papousek (2007), Orlinsky and Howard (1986) contend that the "non-verbal, prerational stream of expression that binds the infant to its parent continues throughout life to be a primary medium of intuitively felt affective-relational communication between persons" (p. 343). And so there are direct commonalities between the spontaneous responses of the maternal intuition of a psychobiologically attuned primary caregiver and the intuitive therapist's sensitive countertransferential responsiveness to the patient's unconscious nonverbal affective bodily based implicit communications.

In the neuroscience literature, Volz and von Cramon (2006) conclude that intuition is related to the unconscious and is "often reliably accurate." It is derived from stored nonverbal representations, such as "images, feelings, physical sensations, metaphors" (note the similarity to primary process cognition). Intuition is expressed not in literal language but is "embodied" in a "gut feeling" or in an initial guess that subsequently biases our thought and inquiry. "The gist information is realized on the basis of the observer's implicit knowledge rather than being consciously extracted on the basis of the observer's explicit knowledge" (p. 2084).

With direct relevance to the concept of somatic countertransference, cognitive neuroscience models of intuition are highlighting the adaptive capacity of "embodied cognition." Allman et al. (2005) assert, "We experience the intuitive process at a visceral level. Intuitive decision-making enables us to react quickly in situations that involve a high degree of uncertainty which commonly involve social interactions" (p. 370). These researchers demonstrate that right prefrontal-insula and anterior cingulate relay a fast intuitive assessment of complex social situations in order to allow the rapid adjustment of behavior in quickly changing and therefore uncertain social situations. This lateralization is also found in a neuroimaging study by Bolte and Goschke (2005), who suggest that right hemisphere association areas play a special role in intuitive judgments.

In parallel psychoanalytic work, Marcus (1997) observes, "The analyst, by means of reverie and intuition, listens with the right brain to the analysand's right brain" (p. 238). Stern (2004) proposes that the clinician can focus his or her attention on brief moments and intuitively grasp the relational and emotional essence of that present moment, without being verbalized. Other clinicians hypothesize that the intuition of an experienced expert therapist lies fundamentally in a process of unconscious *pattern* matching (Rosenblatt & Thickstun, 1994), and that this pattern recognition follows a nonverbal path, because verbal activity interferes with achieving insight (Schooler & Melcher, 1995). Even more specifically, Bohart (1999) contends that intuition involves the detection of "patterns and rhythms in interaction." But if not verbal stimuli, then which patterns are being intuitively tracked?

Recall that "transference is distinctive in that it depends on early *patterns of emotional attachment* with caregivers" (Pincus et al., 2007), and enactments are powerful expressions of "*unconscious self-states and relational patterns*" (Ginot, 2007). Van Lancker and Cummings (1999) assert, "Simply stated, the left hemisphere specializes in analyzing sequences, while the right hemisphere gives evidence of superiority in processing *patterns*" (p. 95). Indeed, "*Pattern recognition* and comprehension of several types of stimuli, such as faces, chords, complex pitch, graphic images, and voices, has been described as superior in the normal right hemisphere" (Van Lancker Sidtis, 2006, p. 223). Updated models of psychotherapy describe the primacy of "*making conscious the organizing patterns of affect*" (Mohaupt, Holgersen, Binder, & Nielsen, 2006). The intuitive psychobiologically attuned therapist, on a moment-to-moment basis, implicitly focuses his or her countertransferential broad attentional processes upon *patterns* of rhythmic crescendos/decrescendos of the patient's regulated and dysregulated states of affective autonomic arousal (for clinical work with the autonomic nervous system, see Schore, 2009d).

Intuition thereby represents a complex right brain primary process, an affectively charged embodied cognition that is adaptive for "implicit feeling or knowing," especially in moments of relational uncertainty. In the heightened affective moment of an enactment, a rupture in the therapeutic alliance is characterized by a high degree of uncertainty and a density of negative affect. To optimally solve this relational problem on a moment-to-moment basis, the therapist must remain psychobiologically attuned to the patient in a state of right brain evenly suspended attention and at the same time access an intuitive fast, emotional, and effortless right brain decision process to navigate through the stressful intersubjective context.

Welling (2005) offers a phase model, in which the amount of information contained in the intuition increases from one phase to another, resulting in increased levels of complexity. An early "detection phase" related to "functions of arousal and attention" culminates in a "metaphorical solution phase," in which the intuition presents itself in the form of kinesthetic sensations, feelings, images, metaphors, and words. Here the solution, which has an emotional quality, is revealed, but in a veiled, nonverbal form. These descriptions reflect the activity of the right hemisphere, which is dominant for emotional arousal (MacNeilage, Rogers, & Vallortigara, 2009), attention (Raz, 2004; Thiebaut de Schotten et al., 2011), kinesthesia (Naito et al., 2005), imageability (Casanto, 2003), unique modes of perception associated with mental creativity (Asari et al., 2008), the processing of novel metaphors (Mashal, Faust, Hendler, & Jung-Beeman, 2007), and emotional words (Kuchinke et al., 2006).

In contrast to the left brain's deliberate, conscious, analytical search strategies, the right brain generates the subjective experience of insight, whereby a novel solution is computed unconsciously and subsequently emerges into awareness suddenly (Bowden & Jung Beeman, 1998; Kounios & Beeman, 2009; Sandkuhler & Bhattacharya, 2008). *Insight* is defined by the *Compact Oxford English Dictionary of Current English* as "the capacity to gain an accurate and intuitive understanding." McGilchrist's (2009) contrast of the cognitive styles of the two hemispheres applies to the self-exploration process of psychotherapy:

> It has often been said that the left hemisphere is the hemisphere of "linear processing"; its cognitive style is sequential, hence its propensity to linear analysis, or to mechanical construction, taking the bits apart, or putting them together, one by one (p. 446). . . . Cognition in the right hemisphere is not a process of something coming into being through adding piece to piece in a sequence, but of something that is out of focus coming into focus, as a whole. (p. 447)

I suggest that phases of intuitive processing of an implicit self are generated in the subcortical-cortical vertical axis of the therapist's (and patient's) right brain, from the right amygdala, right insula, and right anterior cingulate to the right orbitofrontal system (Figure 4.1; see also Figure A-2 in Schore, 2003a). The latter, the highest level of the right brain, acts as an "inner compass that accompanies the decoding process of intuition" (Welling, 2005). The orbitofrontal system, the "senior executive of the emotional brain," is specialized for contexts of "uncertainty or unpredictability" (Elliott, Dolan, & Frith, 2000). It functions as a dynamic filter of emotional stimuli (Rule, Shimamura, & Knight, 2002) and provides "a panoramic view of the entire external environment, as well as the internal environment associated with motivational factors" (Barbas, 2007). It also acts in nonconscious intuitive processes as "a fast detector and predictor of potential content that utilizes coarse facets of the input" (Volz et al., 2008); responds to novel visual stimuli (Rolls, Browning, Inoue, & Hernadi, 2005); formulates a theory of mind, now defined as "a kind of affective-decision making" (Happaney et al., 2004); and is centrally involved in "intuitive decision-making" (Allman et al., 2005). Recent neuroscience research clearly demonstrates that the right and not left prefrontal areas are active when decisions are required in incompletely specified situations, and that this adaptive role "involves the maintenance of ambiguous mental representations that temper premature overinterpretation by the left hemisphere" (Goel et al., 2006, p. 2245).

I have suggested that the right orbitofrontal cortex and its subcortical and cortical connections represent what Freud described as the preconscious (Schore, 2003a). Alluding to preconscious functions, Welling describes intuition as

> a factory of pieces of thoughts, images, and vague feelings, where the raw materials seem to float around half formless, a world so often present, though we hardly ever visit it. However, some of these floating elements come to stand out, gain strength, or show up repeatedly. When exemplified, they may be easier to recognize and cross the border of consciousness. (2005, p. 33)

Over the course of the treatment, but especially in heightened affective moments of enactments, the psychobiologically attuned clinician accesses this preconscious domain, as does the free-associating, affect-communicating patient. Rather than conscious logical reasoning and technical explicit skills, the clinician's intuitive implicit capacities may be responsible for the negotiated outcome of an affectively charged enactment and may dictate the depth of the therapeutic contact, exploration, and change processes.

IMPLICIT PROCESS CENTRAL TO CHANGE: AFFECT REGULATION

Although enactments are the most stressful moments of the treatment, in an optimal context the therapist can potentially act as an implicit regulator of the patient's conscious and dissociated unconscious affective states. According to Ginot (2007), "This focus on enactments as communicators of affective building blocks also reflects a growing realization that explicit content, verbal interpretations, and the mere act of uncovering memories are insufficient venues for curative shifts" (p. 317). This clearly implies that the resolution of enactments involves more than the standard Freudian idea of making the unconscious conscious by defense interpretations. Yet if not these explicit factors, then what implicit relational experience is essential to the change process, especially in developmentally impaired personalities who access pathological dissociation and are not psychologically minded?

At the most fundamental level the implicit change mechanism must certainly include a conscious or unconscious affective experience that is communicated to an empathic other. But in addition, an optimal intersubjective context provides not only right brain implicit affective communication but also an opportunity for right brain interactive regulation of dysregulated intense affective states, the core of the attachment dynamic. The importance of this connection is stressed by Whitehead (2006): "Every time we make therapeutic contact with our patients we are engaging profound processes that tap into essential life forces in our selves and in those we work with. . . . Emotions are deepened in intensity and sustained in time when they are intersubjectively shared. This occurs at moments of deep contact" (p. 624). Ogden, Pain, Minton, and Fisher (2005) conclude that the psychotherapy change mechanism lies not in verbal exchanges but rather in a background of the empathic clinician's psychobiologically attuned interactive affect regulation, a relational context that allows the patient to safely contact, describe, and eventually regulate his or her inner experience. I suggest that the regulation of stressful and disorganizing high or low levels of affective-autonomic arousal facilitates the repair and reorganization of the right brain, the biological substrate of the human unconscious.

It is now clear that affective processes lie at the core of the implicit self, and that a deeper understanding of affect is closely tied to the problem of the regulation of these bodily based processes. The essential adaptive capacity of emotion regulation can be defined as "the process of initiating, maintaining, modulating, or changing the occurrence, intensity, or duration of internal feeling states, emotion-related physiological processes, and the behavioral concomitants of emotion" (Eisenberg et al., 2001, p. 1114). Affect regulation—a central mechanism of development, psychopathogenesis, and the change process of psychotherapy—is usually defined as a set of conscious control processes by which we influence, consciously and voluntarily, the conscious emotions we have, and how we experience and express them (e.g., Ochsner & Gross, 2005). But, as developmental attachment studies clearly show, right brain interactive implicit affect regulation occurs on nonconscious levels. Clinicians vary not only in the implicit capacity of negative and positive affect tolerance but also in the ability to implicitly regulate positive and negative affect states (Schore & Schore, 2008).

In a groundbreaking article in the clinical psychology literature, Greenberg (2007) describes a "self-control" form of emotion regulation involving higher levels of cognitive executive function that allows individuals "to change the way they feel by consciously changing the way they think" (p. 415). This explicit form of affect regulation is performed by the verbal left hemisphere, and unconscious bodily based emotion is usually not addressed. This mechanism is at the core of verbal-analytic understanding and controlled reasoning, heavily emphasized in therapeutic models of not only classical psychoanalysis but also cognitive-behavioral therapy. In contrast to this conscious emotion regulation system, Greenberg describes a second, more fundamental implicit affect regulatory process performed by the right hemisphere. This system rapidly and automatically processes facial expression, vocal quality, and eye contact in a relational context. Therapy attempts not control but the "acceptance or facilitation of particular emotions," including "previously avoided emotion," in order to allow the patient to tolerate and transform them into "adaptive emotions." Citing my work, he asserts, "it is the building of implicit or automatic emotion regulation capacities that is important for enduring change, especially for highly fragile personality-disordered clients" (2007, p. 416).

Both scientists and clinicians now assert that affect dysregulation is a fundamental mechanism of all psychiatric disorders, and that an impaired ability to regulate the intensity of affect is the most enduring consequence of early relational trauma. This deficit in implicit affect regulation underpins later problems in emotional and interpersonal functioning. Due to early forming, inefficient coping strategies, self-pathologies and personality disorders, especially in periods of relational stress, experience under- and/or overregulation of affects. An inability in solving social problems with right brain, implicit emotional regulating functions is frequently accompanied by an overreliance on left brain, explicit analytic reasoning. The limitation of this hemispheric strategy is described by Keenan et al. (2005): "the left hemisphere often fills in information that it is unaware of. . . . However, the filling in of left hemisphere does not require insight, self-awareness, or any higher-order state. The left hemisphere appears to do so in a rather blind manner" (p. 702). In contrast, the right hemisphere has the ability to see the "big picture" and "find the thread that unites" (Drago et al., 2009, p. 141). Heilman, Nadeau, and Beversdorf (2003) observe, "A possible method of resolving a previously unsolved problem is to see this problem 'in a new light' and a means of seeing a problem in a new light is to use a different form of knowledge and a different cognitive strategy that might be mediated by the hemisphere that is opposite to the one previously used" (p. 374).

Due to ongoing therapeutic right brain interactive regulation of arousal and affect, the patient's implicit sense of safety and trust increases, and ruptures of the attachment bond are now more easily negotiated. These negotiations involve not only nonverbal but also verbal affective communications, especially in spontaneous expressions that occur in the intimate context of a regulated heightened affective moment. It has been assumed in the psychoanalytic and broader psychotherapeutic literature that all forms of language reflect left hemispheric functioning. The processing of both positive and negative emotional words activates the right and not left prefrontal cortex (Kuchinke et al., 2006). In a recent review Ross and Monnot conclude, "Thus, the traditional concept that language is a dominant and lateralized function of the left hemisphere is no longer tenable" (2008, p. 51). They report,

> Over the last three decades, there has been growing realization that the right hemisphere is essential for language and communication competency and psychological well-being through its ability to modulate affective prosody and gestural behavior, decode connotative (non-standard) word meanings, make thematic inferences, and process metaphor, complex linguistic relationships and non-literal (idiomatic) types of expressions. (p. 51)

This right brain mechanism underlies Joseph's clinical observation: "In my experience, fresh and heartfelt metaphorical language or direct, straightforward, and even blunt language is often the most direct route to truth, richness, and honesty. That is a type of language that often evokes an emotional outpouring from others" (2008, p. 253). As opposed to left brain neutral, detached secondary process language, this emotional language is saturated in right brain nonverbal prosodic, facial, and gestural communications.

Even more than the late-acting rational, analytical, and verbal left mind, the growth-facilitating psychotherapeutic relationship needs to directly access the deeper psychobiological strata of the implicit regulatory structures of both the patient's and the clinician's right brain–mind–body. Effective psychotherapy of attachment pathologies and severe personality disorders must focus on unconscious affect and the survival defense of pathological dissociation, "a structured separation of mental processes (e.g., thoughts, emotions, conation, memory, and identity) that are ordinarily integrated" (Spiegel & Cardeña, 1991, p. 367). The clinical precept that unregulated, overwhelming traumatic feelings cannot be adaptively integrated into the patient's emotional life is the expression of a dysfunction of "the right hemispheric specialization in regulating stress- and emotion-related processes" (Sullivan & Dufresne, 2006, p. 55).

As described earlier, this dissociative deficit specifically results from a lack of integration of the right-lateralized limbic-autonomic circuits of the emotional brain (see Figure 4.1). A psychotherapeutic increase of interconnectivity within the unconscious system of the implicit self thus promotes the complexity of defenses, right brain coping strategies for regulating stressful bodily based affects that are more flexible and adaptive than pathological dissociation. This structural maturation of the right-lateralized vertical axis is expressed in further development of the right brain core of the self and its central involvement in "patterns of affect regulation that integrate a sense of self across state transitions, thereby allowing for a continuity of inner experience" (Schore, 1994, p. 33). This right brain therapeutic mechanism supports the integration of what Bromberg (2006) calls dissociated "not-me" states into the implicit self.

REGULATED ENACTMENTS, CORRECTIVE EMOTIONAL EXPERIENCES, AND EXPANSION OF THE RIGHT BRAIN IMPLICIT SELF

Recall Ginot's (2007) assertion that enactments "generate interpersonal as well as internal processes eventually capable of promoting integration and growth." Indeed, long-term affectively focused psychotherapy can generate corrective emotional experiences. In classical writings, Alexander and French posited,

> In all forms of etiological psychotherapy, the basic therapeutic principle is the same: To re-expose the patient, under more favorable circumstances, to emotional situations which he could not handle in the past. The patient, in order to be helped, must undergo a corrective emotional experience suitable to repair the traumatic influence of previous experiences. (1946, p. 46)

Recent data from developmental affective neuroscience and traumatology now clearly suggest that corrective emotional experiences of the psychotherapeutic change process involve not just cathartic discharge but right brain interactive regulation of affect.

Regulated enactments positively alter the developmental growth trajectory of the right brain and facilitate the top-down and bottom-up integration of its corti-cal and subcortical systems (Schore, 2003a). These enhanced right amygdala-ventral prefrontolimbic connections allow therapeutic affectively charged "now moments" of lived interactive experience to be integrated into autobiographical memory. Autobiographical memory, an output of the right brain, is the highest memory system that consists of personal events with a clear relation to time, space, and context. In this right brain state of autonoetic consciousness, the expe-riencing self represents emotionally toned memories, thereby allowing for "sub-jective time travel" (Kalbe, Brand, Thiel, Kessler, & Markowitsch, 2008) and the capacity to project the self into the future. This developmental progression is re-flected in a functional expansion in implicit self-regulation, affect, communica-tion, and cognition, essential functions of the right brain, the locus of "the highest human mental function, responsible for creativity and integration of past, present, and future experience" (Rotenberg, 2004, p. 864).

Current neuroscientific models view creativity as the production of an idea that is both novel and useful in a particular social setting (Flaherty, 2005). Re-searchers now conclude that although the left hemisphere is specialized for cop-ing with predictable representations and strategies, the right predominates for coping with and assimilating novel situations (Podell, Lovell, & Goldberg, 2001) and ensures the formation of a new program of interaction with a new environ-ment (Ezhov & Krivoschekov, 2004). Indeed,

> The right brain possesses special capabilities for processing novel stimuli. . . . Right-brain problem solving generates a matrix of alternative solutions, as contrasted with the left brain's single solution of best fit. This answer matrix remains active while alternative solutions are explored, a method suitable for the open-ended possibili-ties inherent in a novel situation. (Schutz, 2005, p. 13)

These right brain data are directly relevant to recent psychoanalytic models of the change process. D. B. Stern (1997) states effective psychotherapy is less a bringing to light preexisting truth than perceiving and interpreting novelty. Bromberg emphasizes the critical role of therapeutic "safe surprises":

> Interpersonal novelty is what allows the self to grow because it is unanticipated by both persons, it is organized by what takes place between two minds, and it belongs to neither person alone. . . . It is through the novelty and surprise of this reciprocal process that the therapeutic action of psychoanalysis takes shape, and it may well be what accounts for the enhanced spontaneity and flexibility of a patient's person-ality structure that results from a successful analysis. (2009, pp. 89–90)

Psychoanalysis has a long history of exploring the role of the unconscious in creativity (Kris, 1952; Reik, 1948), and current authors have applied these ideas to the problem of the clinician's capacity for interpersonal novelty and creativity (Arnold, 2007; Horner, 2006). I suggest that the clinician's creativity, a right hemispheric process (Grabner et al., 2007; Jausovec & Jausovec, 2000; Mihov,

Denzler, & Forster, 2010) is an essential element of clinical expertise, and that basic research on this individual difference variable applies to psychotherapists. Summarizing this body of studies, Ansburg and Hill (2003) assert that highly creative (as opposed to analytic) thinkers are more likely to produce nonconsciously primed solutions, gather information using diffuse instead of focused attentional processes that occur beneath awareness, sample a wider range of environmental input, and generate innovative connections when they unwittingly encounter a trigger in the environment. They conclude, "Instead of relying solely on explicit memory processes, creative individuals may be able to take better advantage of their implicit memory processes" (2003, p. 1149).

The relational neuropsychoanalytic perspective of regulation theory suggests that an optimal therapeutic experience can also expand the patient's right brain implicit creative functions. Indeed, the right hemisphere is more critical than the left in learning a new task and building an experiential base (Shrira & Martin, 2005). Heightened affective moments are potential mediators of the therapeutic change process, and thus the emotion-processing right brain, the psychobiological substrate of the human unconscious, is the site of both an implicit enactment and a corrective emotional experience. According to Friedman and Natterson,

> Enactments are interactions of analysand and analyst with communicative and resistive meanings that lead to valuable insight and can constitute corrective emotional experiences. Enactments that are recognized and defined become valuable dramatizing moments that have condensing, clarifying, and intensifying effects upon consciousness. (1999, p. 220)

Echoing this principle in the clinical psychology literature, Hayes and her colleagues conclude,

> Although change can happen in a gradual and linear way, there is increasing evidence across disciplines that it can also occur in discontinuous and nonlinear ways. This latter type of change is often preceded by an *increase in variability and a destabilization or loosening of old patterns that can be followed by system reorganization.* In post-traumatic growth, life transition, and psychotherapy, destabilization often occurs in the context of emotional arousal which, when accompanied by emotional processing and meaning-making, seems to contribute to better outcomes. (2007, p. 721, my italics)

This description of the change process directly applies to the enactments that arise in the psychotherapy of patients with a history of relational attachment trauma and pathological dissociation (Ginot, 2009; Schore, 2007, 2009b). Indeed, research now indicates that psychotherapy is superior to pharmacotherapy in patients with a history of early childhood trauma (Nemeroff et al., 2003) and that long-term psychodynamic therapy is effective in treating personality disorders and chronic mental disorders (Leichsenring & Rabung, 2008). Ultimately, effective psychotherapeutic treatment of early evolving self-pathologies (such as severe personality disorders) can facilitate changes in the right brain, including alterations of the internal working model and more effective coping strategies for affect regulation. This interpersonal neurobiological mechanism allows optimal treatment to potentially transform "insecure" into "earned secure" attachments.

It is certainly true that the clinician's left brain conscious mind is an important contributor to the treatment process. But perhaps more than other treatment modalities, psychodynamic psychotherapeutic models are now intensively focusing upon the critical functions of the therapist's "unconscious right mind." The right hemisphere plays a dominant role in the processing of self-relevant information, affective theory of mind (Schore, 2003b), empathy (Schore, 1994; Shamay-Tsoory, Tomer, Berger, & Aharon-Peretz, 2003), as well as in mentalizing (Ohnishi et al., 2004), all aspects of the treatment process. A body of studies now indicates that psychotherapy induces changes in the brain. Glass (2008) summarizes these findings: "Recent research in brain imaging, molecular biology, and neurogenetics has shown that psychotherapy changes brain function and structure. Such studies have shown that psychotherapy effects regional cerebral blood flow, neurotransmitter metabolism, gene expression, and persistent modifications in synaptic plasticity" (p. 1589).

The growth-facilitating environment of the therapeutic relationship can promote the experience-dependent maturation of the right brain implicit self. Psychoneurobiological reorganizations of the right brain human unconscious underlie Alvarez's (2005) assertion: "Schore points out that at the more severe levels of psychopathology, it is not a question of making the unconscious conscious: rather it is a question of restructuring the unconscious itself" (p. 171). The implicit functions of the emotional right brain are essential to the self-exploration process of psychotherapy, especially of unconscious affects that can be potentially integrated into a more complex implicit sense of self. At the most fundamental level, the work of psychotherapy is not defined by what the therapist explicitly, objectively *does* for the patient, or *says* to the patient. Rather the key mechanism is how to implicitly and subjectively *be* with the patient, especially during affectively stressful moments when the "going-on-being" of the patient's implicit self is dis-integrating in real time.

REFERENCES

Aftanas, L. I., & Varlamov, A. A. (2007). Effects of alexithymia on the activity of the anterior and posterior areas of the cortex of the right hemisphere in positive and negative emotional activation. *Neuroscience and Behavioral Physiology, 37,* 67–73.

Alexander, F., & French, T. M. (1946). *Psychoanalytic therapy: Principles and application.* New York: Ronald Press.

Allman, J. M., Watson, K. K., Tetreault, N. A., & Hakeem, A. Y. (2005). Intuition and autism: A possible role for Von Economo neurons. *Trends in Cognitive Sciences, 9,* 367–373.

Alvarez, A. (2006). Some questions concerning states of fragmentation: Unintegration, under-integration, disintegration, and the nature of early integrations. *Journal of Child Psychotherapy, 32,* 158–180.

Ammaniti, M., & Trentini, C. (2009). How new knowledge about parenting reveals the neurobiological implications of intersubjectivity: A conceptual synthesis of recent research. *Psychoanalytic Dialogues, 19,* 537–555.

Andrade, V. M. (2005). Affect and the therapeutic action in psychoanalysis. *International Journal of Psychoanalysis, 86,* 677–697.

Ansburg, P. I., & Hill, K. (2003). Creative and analytic thinkers differ in their use of attentional resources. *Personality and Individual Differences, 34,* 1141–1152.

Arnold, K. (2007). The creative unconscious, the unknown self, and the haunting melody: Notes on Reik's theory of inspiration. *Psychoanalytic Review, 94,* 431–445.

Aron, L. (1998). The clinical body and the reflexive mind. In L. Aron & F. Sommer Anderson (Eds.), *Relational perspectives on the body* (pp. 3–37). Hillsdale, NJ: Analytic Press.

Asari, T., Konishi, S., Jimura, K., Chikazoe, J., Nakamura, N., & Miyashita, Y. (2008). Right temporopolar activation associated with unique perception. *NeuroImage, 41,* 145–152.

Bach, S. (2008). On digital consciousness and psychic death. *Psychoanalytic Dialogues, 18,* 784–794.

Barbas, H. (2007). Flow of information for emotions through temporal and orbitofrontal pathways. *Journal of Anatomy, 211,* 237–249.

Bargh, J. A., & Morsella, E. (2008). The unconscious mind. *Perspectives on Psychological Science, 3,* 73–79.

Beebe, B., Jaffe, J., Markese, S., Buck, K., Chen, H., Cohen, P., et al. (2010). The origins of 12-month attachment: A microanalysis of 4-month mother-infant interaction. *Attachment & Human Development, 12,* 3–142.

Benowitz, L. I., Bear, D. M., Rosenthal, R., Mesulam, M-M., Zaidel, E., & Sperry, R. W. (1983). Hemispheric specialization in nonverbal communication. *Cortex, 19,* 5–11.

Blonder, L. X., Bowers, D., & Heilman, K. M. (1991). The role of the right hemisphere in emotional communication. *Brain, 114,* 1115–1127.

Bohart, A. C. (1999). Intuition and creativity in psychotherapy. *Journal of Constructivist Psychology, 12,* 287–311.

Bolte, A., & Goschke, T. (2005). On the speed of intuition: Intuitive judgments of semantic coherence under different response deadlines. *Memory & Cognition, 33,* 1248–1255.

Boucouvalas, M. (1997). Intuition: The concept and the experience. In R. D. Floyd & P. S. Arvidson (Eds.), *Intuition: The inside story* (pp. 39–56). New York: Routledge.

Bowden, E. M., & Jung Beeman, M. (1998). Getting the right idea: Semantic activation in the right hemisphere may help solve insight problems. *Psychological Science, 9,* 435–440.

Bowlby, J. (1991, Autumn). The role of the psychotherapist's personal resources in the therapeutic situation. In *Tavistock Gazette.*

Brancucci, A., Lucci, G., Mazzatenta, A., & Tommasi, L. (2009). Asymmetries of the human social brain in the visual, auditory and chemical modalities. *Philosophical Transactions of the Royal Society of London B, 364,* 895–914.

Bromberg, P. M. (2006). *Awakening the dreamer: Clinical journeys.* Mahwah, NJ: Analytic Press.

Bromberg, P. M. (2009). Truth, human relatedness, and the analytic process: An interpersonal/relational perspective. *International Journal of Psychoanalysis, 90,* 347–361.

Bromberg, P. M. (2011). *The shadow of the tsunami and the growth of the relational mind.* New York: Routledge.

Buchanan, T. W., Tranel, D., & Adolphs, R. (2006). Memories for emotional autobiographical events following unilateral damage to medial temporal lobe. *Brain, 129,* 115–127.

Buchner, A., & Wippich, W. (1998). Differences and commonalities between implicit learning and implicit memory. In M. A. Stadler & P. A. Frensch (Eds.), *Handbook of implicit learning* (pp. 3–46). Thousand Oaks, CA: Sage.

Bugental, J. F. (1987). *The art of the psychotherapist.* New York: Norton.

Buklina, S. B. (2005). The corpus callosum, interhemispheric interactions, and the function of the right hemisphere of the brain. *Neuroscience and Behavioral Physiology, 35,* 473–480.

Burgoon, J. K. (1985). Nonverbal signals. In M. L. Knapp & C. R. Miller (Eds.), *Handbook of interpersonal communication* (pp. 344–390). Beverly Hills, CA: Sage.

Carretie, L., Hinojosa, J. A., Mercado, F., & Tapia, M. (2005). Cortical response to subjectively unconscious danger. *NeuroImage, 24,* 615–623.

Casanto, D. (2003). Hemispheric specialization in prefrontal cortex: Effects of verbalizability, imageability and meaning. *Journal of Neurolinguistics, 16,* 361–382.

Cerqueira, J. J., Almeida, O. F. X., & Sousa, N. (2008). The stressed prefrontal cortex. Left? Right! *Brain, Behavior, and Immunity, 22,* 630–638.

Chiron, C, Jambaque, I., Nabbout, R., Lounes, R., Syrota, A., & Dulac, O. (1997). The right brain hemisphere is dominant in human infants. *Brain, 120,* 1057–1065.

Chused, J. F. (2007). Nonverbal communication in psychoanalysis: Commentary on Harrison and Tronick. *Journal of the American Psychoanalytic Association, 55,* 875–882.

Cortina, M., & Liotti, G. (2007). New approaches to understanding unconscious processes: Implicit and explicit memory systems. *International Forum of Psychoanalysis, 16,* 204–212.

Davies, J. M. (2004). Whose bad objects are we anyway? Repetition and our elusive love affair with evil. *Psychoanalytic Dialogues, 14,* 711–732.

Decety, J., & Chaminade, T. (2003). When the self represents the other: A new cognitive neuroscience view on psychological identification. *Consciousness and Cognition, 12,* 577–596.

Derryberry, D., & Tucker, D. M. (1994). Motivating the focus of attention. In P. M. Niedenthal & S. Kiyayama (Eds.), *The heart's eye: Emotional influences in perception and attention* (pp. 167–196). San Diego, CA: Academic Press.

Devinsky, O. (2000). Right cerebral hemispheric dominance for a sense of corporeal and emotional self. *Epilepsy & Behavior, 1,* 60–73.

Dijksterhuis, A., & Meurs, T. (2006). Where creativity resides: The generative power of unconscious thought. *Consciousness and Cognition, 15,* 135–146.

Dijksterhuis, A., & Nordgren, L. F. (2006). A theory of unconscious thought. *Perspectives on Psychological Science, 1,* 95–109.

Dorpat, T. L. (2001). Primary process communication. *Psychoanalytic Inquiry, 3,* 448–463.

Drago, V., Foster, P. S., Okun, M. S., Haq, I., Sudhyadhom, A., Skidmore, F. M., et al. (2009). Artistic creativity and DBS: A case report. *Journal of the Neurological Sciences, 276,* 138–142.

Dutra, L., Bureau, J.-F., Holmes, B., Lyubchik, A., & Lyons-Ruth, K. (2009). Quality of early care and childhood trauma. A prospective study of developmental pathways to dissociation. *Journal of Nervous and Mental Disease, 197,* 383–390.

Eisenberg, N., Cumberland, A., Spinard, T. L., Fabes, R. A., Shepard, S. A., Reiser, M., et al. (2001). The relations of regulation and emotionality to children's externalizing and internalizing problem behavior. *Child Development, 72*, 1112–1134.

Elliott, R., Dolan, R. J., & Frith, C. D. (2000). Dissociable functions in the medial and lateral orbitofrontal cortex: Evidence from human neuroimaging studies. *Cerebral Cortex, 10*, 308–317.

Ezhov, S. N., & Krivoschekov, S. G. (2004). Features of psychomotor responses and inter-hemispheric relationships at various stages of adaptation to a new time zone. *Human Physiology, 30*, 172–175.

Flaherty, A. W. (2005). Frontotemporal and dopaminergic control of idea generation and creative drive. *Journal of Comparative Neurology, 493*, 147–153.

Freud, S. (1957). The unconscious. In J. Strachey (Ed. & Trans.), *The standard edition of the complete psychological works of Sigmund Freud* (Vol. 14, pp. 159–205). London: Hogarth Press. (Original work published 1915)

Freud, S. (1961 & 1963) Introductory lectures on psycho-analysis. In J. Strachey (Ed. & Trans.), *The standard edition of the complete psychological works of Sigmund Freud* (Vol. 19, pp. 12–63). London: Hogarth Press. (Original work published 1916–1917)

Friedman, R. J., & Natterson, J. M. (1999). Enactments: An intersubjective perspective. *Psychoanalytic Quarterly, 68*, 220–247.

Gainotti, G. (2006). Unconscious emotional memories and the right hemisphere. In M. Mancia (Ed.), *Psychoanalysis and neuroscience* (pp. 151–173). Milan, Italy: Springer.

Ginot, E. (2007). Intersubjectivity and neuroscience. Understanding enactments and their therapeutic significance within emerging paradigms. *Psychoanalytic Psychology, 24*, 317–332.

Ginot, E. (2009). The empathic power of enactments. The link between neuropsychological processes and an expanded definition of empathy. *Psychoanalytic Psychology, 26*, 290–309.

Glass, R. M. (2008). Psychodynamic psychotherapy and research evidence. Bambi survives Godzilla? *The Journal of the American Medical Association, 300*, 1587–1589.

Goel, V., Tierney, M., Sheesley, L., Bartolo, A., Vartanian, O., & Grafman, J. (2007). Hemispheric specialization in human prefrontal cortex for resolving certain and uncertain inferences. *Cerebral Cortex, 17*, 2245–2250.

Grabner, R. H., Fink, A., & Neubauer, A. C. (2007). Brain correlates of self-related originality of ideas: Evidence from event-related power and phase-locking changes in the EEG. *Behavioral Neuroscience, 121*, 224–230.

Greenberg, L. S. (2007). Emotion coming of age. *Clinical Psychology Science and Practice, 14*, 414–421.

Happaney, K., Zelazo, P. D., & Stuss, D. T. (2004). Development of orbitofrontal function: Current themes and future directions. *Brain and Cognition, 55*, 1–10.

Hayes, A. M., Laurenceau, J-P., Feldman, G., Strauss, J. L., & Cardaciotto, L. (2007). Change is not always linear: The study of nonlinear and discontinuous patterns of change in psychotherapy. *Clinical Psychology Review, 27*, 715–723.

Heilman, K. M., Nadeau, S. E., & Beversdorf, D. O. (2003). Creative innovation: Possible brain mechanisms. *Neurocase, 9*, 369–379.

Horner, A. J. (2006). The unconscious and the creative process. *Journal of the American Academy of Psychoanalysis and Dynamic Psychiatry, 34*, 461–469.

Hugdahl, K. (1995). Classical conditioning and implicit learning: The right hemisphere hypothesis. In R. J. Davidson & K. Hugdahl (Eds.), *Brain asymmetry* (pp. 235–267). Cambridge, MA: MIT Press.

Hutterer, J., & Liss, M. (2006). Cognitive development, memory, trauma, treatment: An integration of psychoanalytic and behavioural concepts in light of current neuroscience research. *Journal of the American Academy of Psychoanalysis and Dynamic Psychiatry*, 34, 287–302.

Jausovec, N., & Jausovec, K. (2000). Differences in resting EEG related to ability. *Brain Topography*, 12, 229–240.

Joseph, L. (2008). Review of *The present moment in psychotherapy and everyday life*, by Daniel Stern. *Psychoanalysis and Psychotherapy*, 24, 251–254.

Kalbe, E., Brand, M., Thiel, A., Kessler, J., & Markowitsch. (2008). Neuropsychological and neural correlates of autobiographical deficits in a mother who killed her children. *Neurocase*, 14, 15–28.

Keenan, J. P., Rubio, J., Racioppi, C., Johnson, A., & Barnacz, A. (2005). The right hemisphere and the dark side of consciousness. *Cortex*, 41, 695–704.

Kestenberg, J. (1985). The flow of empathy and trust between mother and child. In E. J. Anthony & G. H. Pollack (Eds.), *Parental influences in health and disease* (pp. 137–163). Boston: Little Brown.

Kounios, J., & Beeman, M. (2009). The *aha!* moment. The cognitive neuroscience of insight. *Current Directions in Psychological Science*, 18, 210–216.

Kringelbach, M. L., Lehtonen, A., Squire, S., Harvey, A. G., Craske, M. G., Holliday, I. E., et al. (2008). A specific and rapid neural signature for parental instinct. *PLoS ONE*, 3, e1664.

Kris, E. (1952). *Psychoanalytic explorations in art*. New York: International Universities Press.

Kuchinke, L., Jacobs, A. M., Vo, M. L. H., Conrad, M., Grubich, C., & Herrmann, M. (2006). Modulation of prefontal cortex activation by emotional words in recognition memory. *NeuroReport*, 17, 1037–1041.

Kuo, W-J., Sjostrom, T., Chen, Y-P., Wang, Y-H., & Huang, C-Y. (2009). Intuition and deliberation: Two systems for strategizing in the brain. *Science*, 324, 519–522.

Lane, R. D., Ahern, G. L., Schwartz, G. E., & Kaszniak, A.W. (1997). Is alexithymia the emotional equivalent of blindsight? *Biological Psychiatry*, 42, 834–844.

Lanius, R. A., Williamson, P. C., Bluhm, R. L., Densmore, M., Boksman, K., Neufeld, R. W. J., et al. (2005). Functional connectivity of dissociative responses in posttraumatic stress disorder: A functional magnetic resonance imaging investigation. *Biological Psychiatry*, 57, 873–884.

LeDoux, J. (2002). *Synaptic self: How our brains become who we are*. New York: Viking.

Leichsenring, F., & Rabung, S. (2008). Effectiveness of long-term psychodynamic psychotherapy. A meta-analysis. *The Journal of the American Medical Association*, 300, 1551–1565.

Lichtenberg, J. D., Lachmann, F. M., & Fosshage, J. L. (1996). *The clinical exchange*. Mahwah, NJ: Analytic Press.

Lieberman, M. D. (2000). Intuition: A social neuroscience approach. *Psychological Bulletin*, 126, 109–137.

Loewenstein, R. J. (1996). Dissociative amnesia and dissociative fugue. In L. K. Michaelson & W. J. Ray (Eds.), *Handbook of dissociation: Theoretical, empirical, and clinical perspectives* (pp. 307–336). New York: Plenum.

Lyons-Ruth, K. (2000). "I sense that you sense that I sense . . . ": Sander's recognition process and the emergence of new forms of relational organization. *Infant Mental Health Journal*, 21, 85–98.

Lyons-Ruth, K. (2005). The two-person unconscious: Intersubjective dialogue, enactive representation, and the emergence of new forms of relational organization. In L. Aron & A. Harris (Eds.), *Relational psychoanalysis* (Vol. II, pp. 2–45). Hillsdale, NJ: Analytic Press.

MacNeilage, P. F., Rogers, L., & Vallortigara, G. (2009). Origins of the left and right brain. *Scientific American, 301,* 160–167.

Mancia, M. (2006). Implicit memory and early unrepressed unconscious: Their role in the therapeutic process (How the neurosciences can contribute to psychoanalysis). *International Journal of Psychoanalysis, 87,* 83–103.

Marcus, D. M. (1997). On knowing what one knows. *Psychoanalysis Quarterly, 66,* 219–241.

Markowitsch, H. J., Reinkemeier, A., Kessler, J., Koyuncu, A., & Heiss, W.-D. (2000). Right amygdalar and temperofrontal activation during autobiographical, but not fictitious memory retrieval. *Behavioral Neurology, 12,* 181–190.

Maroda, K. J. (2005). Show some emotion: Completing the cycle of affective communication. In L. Aron & A. Harris (Eds.), *Revolutionary connections. Relational psychoanalysis. Vol. II. Innovation and expansion* (pp. 121–142). Hillsdale, NJ: Analytic Press.

Mashal, N., Faust, M., Hendler, T., & Jung-Beeman, M. (2007). An fMRI investigation of the neural correlates underlying the processing of novel metaphoric expressions. *Brain and Language, 100,* 115–126.

McGilchrist, I. (2009). *The master and his emissary.* New Haven CT: Yale University Press.

McGilchrist, I. (2010). Reciprocal organization of the hemispheres. *Dialogues in Clinical Neuroscience, 12,* 503–515.

McLaughlin, J. T. (1991). Clinical and theoretical aspects of enactment. *Journal of the American Psychoanalytic Association, 39,* 595–614.

Mihov, K. M., Denzler, M., & Forster, J. (2010). Hemispheric specialization and creative thinking: A meta-analytic review of lateralization of creativity. *Brain and Cognition, 72,* 442–448.

Minagawa-Kawai, Y., Matsuoka, S., Dan, I., Naoi, N., Nakamura, K., & Kojima, S. (2009). Prefrontal activation associated with social attachment: Facial-emotion recognition in mothers and infants. *Cerebral Cortex, 19,* 284–292.

Mohaupt, H., Holgersen, H., Binder, P-E., & Nielsen, G. H. (2006). Affect consciousness or mentalization? A comparison of two concepts with regard to affect development and affect regulation. *Scandinavian Journal of Psychology, 47,* 237–244.

Morris, J. S., Ohman, A., & Dolan, R. J. (1998). Conscious and unconscious emotional learning in the human amygdala. *Nature, 393,* 467–470.

Naito, E., Roland, P. E., Grefkes, C., Choi, H. J., Eickhoff, S., Geyer, S., et al. (2005). Dominance of the right hemisphere and role of Area 2 in human kinesthesia. *Journal of Neurophysiology, 93,* 1020–1034.

Narvaez, D. (2010). Moral complexity: The fatal attraction of truthiness and the importance of mature moral functioning. *Perspectives in Psychological Science, 5,* 163–181.

Nemeroff, C. B., Heim, C. M., Thase, M. E., Klein, D. N., Rush, A. J., Schatzberg, A. F., et al. (2003). Differential responses to psychotherapy versus pharmacotherapy in patients with chronic forms of major depression and childhood trauma. *Proceedings of the National Academy of Sciences of the United States of America, 100,* 14293–14296.

Ochsner, K. N., & Gross, J. J. (2005). The cognitive control of emotion. *Journal of Cognitive Neuroscience, 9,* 242–249.

Ogden, P., Pain, C., Minton, K., & Fisher, J. (2005). Including the body in mainstream psychotherapy for traumatized individuals. *Psychologist-Psychoanalyst, XXV,* 19–24.

Ohnishi, T., Moriguchi, Y., Matsuda, H., Mori, T., Hirakata, M., Imabayashi, E., et al. (2004). The neural network for the mirror system and mentalizing in normally developed children: An fMRI study. *NeuroReport, 15*, 1483–1487.

Orlinsky, D. E., & Howard, K. I. (1986). Process and outcome in psychotherapy. In S. L. Garfield & A. E. Bergin (Eds.), *Handbook of psychotherapy and behavior change* (3rd ed.) (pp. 311–381). New York: Wiley.

Papousek, M. P. (2007). Communication in early infancy: An arena of intersubjective learning. *Infant Behavior & Development, 30*, 258–266.

Pincus, D., Freeman, W., & Modell, A. (2007). A neurobiological model of perception. Considerations for transference. *Psychoanalytic Psychology, 24*, 623–640.

Plakun, E. M. (1999). Making the alliance and taking the transference in work with suicidal patients. *Journal of Psychotherapy Practice and Research, 10*, 269–276.

Podell, K., Lovell, M., & Goldberg, E. (2001). Lateralization of frontal lobe functions. In S. P. Salloway, P. E. Malloy, & J. D. Duffy (Eds.), *The frontal lobes and neuropsychiatric illness* (pp. 83–89). London: American Psychiatric Publishing.

Raz, A. (2004). Anatomy of attentional networks. *Anatomical Records, 281B*, 21–36.

Reik, T. (1948). *Listening with the third ear: The inner experience of a psychoanalyst.* New York: Grove Press.

Renik, O. (1993). Countertransference enactment and the psychoanalytic process. In M. J. Horowitz, O. F. Kernberg, & E. M. Weinshel (Eds.), *Psychic structure and psychic change: Essays in honor of Robert S. Wallerstein* (pp. 135–158). Madison CT: International Universities Press.

Rizzuto, A-M. (2008). The talking cure and the analyst's intentions. *Psychoanalytic Review, 95*, 729–749.

Rolls, E. T., Browning, A. S., Inoue, K., & Hernadi, J. (2005). Novel visual stimuli activate a population of neurons in the primate orbitofrontal cortex. *Neurobiology of Learning and Memory, 84*, 111–123.

Rosenblatt, A. D., & Thickstun, J. T. (1994). Intuition and consciousness. *Psychoanalytic Quarterly, 63*, 696–714.

Ross, E. D., & Monnot, M. (2008). Neurology of affective prosody and its functional-anatomic organization in right hemisphere. *Brain and Language, 104*, 51–74.

Rotenberg, V. S. (2004). The ontogeny and asymmetry of the highest brain skills and the pathogenesis of schizophrenia. *Behavioral and Brain Sciences, 27*, 864–865.

Rule, R. R., Shimamura, A. P., & Knight, R. T. (2002). Orbitofrontal cortex and dynamic filtering of emotional stimuli. *Cognition, Affective, & Behavioral Neuroscience, 2*, 264–270.

Russell, P. (1998). The role of paradox in the repetition compulsion. In J. G. Teicholz & D. Kriegman (Eds.), *Trauma, repetition, and affect regulation: The work of Paul Russell* (pp. 1–22). New York: Other Press.

Ryan, R. (2007). *Motivation and emotion*: A new look and approach for two reemerging fields. *Motivation and Emotion, 31*, 1–3.

Sandkuhler, S., & Bhattacharya, J. (2008). Deconstructing insight: EEG correlates of insightful problem solving. *PLoS ONE, 3*, e1459.

Sato, W., & Aoki, S. (2006). Right hemisphere dominance in processing unconscious emotion. *Brain and Cognition, 62*, 261–266.

Schooler, J., & Melcher, J. (1995). The ineffability of insight. In S. T. Smith, T. B. Ward, & R. A. Finke (Eds.), *The creative cognition approach* (pp. 27–51). Cambridge, MA: MIT Press.

Schore, A. N. (1994). *Affect regulation and the origin of the self.* Mahwah, NJ: Erlbaum.

Schore, A. N. (2000). Attachment and the regulation of the right brain. *Attachment and Human Development, 2,* 23–47.

Schore, A. N. (2001). The effects of relational trauma on right brain development, affect regulation, and infant mental health. *Infant Mental Health Journal, 22,* 201–269.

Schore, A. N. (2002). Dysregulation of the right brain: A fundamental mechanism of traumatic attachment and the psychopathogenesis of posttraumatic stress disorder. *Australian and New Zealand Journal of Psychiatry, 36,* 9–30.

Schore, A. N. (2003a). *Affect regulation and the repair of the self.* New York: Norton.

Schore, A. N. (2003b). *Affect dysregulation and disorders of the self.* New York: Norton.

Schore, A. N. (2005). A neuropsychoanalytic viewpoint. Commentary on paper by Steven H. Knoblauch. *Psychoanalytic Dialogues, 15,* 829–854.

Schore, A. N. (2007). Review of *Awakening the dreamer: Clinical journeys* by Philip M. Bromberg. *Psychoanalytic Dialogues, 17,* 753–767.

Schore, A. N. (2009a, August 8). *The paradigm shift: The right brain and the relational unconscious.* Invited plenary address, 2009 Convention of the American Psychological Association, Toronto, Canada. Retrieved September 16, 2009, from http://www.allanschore.com/pdf/SchoreAPAPlenaryFinal09.pdf

Schore, A. N. (2009b). Relational trauma and the developing right brain: An interface of psychoanalytic self psychology and neuroscience. *Annals of the New York Academy of Sciences, 1159,* 189–203.

Schore, A. N. (2009c). Attachment trauma and the developing right brain: Origins of pathological dissociation. In P. F. Dell & J. A. O'Neil (Eds.), *Dissociation and the dissociative disorders: DSM-V and beyond* (pp. 107–141). New York: Routledge.

Schore, A. N. (2009d). Right brain affect regulation: An essential mechanism of development, trauma, dissociation, and psychotherapy. In D. Fosha, D. Siegel, & M. Solomon (Eds.), *The healing power of emotion: Affective neuroscience, development, & clinical practice* (pp. 112–144). New York: Norton.

Schore, J. R., & Schore, A.N. (2008). Modern attachment theory: The central role of affect regulation in development and treatment. *Clinical Social Work Journal, 36,* 9–20.

Schutz, L. E. (2005). Broad-perspective perceptual disorder of the right hemisphere. *Neuropsychology Review, 15,* 11–27.

Shamay-Tsoory, S. G., Tomer, R., Berger, B. D., & Aharon-Peretz, J. (2003). Characterization of empathy deficits following prefrontal brain damage: The role of the right ventromedial prefrontal cortex. *Journal of Cognitive Neuroscience, 15,* 324–337.

Shrira, I., & Martin, L. L. (2005). Stereotyping, self-affirmation, and the cerebral hemispheres. *Personality & Social Psychology Bulletin, 31,* 846–856.

Siegel, D. J. (1999). *The developing mind: Toward a neurobiology of interpersonal experience.* New York: Guilford Press.

Sim, T-C., & Martinez, C. (2005). Emotion words are remembered better in the left ear. *Laterality, 10,* 149–159.

Spiegel, D., & Cardeña, E. (1991). Disintegrated experience: The dissociative disorders revisited. *Journal of Abnormal Psychology, 100,* 366–378.

Spitzer, C., Wilert, C., Grabe, H-J., Rizos, T., & Freyberger, H. J. (2004). Dissociation, hemispheric asymmetry, and dysfunction of hemispheric interaction: A transcranial magnetic approach. *Journal of Neuropsychiatry and Clinical Neurosciences, 16,* 163–169.

Spitzer, C., Barnow, S., Freyberger, H. J., & Grabe, H. J. (2007). Dissociation predicts symptom-related treatment outcome in short-term inpatient psychotherapy. *Australian and New Zealand Journal of Psychiatry, 41,* 682–687.

Stern, D. B. (1997). *Unformulated experience: From dissociation to imagination in psychoanalysis.* Hillsdale, NJ: Analytic Press.

Stern, D. N. (2004). *The present moment in psychotherapy and everyday life.* New York: Norton.

Stern, D. N. (2005). Intersubjectivity. In E. S. Person, A. M. Cooper, & G. O. Gabbard (Eds.), *Textbook of psychoanalysis* (pp. 77–92). Washington, DC: American Psychiatric Publishing.

Stern, D. N., Bruschweiler-Stern, N., Harrison, A. M., Lyons-Ruth, K., Morgan, A. C., Nahum, J. P., et al. (1998). The process of therapeutic change involving implicit knowledge: Some implications of developmental observations for adult psychotherapy. *Infant Mental Health Journal, 19,* 300–308.

Sullivan, R. M., & Dufresne, M. M. (2006). Mesocortical dopamine and HPA axis regulation: Role of laterality and early environment. *Brain Research, 1076,* 49–59.

Thiebaut de Schotten, M., Dell'Acqua, F., Forkel, S. J., Simmons, A., Vergani, F., Murphy, D. G. M., & Catani, M. (2011). A lateralized brain network for visuospatial attention. *Nature Neuroscience, 14,* 1245–1246.

Tschacher, W., Schildt, M., & Sander, K. (2010). Brain connectivity in listening to affective stimuli: A functional magnetic resonance imaging (fMRI) study and implications for psychotherapy. *Psychotherapy Research, 20,* 576–588.

Tucker, D. M., & Moller, L. (2007). The metamorphosis. Individuation of the adolescent brain. In D. Romer & E .F. Walker (Eds.), *Adolescent psychopathology and the developing brain. Integrating brain and prevention science* (pp. 85–102). Oxford, UK: Oxford University Press.

Uddin, L. Q., Molnar-Szakacs, I., Zaidel, E., & Iacoboni, M. (2006). rTMS to the right inferior parietal lobule disrupts self-other discrimination. *Social Cognitive and Affective Neuroscience, 1,* 65–71.

Van Lancker, D., & Cummings, J. L. (1999). Expletives: Neurolinguistic and neurobehavioral perspectives on swearing. *Brain Research Reviews, 31,* 83–104.

Van Lancker, D., & Cummings, J. L. (2006). Where in the brain is nonliteral language? *Metaphor and Symbol, 21,* 213–244.

Volz, K. G., & von Cramon, D. Y. (2006). What neuroscience can tell about intuitive processes in the context of perceptual discovery. *Journal of Cognitive Neuroscience, 18,* 2077–2087.

Volz, K. G., Rubsamen, R., & von Cramon, D. Y. (2008). Cortical regions activated by the subjective sense of perceptual coherence of environmental sounds: A proposal for a neuroscience of intuition. *Cognitive Affective & Behavioral Neuroscience, 8,* 318–328.

Welling, H. (2005). The intuitive process: The case of psychotherapy. *Journal of Psychotherapy Integration, 15,* 19–47.

Whitehead, C. C. (2006). Neo-psychoanalysis: A paradigm for the 21st century. *Journal of the Academy of Psychoanalysis and Dynamic Psychiatry, 34,* 603–627.

Zanocco, G., De Marchi, A., & Pozzi, F. (2006). Sensory empathy and enactment. *International Journal of Psychoanalysis, 87,* 145–158.

CHAPTER 5

Therapeutic Enactments: Working in Right Brain Windows of Affect Tolerance

Over the course of my writings I continue to elaborate on and expand the clinical applications of regulation theory's developmental and interpersonal neurobiological models. This body of work indicates that the right brain is dominant in psychotherapy, and that the integration of recent scientific studies into updated models of psychotherapeutic action allows for a deeper understanding of underlying change processes. In my very first book (Schore, 1994), I offered speculations on "developmental affect theory and the mechanisms of psychotherapeutic change," a theme that runs throughout my subsequent books, articles, and chapters. In this work I offer a further contribution toward elucidating the psychological and biological change mechanisms that are activated in the rapid, elusive, and complex clinical phenomenon of therapeutic enactment.

In my second book, *Affect Regulation and the Repair of the Self* (2003b), I cited Strupp's (1989) classic psychotherapy research:

> By all odds, the greatest challenge facing the therapist is the skillful management of enactments that often put the therapist on the defensive, evoke boredom, irritation, anger, and hostility and in other respects "put pressure" on the therapist to behave in ways that are incompatible with his or her stance as an empathic listener and clarifier. (p. 719)

Enactments represent the most stressful moments of the treatment. To cite but one clinical example, Knox (2010) describes a dramatic and critical affectively charged moment that occurred in an ongoing psychotherapy process:

The patient had, over a number of consecutive sessions, been complaining that she had no sense of my emotional presence for her, that I was distant and that my technique was inadequate, making me utterly useless to her. She persistently goaded me to tell her how I felt. This had the effect of making me even more tight-lipped and resistant to what I experienced as a ruthless whinging attack on me both as a person and as her analyst. Eventually, I could no longer hold my temper, and I told her exactly what I felt—how much I didn't look forward to her coming, how I hated her and her endless demands on me, and how deeply I cherished the thought of her ending her analysis. This was not beautiful, poetic or musical, but full of raw emotion. The patient burst into deep sobs for some minutes. When she recovered the power of speech she said, "Thank God. You've come back from the dead." With hindsight I believe that, at a completely unconscious level, I had taken in and digested something of her of which both she and I were unconscious. What I gave her was digested in the sense that I had incorporated it into myself, and combined it with some aspect of me deeper than my consciousness, before giving it back to her. . . . (George Bright, unpublished paper, cited in Knox, 2010, p. 120)

The conceptual understanding as well as the clinical processing of enactments is now undergoing a major transformation. In 1994 Glen Gabbard began an American Psychoanalytic Association panel on "Enactment of Boundary Violations" by reading Freud's letter to Jung that he had not yet acquired "the necessary objectivity" for the work:

You still get involved, giving a good deal of yourself and expecting the patient to give something in return. Permit me, speaking as the venerable old master, to say that this technique is invariably ill-advised and that . . . it is best to remain reserved and purely receptive. We must never let our poor neurotics drive us crazy. I believe an article on "countertransference" is sorely needed; of course, we could not publish it. . . . (McGuire, 1974, pp. 475–476)

Gabbard concluded by arguing that if we are to *prevent destructive enactments of boundary violations,* we must begin with a psychoanalytic understanding of how such enactments evolve (Keenan, 1995). In parallel writings, Renik (1993) asserted that in order to appreciate the value of enactment, clinicians must change the way they think about the therapeutic action of the treatment. In this same time period Chused (1991) offered a classical conception of an enactment, which posited that its origins were to be found within the psyche of patient, who is attempting to re-create the past and gain gratification, a motive that is counterproductive. In subsequent writings she asserted that a therapeutic moment occurs when the clinician thwarts an enactment and provides a correct interpretation instead (Chused, 1997).

By the end of the 1990s theoretical and clinical models had evolved from a one-person intrapsychic to a two-person relational psychology, and this trend was echoed in updated conceptions of enactments. In 1997 I wrote that although early painful experiences are usually buried in deep layers of the unconscious, in certain heightened affective moments, interpersonal stressors within the transfer-ence-countertransference relationship instantly rupture the attachment bond between patient and therapist.

> This sudden shattering of the therapeutic alliance . . . induces the entrance into consciousness of a chaotic state associated with early traumatic experiences that is stored in implicit (Siegel, 1995) procedural memory. . . . Sander (1992) refers to a "mutuality of influence," "a thinking that is oriented as much around the way the patient's signals influence therapist state as around therapist on patient state" (p. 583). This dialectical mechanism is especially prominent during stressful ruptures of the working alliance that occur during "enactments," defined as those "events occurring within the dyad that both parties experience as being the consequence of behavior in the other. (McLaughlin, 1991, p. 611; Schore, 1997a, pp. 47–48)

In 1998 Maroda was describing enactment as a therapeutic context in which the patient's and the therapist's pasts converge: "Enactment is an affectively driv-en repetition of converging emotional scenarios from the patient's and the ana-lyst's lives" (p. 520). Foreshadowing later studies of the importance of nonverbal communications in enactments, she noted these difficult clinical phenomena may be expressed not only in dramatic action but also in silence or gesture:

> Behaviorally, it may take the form of a heated argument, a sadomasochistic ex-change, a spontaneous hug or other physical gesture, a shortening or lengthening of a session, a failure to collect the fees, an unexpected dissolution into tears, or a withdrawal into silent rejection. (Maroda, 1998, p. 519)

It should be recalled that up through the early 1990s the problem of trauma was not addressed (if not ignored) in all clinical models. With the incorporation of modern trauma theory into updated clinical models (especially advances in the developmental mechanisms of attachment trauma and its enduring impact on brain development, emotional processes, and stress regulation), theoretical understandings of enactment became more complex, yet more specific. As op-posed to earlier conceptions that viewed enactments as technical mistakes, it was now held,

> It is not merely an affectively driven set of behaviors, it is necessarily a repetition of past events that have been buried in the unconscious due to associated unmanage-able or unwanted emotion. . . . *It is his or her chance to relive the past, from an af-fective standpoint, with a new opportunity for awareness and integration.* (Maroda, 1998, p. 520, my emphasis)

In a further break from classical ideas, Maroda (1998) described "just how ubiquitous it is and how equally inevitable is the evocation of the analyst's past in terms of re-creating an emotional scenario" (p. 531). Thus, she argued that earlier clinical advice about avoiding enactments was senseless. Echoing this,

Friedman and Natterson (1999) referred to enactments as "intersubjective inevitabilities."

Over this same time period the clinical literature began to incorporate emotion into clinical models of enactment. In 1992 a panel of the American Psychoanalytic Association concluded that all enactments contain two essential elements: the stimulation of strong, unconscious affects and some resulting behavior. By the end of the decade Maroda (1998) contended that enactments involve the experience of *unconsciously strong or even overwhelming affect*. In a groundbreaking article she concluded that "Although it necessarily involves action, enactment is essentially an affective event" (p. 531). By this time affect was so central that she warned, "Failing to appreciate the emotional intensity of enactment constitutes its inevitability, rather than a particular behavior, could lead to irresponsible acts on the part of therapists" (p. 532).

I suggest that in the ensuing time period, over the last 10 years, due to the emergence of a truly interdisciplinary perspective, we now possess a substantial increase in knowledge of the complex clinical phenomena embedded in an enactment, one that speaks directly to Gabbard's and Renik's call for not only a deeper psychoanalytic but also a neuropsychoanalytic understanding of enactments. In fact I will argue that the ongoing enriched dialogue between science and clinical practice is producing a paradigm shift that is expanding our therapeutic approaches to enactment and our theoretical understandings of the change process of psychotherapy. In the next section of this chapter, I explicate in some detail how regulation theory integrates new scientific knowledge of right brain emotional processes with advances in psychodynamic clinical approaches, and how this modern neuropsychoanalytic perspective radically alters our clinical approach to the stressful, heightened affective moments of enactments. This paradigm shift is also emphasizing the tight linkage between the science and the art of psychotherapy.

THE PARADIGM SHIFT INFORMS UPDATED CLINICAL CONCEPTIONS OF ENACTMENTS

Paradigm shift: Regulation theory's neuropsychoanalytic model of unconscious emotions deepens our understanding of enactments.

In 2009 I was invited to deliver a plenary address, "The Paradigm Shift: The Right Brain and the Relational Unconscious," to the annual American Psychological Association Convention in Toronto. Although the transformation of a dominant scientific paradigm impacts all disciplines, with respect to psychotherapy, the shift is from conscious cognition to unconscious emotion. In the 1960s and 1970s, psychology was dominated by a behavioral paradigm, and it lead to the expression of a behavioral model of psychotherapy. This transformed into a cognitive model in the 1980s and 1990s, and the emergence of cognitive psychotherapy. At present strong links are being forged between psychology and biology. Due to the change in paradigm, recent developmentally oriented psychodynamic models of psychotherapy such as affect regulation therapy (ART) are placing affect and psychobiological processes at center stage, and viewing implicit, unconscious relational functions at the core of the therapeutic change mechanisms, including the change process activated within an enactment.

Though long devalued by science, psychoanalysis, and indeed conscious and unconscious cultural forces, an enormous amount of current experimental and clinical data supports the psychobiological organizing principle that emotional processes are essential to organismic survival. Due to the massive increase in studies in affective neuroscience over the last two decades, there is now widespread agreement that emotional processing is no longer thought of as a fundamentally disorganizing force that needs to be suppressed, but rather as an adaptive process of rapid appraisals of events that are important to individual, and a survival mechanism that allows for flexibility of responses to changes in the environment. This processing of bodily based emotional information is essential to well-being, because it is necessary for both avoidance of danger and approach toward successful social interactions. Furthermore, these subjective states generate fundamental relational meanings that have adaptive significance. Lane (2008) summarizes the current view:

> Primary emotional responses have been preserved through phylogenesis because they are adaptive. They provide an immediate assessment of the extent to which goals or needs are being met in interaction with the environment, and they reset the organism behaviorally, physiologically, cognitively, and experientially to adjust to these changing circumstances. (p. 225)

The ongoing "emotional revolution" in all fields of mental health has clearly impacted our understanding of enactments as relational contexts for the expression of "primary emotional responses." But as Maroda (1998) pointed out, these therapeutic moments involve a dysregulation of emotions, especially their intensity (*overwhelming affect*). From the psychoanalytic perspective, she added that enactments contain expressions of not only conscious but also *unconsciously strong affect*. This seminal observation clearly indicates that the clinical phenomenon of the heightened affective moment of an enactment cannot be understood without a theory of unconscious processes. For over a century psychoanalysis, "the scientific study of the unconscious mind" (Brenner, 1980), has provided such a theory. Although disconnected from the other sciences for most of the last century, psychoanalysis is now experiencing a rapprochement and indeed a mutually enriching dialogue with its neighboring disciplines, including neuroscience (Schore, 1996). By 2008 Bargh and Morsella asserted that "Freud's model of the unconscious as the primary guiding influence over every day life, even today, is more specific and detailed than any to be found in contemporary cognitive or social psychology" (p. 73). And in a breakthrough article in 2010, Shedler offered a strong body of evidence to argue that "blanket assertions that psychodynamic approaches lack scientific support are no longer defensible" (p. 106), and that "increased awareness of implicit or unconscious mental life—is the core defining feature of psychoanalysis and psychoanalytic therapy" (p. 104).

Over the last two decades psychoanalysis has returned to its roots and the fundamental questions about unconscious affect and motivation that lie at the core of the field, first addressed by Freud in his *Project for a Scientific Psychology* (1895/1966). The creation of modern neuropsychoanalysis has thus acted as a major integrative force within the field itself. Toward that effort, in 1997 I suggested that the early maturing right brain is isomorphic with the developing unconscious system described by not only Freud but also various psychoanalytic observers (Schore, 1997b). Since then I continue to cite a burgeoning amount of interdisciplinary research indicating that the right-lateralized "emotional brain" represents the biological substrate of Freud's unconscious, which is now conceptualized as a "relational unconscious." As opposed to other neuroscientific disciplines, neuropsychoanalysis highlights not only conscious but also unconscious (implicit) emotion, including the *unconsciously strong or even overwhelming affect* expressed in enactments. Almost 100 years ago Freud (1915/1957) speculated, "Unconscious ideas continue to exist after repression as actual structures in the system *Ucs*, whereas all that corresponds in that system to unconscious affects is a potential beginning which is prevented from developing" (p. 178).

Indeed, recent neuroscience now confirms the importance of unconscious affects. Mlot (1998), writing in the journal *Science*, reported on studies showing that unconscious, implicit processing of emotional stimuli is specifically associated with activation of the right, not the left, hemisphere. More specifically Price (2005) asserted, "the enhanced memory for emotional experiences may proceed at a relatively subconscious level, without clear awareness" (p. 135). At this same time neuroscientists were describing "Right hemispheric dominance in processing of *unconscious negative emotion*" (Sato & Aoki, 2006) and "cortical response to subjectively *unconscious danger*" (Carretie, Hinojosa, Mercado, & Tapia, 2005).

In previous neuropsychoanalytic contributions, I have demonstrated that the implicit communication of regulated affective states in attachment communications between the right brains of the infant–mother dyad is best described as "intersubjectivity." The neurobiological correlate of this intersubjectivity principle is expressed in the dictum "the self-organization of the developing brain occurs in the context of a relationship with another self, another brain" (Schore, 1996, p. 60). But during this same period of the infant's right brain development, stressful dysregulated attachment transactions also imprint right-lateralized circuits for coping with dysregulated relational stress. By this interpersonal neurobiological mechanism, early relational trauma is encoded in implicit-procedural memory. Relational trauma thereby negatively impacts the developmental trajectory of the right hemisphere, dominant for detecting threat, for enabling an organism to cope actively and passively with emotional stress, and for control of vital functions supporting survival.

According to the regulation model of psychopathogenesis, these relational deficits are later expressed in the therapeutic alliance, and so therapeutic enactments represent reexpressions in real time of early forming right brain automatic survival mechanisms. More specifically, enactments are dialogically re-created in right brain–to–right brain transference-countertransference communications, interactions occurring between the patient's relational unconscious and the therapist's relational unconscious. Mirroring this conceptualization, Maroda (1998) states, "Enactment is a dynamic, naturally occurring manifestation of the transference and countertransference merging into a living entity, making the past alive in the present" (p. 530).

Confirming the paradigm shift from conscious cognition to unconscious emotion and the early origins of enactments, current neuroscience now reveals that "The right hemisphere develops a specialization for cognitive functions of a more ancient origin and the left for a specialization for functions of more modern origin" (Howard & Reggia, 2007, p. 121). Echoing this, Panksepp (2008, p. 51) observes, "Cognitive science must re-learn that ancient emotional systems have a power that is quite independent of neocortical cognitive processes." The ancient emotional system that is activated during an enactment is a right-lateralized cortical-subcortical system. Note that not only right cortical but also right subcortical processes in the medial temporal lobe are expressed in therapeutic moments of strong, overwhelming affect (Buchanan, Tranel, & Adolphs, 2006; Simian-Tov et al., 2008). As opposed to the left anterior temporal lobe that is associated with semantic memory, the right anterior temporal lobe is the storehouse of personal, episodic emotional memories (Olson, Plotzker, & Ezzyat, 2007). Citing a number of studies, Engdahl et al. (2010, p. 1) report that "electrical stimulation of the temporal cortex in awake human subjects, mostly in the right hemisphere, can elicit the re-*enactment* and re-living of past experiences" (my emphasis).

Paradigm shift: Regulation theory's model of relational trauma and dissociation deepens our understanding of enactments.

In accord with a developmentally focused model of psychotherapy, enactments are more common in severe psychopathologies, specifically those that contain histories of attachment trauma (Schore, 2009d). According to Borgogno and Vigna-Taglianti (2008),

> In patients whose psychic suffering originates in . . . preverbal trauma . . . transference occurs mostly at a more primitive level of expression that involves in an unconscious way . . . not only the patient but also the analyst. . . . These more archaic forms of the transference-countertransference issue—which frequently set aside verbal contents—take shape in the analytical setting through actual mutual enactments. (p. 314)

Instead of being obstacles to the treatment, enactments offer "a way of reaching deeply into traumatized areas" (Cassorla, 2008, p. 158). In order to form this deep connection, "The patient must be able to stimulate something in the [therapist] that is equally primitive and split off, so that they can relive the drama in a real way together. . . . Enactment thus involves mutual stimulations of repressed affective experience, ideally with the patient taking the lead" (Maroda, 1998, p. 520). In light of the fact that a modern theory of relational trauma is now available (Schore, 2009d), the current paradigm shift also applies to defenses; and so the field is now moving from repression to dissociation in understanding the dynamics of enactments.

There is current agreement on the following: that the essential effect of trauma is "the disruption of the continuity of being (*the 'illusion of being one self'*)" (Pizer, 1998, pp. 141–142, my italics), that trauma represents the "event(s) that cause dissociation" (Howell, 2005), and that in dissociative states the mind/brain tries to avoid self-annihilation by protecting the inner world from the existence of the outside (Bromberg, 2011). According to Donnel Stern (2009),

> It is by now a clinical truism that experience dissociated in the strong sense—dissociated with unconscious defensive purpose—does not simply disappear into some untended part of the mind, but is instead repetitively externalized, unconsciously enacted in relationship (Bromberg, 1998, 2006; Davies, 1997; Pizer, 1998; Stern, 2006). Enactments are more or less stereotyped, rigid, constricted, and highly selective ways of behaving and experiencing. (p. 661)

In a number of writings I have suggested that pathological dissociation represents an early forming bottom-line right brain survival defense of the implicit self against overwhelming, unbearable, painful emotional experiences, including those generated in relational attachment trauma (Schore, 2001b, 2002, 2009b). Dissociation has been described as detachment from unbearable situations, the escape when there is no escape, the last resort defensive strategy, and it can be manifested as a freeze response or a collapsed state. This fundamental defense to the memory of the arousal dysregulation of an overwhelming negative affective state blocks intense emotional pain from entering conscious awareness, and thereby instigates an altered state of consciousness. In the words of Emily Dickinson (1862),

> There is a pain—so utter—
> It swallows substance up—
> Then covers the Abyss with Trance—
> So memory can step
> Around—across—upon it—
> As one within a Swoon—
> Goes safely—where an open eye—
> Would drop Him—Bone by Bone

Pathological dissociation, an enduring outcome of early relational trauma, is manifest in a maladaptive highly rigid, closed right brain system. This system's implicit visual, auditory, and tactile sensory perceptual functions—performed by the temporoparietal areas of the posterior right cortical hemisphere that "plays a key role in perception and awareness" (Papeo, Longo, Feurra, & Haggard, 2010)—are radically altered in trauma. A body of research now demonstrates that "Psychic suffering seems to correspond quite often with a reduced sensory memory processing" (Menning, Renz, Seifert, & Maercker, 2008, p. 31). Note Dickinson's observation that an "open eye" (vision, the major sensory perceptual modality for processing threat in the external environment) must be radically altered in the dissociative defense of "detachment from an unbearable situation." Bromberg (2011) observes that the essence of dissociation is that it alters perceptual experience—and thereby drains the interpersonal context of personal meaning.

Bromberg (2011) also notes that in dissociation the ordinary links between symbolic and subsymbolic communication have been broken—at least for a while. Neurobiologically this translates to a disconnection between higher right cortical (symbolic) and lower right subcortical (subsymbolic) systems. Dissociation thus reflects the inability of the right brain cortical-subcortical implicit self-system to recognize and process the perception of external stimuli (exteroceptive information coming from the relational environment) and on a moment-to-moment basis integrate them with internal stimuli (interoceptive information from the body, somatic markers, the "felt experience"). This failure of integration of the higher right hemisphere with the lower right brain and disconnection of the central nervous system from the autonomic nervous system induce an instant collapse of both subjectivity and intersubjectivity. Stressful affects, especially those associated with emotional pain, are thus not experienced in consciousness; they are associated with what Bromberg (2006) terms "not-me" self-states.

It is important to emphasize that dissociation involves more than an alteration of mental processes, but rather mind–body disconnections. Kalsched (2005, p. 174) describes operations of defensive dissociative processes used by the child during a traumatic experience by which "Affect in the body is severed from its corresponding images in the mind and thereby an unbearably painful meaning is obliterated." There is now agreement that "traumatic stress in childhood could lead to self-modulation of painful affect by directing attention away from internal emotional states" (Lane, Ahern, Schwartz, & Kaszniak, 1997, p. 840). The right hemisphere is dominant not only for regulating affects but also for maintaining a coherent sense of one's body (Tsakiris, Costantini, & Haggard, 2008), for attention (Baijal & Srinivasan, 2011; Helton, Kern, & Walker, 2009; Raz, 2004), and for pain processing (Carrasquillo & Gereau, 2008; Geha et al., 2008; Ji & Neugebauer, 2009; Ploner, Gross, Timmermann, Pollok, & Schnitzler, 2006; Schon et al., 2008; Symonds, Gordon, Bixby, & Mande, 2006). And so the right brain strategy of dissociation represents the ultimate defense for blocking emotional bodily based pain. The endpoint of chronically experiencing catastrophic states of relational trauma in early life is therefore a progressive impairment of the ability to adjust, take defensive action, or act on one's own behalf, and a blocking of the capacity to register affect and pain, all critical to survival.

At all points of the life span, although dissociation represents an effective short-term strategy, it is detrimental to long-term functioning, specifically by preventing exposure to potential relational learning experiences embedded in intimate intersubjective contexts that are necessary for emotional growth. As Bromberg notes, the function of pathological dissociation is to act as an "early warning system" that anticipates potential affect dysregulation by anticipating trauma before it arrives. If early trauma is experienced as "psychic catastrophe," dissociation represents "a submission and resignation to the inevitability of overwhelming, even psychically deadening danger" (see references in Schore, 2003a, 2009a). In addition, this closed system responds to even low levels of intersubjective relational stress with an instant switch from sympathetic hyperarousal into the survival response of defensive parasympathetic, dorsal vagal hypoarousal and heart rate deceleration (see Schore, 2009a). This results in moments of "psychic death" and an inability to sustain an inner sense of "aliveness" (Bach, 2008). McGilchrist (2009) describes dissociation as "a relative hypofunction of the right hemisphere." This psychobiological survival defense becomes characterological in personalities who experience attachment trauma in early development.

The fragile unconscious system of such personalities is susceptible to not only hypermetabolic hyperarousal but also mind–body hypometabolic collapse. The latter is manifest in a sudden loss of energy-dependent synaptic connectivity within the right brain, expressed in an instant implosion of the implicit self, a rupture of self-continuity, and a loss of an ability to experience a particular conscious affect. This collapse of the implicit self is signaled by the cognitions of hopelessness and helplessness. Because the right hemisphere mediates the communication and regulation of emotional states, the rupture of intersubjectivity is accompanied by an instant dissipation of safety and trust, a common occurrence in enactments that occur in the treatment of the right brain deficits of severe personality disorders (see chapter 3).

Confirming this model, Lanius and her colleagues (2005), in a functional magnetic resonance imaging study of traumatized (post-traumatic stress disorder, PTSD) patients, show right hemispheric activation during dissociation. These authors conclude that patients dissociate in order to escape from the overwhelming emotions associated with the traumatic memory. Using transcranial magnetic stimulation, Spitzer et al. (2004) similarly report dissociation is associated with right hemisphere dysfunction in the form of lack of integration in the presence of emotionally distressing or threatening stimuli. Enriquez and Bernabeu (2008) offer research showing "dissociation is associated with dysfunctional changes in the right hemisphere which impair its characteristic dominance over emotional processing" (pp. 272–273). As an example, these authors document that although high dissociators retain an ability for processing left hemispheric verbal stimuli, they show deficits in right hemispheric perception of the emotional tone of voice (prosody).

More recently, Helton, Dorahy, and Russell (in press) report that high dissociators have difficulty in specifically coordinating activity within the right hemisphere, and that such deficits become evident when this hemisphere is "loaded with the combined effects of a sustained attention task and negative emotional stimuli. . . . Thus, the integration of experiences, which rely heavily on right hemispheric activation (e.g., negative emotion, sense of self with reference to the experience) may be compromised in high dissociators." These findings are echoed in current neurological research. Brand et al. (2009) and Stanilou, Markowitsch, and Brand (2010) document right temporofrontal hypometabolism in cases of dissociative amnesia, which is clinically expressed as an inability to recall important personal information of a traumatic nature; a failure of integration of consciousness, emotion, and cognition; and a "constricted self."

A number of recent clinical authors hold that enactments are specifically related to dissociation. D. B. Stern (2008) argues that enactments are the only means of encountering dissociated aspects of the patient. These clinical encounters offer an opportunity to "understand the unconscious aspect of the patient on him, and then to use his knowledge of this impact, and of his own disequilibrium, to grasp parts of the patient's experience that the patient has no way to put into words" (p. 402). This impact is not only on the therapist's mind but also in his or her body. Lebovici defines enactment as something "achieved in a truly extraordinary moment in which the analyst feels in his own body an act which remains experienced and not acted out" (cited in Zanocco, De Marchi, & Pozzi, 2006, p. 149). Zanocco et al. contrast acting out with the undoing of repression: "Enactment, by contrast is related to primitive unconscious elements which find in their act their first expression and which involve both the analyst and patient, precisely because of the particular relationship that is formed between them" (p. 150).

The bodily based unconscious communications of dissociated affects embedded in an enactment are transmitted and received through right brain–to–right brain channels. McGilchrist (2009) observes, "The right hemisphere, is . . . more closely in touch with emotion and the body (therefore with the neurologically 'inferior' and more ancient regions of the central nervous system). . ." (p. 437). Enactments, "a particular form of expression related to processes and dynamics originating in the primitive functioning of the mind" (Zanocco et al., 2006, p. 150), thus represent reexpressions of early right brain attachment dysregulations of *mind and body*, of both the central nervous system (CNS) and the sympathetic and parasympathetic branches of the autonomic nervous system (ANS), the "physiological bottom of the mind" (Jackson, 1931). In the enactment the patient experiences more than mental distress, but a rupture of the integration of psychic and somatic experience, what Winnicott (1949/1975a) called psyche-soma, and thereby self-wholeness.

Thus an enactment, a right brain–to–right brain traumatic intersubjective context characterized by "unconsciously strong or even overwhelming affect," equated with Freud's (1915/1957, p. 178) "unconscious affect," involves a release of dissociated not repressed unconscious affect. According to Cassorla (2008) enactment "discharges" occur that "involve both members of the analytical dyad without their being conscious of the fact" (p. 164). Before the affective eruption, the underlying traumatic situation in the patient's life "is frozen and unable to manifest itself openly" (p. 171), (note allusion to a traumatic freeze response, Schore 2009a). But at the moment of an enactment there is a state shift, "a revival of the trauma, which had been frozen," which "releases the plugged anxiety, with both seizing abruptly the analytical field" (p. 171). What is released (discharged) is sympathetic hyperarousal that lies beneath parasympathetic dorsal vagal inhibition. I have argued that the dissociative defense represents the major counterforce to the emotional-motivational aspects of the change process in psychotherapy, and that a graded lowering of this defense and release of negative affect represent a stressful yet valuable opportunity for change. Cassorla (2008) notes that with this shift the acute enactment now serves as a catalyst to move the therapeutic process forward.

Sands (2010) elegantly describes the critical nature of these moments in the treatment process:

> When our ongoing treatment of a trauma survivor is "working," there will come a time when dissociative structure begins to loosen and dissociative defenses begin to fail. There develops a "crisis" in the treatment—a time when the patient feels precariously poised on the edge of a precipice and suddenly, desperately, needs not only our help *but our very being* to sustain her. It is these moments that can make or break a treatment. (p. 369, my italics)

Paradigm shift: Regulation theory views enactments as potential context of therapeutic change.

A more complex model of the mechanisms that underlie clinical enactments allows for not only more effective therapeutic interventions but also a deeper theoretical understanding of the change process. Citing my work, Ginot (2007) asserts, "Increasingly, enactments are understood as powerful manifestations of the intersubjective process and as inevitable expressions of complex, though largely unconscious self-states and relational patterns" (p. 317). Such intense transference-countertransference affective *entanglements* "bring to life and consequently alter implicit memories and attachment styles," but at the same time "generate interpersonal as well as internal processes eventually capable of promoting integration and growth" (pp. 317–318, my italics).

Although I have written about therapeutic heightened affective moments for some time, I recently expanded these ideas into a formal regulation theory model of the change mechanism embedded in mutual enactments (Schore, 2009b, 2010). Summarizing this work, the following developmental organizing principles lie at the core of the clinical model. Early growth-inhibiting social-emotional environments negatively influence the ontogeny of right brain homeostatic self-regulatory and attachment systems. During pre- and postnatal critical periods of right brain cortical-subcortical connections, unrepaired states of dysregulated hyperarousal and hypoarousal epigenetically shape an enduring lowered limbic-autonomic threshold for emotional turbulence, a reduced threshold for dissociation, and a hyperreactivity to novelty in the environment.

The patient brings into treatment an enduring imprint of attachment trauma: an impaired capacity to regulate stressful affect and an overreliance on the affect-deadening defense of pathological dissociation. Under relational stress, this affect dysregulation deficit is characterologically expressed in a tendency toward low-threshold, high-intensity emotional reactions followed by slow return to baseline. Highs and lows are too extreme, too prolonged, or too rapidly cycled and unpredictable. Patients with histories of attachment trauma (i.e., personality disorders) thus contain unconscious insecure working models that automatically trigger right brain stress responses at low thresholds of ruptures of the therapeutic alliance. In addition to their hypersensitivity to even low levels of interpersonal threat (narcissistic injuries), they also frequently experience enduring states of high-intensity negative affect and defensively dissociate at lower levels of stressful arousal.

As previously mentioned, the stressful psychobiological dynamics of attachment trauma are *reenacted* in right brain intersubjective bodily based affective communications within the co-created therapeutic alliance (the relational unconscious of the patient implicitly communicates with the relational unconscious of the therapist). In heightened affective moments of enacted transference-countertransference ruptures, communication of intense negative right brain bodily based unconscious affects dysregulates both members of the therapeutic dyad. Enactments thus represent expressions of dyadic affect-arousal dysregulation, a relational context in which both are in a stressful state of dysregulated organismic homeostasis.

This neuropsychoanalytic model of implicit affective (as opposed to explicit cognitive) change attempts to describe the structure-function relationships of right brain development over the life span, including the brain development fostered by effective psychotherapy. It thus generates a clinically relevant and experimentally testable conceptualization of the "curative" process of psychotherapy, especially the changes induced by ART, that is, developmental, affectively focused psychodynamic psychotherapy. Writing on the efficacy of psychodynamic psychotherapy, Shedler (2010) observes, "The essence of psychodynamic therapy is exploring those aspects of self that are not fully known, especially as they are manifested and potentially influenced in the therapy relationship" (p. 98). The current psychodynamic therapeutic perspective focuses on "affect and the expression of emotion"; on the "exploration of attempts to avoid distressing thoughts and feelings"; and on development, whereby "past experience, especially early experiences of attachment figures, affects our relation to, and experience of, the present" (p. 99).

From a modern psychoanalytic affect regulation (ART as opposed to cognitive-behavioral, CBT) perspective, enactments represent essential therapeutic contexts that potentially allow for the revelation of parts of the self that are not fully known (dissociated "not-me states"). Echoing the paradigm shift from conscious cognition to unconscious affect, this clinical approach encourages not the control of emotion, but the exploration of the patient's full emotional range, including distressing affects associated with early experience that are consciously and *unconsciously avoided*, and thereby on the affect-deadening defense of dissociation. The patient's growth from a constriction to an expansion of adaptive right brain affective functions is a central feature of the clinical work.

With this introduction in mind, in the following sections of this chapter I offer a detailed neuropsychoanalytic model of working with enactments, heightened affective moments of the treatment that have been the most difficult to conceptualize as well as to treat. The temporal context of the intensely affective moment of a "spontaneous" enactment is what Stern (2004) terms a "now moment":

> Now moment is a present moment that suddenly arises in a session as an emergent property of the moving along process. *It is an affectedly charged moment because it puts the nature of the patient–therapist relationship into question.* This usually involves bumping up against or threatening to break the habitual framework or "rules" of how they work together and are together. What is at stake is how they will be with each other. The level of anxiety in the patient and therapist rises. They are both pulled forcefully into the present. The therapist feels that a routine technical response will not suffice. This adds to his or her own anxiety. A crisis that needs resolution has been created. (2004, p. 245, my italics)

Notice I am speaking of "moments," clearly implying that a number of enactments (and not a single event) occur over the course of treatment.

An essential tenet of the interdisciplinary perspective of regulation theory is that current knowledge about the interpersonal neurobiology of the right brain implicit self, the biological substrate of the human unconscious, can uniquely deepen our understanding of the contributions of both the patient and the therapist both in an enactment and in the unfolding of the "therapeutic action." This neurobiologically based clinical model of enactments, which I offer to researchers as well as to clinicians, applies not only to the treatment of attachment trauma but also to all attachment histories, and it addresses the following problems:

How can an attachment relationship of communication and regulation of conscious and unconscious painful affect and dysregulated arousal be established within the therapeutic alliance?

Can alliance ruptures of enactments be repaired? That is, can states of hyper- and hypoarousal be communicated, shared, and interactively regulated?

As opposed to a cognitive focus of treatment (how can a repressed unconscious cognition be transformed into a conscious cognition?), this affectively focused model attempts to ask the question, how can an unconscious (dissociated) affect be transformed into a conscious affect?

How can treatment alter developmental deficits in the patient's right brain functions in the human stress response, including its implicit, rapid capacity for detecting threat and coping actively and passively with stress?

Can a responsive relational context within the co-created therapeutic alliance reduce a dissociative defense, alter stress response threshold set points, and increase affect tolerance and affect regulation?

What interpersonal neurobiological mechanisms allow regulated enactments to induce an expansion of the patient's right brain and an increase in the complexity of both negative (painful) and positive (pleasurable) affective processing?

How can the integrative functions of the right brain (the "emotional," "social" brain) change within the growth-facilitating relational environment co-created within the therapeutic relationship?

An integration of the recent interdisciplinary scientific data on emotion, trauma, and therapeutic change in this section clearly suggests a paradigm shift in the conceptualization of clinical enactments. This advance allows for a more comprehensive understanding of specifically how regulated enactments represent a central mechanism of therapeutic action, especially for patients who have experienced early relational attachment trauma, whether they are infants, children, or adults. The following is directly relevant to clinical work with personality disorders, especially borderline patients who present with an attachment history of heavy psychic suffering and right hemispheric structural and functional deficits (Dinn et al., 2004; Driessen et al., 2009; Irle, Lange, & Sachsse, 2005; Meares, Schore, & Melkonian, 2011; Merkl et al., 2010; Ruocco, 2005). Yet these clinical ideas, grounded in interpersonal neurobiology and traumatology, apply to all patients.

In his most recent book, *The Shadow of the Tsunami and the Growth of the Relational Mind*, Bromberg (2011) argues that therapeutic joint processing of enactments

> allows one's work with so-called "good" analytic patients to become more powerful because it provides a more experience-near perspective from which to perceptually engage clinical phenomena that are immune to interpretation, such as "intractable resistance" and "therapeutic stalemate." Further, it . . . allows [therapists] to use their expertise with a wide spectrum of personality disorders often considered "difficult" or "unanalyzable," such as individuals diagnosed as borderline, schizoid, narcissistic, and dissociative. (pp. 161–162)

I am very familiar with this book, because I wrote its Foreword, which can be used as a reader's guide that broadly translates Bromberg's numerous clinical vignettes of enactments in terms of my regulation theory (Schore, 2011b). In parallel to the following discussion of the interpersonal neurobiological mechanisms that underlie enactments, I refer the reader to that work for numerous clinical descriptions of these heightened affective moments, as well as to the clinicians I repeatedly cite in the upcoming sections of this chapter.

PROJECTIVE IDENTIFICATION AS THE NONVERBAL COMMUNICATION SYSTEM OF ENACTMENTS

In this section of the chapter I use regulation theory to describe in a more experience-near fashion the intersubjective psychobiological communications that occur between patient and therapist within an enactment. This theoretical perspective integrates psychology and biology, and thereby models the essential nonconscious interpersonal neurobiological mechanisms that are activated in these critical moments of the treatment process. Over the course of the psychotherapy, aspects of the patient's implicit self that are dissociated—including overwhelming, distressing affective states that are avoided, kept out of consciousness, and thereby hidden from the higher centers of the implicit self—can become more fully known in these heightened affective moments. In recent relational clinical models, enactments are understood as intense affective eruptions within the therapeutic relationship that are part of the ongoing therapeutic process, and not due to a failing of the patient or the psychological makeup and approach of the clinician. Congruent with the idea that enactment is "an affectively driven repetition of converging emotional scenarios from the patient's and the analyst's lives" (Maroda, 1998, p. 520), ongoing research now clearly demonstrates, "There is a growing consensus in the field of psychotherapy that the personalities of the client and the therapist, together with the therapeutic relationship, play a critical role in psychotherapy processes and outcomes" (Romano, Fitzpatrick, & Janzen, 2008, p. 495).

Magnavita (2006) notes, "The process of psychotherapy uses relational factors to stimulate healing and growth. The quality of the therapeutic relationship is probably the most robust aspect of therapeutic outcome" (p. 888). There is now agreement that the clinician's ability to co-create a working alliance with a particular patient is a central determinant of therapeutic effectiveness. Writing in the clinical research literature, Ackerman, Hilsenroth, and Knowles (2005) offer the following description of the early phases of the therapeutic alliance:

> The therapist's use of psychodynamic-interpersonal activities in the beginning of treatment (e.g., encouraging the experience and exploration of uncomfortable feelings, allowing the patient to initiate discussion of salient themes, and focusing on in-session relational themes between the therapist and the patient) may inform the patient that the therapist is willing (and able) to help address issues that have been previously avoided. The willingness of the patient to experience and explore affect, as well as initiate discussion, may broaden the therapist's perception of the patient as even more actively engaged and lend momentum to the developing therapeutic alliance. (p. 229)

In the early phases of treatment, right brain–to–right brain communications solidify the therapeutic alliance and increase the positive transference (Schore, 1994, 2003b). This co-created emotional bond enables the patient, at an unconscious level, to experience increasing trust and safety, thereby allowing defenses to be lowered. In my first book I described,

> The therapist's focus is on the empathic grasp of the experiential state of the patient. . . . As a result the patient establishes an "archaic bond" with the therapist and thereby facilitates the revival of the early phases at which his psychological development has been arrested (Kohut, 1984). It is known that the emotional bond between the patient and therapist, manifested in the working alliance, promotes the exploration of the individual's internal experience and affective state. This strongly felt bond enables the patient to confront inner states associated with frightening aspects of the self. (Schore, 1994, p. 449)

According to Bowlby (1988), the burgeoning therapeutic relationship also reactivates the patient's unconscious expectations about the responsiveness and emotional availability of others, including the therapist. In 1990 in his last interview, Bowlby specifically stated, "Emotion is nonverbal communication of basic but very powerful attitudes of mind and potential action" (Tondo, 2011, p. 167). Ongoing psychobiologically attuned right brain communications within the dyad facilitate the reexpression of the patient's early traumatic attachment experiences with the mother, stored in an internal working model and expressed in right brain nonverbal implicit/procedural autobiographical memory. Gainotti (2006) observes, "the right hemisphere may be crucially involved in those unconscious memories which must be reactivated and reworked during the . . . treatment" (p. 167).

This is a difficult but essential task in the treatment of patients with a history of relational trauma. Krystal (2002) points out that because the registration of the traumatic state is on a preverbal, sensorimotor level, no language is available for the presentation of the memory. He describes why this work is so challenging:

> Traumatic memories are not repressed in the ordinary sense of the word. Something worse happens to them. They are repudiated. Freud used the word *verwerfung* instead the verb *verdrangung*, meaning "to repress." Their return to consciousness may produce a life-threatening situation and/or a sanity-threatening situation. Some traumatic perceptions are not compatible with the survival of the self and are never registered consciously or in a form that is recoverable by any normal means; and these are the *memories that cannot be remembered or forgotten*. . . . It is not just because the past involved enforced passivity, submission, and surrender, but because *the emotional regression to certain infantile forms of relatedness causes an evocation of the infantile and childhood trauma encapsulated within their memories of the major trauma.* (2002, p. 217, my italics)

The re-evocation of the unconscious memories of infantile trauma and relatedness occurs in an enactment, and it is marked by an intense negative transference. Bromberg (2006) describes enactment as "reliving." He suggests that because trauma cannot be narratively represented in memory, developmental trauma is unsymbolized by language and cannot be spoken "about" as material, but rather relived as part of the telling. In her most recent book Maroda (2010) describes how during an enactment both therapist and patient are simultaneously experiencing strong, unacceptable emotions originating in each of their pasts, and both express these in their relationship. She further notes that enactment occurs when the patient unconsciously stimulates a strong, unplanned response by the therapist. Maroda postulates that to fit the definition of enactment, both therapist and patient need to be unaware of what they are stimulating in each other until some untoward event occurs. This untoward event, she says, specifically occurs in a mutual projective identification. Thus Gainotti's "reactivation," Bromberg's "reliving," and Krystal's "emotional regression" and "evocation" of the developmental trauma occur not within a spoken objective verbal narrative between patient and therapist but within the intersubjective nonverbal communication of a negative affectively charged projective identification.

Klein (1946) originally defined projective identification as a process wherein largely unconscious information is projected from the sender to the recipient. Although this primitive process of communication between the unconscious of one person and the unconscious of another begins in early development, it continues throughout life. In updated clinical conceptions, B. Joseph (1997) stresses that "projective identification is, by its very nature, a kind of communication" (p. 103); and Adler and Rhine (1992) assert that projective identification involves the projection of *affects* associated with self and object representations.

In *Affect Regulation and the Repair of the Self*, I offered a chapter, "Clinical Implications of a Psychoneurobiological Model of Projective Identification" (Schore, 2003b). In that work I proposed that the communication in enactments occurs by mutual projective identification, a right brain–to–right brain transaction in which events occurring within the dyad are experienced by both parties as being the consequence of behavior in the other. A large body of studies indicates that the therapist's right brain plays a dominant role in spontaneous emotional communication (Blonder, Bowers, & Heilman, 1991) and in the unconscious processing of emotional stimuli (Mlot, 1998). This conception clearly implies that unconscious systems interact with other unconscious systems, and that both receptive and expressive properties determine their communicative capacities. In the chapter I offered a slow motion analysis of the rapid dyadic unconscious psychobiological communications that occur in such clinical heightened affective moments. These right brain transmissions occur within milliseconds, in the temporal domain of Daniel Stern's (2004) "present moment," an event that lasts 4 seconds or less. The dyadic psychobiological mechanism of projective identification allows for the detection and reception of unconscious affects on both sides of the dyad.

Furthermore, in the 2003 chapter I concluded,

> Current developmental models thus emphasize the fact that projective identification, both in the developmental and the therapeutic situations, is not a unidirectional, but a bi-directional process in which both members of an emotionally communicating dyad act in a context of mutual reciprocal influence. Although projective identification arises in the emotional communications within the mother–infant dyad, this "primitive" process plays an essential role in "the communication of affective experiences" in all later periods of development (Modell, 1994). These communications, however, have unique operational properties and occur in specified contexts. Authors are emphasizing that projective identification constitutes a mode of "primitive joint action" mediated by nonverbal signs (Leiman, 1994). (Schore, 2003b, pp. 65–66)

It is important to note that the term *projective identification* has also been used to describe a primitive unconscious defense mechanism that is a central focus of the treatment of child and adult developmental psychopathologies. In a number of writings I have described defensive projective identification as an early organizing unconscious psychoneurobiological coping strategy for regulating right brain–to–right brain communications, especially of intense affective states. At all points in the life span defensive projective identification, a right brain survival mechanism for coping with interactively generated overwhelming traumatic affects, is activated in response to subjectively perceived social stimuli that potentially trigger imminent dysregulation.

The use of a unique and restricted set of defenses in severely disturbed personalities has been long noted in the clinical literature. Indeed a primary goal of treatment of such patients is to help them replace excessive use of projective identification with more mature defensive operations. Boyer (1990) describes a group of patients who have experienced an early defective relationship with the mother that results in a grossly deficient ego structure. Their excessive use of projective identification

> very heavily influences their relationships with others as well as their psychic equilibrium. Their principal conscious goal in therapy is to relieve themselves immediately of tension. Often they greatly fear that the experience of discomfort is intolerable and believe that failure to rid themselves of it will lead to physical or mental fragmentation or dissolution. (p. 304)

In the 2003 chapter I described an attachment scenario of relational trauma in which an early defective relationship with the mother induces a deficient regulatory structure in the developing infant. Whenever he or she nonconsciously senses imminent attachment trauma, the stressed infant (child, adolescent, adult), with only primitive abilities to cope with the overwhelming arousal induced by relational stress and at the limit of his or her fragile regulatory capacities, experiences intense affect dysregulation, projects a distressing emotional communication, and then instantly dissociates. This strategy, because it is imprinted into developing right brain limbic-autonomic circuits, becomes characterological, and represents a psychobiological mechanism by which intolerable psychic-physical discomfort and tension are instantly inhibited.

These survival mechanisms are "reenacted" in the affective relationship between patient and therapist. Modell (1993) states that in projective identification, "affects that are associated with the patient's past traumatic relationships are . . . projected onto the therapist, so that these affects are also experienced by the therapist" (p. 148). Sands (1997) points out that certain patients use projective identification because they seek to bring into the therapeutic relationship affective experience that was encoded under traumatic conditions or because it pertains to a preverbal period of life, and therefore remains unsymbolized. She offers the important observation that because such experience remains in somatosensory or iconic form, it must be communicated in like manner.

Congruent with this idea, I have suggested that because affects are psychobiological phenomena and the self is bodily based, the coping strategy of projective identification represents not conscious verbal-linguistic behaviors but unconscious, nonverbal *mind–body communications*. The right brain is centrally involved in unconscious activities; and just as the left brain communicates its states to other left brains via conscious linguistic behaviors, so the right brain nonverbally communicates its unconscious states to other right brains *that are tuned to receive these communications*.

Until recently the concept of unconscious nonverbal (as opposed to conscious verbal) communication has remained within the province of psychoanalysis, but at present other sciences are now investigating this fundamental form of communication. In the journal *Nature* (2009), Buchanan describes "secret signals":

> A person's responses can often be explained by "non-linguistic behaviours of other people and simple instincts for social display and response, without any recourse to conscious cognition. . . . This "second channel" of human communication acts in parallel with that based on rational thinking and verbal communication, and it is much more important in human affairs than most people like to think. . . . It is incredibly naïve . . . to take conscious verbal communications as the primary way that people respond to each other. (pp. 528–529)

This channel of communication processes social signals that are expressed in intonation, fluctuating pace and amplitude of voice, and upper-body movements, and in "mirroring," "which occurs when one participant subconsciously copies another's prosody and gesture" (p. 529). The outputs of this channel are an expression of "a more archaic brain system for non-linguistic social signals" (p. 529). I suggest that this "second" channel of not left but right brain commu-

nication is activated in enactments and expressed in a mutual projective identification of unconscious information. Zanocco et al. (2006) observe that during
an enactment clinicians "will catch themselves making a gesture, changing posture or simply modifying the tone of their voices" (p. 150). These heightened
affective moments represent an alignment of what Zeddies (2000) calls the
"nonlinguistic dimension" of the "relational unconscious" of both the therapist
and the patient.

Migone (1995) holds that instances of projective identification occur in "intimate or close relationships, such as the mother–child relationship or the
patient–analyst relationship" (p. 626). In both, rapid dyadic unconscious psychobiological communications occur within milliseconds. These subliminal right
brain communications, imprinted in the attachment relationship between the
infant and the primary caregiver, are transmitted through the same right brain
nonverbal mechanism between the patient and the clinician. Recall Bowlby's
(1969) assertion that nonverbal mother–infant attachment communications are
"accompanied by the strongest of feelings and emotions," and occur within a
context of "facial expression, posture, tone of voice, physiological changes, tempo of movement, and incipient action" (p. 120). There is now extensive neurobiological data demonstrating the critical role of the early maturing right brain
in the infant's developing capacity to process the auditory prosodic aspects of the
human voice (Grossmann, Fitzpatrick, & Janzen, 2010), the visual response to a
female face (Grossmann, Johnson, Farroni, & Csibra, 2007), and the ability to
express communicative gestures (Montirosso, Borgatti, & Tronick, 2010).

Indeed, regulated attachment communications in critical periods of infancy
imprint the circuits of the right brain that support the adaptive capacity to process
social-emotional information over the ensuing stages of childhood, adolescence,
and adulthood. In recent writings neuroscientists are characterizing the unique
adaptive functions of this system: "Pattern recognition and comprehension of several types of stimuli, such as faces, chords, complex pitch, graphic images, and
voices, has been described as superior in the normal right hemisphere" (Van
Lancker Sidtis, 2006, p. 223). Describing the capacities of the right-lateralized
"social brain," Brancucci, Lucci, Mazzatenta, & Tommasi (2009) conclude,
"The neural substrates of the perception of voices, faces, gestures, smells and
pheromones, as evidenced by modern neuroimaging techniques, are characterized by a general pattern of right-hemispheric functional asymmetry" (p. 895).
During enactments dysregulated states of insecure attachment communicated in
mutual projective identifications utilize this same system.

INTERPERSONAL NEUROBIOLOGY OF
RIGHT BRAIN UNCONSCIOUS COMMUNICATIONS
IN ENACTMENTS

According to Zanocco et al. (2006), enactments are processes and dynamics originating in the primitive functioning of the mind, and they allow the therapist to
access a way of interacting with patients who are not able to give representation

to their instinctual impulses. Enactments represent "an unconscious mental activity which does not follow the rules of conscious activity. There is no verbal language involved. Instead, there is a production of *images* that do not seem to follow any order, and, even less, any system of logic" (p. 145, my italics). These authors further suggest that this form of interaction is mediated not by secondary but by primary process mechanisms. Dorpat (2001) observes, "Intuitions, *images*, and emotions derived chiefly from the primary process system provide an immediate and prereflective awareness of our vital relations with both ourselves and others" (p. 450).

In earlier work I proposed that the transmissions of the relational unconscious are mediated by right brain primary process communications, including visual-facial, auditory-prosodic, and tactile-gestural signaling (Schore, 1994). Consonant with this model, Dorpat (2001) argues that "affective and object-relational information is transmitted predominantly by primary process communication," and that it is expressed in "nonverbal communication" including "both body movements (kinesics), posture, gesture, facial expression, voice inflection, and the sequence, rhythm, and pitch of the spoken words" (p. 451). Recall that enactments "frequently set aside verbal contents." During these heightened affective moments the sensitive psychobiologically attuned therapist is processing not left brain rational, explicit secondary process but right brain emotional, implicit primary process nonverbal communications. Weinberg (2000) points out, "Emotions are closely associated with the right hemisphere. . . . *Words can name emotions, but they cannot convey the essence of emotional experience*" (p. 801, my italics). These data clearly mean that explicit, conscious, verbal voluntary responses are inadequate to prevent, facilitate, or metabolize implicit emotional enactments.

It is important to point out that the right brain is composed of both "higher" cortical (cerebral hemispheric) and "lower" subcortical areas. The lower subcortical levels of the right brain (the deep unconscious; e.g., the amygdala, insula, and hippocampus within the temporal lobe, hypothalamus, brain stem, etc.) contain all the major motivational systems (including attachment, fear, sexuality, play, aggression, shame, disgust, etc.) and generate the somatic autonomic expressions and arousal intensities of all emotional states. The "higher" dual-circuit orbitofrontal system (Schore, 2003a), which I equate with Freud's "preconscious," functions as a dynamic filter of emotional stimuli, provides a panoramic view of the entire external and internal environment that is associated with motivational factors, and formulates a kind of affective decision making (see chapter 4). At the orbitofrontal level, cortically processed information concerning the external environment (visual, auditory, and tactile stimuli processed by the posterior sensory areas of the right hemisphere) is integrated with subcortically processed information regarding the internal visceral environment (such as concurrent changes in the emotional or bodily self-state). This thereby enables incoming regulatory information to induce a switch to a particular motivational and affective self-state (Schore, 2003a).

In current neurobiological writings on the role of the amygdala in "the affective regulation of body, brain, and behavior," Mirolli, Mannella, and Baldassarre (2010) characterize these adaptive switching functions:

> The capacity for survival and reproduction of organisms depends on several different abilities, for example, the ability to find food and water, the ability to prevent that the body gets damaged (and to recover from what happens), the ability to find a sexual partner willing to copulate and reproduce, the ability to escape from predators, the ability to find a suitable place for resting and sleeping, and so on. If an agent has to satisfy all these needs, a crucial "meta-ability" is required, namely the ability to manage the interactions between all these activities. In particular, in *each moment* the organism must solve the problem of establishing the need to which it should attend. Affective systems allow organisms to solve precisely this problem, that is, to choose which is the activity that has to be accomplished in each moment. (p. 216)

This critical "meta-ability" is an output of the orbitofrontal system, the "senior executive of the emotional brain," which performs an essential adaptive function—the relatively fluid switching of internal bodily based emotional and motivational states in response to moment-to-moment changes in the external environment that are nonconsciously appraised to be personally meaningful. In this manner the stress-regulating orbitofrontal system neurobiologically maintains the capacity of "positive emotionality," a personality trait associated with resilience (Volkow et al., 2010). Resilience, a function mediated by the ventromedial prefrontal cortex (Katz et al., 2009; Stevenson et al., 2008), is an outcome of the optimal early attachment experiences that shape this regulatory system. In more poetic terms, this system provides *"a strong foundation when the winds of change shift."*

In basic research on orbitofrontal functions in appropriately adapting and rapidly modifying emotions on a moment-to-moment basis, Reekie, Braesicke, Man, and Roberts (2008) conclude,

> Successful adaptation to changes in an (individual's) emotional and motivational environment depends on behavioral flexibility accompanied by changes in bodily responses, e.g., autonomic and endocrine, which support the change in behavior. . . . [T]he orbitofrontal cortex is pivotal in the flexible regulation and coordination of behavioral and autonomic responses during adaptation. (p. 9787)

With optimal maturation, the higher orbitofrontal limbic-autonomic levels of the right hemisphere, the locus of Bowlby's attachment system (Schore, 1994), can function as the brain's most complex affect and stress regulatory system. They can generate a conscious emotional state that reflects the affective interoceptive expression of each motivational system.

Patients with psychopathologies in affect regulation manifest orbitofrontal dysfunctions and thereby deficits in these adaptive capacities. In important neurophysiological studies of psychoanalytic defense mechanisms, Northoff, Bermpohl, Schoeneich, and Boeker (2007) report,

[W]e assume that the orbitofrontal cortex plays a crucial role in constituting more mature and cognitively guided defense. . . . Dysfunction in this region . . . might make the constitution of cognitively guided defense mechanisms impossible. This, in turn, might induce regressive processes with the consecutive predominance of rather immature and emotionally guided defense mechanisms like splitting, projective identification, denial and psychotic introjection/projection. For example, one would suspect dysfunction in the orbitofrontal cortex in patients with a borderline personality, where projective identification predominates. (p. 148)

Enactments, common in psychotherapy with borderline patients. potentially allow for the reorganization of cortical (orbitofrontal)-subcortical (amygdala) connectivity.

I suggest that during enactments the clinician's right-lateralized orbital prefrontal corticolimbic system must be temporarily taken "off-line'" in order to receive the patient's deep projective identifications. The fact that both the right cortical and right subcortical subsystems process relational and affective cues clearly suggests discrete systems of right cortical ("preconscious") communications and right subcortical ("deep unconscious") communications within close relationships. The latter is activated in the projective identifications of a stressful enactment. Indeed, both the right brain fear system and the right brain attachment system are activated in an enactment. Bromberg (2011) argues that enactments, the reliving of attachment-related developmental trauma in a patient's past, activate the patient's brain's "fear system" via triggering of a "smoke detector." I would add so is the clinician's "fear system."

It is important to note that this fear state may not reach conscious awareness. Neuroscience now concludes that fear "is not necessarily conscious; a fearful response may be evoked even when one is not fully aware of being 'afraid'" (Price, 2005, p. 135). A large body of studies reports that specifically the right amygdala specializes in "unseen fear" (Morris, Ohman, & Dolan, 1999), fear conditioning (Morris & Dolan, 2004), the unconscious perception of ambiguously threatening stimuli, which sustains excessive monitoring behavior and an intolerance for uncertainty (Ohrmann et al., 2007), and in unconscious emotional learning (Morris, Ohman, & Dolan, 1998). The patient's right amygdaloid subcortical system is thus unconsciously mobilized as a "smoke detector" in ambiguous intersubjective contexts that activate potentially overwhelmingly dysregulated, and therefore dangerous, dissociated affects.

The early developing right amygdala is imprinted by intense states of fear-terror associated with attachment trauma. This generates not only projective identification but also the defensive coping strategy of pathological dissociation, which blocks the conscious awareness of overwhelming affects and induces enduring deficits in mind and body (Schore, 2009a). The communications within mutual defensive projective identifications thus represent not right cortical–to–right cortical communications but right subcortical–to–right subcortical bodily based limbic-autonomic communications. During an enactment this latter system of communication between the deep unconscious of the patient and the deep unconscious of the therapist allows for the unconscious reception of a defensive projective identification, the detection of a dissociated affect, the synchronization of autonomic states, and the mutual amplification of arousal by an interpersonal resonance amplification of the "unconsciously strong or even overwhelming affect." What would this look like clinically?

In a very recent clinical paper, Sands (2010) describes "dissociative unconscious communication":

> This form of implicit communication, an emergent property of the analytic process, is characterized by a powerful and visceral resonance between patient and analyst, as something dissociated in the patient *grabs hold of* and enters into deep communion with something dissociated in the analyst and opens up a channel of unconscious empathy. . . . Then, during the rapid sequence of reciprocal interactions that follow, the unconscious affective communications become amplified within the intersubjective field to the point of intolerability. Patient and analyst become joined in a momentary traumatic state. . . . (p. 365, my italics)

She offers the following case illustration in which the patient's report of a dream elicits a dissociative unconscious communication.

The patient, Lillian, arrives looking pale and drawn, saying she has "blunted feelings." She talks for a few minutes, then says, "I had another one of those icky dreams. I HATE my dreams." Lillian (at this point in treatment) feels persecuted by her dreams, as well as by many other things in life. She has little curiosity about her dreams beyond railing at them for being so disagreeable. She tells me the following dream looking irritated but with little other affect:

> I'm in some kind of a downtown bar situation with [two neighbors she knows slightly]. Police come up and give breathalyzer tests, and it turns out both are legally intoxicated and will be going to jail. One goes around the corner and takes a gun to his head and kills himself. Then the other one goes into my house and in the hall facing the bathroom. takes a gun out and blows his brains out. My concern is not him but how icky it is. So I avoid going home, but then when I do go home I find him all crumpled up and blood all over. I call the police, but they say it's not an emergency, that they'll be there in 3 to 5 hours. I say, "But I don't want to have to look at him. Can I put a sheet over him?" They say, "Well, maybe, but don't disturb the crime scene." They leave me dangling. And he's in rigor mortis now, a hunk of bloody tissue.

When Lillian says a "hunk of bloody tissue," I see the *horrific image* rise up before me in the most intensely visual and vivid way, as if it were my own dream. I suddenly feel *hot, slightly nauseated, and dizzy*. I stare at her dumbly for a few moments, unable to find any words. She notes my reaction but then hurries on to talk about her shame about not being more concerned about the dead man. I stop her, saying something like, "Wait, wait . . .

that image of the hunk of bloody tissue . . . it's so *awful* . . . and it's right there in your *house*." I watch her tune into me and get hit by my state. She tears up, then just as quickly says angrily and bitterly, "OK. So *now* you get it. The story of my life! . . . It was SO bad!" She cries for a few minutes, and then goes on to talk about having had to live day in and day out with her violent, mentally ill, sexually abusive mother, and later on she also finds herself discussing that ugly, disgusting part of her that she repeatedly and violently kills off internally. (Sands, 2010, pp. 362–363)

Citing my work on right brain cortical-subcortical communications, Sands speculates that the traumatic imagery of the dream is encoded in "right amygda-loidal memory," and that dissociative unconscious communications represent "right to right amygdala projective communications (Schore, personal communication)" (pp. 366–367). In her discussion of this case, Sands also refers to a "fascinating" paper by Eshel (2006) on the patient's use of "telepathic dreams" in order to contact the therapist to prevent collapse into a state of early traumatic abandonment. In the neuroscience literature there is now consensus that "The right hemisphere operates in a more free-associative, primary process manner, typically observed in states such as dreaming or reverie" (Grabner, Fink, & Neubauer, 2007, p. 228). Recall Freud's (1933/1965) speculation that sleep is especially suitable for the reception of emotionally intense "telepathic" communications, and Jung's assertion that "telepathic phenomena are undeniable facts" (1902/1977, p. 135).

In an intriguing contribution on 19th- through 21st-century therapeutic approaches to cases of childhood trauma and pathological dissociation, Platt (2009) cites my model of right brain–to–right brain unconscious communications within the therapeutic dyad. She states that this same right brain limbic mechanism lies at the core of two other related phenomena that are associated with such cases, telepathic and paranormal communication. Platt describes a functional MRI investigation of telepathy by Venkatasubramanian et al. (2008) showing right parahippocampal activity. This research echoes an earlier SPECT study by Persinger's group demonstrating right parietotemporal activation during the processing of paranormal information (Roll, Persinger, Webster, Tiller, & Cook, 2002). Both the right-lateralized parahippocampal and amygdala subcortical limbic structures are located within the right temporal lobe. In summary, these clinical and research data support my earlier proposal that the unconscious, spontaneous emotional communication within enactments represents "a conversation between limbic systems" (Schore, 2003b).

ENACTMENTS EXPRESSED IN RIGHT BRAIN–TO–RIGHT BRAIN TRANSFERENCE-COUNTERTRANSFERENCE TRANSACTIONS

In recent work I have expanded my regulation theory formulation that during an enactment unconscious bodily based dysregulated affects are transacted in the transference-countertransference relationship as moment-to-moment, right brain–to–right brain bodily based nonverbal visual-facial, auditory-prosodic attachment communications, as well as in gestures and body language (Schore, 2011a, 2011b). Valent (1999) states, "Transference-countertransference may be the only way infants or severely traumatized persons can communicate their stories of distress, and are therefore central tools for discerning unprocessed or defended events" (p. 73). In this manner experiences of relational attachment trauma are *reenacted* in implicit affective communications within the transference-countertransference relationship.

Transference, now common to all forms of psychotherapy, can be defined as "an established pattern of relating and emotional responding that is cued by something in the present, but oftentimes calls up both an affective state and thoughts that may have more to do with past experience than present ones" (Maroda, 2005, p. 134). Note the similarity of this description to the functions of the right hemisphere:

> The right hemisphere holds representations of the emotional states associated with events experienced by the individual. When that individual encounters a familiar scenario, representations of past emotional experiences are retrieved by the right hemisphere and are incorporated into the reasoning process. (Shuren & Grafman, 2002, p. 918)

This hemisphere also contains imprints of past experiences of early overwhelming traumatic painful affect, expressed in an intense negative transference.

The quintessential context for an enactment is thus a right brain transferential-countertransferential nonverbal communication of a dysregulated emotional state, a moment of shared overwhelming, yet unconscious negative affect. This affective communication occurs beneath the words, at implicit levels of the therapeutic relationship; and it represents *an interaction between the patient's emotional vulnerability and the therapist's emotional availability*. In earlier work I suggested that in these critical moments the therapist's emotional disengagement and deflection of the projected negative state intensify the patient's interactive dysregulation, including the iatrogenic reinforcement of the patient's dissociative defense, a not uncommon occurrence (Schore, 2003b). Maroda (1998) offers the important observation: "What is the point of withholding emotion and thwarting the patient in his quest for affective communication? . . . He will only have to up the ante next time, until he finally gets an emotional response or gives up in despair and subsequent depressed withdrawal" (p. 83). Effective clinical work in dyadic enactments thus implies a profound commitment by both therapeutic participants and a deep emotional involvement on the therapist's part (Tutte, 2004). The challenge to the clinician is, can she "receive and read" these stressful unconscious communications? Put another way, can she access a state of right brain receptivity for processing defensive projective identification? This same question is addressed in the clinical query, during the stressful enactment, can she "take the negative transference"?

On this essential clinical matter, Ginot (2009) states, "The analyst's sensitivity, or her right brain readiness to be fully attuned to nonverbal communication, is a necessary therapeutic skill. Becoming entangled in an enactment, although at first out of awareness, is a surprising facet of such sensitivity" (p. 297). Note the paradigm shift, as earlier models held that the therapist's technical mistakes and insensitivity triggered the enactment. In a recent work, Schore and Schore (2008) discuss the clinician's sensitivity as a central component of clinical expertise. Sensitivity is defined as "susceptible to the attitudes, feelings, or circumstances of others; *registering very slight differences or changes of emotion*" (*American Heritage Dictionary*). In line with this we have suggested that "the sensitive clinician's oscillating attentiveness is focused on barely perceptible cues that signal a change in state, and on nonverbal behaviors and shifts in affects" (Schore & Schore, 2008, p. 17). Bugental (1987) stresses the importance of the clinician's "disciplined sensitivity" and ability to "learn to experience finer and finer distinctions or nuances."

These affective communications within the transference–countertransference right brain communications impact not only mental but also psychobiological systems in both the patient and the therapist. The intersubjective transactions between empathic clinician and patient include more than two minds, but *two bodies*. Mathew (1998) evocatively portrays this omnipresent implicit process of bodily communications:

> The body is clearly an instrument of physical processes, an instrument that can hear, see, touch and smell the world around us. This sensitive instrument also has the ability to tune in to the psyche: to listen to its subtle voice, hear its silent music and search into its darkness for meaning. (p. 17)

Aron (1998) observes, "patient and [therapist] mutually regulate each other's behaviors, enactments, and states of consciousness such that each gets under the other's skin, each reaches into the other's guts, each is breathed in and absorbed by the other . . . the analyst must be attuned to the nonverbal, the affective . . . to his or her bodily responses" (p. 26).

Thus, during an enactment the patient's bodily based transferential nonverbal communications elicit somatic countertransferential responses in the sensitive psychobiologically attuned clinician. This neuropsychoanalytic conception follows the clinical principle, "Every transference situation provokes a countertransference situation" (Racker, 1968). That said, just as the transferences of patients with early attachment trauma are more dysregulated, so are the countertransferences they induce. McDougall (1978) asserts that the patient who has suffered preverbal traumas transmits "primitive communications" that induces distressing countertransferential emotional states in the clinician. There is now consensus that reenactments generate the most intense countertransference reactions in empathic psychotherapists.

In my first book I proposed,

> Countertransferential processes are currently understood to be manifest in the capacity to recognize and utilize the sensory (visual, auditory, tactile, kinesthetic, and olfactory) and affective qualities of imagery which the patient generates in the psychotherapist . . . countertransference dynamics are appraised by the therapist's observations of his own visceral reactions to the patient's material. (Schore, 1994, p. 451)

These countertransferential reactions also occur in response to communications of the patient's state of "subjectively unconscious danger":

> Unconsciously perceived negative images (angry faces) elicit significant cognitive, vegetative, and motor responses. For example, these stimuli increase skin conductance response, influence facial expression, facilitate the detection of forthcoming events, and negatively affect the subjective evaluation of other elements of the environment. (Carretie et al., 2005, p. 615)

Furthermore, the conception of countertransference as a purely receptive state is now being altered by two types of models: Updated clinical models describe a two-way reciprocal interaction between the relational unconscious of the patient and that of the therapist; and neuropsychoanalytic models describe spontaneous right brain–to–right brain, face-to-face communications of fast-acting, automatic regulated and dysregulated bodily based emotional states within the therapeutic dyad. In other words, countertransferential reactions are continually implicitly expressed and communicated back to the patient. Over 25 years ago Casement offered this radical idea: "It is usual for therapists to see themselves as trying to understand the unconscious of the patient. What is not always acknowledged is that the patient also reads the unconscious of the therapist, knowingly or unknowingly" (1985, p. 3).

Although there is some clinical literature on the impact of the patient's face on the therapist, there is little to none on the impact of the clinician's facial communications on the patient, and on the unconscious face-to-face transference-countertransference nonverbal dialogue that they co-construct. In a remarkable, indeed brilliant, contribution, Searles (1984–1985) describes the critical role of the analyst's face in the treatment of borderline and schizophrenic patients. Offering detailed observations of face-to-face transactions in a number of case vignettes, he persuasively argues that "the analyst's facial expressions are a highly and often centrally, significant dimension of psychoanalysis and psychoanalytic psychotherapy, a dimension that has been largely neglected, nonetheless, in the literature" (p. 48). Searles describes working with a 40-year-old woman with borderline personality functioning:

I found that the work went best if I were very sparing with my interpretations . . . any interpretation I ventured was too likely to be utilized by this very glib woman in the service of her resistance. (She used words primarily for unconscious defensive purposes, to keep her affects largely dissociated and to protect herself from any strong felt emotional bond with me.) Meanwhile . . . I found that *her attunement to my face proved to be a far more emotionally significant avenue for the development and unfolding of the transference, than did the realm of words on the part of either of us.* (p. 64, my italics)

In another case with a borderline man in his twenties, Searles (1984–1985) notes that "the work was quite stressful for me because of the extent to which he was attuned to my facial expressions" (p. 51). This occurred especially in moments that triggered "his unconscious perception of me as the personification of person(s) from his past who had appreciable difficulties in ego integration, person(s) who were contributory sources of his own sickest introjects" (p. 53).

In my work with him, as that with a number of other patients of varying degrees of illness, I found evidence of his unconsciously identifying, in his facial expressions, with my own, as he perceived (largely *unconsciously*) mine to be. That is, on occasion he would endeavor to quote or paraphrase something I had said in an earlier session, and his facial expressions (and other aspects of his demeanor), in his efforts to do this, gave me to understand that he was unconsciously quoting or paraphrasing, as it were, not merely my words but my facial expressions (and other nonverbal aspects of my demeanor) in my making of those comments. (p. 52)

Searles concludes, "in the core phase of the work with any one patient, each of the two participants' facial expressions 'belong,' in a sense, as much to the other as to oneself" (p. 60).

This unconscious, bidirectional right brain–to–right brain mechanism, which acts at levels beneath conscious awareness of either member of the therapeutic dyad, explains Geller's distinction between (explicit) "knowing about" and (implicit) "experiential knowing."

Patients have two potential sources of knowledge about their therapists: knowledge that is dependent on what the therapist chooses to verbally reveal and the knowledge that is dependent on receiving the information that is available to the senses during therapy sessions. . . . Therapists have less conscious awareness of and control over the messages conveyed by their characteristic level of expressivity than over the messages conveyed by intentional disclosures. . . . Analogously, patients have far less awareness of what they are learning about their therapists by receiving information during therapy sessions. In other words, the knowledge that patients acquire from encounters with the "perceptual reality" of their therapist often remains at a tacit or subliminal level. . . . Consequently, a patient may know much

more than he or she knows about the therapist than either of them is willing to acknowledge. (2003, pp. 549–550)

A similar differentiation is highlighted in the neuroscience literature, in
which authors assert, "It appears clear that social perception based on nonverbal cues would depend mostly on the right hemisphere, as the left is ruled
out of the story due to its major implication in linguistic processing" (Brancucci et al., 2009, p. 896). In the heightened affective moment of an enactment, the therapist's right (and not left) brain receptivity to the patient's
emotional communications is essential because "The right hemisphere, in fact,
truly interprets the mental state not only of its own brain, but the brains (and
minds) of others" (Keenan, Rubio, Racioppi, Johnson, & Barnacz, 2005, p.
702). I would add that this process includes not only the brain and mind but
also the body of others.

This right brain–to–right brain psychobiological mechanism is highly activated in an enactment. It allows for the detection of bodily based unconscious
affects and underlies the premise that "an enactment, by patient or analyst, could
be evidence of something which has not yet been 'felt' by them" (De Marchi,
cited in Zanocco et al., 2006, p. 153). The first medium in which transmitted
somatically dissociated material is "felt" is in the somatic countertransference,
where it must be tolerated and recognized by the clinician. Ginot (2009) offers
this important observation:

> By allowing implicit relational and emotional patterns to be *fully experienced* with-
> in the [therapeutic] process, enactment enables both participants, and especially
> the [therapist], to attain an unmediated connection with what cannot yet be verbal-
> ized, a connection that essentially construes an empathic resonance. (p. 290, my
> italics)

It is important to emphasize that maintaining empathic resonance during an
enactment is clinically difficult, because it occurs during a stressful breach in the
transference-countertransference relationship and a rupture of the therapeutic
alliance. This rupture can be generated not only by the patient's right brain affective defensive strategies but also by the therapist's mis-attuned left brain cognitive "resistance interpretation" of the patient's defense. Valliant (1994) notes, "By
thoughtlessly challenging irritating, but partly adaptive, immature defenses, a
clinician can evoke enormous anxiety and depression in a patient and the rupture the alliance" (p. 49).

Echoing the definition of enactment, in clinical studies Aspland, Llewelyn,
Hardy, Barkman, and Stiles (2008) note ruptures are "points of emotional disconnection between client and therapist that create a negative shift in the quality of the therapeutic alliance" (p. 699); and they act as "episodes of covert or
overt behavior that trap both participants in negative complementary interac-

tions" (p. 700). But Aspland et al. also highlight the importance of therapists explicitly recognizing and acknowledging problems in the relationship. Indeed, they conclude ruptures can have positive consequences if successfully resolved: "Therapists' ability to attend to ruptures emerged as an important clinical skill" (p. 699).

In classical work, Safran and Muran (1996) defined ruptures as "deteriorations in the relationship between therapist and patient" indicated by "patient behaviors or communications that are interpersonal markers indicating critical points in therapy for exploration" (p. 477). During these most stressful moments of the treatment, marked by "a negative shift in the quality of the therapeutic alliance," the therapist's expertise is expressed in an ability to maintain a right brain–to–right brain intersubjective connection during enactment ruptures. But first the clinician must be able to recognize not only his or her countertransferential responses but also his or her own defenses against overwhelming affects—no easy matter. Making this work even more emotionally challenging, Renik (1993) notes enactments cannot be recognized until one is already in them. The reenacting of early representations of "bad objects" is accompanied by dysregulated affects, and these are experienced at the regulatory boundaries of the clinician's affect tolerance, thereby triggering defenses. Russell (1998) offers the provocative assertion, "The most important source of resistance in the treatment process is the therapist's resistance to what the patient feels" (p. 19).

OVERWHELMING AFFECTS IN ENACTMENT ACCOMPANIED BY DISSOCIATIVE DEFENSE

Especially in the treatment of patients with developmental disorders, relational trauma induces not only intensely negative affects but also unique defenses to cope with the severe arousal dysregulation associated with attachment trauma. Applying this principle to the therapeutic context, an essential factor in the dynamic of an enactment is the defensive stress-regulating coping strategy used in the heightened affective moment not only by the patient but also by the clinician. According to regulation theory, defense mechanisms are implicit coping strategies acquired in early attachment transactions, forms of emotional regulation strategies for avoiding, minimizing, or converting affects that are too difficult to tolerate (Schore, 2003a). Importantly, a relational perspective would theorize that the *interaction* between the patient's and therapist's unconscious defenses would act as a potent mechanism in not only the co-creation but also the resolution of an enactment. Boesky (1990) concludes, "the manifest form of a resistance is even sometimes unconsciously negotiated by both patient and analyst" (p. 572). An interpersonal neurobiological model of the nonconscious communication of right brain–to–right brain coping strategies would thus describe the synergistic, defense-amplifying effects of the therapist's transient or enduring countertransferential affective "mindblindness" and the patient's negatively biased transferential expectation of mis-attunement in the co-creation of an enactment. Gans (2011) notes, "Perhaps the most difficult situations involving unwitting self disclosures occur when patient and therapist blind spots intersect" (p. 235).

In an elegant description Bromberg (2006) observes,

> It is the enacted piece of each partner's impact on the other that makes the royal road a bumpy one and makes all too evident that the raw material from which the road is constructed is drawn from the unconscious not only of the patient but also the analyst. (p. 87)

What play out in the intersubjective field at the moment of an enactment are not only stressful aspects of both the patient's and the therapist's past histories but also the coping mechanisms used by each in their early histories. As we move toward modeling the therapeutic alliance with a two-person psychology, we must also use a relational perspective to understand the unconscious communication of projective identification and the interaction between the patient's and the therapist's defenses. As pointed out earlier, the key defense in an enactment (and trauma) is not repression but dissociation (see Schore 2003b on the relationship between projective identification and dissociation). Again, Bromberg (2006) describes the potential intensity of the dysregulation that accompanies dissociated attachment trauma:

> One could even suggest that the impact of trauma leads to the most rigid dissociative mental structure when one of the resulting disjunctive states is highly organized by the attachment-related core-self, and the trauma threatens its violation. In such instances, the threat of affective destabilization carries with it a potential identity crisis. (p. 99)

Recall that at the moment of an enactment there is "a revival of the trauma, which had been frozen," but now "releases the plugged anxiety, with both seizing abruptly the analytical field" (Cassorla, 2008, p. 171). Earlier in this chapter I suggested that this freeze response involves a dissociated (and not repressed) intense affect. Patients with early attachment trauma characterologically use pathological dissociation, and so clinicians need to be informed about this early forming bottom-line right brain passive survival defense against overwhelming, unbearable, painful emotional experiences, including those first generated in attachment trauma. Distinguishing between early forming dissociative defenses and late-forming repressive defenses, Diseth (2005) writes,

> As a defense mechanism, dissociation has been described as a phenomenon quite different from repression. Repression has been considered an unconscious mechanism, placing unwanted feelings away from the conscious mind because of shame, guilt or fear. [p. 81] . . . However, in order to repress, you must to some degree have processed the feelings, recognized their nature and the taboos connected to such feelings. Dissociation is about not having processed the inputs at all. (p. 82)

According to Nemiah (1989),

> In Janet's view dissociation resulted from the *passive* falling away of mental contents from an ego that was too weak to retain them in consciousness, whereas, for Freud, dissociation was the result of the *active* repression of undesirable and emotionally painful mental contents by an ego that was strong enough to banish them from conscious awareness. (p. 1528)

With respect to the psychotherapeutic context, the clinical research of Spitzer, Barnow, Freyberger, & Grabe (2007) shows that insecurely attached dissociative patients dissociate as a response to negative emotions arising in psychodynamic psychotherapy, leading to a less favorable treatment outcome. In the clinical literature Sands (1994) writes, "Dissociative defenses serve to regulate relatedness to others. . . . The dissociative patient is attempting to stay enough in a relationship with the human environment to survive the present while, at the same time, keeping the needs for more intimate relatedness sequestered but alive" (p. 149). Spiegel (2006) concludes, "These patients are difficult to treat. . . . The therapist needs to interact directly with all elements of the patient's emotional world. One has to participate in a real enough relationship with the patient so that one comprehends the patient's world . . . " (p. 567).

Returning to the moment of the release of frozen emotion in an enactment, current relational models also apply to defenses on both sides of the therapeutic alliance. Cassorla (2008, p. 164) states that enactment "discharges" involve "both members of the analytical dyad without their being conscious of the fact," and that this may act as a catalyst to move the therapeutic process *forward*. Thus, to understand the outcome of an enactment, we must take into account not only the patient's but also the clinician's dissociative response. The therapist's ability not to dissociate from the patient's communication of overwhelming negative affect is key here. In this heightened affect moment, will the therapist retain an empathic resonance or defensively dissociate? Ginot (2009) highlights the critical nature of these moments:

> As these interactions might give expression to dissociated painful, angry, and defensive self-states, the empathic aspects in enactments do not depend on the [therapist's] ability to experience empathy for the patient's difficulties. The empathic component is found in the [therapist's] readiness and ability to resonate with what is not verbalized but nonconsciously transmitted nonetheless. (p. 300)

Referring to potential defense-inducing effects of these heightened affective moments, Bromberg (2006) warns,

> Clinically, the phenomenon of dissociation as a defense against self-destabilization . . . has its greatest relevance during enactments, a mode of clinical engagement that requires an analyst's closest attunement to the unacknowledged affective shifts in his own and the patient's self-states. (p. 5)

In light of the principle that enactment can be a turning point in therapy at moments when the therapeutic relationship is characterized by a mode of resistance/counterresistance, these transactions call for the most complex clinical skills of the therapist. On the one hand, Merten et al. (1996) state that poor outcome is "the result of the linkage of the therapist's affective relationship regulation to the unconscious signals of the patient which leads to a stabilization of the patient's conflictive [defensive] structure" (p. 210). On the other hand, if the therapist is does not disengage, dissociate, and interpret but stays in a mode of right brain openness, he or she can participate in what Sands (2010) calls "dissociative unconscious communication." Kantrowitz (1999) asserts that when patient and therapist are able to overcome resistance to engagement, an "intense affective engagement takes place." Thus I have suggested that a spontaneous co-created enactment can evolve into two potential outcomes (Schore, 2003b):

> It can either blindly repeat a familiar pathological object relation through the therapist's deflection of projected negative states and intensification of interactive dysregulation and defensiveness

Or

> [It can] creatively provide a novel relational experience via the therapist's autoregulation of projected negative states and via interactive repair act as an implicit regulator of patient's conscious and dissociated unconscious affective states.

In the next section I offer thoughts on working with the enactment change mechanism at the edges of the regulatory boundaries of right brain windows of affect tolerance.

CLINICAL ENACTMENTS: WORKING IN RIGHT BRAIN WINDOWS OF AFFECT TOLERANCE WITHIN INTERSUBJECTIVE FIELDS

The nonconscious affective intersubjective communications and psychobiological dynamics of an enactment occur within and between the patient's and the therapist's right brain windows of affect tolerance. In recent work (Schore, 2009b), I have proposed that enactments occur at the *edges of the regulatory boundaries of affect tolerance,* or what Lyons-Ruth describes as the "fault lines" of self-experience where "interactive negotiations have failed, goals remain aborted, negative affects are unresolved, and conflict is experienced" (2005, p. 21). Yet these fault lines are also the site of potential therapeutic growth. In terms of nonlinear dynamics systems theory, the edges of affect tolerance also represent "the edge of chaos."

In the most comprehensive and clinically relevant nonlinear modeling of intersubjectivity to date, Marks-Tarlow (2011) states that at the edges of affect tolerance "the coupled therapist/patient system self-organizes implicitly towards the edge of chaos" (p. 120). She describes the therapist's left-to-right shift that allows for his or her participation in the co-creation of the therapeutic alliance:

> As we surrender to deep involvement with our patients, a certain level of autonomy takes over as the two systems become coupled in self-organized fashion, largely beneath the realm of awareness. The resulting therapist/patient system takes on a life of its own as it moves away from equilibrium, toward the edge of chaos, the territory in between and fertile for a switch to somewhere new. (p. 125)

With respect to the edge of chaos, Marks-Tarlow (2011) explains,

> Here the word "chaos" is meant not in the everyday sense of being random or structureless, but rather in the technical, scientific sense where hidden order is invisibly tucked beneath what may appear random on the surface. . . . Many if not most complex systems in nature self-organize toward the edge of chaos, which is a highly fertile zone, where system reorganization is possible. (p. 120)

Marks-Tarlow (2011) further asserts that when the dyad is "working near the edges of our affect tolerance," a context in which both the patient and the clinician are "safe but not too safe" (Bromberg, 2006), the most significant therapeutic change occurs. Systems poised at the edge of chaos show "sensitive dependence on initial conditions," meaning that "the tiniest, microscopic change in an underlying system value can escalate rapidly and unpredictably to tremendous, macroscopic proportions" (p. 121). In these "transformative moments" the "evolution towards disequilibrium at the edge of chaos" also allows for the possibility of an expansion of the regulatory boundaries (p. 120).

Marks-Tarlow (2011) describes the challenge to such work: "this fertile place is also a dangerous one, just as capable of potential annihilation when things break down as of potential creation when things break through" (p. 120). But work at the edge of chaos also allows for unique possibilities for therapeutic growth. "Whether it is in the form of brains, individual people, or coupled relationships, systems poised at the critical edge of chaos are healthiest because they are most flexible, adaptable, and responsive to environmental change" (p. 121). She further states that these chaotic clinical phenomena occur at a "boundary zone of negotiation between self and other constituting intersubjective space" (p. 122), what she calls "the edges of the psyche." I suggest that in order to sustain this conjoint work at the "intimate edge" (Ehrenberg, 1992), both members of the therapeutic dyad must be in a state of emotion-processing right brain dominance. Citing basic research, McGilchrist (2010) observes,

> The right hemisphere alone attends to the peripheral field of vision from which new experiences tend to come; only the right hemisphere can direct attention to what comes to us from the edges of awareness, regardless of side. (p. 506)

The edges of the regulatory boundaries of affect tolerance constitute an area of the patient's immature or delayed right brain emotional development, an affective version of Vygotsky's (1978) cognitive "zone of proximal development" that is occupied by "processes that are currently in a state of formation." Vygotsky speculated, "The zone of proximal development defines those functions that have not yet matured but are in the process of maturation, functions that will mature tomorrow but are currently in an embryonic state" (p. 86). Social learning experiences create this zone by arousing a "variety of internal developmental processes that are able to operate *only when the [individual] is interacting with people*" (p. 90, my emphasis).

These edges of the regulatory boundaries represent not only a "zone of proximal emotional development" but also Winnicottian (1951/1975b) "transitional space," located in the right hemisphere (Weinberg, 2000), which has been developmentally altered by unbearable relational trauma and "unconsciously strong or even overwhelming affect." Wilkinson (2010) discusses

> Ferenczi's interest in exploring the degree of tension that a patient could tolerate and his assertion that to work *at the edge of what was bearable* could bring about therapeutic results. If we look at the work of Ogden et al. (2006) and of Schore concerning the appropriate level of arousal, we find that this latter assertion of Ferenczi has a curiously modern ring to it. (p. 149)

Recall Maroda's (1998) assertion that the therapist must attend to the overwhelming emotional *intensity* of an enactment, that is, the altered state of arousal.

There is now wide acceptance within affective science that emotion is composed of two dimensions: arousal (intensity, energy, calm–excited) and valence (positive–negative, pleasant–unpleasant, approach–avoidance of discrete emotions) (Lang, 1995; Robinson & Compton, 2006; Russell, 1980). Neuroscientists now contend that the most basic level of regulatory processes is the regulation of arousal (Tucker, Luu, & Pribram, 1995), and that the right hemisphere is dominant for arousal processes (Aston-Jones, Foote, & Bloom, 1984). This is in large part through the action of arousal-inducing noradrenaline neurons in the locus coeruleus (Aston-Jones, Rajkowski, Kubiak, Valentino, & Shipley, 1996). In my developmental writings I have emphasized that early attachment dynamics fundamentally represent the interactive regulation of not the valence but the autonomic and central arousal level of the infant's affective state (Schore, 1994). At the most basic level, the primary caregiver modulates the child's energetic state, as arousal levels are known to be associated with changes in metabolic energy (Gonzalez-Lima & Scheich, 1985).

Throughout all stages of development, affect dysregulation refers not to a discrete emotion that is inappropriate to a particular relational context, but to the inability to regulate the arousal intensity of the state, especially ultra-high or ultra-low arousal; that is, significantly increased or reduced physiological reactivity and metabolic energy that accompanies an intensely painful and potentially traumatic state. The same mechanism operates in therapeutic enactments, and clinical interventions are now shifting from altering affective valence to regulating arousal. In line with this I have suggested that self-destabilization of the emotional right brain in clinical enactments can take one of two forms: high-arousal explosive fragmentation or low-arousal implosion of the implicit self (see chapter 3, Figure 3.7). What more can neuroscience tell us about the neurobiology of enactments?

A large body of research now shows that "The right and left human brain hemispheres differ in macrostructure, ultrastructure, physiology, chemistry, and control of behavior" (Braun et al., 2002, p. 97). It is now accepted that functional lateralization is crucial for brain efficiency because it enhances neural capacity by allowing separate, parallel, and specialized processing in the two hemispheres (Vallortigara, 2006). Under low stress conditions the left brain inhibits right brain emotional expression, but as stress increases the right becomes dominant (Cerqueira, Almeida, & Sousa, 2008; Schore, 1994). The right hemisphere is dominant not only for anxious arousal (somatic anxiety or panic) (Nitschke, Heller, Palmieri, & Miller, 1999) but also for "regulating stress—and emotion-related processes" (Sullivan & Dufresne, 2006).

Perez-Cruz, Simon, Czeh, Flugge, and Fuchs (2009) report the reaction of the medial prefrontal cortex to stress is lateralized, in that *responses to "minor challenges" stimulate the left hemisphere whereas "severe stress" activates the right medial prefrontal cortex*. Citing Sullivan's (2004) pioneering work on hemispheric asymmetry in stress processing, Czeh, Perez-Cruz, Fuchs, and Flugge (2008) describe,

> [W]hen an [individual] is exposed to a mildly stressful challenge, the initial coping attempt is accompanied by activation of the left prefrontal cortex (the left prefrontal cortex is less emotional and more motor dominant than the right prefrontal cortex). Because most normal life stressors are manageable, the left prefrontal dominance successfully deals with mildly challenging situations without the need to activate the right prefrontocortex. However, when attempts to cope with the stress fail, activity in the stress-sensitive right prefrontal cortex will be dominant. (p. 7)

This right lateralization of severe (and chronic) stress associated with significant alterations of the intensity of arousal has been documented by other researchers. Studying lateralized involvement of the cortical hemispheres in affect and psychopathology, Papousek, Schulter, and Lang (2009) conclude, "Both the tendency to withdraw and emotional arousal seemed to produce relative advantages for cognitive performance that are more strongly represented in the right than left prefrontal cortex" (p. 510). In a recent overview, MacNeilage, Rogers, and Vallortigara (2009) assert, "The left hemisphere of the vertebrate brain was originally specialized for the control of well-established patterns of behavior under *ordinary and familiar circumstances*. In contrast, the right hemisphere (is) the primary seat of *emotional arousal*" (p. 160, my emphasis).

Consonant with the neurobiological literature, psychological and psychiatric research is moving from studies of individuals in "familiar circumstances," "minor challenges," and "optimal" (mid-range, neutral) arousal to current studies on trauma ("severe stress" and intense emotional arousal) and the right brain's unconscious detection of stressful, unexpected stimuli inducing states of hyperarousal and/or hypoarousal and a rapid response to danger. As previously mentioned, this paradigm shift is also being incorporated into clinical models. From these data I deduce that earlier models of a single window of affect tolerance (e.g., Corrigan, Fisher, & Nutt, 2010; Siegel, 1999) are imprecise. Rather, there are multiple windows—each hemispheric system has unique windows of arousal tolerance.

The left hemisphere window of tolerance represents an optimal range of arousal for "behavior under ordinary and familiar circumstance" (see Figure 5.1). This means voluntary, controlled behavior; explicit, conscious thought; analytical processing; cold cognition; mild and "pleasant" affect; and verbal communication. These "cognitive and behavioral" functions depend upon a moderate rather than a high- or low-arousal range, and are represented by a classical "inverted U." This window of optimal verbal processing and overt behavioral expression is consciously regulated by the left dorsolateral prefrontal cortex. Current counseling and CBT cognitive insight-driven clinical models operate in this arousal range and focus on changing these left brain functions.

In contrast, the right hemisphere, which is dominant for "emotional arousal" and high-arousal emotional states (Heller, 1993), sustains arousal levels optimal for involuntary behavior; implicit, unconscious activities; synthetic-integrative

FIGURE 5.1.   Left brain window of tolerance.

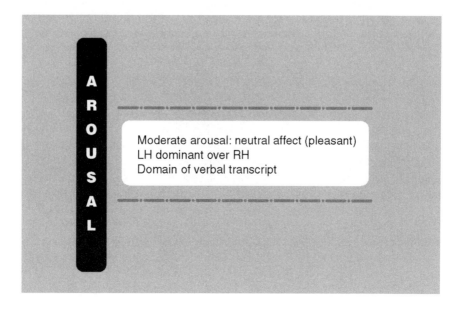

A
R
O
U
S
A
L

Moderate arousal: neutral affect (pleasant)
LH dominant over RH
Domain of verbal transcript

processing; hot cognition; nonverbal communication; and the human stress response. This is the domain of the right orbitofrontal (ventromedial) prefrontal cortex and unconscious affect regulation and, therefore, of affect regulation therapy. Long-term treatment offers a potential to alter right-lateralized, unconscious internal working models of attachment that encode strategies of affect regulation. The right brain's different range of arousal tolerance allows this system to sustain its nonconscious psychobiological survival functions under stress. As opposed to the left, it can operate at a window of very high, stressful sympathetic energy-expending autonomic hyperarousal, or a window of very low, stressful parasympathetic energy-conserving dissociation-autonomic hypoarousal (Figure 5.2).

In the heightened affective moments of clinical enactments, the developmentally oriented psychoanalytic perspective of ART operates in this psychoneurobiological domain. In such work as the co-created therapeutic alliance between patient and therapist stabilizes the patient's attachment system is reactivated. This is accompanied by not only an incrementally burgeoning implicit sense of safety and trust but also a re-experiencing of right brain autobiographical-episodic memories (Brand & Markowitsch, 2008; Markowitsch, Reinkemeier,

FIGURE 5.2. Right brain windows of affect tolerance. Note dysregulation above and below the windows of affect tolerance.

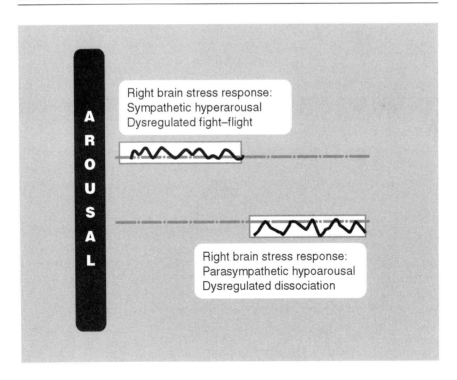

Kessler, Koyuncu, & Heiss, 2000). Mancia (2006) describes, "The discovery of the implicit memory has extended the concept of the unconscious and supports the hypothesis that this is where the emotional and affective—sometimes traumatic—presymbolic and preverbal experiences of the primary mother–infant relations are stored" (p. 83). These reenacted state-dependent traumatic implicit-procedural memories are encoded in high- (hyperarousal) and low- (hypoarousal) arousal states, marked by dysregulated sympathetic and parasympathetic dominant affective states.

Both members of the therapeutic dyad must utilize right brain systems to access this hyperarousal or hypoarousal state-dependent memory system. In earlier work I wrote,

> In light of the related principles of state-dependent learning of affectively charged information (Reus, Weingartner, & Post, 1979)—that retrieval of information is minimal when the subject's current state differs from that in which the information was acquired, and state-dependent recall (Bower, 1981)—that achieving a particular bodily state is necessary in order to access certain cognitions, switching between states allows for a full range of access to qualitatively different affectively laden autobiographical memories and various psychobiological motivations. . . . This allows for an opportunity for state-dependent learning in states that are usually defended against and avoided. (Schore, 1994, p. 364)

These avoided states include states of hyperarousal and dissociative hypoarousal associated with early experiences of relational trauma, such as abuse and neglect.

These relationships are depicted in Figure 5.3. A central zone reflects operations of both left and right hemispheric activities in neutral, pleasant affect. The left is thus dominant in states of moderate arousal and autonomic balance. The middle band of neutral affect is bounded by (1) an upper band of right hemispheric sympathetic, dominant, energy-expending, high-arousal affects associated with tight engagement with the environment (e.g., emotional flooding, apprehensive vigilance, rage, terror); and (2) a lower band of right hemispheric parasympathetic, dominant, energy-conserving, low-arousal affects and disengagement from the external environment (e.g., dissociation, disgust, flat affect, numbing, deadness, helplessness and hopelessness). The right hemispheric arousal windows are the intersubjective domains of high- and low-arousal enactments.

Recall that enactments express "unconscious overwhelming affect," equated with dissociated affect. As mentioned earlier, Cassorla (2008) observes that before the enactment the traumatic situation "is *frozen* and unable to manifest itself openly," but at the moment of the enactment there is a state shift, "a revival of the trauma, which had been *frozen*," that "releases the plugged anxiety." Freezing is expressed in terrified muteness and paralysis (left brain motor and verbal inhibition) and frozen defensive responses (frozen fight or frozen flight). This simultaneous massive activation of the sympathetic and dorsal vagal, parasympa-

FIGURE 5.3.   Windows of affect tolerance associated with right brain sympathetic hyper-arousal and parasympathetic hypoarousal enactments. Note regulation within windows, but dysregulation at extremes of arousal.

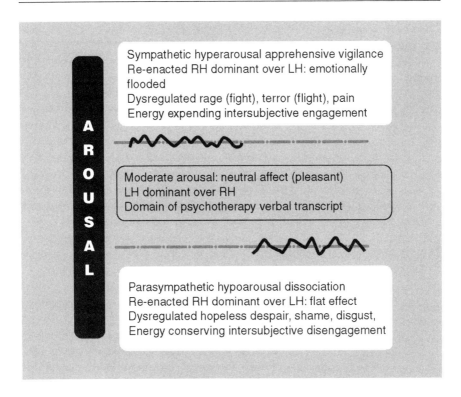

thetic nervous systems induces a state of high-arousal immobility and is accompanied by associated somatic memories. In previous work I have described the importance of the freeze response in trauma processing and neurobiologically characterized it as a co-activation of dorsal vagal, parasympathetic, dominant hypoarousal over sympathetic hyperarousal (Schore, 2009a). There is an oscillation between the upper and lower right brain windows of affect tolerance. In terms of Porges' polyvagal model, the patient oscillates between states of danger and life threat (see chapter 3, Figures 3.1 and 3.5).

The windows of affect tolerance of the "emotional," "social" right brain thus refer to optimal ranges of arousal for different right brain affects and motivational states, which vary in arousal intensity (e.g., high: sympathetic arousal—terror, rage, joy; low: parasympathetic arousal—shame, disgust, hopeless despair, etc.). Yet each window of affect tolerance has its limits, a range within which it sustains a regulated affect. Dysregulated stress responses are triggered at the upper limit of the edge of a regulatory boundary zone (the arrowheads that meet the edges of the white boxes in Figure 5.4). The white boxes represent dysregulated stress responses, wherein the severe arousal (energetic-metabolic) alterations uncouple the cortical and subcortical components of the right brain. These neurobiological events would be expressed in high-arousal explosive fragmentation versus low-arousal implosion of the implicit self.

As I have noted in previous writings, the clinical principle of working at the regulatory boundaries is expressed in this dictum: The sensitive empathic therapist allows the patient to re-experience highly stressful dysregulating affects in *affectively tolerable doses in the context of a safe environment,* so that overwhelming traumatic feelings can be regulated and integrated into patient's emotional life (Schore, 2003b). This therapeutic principle is grounded in developmental neurobiological evidence that "graded stress inoculation"—early exposure to mildly stressful challenging experiences—promotes myelination of the ventromedial cortex that controls arousal regulation (Katz et al., 2009).

This affect principle is also anchored in clinical models. Clearly implying that the patient must consciously endure some affective stress, Bromberg (2006) points out the therapeutic relationship must "feel safe but not perfectly safe." Therapy that always stays in the left brain window of mild to moderate levels of

FIGURE 5.4.   Clinical work at the edges of dual right brain regulatory boundaries.

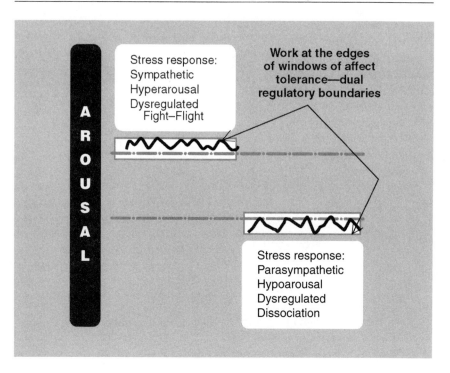

arousal would therefore be "too safe" and would not access stressful affects and potential subsequent regulation.

The windows of right brain affect tolerance are also the site of the generation of an intersubjective field. In my first book, building upon the principle that the right cortical hemisphere is dominant for "subjective emotional experiences" (Wittling & Roschmann, 1993), I described the co-creation of a right brain–to–right brain intersubjective interactive affect communicating and regulating system within the patient–therapist relationship:

> Affect, especially unconscious affect, is the focus of the psychoanalytically-oriented treatment of primitive emotional disorders. This affect is transacted between the therapist and patient in transference-countertransference communications. In such transactions the empathic therapist is psychobiologically attuned to patient's internal state. In the initial stages of treatment this allows for the creation of an intersubjective field. (Schore, 1994, p. 473)

Recall there are two intersubjective fields, each with unique transference-countertransference psychobiological dynamics (see chapter 3, Tables 3.1 and 3.2). In Figure 5.4 the two purple segments represent the following: the patient's contribution to a sympathetic, dominant, high-energy intersubjective field that processes state-dependent implicit memories of object relational–attachment transactions in high-arousal enactments (e.g, experiences of relational abuse); and a parasympathetic, dominant, low-energy intersubjective field that processes state-dependent implicit memories of object relational–attachment transactions in low-arousal enactments (e.g., experiences of relational neglect).

The therapeutic dyad's entrances and exits into the regulatory boundaries reflect their implicit expressions of engagement and disengagement within the right brain windows of affect tolerance:

> The two right brain systems that process unconscious attachment-related information within the co-constructed intersubjective field of the patient and therapist are temporally co-activated and coupled, de-activated and uncoupled, or re-activated and re-coupled. The unconscious minds and bodies of two self systems are connected and co-regulating, disconnected and autoregulating, or reconnected and again mutually regulating their activity. (Schore, 2003b, p. 52)

In chapter 3, I offered a model of the co-construction of an intersubjective field, whereby the therapist's right brain window of affect tolerance is spatiotemporally synchronized with that of the patient. Visualize Figure 5.5 of the patient in front of and aligned with Figure 5.5 of the patient, as in a face-to-face communication. At the edges of the mutually reflecting windows, the regulatory boundaries, the psychobiologically attuned empathic therapist, on a moment-to-moment basis, implicitly tracks and matches patterns of rhythmic crescendos/decrescendos of the patient's regulated and dysregulated states of autonomic arousal with his or her own crescendos/decrescendos. The affect-processing win-

FIGURE 5.5.   Resonance-amplification mechanism of co-created intersubjective fields.

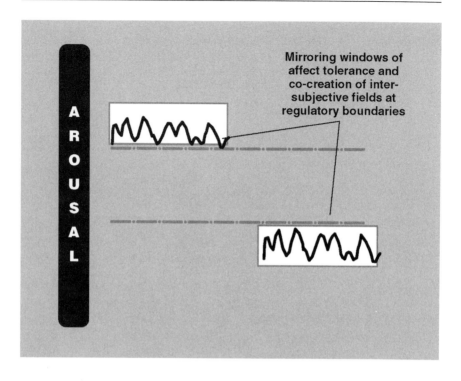

dows of both are mirrored and in a state of resonance. When patterns of synchronized rhythms (dynamic pattern changes within the white rectangles) are in interpersonal resonance, this right brain–to–right brain "specifically fitted interaction" generates amplified energetic processes of affective arousal within the co-created intersubjective field. This interpersonal neurobiological mechanism allows the field to "reshaped" and "enlarged" (D. N. Stern, 2005). Note the expansion of the area within the white rectangles shown in Figure 5.5 as compared to that shown in Figure 5.4.

Whitehead (2005) describes the effect of this resonance-amplification mechanism within an intersubjective field: "*Emotions are deepened in intensity and sustained in time when they are intersubjectively shared. This occurs at moments of deep contact*" (p. 624, my italics). In terms of regulation theory, intersubjective psychobiological resonance between the patient's relational unconscious and the clinician's relational unconscious produces an amplification of arousal and affect, and so affects are deepened in intensity and sustained in time. In earlier work I described

When a psychobiologically attuned dyad co-creates a resonant context within an attachment transaction, the behavioral manifestation of each partner's internal state is monitored by the other, and this results in the coupling between the output of one partner's loop and the input of the other's to form a larger feedback configuration. (Schore, 2001a, p. 19)

This same right brain–to–right brain resonance arousal-energetic amplification mechanism allows for the implicit (Greenberg, 2007) unconscious (Williams, Bargh, Nocera, & Gray, 2009) regulation of nonconscious dissociated affects embedded in enactments. As I have proposed:

> The empathically resonating therapist's matching of the rhythmic crescendos and decrescendos of her subjective state with the patient's represents the psychobiological attunement of her felt sense to the patient's felt sense. The key to working with dissociated affect is the co-creation of an amplified stronger signal of the felt sense—the therapist serves as a source of autonomic feedback of the patient's dissociated unconscious affect, thereby allowing the therapeutic alliance to amplify the intensity and duration of an unconscious affect long enough for it to enter into consciousness. (Schore, 2003b, p. 82)

This increase of emotional intensity (increased energetic arousal) results from interactive affect regulation. It allows dissociated bodily based affects beneath levels of awareness to emerge into consciousness of both members of the co-created intersubjective field.

Thus, the therapist's ability to stay in a right brain dominant state is essential to the optimal interactive repair and resolution of an enactment. The right brain–to–right brain mechanism that is accessed for the negotiation of a collision of subjectivities in an enactment is essentially the same as the developmental process that Beebe and Lachmann (1994) call "disruption and repair," and Tronick (1989) terms "interactive repair" following a dyadic mis-attunement. Unlike the patient's earlier experiences, this relational repair process allows him or her to cope with stressful negatively charged affects and to gain self-regulatory skills in the form of maintaining persistent efforts to overcome interactive stress. The therapist's maintenance of a right brain state is essential for another reason. In chapter 4, I described how the effective clinician negotiates these dysregulated affective moments within the co-created intersubjective field not by explicit, linear, left brain, verbal secondary process cognition, but by implicit, nonlinear, right brain, nonverbal primary process clinical intuition. In order to co-participate in a regulated enactment, the therapist on a moment-to-moment basis must retain a right brain–to–right brain connection with the patient and at the same time access a rapid, emotional, and embodied right brain intuitive decision process to navigate through the relational uncertainty of the enactment.

In other words, the dyadic resolution of the intensely heightened affective moment of an enactment represents the evolution of what Stern (2004) terms a "now moment," defined as an affectively charged moment that puts the nature of the patient–therapist relationship into question, into a "moment of meeting":

Moment of meeting is a present moment between two participants that potentially resolves the crisis created by a now moment. It thereby reshapes the intersubjective field and alters the relationship. It is called forth as an emergent property from the micro-context of the now moment and must be exquisitely sensitive to this context. It involves a response to the crisis that is well fitted to the specificity of that particular crisis. *It cannot be a general technical response but must be a specific authentic one that carries the therapist's personal signature, so to speak.* This is necessary because there is an interpersonal sharing in this moment that alters the intersubjective field between the two. The affectively charged sharing expands the intersubjective field so that their relationship as mutually sensed is suddenly different from what it was before the moment of meeting. This change in the intersubjective field does not require verbalization or narration to be effective and lasting. (Stern, 2004, p. 244, my italics)

A great deal has been written about the need, especially in certain stressful moments of the treatment of the therapist, to offer not a classical transference interpretation but the self-revelation of an authentic response to the patient's affective communication. Lichtenberg and colleagues (1996, pp. 213–214) describe the importance of an analytic communication that deviates from the more customary therapeutic interventions, what they term "disciplined spontaneous engagements." These events occur "at a critical juncture in analysis" and are usually prompted by some breach or miscommunication that requires "a human response." Although there is a danger of "exchanges degenerating into mutually traumatizing disruptions" that "recreate pathogenic expectations," the clinician's communications signal a readiness to participate authentically in the immediacy of an enactment. This is spontaneously expressed in the clinician's facial expressions, gestures, and unexpected comments that result from an "unsuppressed emotional upsurge"; and they provide "intense moments that opened the way for examination of the role enactments into which the analyst had fallen unconsciously."

The authentic self-revelation of the clinician's "personal signature" is also an expression of his or her right brain state. According to Ginot (1997), self-disclosure is not directed toward promoting a sense of intimacy through similar shared experience, but a revealing of emotional data growing from and organically related to the intersubjective matrix. Echoing this, Quillman (2011) asserts that the therapist's self-disclosure communicates his or her somatic and/or affective experience of the here-and-now interaction with the patient, not to be confused with disclosure of the therapist's personal history or experiences outside the therapy hour. Maroda (1998) stresses the clinical principle that during an enactment the therapist's affective participation must be real, or the patient could not continue:

Believing that giving the patient an emotionally honest response, in the moment, is essentially therapeutic—provided that the analyst expresses herself clearly and responsibly the majority of the time—is at the heart of accepting enactment as inevitable and potentially useful. Accepting that patient and analyst are fated to move each other in mysterious and unplanned ways leaves room for accepting being both the recipient and the stimulator of intense, unexpected emotion. And this accep-tance leaves further room for exploring the most therapeutic ways in which to work through the re-created scenes from the past. (p. 534)

Over the course of long-term treatment, the co-regulated psychophysiology of sympathetic, dominant, high-arousal enactments (collisions of engaged subjec-tivities) and parasympathetic, dominant, low-arousal enactments (mutual disen-gagements) is played out in the two intersubjective fields of psychobiological attunement, rupture, and interactive repair. Effective clinical work within an en-actment at the edges of the regulatory boundaries thus mobilizes an intersubjec-tive context that potentially facilitates an incremental expansion of right brain tolerance for high- or low-intensity affects. This broadened and deepened capac-ity to consciously experience a wide array of both negative and positive affects is a major goal of ART.

THERAPEUTIC CHANGE: REGULATED ENACTMENTS AND INTEGRATION OF THE RIGHT BRAIN

This chapter suggests that although enactments are the most stressful moments of the treatment, in an optimal co-created therapeutic alliance the clinician can potentially act as an implicit regulator of the patient's conscious and unconscious affective states. Dyadic enactments trigger the reappearance of highly dysregulat-ing, and therefore dissociated, unconscious emotional experiences that resonate with the original infant–mother attachment history on both sides of the thera-peutic alliance. Yet these stressful, heightened affective moments that allow for encountering dissociated aspects of the patient (Stern, 2008) also act as "affective building blocks" in "curative shifts" (Ginot, 2007).

Over the stages of the treatment, in order to work effectively with enactments, the sensitive, empathic clinician's monitoring of unconscious psychobiological process, rather than conscious verbal content, facilitates right brain attention to and matching of the patient's implicit affective-arousal states. In turn, these col-laborations of the therapist's and client's subjectivities allow for right brain com-munications of dysregulated affective states. These heightened affective moments also afford an opportunity for interactive affect regulation, the core of the attach-ment mechanism. Recall that the attachment process of psychobiological inter-active regulation of dysregulated conscious, and especially unconscious, affective states is an essential therapeutic mechanism (Schore, 1994, 2003a, 2003b). *Im-plicit affect regulation (and not mentalization) is essential to working with rela-tional trauma and the early forming defense of dissociation.*

In the preceding chapters I have cited Greenberg's (2007) differentiation of two forms of affect regulation. Earlier I offered the dual hemispheric model of stress regulation of Czeh et al. (2008), wherein the hemispheres are preferentially associated with distinct stages and strategies of coping with stressful experiences of varying intensities. The dorsolateral prefrontal and orbitofrontal (ventromedial) systems are known to inhibit each other's functions. Under moderate to severe stress, unconscious, implicit affect regulation is mobilized by the orbitofrontal and prefrontal systems of the right cortical hemisphere, which unlike the non-limbic dorsolateral prefrontal cortex, has direct limbic connections with subcortical amygdaloid nuclei and thereby can facilitate the transformation of "previously avoided emotions" into regulated and tolerated "adaptive emotions." In contrast, under mild stress conscious, explicit emotion regulation associated with "self-control" is performed by the left cortical hemisphere. It involves higher levels of cognitive (mainly left dorsolateral prefrontal cortical) executive function that allow individuals "to change the way they feel by consciously changing the way they think" (p. 415).

This left-lateralized prefrontal system is known to act in the cognitive control of the semantic retrieval of details about past events (Badre & Wagner, 2007) and in the cognitive retrieval of declarative memory (Danker, Gunn, & Anderson, 2008). It is therefore the major target of therapeutic action of psychological counseling, mentalization, and CBT. Fonagy and his colleagues report an fMRI study showing mentalization is associated with activation of the left inferior frontal gyrus, left posterior superior temporal sulcus, and left temporoparietal junction (Nolte et al., 2010). Studies show that depressed patients with greater left hemisphere superiority for verbal processing are better able to use the language-dominant hemisphere in learning to reinterpret life events and therefore show a more favorable outcome to CBT (Bruder et al., 1997). Very recent research on cognitive therapy, which involves "learning to interrupt automatic sustained emotional processing," reveals that it is more effective only with lower levels of depression, and that it focuses on the left dorsolateral prefrontal cortex associated with "regulatory control" (Siegle, Steinhauer, Friedman, Thompson, & Thase, 2011).

In support of this dual regulation model, research in neuroscience now demonstrates that the "supervisory" functions of the prefrontal cortex can be differentiated between

> cognitive control or "cold" executive function, which flexibly regulates thoughts and actions in the presence of competing goals (Durston & Casey, 2006; Miller & Cohen, 2001), and affective control or "hot" executive function, which strategically controls feelings in the service of a goal (Dahl, 2003; Kerr & Zelazo, 2004). Studies in neuroimaging and neuropsychology have shown that cognitive and affective control associate with different but interacting subregions of the prefrontal cortex—the dorsolateral prefrontal cortex and the orbitofrontal/ventromedial prefrontal cortex, respectively. (Johnson et al., 2008, p. 715)

In earlier work (Schore, 1994), I have proposed that the dorsolateral prefrontal cortex is expanded in the left hemisphere, where it performs an executive cognitive control function, whereas the orbitofrontal prefrontal cortex is expanded in the right hemisphere, where it performs an executive affective function. Extrapolating these data to the psychotherapeutic context, "cold" cognitive systems dependent upon the dorsolateral prefrontal cortical systems dominate within the left hemispheric window of tolerance (Figure 5.1), whereas "hot" affective and emotional systems dominate within the right hemispheric windows of tolerance (Figure 5.2).

It is important to note that research from cognitive science has overemphasized studies on conscious, voluntary cognitive strategies including rationalization, reappraisal, and suppression (e.g., Gross, 1999). Conscious, explicit emotion regulation has been adopted into the core of the change models of cognitive-behavioral therapy, which dictate that "Individuals can become more functional and adaptive by intentionally modifying their cognitive and behavioral responses to the circumstances they face" (Beck & Dozois, 2011, p. 400). Indeed the central mechanism of cognitive therapy is "effortful" top-down processing, defined as "a slow, deliberate, explicit and strategic form of rational processing that uses rule-based knowledge to guide the information processing system" (Clark & Beck, 2010, p. 418).

A significant number of studies in basic cognitive science, however, have demonstrated the limitations of the self-control form of self-regulation. In 2000 Muraven and Baumeister summarized the extant literature and concluded the following: that self-control consumes a limited resource and can be costly and draining, that sustained self-control efforts such as vigilance degrade over time, and that when used in "coping with stress" and "regulating negative affects," subsequent attempts at self-control are likely to fail. They concluded,

> People have only a limited capacity to control and alter their behavior, and this capacity appears to be vulnerable to depletion in the aftermath of strenuous use. When people find themselves in circumstances that make strong, novel demands for self-control . . . they may find that their self-control breaks down in other, unrelated spheres. (Muraven & Baumeister, 2000, p. 256)

The reason for this lies in underlying neurobiological mechanisms. Carter (1999) observes, "Our conscious control over emotions is weak, and feelings often push out thinking, whereas thinking fights mainly a losing battle to banish emotions. . . . The connections from the emotional systems to the cognitive systems are stronger than the connections that run the other way" (p. 98).

On the other hand, more recent studies in affective science are exploring the unique functions of implicit, unconscious affect regulation, a focus of ART. In overviewing the literature, Williams et al. (2009) contrast the efficiency of unconscious emotion regulation in coping with regulatory challenges versus conscious (volitional and effortful) emotion regulation. These authors assert that due to the serial nature of conscious processing and limited capacity of working memory "conscious attempts at emotion regulation are difficult" (p. 847), and that "when people attempt to control their emotions, they often fail" (p. 853). On the other hand, nonconscious emotion regulation, defined as "the unintentional, automatic, and relatively effortless control of one's exposure to, processing of, and response to emotionally evocative events" (p. 848), is not subject to the same memory and attention limitations, and therefore is better suited for individuals to access in navigating their emotional lives. They assert:

> The present results have important implications for people's ability to withstand the emotion regulatory challenges they routinely face in daily life . . . there are common conditions of daily life, such as distraction, *arousal, stress,* and time pressure (i.e., cognitive load), under which conscious processes are unable to operate but nonconscious processes can. (Williams et al., 2009, p. 853, my italics)

In summarizing the meaning of this work they state, "there is no question that nonconscious processes operate more efficiently than conscious processes" (p. 848).

Clinical enactments represent highly stressful contexts of altered arousal and unconsciously strong, overwhelming affect, and so they are refractory to conscious, voluntary, verbal strategies of emotion regulation. The stressful affect dysregulation of reenacted relational trauma reflects a failure of right brain implicit, unconscious affect regulation that cannot be compensated by left brain regulatory (control) processes. Thus, effective treatment of these cases does not involve a replacement of right brain unconscious emotion regulation by left brain conscious verbal explicit emotion-regulation strategies, but the experience-dependent maturation and expansion of a more complex and resilient right brain nonverbal implicit affect communication and regulation system within a growth-facilitating therapeutic environment. Basic research shows that stress inoculation facilitates the myelination of not the dorsolateral but orbitofrontal cortex and its essential role in resilience (Katz et al., 2009).

Sassenfeld (2008) describes a "relational theory of psychotherapeutic change" that emphasizes

> a potential therapeutic action moving toward transformation of implicit interactive processes. Without denying the relevance of better-known change mechanisms (such as making the unconscious conscious through mutative verbal interpretations), the work . . . has shown that in-session micro-changes can be related to small but significant modifications of the nonverbal interaction of patient and therapist. (p. 5)

Consonant with this proposal Greenberg states, "it is the building of implicit or automatic emotion regulation capacities that is important for enduring change, especially for highly fragile personality-disordered clients" (2007, p. 416). I agree, because only the latter system, explored in ART, is effective in dealing with relational trauma; the emotional right (and not left) hemisphere generates a "threat-based regulatory style" (Nitschke et al., 1999). In terms of psychotherapy, change is not so much about increasing the left's reasoned control over emotion, as it is the expansion of affect tolerance and regulation of the right-lateralized "emotional brain" and the human relatedness of the right-lateralized "social brain."

In chapter 3, I described how the "affective building blocks of enactments" (Ginot, 2007) co-created at the edges of windows of affect tolerance induce more complex forms of implicit affect regulation, and in chapter 4 how "corrective emotional experiences" (Alexander & French, 1946) allow for a maturational advance of the right brain implicit self. In Figure 3.9 I depicted the psychotherapeutic changes from the original constricted windows to expanded windows of affect tolerance, which in turn allow for a wider range of more intense affects and motivational states. Recall that the patient's increased ability to consciously experience and communicate a wider range of positive and negative affects is due to a developmental advance in the capacities to both autoregulate and interactively regulate affective arousal. This experience-dependent maturation of adaptive self-regulation is in turn reflected in the appearance of more complex emotions that result from the simultaneous blending of different affects, and in an expansion in the "affect array." Furthering these ideas I now offer more thoughts on what this psychotherapeutic expansion in affect tolerance and affect regulation looks like clinically.

As previously described, at the outset of the treatment the patient with a history of relational trauma presents with a chronically elevated or diminished resting state of arousal and a significantly lowered threshold for irritability, agitation, and affective outbursts. This high neurobiological threat sensitivity is accompanied by a constant state of increased vigilance resulting in more easily triggered states of fear in ambiguous situations and a low tolerance for uncertainty (Ohrmann et al., 2007). The deficit in affect regulation is expressed in a tendency toward low-threshold, high-intensity emotional reactions followed by slow return to baseline: Highs and lows are too extreme, too prolonged, or too rapidly cycled and unpredictable. Due to a lowered right-lateralized limbic-autonomic threshold for emotional turbulence, reduced threshold for dissociation, and hyperreactivity to novel environmental events, the patient reacts more strongly to even small stressors, such as mis-attunements within the therapeutic alliance; defensively dissociates at lower levels of stressful arousal; and avoids novelty, thereby precluding the learning of new psychotherapeutic emotional experiences.

But as the work progresses, especially in long-term ART, the plasticity of these implicit right brain affect and stress regulatory functions is optimized. Within numerous enactments right brain–to–right brain regulated attachment communications between patient and therapist co-create a dynamic, mutually interacting intersubjective field. This co-constructed dyadic system contingently provides affectively tolerable doses of relational stress in the context of a safe environment (graded stress inoculation), so that overwhelming traumatic feelings can be regulated and integrated into the patient's emotional life. The psychobiological context of the therapeutic alliance thus acts a predictable, trustworthy, growth-facilitating relational environment that allows the patient to, over time, reduce the dissociative defense and vigilance, raise the stress response threshold set point, and increase affect tolerance of regulation. Recall Bromberg's (2006) assertion that "The therapy proceeds . . . with the therapist's job being to try to enable the processing to be safer and safer so that the person's tolerance for potential flooding of affect goes up" (p. 79).

This advance in emotional development is characterized by Lane's (2008) work on implicit emotional processes. He contrasts the individual functioning at a lower level of emotional development who is more likely to behave impulsively and be less aware of feeling, especially in "the context of high arousal emotions," with one who possesses a higher level of emotional awareness and a capacity to be "better able to tolerate and consciously process intense emotions" (p. 220). Lane observes, "This may be understood as a greater ability among more highly aware individuals to be cognizant of their own emotional reactions *in the context of high arousal* and to anticipate and evaluate the consequences of their actions in advance of their behavioral expression" (p. 220, my italics). This more complex emotional awareness is also expressed in an increased attention to internal and external emotion cues, a function that is highly adaptive because "the subsequent cognitive processing of this information can contribute to ongoing emotional development" (p. 219). I would add that this progression of emotional development also occurs with an expanded tolerance of consciously experiencing not just high- but low-arousal emotions.

In light of the fact that relational trauma generates a personality that is hyperreactive and avoidant of novel environmental events, effective psychotherapy not only would increase the regulation of negative affective arousal but also would scaffold an increased capacity for regulation of positive affective arousal and an ability to tolerate the novelty and uncertainty that accompanies new emotional experiences, such as those associated with intimacy. In chapter 4, I discussed Bromberg's concept of therapeutic moments of "safe surprises" in the treatment of dissociation. In patients with a history of relational trauma, therapeutic regulated enactments may act as intersubjective contexts that transform the patient's affective response to interpersonal novelty from negative startle to positive surprise. This shift may represent changes in the subcortical amygdala, since this structure is involved in both startle (Davis, 1989) and surprise (Holland & Gallagher, 2006). Both clinical observers and emotion researchers hold that the processing of novel information is accompanied by the positive affect of surprise, an emotion that is associated with a response to the unexpected. Enactments represent a heightened affective moment in which what is unconscious emerges into consciousness, and Reik (1948) postulates that when unconscious material becomes conscious it emerges as "surprise." The positive arousal of surprise is also central to all forms of exploration and play, a common outcome of the increased safety and trust that is co-created in negotiated, regulated enactments.

Recall Winnicott's (1971) dictum: "Psychotherapy is done in the overlap of the two play areas, that of the patient and that of the therapist. If the therapist cannot play, then he is not suitable for the work. If the patient cannot play, then something needs to be done to enable the patient to become able to play" (p. 54). In my first book I suggested that spontaneous play transforms an environment into an enriched environment, one that facilitates processing of novel information and thereby improves learning capacity, including social-emotional learning (Schore, 1994). Thus a corrective emotional experience can take the form not only of reducing negative affect but also of increasing the patient's capacity for the positive affects that accompany intersubjective play and the curiosity that drives psychotherapeutic internal exploration. The novelty of dyadically negotiating enactments is thus a potential source of surprise and co-created play experiences, and thereby a psychotherapeutic growth-facilitating environment for the expansion of the tolerance of positive arousal and thereby the capacity for intimacy. Marks-Tarlow (2010) and Levy (2011) are now describing the essential role of right brain processes in play experiences. More than anyone else, Panksepp (1998) has persuasively argued that play is a basic motivational system, on a par with fear, aggression, and sexuality.

At the beginning of this chapter, I cited Ginot's (2007) assertion that enactments "generate interpersonal as well as internal processes eventually capable of promoting *integration* and growth," and Maroda's (1998) proposal that these heightened affective moments provide "a new opportunity for awareness and *integration.*" If pathological dissociation, an essential element of enactments, represents a *dis-integration* and disconnection between higher right cortical and lower right subcortical systems, regulated enactments facilitate the top-down and bottom-up *integration* of right cortical and subcortical systems, including increased interconnectivity between the limbic system and the autonomic nervous system (see right side of Figure 4.1). The dorsal vagal inhibition of sympathetic arousal that underlies dissociation engenders a "metabolically conservative immobilized state mimicking death," "dead spots" in subjective experience, and an inability to sustain an inner sense of "aliveness" (Bach, 2008; Porges, 1997). In contrast, the interactive regulation and resonance-amplification mechanisms within a therapeutic enactment release regulated sympathetic arousal from dorsal vagal energy inhibition. This dis-inhibition is accompanied by an increased generation of metabolic energy, a shift out of a hypometabolic dissociated state, and a burst of vitality affects, ultimately allowing dormant parts of the patient's self to "wake up" and "come alive" (Sands, 2010).

Earlier I cited very recent studies demonstrating that the overutilization of dissociation induces dysfunctional changes in the right hemisphere, which impair its characteristic dominance for emotional processing (Enriquez & Bernabeu, 2008), and that the chronic use of this defense interferes with the *integration of experiences* and sense of self that rely heavily on right hemispheric activation (Helton, Dorahy, & Russell, in press). Thus, the dyadic diminution of the autoregulatory dissociative defense in therapeutic enactments allows for the interactive regulation of stressful and disorganizing high or low levels of affective-autonomic arousal and an expansion of the capacity to allow affective experiences into conscious awareness and to integrate them into autobiographical memory. This advance in adaptive capacity reflects an increased connectivity and reorganization of the right hemispheric specialization in regulating stress- and emotion-related processes (Cerqueira et al., 2008; Sullivan & Dufresne, 2006). Indeed, neuroscience research now indicates that the right hemisphere is significantly more interconnected than the left hemisphere and thereby plays a "leading role" for "*integration* tasks" (Iturria-Medina et al., 2011, p. 56, my italics).

The chronic use of the survival strategy of pathological dissociation is associated with a dis-integration of the right brain emotional-corporeal implicit self. Recall that the essential effect of trauma is the disruption of the 'illusion of being one self'" (Pizer, 1998). According to McGilchrist (2009), "Dissociation is . . . the fragmentation of what should be experienced as a whole—the mental separation of components of experience that would ordinarily be processed together . . . suggesting a right hemisphere problem" (p. 236). Overviewing a voluminous body of research, he states that an *efficient* right hemisphere is dominant for "integration." In contrast to the left hemisphere,

> [T]he right hemisphere has a greater degree of myelination, facilitating swift transfer of information between the cortex and the centres below the cortex, and greater connectivity in general. . . . At the experiential level it is also better able to integrate perceptual processes, particularly binding together different kinds of information from different senses . . . this means bringing together in consciousness different elements, including information from the ears, eyes, and other sensory organs, and from memory, so as to generate the richly complex but coherent, world which we experience. (2009, p. 42)

Furthering this idea, McGilchrist offers the observation that "the representation of the two hemispheres is not equal, and that while both contribute to our knowledge of the world, which therefore needs to be synthesized, one hemisphere, the right hemisphere, has precedence, in that it understands the knowledge that the other comes to have, and is alone able to synthesize what *both* know into a useable whole" (2009, p. 176).

Affect regulation therapy—the psychodynamic, affectively focused treatment of early relational trauma—attempts to alter the developmental trajectory of an *inefficient* and indeed developmentally impaired right hemisphere, one that cannot swiftly transfer information between the cortex and the centers below the cortex. Enactments, heightened affective moments of the therapy process, represent critical opportunities for the treatment of relational trauma and an expansion of the adaptive affective and stress regulatory functions of the right brain. The fundamental goal of "long-term" psychotherapy is to facilitate the experience-dependent maturation of the "emotional" right hemisphere, which, according to McGilchrist (2009), "has the most sophisticated and extensive, and quite possibly most lately evolved, representation in the prefrontal cortex, the most highly evolved part of the brain" (p. 437).

As this chapter shows, a growing number of clinical authors and researchers are now exploring and creating updated, neurobiologically informed, trauma-focused models of treatment of a spectrum of early forming developmental disorders that show right brain deficits. As an example, my colleagues and I have recently published an event-related potential study showing right hemispheric maturational failures in borderline personality disorder (Meares, Schore, & Melkonian, 2011). This work offers experimental data that reflect impeded maturation of right fronto-medial regulatory systems due to a history of "traumatic attachments." Applying these findings to the psychotherapeutic context, we suggest that a major role in treatment is played by an engagement between therapist and patient that is expressed in the emotional, nonverbal, and analogical "language" of the right hemisphere. By abstracting these results to other disorders that have their origins in relational trauma, I propose that the growth-facilitating environment of developmentally oriented affect regulation therapy can allow for the experience-dependent maturation of more complex right-lateralized orbito-frontal-cingulate-insula-amygdala circuits. *Over the course of long-term treatment, more complex psychic structure evolves, which in turn can process more right brain complex functions (empathy, intersubjectivity, affect tolerance, and stress regulation).*

Although this psychotherapy is challenging (for both the patient and therapist), the ultimate payoff is substantial. Searles (1993), who has contributed greatly to our understanding of working with more severely disturbed patients, contends, "I want to emphasize, too, that the growth processes of integration and differentiation occur, in any prolonged and successful psychotherapeutic endeavour, not only in the patient, but also to a significant degree in the therapist himself; the growth process is a genuinely mutual one" (p. 316). Even more than a relief of chronic suffering and isolation, the shared deeply human context that lies at the core of effective treatment can expand the essential adaptive functions of the right brain, the biological substrate of the human unconscious described by Freud.

In his masterly and broad-ranging review of laterality research, McGilchrist (2009) documents the assertion that the right (and not left) hemisphere is dominant for

> [E]mpathy and intersubjectivity as the ground of consciousness; the importance of an open, patient attention to the world, as opposed to a willful, grasping attention; the implicit or hidden nature of truth; the emphasis on process rather than stasis, the journey being more important than the arrival; the primacy of perception; the importance of the body in constituting reality; an emphasis on uniqueness; the objectifying nature of vision; the irreducibility of all value to utility; and creativity as an unveiling (no-saying) process rather than a willfully constructive process. (p. 177)

> The right hemisphere . . . yields a world of individual, changing, evolving, interconnected, implicit, incarnate, living beings within the context of the lived world, but in the nature of things never fully graspable, always imperfectly known—and to this world it exists in a relationship of care. (p. 174)

Note that this description also applies to the patient–therapist right brain–to–right brain processes that create the therapeutic relationship, to regulation theory's central tenet that the right hemisphere is dominant not only in the mechanism of change but also in the outcome of treatment, and to the art of psychotherapy.

REFERENCES

Ackerman, S. J., Hilsenroth, M. J., & Knowles, E. S. (2005). Ratings of therapist dynamic activities and alliance early and late in psychotherapy. *Psychotherapy: Theory, Research, Training, 42,* 225–231.

Adler, G., & Rhine, M. W. (1992). The selfobject function of projective identification. In N. G. Hamilton (Ed.), *From inner sources: New directions in object relations psychotherapy* (pp. 139–162). Northvale, NJ: Jason Aronson.

Alexander, F., & French, T. M. (1946). *Psychoanalytic therapy: Principles and application.* New York: Ronald Press.

American Psychoanalytic Association Panel on Enactment. (1992). Enactments in psychoanalysis, reported by M. Johan, M.D. *Journal of the American Psychoanalytic Association, 40,* 827–841.

Aron, L. (1998). The clinical body and the reflexive mind. In L. Aron & F. Sommer Anderson (Eds.), *Relational perspectives on the body* (pp. 3–37). Hillsdale, NJ: Analytic Press.

Aspland, H., Llewelyn, S., Hardy, G. E., Barkham, M., & Stiles, W. (2008). Alliance rupture resolution in cognitive-behavior therapy: A preliminary task analysis. *Psychotherapy Research, 18,* 699–710.

Aston-Jones, G., Foote, S. L., & Bloom, F. E. (1984). Anatomy and physiology of locus coeruleus neurons: Functional implication. *Frontiers of Clinical Neuroscience, 2,* 92–116.

Aston-Jones, G., Rajkowski, J., Kubiak, P., Valentino, R. J., & Shipley, M. T. (1996). Role of the locus coeruleus in emotional activation. *Progress in Brain Research, 107,* 379–402.

Bach, S. (2008). On digital consciousness and psychic death. *Psychoanalytic Dialogues, 18,* 784–794.

Badre, D., & Wagner, A. D. (2007). Left ventrolateral prefrontal cortex and the cognitive control of memory. *Neuropsychologia, 45,* 2883–2901.

Baijal, S., & Srinivasan, N. (2011). Emotional and hemispheric asymmetries in shifts of attention: An ERP study. *Cognition & Emotion, 25,* 280–294.

Bargh, J. A., & Morsella, E. (2008). The unconscious mind. *Perspectives on Psychological Science, 3,* 73–79.

Beck, A. Y., & Dozois, D. J. A. (2011). Cognitive therapy: Current status and future directions. *Annual Review of Medicine, 62,* 397–409.

Beebe, B., & Lachmann, F. M. (1994). Representations and internalization in infancy: Three principles of salience. *Psychoanalytic Psychology, 11,* 127–165.

Blonder, L. X., Bowers, D., & Heilman, K. M. (1991). The role of the right hemisphere in emotional communication. *Brain, 114,* 1115–1127.

Boesky, D. (1990). The psychoanalytic process and its components. *Psychoanalytic Quarterly, 59,* 550–584.

Borgogno, F., & Vigna-Taglianti, M. (2008). Role-reversal: A somewhat neglected mirror of heritages of the past. *American Journal of Psychoanalysis, 68,* 313–328.

Bower, G. H. (1981). Mood and memory. *American Psychologist, 36,* 129–148.

Bowlby, J. (1969). *Attachment and loss; Vol. 1. Attachment.* New York: Basic Books.

Bowlby, J. (1988). Attachment, communication, and the therapeutic process. In J. Bowlby (Ed.), *A secure base: Clinical applications of attachment theory.* London: Routledge.

Boyer, L. B. (1990). Countertransference and technique. In L. B. Boyer & P. L. Giovacchini (Eds.), *Master clinicians on treating the regressed patient* (pp. 303–324). Northvale, NJ: Jason Aronson.

Brancucci, A., Lucci, G., Mazzatenta, A., & Tommasi, L. (2009). Asymmetries of the human social brain in the visual, auditory and chemical modalities. *Philosophical Transactions of the Royal Society B, 364,* 895–914.

Brand, M., Eggers, C., Reinhold, N., Fujiwara, E., Kessler, J., Heiss, W-D., et al. (2009). Functional brain imaging in 14 patients with dissociative amnesia reveals right inferolateral prefrontal hypometabolism. *Psychiatry Research: Neuroimaging, 174,* 32–39.

Brand, M., & Markowitsch, H. J. (2008). The role of the prefrontal cortex in episodic memory. In E. Dere, A. Easton, L. Nadel, & J. P. Huston (Eds.), *Handbook of behavioral neuroscience: Episodic memory research* (Vol. 18, pp. 317–342). Amsterdam: Elsevier.

Braun, C. M. J., Boulanger, Y., Labelle, M., Khiat, A., Dumont, M., & Mailloux, C. (2002). Brain metabolic differences as a function of hemisphere, writing hand preference, and gender. *Laterality, 7,* 97–113.

Brenner, C. (1980). A psychoanalytic theory of affects. In R. Plutchik & H. Kellerman (Eds.), *Emotion: Theory, research and experience* (vol. 1). New York: Academic Press.

Bromberg, P. M. (1998). *Standing in the spaces: Essays on clinical process, trauma, and dissociation.* Hillsdale, NJ: Analytic Press.

Bromberg, P. M. (2006). *Awakening the dreamer: Clinical journeys.* Mahwah, NJ: Analytic Press.

Bromberg, P. M. (2011). *The shadow of the tsunami and the growth of the relational mind.* New York: Routledge.

Bruder, G. E., Stewart, J. W., Mercier, M. A., Agosti, V., Leite, P., Donovan, S., et al. (1997). Outcome of cognitive-behavioral therapy for depression: Relation to hemispheric dominance for verbal processing. *Journal of Abnormal Psychology, 106,* 138–144.

Buchanan, M. (2009). Secret signals. *Nature, 457,* 528–530.

Buchanan, T. W., Tranel, D., & Adolphs, R. (2006). Memories for emotional autobiographical events following unilateral damage to medial temporal lobe. *Brain, 129,* 115–127.

Bugental, J. F. (1987). *The art of the psychotherapist.* New York: Norton.

Carrasquillo, Y., & Gereau, R. W. (2008). Hemispheric lateralization of a molecular signal for pain modulation in the amygdala. *Molecular Pain, 4,* 24.

Carretie, L., Hinojosa, J. A., Mercado, F., & Tapia, M. (2005). Cortical response to subjectively unconscious danger. *NeuroImage, 24,* 615–623.

Carter, R. (1999). *Mapping the mind.* Berkeley: University of California Press.

Casement, P. (1985). *Learning from the patient.* New York: Guilford Press.

Cassorla, R. M. (2008). The analyst's implicit alpha function, trauma and enactment in the analyst's borderline patients. *International Journal of Psychoanalysis, 89,* 161–180.

Cerqueira, J. J., Almeida, O. F. X., & Sousa, N. (2008). The stressed prefrontal cortex. Left? Right! *Brain, Behavior, and Immunity, 22,* 630–638.

Chused, J. (1991). The evocative power of enactments. *Journal of the American Psychoanalytic Association, 39,* 615–640.

Chused, J. (1997). Discussion of "Observing-participation, mutual enactment, and the new classical models," by Irwin Hirsch, Ph.D. *Contemporary Psychoanalysis, 33,* 263–277.

Clark, D. A., & Beck, A. T. (2010). Cognitive theory and therapy of anxiety and depression: Convergence with neurobiological findings. *Trends in Cognitive Sciences, 14,* 418–424.

Corrigan, F. M., Fisher, J. J., & Nutt, D. J. (2011). Autonomic dysregulation and the Window of Tolerance model of the effects of complex emotional trauma. *Journal of Psychopharmacology, 25,* 17–25.

Czeh, B., Perez-Cruz, C., Fuchs, E., & Flugge, G. (2008). Czeh, B., Perez-Cruz, C., Fuchs, E., & Flugge, G. (2008). Chronic stress-induced cellular changes in the medial prefrontal cortex and their potential clinical implications: Does hemisphere location matter? *Behavioural Brain Research, 190,* 1–13.

Dahl, R. E. (2003). The development of affect regulation: Bringing together basic and clinical perspectives. *Annals of the New York Academy of Sciences, 1008,* 183–188.

Danker, J. F., Gunn, P., & Anderson, J. R. (2008). A rational account of memory predicts left prefrontal activation during controlled recall. *Cerebral Cortex, 18,* 2674–2685.

Davies, J. M. (1997). Dissociation and therapeutic enactment. *Gender and Psychoanalysis, 2,* 241–257.

Dickinson, E. (1862). There is a pain—so utter. In T. H. Johnson (Ed.), *The complete poems of Emily Dickinson.* Cambridge, MA: The Belknap Press of Harvard University.

Dinn, W. M., Harris, C. L., Aycicegi, A., Greene, P. B., Kirkley, S. M., & Reilly, C. (2004). Neurocognitive function in borderline personality disorder. *Progress in Neuro-Psychopharmcology & Biological Psychiatry, 28,* 329–341.

Diseth, T. H. (2005). Dissociation in children and adolescents as reaction to trauma—An overview of conceptual issues and neurobiological factors. *Nordic Journal of Psychiatry, 59,* 79–91.

Dorpat, T. L. (2001). Primary process communication. *Psychoanalytic Inquiry, 3,* 448–463.

Driessen, M., Wingenfeld, K., Rullkoettter, N., Mensebach, C., Woermann, F. G., Mertens, M., et al. (2009). One-year functional magnetic resonance imaging follow-up study of neural activation during the recall of unresolved negative life events in borderline personality disorder. *Psychological Medicine, 39,* 507–516.

Durston, S., & Casey, B. J. (2006). What have we learned about cognitive development from neuroimaging? *Neuropsychologia, 44,* 2149–2157.

Ehrenberg, D. (1992). *The intimate edge. Extending the reach of psychoanalytic interaction.* New York: Norton.

Engdahl, B., Leuthold, A. C., Tan, H-R. M., Lewis, S. M., Winkowski, A. M., Dikel, T. N., et al. (2010). Post-traumatic stress disorder: A right temporal lobe syndrome? *Journal of Neural Engineering, 7,* 1–8.

Enriquez, P., & Bernabeu, E. (2008). Hemispheric laterality and dissociative tendencies: Differences in emotional processing in a dichotic listening task. *Consciousness and Cognition, 17,* 267–275.

Eshel, O. (2006). Where are you, my beloved? On absence, loss and the enigma of telepathic dreams. *International Journal of Psychoanalysis, 87,* 1603–1627.

Freud, S. (1957). The unconscious. In J. Strachey (Ed. & Trans.), *The standard edition of the complete psychological works of Sigmund Freud* (Vol. 14, pp. 166–204). London: Hogarth Press. (Original work published 1915)

Freud, S. (1965). New introductory lectures on psychoanalysis. New York: Norton. (Original work published 1933)

Freud, S. (1966). Project for a scientific psychology. In J. Strachey (Ed. & Trans.), *The standard edition of the complete psychological works of Sigmund Freud* (Vol. 1, pp. 295–397). London: Hogarth Press. (Original work published 1895)

Friedman, R. J., & Natterson, J. M. (1999). Enactments: An intersubjective perspective. *Psychoanalytic Quarterly, 68*, 220–247.

Gainotti, G. (2006). Unconscious emotional memories and the right hemisphere. In M. Mancia (Ed.), *Psychoanalysis and neuroscience* (pp. 151–173). Milan, Italy: Springer.

Gans, J. S. (2011). Unwitting self-disclosure in psychodynamic psychotherapy: Deciphering their meaning and accessing the pain within. *International Journal of Group Psychotherapy, 61*, 219–237.

Geha, P. Y., Baliki, M. N., Harden, R. N., Bauer, W. R., Parrish, T. B., & Apkarian, A. V. (2008). The brain in chronic CRPS pain: Abnormal gray-white matter interactions in emotional and autonomic regions. *Neuron, 60*, 570–581.

Geller, J. D. (2003). Self-disclosure in psychoanalytic–existential therapy. *Journal of Clinical Psychology, 59*, 541–554.

Ginot, E. (1997). The analyst's use of self, self-disclosure, and enhanced integration. *Psychoanalytic Psychology, 14*, 365–381.

Ginot, E. (2007). Intersubjectivity and neuroscience. Understanding enactments and their therapeutic significance within emerging paradigms. *Psychoanalytic Psychology, 24*, 317–332.

Ginot, E. (2009). The empathic power of enactments. The link between neuropsychological processes and an expanded definition of empathy. *Psychoanalytic Psychology, 26*, 290–309.

Gonzalez-Lima, F., & Scheich, H. (1985). Ascending reticular activating system in the rat: A 2-deoxyglucose study. *Brain Research, 344*, 70–88.

Grabner, R.H., Fink, A., & Neubauer, A.C. (2007). Brain correlates of self-rated originality of ideas: Evidence from event-related power and phase-locking changes in the EEG. *Behavioral Neuroscience, 121*, 224–230.

Greenberg, L. S. (2007). Emotion coming of age. *Clinical Psychology Science and Practice, 14*, 414–421.

Gross, J. J. (1999). Emotion regulation; past, present, future. *Cognition and Emotion, 13*, 551–573.

Grossmann, T., Johnson, M. H., Farroni, T., & Csibra, G. (2007). Social perception in the infant brain: Gamma oscillatory activity in response to eye gaze. *Social Cognitive and Affective Neuroscience, 2*, 284–291.

Grossmann, T., Oberecker, R., Koch, S. P., & Friederici, A. D. (2010). The developmental origins of voice processing in the human brain. *Neuron, 65*, 852–858.

Heller, W. (1993). Neuropsychological mechanisms of individual differences in emotion, personality, and arousal. *Neuropsychology, 7*, 1–14.

Helton, W. S., Dorahy, M. J., & Russell, P. N. (in press). Dissociative tendencies and right-hemisphere processing load: Effects on vigilance performance. *Consciousness and Cognition.*

Helton, W. S., Kern, R. P., & Walker, D. R. (2009). Tympanic membrane temperature, exposure to emotional stimuli and the sustained attention to response task. *Journal of Clinical and Experimental Neuropsychology, 31,* 611–616.

Holland, P. C., & Gallagher, M. (2006). Different roles for amygdala central nucleus and substantia innominata in the surprise-induced enhancement of learning. *Journal of Neuroscience, 26,* 3791–3797.

Howard, M. F., & Reggia, J. A. (2007). A theory of the visual system biology underlying development of spatial frequency lateralization. *Brain and Cognition, 64,* 111–123.

Howell, E. (2005). *The dissociative mind.* Hillsdale, NJ: Analytic Press.

Irle, E., Lange, C., & Sachsse, U. (2005). Reduced size and abnormal asymmetry of parietal cortex in women with borderline personality disorder. *Biological Psychiatry, 57,* 173–182.

Iturria-Medina, Y., Perez Fernandez, A., Morris, D. M., Canales-Rodriguez, E. J., Haroon, H. A., Garcia Penton, L., et al. (2011). Brain hemispheric structural efficiency and interconnectivity rightward asymmetry in human and nonhuman primates. *Cerebral Cortex, 21,* 56–67.

Jackson, J. H. (1931). *Selected writings of J. H. Jackson: Vol. I.* London: Hodder and Soughton.

Ji, G., & Neugebauer, V. (2009). Hemispheric lateralization of pain processing by amygdala neurons. *Journal of Neurophysiology, 102,* 2253–2264.

Johnson, C. A., Xiao, L., Palmer, P., Sun, P., Wang, Q., Wei, Y., et al. (2008). Affective-decision making deficits, linked to a dysfunctional ventromedial cortex, revealed in 10th grade Chinese adolescent binge drinkers. *Neuropsychologia, 46,* 714–726.

Joseph, B. (1997). Projective identification. In R. Schafer (Ed.), *The contemporary Kleinians of London* (pp. 100–116). Madison, CT: International Universities Press.

Jung, C. G. (1977). *Psychology and the occult* (R. F. C. Hull, Trans). Princeton, NJ: Princeton University Press. (Original work published 1902)

Kalsched, D. (2005). Hope versus hopelessness in the psychoanalytic situation and Dante's *Divine Comedy. Spring, 72,* 167–187.

Kantrowitz, J. (19998). The role of the preconscious in psychoanalysis. *Journal of the American Psychoanalytic Association, 47,* 65–89.

Keenan, J. P., Rubio, J., Racioppi, C., Johnson, A., & Barnacz, A. (2005). The right hemisphere and the dark side of consciousness. *Cortex, 41,* 695–704.

Katz, M., Liu, C., Schaer, M., Pasker, K. J., Ottet, M-C., Epps, A., et al. (2009). Prefrontal plasticity and stress inoculation-induced resilience. *Developmental Neuroscience, 31,* 293–299.

Keenan, M. C. (1995). Enactments of boundary violations. *Journal of the American Psychoanalytic Association, 43,* 853–868.

Kerr, A., & Zelazo, P. D. (2004). Development of "hot" executive function: The children's gambling task. *Brain and Cognition, 55,* 148–157.

Klein, M. (1946). Notes on some schizoid mechanisms. *International Journal of Psychoanalysis, 27,* 99–110.

Knox, J. (2010). *Self-agency in psychotherapy: Attachment, autonomy, and intimacy.* New York: Norton.

Kohut, H. (1984). *How does analysis cure?* Chicago: University of Chicago Press.

Krystal, H. (2002). What cannot be remembered or forgotten. In J. Kauffman (Ed.), *Loss of the assumptive world: A theory of traumatic loss* (pp. 213–219). New York: Psychology Press.

Lane, R. D. (2008). Neural substrates of implicit and explicit emotional processes: A unifying framework for psychosomatic medicine. *Psychosomatic Medicine, 70,* 214–231.

Lane, R. D., Ahern, G. L., Schwartz, G. E., & Kaszniak, A. W. (1997). Is alexithymia the emotional equivalent of blindsight? *Biological Psychiatry, 42,* 834–844.

Lang, P. J. (1995). The emotion probe. Studies of motivation and attention. *American Journal of Psychology, 50,* 372–385.

Lanius, R. A., Williamson, P. C., Bluhm, R. L., Densmore, M., Boksman, K., Neufeld, R. W. J., et al. (2005). Functional connectivity of dissociative responses in posttraumatic stress disorder: A functional magnetic resonance imaging investigation. *Biological Psychiatry, 57,* 873–884.

Leiman, M. (1994). Projective identification as early joint action sequences: A Vygotskian addendum to the procedural sequence object relations model. *British Journal of Medical Psychology, 67,* 97–106.

Levy, A. J. (2011). Neurobiology and the therapeutic action of psychoanalytic play therapy with children. *Clinical Social Work Journal, 39,* 50–60.

Lichtenberg, J. D., Lachmann, F. M., & Fosshage, J. L. (1996). *The clinical exchange.* Mahwah, NJ: Analytic Press.

Lyons-Ruth, K. (2005). The two-person unconscious: Intersubjective dialogue, enactive representation, and the emergence of new forms of relational organization. In L. Aron & A. Harris (Eds.), *Relational psychoanalysis: Vol. II. Innovation and expansion* (pp. 2–45). Hillsdale, NJ: Analytic Press.

MacNeilage, P. F., Rogers, L., & Vallortigara, G. (2009). Origins of the left and right brain. *Scientific American, 301,* 160–167.

Magnavita, J. J. (2006). In search of the unifying principles of psychotherapy: Conceptual, empirical, and clinical convergence. *American Psychologist, 61,* 882–892.

Mancia, M. (2006). Implicit memory and early unrepressed unconscious: Their role in the therapeutic process (How the neurosciences can contribute to psychoanalysis). *International Journal of Psychoanalysis, 87,* 83–103.

Markowitsch, H. J., Reinkemeier, A., Kessler, J., Koyuncu, A., & Heiss, W.-D. (2000). Right amygdalar and temperofrontal activation during autobiographical, but not fictitious memory retrieval. *Behavioral Neurology, 12,* 181–190.

Marks-Tarlow, T. (2010). The fractal self at play. *American Journal of Play, 3,* 31–62.

Marks-Tarlow, T. (2011). Merging and emerging: A nonlinear portrait of intersubjectivity during psychotherapy. *Psychoanalytic Dialogues, 21,* 110–127.

Maroda, K. J. (1998). Enactment. When the patient's and analyst's pasts converge. *Psychoanalytic Psychology, 15,* 517–535.

Maroda, K. J. (2005). Show some emotion: Completing the cycle of affective communication. In L. Aron & A. Harris (Eds.), *Revolutionary connections. Relational psychoanalysis: Vol. II. Innovation and expansion* (pp. 121–142). Hillsdale, NJ: Analytic Press.

Maroda, K. (2010). *Psychodynamic techniques. Working with emotion in the therapeutic relationship.* New York: Guilford Press.

Mathew, M. (1998). The body as instrument. *Journal of the British Association of Psychotherapists, 35,* 17–36.

McDougall, J. (1978). Countertransference and primitive communication. In J. McDougall, *Plea for a measure of abnormality* (pp. 247–298). New York: International Universities Press.

McGilchrist, I. (2009). *The master and his emissary*. New Haven CT: Yale University Press.

McGilchrist, I. (2010). Reciprocal organization of the hemispheres. *Dialogues in Clinical Neuroscience, 12*, 503–515.

McGuire, W. (Ed.). (1974). *The Freud/Jung letters: The correspondence between Sigmund Freud and C. G. Jung*. Princeton, NJ: Princeton University Press.

McLaughlin, J. T. (1991). Clinical and theoretical aspects of enactment. *Journal of the American Psychoanalytic Association, 39*, 595–614.

Meares, R., Schore, A. N., & Melkonian, D. (2011). Is borderline personality a particularly right hemispheric disorder? A study of P3A using single trial analysis. *Australian and New Zealand Journal of Psychiatry, 45*, 131–139.

Menning, H., Renz, A., Seifert, J., & Maercker, A. (2008). Reduced mismatch negativity in posttraumatic stress disorder: A compensatory mechanism for chronic hyperarousal? *International Journal of Psychophysiology, 68*, 27–34.

Merkl, A., Ammelburg, N., Aust, S., Roepke, S., Reinecker, H., Trahms, L., et al. (2010). Processing of visual stimuli in borderline personality disorder: A combined behavioural and magnetoencephalographic study. *International Journal of Psychophysiology, 78*, 257–264.

Merten, J., Anstadt, T., Ullrich, B., Krause, R., & Buchheim, P. (1996). Emotional experience and facial behavior during the psychotherapeutic process and its relation to treatment outcome: A pilot study. *Psychotherapy Research, 6*, 198–212.

Migone, P. (1995). Expressed emotion and projective identification: A bridge between psychiatric and psychoanalytic concepts? *Contemporary Psychoanalysis, 31*, 617–640.

Miller, E. K., & Cohen, J. D. (2001). An integrative theory of prefrontal cortex function. *Annual Review of Neuroscience, 24*, 167–202.

Mirolli, M., Mannella, F., & Baldassarre, G. (2010). The roles of the amygdala in the affective regulation of body, brain, and behaviour. *Connection Science, 22*, 215–245.

Mlot, C. (1998). Probing the biology of emotion. *Science, 280*, 1005–1007.

Modell, A. H. (1993). *The private self*. Cambridge, MA: Harvard University Press.

Modell, A. H. (1994). Fairbairn's structural theory and the communication of affects. In J. S. Grotstein & D. B. Rinsley (Eds.), *Fairbairn and the origins of object relations* (pp. 195–207). New York: Guilford Press.

Montirosso, R., Borgatti, R., & Tronick, E. (2010). Lateral asymmetries in infants' regulatory and communicative gestures. In R. A. Lanius, E. Vermetten, & C. Pain (Eds.), *The impact of early life trauma on health and disease* (pp. 103–111). Cambridge, UK: Cambridge University Press.

Morris, J. S., & Dolan, R. J. (2004). Dissociable amygdala and orbitofrontal responses during reversal fear conditioning. *NeuroImage, 22*, 372–380.

Morris, J. S., Ohman, A., & Dolan, R. J. (1998). Conscious and unconscious emotionbal learning in the human amygdala. *Nature, 393*, 467–470.

Morris, J. S., Ohman, A., & Dolan, R. J. (1999). A subcortical pathway to the right amygdala mediating "unseen" fear. *Proceedings of the National Academy of Sciences of the United States of America, 96*, 1680–1685.

Muraven, M., & Baumeister, R. F. (2000). Self-regulation and depletion of limited resources: Does self-control resemble a muscle? *Psychological Bulletin, 126*, 247–259.

Nemiah, J. C. (1989). Janet redivivus: The centenary of l'automatisme psychologique. *American Journal of Psychiatry, 146*, 1527–1529.

Nitschke, J. B., Heller, W., Palmieri, P. A., & Miller, G. A. (1999). Contrasting patterns of brain activity in anxious apprehension and anxious arousal. *Psychophysiology, 36*, 628–637.

Nolte, T., Hudac, C., Mayes, L. C., Fonagy, P., Blatt, S. J., & Pelphrey, K. (2010). The effect of attachment-related stress on the capacity to mentalize: An fMRI investigation of the biobehavioral switch model. *Journal of the American Psychoanalytic Association, 58*, 566–573.

Northoff, G., Bermpohl, F., Schoeneich, F., & Boeker, H. (2007). How does your brain constitute defense mechanisms? First-person neuroscience and psychoanalysis. *Psychotherapy and Psychosomatics, 76*, 141–153.

Ogden, P., Minton, K., & Pain, C. (2006). *Trauma and the body: A sensorimotor approach to psychotherapy*. New York: Norton.

Olson, I.R., Plotzker, & Ezzyat, Y. (2007). The enigmatic temporal pole: a review of findings on social and emotional processing. *Brain, 130*, 1718-1731.

Ohrmann, P., Rauch, A. V., Bauer, J., Kugel, H., Aroit, V., Heindel, W., et al. (2007). Threat sensitivity as assessed by automatic amygdala response to fearful faces predicts speed of visual search for facial expression. *Experimental Brain Research, 183*, 51–59.

Panksepp, J. (1998). *Affective neurosciences: The foundations of human and animal emotions*. Oxford, UK: Oxford University Press.

Panksepp, J. (2008). The power of the word may reside in the power of affect. *Integrative Psychological and Behavioral Science, 42*, 47–55.

Papeo, L., Longo, M. R., Feurra, M., & Haggard, P. (2010). The role of the right temporoparietal junction in intersensory conflict: Detection or resolution? *Experimental Brain Research, 206*, 129–139.

Papousek, I., Schulter, G., & Lang, B. (2009). Effects of emotionally contagious films on changes in hemisphere-specific cognitive performance. *Emotion, 9*, 510–519.

Perez-Cruz, C., Simon, M., Czeh, B., Flugge, G., & Fuchs, E. (2009). Hemispheric differences in basilar dendrites and spines of pyramidal neurons in the rat prelimbic cortex: Activity- and stress-induced changes. *European Journal of Neuroscience, 29*, 738–747.

Pizer, S. (1998). *Building bridges: Negotiating paradox in psychoanalysis*. Hillsdale, NJ: Analytic Press.

Platt, C. B. (2009). The medium and the matrix. Unconscious information and the therapeutic dyad. *Journal of Consciousness Studies, 16*, 55–76.

Ploner, M., Gross, J., Timmermann, L., Pollok, B., & Schnitzler, A. (2006). Pain suppresses spontaneous brain rhythms. *Cerebral Cortex, 16*, 537–540.

Porges, S. W. (1997). Emotion: An evolutionary by-product of the neural regulation of the autonomic nervous system. *Annals of the New York Academy of Sciences, 807*, 62–77.

Price, J. L. (2005). Free will versus survival: Brain systems that underlie intrinsic constraints on behavior. *Journal of Comparative Neurology, 493*, 132–139.

Quillman, T. (2011, January 18). Neuroscience and therapist self-disclosure: Deepening right brain to right brain communication between therapist and patient. *Clinical Social Work Journal*, 1–9.

Racker, H. (1968). *Transference and countertransference*. New York: International Universities Press.

Raz, A. (2004). Anatomy of attentional networks. *Anatomical Records, 281B*, 21–36.

Reekie, Y. L., Braesicke, K., Man, M. S., & Roberts, A. C. (2008). Uncoupling of behavioral and autonomic responses after lesions of the primate orbitofrontal cortex. *Proceedings of the National Academy of Sciences of the United States of America, 105, 9787–9792.

Reik, T. (1948). *Listening with the third ear: The inner experience of a psychoanalyst.* New York: Grove Press.

Renik, O. (1993). Analytic interaction: Conceptualizing technique in light of the analyst's irreducible subjectivity. *Psychoanalytic Quarterly, 62,* 553–571.

Reus, V. I., Weingartner, H., & Post, R. M. (1979). Clinical implications of state dependent learning. *American Journal of Psychiatry, 136,* 927–931.

Robinson, M. D., & Compton, R. J. (2006). The automaticity of affective reactions: Stimulus valence, arousal, and lateral spatial attention. *Social Cognition, 24,* 469–495.

Roll, W. G., Persinger, M. A., Webster, D. L., Tiller, S. G., & Cook, C. M. (2002). Neurobehavioral and neurometabolic (SPECT) correlates of paranormal information: Involvement of the right hemisphere and its sensitivity to weak complex magnetic fields. *International Journal of Neuroscience, 112,* 197–224.

Romano, V., Fitzpatrick, M., & Janzen, J. (2008). The secure-base hypothesis; global attachment, attachment to counselor, and session exploration in psychotherapy. *Journal of Counseling Psychology, 55,* 495–504.

Ruocco, A. C. (2005). The neuropsychology of borderline personality disorder: A meta-analysis and review. *Psychiatry Research, 137,* 191–202.

Russell, J. (1980). A circumplex model of affect. *Journal of Personality and Social Psychology, 39,* 1161–1178.

Russell, P. (1998). The role of paradox in the repetition compulsion. In J. G. Teicholz & D. Kriegman (Eds.), *Trauma, repetition, and affect regulation: The work of Paul Russell* (pp. 1–22). New York: Other Press.

Safran, J. D., & Muran, J. C. (1996). The resolution of ruptures in the therapeutic alliance. *Journal of Consulting and Clinical Psychology, 64,* 447–458.

Sander, L. W. (1992). Letter to the editor. *International Journal of Psychoanalysis, 73,* 582–584.

Sands, S. (1994). What is dissociated? *Dissociation, 7,* 145–152.

Sands, S. (1997). Self psychology and projective identification—whither shall they meet? A reply to the editors (1995). *Psychoanalytic Dialogue, 7,* 651–668.

Sands, S. (2010). On the royal road together: The analytic function of dreams in activating dissociative unconscious communication. *Psychoanalytic Dialogues, 20,* 357–373.

Sassenfeld, A. (2008). The body in Jung's work: Basic elements to lay the foundation for a theory of technique. *The Journal of Jungian Theory and Practice, 10,* 1–13.

Sato, W., & Aoki, S. (2006). Right hemisphere dominance in processing unconscious emotion. *Brain and Cognition, 62,* 261–266.

Schon, D., Rosenkranz, M., Regelsberger, J., Dahme, B., Buchel, C., & von Leupoldt, A. (2008). Reduced perception of dyspnea and pain after right insular cortex lesions. *American Journal of Respiratory and Critical Care Medicine, 178,* 1173–1179.

Schore, A. N. (1994). *Affect regulation and the origin of the self.* Mahwah, NJ: Erlbaum.

Schore, A. N. (1996). The experience-dependent maturation of a regulatory system in the orbital prefrontal cortex and the origin of developmental psychopathology. *Development and Psychopathology, 8,* 59–87.

Schore, A. N. (1997a). Interdisciplinary developmental research as a source of clinical models. In M. Moskowitz, C. Monk, C. Kaye, & S. Ellman (Eds.), *The neurobiological and developmental basis for psychotherapeutic intervention* (pp. 1–71). Northvale, NJ: Jason Aronson.

Schore, A. N. (1997b). A century after Freud's *Project*: Is a rapprochement between psychoanalysis and neurobiology at hand? *Journal of the American Psychoanalytic Association, 45,* 807–840.

Schore, A. N. (2001a). The effects of a secure attachment relationship on right brain development, affect regulation, and infant mental health. *Infant Mental Health Journal, 22,* 7–66.

Schore, A. N. (2001b). The effects of relational trauma on right brain development, affect regulation, and infant mental health. *Infant Mental Health Journal, 22,* 201–269.

Schore, A. N. (2002). Dysregulation of the right brain: A fundamental mechanism of traumatic attachment and the psychopathogenesis of posttraumatic stress disorder. *Australian and New Zealand Journal of Psychiatry, 36,* 9–30.

Schore, A. N. (2003a). *Affect dysregulation and disorders of the self.* New York: Norton.

Schore, A. N. (2003b). *Affect regulation and the repair of the self.* New York: Norton.

Schore, A. N. (2009a). Attachment trauma and the developing right brain: Origins of pathological dissociation. In P. F. Dell & J. A. O'Neil (Eds.), *Dissociation and the dissociative disorders: DSM-V and beyond* (pp. 107–141). New York: Routledge.

Schore, A. N. (2009b). Right brain affect regulation: An essential mechanism of development, trauma, dissociation, and psychotherapy. In D. Fosha, D. Siegel, & M. Solomon (Eds.), *The healing power of emotion: Affective neuroscience, development, & clinical practice* (pp. 112–144). New York: Norton.

Schore, A. N. (2009c, August 8). *The paradigm shift: The right brain and the relational unconscious.* Invited plenary address, 2009 Convention of the American Psychological Association, Toronto, Canada. Retrieved September 16, 2009, from http://www.allan schore.com/pdf/SchoreAPAPlenaryFinal09.pdf

Schore, A. N. (2009d). Relational trauma and the developing right brain: An interface of psychoanalytic self psychology and neuroscience. *Annals of the New York Academy of Sciences, 1159,* 189–203.

Schore, A. N. (2010). The right brain implicit self: A central mechanism of the psychotherapy change process. In J. Petrucelli (Ed.), *Knowing, not-knowing and sort of knowing: Psychoanalysis and the experience of uncertainty* (pp. 177–202). London: Karnac.

Schore, A. N. (2011a). The right brain implicit self lies at the core of psychoanalysis. *Psychoanalytic Dialogues, 21,* 75–100.

Schore, A. N. (2011b). Foreword to *The shadow of the tsunami and the growth of the relational mind*, by Philip M. Bromberg. New York: Routledge.

Schore, J., & Schore, A. (2008). Modern attachment theory: The central role of affect regulation in development and treatment. *Clinical Social Work Journal, 36,* 9–20.

Searles, H. F. (1984–1985). The role of the analyst's facial expressions in psychoanalysis and psychoanalytic therapy. *International Journal of Psychoanalytic Psychotherapy, 10,* 47–73.

Searles, H. F. (1993). Integration and differentiation in schizophrenia. In *Collected papers on schizophrenia and related subjects*. London: Karnac.

Shedler, J. (2010). The efficacy of psychodynamic psychotherapy. *American Psychologist, 65,* 98–109.

Shuren, J. E., & Grafman, J. (2002). The neurology of reasoning. *Archives of Neurology, 59,* 916–919.

Siegel, D. J. (1995). Memory, trauma, and psychotherapy: A cognitive science view. *Journal of Psychotherapy Practice and Research, 4,* 93–122.

Siegal, D. J. (1999). *The developing mind: Toward a neurobiology of interpersonal experience*. New York: Guilford Press.

Siegle, G. J., Steinhauer, S. R., Friedman, E. S., Thompson, W. S., & Thase, M. E. (2011). Remission prognosis for cognitive therapy for recurrent depression using the pupil: Utility and neural correlates. *Biological Psychiatry, 69*, 726–733.

Simian-Tov, T., Papo, D., Gadoth, N., Schonberg, T., Mendelsohn, A., Perry, D., et al. (2008). Mind your left: Spatial bias in subcortical fear processing. *Journal of Cognitive Neuroscience, 21*, 1782–1789.

Spiegel, D. (2006). Recognizing traumatic dissociation. *American Journal of Psychiatry, 163*, 566–568.

Spitzer, C., Barnow, S., Freyberger, H. J., & Grabe, H. J. (2007). Dissociation predicts symptom-related treatment outcome in short-term inpatient psychotherapy. *Australian and New Zealand Journal of Psychiatry, 41*, 682–687.

Spitzer, C., Wilert, C., Grabe, H-J., Rizos, T., & Freyberger, H. J. (2004), Dissociation, hemispheric asymmetry, and dysfunction of hemispheric interaction: A transcranial magnetic approach. *Journal of Neuropsychiatry and Clinical Neurosciences, 16*, 163–169.

Stanilou, A., Markowitsch, H. J., & Brand, M. (in press). Psychogenic amnesia—A malady of the constricted self. *Consciousness and Cognition*.

Stern, D. B. (2006). Opening what has been closed, relaxing what has been clenched: Dissociation and enactment over time in committed relationships. *Psychoanalytic Dialogues, 16*, 747–761.

Stern, D. B. (2008). On having to find to know how to look for: Two perspectives on reflection. In J. E. Jurist, A. Slade, & S. Burger (Eds.), *Mind to mind: Infant research, neuroscience, and psychoanalysis* (pp. 398–413). New York: Other Press.

Stern, D. B. (2009). Dissociation and unformulated experience: A psychoanalytic model of mind. In P. F. Dell & J. A. O'Neil (Eds.), *Dissociation and the dissociative disorders: DSM–V and beyond* (pp. 653–663). New York: Routledge.

Stern, D. N. (2004). *The present moment in psychotherapy and everyday life*. New York: Norton.

Stern, D. N. (2005). Intersubjectivity. In E. S. Person, A. M. Cooper, & G. D. Gabbard (Eds.), *Textbook of psychoanalysis* (pp. 77–92.) Washington, DC: American Psychiatric Publishing.

Stevenson, C. W., Halliday, D. M., Marsden, C. A., & Mason, R. (2008). Early life programming of hemispheric lateralization and synchronization in the adult medial prefrontal cortex. *Neuroscience, 155*, 852–863.

Strupp, H. H. (1989). Psychotherapy: Can the practitioner learn from the researcher? *American Psychologist, 44*, 717–724.

Sullivan, R. M. (2004). Hemispheric asymmetry in stress processing in rat prefrontal cortex and the role of mesocortical dopamine. *Stress, 7*, 131–143.

Sullivan, R. M., & Dufresne, M. M. (2006). Mesocortical dopamine and HPA axis regulation: Role of laterality and early environment. *Brain Research, 1076*, 49–59.

Symonds, L. L., Gordon, N. S., Bixby, J. C., & Mande, M. M. (2006). Right-lateralized pain processing in the human cortex: An fMRI study. *Journal of Neurophysiology, 95*, 3823–3830.

Tondo, L. (2011). Interview with John Bowlby, M.D. *Clinical Neuropsychiatry, 8*, 159–171.

Tronick, E. Z. (1989). Emotions and emotional communication in infants. *American Psychologist, 44,* 112–119.

Tsakiris, M., Costantini, M., & Haggard, P. (2008). The role of the right tempero-parietal junction in maintaining a coherent sense of one's body. *Neuropsychologia, 46,* 3014–3018.

Tucker, D. M., Luu, P., & Pribram, K. H. (1995). Social and emotional self-regulation. *Annals of the New York Academy of Sciences, 769,* 213–239.

Tutte, J. C. (2004). The concept of psychical trauma: A bridge in interdisciplinary space. *International Journal of Psychoanalysis, 85,* 897–921.

Valent, P. (1999). *Trauma and fulfillment therapy: A wholist framework.* Philadelphia: Brunner/Mazel.

Valliant, G. E. (1994). Ego mechanisms of defense and personality psychopathology. *Journal of Abnormal Psychology, 103,* 44–50.

Vallortigara, G. (2006). The evolutionary psychology of left and right: Costs and benefits of lateralization. *Developmental Psychobiology, 48,* 418–427.

Van Lancker Sidtis, D. (2006). Where in the brain is nonliteral language? *Metaphor and Symbol, 21,* 213–244.

Venkatasubramanian, G., Jayakumar, P. N., Hongasandra, R. N., Nagaraja, D., Deeptha, R., & Ganadadhar, B. N. (2008). Investigating paranormal phenomena: Functional brain imaging of telepathy. *International Journal of Yoga, 1,* 66–71.

Volkow, N. D., Tomasi, D., Wang, G-J., Fowler, J. S., Telang, F., Goldstein, R. Z., et al. (2011). Positive emotionality is associated with baseline metabolism in orbitofrontal cortex and in regions of the default network. *Molecular Psychiatry, 16,* 818–825.

Vygotsky, L. S. (1978). *Mind in society.* Cambridge, MA: Harvard University Press.

Weinberg, I. (2000). The prisoners of despair: Right hemisphere deficiency and suicide. *Neuroscience and Biobehavioral Reviews, 24,* 799–815.

Whitehead, C. C. (2006). Neo-psychoanalysis: A paradigm for the 21st century. *Journal of the Academy of Psychoanalysis and Dynamic Psychiatry, 34,* 603–627.

Wilkinson, M. (2010). *Changing minds in psychotherapy. Emotion, attachment, trauma & neurobiology.* New York: Norton.

Williams, L. E., Bargh, J. A., Nocera, C. C., & Gray, J. R. (2009). The unconscious regulation of emotion: Nonconscious reappraisal goals modulate emotional reactivity. *Emotion, 9,* 847–854.

Winnicott, D. W. (1971). *Playing and reality.* New York: Routledge.

Winnicott, D. W. (1975a). Mind and its relation to the psyche-soma. In *Through pediatrics to psychoanalysis: Collected papers* (pp. 243–254). London: Hogarth Press. (Original work published 1949)

Winnicott, D. W. (1975b). Transitional objects and transitional phenomena. In *Through pediatrics to psychoanalysis: Collected papers* (pp. 229–242). London: Hogarth Press. (Original work published 1951)

Wittling, W., & Roschmann, R. (1993). Emotion-related hemisphere asymmetry: Subjective emotional responses to laterally presented films. *Cortex, 29,* 431–448.

Zanocco, G., De Marchi, A. D., & Pozzi, F. (2006). Sensory empathy and enactment. *International Journal of Psychoanalysis, 87,* 145–158.

Zeddies, T. J. (2000). Within, outside, and in between. The relational unconscious. *Psychoanalytic Psychology, 17,* 467–487.

PART II

DEVELOPMENTAL
AFFECTIVE
NEUROSCIENCE AND
DEVELOPMENTAL
NEUROPSYCHIATRY

Attachment, Affect Regulation, and the Developing Right Brain: Linking Developmental Neuroscience to Pediatrics

We are now in the midst of an exciting period in science and medicine. A powerful engine driving this progression of knowledge is the recent remarkable advance in biotechnology, especially imaging technologies. Noninvasive studies of organ systems have substantially increased our understanding of the biological processes that underlie various diseases of the body, whereas neuroimaging research of both psychological functions and psychiatric conditions has generated more complex models of the normal and abnormal operations of the human mind. Yet another catalyst of the continuing dramatic increase in information is the rapid expansion of collaborative interdisciplinary research. The current emphasis on integrating the perspectives of different disciplines into testable and clinically relevant psychobiological models of human function and dysfunction has facilitated a more rapid transfer of information from the basic to the clinical sciences. Of particular interest to pediatrics, this same time period has seen an explosion of both developmental neurobiology and interdisciplinary infant research, which has deepened our knowledge of very early childhood. In this chapter I will suggest that those updated models of early development that integrate developmental neuroscience, developmental psychology, developmental biology, and child psychiatry have direct relevance to pediatrics' interests in the normal and abnormal functions of the developing child's mind and body.

The *New Shorter Oxford English Dictionary* defines pediatrics as "the branch of medical science that deals with childhood and the diseases of children." The field specializes in the diseases commonly found in the early stages of human development that are characterized by active states of growth. We know that the biology of growing tissues and the psychology of an immature yet evolving mind and body are qualitatively different from those of a mature organism. The infant or child's immature immune system is particularly vulnerable to pathogens that assault developing organs, as well as to psychopathological forces that threaten developing brain–mind–body systems. Despite the different origins of these stressors, both trigger common adaptive and maladaptive alterations of an immature organism's evolving psychobiological coping mechanisms in order to respond to internal pathogenic organisms and external psychopathogenic forces.

The concept of "disease" represents an inability of internal regulatory mechanisms to adequately adapt to stressors and maintain organismic homeostasis. Indeed, there is a growing consensus that human disease states fundamentally involve a dysregulation of an organism's psychobiological stress coping systems. It is important to remember that in infancy, the individual's unique set of coping mechanisms, which is a product of the interaction of its genotype and its experiences with the early environment, is in the process of developing. During early critical periods, growth-inhibiting environments can epigenetically alter the developmental trajectory of these coping systems.

But the medical specialty of pediatrics' self-definition also states its essential interest in not just diseases of children but also "childhood," a stage of development before maturation, before adulthood. The clear implication is that normal processes of development are also an essential part of the knowledge base of pediatrics (Zuckerman, Augustyn, & Parker, 2001). One of the fundamental tenets of all of the developmental sciences is that the early life events have an inordinate influence on literally everything that follows. A spectrum of disciplines— from developmental neurochemistry and neurobiology through developmental psychology and infant psychiatry—share the common principle that the beginnings of living systems indelibly set the stage for every aspect of an organism's internal and external functioning throughout the life span. The interdisciplinary nature of the developmental sciences is now serving as a convergence point for models integrating structure and function, brain, body, and mind.

A paradigm shift is currently occurring in the basic sciences that underlie the applied medical science of pediatrics, the area of medicine that focuses upon early development. Research in developmental biology and physiology now strongly supports a model of the "developmental origins of health and disease" (Gluckman & Adler, 2004). Although the role of early expressed genetic factors is an essential focus of current study, it has become clear that genes do not specify behavior absolutely; prenatal and postnatal environmental epigenetic factors play critical roles in these developmental origins. The social environment, particularly the one created together by the mother and infant, directly affects gene–environment interactions and so has long-enduring effects (Suomi, 2004). The newer interdisciplinary models, therefore, detail the mechanisms by which "mother nature meets mother nurture" (Crabbe & Phillips, 2003). Complementing this conception of the nature–nurture problem, studies in neuroscience indicate that development represents an experiential shaping of genetic potential and that early experiences with the social environment are critical to the maturation of brain tissue. Thus, nature's potential can be realized only as it is facilitated by nurture (Cicchetti & Tucker, 1994).

In parallel advances in developmental psychology and child psychiatry, attachment theory—initially proposed more than 40 years ago by John Bowlby (1969) as a conception of the mother–infant relationship—has become the dominant model of human social-emotional development available to researchers and clinicians. In his attempt to integrate psychiatry, psychology, and psychoanalysis with behavioral biology, Bowlby speculated that the attachment system, an evolutionary mechanism common to both humans and animals, ultimately would be located in specific areas of the brain (Schore, 2000a). Updated models of attachment theory that emphasize both emotional and social functions and neurobiological structures now are interfacing with developmental neuroscience to generate a large body of interdisciplinary studies.

This recent information on the developmental origins of health and disease can be translated directly into clinical practice. It has both expanded the amount of factual knowledge and altered the theoretical constructs that model the diagnoses and treatments of a variety of psychological and physical disorders of childhood. These advances are, in turn, directly relevant to pediatricians' interest in the normal and abnormal functions of the developing child's mind and body. The common ground of the expanding body of knowledge in the developmental sciences, therefore, can strengthen the ties of pediatrics to the allied fields that border it: developmental neurology, child psychiatry, and developmental psychology.

This ongoing paradigm shift, occurring in the basic and applied sciences, is expressed in three converging themes. The first theme arises from the wealth of neurobiological data that became available in the last decade, the "decade of the brain." Contemporary neuroscience is becoming very interested in the early development of the brain and indeed in the process of development itself. Developmental theoreticians are asserting that the most powerful conception of development may come from a deeper understanding of the brain's own self-organizing operations. An intense focus has been upon the human brain growth spurt, which begins in the last trimester of pregnancy and continues to 18 to 24 months of age. The myelinization of the brain is so rapid and extensive at this time that the brain takes on an "adult-like" appearance at the end of the first year (Paus, Collins, Leonard, & Zijdenbos, 2001). Neuroscientists are concluding that the accelerated growth of brain structure during critical periods of infancy is experience-dependent and influenced by social forces, whereas neuropsychiatrists are referring to the social construction of the human brain and positing that the cellular architecture of the cerebral cortex is sculpted by input from the social environment embedded in the early attachment relationships. In my writings I have suggested that a central concept of the disciplines of developmental affective and social neuroscience is expressed in this principle: "the self-organization of the developing brain occurs in the context of a relationship with another self, another brain" (Schore, 1996, p. 60).

Furthermore, more than ever before we now are aware of the importance of the fact that "the brain" is actually a system of two brains, each with very different structural and functional properties. Of particular interest to both prenatal and perinatal biology and pediatrics is the right brain. This early developing right brain is in a growth spurt in the first 2 years, before the verbal left, and is dominant in the first 3 years of human life (Chiron et al., 1997; Schore, 1994). This growth is not totally encoded in the genome, but is indelibly shaped by the emotional communications within attachment transactions. In light of the fact that the right hemisphere is dominant for the emotional and corporeal self (Devinsky, 2000), the social experience-dependent maturation of the right brain in human infancy is equated with the early development of the self (Schore, 1994). The development of the brain–mind–body in infancy, the origin of the self, is essentially a reflection of the development of the right brain and its emergent embodied survival functions. Thus, current studies of how the first human relationship permanently impacts the early developing right brain represent explorations of the *terra incognita* of the essential beginnings of the human experience.

The second theme of the interdisciplinary paradigm shift emerges from ongoing transformations within psychology, psychiatry, and neuroscience. All subdisciplines within psychology, from developmental psychology through abnormal psychology, are changing their focus from cognition to emotion. Developmental psychological research suggests that, more so than the development of complex cognitions, the attainment of an attachment bond of emotional communication and the maturation of affects represent the key events in infancy. Hence, models have moved from Piagetian theories of cognitive development to psychobiological models of social-emotional development. Clinical psychology and psychiatry are moving from cognition to emotion as a central force in psychopathology and psychotherapy.

This emphasis on emotion is also reflected in two areas: the emergence of affective neuroscience and its focus on the specializations of the right hemisphere for processing affective states, as well as psychiatry's current intense interest in the emotion-processing limbic system. This is the brain system that derives subjective information in terms of emotional feelings that guide behavior and functions to allow the individual to adapt to a rapidly changing environment and organize new learning. Indeed pediatrics too has appreciated neuroscience's close attention to the brain systems that process social and emotion information. Gorski (2001) has argued that such information is essential to pediatric practice, asserting treating children's emotional health and development is the central focus of pediatric primary care.

The third theme of the paradigm shift revolves around one of the few theoretical constructs that lies at the core of literally every biological and psychological discipline—self-regulation. The process of development itself is now thought to fundamentally represent a progression of stages in which emergent, adaptive self-regulatory structures and functions enable qualitatively new interactions between the individual and the social environment. We now know that emotions are the highest order, direct expression of bioregulation in complex organisms, that the maturation of the neural mechanisms involved in self-regulation is experience-dependent, and that these critical experiences are the early social experiences embedded in the attachment relationship.

In other words, attachment relationships are essential because they facilitate the development of the brain's self-regulatory mechanism. Furthermore, studies now reveal that these essential self-regulatory structures are located in the right brain. Consensus currently indicates that attachment can be fundamentally defined as the dyadic regulation of emotion, that the attainment of the self-regulation of affect is a major developmental achievement, and that normal development fundamentally represents the enhancement of self-regulation.

The three trends of the paradigm shift—new data from studies of right brain development, an emphasis on emotion, and models of self-regulation—are converging to produce clinical models that are directly relevant to pediatrics; specifically, these are models of the development of childhood mental health and mental illness. The mission statement of the American Academy of Pediatrics states its commitment to "the attainment of optimal physical, mental, and social health for all infants, children, adolescents, and young adults." It is interesting to note that another medical specialty, psychiatry, is also extremely interested in mental health. In an issue of the *American Journal of Psychiatry*, Vaillant (2003) argues that psychiatry needs to model not only mental illness but also positive mental health. He suggests that the most important single dimension of mental health is the evolution of emotional and social intelligence, an adaptive capacity that is mediated by progressive brain myelinization.

In a parallel formulation, the interdisciplinary field of infant mental health is now focusing upon "infant social-emotional development, caregiver–infant interactions, contextual and cultural influences on infant and family development, and all conditions that place infants and/or their families at risk for less than optimal development" (Schore, 2001b, p. 9). In a special edition of the *Infant Mental Health Journal* that I edited entitled "Contributions from the Decade of the Brain to Infant Mental Health" (Schore, 2001a), my colleagues and I offered a series of articles demonstrating that early interpersonal relationships, *for better or worse*, profoundly and indelibly impact the psychological, physiological, and neurobiological aspects of the early development of the self.

With this introduction in mind, I will use the perspective of regulation theory (Schore, 1994, 2003a, 2003b) to discuss and interpret recent studies on attachment, affect regulation, and development of the right brain. I will suggest that the development of self-regulation is central to the emergence of infant physical, mental, and social-emotional health, and that current information from attachment theory and developmental neuroscience is highly relevant to the interests of pediatrics in the normal and abnormal functions of the developing child's mind and body.

INTERACTIVE AFFECT REGULATION
AS A FUNDAMENTAL MECHANISM OF
ATTACHMENT DYNAMICS

For the human infant, the fundamental interrelated goals of the first year of life are the co-creation of an attachment bond of emotional communication with the primary caregiver and the development of self-regulation. As opposed to earlier models that emphasized cognitive development, it is now thought that learning how to communicate represents perhaps the most important developmental process to take place during human infancy. What do we know about the relationships between the earliest development of socioemotional communication, interactive regulation, and the creation of a secure attachment?

From birth onward, the infant is using his or her expanding coping capacities to interact with the social environment. In the earliest proto-attachment experiences, the infant is utilizing his or her maturing motor and developing sensory capacities, especially smell, taste, and touch, to interact with the social environment (Van Toller & Kendal-Reed, 1995; Weller & Feldman, 2003). But by 8 weeks there is a dramatic progression of social and emotional capacities. Within episodes of mutual gaze, the mother and infant engage in intuitive and nonconscious facial, vocal, and gestural preverbal communications; and these highly arousing, affect-laden face-to-face interactions allow the infant to be exposed to high levels of social and cognitive information. The mother makes herself contingent, easily predictable, and manipulatable by the infant; and in order to regulate the high positive arousal, the dyad synchronizes the intensity of their affective behavior within lags of split seconds. These episodes of "affect synchrony" occur in the first expression of social play and generate increasing levels of the positive affects of joy and excitement. In this interactive matrix both partners match states and then simultaneously adjust their social attention, stimulation, and accelerating arousal to each other's responses. According to Lester, Hoffman, and Brazelton (1985, p. 24) "synchrony develops as a consequence of each partner's learning the rhythmic structure of the other and modifying his or her behavior to fit that structure."

In this process of "contingent responsivity," not only the tempo of their engagement but also their disengagement and reengagement are coordinated. The more the empathic mother tunes her activity level to the infant during periods of social engagement, the more she allows the infant to recover quietly in periods of disengagement; and the more she attends to the child's reinitiating cues for reengagement, the more synchronized their interaction. The caregiver thus facilitates the infant's information processing by adjusting the mode, amount, variability, and timing of the onset and offset of stimulation to the infant's unique, temperamentally determined integrative capacities. These interactively regulated synchronized interactions promote the infant's regulatory capacities and are fundamental to his or her healthy affective development.

In order to enter into this communication, the mother must be psychobiologically attuned not so much to the child's overt behavior as to the reflections of the rhythms of his or her internal state, enabling the dyad to co-create "mutual regulatory systems of arousal." In order to act as a regulator of the infant's arousal, the mother must be able to regulate her own arousal state. The burgeoning capacity of the infant to experience increasing levels of accelerating, positive arousal states is thus at this stage amplified and externally regulated by the primary caregiver. It also depends upon the mother's capacity to engage in an interactive emotion-communicating mechanism that generates these states in herself and her child. Maternal sensitivity thus acts as an external organizer of the infant's biobehavioral regulation.

But the primary caregiver is not always attuned—developmental research shows frequent moments of mis-attunement in the dyad, ruptures of the attachment bond. In early development an adult provides much of the necessary modulation of infant states, especially after a state disruption and across a transition between states; and this allows for the development of self-regulation. Again, the key to this is the caregiver's capacity to monitor and regulate her own affect, especially negative affect. In this essential regulatory pattern of "interactive repair," the "good-enough" caregiver who induces a stress response in her infant through a mis-attunement, re-invokes in a timely fashion her psychobiologically attuned regulation of the infant's negative affect state. The process of re-experiencing positive affect following negative experience allows the child to learn that negative affect can be tolerated and that relational stress can be regulated. Infant resilience emerges from an interactive context in which the child and parent transition from positive to negative and back to positive affect. In fact, resilience in the face of stress is an ultimate indicator of attachment and therefore adaptive regulatory capacities and infant mental health.

The dual regulatory processes of affect synchrony, which creates states of positive arousal, and interactive repair, which modulates states of negative arousal, are the fundamental building blocks of attachment and its associated emotions. These arousal-regulating transactions, which continue throughout the first year, underlie the formation of an attachment bond and thereby the interactive regulation of emotions between the infant and the primary caregiver. An essential attachment function is to promote the synchrony or regulation of biological and behavioral systems on an organismic level. Indeed, psychobiological attunement and the interactive mutual entrainment of physiological rhythms are fundamental processes that mediate attachment, and thus attachment is a primary mechanism of the regulation of biological synchronicity between and within organisms.

These data clearly suggest that affect regulation is not just the reduction of affective intensity, or the dampening of negative emotion. It also involves an amplification, an intensification of positive emotion; this condition is necessary for more complex self-organization. The psychobiologically attuned mother of the securely attached child not only minimizes the infant's negative states in comforting transactions but also maximizes his or her positive affective states in interactive play. Regulated affective interactions with a familiar, predictable primary caregiver create not only a sense of safety but also a positively charged curiosity that fuels the burgeoning self's exploration of novel socioemotional and physical environments. This ability is a marker of adaptive infant mental health.

INTERPERSONAL NEUROBIOLOGY OF RIGHT BRAIN–TO–RIGHT BRAIN ATTACHMENT COMMUNICATIONS

A fundamental theme of the current paradigm shift in conceptualizations of human infancy is articulated in the principle that learning how to communicate emotional states is an essential developmental process. Due to the fact that these communications are totally nonverbal and intersubjective, until recently it was thought that their underlying mechanisms were unavailable for experimental analysis. It is here, however, where developmental neurobiology and psychobiology have offered important contributions. This research reveals that during optimal moments of bodily based affective communications, the primary caregiver's exogenous sensory stimulation coincides with the infant's endogenous organismic rhythms. This concurrence allows the empathically resonating mother to appraise the nonverbal expressions of her infant's internal arousal and psychobiological states, regulate them, and then communicate them back to the infant.

Basic research in developmental neuroscience is consonant with the psychological models of early human mother–infant communication described in the preceding section. Coordinated visual eye-to-eye messages, auditory prosodic vocalizations, and tactile and body gestures serve as a channel of communicative signals that induce instant emotional effects; namely, the positive affects of excitement and pleasure build within the dyad. According to Trevarthen (1993), the intrinsic regulators of human brain growth in a child are specifically adapted to be coupled, by emotional communication, to the regulators of adult brains.

A general principle of development dictates that attachment communications are built into the nervous system and induce substantial changes in the developing brain. But specifically what parts of the brain are impacted by the interactive regulation embedded within various types of visual, auditory, and tactile attachment communications? Keeping in mind that *the brain* actually represents two unique hemispheric processing systems, a substantial body of research indicates that the right hemisphere begins a critical period of maturation before the left. Neuroanatomical studies show that this hemisphere is more advanced than the left in surface features from about the 25th gestational week, and this advance persists until the left hemisphere shows a postnatal growth spurt starting in the second year (Trevarthen, 1996). Indeed, neuroimaging studies demonstrate the following: The mass of the brain increases rapidly during the first 2 years, normal adult appearance is seen at 2 years, all major fiber tracts can be identified by age 3, and infants under 2 years show higher right than left hemispheric volumes (Matsuzawa et al., 2001).

Earlier I mentioned that the burgeoning field of developmental affective neuroscience is now focusing upon the unique roles of the right hemisphere in emotional development. This work emphasizes that learning how to communicate and the evolution of self-regulation are at the core of human infancy, and it posits that the self-organization of the developing brain occurs in the context of a relationship between an infant brain and an adult brain. Developmental neurobiology is thus fundamentally an interpersonal neurobiology of right brain–to–right brain communications. Indeed, it is now established that although the left hemisphere mediates most language functions, the right hemisphere is more important to the broader aspects of communication.

In support of this right brain–to–right brain communication model, developmental neuroscientists have observed that a milestone for normal development of the infant brain occurs at about 8 weeks. This is the onset of a critical period during which the following occur: Synaptic connections in the occipital cortex are modified by visual experience (Yamada et al., 2000); infants as young as 2 months show right hemispheric activation when exposed to a woman's face; and particular areas of the right hemisphere are timed to be in a plastic and receptive state at the very time when polysensory information that emanates from faces is being attended to most intensely by the infant (Tzourio-Mazoyer et al., 2002). During synchronized face-to-face transactions, patterns of information emanating from the caregiver's face—especially of low visual and auditory frequencies—are specifically processed by the infant's right hemisphere.

Over the first year regulated and dysregulated emotional communications embedded within mutual gaze transactions are etched into rapidly developing right-lateralized structures that are specialized for assessing familiar faces, gaze direction, and processing visual, auditory, and tactile emotional communicative signals. The right cerebral cortex is dominant for the infant's processing of individual faces, recognition of arousal-inducing maternal facial expressions, and response to the prosody of "motherese." In fact, it is now asserted that the development of the capacity to efficiently process information from faces requires visual input to the right (and not left) hemisphere during infancy (Le Grand, Mondloch, Maurer, & Brent, 2003). Complementing this the mother's mature right hemisphere is faster than the left in performing valence-dependent, automatic, pre-attentive appraisals of emotional facial expressions, in responding to the positive aspects of facial expressions, visual stimuli, and touch and smell, and in assessing visual or auditory emotional communicative signals.

In terms of the auditory aspects of attachment communications, studies reveal that the human maternal response to an infant's cry, a fundamental behavior of the attachment dynamic, is accompanied by an activation of the mother's right brain, and that engrams related to emotional voices are more strongly imprinted into the infant's early maturing, more active right hemisphere (Lorberbaum et al., 2002). And with respect to tactile communications, research demonstrates that most human females show a tendency toward cradling infants on the left side of their body, and that this left-cradling tendency facilitates the flow of affective information from the infant via the left ear and eye to the center of emotional decoding in the mother's right hemisphere (Manning et al., 1997). In this manner, "The emotional experience of the infant develops through the sounds, images, and pictures that constitute much of an infant's early learning experience, and are disproportionately stored or processed in the right hemisphere during the formative stages of brain ontogeny" (Semrud-Clikeman & Hynd, 1990, p. 198).

These moments of imprinting, the very rapid form of learning that irreversibly stamps early experience with the social environment upon the developing nervous system, are central to attachment bond formation. The fact that the early imprinting of the dual attachment regulatory processes of affect synchrony that modulates states of positive arousal and interactive repair that modulates states of negative arousal impacts the developmental trajectory of the right brain and therefore the individual over the rest of the life span is explained by the finding that attachment experiences are "affectively burnt in" the infant's rapidly developing right brain.

ATTACHMENT, AFFECT REGULATION, AND THE ORGANIZATION OF RIGHT BRAIN REGULATORY SYSTEMS

Another productive example of the current paradigm shift in the developmental sciences is the proliferation of interdisciplinary studies exploring the neurobiological mechanisms that underlie the regulatory functions of attachment. In his earliest formulation, Bowlby (1969) speculated that the control system that mediated attachment behavior is located in the brain, specifically in the emotion-processing limbic system and the frontal lobes. Subsequent theoreticians hypothesized that the mother initially provides an external regulating mechanism for the infant's immature neurobiological processes, but at some point in development the infant becomes self-regulating through the maturation of internal regulatory mechanisms entrained to the stimuli provided by the mother.

Continuing and expanding upon this theoretical connection between attachment and regulation, in my 1994 book *Affect Regulation and the Origin of the Self*, I integrated data from developmental psychology and developmental neurobiology in order to specify the timing and location of the neuroanatomical systems imprinted by attachment experiences. In that volume I proposed that the neurobiological maturation of regulatory circuits in the infant's early developing right brain is significantly influenced by the social-emotional experiences embedded in the attachment relationship with the primary caregiver, and that the control system for attachment is centered in the right frontal lobe.

Over the course of the last 10 years and the ensuing "decade of the brain," a rapidly growing body of interdisciplinary studies has documented, at a remarkable level of detail, the impact of the presence or absence of maternal visual, vocal, and tactile emotional stimuli on the infant's brain development, and thereby its emotional, social, and cognitive capacities (or deficits) in later life.

Thus, current authors describe moments of attachment imprinting: "When the child is held and hugged, brain networks are activated and strengthened and firing spreads to associated networks; when the child is sung to, still other networks are strengthened to receive sounds and interpret them as song. The repeated appearance of the mother provides a fixation object as in imprinting" (Epstein, 2001, p. 43). These studies are detailing how even subtle affect regulating transactions permanently alter activity levels in the child's maturing brain.

Furthermore, basic research on the neurobiology of attachment is revealing how the mother functions in the short term as a regulator of alterations within the child's internal homeostasis, and in the long term of his or her emerging capacity to adaptively cope with the social-emotional environment (Ovtscharoff & Braun, 2001). This is due to the fact that mother–infant attachment interactions critically impact developing limbic circuits in the infant brain, thereby inducing enduring emotional and cognitive changes. In light of the facts that the human limbic system undergoes extensive myelination in the first year and a half, and that the early maturing right hemisphere—which is deeply connected into the limbic system—is in a growth spurt at this time, attachment experiences with the social-emotional environment specifically impact developing limbic and cortical areas of the right brain. Indeed, the spontaneous emotional communication between mother and infant has been described as "a conversation between limbic systems" (see Schore, 2003a).

In his initial outline of attachment theory, Bowlby hypothesized that a succession of increasingly complex regulatory systems involving the limbic system and brain arousal areas mediate attachment processes. The neuroscience literature now refers to the "rostral limbic system," a hierarchical sequence of interconnected limbic areas in amygdala, anterior cingulate, insula, and orbital cortex, and a "circuit of emotion regulation" consisting of amygdala, anterior cingulate, and orbital frontal cortex. Based upon the principle of caudal to rostral brain development, I have offered a model of the early experience-dependent maturation of the limbic system, and proposed a sequence of regulatory systems that are imprinted by more complex attachment communications and thereby evolve over the first 2 years of human infancy (Schore, 2001b, 2003a). The optimal formation of these brain areas essential to the child's emotional development is thus dependent upon the interactive regulation embedded within the attachment communications of the mother–infant relationship.

At birth only the amygdala, a primitive subcortical limbic regulatory system that appraises crude information about external stimuli and modulates autonomic and arousal systems is online. The right amygdala processes olfactory stimuli within the mother–perinatal infant relationship, and mediates the infant's recognition of the mother's scent as well as the mother's recognition of neonates through olfactory cues. At 8 weeks the onset of a critical period for the development of the anterior cingulate commences, allowing this system to regulate play and separation behaviors, laughing and crying vocalizations, face representations, and the modulation of autonomic activity. The first year is also a critical period of experience-dependent maturation of the right insula, a structure within the temporal lobes that is essentially involved in the subjective awareness of inner body feelings and emotionality, and the right parietal cortex, a posterior cortical area involved in the representation of the physical self and the ability to distinguish self from others.

By the last quarter of the first year, the orbital (ventromedial) areas of the frontal lobes enter a critical period of growth that continues through the middle of the second year. The orbitofrontal cortex, the hierarchical apex of the limbic system, acts at the highest level of control of behavior, especially in relation to emotion, and is identical to Bowlby's control system of attachment. I have suggested that in mutual gaze transactions the mother is downloading programs from her limbic system into the child's developing limbic system. A recent fMRI study by Nitschke and colleagues (2004) of mothers viewing a photograph of their own infant shows maximal brain activation in the mother's orbitofrontal cortex, especially on the right side. These authors conclude the following: that this cortex plays a critical role in the representation of attachment-related positive affect as described by Bowlby, that it linearly tracks the intensity of positive emotions that underlie maternal attachment, and that individual variations in orbitofrontal activation to infant stimuli reflect an important dimension of maternal attachment.

Other studies demonstrate that the right prefrontolimbic areas play a primary role in the appraisal of biologically meaningful exteroceptive and interoceptive self-related information and in the integration of internal physiological states with salient environmental cues, processes central to the attachment mechanism. This right cerebral hemisphere is centrally involved in regulating the hypothalamic-pituitary-adrenal (HPA) axis and in activating physiological stress responses (Wittling, 1997). More than any other area of the human prefrontal lobes, the right orbitofrontal cortex is most directly linked to the brain's stress regulatory system (Sullivan & Gratton, 2002). Recall, the regulation of stressors in social relationships modifies prefrontal maturation, and in this manner a secure attachment facilitates the transfer of regulatory capacities from caregiver to infant. Thus, on a fundamental level, the attachment relationship between the child and the primary caregiver is formative because it promotes the development of the brain's major self-regulatory mechanisms.

More specifically, the attachment relationship mediates the dyadic regulation of both positive and negative emotion via the maternal interactive regulation of the infant's postnatally developing autonomic nervous system (ANS). Optimally regulated communications embedded in secure attachment experiences thus imprint the connections between the postnatally maturing CNS limbic system that processes and regulates social-emotional stimuli and the ANS that generates the somatic aspects of emotion. A growing body of work now reveals that the right hemisphere is deeply connected into the ANS and that it, more so than the left, controls both sympathetic and parasympathetic responses (Spence, Shapiro,

& Zaidel, 1996). The hypothalamus, the head ganglion of the ANS, is right lateralized, and the hypothalamic nuclei are considerably larger on the right side of the human brain. This hemisphere is dominant for the production of corticotropin releasing factor and the glucocorticoid cortisol, the neurohormones that mediate stress coping responses. There is now convincing evidence to show the following: that the infant's relationship with the mother regulates the development of the hypothalamic-pituitary-adrenal (HPA) axis (Gunnar & Donzella, 2002), that neonatal social behavior associated with the HPA axis increases right hemisphere dominance (Tang, Reeb, Romeo, & McEwen, 2003), and that perinatal distress leads to a blunting of the stress response in the right (and not left) prefrontal cortex that is manifested in adulthood (Brake, Sullivan, & Gratton, 2000).

For the rest of the life span, the right brain is dominant for the regulation of fundamental physiological, endocrinological, immunological, and cardiovascular functions and thereby the control of vital functions supporting survival and enabling the organism to cope actively and passively with stress. A growing body of data underscores a strong association between alterations in maternal–infant interactions, early programming of the HPA, pre- and postnatal critical periods of brain development, and adult health and disease (Matthews, 2002). This work is paralleled by studies linking attachment, stress, and disease (Maunder & Hunter, 2001; Schmidt, Nachtigall, Wuethrich-Martone, & Strauss, 2002) and childhood attachment and adult cortisol and cardiovascular function (Luecken, 1998), and research showing the right hemisphere plays a unique role for pain sensitivity and negative affect (Pauli, Wiedemann, & Nickola, 1999). Assets or limitations of right brain survival functions thus impact not just "psychological" but essential organismic "psychobiological" capacities of coping with both emotional disturbance and physical disease. These regulatory capacities, an outcome of optimal attachment experiences, are surely critical indices of adaptive physical as well as mental health.

SECURE ATTACHMENT, OPTIMAL RIGHT BRAIN MATURATION, AND THE INTERPERSONAL NEUROBIOLOGICAL ORIGINS OF MENTAL HEALTH

At the outset of this contribution I proposed that three trends of the ongoing paradigm shift in the developmental sciences—studies of right brain development, research on emotion, and models of self-regulation—are converging to produce psychoneurobiologically informed models of human infancy that are clinically relevant to pediatrics. These interdisciplinary streams are expressed in conceptions of the dynamics of attachment bond formation, wherein optimally co-regulated emotional communications facilitate the self-organization and increased complexity of the infant's right brain. The cortical and subcortical systems of the infant's right brain become tuned to dynamically self-organize upon perceiving certain patterns of exteroceptive social information, namely the visual, auditory, and tactile stimuli emanating from the smiling and joyful, and soothing and calming face, as well as the expressive body of a loving mother.

To date, the fundamental importance of positive emotions to early development has not been appreciated. Current attachment studies describe that the baby becomes attached to the regulating caregiver who not only minimizes negative affect but also expands opportunities for positive affect, and neuroscience research reveals that positive affects are critical to brain growth. According to Nitschke et al. (2004, p. 583, italics added), "*Positive affect elicited in a mother toward her newborn may be one of the most powerful and evolutionarily preserved forms of positive affect in the emotional landscape of human behavior.*" Other researchers have noted that "the positive emotional exchange resulting from autonomy-supportive parenting involves participation of right hemispheric cortical and subcortical systems that participate in global, tonic emotional modulation" (Ryan, Kuhl, & Deci, 1997, p. 719). An expanding body of research indicates that the major systems that modulate a broad array of intense positive and negative emotional states and regulate attachment functions in infancy and the later stages of life are located in the right hemisphere.

As a result of his or her interaction with caregivers, the infant forms internal working models of attachment that are stored in right-lateralized nonverbal implicit-procedural memory. These interactive representations encode strategies of affect regulation and contain coping mechanisms for maintaining basic regulation and positive affect in the face of environmental challenge. Security of attachment fundamentally relates to a physiological coding of an expectation that during times of stress homeostatic disruptions will be set right. Subsequent to the child's attachment to the mother in the first year, the child forms another attachment, in the second year, to the father. This allows the child to have affect-attuning and arousal-regulating experiences with two different types of caregivers. The infant's ability to develop more complex self-regulatory coping capacities and to regulate stressful alterations of psychobiological state via interactive regulation in interconnected contexts or autoregulation in autonomous contexts, emerges out of his or her affect-regulating experiences with the early social environment.

In all later interpersonal functioning this right hemispheric representation of a secure working model, acting at levels beneath conscious awareness, is accessed to appraise, interpret, and regulate socioemotional information and thereby guide future action in familiar and novel interpersonal environments. For the rest of the life span the right hemisphere—imprinted and organized by early relational experiences—is dominant for the nonconscious reception, expression, and communication of emotion. These are essential functions for co-creating and maintaining social and especially intimate relationships (Blonder, Bowers, & Heilman, 1991; Borod et al., 1998; Dimberg & Petterson, 2000; George et al., 1996). Furthermore, studies also suggest that the interactive regulation of attachment psychobiology and right brain neuropsychology represent the substrate of three other capacities that are critical to human interactions: trust, empathy, and moral development (Perry et al., 2001; Shamay-Tsoory, Tomer, Berger, & Aharon-Peretz, 2003; Winston, Strange, O'Doherty, & Dolan, 2002).

Most importantly, in addition to self-regulation, the right hemisphere is specialized for generating self-awareness and self-recognition and for the processing of "self-related material" (Decety & Chaminade, 2003; Keenan, Nelson, O'Connor, & Pascual-Leone, 2001). Reviewing the behavioral neurology literature, Devinsky (2000) posits an evolutionary role of the right hemisphere in the following adaptive functions: identifying a corporeal image of self and its relation to the environment; distinguishing self from nonself; recognizing familiar members of a species, as well as other familiar organisms, items, and places; emotionally understanding and reacting to bodily and environment stimuli; recalling autobiographical information; appraising environmental reality; and maintaining a coherent, continuous, and unified sense of self. Notice that all of these critical adaptive functions are present by the second year of life, the end of the right brain growth spurt, and that all are essential neuropediatric components of the earliest manifestation of mental health.

In an address to Head Start, "Parent–Infant Communications and the Neurobiology of Emotional Development" (Schore, 2000b) and in an article in the *Infant Mental Health Journal*, the official publication of the World Association for Infant Mental Health, entitled "The Effects of a Secure Attachment Relationship on Right Brain Development, Affect Regulation, and Infant Mental Health" (Schore, 2001a), I have argued that the earliest expression of mental health reflects the adaptive or maladaptive functioning of the right brain, the neurobiological locus of the emotional self.

Although the right brain reorganizes at later points of the life span, conditions of its early evolution in the brain growth spurt have an enormous impact on its trajectory over subsequent stages of development. The experience-dependent maturation of its regulatory limbic-autonomic circuits is significantly influenced by the social-emotional experiences embedded in the attachment relationship with the primary caregiver. A compelling amount of experimental research and clinical studies now definitively show that stressful dysregulating interactions with the early social environment lay the groundwork for an insecure attachment, right brain dysfunction, limbic-autonomic deficits, and the development of a predisposition to later-forming psychiatric disorders. (See Schore, 1994, 2003a for an extensive discussion of the neurobiology of psychopathogenesis.)

The principle that early disruption of the mother–infant attachment relationship negatively impacts brain plasticity and predisposes to later-forming psychopathology is now well established (Cirulli, Berry, & Alleva, 2002; Schore, 1994; 2001b, 2002; Siegel, 1999). Lyons and his colleagues (2002, p. 51) state, "theories of human development suggest that stressful experiences in social relationships modify prefrontal maturation (Schore, 1996)," and demonstrate that conditions impacting early maternal variability in infancy produce "significant differences in right but not left adult prefrontal volumes, with experience-dependent asymmetric variation most clearly expressed in ventral medial cortex measured in vivo by magnetic resonance imaging" (p. 51). And in basic research Helmeke et al. conclude, "Positive (formation of emotional attachment) or negative (e.g., maternal separation or loss) emotional experience may carve a permanent trace into a still developing neuronal network of immature synaptic connections, and thereby can extend or limit the functional capacity of the brain during later stages of life" (Helmeke, Ovtscharoff, Poeggel, & Braun, 2001, p. 717).

The ongoing paradigm shift in the developmental sciences is expressed in the fundamental principles that the maturation of affects represents the key event in infancy, and that the attainment of the essential adaptive capacity for the self-regulation of affect is a major developmental achievement. The increasing appreciation of the profound and indelible impact of early interpersonal relationships on the psychological, physiological, and neurobiological aspects of the early development of the self substantially alters our view of human infancy. In the middle of the last century, the pediatrician-psychoanalyst Donald Winnicott (1960) asserted that there is no infant without the mother. Echoing that conception, a recent National Institute of Child Health & Human Development (NICHD) study (2004) concludes, "Self-regulation in infancy is best conceptualized as a quality of the infant–caregiver relationship, rather than a characteristic of the infant alone" (p. 43). In parallel studies neuroscience now reveals that regulated attachment experiences facilitate the brain's major regulatory systems that are located in the right brain.

Psychobiological markers that assess attachment relationships, affect regulation, the right brain, and infant mental health thus need to be included in the diagnostic armamentarium of the practicing pediatrician This knowledge allows the clinician to understand more deeply the system of nonverbal communication and interactive regulation that lies at the core of the mother–infant relationship, a fundamental element of the child's developmental matrix. Furthermore, regulation theory applies not only to the mother–infant relationship but also to the clinician–patient relationship (Schore, 1994, 2003b). According to Adler (2002), the art of the doctor–patient relationship, which involves the physician's empathy and the capacity for responsive listening, "entails establishing the same kind of person-to-person attunement that is essential to the development of the newborn (Schore, 1994)" (p. 887).

These progressions of knowledge offer clinically relevant models of the earliest manifestations of normal and abnormal development. Adaptive infant mental health can be fundamentally defined as the earliest expression of efficient and resilient right brain strategies for regulating both negative and positive affective states and for coping with novelty and stress. The formation of an increasingly complex emotion-communicating system allows for an expanding ability to flexibly switch internal bodily based affective states in response to perceived changes in the external social environment via autoregulation or interactive regulation, and thereby the maintenance of a cohesive sense of self in both autonomous and interconnected contexts. On the other hand, maladaptive infant mental health is manifested in prolonged, frequent, and intense episodes of affect dysregulation (Schore, 2001c). This deficit of coping mechanisms is expressed in the perseveration of negative affect and an inability to respond to demands of the dynamically changing social environment in a timely manner. The former is a resilience factor for coping with the psychobiological stressors inherent in social interactions at later stages of the life cycle; the latter is a risk factor for interruptions of developmental processes and a vulnerability to the coping deficits that define later-forming psychopathologies. These conceptions directly relate to what the American Academy of Pediatrics terms "the attainment of optimal physical, mental, and social health for all infants" and thereby the primordial expression of health in "children, adolescents, and young adults."

REFERENCES

Adler, H. M. (2002). The sociophysiology of caring in the doctor–patient relationship. *Journal of General Internal Medicine, 17,* 883–890.

American Academy of Pediatrics. Core values, vision, and mission statement. Retrieved September 6, 2011, from http://www.aap.org/member/memcore.htm

Blonder, L. X., Bowers, D., & Heilman, K. M. (1991). The role of the right hemisphere in emotional communication. *Brain, 114,* 1115–1127.

Borod, J., Cicero, B. A., Obler, L. K., Welkowitz, J., Erhan, H. M., Santschi, C., et al. (1998). Right hemisphere emotional perception: Evidence across multiple channels. *Neuropsychology, 12,* 446–458.

Bowlby, J. (1969). *Attachment and loss: Vol. 1. Attachment.* New York; Basic Books.

Brake, W. G., Sullivan, R. M., & Gratton, A. (2000). Perinatal distress leads to lateralized medial prefrontal cortical dopamine hypofunction in adult rats. *Journal of Neuroscience, 20,* 5538–5543.

Chiron, C., Jambaque, I., Nabbout, R., Lounes, R., Syrota, A., & Dulac, O. (1997). The right brain hemisphere is dominant in human infants. *Brain, 120,* 1057–1065.

Cicchetti, D., & Tucker D. (1994). Development and self-regulatory structures of the mind. *Development and Psychopathology, 6,* 533–549.

Cirulli, F., Berry, A., & Alleva, E. (2002). Early disruption of the mother–infant relationship: Effects on brain plasticity and implications for psychopathology. *Neuroscience and Biobehavioral Reviews, 27,* 73–82.

Crabbe, J. C., & Phillips, T. J. (2003). Mother nature meets mother nurture. *Nature Neuroscience, 6,* 440–442.

Decety, J., & Chaminade, T. (2003). When the self represents the other: A new cognitive neuroscience view on psychological identification. *Consciousness and Cognition, 12,* 577–596.

Devinsky, O. (2000). Right cerebral hemisphere dominance for a sense of corporeal and emotional self. *Epilepsy & Behavior, 1,* 60–73.

Dimberg, U., & Petterson, M. (2000). Facial reactions to happy and angry facial expressions: Evidence for right hemisphere dominance. *Psychophysiology, 37,* 693–696.

Epstein, H. T. (2001). An outline of the role of brain in human cognitive development. *Brain Cognition, 45,* 44–51.

George, M. S., Parekh, P. I., Rosinsky, N., Ketter, T. A., Kimbrell, T. A., Heilman, K. M., et al. (1996). Understanding emotional prosody activates right hemispheric regions. *Archives of Neurology, 53,* 665–670.

Gluckman, P. D., & Adler, H. M. (2004). Living with the past: Evolution, development, and patterns of disease. *Science, 305,* 1733–1736.

Gorski, P. (2001). Contemporary pediatric practice: In support of infant mental health (imaging and imagining). *Infant Mental Health Journal, 22,* 188–200.

Gunnar, M. R., & Donzella, B. (2002). Social regulation of the cortisol levels in early human development. *Psychoneuroendocrinology, 27,* 199–220.

Helmeke, C., Ovtscharoff, W., Jr., Poeggel, G., & Braun, K. (2001). Juvenile emotional experience alters synaptic inputs on pyramidal neurons in the anterior cingulate cortex. *Cerebral Cortex, 11,* 717–727.

Keenan, J. P., Nelson, A., O'Connor, M., & Pascual-Leone, A. (2001). Self-recognition and the right hemisphere. *Nature, 409,* 305.

Le Grand, R., Mondloch, C., Maurer, D., & Brent, H. P. (2003). Expert face processing requires visual input to the right hemisphere during infancy. *Nature Neuroscience, 6,* 1108–1112.

Lester, B. M., Hoffman, J., & Brazelton, T. B. (1985). The rhythmic structure of mother–infant interaction in term and preterm infants. *Child Development, 56,* 15–27.

Lorberbaum, J. P., Newman, J. D., Horwitz, A. R., Dubno, J. R., Lydiard, R. B., Hamner, M. B., et al. (2002). A potential role for thalamocingulate circuitry in human maternal behavior. *Biological Psychiatry, 51,* 431–445.

Luecken, L. J. (1998). Childhood attachment and loss experiences affect adult cardiovascular and cortisol function. *Psychosomatic Medicine, 60,* 765–772.

Lyons, D. M., Afarian, H., Schatzberg, A. F., Sawyer-Glover, A., & Moseley, M. E. (2002). Experience-dependent asymmetric maturation in primate prefrontal morphology. *Experimental Brain Research, 136,* 51–59.

Manning, J. T., Trivers, R. L., Thornhill, R., Singh, D., Denman, J., Eklo, M. H., et al. (1997). Ear asymmetry and left-side cradling. *Evolution and Human Behavior, 18,* 327–340.

Matsuzawa, J., Matsui, M., Konishi, T., Noguchi, K., Gur, R. C., Bilker, W., et al. (2001). Age-related changes of brain gray and white matter in healthy infants and children. *Cerebral Cortex, 11,* 335–342.

Matthews, S. G. (2002). Early programming of the hypothalamo-pituitary-adrenal axis. *Trends in Endocrinology and Metabolism, 13,* 373–380.

Maunder, R. G., & Hunter, J. J. (2001). Attachment and psychosomatic medicine: Developmental contributions to stress and disease. *Psychosomatic Medicine, 63,* 556–567.

NICHD Early Child Care Research Network. (2004). Affect dysregulation in the mother–child relationship in the toddler years: Antecedents and consequences. *Development and Psychopathology, 16,* 43–68.

Nitschke, J. B., Nelson, E. E., Rusch, B. D., Fox, A. S., Oakes, T. R., & Davidson, R. J. (2004). Orbitofrontal cortex tracks positive mood in mothers viewing pictures of their newborn infants. *NeuroImage, 21,* 583–592.

Ovtscharoff, W., Jr., & Braun, K. (2001). Maternal separation and social isolation modulate the postnatal development of synaptic composition in the infralimbic cortex of *octodon degus*. *Neuroscience, 104,* 33–40.

Pauli, P., Wiedemann, G., & Nickola, M. (1999). Pain sensitivity, cerebral laterality, and negative affect. *Pain, 80,* 359–364.

Paus, T., Collins, A. C., Leonard, B., & Zijdenbos, A. (2001). Maturation of white matter in the human brain: A review of magnetic resonance studies. *Brain Research Bulletin,* 54, 255–266.

Perry, R. J., Rosen, H. R., Kramer, J. H., Beer, J. S., Levenson, R. L., & Miller, B. L. (2001). Hemispheric dominance for emotions, empathy, and social behavior: Evidence from right and left handers with frontotemporal dementia. *Neurocase,* 7, 145–160.

Ryan, R. M., Kuhl, J., & Deci, E. L. (1997). Nature and autonomy: An organizational view of social and neurobiological aspects of self-regulation in behavior and development. *Development and Psychopathology,* 9, 701–728.

Schmidt, S., Nachtigall, C., Wuethrich-Martone, O., & Strauss, B. (2002). Attachment and coping with chronic disease. *Journal of Psychosomatic Research,* 53, 763–773.

Schore, A. N. (1994). *Affect regulation and the origin of the self.* Mahwah, NJ: Erlbaum.

Schore, A. N. (1996). The experience-dependent maturation of a regulatory system in the orbital prefrontal cortex and the origin of developmental psychopathology. *Development and Psychopathology,* 8, 59–87.

Schore, A. N. (2000a). Attachment and the regulation of the right brain. *Attachment & Human Development,* 2, 23–47.

Schore, A. N. (2000b). Plenary address: Parent–infant communications and the neurobiology of emotional development. In *Proceedings of Head Start's Fifth National Research Conference, Developmental and Contextual Transitions of Children and Families. Implications for Research, Policy, and Practice* (pp. 49–73). Washington, DC: Department of Health and Human Services.

Schore, A. N. (Ed.). (2001a). Contributions from the decade of the brain to infant mental health. *Infant Mental Health Journal,* 22, 1–269.

Schore, A. N. (2001b). The effects of a secure attachment relationship on right brain development, affect regulation, and infant mental health. *Infant Mental Health Journal,* 22, 7–66.

Schore, A. N. (2001c). The effects of relational trauma on right brain development affect regulation, and infant mental health. *Infant Mental Health Journal,* 22, 201–269.

Schore, A. N. (2002). Dysregulation of the right brain: A fundamental mechanism of traumatic attachment and the psychopathogenesis of posttraumatic stress disorder. *Australian and New Zealand Journal of Psychiatry,* 36, 9–30.

Schore, A. N. (2003a). *Affect dysregulation and disorders of the self.* New York: Norton.

Schore, A. N. (2003b). *Affect regulation and the repair of the self.* New York: Norton.

Semrud-Clikeman, M., & Hynd, G. W. (1990). Right hemisphere dysfunction in nonverbal learning disabilities: Social, academic, and adaptive functioning in adults and children. *Psychological Bulletin,* 107, 196–209.

Shamay-Tsoory, S. G., Tomer, R., Berger, B. D., & Aharon-Peretz, J. (2003). Characterization of empathy deficits following prefrontal brain damage: The role of the right ventromedial prefrontal cortex. *Journal of Cognitive Neuroscience,* 15, 324–337.

Siegel, D. J. (1999). *The developing mind: Toward a neurobiology of interpersonal experience.* New York: Guilford Press.

Spence, S., Shapiro, D., & Zaidel E. (1996). The role of the right hemisphere in the physiological and cognitive components of emotional processing. *Psychophysiology,* 33, 112–122.

Sullivan, R. M., & Gratton, A. (2002). Prefrontal cortical regulation of hypothalamic-pituitary-adrenal function in the rat and implications for psychopathology: Side matters. *Psychoneuroendocrinology,* 27, 99–114.

Suomi, S. J. (2004). How gene–environment interactions can influence emotional development in Rhesus monkeys. In C. Garcia-Coll, E. L. Bearer, & R. M. Lerner (Eds.), *Nature and nurture: The complex interplay of genetic and environmental influences on human behaviour and development* (pp. 35–51). Mahwah, NJ: Erlbaum.

Tang, A. C., Reeb, B. C., Romeo, R. D., & McEwen, B. S. (2003). Modification of social memory, hypothalamic-pituitary-adrenal axis, and brain asymmetry by neonatal novelty exposure. *Journal of Neuroscience, 23,* 8254–8260.

Trevarthen, C. (1993). The self born in intersubjectivity: The psychology of an infant communicating. In U. Neisser (Ed.), *The perceived self: Ecological and interpersonal sources of self-knowledge* (pp. 121–173). New York: Cambridge University Press.

Trevarthen, C. (1996). Lateral asymmetries in infancy: Implications for the development of the hemispheres. *Neuroscience and Biobehavioral Reviews, 20,* 571–586.

Tzourio-Mazoyer, N., de Schonen, S., Crivello, F., Reutter, B., Aujard, Y., & Mazoyer, B. (2002). Neural correlates of woman face processing by 2-month-old infants. *NeuroImage, 15,* 454–461.

Vaillant, G. E. (2003). Mental health. *American Journal of Psychiatry, 160,* 1373–1384.

Van Toller, S., & Kendal-Reed, M. (1995). A possible protocognitive role for odor in human infant development. *Brain and Cognition, 29,* 275–293.

Weller, A., & Feldman, R. (2003). Emotion regulation and touch in infants: The role of cholecystokinin and opioids. *Peptides, 24,* 779–788.

Winnicott, D W. (1960). The theory of parent–infant relationship. In *The maturational processes and the facilitating environment.* New York: International Universities Press.

Winston, J. S., Strange, B. A., O'Doherty, J. O., & Dolan, R. J. (2002). Automatic and intentional brain responses during evaluation of trustworthiness of faces. *Nature Neuroscience, 5,* 277–283.

Wittling, W. (1997). The right hemisphere and the human stress response. *Acta Physiologica Scandinavica, Supplement, 640,* 55–59.

Yamada, H., Sadato, N., Konishi, Y., Muramoto, S., Kimura, K., Tanaka, M., et al. (2000). A milestone for normal development of the infantile brain detected by functional MRI. *Neurology, 55,* 218–223.

Zuckerman, B., Augustyn, M., & Parker, S. (2001). Child development in pediatrics. *Archives of Pediatric and Adolescent Medicine, 155,* 1294–1295.

CHAPTER 7

How Elephants Are Opening Doors: Developmental Neuroethology, Attachment, and Social Context

With Gay Bradshaw

Recalling the work of Niko Tinbergen, a number of authors are now encouraging renewed interdisciplinary efforts in the analysis of behavior (Linklater, 2004; Taborsky, 2006). Tinbergen considered that attention to all four analytical levels informing behavior—evolution, development, causation, and function—was necessary to create conceptual and methodological coherency (Tinbergen, 1963). Along these lines, Bateson (2003) suggests that ethology should return to Tinbergen's "how" and "why" questions: to fundamental problems of understanding mechanisms involved in the development and control of behavior. Citing developmental neuroscience studies on social learning (learning from observing another's behavior) in early brain development, Bateson calls for an integrated approach to behavioral biology with attention to "the features of the stimuli that start off the formation of the social attachment [and] the establishment of a representation of that combination of features and the linking of such a representation to the system controlling social behavior" (2003, p. 12).

Ethology is not alone in its renewed interest in attachment (i.e., caregiver–infant bonding; Stamps, 2003). Over the past decade, psychology and neuroscience have intensively studied the link between social attachment and their neural substrates. This focus has created unifying models of developmental neuroethology for humans and animals. It has also contributed to significant changes in how development and behavior are understood (Davidson, Scherer, & Hill Goldsmith, 2003). Together, ethology, psychology, and neuroscience appear to be converging on trans-species models of brain and behavior.

Each field brings a critical dimension to understanding how developmental context contributes to particular behavioral outcomes: ethology in its underscoring of social systems of behavior and contexts (e.g., ontogenetic niche; West & King, 1987), psychology in its emphasis on socio-affective attachment transactions (e.g., Schore, 1994), and neuroscience in its explication of the coupled development of brain and social behavior (e.g., Curley & Keverne, 2005; Sapolsky, 2004). Here, we review the relationship between attachment and behavior outcomes at this interdisciplinary confluence with emphasis on underlying neuroethological mechanisms.

The opportunity to illustrate this disciplinary intersection comes from a somewhat unanticipated source: atypical behavior and developmental compromise in wild African elephants. Since the 1990s, significant changes from statistically normative behavior of wild elephants have been observed and linked to stressors that disrupt social processes: culls (systematic killing to control populations), poaching, herd manipulation, habitat fragmentation, and translocation (Bradshaw, Schore, Poole, Moss, & Brown, 2005; Owens & Owens, 2009; Slotow, van Dyk, Poole, & Klocke, 2000). Whereas developmental contexts and the effects of social disruptions on behavior are extensively documented for multiple species in clinical and *ex situ* studies (Silk, Scherer, & Hill Goldsmith, 2003; Topal et al., 2005), what has not been studied or hitherto observed, except for the most part as anecdotal, are these phenomena in free-ranging species. Excluding a few exceptions (e.g., primate infanticide; Hausfater & Blaffer Hrdy, 1984), abnormal behavior in the wild is sparsely studied.

Integrating ethology and psychology is nothing novel. Tinbergen himself spoke about the two disciplines differing mainly in focus (Tinbergen, 1951), and the seminal work on attachment by psychiatrist John Bowlby (1969) drew directly from ethology. However, until recently, drawing formal inferences from humans and extending them to animals has been judged, at best, as speculative (although exceptions exist; see Wrangham, Wilson, & Muller, 2006). By and large, cognitive and affective elements underlying human behavior models have been considered lacking in other species. New ethological data, brain imaging research, and an understanding of the evolutionary conservation of brain structures and mechanisms have lifted this restriction and lead to species-inclusive models (Berridge, 2003; Bradshaw & Finlay, 2005; Bradshaw & Sapolsky, 2006). Species differences remain and not all issues surrounding comparative study are erased. However, increasingly, the use of a common mammalian model is assumed where species differences are only noted when deemed significant (a convention we follow here).

The primary goal of this review is to describe the coalescence of theories of behavior across disciplines and the emergence of trans-species models of brain and behavior. The neuroethological analysis of nonnormative elephant behavior here illustrates how integrative models of psychobiology and ethology find congruence with what we already know about core psychophysiological homologies among all mammals (and birds; see Jarvis et al., 2005). Aggression (Blanchard & Blanchard, 1984) and attachment (Schore, 2003a, 2003b), both key elements in the elephant narrative, are specific examples whereby such cross-species research is well established. What may have appeared in the past to be behavioral isolates, now make up the fabric of a coherent conceptual framework for describing both humans and animals.

SOCIAL CONTEXT AND DEVELOPMENTAL MECHANISMS

Altricial avian and mammalian young are immersed in a social environment. Parents or alloparents (a set of caretaking affiliated siblings and adults; Lee, 1987) provide the primary external source of sensory input and regulation of all essential developmental processes that interact with genetics and greater environmental conditions (West, King, & White, 2003). Communication modalities of smell, taste, touch, vision, and sound and socio-affective interactions form the sensory matrix in which the infant is embedded, and from which the infant learns how to function (Goldstein, King, & West, 2003). How an organism initially develops in this context affects individual viability and adaptation success over the rest of the life span (Schore, 1994).

Sociality, of which attachment is a central feature, is envisioned as an evolutionary strategy to help maximize fitness in the face of complex social and environmental variability (Dunbar, 1998). Details of social exchange reflect successful adaptations necessary for infant survival through the process of maturation. What and how an individual learns is specific to the species and anticipated environmental demands. However, a great deal of flexibility exists in what and how traits are expressed. Individual survival and mortality depend on variations in rearing behavior, demographics, and environmental surroundings (Ha, Robinette, & Sackett, 1999), which in turn influence how, and to what degree, genetics are expressed (Curley & Keverne, 2005; Sapolsky, 2004).

Attachment is typically the first stage in socialization (Bowlby, 1969). Early social contexts are comprised of multiple dynamic processes having the potential for positive or negative values in terms of ecological and evolutionary significance (Stamps, 2003). Elephant matriarch age, associated with enhanced context, is a significant predictor of the number of calves produced by the family (McComb, Moss, Durant, Sayialel, & Baker, 2001). Levels and quality of sociality among adult females have been positively correlated with infant survival in primates and other species (e.g., elephants: Lee, 1987; baboons: Silk et al., 2003). Socialization quality influences fitness by affecting infant protection, stress levels, resource mobilization, and socio-ecological knowledge (Mesnick, 1997). It is now established that elephants, like humans, great apes, and dolphins, show highly complex behaviors such as self-awareness (mirror self-recognition; Plotnik, de Waal, & Reiss, 2006), an outcome of optimal attachment bonding and right brain development (Schore, 1994).

Social disruptions exceeding a certain level diminish fitness by decreasing the efficacy of social bond functions. Stressors that diminish parent–infant transactions or cause parental energy to divert from foraging, mating, infant care, and group participation (e.g., ecotourism, noise, perceived threats by hunters) are one example (Burke, 2005; Fowler, 1999). Neglectful, stressed, or abusive maternal behavior, hyperaggression, exaggerated fearfulness, infant abandonment, spontaneous abortions, and infanticide are stress-related behaviors that contribute to fitness and population declines (Ha et al., 1999; Owens & Owens, 2009; Silk et al., 2003). Significantly, social context and environmental quality directly map to neurobiological patterns and processes in the developing offspring, processes that are now understood to influence adults as well (Schore, 2003a, 2003b).

Vertebrates, and mammals in particular, share common socially mediated brain and behavioral development patterns (Berridge, 2003). Cortical and limbic structures responsible for processing and controlling emotional and social information and associated psychophysiological and behavioral traits (e.g., attachment, maternal behavior, facial recognition, play and sexual behavior, fear, aggression, extinction learning, and affect regulation) are all highly conserved evolutionarily across species (Fleming, O'Day, & Kraemer, 1999; Panksepp, 1998).

Mammalian brain development is experience-dependent and highly sensitive to environmental change (Meaney, 2001). Transactions between caregivers and offspring guide a finely tuned dialogue between social and neurobiological processes. In conjunction with the infant's own autonomic nervous system (ANS), these exchanges serve as primary regulatory mechanisms that govern behavior throughout life. Socially dominated development coincides with periods of rapid brain growth and neurobiological shaping of evolving affective and neuroendocrinological self-regulatory systems (Helmeke, Ovtscharoff, Poeggel, & Braun, 2001; Schore, 1994; Siegel, 1999). Not only does the caregiver's behavior guide the infant's stress responses through neuroethological patterning, but it does so through tissue-specific effects on gene expression (Meaney & Szyf, 2005).

Early social context parameters directly influence one of the most fundamental structures in behavior regulation—the hypothalamic-pituitary-adrenal (HPA) axis. Repeated HPA axis activation and associated elevated endogenous corticosteroids affected through stress can not only impair gene expression involved in neurogenesis and synaptogenesis (Karten, Olariu, & Cameron, 2005) but also compromise postnatally maturing brain circuits involved in mnemonic, cognitive, and affective regulatory functions (Ladd, Huot, Thrivikraman, Nemeroff, & Plotsky, 2004). Traumatic disruption from a single threatening event alone can create lifelong changes in social learning abilities and neural organization (Wiedenmayer, 2004). Direct (e.g., death of mother) or indirect (e.g., transmitted maternal stress; Francis, Diorio, Liu, & Meaney, 1999) compromise can induce sustained effects on brain plasticity and create a structural vulnerability for psychopathogenesis and even early death (Cirulli, Berry, & Alleva, 2003; Heim & Nemeroff, 1999).

Cross-species studies show that early rearing conditions affect both HPA axis autonomic functions and hemispheric development (Ronsaville et al., 2006). Specifically, neonatal social behavior associated with the HPA axis increases right hemisphere dominance (Tang, Reeb, Romeo, & McEwen, 2003). Preferential hemispheric development is significant because postnatally maturing orbital prefrontal areas in the early developing (Chiron et al., 1997) right brain are centrally involved in attachment, emotion, stress regulation, and the control of social behavior (Henry, 1993; Lyons, Afarian, Shatzberg, Sawyer-Glover, & Mosley, 2002; Sullivan & Dufresne, 2006). Early attachment trauma is thereby "affectively burnt in" the hierarchical apex of the limbic system and the HPA axis, the right frontal lobe (Stuss & Alexander, 1999). Altered sociality therefore translates to altered patterns in core survival functions that govern basic coping behavior and stress regulation abilities. Further, by such mechanisms, relational stress during gestational and postnatal periods can transmit across generations (Dettling, Feldon, & Pryce, 2002).

Stress effects manifest both intra-organismically (e.g., increased vulnerability to disease) and inter-organismically (e.g., asocial and atypical affiliative behaviors) through triggering hyperarousal in the limbic and autonomic nervous systems that support emotional behavior (Schore, 2003a). This is expressed biochemically in elevated levels of arousal-regulating catecholamines, corticotropin-releasing factor, and corticosteroids. It is also expressed behaviorally in one or more ways: a persistent fearful temperament (Adolphs et al., 2004); a diminished capacity to modulate memory, fear, and social judgment (Morris, Ohman, & Dolan, 1999); a predisposition to aggression dysregulation and violence (Rohlfs & Ramirez, 2006); and post-traumatic stress disorder (PTSD; Schore, 2002). Resulting impairment of socio-affective circuits, especially in higher cortical regions, underlie many abnormal and inappropriate emotional responses that express at later stages of life (Poeggel, Nowicki, & Braun, 2005).

Beyond altered behavior and biology of the affected individual, early experiences link evolutionarily. For example, epigenetic mechanisms contributing to brain lateralization and hemispheric specialization can offer an evolutionary advantage in survival (Vallortigara & Rogers, 2005). Ecological and evolutionary fitness are therefore directly related to the early relational quality through the shaping of neuroendocrinological pathways. As recent G × E (gene-by-environment interactions) research indicates (Curley & Keverne, 2005; Suomi, 2004), inheritance and experience are intertwined; and parental care is revealed as a critical agent of natural selection that influences the stabilization or elimination of corticolimbic connections during early critical periods (Schore, 1994). In summary, a psychobiological perspective reveals that stressful changes in context and normative patterns of sociality can have far-reaching and potentially maladaptive consequences. Early relational disruptions including neglect and abuse induce psychophysiological compromise and alterations leading to maladaptive responses to environmental cues later in life that transmit across generations (Ichise et al., 2006; McCormack, Sanchez, Bardi, & Maestripieri, 2006).

ALTERED SOCIAL CONTEXT EFFECTS IN WILD ELEPHANTS

Elephant social contexts are organized in nested sets of sustained relationships revolving around a natal family comprised of a matriarch and female allomothers (Lee, 1987). After weaning, females remain in the natal herd as they learn how to care for younger herd members, whereas young males, between the ages of 9 and 18 years, leave and enter a second phase of socialization in the company of an all-bull group or area (Lee & Moss, 1999).

In contrast to historical patterns and locales today such as Amboseli, Kenya, where herd structure is relatively intact, elephant social contexts are extremely altered as a result of anthropogenic disturbances (Nyakaana, Abe, Arctander, & Siegismund, 2001; Poole, 1989). Starvation, culls (systematic killing to control populations), poaching, habitat reduction and isolation, revenge killings, and translocations have severely altered traditional socialization patterns and skewed elephant demographics significantly (Abe, 1994; Poole, 1989). DNA studies show that selective hunting of older members has been so extensive to cause genetic shifts (Nykaana et al., 2001). In North Luangwa National Park in Zambia, 93% of the population has been killed and allomother contexts are largely absent. Females reproduce at much younger ages (48% of the births were by females less than 14 years compared with a normative mean age of first birth at 16 years). Group size and composition have drastically altered: Thirty-six percent of groups have no adult females, one quarter of the units consists of only a single mother and calf, and 7% of groups are sexually immature orphans (Owens & Owens, 2005, 2009). In Mikumi, Tanzania, 72% of the population was similarly affected; and in Uganda, elephants live in semipermanent aggregations of over 170 animals with many females between the ages of 15 and 25 years having no familial association or hierarchical structure (Aleper & Moe, 2006; Poole, 1989). Infants are largely reared by inexperienced, highly stressed, single mothers without the socio-ecological knowledge, leadership, and support that a matriarch and allomothers provide (Owens & Owens, 2009; Slotow & van Dyk, 2001).

Accompanying highly altered developmental contexts, elephants are exhibiting uncharacteristic behaviors and elevated stress (Table 7.1). Most astounding and statistically significant have been the killing of white (*Diceros bicornis*) and black (*Ceratotherium simu*) rhinoceroses (Slotow et al., 2000). Between 1991 and 2001, young male elephants killed 58 white rhinoceroses and 5 black rhinoceroses in Hluhluwe-Umfolozi National Park (HUP), and from 1992 and 1996, 49 white rhinoceroses in Pilanesberg National Park (PNP; Slotow, Balfour, & Howison, 2001). Prior to these elephant-caused deaths, median rhinoceros mortality was estimated at 3 per year (Slotow & van Dyk, 2001). In both parks,

TABLE 7.1 Elephant Developmental Context Alterations and Associated Behavior
(Eight Locations in Africa)

Location	Behavior	Altered Developmental Context Alteration and Associated Stressor	Reference
Pilanesberg National Park (PNP), SA	Interspecies hyperaggression, nonconsensual interspecies sex, and mortality; decreased affiliative behavior	Cull, translocation, inadequate herd structure, premature weaning	Slotow et al., 2000; Slotow & van Dyk, 2001; Garaï et al., 2004
Hluhluwe-Umfolozi National Park (HUP), SA	Interspecies hyperaggression, nonconsensual interspecies sex, and mortality	Cull, translocation, inadequate herd structure, premature weaning	Slotow et al., 2001; Slotow et al., 2000
Venetia Limpopo Nature Reserve, SA	Intraspecific aggression, decreased affiliative behavior in a confined group of juveniles, nervousness	Cull, translocation, confinement, loss of family, absence of mother figure	Garaï, 1997; EMOA database, 2006
Addo Elephant National Park, SA	Intraspecific hyperaggression and mortality	Extreme population density, patterns of irregular herd structure	Whitehouse & Hall-Martin, 2000; Whitehouse & Kerley, 2002
Zambia	Poor mothering and infant neglect, intraspecific hyperaggression	Severe poaching, single mother–infant, herd structure breakdown	Owens & Owens, 2005, 2009; Poole, 1989
Queen Elizabeth National Park (QENP), Uganda	Poor mothering and infant neglect, intraspecific hyperaggression	Severe poaching, herd structure breakdown	Abe, 1994; Nyakaana et al., 2001; Poole, 1989
Kenya	Apathy, diminished social skills, diminished mothering capabilities	Poaching, culls, accidental separations	D. Sheldrick, pers. comm.
Pongola Game Reserve, SA	Less vigilance toward offspring, no birth helping	Orphans, absence of experienced adult females	EMOA database, 2006

elephant demographics were very skewed. For instance, in HUP all of the 12 males were less than 14 years of age. In addition to the killing, young males were observed to attempt copulation with some of the rhinoceroses. No particular factor could be ascribed to the rhinoceroses that might have lead to the killings (Slotow et al., 2001; Slotow & van Dyk, 2001).

Nonnormative elephant behavior is not unknown, but it has been regarded as a condition of psychophysiological stress of captivity. The following are well doc-umented: infant rejection and neglect, elevated intraspecies and interspecies dysregulated aggression, anhedonia, depression, a suite of socio- and psycho-pathologies, distress vocalizations, movements, immunosuppression, and elevat-ed cortisol levels (Brown, Wielebnowski, & Cheeran, 2005). Now such behaviors associated with attachment disorders and symptoms characteristic of stress re-sponse dysregulation in vertebrates (Schore, 2003a, 2003b) are increasingly ob-served in the wild (Garaï, Slotow, Carr, & Reilly, 2004; Slotow et al., 2001; Slotow, van Dyk, Poole, & Klocke, (2000).

Historically, intraspecies and interspecies violence is uncommon (Hanks, 1979). Even during musth (the period when male elephants exhibit elevated ag-gression and high levels of testosterone and temporal gland secretion), male–male injury and mortality are relatively rare (Amboseli Elephant Trust, 2006). In Amboseli, mortality data over several decades reveal only 3 cases (6.1%) of adult (> 12 years) male–male killings out of 49 incidences where the cause of death was known. In contrast, significant intraspecific aggression is present where ele-phants have undergone intensive culling and confinement. For example, in Addo Elephant National Park in South Africa, intraspecific mortality has been recorded as high as 70% to 90% of adult male elephant deaths (Whitehouse & Kerley, 2002). Other indicators associated with intense socio-ecological distur-bance, including broken tusks and puncture wounds, and elevated corticosteroid metabolite concentrations, have also been observed (Foley, Papageorge, & Was-ser, 2001).

NEUROETHOLOGY OF ATYPICAL ELEPHANT BEHAVIOR

In all cases described, individuals exhibiting abnormal behaviors were either translocated cull orphans or progeny of cull survivors, or they were reared under highly irregular herd structures. The hyperaggressive cull orphans sustained multiple, major attachment disruptions and relational trauma (i.e., loss of moth-er and allomothers, premature weaning, witness to family deaths, herd dissolu-tion, translocation; Slotow et al., 2001) during periods when critical patterning of brain development occurs (Schore, 2003a). Neurobiologically, their hyperag-gression is consistent with an intense state of amygdala-hypothalamic sympathet-ic hyperarousal and a weakened higher right orbitofrontal inhibitory system associated with impaired developmental trauma (Rohlfs & Ramirez, 2006).

The absence of second-phase all-male socialization is also likely to have been a significant factor leading to affective dysregulation. When males join other bulls, they learn how to navigate complex social interactions and regulate sensory-chemical systems of communication that inform appropriate behavior and help provide social order. This all-male developmental phase is coincident with a sec-ond phase of major mammalian brain reorganization (Spear, 2000).

Relational trauma interferes with social learning that informs appropriate responses to environmental stimuli such as the ability to accurately detect species-shared emotional states and conspecific identities (Soltis, Leong, & Savage, 2005). Processes of intraspecies hormone detection are affected through compromise of right hemisphere amygdala-hypothalamic connections central to olfaction, emotional communication, and regulation of fear (Blonder, Bowers, & Heilman, 1991; Schore, 2002; Small et al., 1999). Attempts by young male elephants to copulate with rhinoceroses are behaviors associated with extremely elevated states of central and autonomic arousal when sensory-processing abilities become impaired and induce an inability to differentiate species-specific sexual signals from intraspecies aggressive pheromone signals (Rasmussen & Krishnamurthy, 2000). Behaviorally, such trauma-induced neuroendocrinological compromise is manifested as an abnormal fusion of affective, defensive, fear-motivated rage combined with elements of frustrated intense sexual drive. The adolescent elephants' elevated affective arousal states may have been particularly acute given the premature and sustained musth they entered in the absence of older bulls (Slotow et al., 2000). Although it is not certain whether all rhinoceros deaths were coincident with elephant musth, abnormal musth patterns and peaks in rhinoceros mortality were correlated (Slotow & van Dyk, 2001). The essential developmental roles that mature bulls fill was clearly demonstrated when older bulls introduced to the park quelled the young males' abnormally early musth cycles and interspecies aggression (Slotow et al., 2000).

In cases in which interspecific aggression appears to be absent but intraspecific mortality is high, a different neuroendocrinological paradigm underlying the aggressive behavior may be dominating. In these locations there has also been a history of social disruption, in particular affecting the male hierarchy; but unlike the other parks, these males are descendents, not necessarily direct recipients, of human-caused disturbances, namely severe hunting pressures and irregular herd demographics (Whitehouse & Hall-Martin, 2000). For example, there were only 2 mature bulls out of 11 elephants in the founder population in 1931 and 1 immature male. Between 1931 and 1938, there were 18 births, but by 1940 all 3 founder mature males had been killed. Offspring therefore received no older male socialization. Fence construction around the park perimeter in 1954 eliminated elephant–farmer conflict and the elephant population increased. However, although the herd was able to stabilize, an additional stressor might have been introduced with ever-decreasing habitat relative to population increases. Extraordinarily high levels of male mortality may therefore reflect a combination of factors that have altered normative social contexts: early trauma; abnormal attachment bonding; absence of male socialization; conditions of chronic, elevated stress created by inadequate habitat; and inability to avoid male-on-male conflict.

Developmental disruptions may have been particularly pronounced in males for another reason. Brain development occurs at a significantly slower rate in male mammals relative to females (Schore, 1994; Taylor, 1969) and therefore effects of developmental compromise are accordingly more pronounced. However, affective disorders in female elephants, although often less obvious (i.e., female internalizing versus male externalizing dysregulation; Schore, 2003a), have also been observed (Owens & Owens, 2005, 2009; Slotow, personal communication). Deviations from normal elephant behavior, namely, decreased maternal skills and infant neglect, have been noted particularly in areas where the loss of older social strata has been nearly complete (Table 7.1). The traumatic loss of the mother's psychobiological regulation during critical periods of infant female brain growth alters the developmental trajectory of successive generations (Champoux, Byrne, DeLizio, & Suomi, 1992). Such compromise strikes at the heart of elephant culture where the female natal herd functions as the central organizing process for elephant behavioral development. When the female matures, there is increased likelihood of not only her exhibiting impaired maternal behavior with her own offspring but also enduring deficits of stress regulation (Fleming, O'Day, & Kraemer, 1999; Meaney, 2001).

CONCLUSIONS

We have used abnormal behavior in wild elephants to illustrate how psychological theories of attachment and biological theories of developmental ecology can be used together to explain behavioral outcomes. Like psychology and neuroscience, ethology has shown an increased appreciation for the relationship between social attachment processes and behavioral patterns. Bringing psychology and ethology together with insights from neuroscience provides one way to relate observed behavior with models of endogenous (e.g., brain development) and exogenous (e.g., socio-ecological contexts) processes to better ascertain functional and proximal causation. This conceptual intersection profits all three disciplines.

For instance, only a few ethological studies have investigated the neuroethology of free-ranging social species. On the other hand, neuroscience has yet to fully explore the diversity of social systems involved in various species' social contexts. The well-documented principle that all mammals share a ubiquitous attachment mechanism that shapes a common stress-regulating neurophysiology clearly suggests that the heuristic model presented here applies to other species. An interdisciplinary perspective also contributes to helping effect a much-called-for inclusion of behavior into conservation (Linklater, 2004). Given continued selective pressures by human disruptions that affect biology and behavior in several ways (social learning, neurobiology, and genetics), it is worth considering long-term outcomes. In addition to sharing basic corticolimbic structures with other mammals, the African elephant has an extremely large and convoluted hippocampus, which is responsible for mediating long-term social memory (Hakeem, Hof, Sherwood, Switzer, & Allman, 2005). Disruptions affecting brain mechanisms central to processing socio-ecological knowledge thus affect how well successive generations are able to retain, represent, process, and communicate complex social information necessary for elephant group survival. We speculate that because of compromised maturation of the right brain through relational trauma that is engendered by capture and captivity, some elephants will not show evidence of complex behaviors such as self-recognition (Plotnik et al., 2006). This is a possible explanation for the apparent absence of this ability in some test subjects.

This raises another important point concerning phenotypic plasticity, or its lack, and the ability for elephant culture to restabilize. Elephant conservation measures are beginning to be revised to prevent disruptions to traditional developmental patterns whenever possible (e.g., translocation of family units versus single infants: Litorah, Omondi, Bitok, & Wambwa, 2001; restoration of social strata and age structures: Slotow et al., 2000). However, artificial reconstruction of normative social contexts has often failed to re-create much of the necessary social processes that rely so heavily on cross-generational fidelity (Garaï et al., 2004). The introduction of older bull elephants to quell the young male aggression attenuated symptoms at one park, but had limited success at another (Druce, Pretorius, Druce, & Slotow, 2006; Slotow et al., 2001; Slotow et al., 2000).

In light of developmental neuroethology, this outcome is not surprising. Although there is some evidence of reversibility (Sapolsky, 2004; Schore, 2003b), early attachment failures without adequate compensatory social structures for recovery are associated with a high risk for later disorders (Perry & Azad, 1999). The persistence of stress effects in the neurobiological substrate predicts that its symptoms are likely to resurface when stress or deprivation levels increase beyond a certain point (Schore, 2003a). Sudden changes in behavior or "problem animal" or "rogue" attacks that are increasingly noted are consistent with the etiology of post-traumatic stress disorder "flashbacks" (Bradshaw, Schore, Poole, Moss, & Brown, 2005).

There is a further concern that selection for asocial heritable traits in the absence of normal socialization structures may increase under such conditions of high stress and social disruption. Between 5% and 10% of a natural population in rhesus monkeys exhibited heritable tendencies for stress sensitivity that are correlated with chronic deficits in metabolic serotonin, a neurotransmitter involved in stress modulation. Under conditions of trauma or compromised bonding, these tendencies fail to be ameliorated and result in hyperaggressive behavior (Suomi, 2004): Evidence suggesting that genetic selection processes already affecting elephant populations with skewed population offtake may impose an added risk.

As perturbing as the data from Africa (and, increasingly, Asia) are, the altered behaviors of wild elephants have performed a significant task. They have opened a door that brings ethological, psychological, and neurobiological models together to gain deeper insights into the relationships between developmental contexts and behavior outcomes. The newfound facility to extend bidirectional inference across species brings an increased coherency to behavioral research, something that Tinbergen surely would have appreciated.

REFERENCES

Abe, E. L. (1994). *Behavioral ecology of elephant survivors in Queen Elizabeth National Park, Uganda.* Unpublished doctoral dissertation, Cambridge University, Cambridge, UK.

Adolphs, R. F., Gosselin, T. W., Buchanan, D., Tranel, P., Schyns, P., & Damasio, A. R. (2004). A mechanism for impaired fear recognition after amygdala damage. *Nature, 1433,* 68–72.

Aleper, D., & Moe, S. R. (2006). The African savannah elephant population in Kedepo Valley National Park, Uganda: Changes in size and structure from 1967–2000. *African Journal of Ecology, 44,* 157–164.

Amboseli Elephant Trust. (2006). Amboseli Elephant Research Project. Long-term records. Amboseli, Kenya.

Bateson, P. (2003). The promise of behavioural biology. *Animal Behaviour, 65,* 11–17.

Berridge, K. C. (2003). Comparing the emotional brains of humans and other animals. In R. J. Davidson, K. R. Scherer, & H. Hill Goldsmith (Eds.), *Handbook of affective sciences* (pp. 23–45). Oxford, UK: Oxford University Press.

Blanchard, D. C., & Blanchard, R. J. (1984). Affect and aggression: An animal model applied to human behavior. *Advances in the Study of Aggression, 1,* 1–62.

Blonder, L. X., Bowers, D., & Heilman, K. M. (1991). The role of the right hemisphere in emotional communication. *Brain, 114,* 1115–1127.

Bowlby, J. (1969). *Attachment.* London: Hogarth Press.

Bradshaw, G. A., & Finlay, B. L. (2005). Natural symmetry. *Nature, 435,* 149.

Bradshaw, G. A., & Sapolsky, R. M. (2006, November/December). Mirror, mirror. *American Scientist, 94,* 487–489.

Bradshaw, G. A., Schore, A. N., Poole, J. H., Moss, C. J., & Brown, J. L. (2005). Elephant breakdown. *Nature, 433,* 807.

Brown, J. L., Wielebnowski, N., & Cheeran, J. C. (2005). Evaluating stress and wellbeing in elephants: Are we doing all we can do to make sure elephants are well cared for? In C. Wemmer & C. Christen (Eds.), *Never forgetting: Elephants and ethics* (pp. 56–61). Baltimore: Johns Hopkins University Press.

Burke, T. (2005). *The effect of human disturbance on elephant behaviour, movement dynamics, and stress in a small reserve: Pilanesberg National Park.* Unpublished master's thesis, University of KwaZulu-Natal, Durban, South Africa.

Champoux, M., Byrne, E., DeLizio, R., & Suomi, S. J. (1992). Motherless mothers revisited: Rhesus maternal behavior and rearing history. *Primates, 33,* 251–255.

Chiron, C., Jambaque, I., Nabbout, R., Lounes, R., Syrota, A., & Dulac, O. (1997). The right brain hemisphere is dominant in human infants. *Brain, 120,* 1057–1065.

Cirulli, F., Berry, A. & Alleva, E. (2003). Early disruption of the mother–infant relationship: Effects on brain plasticity and implications for psychopathology. *Neurosciences and Behavioural Review, 27,* 73–82.

Curley, J. P., & Keverne, E. P. (2005). Genes, brains, and mammalian social bonds. *Trends in Ecology and Evolution, 20,* 561–567.

Davidson, R. J., Scherer, K. R., & Hill Goldsmith, H. (Eds.). (2003). *The handbook of affective neuroscience.* Oxford, UK: Oxford University Press.

Dettling, A. C., Feldon, J., & Pryce, C. R. (2002). Repeated parental deprivation in the infant Common Marmoset (*Callithrix,* Primates) and analysis of its effects on early development. *Biological Psychiatry, 52,* 1037–1046.

Druce, H., Pretorius, K., Druce, D., & Slotow, R. (2006). The effect of mature elephant bull introduction of ranging patterns of resident bulls: Phinda Private Game Reserve, South Africa. *Koedoe, 49*, 77–84.

Dunbar, R. I. M. (1998). The social brain hypothesis. *Evolutionary Anthropology, 6*, 178–190.

Elephant Management and Owners Association (EMOA) Database. (2006). Valwaater, South Africa.

Fleming, A. S., O'Day, D. H., & Kraemer, G. W. (1999). Neurobiology of mother–infant interactions: Experience and central nervous system plasticity across development and generations. *Neuroscience and Biobehavioral Reviews, 23*, 673–685.

Foley, C. A. H., Papageorge, S., & Wasser, S. K. (2001). Nonreproductive stress and measures of socio-ecological pressures in free-ranging African elephants. *Conservation Biology, 15*, 1134–1142.

Fowler, G. S. (1999). Behavioral and hormonal responses of Magellanic penguins (*Spheniscus magellanicus*) to tourism and nest site visitation. *Biological Conservation, 90*, 143–149.

Francis, D. J., Diorio, D., Liu, D., & Meaney, M. J. (1999). Nongenomic transmission across generations of maternal behaviour and stress responses in the rat. *Science, 286*, 1155–1158.

Garaï, M. E. (1997). *The development of social behavior in translocated juvenile elephants* (Loxodonta africanus). Unpublished doctoral dissertation, University of Pretoria, South Africa.

Garaï, M. E., Slotow, R. Carr, D., & Reilly, B. (2004). Elephant reintroductions to small fenced reserves in South Africa. *Pachyderm, 37*, 28–36.

Goldstein, M. H., King, A. P., & West, M. J. (2003). Social interaction shapes babbling: Testing parallels between birdsong and speech. *Proceedings of the National Academy of Sciences of the United States of America, 100*, 8030–8035.

Ha, J. C., Robinette, R. L., & Sackett, G. P. (1999). Social housing and pregnancy outcome in captive pigtailed macaques. *American Journal of Primatology, 47*, 153–163.

Hakeem, A. Y., Hof, O. R., Sherwood, C. C., Switzer, R. C., III, & Allman, J. M. (2005). Brain of the African elephant (*Loxodonta africana*): Neuroanatomy from magnetic resonance images. *Anatomical Record, 287A*, 1117–1127.

Hanks, J. (1979). *A struggle for survival: The elephant problem*. Cape Town, South Africa: Struik.

Hausfater, G., & Blaffer Hrdy, S. (Eds.). (1984). *Infanticide: Comparative and evolutionary perspectives*. New York: Aldine.

Heim, C., & Nemeroff, C. B. (1999). The impact of early adverse experiences on brain systems involved in the pathophysiology of anxiety and affective disorders. *Biological Psychiatry, 46*, 1509–1522.

Helmeke, C., Ovtscharoff, W., Jr., Poeggel, G., & Braun, K. (2001). Juvenile emotional experience alters synaptic inputs on pyramidal neurons in the anterior cingulate cortex. *Cerebral Cortex, 11*, 717–727.

Henry, J. P. (1993). Psychological and physiological responses to stress: The right hemisphere and the hypothalamo-pituitary-adrenal axis, an inquiry into problems of human bonding. *Integrative Physiological and Behavioural Science, 28*, 369–387.

Ichise, M., Vines, D. C., Gura, T., Anderson, G. M., Suomi, S. J., Higley, J. D., et al. (2006). Effects of early life stress on [^{11}A] DASB positron emission tomography imaging of serotonin transporters in adolescent peer- and mother-reared rhesus monkeys. *Journal of Neuroscience, 26,* 4638–4643.

Jarvis, E., Güntürkün, O., Bruce, L., Csillag, A., Karten, H., Kuenzel, W., et al. (2005). Avian brains and a new understanding of vertebrate brain evolution. *Nature Reviews Neuroscience, 6,* 151–159.

Karten, Y. J. G., Olariu, A., & Cameron, H. A. (2005). Stress in early life inhibits neurogenesis in adulthood. *Trends in Neuroscience, 28,* 171–172.

Ladd, C. O., Huot, R. L., Thrivikraman, K. V., Nemeroff, C. B., & Plotsky, P. (2004). Long-term adaptations in glucocorticoid receptor and mineralocorticoid receptor mRNA and negative feedback on the hypoathalamo-pituitary-adrenal axis following maternal separation. *Biological Psychiatry, 55,* 367–375.

Lee, P. C. (1987). Allomothering among African elephants. *Animal Behaviour, 35,* 278–291.

Lee, P. C., & Moss, C. N. (1999). The social context for learning and behavioural development among wild African elephants. In H. O. Box & K. R. Gibson (Eds.), *Mammalian social learning* (pp. 102–125). Cambridge, MA: Cambridge University Press.

Linklater, W. L. (2004). Wanted for conservation research: Behavioral ecologists with a broader perspective. *BioScience, 54,* 352–360.

Litoroh, M., Omondi, P., Bitok, E., & Wambwa, E. (2001). Two successful elephant translocations in Kenya. *Pachyderm, 31,* 74.

Lyons, D. M., Afarian, H., Shatzberg, A. F., Sawyer-Glover, A., & Mosley, M. E. (2002). Experience-dependent asymmetric variation in primate prefrontal morphology. *Behavioural Brain Research, 136,* 51–59.

McComb, K. C., Moss, C., Durant, S., Sayialel, S., & Baker, L. (2001). Matriarchs as repositories of social knowledge. *Science, 292,* 491–494.

McCormack, K., Sanchez, M. M., Bardi, M., & Maestripieri, D. (2006). Maternal care patterns and behavioral development of rhesus macaque abused infants in the first 6 months of life. *Developmental Psychobiology, 48,* 537–540.

Meaney, M. J. (2001). Maternal care, gene expression, and the transmission of individual differences in stress reactivity across generations. *Annual Reviews of Neuroscience, 24,* 1161–1192.

Meaney, M. J., & Szyf, M. (2005). Maternal care as a model for experience-dependent chromatin plasticity? *Trends in Neurosciences, 28,* 456–463.

Mesnick, S. L. (1997). Sexual alliances: Evidence and evolutionary implications. In P. A. Gowaty (Ed.), *Feminism and evolutionary biology: Boundaries, intersections and frontiers* (pp. 207–260). New York: Chapman & Hall.

Morris, J. S., Ohman, A., & Dolan, R. J. (1999). A subcortical pathway to the right amygdala mediating "unseen" fear. *Proceedings of the National Academy of Sciences of the United States of America, 96,* 1680–1685.

Nyakaana S., Abe, E. L., Arctander, P., & Siegismund, H. R. (2001). DNA evidence for elephant social behaviour breakdown in Queen Elizabeth National Park, Uganda. *Animal Conservation, 4,* 231–237.

Owens, D., & Owens, M. (2005, July). Comeback kids: Elephant "single moms" are struggling to recreate family life after the traumatic years of poaching. *Natural History,* p. 34.

Owens, D., & Owens, M. (2009). Early age reproduction in female elephants after severe poaching. *African Journal of Ecology, 47,* 214–222.

Panksepp, J. (1998). *Affective neurosciences: The foundations of human and animal emotions.* Oxford, UK: Oxford University Press.

Perry, B. D., & Azad, I. (1999). Post-traumatic stress disorders in children and adolescents. *Current Opinion in Pediatrics, 11*, 121–132.

Plotnik, J. M., de Waal, F. B. M., & Reiss, D. (2006). Self-recognition in an Asian elephant. *Proceedings of the National Academy of Sciences of the United States of America, 103*, 17053–17057.

Poeggel, G., Nowicki, L., & Braun, K. (2005). Early social environment interferes with the development of NADPH-diaphorase-reactive neurons in the rodent orbital prefrontal cortex. *International Journal of Neurobiology, 62*, 42–46.

Poole, J. H. (1989). The effects of poaching on the age structures and social and reproductive patterns of selected East African elephant populations. In *The ivory trade and the future of the African elephant: Volume II. Technical reports.* Prepared for the 7th CITES Conference of the Parties (pp. 1–73). Nairobi, Kenya.

Rasmussen, L. E. L., & Krishnamurthy, V. (2000). How chemical signals integrate Asian elephant society: The known and the unknown. *Zoo Biology, 19*, 405.

Rohlfs, P., & Ramirez, J. M. (2006). Aggression and brain asymmetries: A theoretical overview. *Aggression and Violent Behavior, 11*, 283–297.

Ronsaville, D. S., Municchi, G., Laney, C., Cizza, G., Meyer, S. E., Haim, A., et al. (2006). Maternal and environmental factors influence the hypothalamic–pituitary–adrenal axis response to corticotropin-releasing hormone infusion in offspring of mothers with or without mood disorders. *Development and Psychopathology, 18*, 173–194.

Sapolsky, R. (2004). Mothering style and methylation. *Nature Neuroscience, 7*, 791–792.

Schore, A. N. (1994). *Affect regulation and the origin of the self.* Mahwah, NJ: Erlbaum.

Schore, A. N. (2002). Dysregulation of the right brain: A fundamental mechanism of traumatic attachment and the psychopathogenesis of posttraumatic stress disorder. *Australian and New Zealand Journal of Psychiatry, 36*, 9–30.

Schore, A. N. (2003a). *Affect dysregulation and disorders of the self.* New York: Norton.

Schore, A. N. (2003b). *Affect regulation and the repair of the self.* New York: Norton.

Siegel, D. J. (1999). *The developing mind: Toward a neurobiology of interpersonal experience.* New York: Guilford Press.

Silk, J. B., Alberts, S. C., & Altmann, J. (2003). Social bonds of female baboons enhance infant survival. *Science, 302*, 1231–1234.

Slotow, R., Balfour, D., & Howison, O. (2001). Killing of black and white rhinoceroses by African elephants in Hluhluhe-Umfolozi, South Africa. *Pachyderm, 31*, 14–20.

Slotow, R., & van Dyk, G. (2001). Role of delinquent young "orphan" male elephants in high mortality of white rhinoceros in Pilanesberg National Park, South Africa. *Koedoe, 44*, 85–94.

Slotow, R., van Dyk, G., Poole, J., & Klocke, A. (2000). Older bull elephants control young males. *Nature, 408*, 425–426.

Small, D. N., Zald, D. H., Jones-Gotman, M., Zatorre, R. J., Pardo, J. V., Frey, S., et al. (1999). Human cortical gustatory areas: A review of functional neuroimaging data. *NeuroReport, 10*, 7–14.

Soltis, J., Leong, K., & Savage, A. (2005). African elephant vocal communication II: Rumble variation reflects the individual identity and emotional state of callers. *Animal Behaviour, 70*, 589–599.

Spear, L. P. (2000). The adolescent brain and age-related behavioral manifestations. *Neuroscience and Biobehavioral Reviews, 24*, 417–463.

Stamps, J. (2003). Behavioural processes affecting development: Tinbergen's fourth question comes of age. *Animal Behaviour, 66*, 1–13.

Stuss, D. T., & Alexander, M. P. (1999). Affectively burnt in: One role of the right frontal lobe. In E. Tulving (Ed.), *Memory, consciousness, and the brain: The Talin Conference* (pp. 215–227). Philadelphia: Psychology Press.

Sullivan, R. M., & Dufresne, M. M. (2006). Mesocortical dopamine and HPA axis regulation: Role of laterality and early environment. *Brain Research, 1076*, 49–59.

Suomi, S. J. (2004). How gene–environment interactions can influence emotional development in Rhesus monkeys. In C. E. Garcia-Coll, E. L. Bearer, & R. M. Lerner (Eds.), *Nature and nurture: The complex interplay of genetic and environmental influences on human behaviour and development* (pp. 35–51). Mahwah, NJ: Erlbaum.

Taborsky, M. (2006). Ethology into a new era. *Ethology, 112*, 1–6.

Tang, A. C., Reeb, B. C., Romeo, R. D., & McEwen, B. S. (2003). Modification of social memory, hypothalamic-pituitary-adrenal axis, and brain asymmetry by neonatal novelty exposure. *Journal of Neuroscience, 23*, 8254–8260.

Taylor, D. C. (1969). Differential rates of cerebral maturation between sexes and between hemispheres. *Lancet, 19*, 140–142.

Tinbergen, N. S. (1951). *The study of instinct.* London: Clarendon Press.

Tinbergen, N. S. (1963). On aims and methods of ethology. *Zeitschrift fur Tierpsychologie, 20*, 410–433.

Topal, J., Gacsi, M., Miklosi, A., Viranyi, Z., Kubinyi, E., & Csanyi, V. (2005). Attachment to humans: A comparative study on hand-reared wolves and differently socialized dog puppies. *Animal Behaviour, 70*, 1367–1375.

Vallortigara, G., & Rogers, L. J. (2005). Survival with an asymmetrical brain: Advantages and disadvantages of cerebral lateralization. *Behavioral and Brain Sciences, 28*, 575–633.

West, M. J., & King, J. A. (1987). Settling nature and nurture into an ontogenetic niche. *Developmental Psychobiology, 20*, 549–562.

West, M. J., King, J. A., & White, D. (2003). The case for developmental ecology. *Animal Behavior, 66*, 617–622.

Whitehouse, A. M., & Hall-Martin, A. J. (2000). Elephants in Addo Elephant National Park, South Africa: Reconstruction of the population's history. *Oryx, 34*, 46–55.

Whitehouse, A. M., & Kerley, G. I. H. (2002). Retrospective assessment of long-term conservation management of elephants in Addo Elephant National Park, South Africa. *Oryx, 36*, 243–248.

Wiedenmayer, C. P. (2004). Adaptations or pathologies? Long-term changes in brain and behaviour after a single exposure to severe threat. *Neurosciences and Behavioural Reviews, 28*, 1–12.

Wrangham, R. W., Wilson, M. L., & Muller, M. N. (2006). Comparative rates of violence in chimpanzees and humans. *Primates, 47*, 14–26.

CHAPTER 8

Attachment Trauma and the Developing Right Brain: Origins of Pathological Dissociation

The concept of dissociation has a long history of bridging psychiatry, psychology, and neurology. Because it is inextricably linked to the concept of trauma, theoretical and clinical models of dissociation have spanned the psychological and biological realms. Although the relationship between trauma early in the life span and dissociation was noted at the end of the 19th century, it is only recently that a developmental perspective has been used as a source of deeper understanding of the etiological mechanisms that underlie dissociation and dissociative disorders. Thus the problem of dissociation, like a broad spectrum of other clinical phenomena, is now being viewed through an interdisciplinary lens.

There is a growing appreciation that developmental models can make unique contributions to one of the fundamental problems of the human condition, psychopathogeneis. This applies to the problem of dissociation, which offers "potentially very rich models for understanding the ontogeny of environmentally produced psychiatric conditions" (Putnam, 1995, p. 582). In the following I will suggest that regulation theory (Schore, 1994, 2003a, 2003b)—which integrates developmental affective neuroscience, attachment theory, and psychiatry—can provide such models. Toward that end I will present the following: recent observations on infant behavior from developmental psychology, current data on brain development from neuroscience, updated basic research in biological psychiatry on stress mechanisms, and new information on the essential functions of the autonomic nervous system from developmental psychobiology in order to offer an interdisciplinary model of the etiology of pathological dissociation, as well as the psychoneurobiological mechanisms that underlie dissociation. As a paradigm case of dissociative disorder, I will use post-traumatic stress disorder, an Axis I environmentally produced psychiatric disorder. I will discuss the earliest expression of pathological dissociation in human infancy and its enduring impact on the experience-dependent maturation of the right brain, including the characterological use of dissociation at later points of interpersonal stress.

INTRODUCTION

Although an important distinction is made between nonpathological and pathological experiences of dissociation (Waller, Putnam, & Carlson, 1996), the focus of this chapter will be on the latter. Dissociation is defined in the *Diagnostic and Statistical Manual of Mental Disorders* (*DSM-IV*) as "a disruption in the usually integrated functions of consciousness, memory, identity, or perception of the environment" (American Psychiatric Association, 1994. In a parallel conception, the latest edition of the *International Classification of Diseases* (*ICD-10*) describes dissociation as "a partial or complete loss of the normal integration between memories of the past, awareness of identity and immediate sensations, and control of body movements" (World Health Organization, 1992). Notice that although both definitions stress a deficit in integration, only the second classification system refers to an alteration of bodily processes. And in another widespread definition, Spiegel and Cardeña characterize dissociation as "a structured separation of mental processes (e.g., thoughts, emotions, conation, memory, and identity) that are ordinarily integrated" (1991, p. 367). In contrast to the other sources, these authors include *emotion* in their definition.

The concept of dissociation, one of the most enduring in modern psychiatry, traces directly back to the work of Pierre Janet in the late 19th century. Janet (1887, 1889) defined (pathological) dissociation as a phobia of memories, expressed as excessive or inappropriate physical responses to thought or memories of old traumas. This dissociation of cognitive, sensory, and motor processes is adaptive in the context of overwhelming traumatic experience, and yet such unbearable emotional reactions result in an altered state of consciousness. Janet also described an *"abaissement du niveau mental"*: a lowering of the mental level, a regression down a hierarchy to a state that is constricted and disunified. Furthermore, Janet speculated that dissociation was the result of a *deficiency of psychological energy*. Due to early developmental factors, the quantity of psychological energy is lowered below a critical point, and thus individuals with pathological dissociation are deficient in binding together all their mental functions into an organized unity under the control of the self.

Following Charcot's work (1887), Janet also posited that a history of early trauma plays a fundamental role in the psychopathogenic origins of hysteria. Freud (1893/1955), who cited Janet in his early pre-psychoanalytic work, defined dissociation as a splitting of consciousness, frequently associated with bizarre physical symptoms. Although in his early writings Freud accepted the idea that developmental trauma is related to the characterological use of pathological dissociation, he later moved away from this idea and instead posited that repression, and not dissociation, was the primary mechanism of psychopathogenesis.

Summarizing the essentials of Janet's model, van der Kolk, Weisaeth, and van der Hart state:

> Janet proposed that when people experience "*vehement emotions*," their minds may become incapable of matching their *frightening experiences* with existing cognitive schemes. As a result the memories of the experience cannot be integrated into personal awareness; instead, they are split off [dissociated] from consciousness and voluntary control . . . extreme *emotional arousal* results in failure to integrate traumatic memories. . . . The memory traces of the trauma linger as unconscious "fixed ideas" that cannot be "liquidated". . . they continue to intrude as terrifying perceptions, obsessional preoccupations, and *somatic reexperiences*. (1996, p. 52, my italics)

Janet also speculated that traumatized individuals "seem to have lost their capacity to assimilate new experiences as well. It is . . . as if their personality development has stopped at a certain point, and cannot enlarge any more by the addition of new elements" (1911, p. 532). Translating the concept of personality into contemporary terms, van der Kolk, van der Hart, and Marmar conclude that "'Dissociation' refers to a compartmentalization of experience: Elements of a trauma are not integrated into a unitary whole or an integrated sense of *self*" (1996, p. 306, my italics).

At the very dawn of modern psychiatry, every major pioneer of the concept of dissociation, including not only Janet and Freud but also Charcot and Hughlings Jackson, was also interested in the underlying neurology of the phenomenon; that is, understanding dissociation in terms of structure-function relationships. Indeed, as noted by Devinsky (2000), late 19th-century clinicians linked specifically the right hemisphere with emotion (Luys, 1881) and dissociative phenomena (Myers, 1885; Richer, 1881). He cites Jackson's (1874/1958b) work on the duality of the brain, and the role of the right hemisphere in "emotional" speech, as opposed to "voluntary expression and conscious awareness of propositional speech" of the left hemisphere. Dissociative psychopathology continues to be of great interest to the epilepsy literature. Patients with intractable epilepsy show high rates of "dissociative convulsions" (De Wet, Mellers, Gardner, & Toone, 2003), and "dissociative pseudoseizures" are common sequelae of traumatic experiences (Harden, 1997), especially in patients with histories of sexual and physical abuse (Alper et al., 1997) and diagnoses of personality disorders and depression (Bowman & Markand, 1996).

Writing in the current neurological and neuropsychiatry literatures, Brown and Trimble (2000) refer back to the work of Janet and Freud and conclude that we now need to move beyond a purely descriptive approach: "The first goal must be to provide a precise definition of dissociation based on a conceptually coherent and empirically justified account of the processes underlying these phenomena" (p. 288). Other investigators are asserting "a precise definition of the term 'dissociation' must be established, based on a coherent and empirically checkable concept. Furthermore, it is important to discover the primary pathophysiologic mechanism that leads to the dissociative symptoms, using neurobiological research mechanisms" (Prueter, Schultz-Venrath, & Rimpau, 2002, p. 191).

Over the last few decades a small number of authors have offered neurobiological models of dissociation. Although these studies vary in terms of different psychiatric and neurological populations, all have been done on adults. Whitlock (1967) and Ludwig (1972) suggested that the primary pathophysiological mechanism involved in the creation and maintenance of dissociative symptoms is an attentional dysfunction resulting from an increase in the corticofugal inhibition of afferent stimulation. As a result of this inhibition, partially processed information fails to be integrated into awareness, thereby generating dissociative symptoms. More recently Krystal, Bremner, Southwick, and Charney (1998), Scaer (2001), and Nijenhuis, van der Hart, and Steele (2002) have offered contributions on the psychobiology of dissociation. And as I will discuss in upcoming sections, current neuroimaging research is adding greatly to our knowledge of the structure-function relationships of dissociation, though these too currently focus only on mature brain systems.

In psychological studies of adults, Loewenstein notes that "Dissociation is conceptualized as a basic part of the psychobiology of the human trauma response: a protective activation of altered states of consciousness in reaction to overwhelming psychological trauma" (1996, p. 312). And in neuropsychiatric research on adult trauma patients, Bremner and his colleagues demonstrate the following: that there are two subtypes of acute trauma response, hyperarousal and dissociation (1999); that dissociation represents an effective short-term strategy that is detrimental to long-term functioning (Bremner & Brett, 1997); and that exposure to extreme stress signals the invocation of neural mechanisms that result in long-term alterations in brain functioning (J. Krystal et al., 1998). Meares also concludes that in all stages "dissociation, at its first occurrence, is a consequence of a 'psychological shock' or high arousal" (1999, p. 1853).

In the following I will offer evidence to show that every one of these observations of dissociation in adults applies to dissociation as it occurs in infants. I will argue that developmental studies can offer not only specific models of how early trauma alters the ontogenetic trajectory and imprints a predisposition for later pathological dissociation, but also a deeper understanding of its underlying neurobiological mechanisms. And I will describe how the current point of contact of development, trauma, and dissociation is attachment theory, "the dominant approach to understanding early socioemotional and personality development during the past quarter-century of research" (Thompson, 1990, p. 145). Disorganized-disoriented insecure attachment, a primary risk factor for the development of psychiatric disorders (Main, 1996), has been specifically implicated in the etiology of the dissociative disorders (Chefetz, 2004; Liotti, 1992; Schore, 1997).

In longitudinal studies, attachment researchers demonstrate an association between traumatic childhood events and proneness to dissociation (Ogawa, Sroufe, Weinfield, Carlson, & Egeland, 1997).

Current models of the neurobiology of attachment are focusing on the impact of both regulated and dysregulated attachment experiences on the formation of the implicit self-system, located in the early maturing right brain (Schore, 1994, 2001a). Researchers are now asserting that an emphasis on fearful arousal and the relational modulation of that arousal lies at the heart of attachment theory, and that relational trauma triggers states of hyperarousal and dissociation in the developing brain. In later sections of this chapter I will cite studies to show that abuse and neglect, the first forms of survival threat to the developing infant, elicit dissociative defenses; these in turn negatively impact the critical growth period of cortical, limbic, brain stem, and autonomic centers in the right brain.

Recent developmental studies strongly support Janet's ideas about early trauma and dissociation, and clearly indicate that experiences with a traumatizing caregiver negatively impact the child's attachment security, stress coping strategies, and sense of self (Crittenden & Ainsworth, 1989; Erickson, Egeland, & Pianta, 1989). There is now a large and convincing body of evidence to show the following: that psychic trauma in childhood results in an arrest of affective development, whereas trauma in adulthood leads to regression in affective development (H. Krystal, 1988); and that the most significant consequence of early relational trauma is the lack of capacity for emotional self-regulation (Toth & Cicchetti, 1998), expressed in the loss of the ability to regulate the intensity and duration of affects (van der Kolk & Fisler, 1994). In total, this chapter presents an argument that these established principles of early emotional development must be incorporated into an overarching model of dissociation.

With this introduction in mind, in this chapter I will discuss how an interdisciplinary perspective can be used to generate a more complex model of dissociation and its role in psychopathogenesis. I will first present a brief overview of the neurobiology of a secure attachment, followed by the neurobiology of infant relational trauma and dissociation, and the developmental neuropsychology of dissociation found in type D disorganized attachment. In the latter sections of the chapter, I will discuss the role of right brain processes in dissociation at later stages of the life span and will end with some speculations about the basic biological mechanisms that mediate dissociation and the implications of this work for *DSM-V*.

THE NEUROBIOLOGY OF A SECURE ATTACHMENT

In the last decade significant advances have occurred in our knowledge of normal and abnormal social and emotional development. The essential task of the first year of human life is now seen as the creation of a secure attachment bond of emotional communication between the infant and the primary caregiver. In order to enter into this communication, the mother must be psychobiologically attuned to the dynamic crescendos and decrescendos of the infant's bodily based internal states of arousal. Within a context of visual-facial, gestural, and auditory-prosodic communications, each partner learns the rhythmic structure of the other and modifies his or her behavior to fit that structure, thereby co-creating a specifically fitted interaction. During mutual gaze episodes of bodily based affective communications, the spatiotemporal patterning of the primary caregiver's exogenous sensory stimulation is synchronized with the spontaneous expressions of the infant's endogenous organismic rhythms. This contingent responsivity allows her to appraise the nonverbal expressions of her infant's internal arousal and affective states, regulate them, and then communicate them back to the infant. To effectively accomplish this interactive regulation, the mother must modulate nonoptimal high *or* low levels of stimulation, which would induce supra-heightened or extremely low levels of arousal in the infant.

Research now clearly demonstrates that the primary caregiver is not always attuned and optimally mirroring, that there are frequent moments of mis-attunement in the dyad, or ruptures of the attachment bond. The disruption of attachment transactions leads to a regulatory failure and an impaired autonomic homeostasis. In this pattern of "interactive repair" following dyadic mis-attunement (Tronick, 1989) or "disruption and repair" (Beebe & Lachmann, 1994), the "good-enough" caregiver who induces a stress response through mis-attunement in a timely fashion reinvokes a re-attunement—a regulation of the infant's negatively charged arousal. This repair process allows the infant to cope with stressful negatively charged affects and to gain self-regulatory skills in the form of maintaining persistent efforts to overcome interactive stress.

If attachment is the regulation of interactive synchrony, attachment stress is defined as an asynchrony in an interactional sequence. In optimal interpersonal contexts a period of reestablished synchrony allows for stress recovery and coping. The regulatory processes of affect synchrony, which co-creates states of positive arousal, and interactive repair, which modulates states of negative arousal, are the fundamental building blocks of attachment and its associated emotions; and resilience in the face of stress is an ultimate indicator of attachment security. Attachment, the outcome of the child's genetically encoded biological predisposition and the particular caregiver environment, thus represents the regulation of biological synchronicity between and within organisms; and imprinting, the learning process that mediates attachment, is defined as synchrony between sequential infant–maternal stimuli and behavior.

Current research supports earlier proposals (Schore, 1994) that the long-enduring effects of the regulation embedded in the attachment relationship are due to their impact on brain development. In a number of writings I have suggested that the attachment mechanism is embedded in right hemisphere–to–right hemisphere regulated affective transactions between the primary caregiver and her infant (Schore, 1994, 2000, 2003a, 2003b). Due to the fact that these affective experiences are occurring in a critical period of right brain development, attachment experiences specifically impact emotion processing cortical and subcortical limbic and autonomic areas of the developing right cerebral hemisphere (Henry, 1993; Schore, 1994; Siegel, 1999; Wang, 1997).

This model accounts for a body of recent developmental neurobiological research. At 2 months of age—the onset of a critical period during which synaptic connections in the developing occipital cortex are modified by visual experience (Yamada et al., 1997; Yamada et al., 2000)—infants show right hemispheric activation when exposed to a woman's face (Tzourio-Mazoyer et al., 2002). The development of the capacity to efficiently process information from faces requires visual input to the right (and not left) hemisphere during infancy (Le Grand, Mondloch, Maurer, & Brent, 2003). Mutual gaze engages face-processing areas of the right hemisphere (Pelphrey, Viola, & McCarthy, 2004; Watanabe, Miki, & Kakigi, 2002); and the tendency of mothers to cradle infants on their left side "facilitates the flow of affective information from the infant via the left ear and eye to the center for emotional decoding, that is, the right hemisphere of the mother" (Manning et al., 1997, p. 327). With respect to the communication of gestural and auditory information, expressive gestures that express inner feeling states activate right hemispheric structures (Gallagher & Frith, 2004). Finally, the maternal response to an infant's cry, a fundamental behavior of the attachment dynamic, is accompanied by activation of the mother's right brain (Lorberbaum et al., 2002).

THE NEUROBIOLOGY OF RELATIONAL TRAUMA

In a relational growth-facilitating environment optimally regulated attachment communications directly influence the maturation of both the postnatally maturing central nervous system (CNS) limbic system, which processes and regulates social-emotional stimuli, and the autonomic nervous system (ANS), which generates the somatic aspects of emotion. In contrast to an emotionally responsive mother who down-regulates and repairs stressful negative arousal and up-regulates and amplifies positive arousal, the caregiver in a relational growth-inhibiting early environment induces traumatic states of enduring negative affect in the child and shows less interactive synchronous play with her infant. Because her attachment is weak, she provides little protection against other potential abusers of the infant, such as the father. This caregiver is inaccessible and reacts to her infant's expressions of emotions and stress inappropriately and/or rejectingly, and therefore shows minimal or unpredictable participation in the various types of arousal-regulating processes. Instead of modulating she induces extreme levels of stimulation and arousal, very high in abuse and/or very low in neglect. And because she provides no interactive repair, the infant's intense negative states last for long periods of time.

More specifically, the infant's psychobiological reaction to trauma is comprised of two separate response patterns, hyperarousal and dissociation (Perry,

Pollard, Blakley, Baker, & Vigilante, 1995; Schore, 1997). The first stage is described by Beebe in her observation of "mutually escalating overarousal" in a disorganized attachment pair:

> Each one escalates the ante, as the infant builds to a frantic distress, may scream, and, in this example, finally throws up. In an escalating overarousal pattern, even after extreme distress signals from the infant, such as ninety-degree head aversion, arching away . . . or screaming, the mother keeps going. (2000, p. 436)

In this initial stage of threat, an alarm or startle reaction is expressed, reflecting activation of the infant's right hemisphere, the locus of the startle mechanism (Bradley, Cuthbert, & Lang, 1996). This triggers a sudden increase of the sympathetic component of the ANS, resulting in significantly elevated heart rate, blood pressure, and respiration. Distress is expressed in crying and then screaming. Crying represents an autonomic response to stress, whereby the nucleus ambiguus of the right vagus excites both the right side of the larynx and the sinoatrial node of the heart (Porges, Doussard-Roosevelt, & Maiti, 1994).

The infant's state of "frantic distress," or fear-terror, is mediated by sympathetic hyperarousal, expressed in increased levels of the brain's major stress hormone, corticotrophin-releasing factor, which in turn regulates sympathetic catecholamine activity (Brown et al., 1982). Hence, brain noradrenaline activity in the locus coeruleus (Aston-Jones, Foote, & Bloom, 1984), as well as adrenaline and dopamine levels are significantly elevated, creating a hypermetabolic state within the developing brain. In addition, increased amounts of vasopressin are expressed; this hypothalamic neuropeptide associated with sympathetic activation is specifically released when an environment is perceived to be unsafe and challenging (Kvetnansky et al., 1989; Kvetnansky et al., 1990).

But a second later-forming reaction to infant trauma is seen in dissociation, in which the child disengages from stimuli in the external world and attends to an "internal" world. Traumatized infants are observed to be "staring off into space with a glazed look." Winnicott (1958) holds that a particular failure of the maternal holding environment causes a discontinuity in the baby's need for "going-on-being"; and Kestenberg (1985) refers to dead spots in the infant's subjective experience, an operational definition of the restriction of consciousness of dissociation. This same response is described by Tronick and Weinberg:

> [W]hen infants' attempts fail to repair the interaction infants often lose postural control, withdraw, and self-comfort. The disengagement is profound even with this short disruption of the mutual regulatory process and break in intersubjectivity. The infant's reaction is reminiscent of the withdrawal of Harlow's isolated monkey or of the infants in institutions observed by Bowlby and Spitz. (1997, p. 66)

The child's dissociation in the midst of terror involves numbing, avoidance, compliance, and restricted affect (the same pattern as for adult post-traumatic stress disorder, or PTSD).

This parasympathetic dominant state of conservation-withdrawal occurs in helpless and hopeless stressful situations in which the individual becomes inhibited and strives to avoid attention in order to become "unseen" (Schore, 1994, 2001b). In this state of passive withdrawal, although levels of the catecholamines noradrenaline and dopamine are reduced, serotonergic activity in the brain stem dorsal raphe nucleus is increased (Tops, Russo, Boksem, & Tucker, 2009). This metabolic shutdown state is a primary regulatory process, used throughout the life span, in which the stressed individual passively disengages in order "to conserve energies . . . to foster survival by the risky posture of feigning death, to allow healing of wounds and restitution of depleted resources by immobility" (Powles, 1992, p. 213). Note the similarity between this parasympathetic shutdown of metabolic energy and Janet's definition of dissociation as *deficiency of psychological energy*. It is this parasympathetic mechanism that mediates the "profound detachment" (Barach, 1991) of dissociation. If early trauma is experienced as "psychic catastrophe" (Bion, 1962), dissociation represents "detachment from an unbearable situation" (Mollon, 1996), "the escape when there is no escape" (Putnam, 1997), and "a last resort defensive strategy" (Dixon, 1998).

The neurobiology of the later-forming dissociative hypoarousal is different from that of the initial hyperarousal response. In this passive state, pain numbing and blunting endogenous opiates (Fanselow, 1986) are elevated. Furthermore, the dorsal vagal complex in the brain stem medulla is rapidly activated, decreasing blood pressure, metabolic activity, and heart rate, despite increases in circulating adrenaline. This elevated parasympathetic arousal, a survival strategy (Porges, 1997), allows the infant to maintain homeostasis in the face of the internal state of sympathetic hyperarousal. It is often overlooked that parasympathetic energy-conserving hypoarousal as well as sympathetic energy-expending hyperarousal represent states of Janetian "extreme emotional arousal."

Vagal tone is defined as "the amount of inhibitory influence on the heart by the parasympathetic nervous system" (Field, Pickens, Fox, Nawrocki, & Gonzalez, 1995). But it now known that there are two parasympathetic vagal systems: a late-developing "mammalian" or "smart" ventral vagal system in the nucleus ambiguus—which allows for the ability to communicate via facial expressions, vocalizations, and gestures via contingent social interactions—and a more primitive early developing "reptilian" or "vegetative" system in the dorsal motor nucleus of the vagus—which acts to shut down metabolic activity during immobilization, death feigning, and hiding behaviors (Porges, 1997). As opposed to the ventral vagal complex, which can rapidly regulate cardiac output to foster engagement and disengagement with the social environment, the dorsal vagal complex "contributes to severe emotional states and may be related to emotional states of 'immobilization' such as extreme terror" (Porges, 1997, p. 75).

There is now agreement that sympathetic nervous system activity manifests in tight engagement with the external environment and a high level of energy mobilization and utilization, whereas the parasympathetic component drives disengagement from the external environment and utilizes low levels of internal energy (Recordati, 2003). The traumatized infant's sudden state switch from sympathetic hyperarousal to parasympathetic dissociation is reflected in Porges' characterization of

> the sudden and rapid transition from an unsuccessful strategy of struggling requiring massive sympathetic activation to the metabolically conservative immobilized state mimicking death associated with the dorsal vagal complex. (1997, p. 75)

H. Krystal also describes the state switch from sympathetic hyperaroused terror into parasympathetic hypoaroused hopelessness and helplessness:

> The switch from anxiety to the catatonoid response is the subjective evaluation of the impending danger as one that cannot be avoided or modified. With the perception of fatal helplessness in the face of destructive danger, one surrenders to it. (1988, pp. 114–115)

As opposed to the nucleus ambiguus, which exhibits rapid and transitory patterns associated with perceptive pain and unpleasantness, the dorsal vagal nucleus shows an involuntary and prolonged characteristic pattern of vagal outflow. This prolonged state of dorsal vagal parasympathetic activation accounts for the extensive duration of "void" states associated with pathological dissociative detachment (Allen, Console, & Lewis, 1999).

DEVELOPMENTAL NEUROPSYCHOLOGY OF DISSOCIATION

How are the trauma-induced neurobiological and psychobiological alterations of the developing right brain to be expressed in the socioemotional behavior of an early traumatized toddler? In a classic study, Main and Solomon (1986) studied the attachment patterns of infants who had suffered trauma in the first year of life. This led to the discovery of a new attachment category, type D, an insecure-disorganized/disoriented pattern, one found in 80% of maltreated infants (Carlson, Cicchetti, Barnett, & Braunwald, 1989) and associated with prenatal and/or postnatal maternal alcohol or cocaine use (Espinosa, Beckwith, Howard, Tyler, & Swanson, 2001; O'Connor, Sigman, & Brill, 1987). Hesse and Main (1999) point out that the disorganization and disorientation of type D attachment phenotypically resembles dissociative states. Main and Solomon (1986) conclude that these infants are experiencing low stress tolerance and that the disorganization and disorientation reflect the fact that the infant, instead of finding a haven of safety in the relationship, is alarmed by the parent. They note that because the infant inevitably seeks the parent when alarmed, any parental behavior that directly alarms an infant should place the child in an irresolvable paradox in which he or she cannot approach, shift attention, or flee. At the most basic level, these infants are unable to generate a coherent active coping strategy to deal with this frightening emotional challenge.

Main and Solomon detailed the uniquely bizarre behaviors these 12-month-old infants show in the Strange Situation procedure. These episodes of interruptions of organized behavior are often brief, frequently lasting only 10 to 30 seconds, yet highly significant. For example, they show a simultaneous display of contradictory behavior patterns, such as "backing" toward the parent rather than approaching face-to-face.

> The impression in each case was that approach movements were continually being inhibited and held back through simultaneous activation of avoidant tendencies. In most cases, however, proximity-seeking sufficiently "over-rode" avoidance to permit the increase in physical proximity. Thus, contradictory patterns were activated but were not mutually inhibited. (1986, p. 117)

Notice the simultaneous activation of the energy-expending sympathetic and energy-conserving parasympathetic components of the ANS.

Maltreated infants also show evidence of apprehension and confusion, as well as very rapid shifts of state during the stress-inducing Strange Situation. Main and Solomon describe the child's entrance into a dissociated state:

> One infant hunched her upper body and shoulders at hearing her mother's call, then broke into extravagant laugh-like screeches with an excited forward movement. Her braying laughter became a cry and distress-face without a new intake of breath as the infant hunched forward. Then suddenly she became silent, blank and dazed. (1986, p. 119)

These behaviors generalize beyond just interactions with the mother. The intensity of the baby's dysregulated affective state is often heightened when the infant is exposed to the added stress of an unfamiliar person. At a stranger's entrance, two infants moved away from both mother and stranger to face the wall, and another "leaned forehead against the wall for several seconds, looking back in apparent terror" (Main & Solomon, 1986). These infants exhibit "behavioral stilling"—that is, "dazed" behavior and depressed affect, behavioral manifestations of dissociation. One infant "became for a moment excessively still, staring into space as though completely out of contact with self, environment, and parent." Another showed "a dazed facial appearance . . . accompanied by a stilling of all body movement, and sometimes a *freezing* of limbs which had been in motion." Yet another "fell face-down on the floor in a depressed posture prior to separation, stilling all body movements." Following up this work, Guedeney and Fermanian (2001) report an infant assessment scale of sustained withdrawal, associated with disorganized attachment, manifested in the following: a *frozen*, absent facial expression; total avoidance of eye contact; immobile level of activity; absence of vocalization; absence of relationship to others; and the impression that the child is beyond reach.

In addition to attachment studies, the state of dissociation has also been explored by developmental researchers using the still-face procedure, an experimental paradigm of traumatic abuse, specifically neglect (see Figure 8.1). In this experimental procedure, the infant is exposed to a severe relational stressor, as the mother, although maintaining eye contact with the infant, suddenly inhibits all vocalization and suspends any spontaneous emotionally expressive facial expression or gesture. This loss of dyadic regulation triggers an initial increase of interactive behavior and arousal in the infant. According to Tronick (2004), the infant's initial state of confusion and fearfulness at the break in connection is manifest in the cognition, "this is threatening." But this is soon followed by sad facial expression, gaze aversion, withdrawal, self-comforting behavior, loss of postural control, withdrawal, and ultimately bodily collapse.

Most interestingly, Tronick (2004) observes that this behavior is accompanied by a "dissipation of the infant's state of consciousness" and a diminishment of self-organizing abilities, which in turn reflect "the disorganization of many of the lower level psychobiological states, such as metabolic systems." Recall that dissociation, a hypometabolic state and a deficiency of psychological energy, has been defined in the *DSM-IV* as "a disruption in the usually integrated functions of consciousness" and described as "a protective activation of altered states of consciousness in reaction to overwhelming psychological trauma" (Loewenstein, 1996, p. 312). Tronick (2004) suggests that infants who have a history of chronic breaks of connections exhibit an "extremely pathological state" of emotional apathy, equated with Spitz hospitalism effects and Romanian orphans who fail to grow and develop. These infants ultimately adopt a communication style described as "stay away; don't connect." This defensive strategy reflects a state of very early forming yet already chronic pathological dissociation associated with loss of ventral vagal and dominance of dorsal vagal parasympathetic states.

Figure 8.1. An infant self-comforting and losing postural control in response to the mother's being still-faced. From Tronick (2004) .

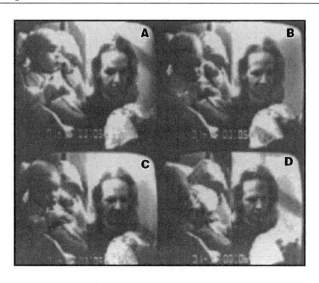

Note that the still-face induction of hyperarousal and dissociation occurs within the maternal–infant face-to-face context. The mother's face is the most potent visual stimulus in the child's world, and it is well known that direct gaze can mediate not only loving but also powerful, aggressive messages. In coding the mother's frightening behavior, Hesse and Main (1999, p. 511) describe, "in non-play contexts, stiff-legged 'stalking' of infant on all fours in a hunting posture; exposure of canine tooth accompanied by hissing; deep growls directed at infant." Thus, during the trauma, the infant is presented with an aggressive expression on the mother's face. The image of this aggressive face, as well as the chaotic alterations in the infant's bodily state that are associated with it, are indelibly imprinted into limbic circuits as a "flashbulb memory," and thereby stored in imagistic procedural memory in the visuospatial right hemisphere, the locus of implicit (Hugdahl, 1995) and autobiographical (Fink et al., 1996; Greenberg et al., 2005; Markowitsch et al., 2000) memory.

But in traumatic episodes the infant is presented with another affectively overwhelming facial expression, a maternal expression of fear-terror. Main and Solomon (1986) note that this occurs when the mother withdraws from the infant as though the infant were the source of the alarm; and they report that dissociated, trancelike, and fearful behavior is observed in parents of type D infants. Current studies show a link between frightening maternal behavior and disorganized infant attachment (Schuengel, Bakermans-Kranenburg, & Van IJzendoorn, 1999). In recent work, Hesse and Main observe that when the mother enters a dissociative state, a fear alarm state is triggered in the infant. The caregiver's entrance into the dissociative state is expressed as "parent suddenly completely 'freezes' with eyes unmoving, half-lidded, despite nearby movement; parent addresses infant in an 'altered' tone with simultaneous voicing and devoicing" (2006, p. 320). In describing the mother as she submits to the freeze state, Hesse and Main note:

> Here the parent appears to have become completely unresponsive to, or even aware of, the external surround, including the physical and verbal behavior of their infant. . . . [W]e observed one mother who remained seated in an immobilized and uncomfortable position with her hand in the air, blankly staring into space for 50 sec. (2006, p. 321)

I suggest that during these episodes the infant is matching the rhythmic structures of the mother's dysregulated states, and that this synchronization is registered in the firing patterns of the stress-sensitive corticolimbic regions of the infant's brain, especially in the right brain, that are in a critical period of growth. It is now established that maternal care influences both the infant's reactivity (Menard, Champagne, & Meaney, 2004) and defensive responses to threat "which serve as the basis for the transmission of individual differences in stress responses from mother to offspring" (Weaver et al., 2004, p. 847). In light of the fact that many of these mothers have suffered from unresolved trauma themselves, this spatiotemporal imprinting of the chaotic alterations of the mother's dysregulated state facilitates the downloading of programs of psychopathogenesis, a context for the intergenerational transmission of both trauma and the dissociative defense against overwhelming and dysregulating affective states that disorganize the nascent self-system.

RIGHT BRAIN PROCESSES AND DISSOCIATION
THROUGHOUT THE LIFE SPAN

In an early history of traumatic attachment, the developing infant/toddler is too frequently exposed to a massively mis-attuning primary caregiver who triggers and does not repair long-lasting, intensely dysregulated states. The growth-inhibiting environment of relational trauma generates dense and prolonged levels of negative affect associated with extremely stressful states of hyperarousal and hypoarousal. And so for self-protective purposes, the child severely restricts the overt expressions of an attachment need for dyadic regulation. The child thus significantly reduces the output of his or her emotion-processing, limbic-centered attachment system. When stressed, defensive functions are rapidly initiated that quickly shift the brain from interactive regulatory modes into long-enduring, less complex autoregulatory modes. These patterns are primitive strategies for survival that remain online for long intervals of time, periods in which the developing brain is in a hypometabolic state, detrimental to the substantial amounts of energy required for critical period biosynthetic processes. This hypometabolic brain state is responsible for dissociative "encoding failures" (Allen et al., 1999) of autobiographical memory of the developing self.

Attachment trauma between the infant and primary caregiver thereby sets the stage for the characterological use of primitive autoregulation, for the continuity of pathological dissociation over all later stages of human development. In accord with this model, Draijer and Langeland (1999) reported that specifically severe early maternal dysfunction is associated with the level of dissociation in psychiatric patients. This finding has been replicated in a study of the effects of childhood traumatization by Roelofs, Keijers, Hoogduin, Naring, and Moene (2002), who show that physical abuse and parental dysfunction by the mother—not the father—is associated with somatoform dissociative experience. In congruent findings, attachment studies reveal that individuals with the type D classification utilize dissociative behaviors in later stages of life (Van IJzendoorn, Schuengel, & Bakermans-Kranenburg, 1999). The characterological use of dissociation by certain personalities is described by Allen and Coyne:

> Although initially they may have used dissociation to cope with traumatic events, they subsequently dissociate to defend against a broad range of daily stressors, including their own posttraumatic symptoms, pervasively undermining the continuity of their experience. (1995, p. 620)

What is maladaptive about this psychic-deadening defense is not only that the individual shifts into dissociation at lower levels of stress but also that it finds difficulty in exiting the state of conservation-withdrawal. During these intervals it is shut down to the external relational environment, and thus totally closed and impermeable to attachment communications and interactive regulation—critical sources of possible further emotional development. Dissociative detachment (Allen et al., 1999) thus becomes an attractor state. Intimate social relationships are habitually appraised at a nonconscious level to be dangerous, because these contexts are always potential triggers of "vehement emotions." The avoidance of emotional connections, especially those containing novel and more complex affective information, prevents emotional learning, which in turn precludes any advances of right brain emotional intelligence (Schore, 2001a) or what Janet (1889) calls an "enlargement" of personality development.

A fundamental question that must be addressed in any developmental model of dissociation is what is the precise mechanism by which the early psychological events of "maltreatment-related" (Beer & De Bellis, 2002) or "pediatric" (Carrion et al., 2001) post-traumatic stress disorder affect the later behavior of the self-system as it develops at further stages of the life cycle? I suggest that a purely psychological conception cannot answer this question, and that a psychoneurobiological perspective that integrates both biological structure and psychological function is required to model how and why pathological dissociation becomes characterological in certain developing personalities.

During the first years of life when the right brain is growing (Trevarthen, 1996) and dominant (Chiron et al., 1997), adverse influences on brain development impact the right brain particularly. In the infant brain, states become traits (Perry, Pollard, Blakley, Baker, & Vigilante, 1995), and so the imprinting of early relational trauma—as well as dissociation, the major defense against attachment trauma—is embedded into the core structure of the evolving right brain. Indeed, there is now evidence to show that early relational trauma is particularly expressed in right hemisphere deficits. Recent studies reveal the following: that maltreated children diagnosed with PTSD manifest right-lateralized metabolic limbic abnormalities (De Bellis et al., 2000); and that adults severely abused in childhood (Raine et al., 2001) and diagnosed with PTSD (Galletly, Clark, McFarlane, & Weber, 2001) show reduced right hemisphere activation during a working memory task. This research supports van der Kolk's (1996) and my own (1997) earlier assertions that the symptoms of PTSD fundamentally reflect an impairment of the right brain, and Spivak et al.'s (1998) proposal that the right hemisphere plays a paramount role in perceptual and cognitive processing and in the regulation of biological responses in PTSD patients.

Neurobiological research thus suggests continuity over the course of the life span of the expression of not only the stress-coping deficits of PTSD but also the use of the primitive defense of pathological dissociation in patients with a history of relational trauma. The principle that severe attachment psychopathologies frequently access this "primitive" mode of autoregulation to cope with Janetian "vehement emotions" can be translated into the clinical tenet that in PTSD in infancy, childhood, and adulthood (and in other early forming severe pathologies of the self), the individual is cut off (disassociated) from experiencing intense affective states. Lane and his colleagues state that "traumatic stress in childhood could lead to self-modulation of painful affect by directing attention away from internal emotional states" (1997, p. 840). The right hemisphere is dominant not only for attachment regulation of affects but also for attention (Raz, 2004) and pain processing (Symonds, Gordon, Bixby, & Mande, 2006). Thus, the right brain strategy of dissociation represents the ultimate defense for blocking emotional pain.

This affective deficit ensues when attachment trauma induces an enduring impairment of what Emde (1983) terms the "affective core," the primordial central integrating structure of the nascent self, and Joseph (1992) describes as the "childlike central core," which maintains the self-image and all associated emotions, cognitions, and memories that are formed during childhood. Joseph localizes this core system in the right brain and limbic system. Recall Devinsky's (2000) assertion that optimal right hemispheric functions allow for the operations of "a coherent, continuous, and unified sense of self," and citation of 19th-century authors who postulated a connection between right hemispheric dysfunction and dissociation.

At the outset of this chapter, I stated my intention to use PTSD as a model system to study pathological dissociation and argued that dissociation as it occurs in adults also applies to dissociation as it occurs in infants. Both developmental (Perry et al., 1995; Schore, 1997) and adult (Bremner et al., 1999) studies support the propositions that there are two subtypes of acute trauma response in PTSD: hyperarousal and dissociative. I suggest that in all stages of life dissociation is a consequence of a "psychological shock" or high arousal (Meares, 1999) and that "at extremely high levels of arousal, coherent integration of sensory information breaks down and dissociative symptoms emerge" (J. Krystal et al., 1998). According to Gadea, Gomez, Gonzalez-Bono, Espert, and Salvador (2005), mild to moderate negative affective experiences activate the right hemisphere, but an intense experience "might interfere with right hemisphere processing, with eventual damage if some critical point is reached" (p. 136). This damage is specifically hyperarousal-induced apoptotic cell death in the hypermetabolic right brain. Thus, via a switch into a hypoarousal, a hypometabolic state allows for cell survival at times of intense stress (Schore, 2003a).

Current neuropsychiatric research indicates that both hyperarousal and dissociative responses are essentially right brain–driven processes. Metzger et al. (2004) report "PTSD arousal symptoms are associated with increased right-sided parietal activation" (p. 324). Similarly, Bonne et al. (2003) document "regional blood flow in right precentral, superior temporal, and fusiform gyri in posttraumatic stress disorder was higher than in healthy controls" (p. 1077), a finding that "may represent continuous preparatory motor activation, reflecting an increased basal level of anxiety and arousal." They suggest, "this may reflect a component common to all survivors of trauma" (p. 1081). Similarly, Rabe, Beauducel, Zollner, Maercker, and Karl (2006) report that PTSD patients show a pattern of right hemisphere activation that is associated with anxious arousal during processing of trauma-specific information. In perhaps the most extensive investigation, Lanius et al. (2004) observe that PTSD patients (as opposed to traumatized patients without PTSD) who experience traumatic memories with heart rate increases (an autonomic indicator of hyperarousal), show a pattern of right brain connectivity of activation of the right posterior cingulate, right caudate, right occipital, and right parietal lobe. They conclude that this right-lateralized pattern "may account for the nonverbal nature of traumatic memory in PTSD subjects" and cite other studies showing that "subjects who had experienced early trauma displayed . . . right dominance during memory recall" (p. 42).

Other recent studies reveal that dissociation in PTSD is also centered in right brain processes. In fMRI research Lanius and her colleagues (2002) studied PTSD patients while they were in a dissociative state, as reflected in a lack of increase in heart rate when exposed to their traumatic script. These authors note that

> activation effects in the superior and middle temporal gyrus, anterior cingulate, medial parietal lobe, and medial frontal gyres in the dissociated PTSD subjects were lateralized to the right side. The possibility that childhood trauma sets the stage for lateralized responses is given credence by report from Schiffer et al. (1995) who showed right hemisphere activation . . . during recall of unpleasant memories in adults with a history of childhood abuse. (p. 309)

They conclude "prefrontal and limbic structures underlie dissociative responses in PTSD" and state that activation of the right superior and middle temporal gyri in dissociated PTSD patients is consistent with a corticolimbic model of dissociation. In a more recent study, Lanius et al. (2005) report predominantly right-hemispheric frontal and insula activation in PTSD patients while they are dissociating; they assert that patients dissociate in order to escape from the overwhelming emotions associated with the traumatic memory, and that dissociation can be interpreted as representing a nonverbal response to the traumatic memory.

Gundel et al. (2004, p. 138) note that dissociating (and alexithymic) patients "have difficulties in integrating aspects of certain neuropsychological functions, namely memories and feelings, into current awareness." They propose that the right anterior cingulate "may represent the structural, neuroanatomical correlate of an active inhibitory system causing a down regulation of emotional processing during the . . . expressive aspects of emotion" (p. 138). Very similar findings are reported by Spitzer et al. (2004) in a transcranial magnetic stimulation study. These researchers state that their data confirm the idea that dissociation may involve

> a lack of integration in the right hemisphere. This corresponds with the idea that the right hemisphere has a distinct role in establishing, maintaining, and process-

ing personally relevant aspects of an individual's world. Thus a right hemispheric dysfunction might result in an altered sense of personally relevant familiarity, which resembles phenomenologically the dissociative symptoms of depersonalization and derealization . . . trauma-related conditions, which themselves are closely-associated with dissociative psychopathology, lack right hemispheric integration. (p. 167)

Citing the *DSM-IV* definition of *dissociation*, Spitzer et al. (2004) conclude, "In dissociation-prone individuals, a trauma that is perceived and processed by the right hemisphere will lead to a 'disruption in the usually integrated functions of consciousness'" (p. 168).

Supporting this right-lateralized model of dissociation, Brand et al. (2009) document right temporofrontal hypometabolism in cases of dissociative amnesia, which is clinically expressed as an inability to recall important personal information of a traumatic nature; a failure of integration of consciousness, emotion, and cognition; and a "constricted self." Overviewing a large body of laterality studies McGilchrist (2009) concludes, "Dissociation is . . . the fragmentation of what should be experienced as a whole—the mental separation of components of experience that would ordinarily be processed together . . . suggesting a right hemisphere problem" (p. 236). Mirroring this, Enriquez and Bernabeu (2008) offer experimental data showing "dissociation is associated with dysfunctional changes in the right hemisphere which impair its characteristic dominance over emotional processing" (pp. 272–273).

DYSREGULATION OF RIGHT-LATERALIZED LIMBIC-AUTONOMIC CIRCUITS AND DISSOCIATION

These studies reflect the ontogenetic development of an early dysregulated system and provide further evidence that prefrontal cortical and limbic areas, particularly of the right hemisphere, are central to dissociative response. More so than the left hemisphere, the right hemisphere is densely interconnected with limbic regions and subcortical areas that generate the physiological aspect of emotions, including fear-terror (Adamec, 1999; Adolphs, Tranel, & Damasio, 2001; Borod, 2000; Gainotti, 2000; Tucker, 1992). Hecaen and Albert (1978) have described the much overlooked importance of hierarchical vertical cortico-subcortical functional systems:

> Cortical neural mechanisms of one hemisphere would be responsible for a particular performance, and subcortical structures connected to these cortical zones would participate in the realization of the performance, creating a complex, corticosubcortical functional system specific to each hemisphere. (p. 414)

This "vertical" model of cortical-subcortical circuits directly applies to models of the right hemisphere, "the emotional brain":

Neural processing of emotions engages diverse structures from the highest to the lowest levels of the neuraxis. On the one hand, high-order association areas are necessary to understand the significance of an emotional situation, and on the other hand, low level structures must be activated to express the emotion through changes in the rhythm of peripheral organs. (Barbas, Saha, Rempel-Clower, & Ghashghaei, 2003)

These vertical circuits also account for the fact that the right hemisphere contains the major circuitry of emotion regulation (Brake, Sullivan, & Gratton, 2000; Porges et al., 1994; Schore, 1994; Sullivan & Dufresne, 2006).

I suggest that dissociation, a primitive coping strategy of affect regulation, is best understood as a loss of vertical connectivity between cortical and subcortical limbic areas within the right hemisphere. In contrast, J. Krystal et al. (1998) emphasize "shifts in interhemispheric processing" and "cortical disconnectivity" between higher frontal and limbic structures. Ontogenetically, however, dissociation appears well before the frontal areas of the cerebral cortex are myelinated and before callosal connections are functional (Bergman, Linley, & Fawcus, 2004; Schore, 2001a). Models of this early appearing defense against organismic threat, like models of PTSD hyperarousal and hypoarousal (Schore, 2002), must move down the neuraxis into the brain stem that generates states of arousal.

In a conception congruent with this vertical model, Scaer postulates that dissociation

is elicited by internal and external cue-specific stimuli, but because the threat itself has not been resolved, internal cues persist without inhibition from external messages of safety, and kindling is triggered in the *cortical, limbic, and brainstem centers.* (2001, p. 84, my italics)

Notice the reference not only to brain stem centers but also to *external and internal* cues, clearly implying top-down and bottom-up processing. It is now accepted that pathological dissociative detachment is a defensive state driven by fear, in which the stressed individual copes by pervasively and diffusely disengaging attention "from both the *outer and inner* worlds" (Allen et al., 1999, p. 164, my italics). In a similar conceptualization Putnam (1997) describes dissociation between "*an observing and experiencing ego.*" However, the dissociation literature has been vague about specifying the exact nature of the "inner world" and the "experiencing ego."

I have suggested that what is "experienced" are bodily states, and that the "inner world," the source of "internal cues," is more so than cognitions, the realm of bodily processes, central components of emotional states (Schore, 1994). According to Allen and his colleagues, "dissociatively detached individuals are not only detached from the environment, but also from the *self*—their *body*, their own actions, and their sense of *identity*" (p. 165, my italics). Recall the *ICD-10* definition of dissociation as "a partial or complete loss of the normal integration between memories of the past, *awareness of identity and immediate sensations, and control of body movements."*

More specifically, recent information about the autonomic nervous system, or what Jackson (1931) called the "physiological bottom of the mind," is central to a deeper understanding of the mind–body alterations of trauma and the mechanism of dissociation (Schore, 2001b, 2002). Indeed, the higher regulatory systems of the right hemisphere form extensive reciprocal connections with not only the limbic but also the sympathetic and parasympathetic branches of the autonomic nervous system (Aftanas, Savotina, Makhnev, & Reva, 2005; Critchley, Elliott, Mathias, & Dolan, 2000; Erciyas, Topaktas, Akyuz, & Dener, 1999; Spence, Shapiro, & Zaidel, 1996; Tucker, 1992; Yoon, Morillo, Cechetto, & Hachinski, 1997). Thereby, these systems control the somatic components of a variety of emotional responses, especially patterns of autonomic physiological responses to social stimuli. Adaptive right brain emotion processing is thus dependent upon the integration of the activities of the central (CNS) and the autonomic (ANS) nervous systems (Hagemann, Waldstein, & Thayer, 2003).

According to Porges at al. (1994), the lower right side of the brain stem that controls the ANS is innervated by the amygdala and unnamed higher limbic structures, and this "vagal circuit of emotion regulation" provides the primary central regulation of homeostasis and physiological reactivity. As the name suggests, Porges' model emphasizes the lower structures in a vertical system. Although he details the brain stem components, he refers to the higher structures as "cortex" that processes information from the social environment. And yet there is a clear implication of a bidirectional system, in which both top-down and bottom-up processes are responsible for adaptive regulatory functioning.

Benarroch (1997) has also described the concept of CNS-ANS limbic-autonomic circuits in his model of a central autonomic network (CAN), an internal regulation system through which the brain controls visceromotor, neuroendocrine, and behavioral responses. Like Porges' model, the CAN is a bidirectional hierarchical system, but here more of the detailed focus is on the higher limbic rather than the lower brain stem structures. The CAN is composed of limbic areas in ventromedial (orbital) prefrontal cortex; anterior cingulate, insula, and amygdala; diencephalic areas in the hypothalamus and brain stem structures in the periaqueductal gray matter; and the nucleus of the solitary tract and nucleus ambiguus in the medulla. Hagemann et al. (2003) characterize the CAN as

> a network of neural structures that generate, receive, and integrate internal and external information in the service of goal-directed behavior and organism adaptability. . . . These structures are reciprocally interconnected such that information flows in both directions—top-down and bottom-up. The primary output of the CAN is mediated through the preganglionic sympathetic and parasympathetic neurons. These neurons innervate the heart via the stellate ganglia and the vagus nerve. (pp. 83–84)

When this network is either completely uncoupled or rigidly coupled, the individual is less able to dynamically assemble the components of the network to meet an environmental challenge and is less adaptive; he or she therefore displays deficits in emotional expression and affect regulation. This finding leads back to the problem of psychopathogenesis—what events could be responsible for such deficits?

Authors are now describing the developmental process of "cerebral maturation in the vertical dimension" (Luu & Tucker, 1996). Both the ANS and the CNS continue to develop postnatally, and the assembly of these limbic-autonomic circuits (Rinaman, Levitt, & Card, 2000) is experience-dependent (Schore, 1994, 2001a). These experiences are provided in attachment transactions of the first and second years, in which the primary caregiver provides complex interpersonal stimuli and interactive affect regulation. Optimal early growth–facilitating environments that promote secure attachments allow for the organization of limbic-autonomic circuits and a right hemispheric limbic-modulated ventral vagal parasympathetic circuit of emotion regulation that mediates both emotion and communication processes (Porges et al., 1994).

Under stress, this complex system exhibits an adaptive capacity to modulate a flexible coping pattern in which homeostatic increases in the activity in one ANS division are associated with decreases in the other. An autonomic mode of coupled reciprocal sympathetic-parasympathetic control is behaviorally expressed in an organism that responds alertly and adaptively to a personally meaningful (especially social) stressor; yet as soon as the context is appraised as safe, it immediately returns to the relaxed state of autonomic balance. Thus, the ANS not only is sensitive to environmental demands and perceived stresses and threats but also will, in a predictable order, rapidly reorganize to different neural-mediated states (Porges, 2001).

In contrast to this developmental scenario is a disorganized-disoriented attachment context, wherein the traumatizing primary caregiver amplifies infant states of dysregulating hyperarousal and/or dissociative hypoarousal. This relational intersubjective context serves as a growth-inhibiting environment for the experience-dependent maturation of CNS-ANS links, which are more extensive on the right side of the brain. In this manner, as the title of this chapter denotes, dysregulation of the developing right brain is associated in the short term with traumatic attachment and in the long term with the psychopathogenesis of dissociation. An extensive apoptotic parcellation of vertical circuits in the developing right brain (especially between the prefrontal and subcortical areas) would lead to an inefficient regulation of the ANS by higher centers in the CNS, functionally expressed as a dissociation of central regulation of sympathetic and hypothalamic-pituitary-adrenal systems (Young, Ross, & Landsberg, 1984). I refer the reader to my previous writings on the neurochemistry of apoptosis and parcellation in the excessive pruning of the dendritic fields of fronto-limbic autonomic circuits (Schore, 1994, 2002, 2003a). My earlier proposal on the vulnerability of dendritic spines in the developing prefrontal cortex to maternal stressors is supported in recent research (Monroy, Hernández-Torres, & Flores, 2010; Pascual & Zamora-León, 2007).

This model of dissociation as a stress-induced disconnect between right brain CNS and ANS systems directly applies to the etiology and psychobiological mechanism of "somatoform dissociation," which is an outcome of early onset traumatization, often involving physical abuse and threat to life by another person. According to Nijenhuis (2000), somatoform dissociation is expressed as a lack of integration of sensorimotor experiences, reactions, and functions of the individual and his or her self-representation. Recall that optimal right hemispheric functions allow for the operations of "a coherent, continuous, and unified sense of self" (Devinsky, 2000).

Psychopathological regulatory systems thus contain poorly evolved CNS-ANS limbic-autonomic switching mechanisms that are inefficient or incapable of uncoupling and recoupling the sympathetic and parasympathetic components of the ANS in response to changing environmental circumstances. This "nonreciprocal mode of autonomic control" (Berntson, Cacioppo, & Quigley, 1991) shows an inability to adapt to stress; and the continued inhibition of internal systems that is inappropriate to a particular environmental situation essentially defines the coping limitations of pathological dissociation. In other words, dissociation reflects the inability of the right brain cortical-subcortical system to recognize and coprocess external stimuli (exteroceptive information coming from the relational environment) and on a moment-to-moment basis integrate them with internal stimuli (interoceptive information from the body, the corporeal self). Neuroscience writers now refer to "a dissociation between the emotional evaluation of an event and the physiological reaction to that event, with the process being dependent on intact right hemisphere function" (Crucian et al., 2000, p. 643).

An immature right brain circuit of emotion regulation would show deficits in "intense emotional-homeostatic processes" (Porges et al., 1994); that is, it would too easily default from fast-acting ventral vagal to slow-acting dorsal vagal systems in moments of "vehement emotions," and thereby be unable to adaptively and flexibly shift internal states and overt behavior in response to stressful external demands. Indeed, the ventral vagal complex is known to be defective in PTSD patients (Sahar, Shalev, & Porges, 2001), and this has been suggested to account for the basal hyperarousal and higher heart rates of these patients (Sack, Hopper, & Lamprecht, 2004). I suggest that under high stress an unstable ventral vagal system could be rapidly displaced by a dorsal vagal system and therefore account for the low heart rate of dissociative hypoarousal.

The disassociation of higher corticolimbic areas of the CAN internal regulation system and Porges' right brain circuit of emotion regulation would preclude top-down control of lower brain stem and autonomic functions and the adaptive integration of CNS exteroceptive and ANS interoceptive information processing. This disinhibition would also release lower control structures in the right amygdala. In classic writings, John Hughlings Jackson (1884/1958a) described this mechanism of the disorganization of the nervous system(s) as *dissolution*: "The higher nervous arrangements inhibit (or control) the lower, and thus, when the higher are suddenly rendered functionless, the lower rise in activity."

What do we now know about these higher control systems? In fact, current neuroimaging research has indicated that the highest level of control (regulatory) structures in the human brain is located in frontolimbic systems of the right hemisphere.

ESSENTIAL ROLE OF RIGHT FRONTOLIMBIC STRUCTURES IN THE REGULATION OF DISSOCIATION

Note that the neuroanatomy of the right brain allows for a reciprocal connection between the highest level of the limbic system, the orbitofrontal and medial frontal cortices, and the lower levels in the brain stem medullary vagal systems, which regulate parasympathetic hypoarousal and dissociation. A similar model is described by Phillips, Drevets, Rauch, and Lane (2003) as a "ventral" regulation system, including orbitofrontal cortex, insula, anterior cingulate, and amygdala. As opposed to a nonlimbic "dorsal" effortful regulation system in the dorsolateral cortex, hippocampus, and other structures involved in explicit processing of the "verbal components of emotional stimuli," this ventral system is important for the implicit identification of the emotional significance of environmental stimuli. It is central to the "automatic regulation and mediation of autonomic responses to emotional stimuli and contexts accompanying the production of affective states" (p. 510).

In previous works I have described a model of dual limbic-autonomic circuits, a hierarchical sequence of interconnected limbic areas in orbitofrontal cortex, insular cortex, anterior cingulate, and amygdala (Schore, 1994, 1996). Research now demonstrates that the organization of dendritic and synaptic networks in the orbitofrontal cortex, the anterior cingulate, and the amygdala is dramatically shaped by early relational emotional experience (Bock, Murmu, Fredman, Leshem, & Braun, 2008; Poeggel, Helmeke, et al., 2003; Schore, 1994). Each component of this "rostral limbic system" interconnects with the others and with brain stem bioaminergic arousal and neuromodulatory systems, including arousal-inducing noradrenaline neurons in the locus coeruleus and nucleus of the solitary tract (Aston-Jones et al., 1984), dopaminergic neurons in the ventral tegmental area, serotonin neurons in the raphe, and hypothalamic neuroendocrine nuclei, which regulate the sympathetic and parasympathetic nervous systems (Schore, 1994, 2003a, 2003b). Of particular importance are the highest levels of this vertical cortical-subcortical system, especially the orbitofrontal cortex, which monitors and controls responses initiated by other brain regions and is involved in the selection and active inhibition of neural circuits associated with emotional responses (Rule, Shimamura, & Knight, 2002). This prefrontal system performs a "hot'" executive function, regulating affect and motivation via control of basic limbic system functions (Zelazo & Muller, 2002).

According to Barbas and her colleagues (2003),

> Axons from orbitofrontal and medial prefrontal cortices converge in the hypothalamus with neurons projecting to brainstem and spinal autonomic centers, linking the highest with the lowest levels of the neuraxis. . . . Descending pathways from orbitofrontal and medial prefrontal cortices [anterior cingulate], which are linked with the amygdala, provide the means for speedy influence of the prefrontal cortex on the autonomic system, in processes underlying appreciation and expression of emotions. . . . Repetitive activation of the remarkably specific and bidirectional pathways linking the amygdala with the orbitofrontal cortex may be necessary for conscious appreciation of the emotional significance of events.

This top-down influence can be either excitatory or inhibitory, the latter expressed in the documented activation of the orbitofrontal cortex in defensive responses (Roberts et al., 2001). Recall Lanius et al.'s (2002) conclusion that prefrontal and limbic structures underlie dissociative responses in PTSD, and Gundel et al.'s (2004) proposal that the right anterior cingulate can act as an inhibitory system that triggers a down regulation of emotional processing, resulting in dissociation; that is, an inability to integrate feelings into conscious awareness.

Indeed, this limbic-autonomic circuit is right lateralized. The right orbitofrontal cortex, the hierarchical apex of the limbic system, comes to act as an executive control function for the entire right brain. The orbitofrontal areas of the right hemisphere are more critical to emotional functions than are those of the left (Tranel, Bechara, & Denburg, 2002). Within the orbitofrontal cortex, the lateral orbital prefrontal areas are specialized for regulating positive emotional states, whereas the medial orbitofrontal areas are specialized for processing negative emotional states (Northoff et al., 2000; Schore, 2001a). The functioning of these two limbic-autonomic circuits, one capped by the lateral orbitofrontal cortex and the other by the medial orbitofrontal cortex (which in earlier writings I termed the excitatory ventral tegmental limbic forebrain-midbrain circuit and the inhibitory lateral tegmental limbic forebrain-midbrain circuits, respectively; Schore, 1994) are organized in attachment experiences of the first and second year.

Optimal maturation of this prefrontolimbic system allows for the highest level of integration of exteroceptive and interoceptive information to take place in the brain. The right orbitofrontal cortex, in conjunction with the right anterior insula, supports a representation of visceral responses accessible to awareness, and provides a substrate for subjective feeling states and emotional depth and awareness (Craig, 2004; Critchley et al., 2004). In contrast to this, recall that pathological dissociation is defined in *ICD-10* as a loss of "awareness of identity and immediate sensations, and control of body movements." Just as secure attachment constrains trauma and dissociation, optimal functioning of the orbitofrontal system opposes somatoform dissociation.

Furthermore, the right prefrontal cortex, the "senior executive of limbic arousal" (Joseph, 1996), is most directly linked to stress-regulatory systems (Brake et al., 2000; Wang et al., 2005); therefore, it is essential for the regulation of the hyperaroused and hypoaroused states that accompany traumatic stress. Right-sided human prefrontal brain activation occurs during acquisition of conditioned fear (Fischer, Andersson, Furmark, Wik, & Fredrickson, 2002); and this cortical-subcortical regulatory mechanism allows for orbitofrontal modulation of the right amygdale, which is specialized for fear conditioning (Baker & Kim, 2004) and processing frightening faces (Adolphs et al., 2001; Whalen et al., 1998). The right amygdala directly projects to the brain stem startle center (Bradley et al., 1996; Davis, 1989), to the locus coeruleus, and to the dorsal motor vagal nucleus (Schwaber, Kapp, Higgins, & Rapp, 1982). And the amygdala's connections with the dorsolateral periaqueductal gray in the brain stem mediate the defensive freeze response (Oliveira, Graeff, Brandao, & Landeira-Fernandez, 2004; Vianna, Graeff, Brandao, & Landeira-Fernandez, 2001). In this manner, the right orbitofrontal cortex "organizes the appropriate cortical and autonomic response based on the implications of . . . sensory information for survival. The orbitofrontal cortex therefore functions as a master regulator for organization of the brain's response to threat" (Scaer, 2001, p. 78).

These data strongly suggest that an individual with an impaired or developmentally immature orbitofrontal system resulting from early relational trauma will be vulnerable to pathological dissociation under stress. LeDoux concludes that without orbital prefrontal feedback regarding the level of threat, the organism remains in an amygdala-driven defensive response state longer than necessary (Morgan & LeDoux, 1995), and that in humans, conditioned fear acquisition and extinction are associated with right hemisphere dominant amygdala function (La Bar, Gatenby, Gore, Le Doux, & Phelps, 1998). Such amygdala-driven startle and fear-freeze responses are intense, because they are totally unregulated by the orbitofrontal (and medial frontal) areas that are unavailable for the correction and adjustment of emotional responses. Indeed, neurological studies of adults confirm that dysfunction of the right frontal lobe is involved in PTSD symptomatology (Freeman & Kimbrell, 2001) and dissociative flashbacks (Berthier, Posada, & Puentes, 2001).

In classic neurological primate research, Ruch and Shenkin (1943) lesioned the orbitofrontal cortex (Brodman area 13) and observed a "definite reduction in emotional expression," and an elimination of fear and aggressive behaviors that were replaced by "gazing into the distance with a blank expression." Neurological patients with orbitofrontal damage show "dissociation among autonomic measures" and an altered response to a startle. Such patients show not an increase but a decrease in heart rate in anticipation of, or in response to, an aversive stimulus (Roberts et al., 2004). This is reminiscent of the deceleration of heart rate that has been observed in traumatized dissociating infants and dissociating adult psychiatric patients.

In support of earlier proposals (Schore, 1994), the following are now accepted: that orbitofrontal maturation is experience-dependent (Neddens, Brandenburg, Teuchert-Noodt, & Dawirs, 2001; Poeggel, Nowicki, & Braun, 2003); that human prefrontal function first emerges early in development, around the end of the first year (Happeney, Zelazo, & Stuss, 2004); and that conditions modifying early maternal variability in infancy produce "significant differences in right but not left adult prefrontal volumes, with experience-dependent asymmetric variation most clearly expressed in ventral medial cortex" (Lyons, Afarian, Schatzberg, Sawyer-Glover, & Moseley, 2002, p. 51). Furthermore, mild early stressful experiences that are challenging but not overwhelming increase myelination in ventromedial (and not dorsolateral) prefrontal cortex, the region that controls arousal regulation and resilience (Katz et al., 2009).

Relational trauma, on the other hand, represents not mild but severe and intensely stressful experience that triggers dissociation. During critical periods extensive hypometabolic states preclude optimal organization and thereby the functional capacity of the highest frontolimbic levels of the right brain. Pathological dissociation reflects an impairment of the affect regulatory functions of the higher centers in the orbitofrontal cortex. Through its connections with the ANS, the orbitofrontal system is implicated in "the representation of emotional information and the regulation of emotional processes" (Roberts et al., 2004, p. 307) and in "the conscious appreciation of the emotional significance of events" (Barbas et al., 2003). In contrast, in the dorsal vagal, parasympathetic dominant state of dissociation, the individual is cut off (disassociated) from both the external and the internal environment; therefore, emotions are not consciously experienced.

Although dissociation is triggered by subcortical mechanisms, it is regulated by higher corticolimbic centers. Pathological dissociation is the product of an inefficient frontolimbic system that cannot regulate the onset and offset of the dissociative response. Rather, for long periods of time, disinhibited lower subcortical centers, especially the right amygdala, drive the dissociative response, a mechanism that reflects a Janetian regression down a hierarchy to a constricted and disunified state. The integration of information from the external world and the internal world (especially "messages of safety") is a product of adequate orbitofrontal activity; and "such integration might provide a way whereby incoming information may be associated with motivational and emotional states to subserve processes such as selective attention and memory formation and retrieval" (Pandya & Yeterian, 1985, p. 51). Loss of orbitofrontal functions that maintain "the integration of past, present, and future experiences, enabling adequate performance in behavioral tasks, social situation, or situations involving survival" (Lipton, Alvarez, & Eichenbaum, 1999, p. 356) is reflected in pathological dissociation, defined in the DSM-IV as "a disruption in the usually integrated functions of consciousness, memory, identity, or perception of the environment." Indeed, patients using pathological dissociation who experience severe alterations of consciousness and loss of identity—dissociative identity disorder—show significant reduction of blood flow and therefore hypoactivation of the orbito-frontal cortices (Sar et al., 2007).

FURTHER SPECULATIONS ON THE BIOLOGICAL
MECHANISM OF DISSOCIATION

In the introduction to this chapter, I cited Prueter et al.'s (2002, p. 191) call for an understanding of the "primary pathophysiologic mechanism that leads to the dissociative symptoms, using neurobiological research mechanisms." Toward that end, in previous sections of this chapter I applied regulation theory to offer a model of the earliest psychobiological expression of dissociation in human infancy. I argued that this basic survival mechanism is a strategy for coping with intense states of energy-expending hyperarousal by shifting into an energy-conserving hypometabolic state, and that this state of hypoarousal—reflected in heart rate deceleration in response to stress—remains unchanged over the life span. This model is based in part on the developmental observations of Main (Hesse & Main, 1999; Main & Solomon, 1986), who asserts that the disorganization and disorientation of type D attachment phenotypically resembles dissociative states, and Tronick (Tronick, 2004; Tronick & Weinberg, 1997), who uses the still-face procedure as an experimental paradigm of traumatic abuse, a threatening interpersonal context that triggers "massive disengagement."

I have suggested that these paradigms used with infants under 1 year of age describe the same state of dissociation described by clinicians as "profound detachment" (Barach, 1991), "detachment from an unbearable situation" (Mollon, 1996), and "dissociative detachment" (Allen et al., 1999). At all points in the life span, the functional aspects of Janetian "extreme emotional arousal" and dissociation reflect a structural alteration in arousal systems in the brain stem associated with a loss of ventral vagal and dominance of dorsal vagal parasympathetic states. In this section I will offer further speculations about the basic biological mechanisms that underlie dissociation.

Studies of dissociation in the developmental literature report that under stress type D infants show "a dazed facial appearance . . . accompanied by a stilling of all body movement, and sometimes a *freezing* of limbs which had been in motion" (Main & Solomon, 1986). These experiences of traumatic freezing are encoded in enduring implicit-procedural memory, representing what Janet termed unconscious "fixed ideas" that cannot be "liquidated." Indeed, the relationship between freeze behavior and dissociation has been noted by authors in a number of disciplines. In psychophysiological research, Porges (1997) describes a trauma-induced "immobilized state" associated with the dorsal vagal complex. In one of the most important psychiatric texts on trauma written in the last century, Henry Krystal (1988) described a traumatic "catatonoid" affective response to "the perception of fatal helplessness in the face of destructive danger." He equates this "pattern of surrender" with the freeze response of animal states of "*cataleptic immobility*." In the trauma literature I have described this behavior in the "frozen watchfulness" observed in the abused child who waits warily for parental demands, responds quickly and compliantly, and then returns to her previous vigilant state, and to the "frozen state" of speechless terror seen in adult PTSD patients (Schore, 2001a).

In parallel neurological writings, Scaer (2001) postulates that dissociation "is initiated by a failed attempt at defensive/escape efforts at the moment of a life threat, and is perpetuated if spontaneous recovery of the resulting *freeze response* is blocked or truncated" (p. 84, my italics). In discussing this state of catatonic immobility and "suspended animation," he concludes,

> If deterrence of the threat through defense or fight fails, the animal enters a state of helplessness, associated by a marked increase in dorsal vagal complex tone, initiating the freeze/immobility response.... The extremes of vagal parasympathetic tone as manifested in the state of dorsal vagal activation, therefore, contribute greatly to the generation of severe emotions, especially those of terror and helplessness. Although freeze/immobility states . . . may be useful for short-term survival, prolongation or repeated activation of that state clearly has serious implications for health and long-term survival. (Scaer, 2001, p. 81)

A number of studies indicate that the freeze response is right lateralized. Primate studies by Kalin, Larson, Shelton, and Davidson (1998) show that freezing in infants, which is elicited by eye contact, correlates with extreme right frontal EEG activity and high basal cortisol levels. Basic research indicates that right parietal lesions are associated with a conditioned freezing deficit (Hogg, Sanger, & Moser, 1998). Human studies (Northoff et al., 2000) show a right lower prefronto-parietal cortical dysfunction in catatonia, a basic somatic defense mechanism associated with "immobilization of anxieties"—a description very similar to dissociation.

But other studies in the developmental literature, those of Tronick, describe not freeze behavior but a collapsed state of "profound disengagement" (see Figure 8.2). Tronick (2004) observes not only a suspension of any spontaneous emotionally expressive facial expression or gesture but also a "dissipation of the infant's state of consciousness," which is ultimately associated with "the disorganization of many of the lower level psychobiological states, such as metabolic system." How does this relate to the characterized freezing just mentioned? Keep in mind that the full manifestation of the fear-freeze response is a late occurring behavior in human infants, in the second half of the first year. But dissociation is seen in the hypoxic human fetus (Reed, Ohel, David, & Porges, 1999) and soon after birth (Bergman et al., 2004).

Again, clues come from studies in basic biology and neuroscience. Citing this literature, Scaer (2001) observes that freeze behavior is a state of alert immobility in the presence of a predator. He points out that freeze may proceed to flight or, if attacked and captured by a predator, to a "*deeper state of freeze*, one associated with apparent unresponsiveness and with marked changes in basal autonomic state" (p. 76, my italics). This state of helplessness, which lasts for up to 30 min-

FIGURE 8.2.   Close-up of the still-face induced collapse. From Tronick (2004) .

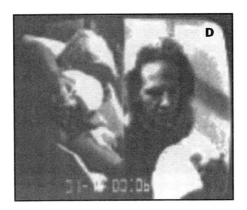

utes, is accompanied by marked bradycardia (heart rate deceleration) and a pronounced state of "deep" parasympathetic vagal tone. Recall that Porges (1997)
describes the involuntary and often prolonged characteristic pattern of vagal outflow from the dorsal vagal nucleus. I equate this with a deep dissociative state,
which, if prolonged, is the psychobiological engine of pathological dissociation.

Other studies in basic biology offer further information about the psychobiological mechanism of this deeper state of freeze. Gabrielsen and Smith (1985)
have explored the physiological responses that underlie basic defenses, defined
as "threat-induced behavior," in all animals. In reaction to an environmental
threat (a predator), an organism can respond in various ways: It can display offensive behavior, aggression (fight), or locomotor flight (associated with a fear
state). Both are associated with increased activity and heart rate tachycardia, reflective of states of sympathetic hyperarousal. In addition to the active defense of
fight–flight, these authors also describe two different types of parasympathetic
passive defenses: freezing and paralysis. These immobile and thus passive forms
of defense differ, in that freezing occurs to visual or auditory stimuli of predator
approach, whereas paralysis occurs in response to strong tactile stimulation by
the predator.

Intriguingly, the organism is alert in freeze, yet "unconscious" in paralysis;
and parasympathetic heart rate deceleration, which Gabrielsen and Smith
(1985) term emotional bradycardia, occurs in both. Biologists have described
this state as "fear bradycardia" or "alarm bradycardia" (Jacobsen, 1979). I suggest
that this differentiation of freeze versus paralysis describes the difference between
Scaer's freeze and deep freeze, and Main's type "D" freezing when the infant is
"alarmed by the parent" versus Tronick's still-face collapse, loss of postural control, and "dissipation of consciousness." In light of the fact that high levels of
dorsal vagal activation are associated with potentially life-threatening bradycardia, these data strongly suggest that lack of maternal interactive repair of infant

dissociative states of deep freeze would be a potent generator of psychopathogenesis. Recall that dissociation represents an effective short-term strategy that is detrimental to long-term functioning (Bremner & Brett, 1997).

Furthermore, Gabrielsen and Smith (1985) refer to another term for the deep freeze state—*feigned death*—a defense mechanism utilized by a number of vertebrates, amphibians, reptiles, birds, and mammals (including humans). In an animal model, the American opossum, a mild threat (the face of a human in this study) elicited freezing and a 12% decrease in heart rate. But a more severe threat (vigorous tactile shaking) induced death feigning and an immediate and more intense heart rate deceleration (46%, or 100 beats per minute decrease!). In a conception congruent with the neurobiological model of dissociation outlined in this chapter, Gabrielsen and Smith (1985) postulate that the suddenness of the depression in heart and respiration rates strongly indicates direct neural control by higher CNS structures on the parasympathetic cardiovascular centers in the medulla, and that this alteration reflects a severe decrease in oxygen consumption and body temperature.

I propose that the freeze response is a dorsal vagal, parasympathetic energy-conserving state coupled with but dominant over a weaker state of energy-expending sympathetic arousal, while in the collapsed state of death feigning the two ANS components are uncoupled. Thus in the deep freeze there is extremely minimal sympathetic activity (low levels of vasopressin, catecholamines, and cortisol) and almost entirely dorsal vagal activation, known to produce massive bradycardia (Cheng, Powley, Schwaber, & Doye, 1999) and a hypometabolic state. Furthermore, the decrease in oxygen consumption in dissociative death feigning is congruent with the role of the caudal hindbrain dorsal vagal system in hypoxic responses (Porges, 2001; Potter & McCluskey, 1986) and in the reptilian diving reflex, an energy-conserving strategy of heart rate deceleration that acts as a "metabolic defense" (Boutilier & St-Pierre, 2000; Guppy & Withers, 1999).

Parasympathetic vagal tone also increases during "entrance into hibernation, a long lasting disengagement from the external environment characterized by decreases in heart rate, breathing frequency, and metabolic rate" (Recordati, 2003, p. 4). The hypometabolic changes in brain plasticity (von der Ohe, Darian-Smith, Garner, & Heller, 2006) and in mitochondrial energy generation (Eddy, Morin, & Storey, 2006) during the hibernation state of torpor (apathy, low responsiveness) may thus be directly related to the neurobiological mechanism of dissociation. This shift into hypoxia also mediates "suspended animation" in developing systems (Padilla & Roth, 2001; Teodoro & O'Farrell, 2003). Entry into a hypometabolic state is a widespread survival strategy used by many organisms when challenged by environmental stress, and it has been characterized as "*putting life on pause*" (Storey & Storey, 2007, my italics). These data support my model of dissociation as a hypometabolic state (Schore, 2001b), a Janetian deficiency of psychological energy.

Note the similarity of this "emotional bradycardia" to the earlier psychoneurobiological portraits of the infant's parasympathetic-driven heart rate deceleration and dissociative response to attachment trauma, Kestenberg's (1985) dead spots in the infant's subjective experience, and Powles' (1992) state of conservation-withdrawal in which the stressed individual passively disengages by "the risky posture of feigning death." In the clinical literature, dissociation is characterized as "a last resort defensive strategy" (Dixon, 1998) and "a submission and resignation to the inevitability of overwhelming, even psychically deadening danger" (Davies & Frawley, 1994, p. 65).

CONCLUSIONS AND IMPLICATIONS FOR *DSM-V*

I began this chapter with a description of the concept of dissociation in the current *DSM-IV*, and I want to end with some thoughts about the implications of this work for the next edition of the *DSM*. We are currently experiencing a period of rapid change within and perhaps more importantly between the theoretical and applied sciences. The future *DSM-V* conception of dissociation should be substantially impacted by the advances in basic science and clinical knowledge that have occurred over "the decade of the brain." The following is a brief synopsis of the relevance of the interdisciplinary information outlined here not only for future research directions but also for models of more effective clinical diagnosis and practice.

This chapter has stressed the importance of not only a developmental understanding of dissociation but also a perspective that integrates biological structure and psychological function. With what we now understand about development and brain-behavior (structure-function) relationships, can we more precisely characterize this classic statement of Classen, Koopman, and Spiegel's?

> Trauma victims who lack the *cognitive and emotional structures* to immediately assimilate the experience use the state of consciousness known as dissociation to escape from the full psychological impact of the event. (1993, p. 29, my italics)

In other words, what is the relationship of cognition and emotion to dissociation, and can we identify these cognitive and emotional structures in known brain systems?

Cognitive Structures and Dissociation

Dissociation is defined in *DSM-IV* as a disruption in the usually integrated functions of consciousness, perception, and memory. Each of these three functions is cognitive, reflecting the dominance of cognition in current psychology, psychiatry, and neuroscience. With respect to memory, it is now well established that this cognitive function is not a single process, which should be reflected in the definition of dissociation in the next edition of the *DSM*. In fact, studies on trauma and dissociation have been an important contributor to the distinction between declarative-explicit-semantic memory and the conscious recall of traumatic experiences, and procedural-implicit-nonverbal memory and the unconscious organization of emotional memories and storage of conditioned sensorimotor traumatic responses. According to Scaer (2001), "Although declarative memory may account for much of the arousal-based cognitive symptoms of PTSD, procedural memory provides the seemingly unbreakable conditioned link that perpetuates the neural cycle of trauma and dissociation" (p. 76).

Recent data from developmental and affective neuroscience also bear upon the importance of implicit-procedural memory in dissociation. It has been noted that "the infant relies primarily on its procedural memory systems" during "the first 2 to 3 years of life" (Kandel, 1999), a period of right hemispheric dominance (Chiron et al., 1997). With respect to the long-term storage of relational trauma, Gaensbauer concludes, "The clinical data, reinforced by research findings, indicate that preverbal children, even in the first year of life, can establish and retain some form of internal representation of a traumatic event over significant periods of time" (2002, p. 259). This early representation is encoded in early maturing nonverbal implicit-procedural memory, before later-maturing verbal explicit-declarative memory processes are operational. Such representations of attachment trauma are encoded as a "frozen whole" (Gendlin, 1970). They include "nonverbal presymbolic forms of relating" that "protect the infant from trauma and continue to be used by patients to avoid retraumatization" (Kiersky & Beebe, 1994, p. 389); that is, the right brain defensive regulatory strategy of dissociation.

A growing body of studies now indicates that "the right hemisphere has been linked to implicit information processing, as opposed to the more explicit and more conscious processing tied to the left hemisphere" (Happaney et al., 2004, p. 7). Recall that pathological dissociative detachment "escapes conscious control and is often experienced passively, as automatic or reflexive" (Allen et al., 1999, p. 163). Although trauma seriously impairs left-lateralized declarative memory and hippocampal function, dissociative mechanisms are efficiently encoded in right-lateralized amygdala-driven implicit memory, which is primarily regulatory, automatized, and unconscious. Much has been written about the memory mechanisms of PTSD, and until recently the focus has been upon deficits in hippocampal function and impairments of conscious explicit memory. Stress-induced elevations of cortisol impair declarative memory (Kirschbaum, Wolf, May, Wippich, & Hellhammer, 1996), and the hippocampal dysfunction observed in PTSD is more lateralized to the left hemisphere (Mohanakrishnan Menon, Nasrallah, Lyons, Scott, & Liberto, 2003).

But current PTSD models are shifting from hippocampus to amygdala, from the explicit memory of places to the implicit memory of faces. Research demonstrates that chronic stress induces contrasting patterns of dendritic remodeling in hippocampal and amygdaloid neurons, leading to a loss of hippocampal inhibitory control, as well as a gain of excitatory control by the amygdala and thereby an imbalance in HPA axis function (Vyas, Mitra, Shankaranarayyana, Rao, & Chattarjai, 2002). This work is complemented by current clinical models of PTSD suggesting the following: that amygdala inhibition of hippocampal function at high levels of arousal mediates the diminution of conscious explicit memory in peritraumatic events (Layton & Krikorian, 2002), and that the amygdala is centrally involved in the consolidation of the traumatic experience and in the storage of perceptual implicit memory for trauma-related information (McNally & Amir, 1996).

It is important to note that more than explicit memory is impaired in dissociation—higher levels of implicit memory associated with intact orbital prefrontal function are also dysfunctional. J. Krystal and his colleagues are describing the disconnection that occurs under extremes of arousal *between* the explicit dorsal regulation system involved in the "verbal components of emotional stimuli" and the implicit ventral regulation system involved in the automatic regulation of emotional stimuli (Phillips et al., 2003). This results in manifestations of cognitive dissociation, but somatic dissociation and indeed the fundamental mechanism of pathological dissociation represent an impairment *within* the ventral regulation system and therefore a deficit in the implicit identification and regulation of autonomic responses and production of affective states.

Two common misunderstandings have confounded the dissociation literature. The first is that consciousness is frequently defined narrowly as reflective consciousness and correlated with left hemispheric verbal functions. But another form of consciousness exists—primary consciousness, which relates visceral and emotional information pertaining to the biological self to stored information processing pertaining to outside reality. Edelman (1989) lateralizes primary consciousness to the right brain. *Somatic dissociation thus fundamentally represents a disruption of primary consciousness.* A second common misunderstanding is that cognition equates to conscious verbal mentation, and because of this the left hemisphere is seen as the sole domain of cognition. But this is untrue. Cognition refers to the faculty of knowledge, but this knowing can be acquired through conscious *and* nonconscious processes. The appraisal of information about the external and internal environment occurs through nonconscious as well as conscious mechanisms.

In fact the right brain appraisal of safety or danger in the social environment is essentially performed implicitly at very fast time frames below conscious awareness (see Schore, 2003b, 2004, 2005). Thus, cognition also refers to the right-lateralized social cognition of face processing, which in a relational intersubjective context allows for the appraisal of exteroceptive social cues. In addition, interoceptive sensitivity (Barrett, Quigley, Moreau, & Aronson, 2004)—the tracking of somatovisceral information coming up from the body—is also a cognitive process. Both of these cognitive functions are operations of the right hemisphere, the locus of implicit learning (Hugdahl, 1995).

Pathological dissociation impairs implicit cognitive appraisals of the external world and the internal world. These data, which reflect a current shift from explicit to implicit memory and from the left to the right hemisphere, need to be incorporated into updated models of dissociation.

Right Brain Emotional Structures and Dissociation

In the present *DSM* clinical manifestations of dissociative disorders include amnesia for autobiographical information and derealization, definitions that like consciousness, memory, and perception reflect a heavy emphasis on cognition. However, another aspect of the current paradigm shift in psychology, psychiatry, and neuroscience is to affect and affect regulation. With this recent work on the primacy of affect, a common convergence of a number of disciplines—including developmental psychology, biological psychiatry, affective neuroscience, and psychoanalysis—indicates that emotion needs to be reincorporated into the DSM-V definition of dissociation. The contemporary revitalization of the work of Janet (Nemiah, 1989; Putnam, 1989; van der Hart, Nijenhuis, & Steele, 2006) clearly implies a return to a model in which "vehement emotions" and "extreme emotional arousal" are central, not secondary, to cognition. A large body of converging clinical studies and experimental research suggests that more so than cognition, *severe affect dysregulation lies at the core of the dis-integration that occurs in the dissociative response to overwhelming traumatic experience.*

The original Janetian conception of dissociation implies that the trigger for dis-integration is an appraisal of an overwhelming traumatic experience and an unbearable emotional reaction. In other words, what is disassociated is the structural system that is centrally involved in rapidly detecting and coping with an overwhelming survival threat and in processing unbearable, potentially dysregulating emotional information. This characterization applies to the right brain, which is dominant for the reception (Adolphs et al., 1996; Anderson & Phelps, 2000; Borod et al., 1998; George et al., 1996; Lucas, Schoenfield-McNeill, Weber, & Ojemann, 2003; Nakamura et al., 1999) and expression (Borod, Haywood, & Koff, 1997; Mandal & Ambady, 2004) of emotion. The right brain dominates as well in responding to preattentive negative emotional stimuli (Kimura, Yoshino, Takahashi, & Nomura, 2004), coping with negative affects (Davidson, Ekman, Saron, Senulis, & Friesen, 1990; Silberman & Weingartner, 1986), and controlling vital functions that support survival and enable the organism to cope with stressors (Wittling & Schweiger, 1993).

The human threat detection system is located in the subcortical areas of the right brain, especially in the right amygdala, which is specialized in the following: for detecting "unseen fear" (Morris, Ohman, & Dolan, 1999), for fear conditioning (Fischer et al., 2002), for stress and emotionally related processes (Scicli, Petrovich, Swanson, & Thompson, 2004), and for the expression of memory of aversively motivated experiences (Coleman-Mensches & McGaugh, 1995). In a study of predator stress-activation of specifically the right amygdala and periaqueductal gray, Adamec, Blundell, and Burton (2003) report, "these data implicate neuroplasticity in right hemispheric limbic circuitry in mediating long-lasting changes in negative affect following brief but severe stress" (p. 1264). The right amygdala is in turn regulated by the right insula, right anterior cingulate, and ultimately right orbitofrontal cortex. This latter prefrontal hierarchical apex of the limbic system is activated in "situations involving survival" (Lipton et al., 1999) and functions as "a master regulator for organization of the brain's response to threat" (Scaer, 2001. Indeed, "the right ventral medial prefrontal cortex plays a primary role in optimizing cautious and adaptive behavior in potentially threatening situations" (Sullivan & Gratton, 2002, p. 69).

Earlier in this chapter I described how secure attachment experiences allow for the maturation of the brain's major regulatory system in the right orbitofrontal cortex. Accordingly, the psychological principle that security of the attachment bond is the primary defense against trauma-induced psychopathology is directly related to the developmental neurobiological tenet that optimal secure attachment experiences facilitate the experience-dependent maturation of a right-lateralized affect regulatory system, which can ultimately efficiently modulate the extreme emotional arousal and vehement emotions of trauma. The capacity to consciously experience regulated negative (and positive) emotional states is profoundly adaptive, because affects act as internal evaluations of what is happening in an encounter with the environment (Lazarus, 1991) and allow for actual or expected changes in events that are important to the individual (Frijda, 1988).

In contrast, the relational context of a disorganized-disoriented insecure attachment acts as a growth-inhibiting environment that generates immature and metabolically inefficient orbitofrontal systems, thereby precluding higher complex forms of affect regulation. Under stress these immature prefrontal corticolimbic systems rapidly disorganize, disinhibiting lower subcortical systems that activate either states of hyperarousal or the primitive defense of dissociation that counterbalances these states. When dissociated from "top-down" orbitofrontal influences, an "exaggerated amygdala" response to masked facially expressed fearful reminders of traumatic events occurs in PTSD patients (Rauch et al., 2000). The characterological use of this "last resort defensive strategy" precludes the capacity to consciously experience affective states, and thereby forfeits their use in adaptive interpersonal and intraorganismic functioning and further emotional development.

The symptomatology of pathological dissociation can thus be conceptualized as a structural impairment of a right brain regulatory system and the resultant functional deficit of affect regulation. The clinical principle that dissociation is detrimental to long-term functioning (Bremner & Brett, 1997) is directly related to the developmental observations that early forming yet enduring disorganized, insecure attachment associated with dissociative states is a primary risk factor for the development of mental disorders (Hesse & Main, 1999; Main, 1996). It is also related to the neuropsychiatric observations that affect dysregulation and right hemisphere dysfunction play a prominent role in all psychiatric disorders (Cutting, 1992; Taylor, Bagby, & Parker, 1997).

Returning to Classen's dictum that individuals who lack the cognitive and emotional structures to assimilate trauma are predisposed to use dissociation, it is important to point out that efficient orbitofrontal function is essential not only for affect regulation but also for "the conscious appreciation of the emotional significance of events" (Barbas et al., 2003). Whereas in normal subjects the right orbitofrontal cortex shows "an enhanced response to consciously perceived, as opposed to neglected fearful faces" (Winston, Vuilleumier, & Dolan, 2003, p. 1827), a dysfunction of the right frontal lobe is seen in PTSD patients exhibiting dissociative flashbacks (Berthier et al., 2001).

The operations of the orbitofrontal system are also critical to the processing of cognitive-emotional interactions (Barbas, 1995). This "thinking part of the emotional brain" (Goleman, 1995) functions as an "internal reflecting and organizing agency" (Kaplan-Solms & Solms, 1996) that is involved in "emotion-related learning" (Rolls, Hornak, Wade, & McGrath, 1994). It acts to "integrate and assign emotional-motivational significance to cognitive impressions; the association of emotion with ideas and thoughts" (Joseph, 1996, p. 427) and "presents an important site of contact between emotional or affective information and mechanisms of action selection (Rogers et al., 1999. These data suggest that the cognitive and emotional structures that are lacking in dissociating trauma victims are located in the right orbitofrontal structure and its cortical and subcortical connections.

Both the current *DSM* and *ICD* definitions of dissociation refer to a traumatic disassociation of a normally integrated system, but neither source identifies this system. In 1994 I described the unique neuroanatomical interconnectivity of the right hemisphere:

> This hemisphere, with dense reciprocal interconnections with limbic and subcortical structures (Tucker, 1981), is specialized to regulate arousal (Levy, Heller, Banich, & Burton, 1983) and to *integrate perceptual processes* (Semmes, 1968). . . . It contains larger cortical areas than the left of intermodal associative zones that *integrate* processing of the three main sensory modalities (Goldberg & Costa, 1981). . . . This right hemisphere, more so than the left, is structurally specialized for greater cross-modal *integration* (Chapanis, 1977; Tucker, 1992), perhaps due to the facts that it contains more myelinated fibers that optimize transfer across regions than the left (Gur et al., 1980), and that it is specialized to represent multiple information channels in parallel (Bradshaw & Nettleton, 1981). (Schore, 1994, p. 308, my italics)

Recent studies demonstrate that when the intracortical connections within this hemisphere are functioning in an optimal manner, it adaptively integrates cross-sensory information and thereby subserves the integration of different representational information systems (Calvert, Hanses, Iversen, & Brammer, 2001; Raij, Utela, & Riita, 2000). However, under the extreme stress of both hyperarousal and hypoarousal, the right cortical hemisphere loses it capacity to integrate posterior sensory processing, thus causing the disruption in the integration of perceptual information depicted in the current *DSM-IV*. But in addition, under these intensely stressful periods, the right brain loses its capacity to act as an integrated vertical cortical-subcortical system.

In this condition, limbic-autonomic information is processed only at the lowest right amygdala level, blocked from access to higher right anterior cingulate and orbitofrontal areas; and so such "partially processed" information (Ludwig, 1972; Whitlock, 1967) cannot be integrated into awareness as a conscious, subjectively experienced emotion. Such "partially processed" somatic information is expresed as what Janet termed "excessive or inappropriate physical responses" and Freud described as "bizzare physical symptoms." The clinical description of dissociation thus describes the loss of this integrative capacity of the vertically organized emotional right brain.

The Right Brain Emotional-Corporeal Self and Somatic Dissociation

DSM-IV uses the term *identity* in its definition of dissociation. The contemporary traumatology literature prefers to use the term *self* (Schore, 1994, 2003a, 2003b). For example, van der Kolk (1996, p. 306) asserts that "Dissociation refers to a compartmentalization of experience: Elements of a trauma are not integrated into a unitary whole or an integrated sense of self." Similarly, in the psychoanalytic literature Kohut (1971) postulates a shattering of the self in trauma survivors, and H. Krystal (1988) states that the focus of treatment in trauma survivors is integration of the self. Developmentalists contend that experiences with a traumatizing caregiver negatively impact the child's attachment security, stress coping strategies, and sense of self (Crittenden & Ainsworth, 1989; Erickson et al., 1989).

The concept of self has also been absorbed into developmental neuroscience. Indeed, the self-organization of the right brain and the origin of the self have been an essential theme of my own writings (Schore, 1994, 2003a, 2003b). A central principle of this work dictates that "The self-organization of the developing brain occurs in the context of a relationship with another self, another brain" (Schore, 1996, p. 60). Decety and Chaminade (2003, p. 578) echo this in their assertion, "The sense of self emerges from the activity of the brain in interaction with other selves." These authors also conclude that "self-awareness, empathy, identification with others, and more generally intersubjective processes, are largely dependent upon . . . right hemisphere resources, which are the first to develop" (p. 591). Indeed the larger neuroscience literature is also very interested in the self. In fact, there is a growing consensus that "The self and personality, rather than consciousness, is the outstanding issue in neuroscience" (Davidson, 2002). Note the relevance of this statement to *DSM-IV*'s overemphasis on consciousness in its definition of dissociation.

It is currently thought that there are dual representations of self, one in each hemisphere. Verbal self-description is mainly a linguistic process associated with a left hemisphere advantage, whereas self-description in terms of affective tone is associated with a right hemisphere advantage (Faust, Kravetz, & Nativ-Safrai, 2004). This dual model is echoed in LeDoux's statement, "That explicit and implicit aspects of the self exist is not a particularly novel idea. It is closely related to Freud's partition of the mind into conscious, preconscious (accessible but not currently accessed), and unconscious (inaccessible) levels" (2002, p. 28). This dichotomy reflects the aforementioned link between the right hemisphere and nonconscious implicit processing, and the left with conscious explicit processing (Happaney et al., 2004). In support of earlier theoretical proposals on the relationship between right hemispheric operations and the implicit self (Schore, 1994), a substantial amount of current research indicates that the right hemisphere is specialized for generating self-awareness and self-recognition, and for the processing of "self-related material" (Craik al., 1999; Decety & Chaminade, 2003; Decety & Sommerville, 2003; Fossati et al., 2004; Frassinetti, Maini, Romualdi, Galante, & Avanzi, 2008; Kaplan, Aziz-Zadeh, Uddin, & Iacoboni, 2008; Keenan, Nelson, O'Connor, & Pascual-Leone, 2001; Keenan, Wheeler, Gallup, & Pascual-Leone, 2000; Kircher et al., 2001; Miller et al., 2001; Morita et al., 2008; Perrin et al., 2005; Platek, Keenan, Gallup, & Mohammed, 2004; Rosa, Lassonde, Pinard, Keenan, & Belin, 2008; Ruby & Decety, 2001; Uddin, Molnar-Szakacs, Zaidel, & Iacoboni, 2006).

According to Miller and his colleagues, "a nondominant frontal lobe process, one that connects the individual to emotionally salient experiences and memories underlying self-schema, is the glue holding together a sense of self" (2001, p. 821). Traumatic overwhelming emotional experiences dissolve this right frontal "glue" function that integrates the self. Keeping in mind the *DSM* definition of dissociation, Stuss and Alexander state that the right prefrontal cortex plays a central role in "the appreciation, integration, and modulation of affective and cognitive information" and serves as "a specific convergence site for all of the neural processes essential to affectively personalize higher order experience of self and to represent awareness of that experience" (1999, p. 223). Clearly, the major debilitating impact of trauma is on this right-lateralized implicit system, *not* on the language functions of the left hemisphere.

Devinsky (2000) argues that the emotion-processing right hemisphere plays an evolutionary role in "maintaining a coherent, continuous, and unified sense of self" and in "identifying a *corporeal* image of self." The concept of self clearly implies more than a mental conception, but rather a psychobiological, right-lateralized bodily based process. Lou et al. (2004) report "a role for the right lateral parietal region in representation of the physical Self" (p. 6831), and Decety and Chaminade (2003) show that the right inferior parietal cortex is involved in somatic experience related to awareness and, therefore, participates in the sense of self. The right temporoparietal junction integrates input from visual, auditory, somaesthetic, and limbic areas, and is thus "a pivotal neural locus for self-processing that is involved in multisensory body-related information processing" (Decety & Lamm, 2007, p. 580). The rostral part of the posterior parietal cortex sends efferents to the insular cortex (Cavada & Goldman-Rakic, 1989). As previously mentioned, the right anterior insula, in conjunction with the right orbitofrontal cortex, generates a representation of visceral responses accessible to awareness, thereby providing a somatosensory substrate for subjective emotional states experienced by the corporeal self (Critchley et al., 2004). This limbic structure, buried in the right temporal lobe, is centrally involved in visceral and autonomic functions that mediate the generation of an image of one's physiological state (Craig, Chen, Bandy, & Reiman, 2000).

These neurobiological data mirror the *ICD-10* description of dissociation as a partial or complete loss of control of body movements. Recall Crucian's (2000) description of a right hemisphere–dependent dissociation between the emotional evaluation of an event and the physiological reaction to that event, and Spitzer et al.'s (2004) observation that the dissociative symptoms of depersonalization reflects a lack of right hemispheric integration. In a study of "out-of-body" experiences, defined as episodes in which "a person's consciousness seems to become detached from the body and take up a remote viewing position," Blanke, Ortigue, Landis, and Seeck (2002, p. 269) report that "the experience of dissociation of self from the body is a result of failure to integrate complex somatosensory and vestibular function" (p. 269). Importantly, right medial temporal lobe activation is seen during the patient's dissociative episode (see Figure 8.3).

Thus, the assertion by neuroscience authors that "impaired self-awareness seems to be associated predominantly with right hemisphere dysfunction" (Andelman, Zuckerman-Feldhay, Hoffien, Fried, & Neufeld, 2004, p. 831) refers to a deficit in the right brain corporeal self during dissociative disruptions of identity. Scaer (2001) concludes that the least appreciated manifestations of traumatic dissociation are in the area of perceptual alterations and somatic symptoms. In earlier work I have offered a model by which attachment trauma alters the development of right-lateralized limbic-autonomic circuits that process visceral-somatic information and set the stage for the characterological predisposition to somatoform dissociation (Schore, 2001b, 2002). This chapter's contribution of regulation theory further elaborates this model and strongly indicates somatoform dissociation must be incorporated into *DSM-V*.

This model also gives important clues for identifying psychobiological markers of this manifestation of pathological dissociation. In previous sections of this

FIGURE 8.3.   Electrodes stimulated at right hemispheric sites trigger depersonalization reactions in a 43-year-old woman with right temporal lobe (starred) epilepsy. The site at which out-of-body experience, body-part illusions, and vestibular responses were induced is designated by the arrow. During these dissociative states, the patient states, "I see myself lying on the bed, from above, but I only see my legs and lower trunk." From Blanke et al., 2002 .

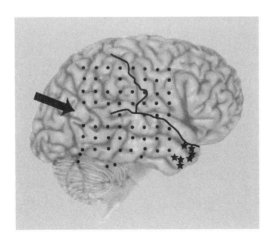

chapter, I have described the hypoarousal and heart rate deceleration of dissociating traumatized human infants and adults, and presented biological data to show that this passive defense mechanism is common to all vertebrates. In this "last resort defensive strategy," significant heart rate deceleration (bradycardia, an abnormal slowness of heart action) occurs in response to survival threat. This rapid shift from a hypermetabolic state of hyperarousal to a hypometabolic state of hypoarousal reflects a significant homeostatic alteration of brain–cardiovascular interactions through higher CNS adjustments of the sympathetic and especially the medullary dorsal vagal, parasympathetic energy-conserving branches of the ANS. The activation of "the escape when there is no escape," of somatic dissociation represents a reorganization of vertical circuits in the right hemisphere, which is dominant for cardiovascular (Erciyas et al., 1999; Yoon, Morillo, Cechetto, & Hachinski, 1997) and survival (Wittling & Schweiger, 1993) functions.

In traumatizing contexts in which active coping mechanisms are blocked or irrelevant and therefore nonadaptive, lateralized limbic-autonomic structures of the central autonomic network (ventromedial prefrontal cortex, anterior cingulate, insula, and amygdala) trigger an instantaneous reorganization of the vagal circuit of emotion regulation on the right side of the brain (Porges et al., 1994), specifically a shift in dominance from ventral vagal to dorsal vagal parasympathetic systems. Older basic research studies revealed orbitofrontal, cingulate, and insula control of bradycardia (Buchanan, Powell, & Valentine, 1984; Hardy & Holmes, 1988; Kaada, 1960). Tracing down this limbic-autonomic vertical circuit, each of these cortical structures, such as the central nucleus of the amygdala, regulates the lateral hypothalamus (Loewy, 1991); the lateral hypothalamus modulates dorsal vagal complex neurons (Jiang, Fogel, & Zhang, 2003); cardiac vagal motoneurons lateralized on right side of the medulla, down the right vagus, regulate the heart (Rentero et al., 2002); and ultimately parasympathetic efferent neurons that are primarily located in the right atrial ganglionated plexus (Stauss, 2003) trigger a hypometabolic response of "emotional bradycardia."

Porges (2001) describes this same pattern of disorganization, which occurs in "posttraumatic stress disorders and the consequences of child abuse":

> [W]hen mobilization strategies (fight–flight behaviors) are ineffective in removing the individual from the stressor and modulating stress, then the nervous system may degrade to a phylogenetically earlier level of organization. . . . (This) may reflect a neural strategy associated with immobilization (e.g. passive avoidance, death feigning, *dissociative states*) that would require a reduction of energy resources. (p. 15, my italics)

In earlier sections of this chapter, I have reported a number of clinical studies that indicate heart rate deceleration (parasympathetic emotional bradycardia) is a psychobiological marker of pathological dissociation. In addition to the work of Lanius et al. (2002), peritraumatic dissociation associated with low heart rate has also been reported by Griffin, Resick, and Mechanic (1997), Koopman et al. (2004), and Williams, Haines, and Sale (2003). In a clinical study, Schmahl and

FIGURE 8.4. As this patient diagnosed with PTSD and borderline personality disorder heard her trauma script, she displayed an intense emotional reaction and an increased heat rate of 7 beats per minute. While listening to an abandonment script, she dissociated. She had the impression that things were moving in slow motion, that things seemed unreal, and that she was watching the situation as an observer. She felt disconnected from her own body and the sense of her body felt changed. During this period, her heart rate fell by 7 beats per minute. After the interview, the dissociative state lasted for a few more minutes. From Schmahl et al., 2002 .

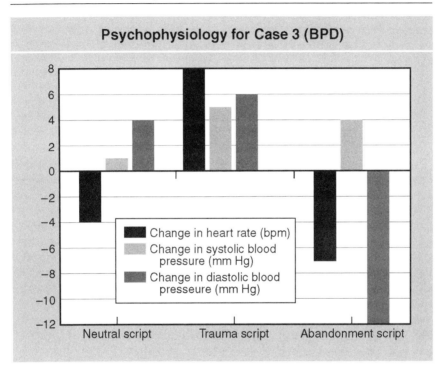

his colleagues (2002) document heart rate decline while a PTSD patient with a history of childhood physical and sexual abuse was dissociating (Figure 8.4).

Very recent studies have shown that the human right insula is activated by perceptual awareness of threat (Critchley, Mathias, & Dolan, 2002), anticipation of emotionally aversive visual stimuli (Simmons, Matthews, Stein, & Paulus, 2004), and harm avoidance (Paulus, Rogalsky, Simmons, Feinstein, & Stein, 2003). In normal functioning, the right insula supports a representation of visceral responses accessible to awareness (Critchley et al., 2004). On the other hand, neurological damage of the right insula in infancy is associated with abnormal bradycardia (Seeck et al., 2003). Increased right insula activity is also found in adult subjects with bradycardia (Volkow et al., 2000). These studies suggest that the right insula may play a key role in somatoform dissociation.

In summary, the developmental and neurobiological data suggest that the next edition of the *DSM* can specify a neuropsychobiological marker for somatic dissociation—heart rate deceleration in response to intersubjective contexts associated with nonconsciously perceived survival threat.

Early Attachment Trauma and the Psychopathogenesis of Dissociation

In the final part of this work, I would like to return to the problem of psychopathogenesis. Over 20 years ago, van der Kolk and van der Hart (1989) and Spiegel and Cardeña (1991) returned to the work of Janet and proposed that dissociation is fundamentally a response to "overwhelming" emotional experience, particularly in childhood. In an overview of the field at the end of the last century, a number of major theoreticians in traumatology echoed this conclusion. Putnam et al. (1996) asserted that "numerous clinical studies have established that elevated levels of dissociation are significantly associated with histories of antecedent trauma" (p. 673); and van der Kolk and his colleagues (1996) stated that "numerous studies have demonstrated a strong relation between trauma and dissociative symptoms" (p. 85). Indeed, a large body of research in the psychiatric and psychological literatures (e.g., Bowman & Markand, 1996; Chu & Dill, 1990; Coons, Bowman, Pellow, & Schneider, 1989; Draijer & Langeland, 1999; Gershuny & Thayer, 1999; Irwin, 1994; Lipschitz, Kaplan, Sorkenn, Chorney, & Asnis, 1996; Merckelbach & Muris, 2001; Mulder, Beautrais, Joyce, & Fergusson, 1998; Nash, Hulsey, Sexton, Harralson, & Lambert, 1993; Sanders, McRoberts, & Tollefson, 1989) and neurological literatures (Alper et al., 1997; Kuyk, Spinhoven, Van Emde Boas, & van Dyck, 1999) now supports the link between childhood trauma and pathological dissociation. Until recently most of these studies have focused primarily on sexual abuse; but currently the role of emotional neglect, physical abuse, and now attachment trauma is being emphasized.

Although these studies are convincing, the precise mechanism of how early trauma transmutes into a later predisposition to pathological dissociation has been unresolved. The important matter of how developmental traumatic psychological experience generates deficits of later adaptive functioning is, however, a central issue of the problem of psychopathogenesis. It is here that an interdisciplinary perspective can provide more detailed and complex models. Developmental psychopathology, an outgrowth of attachment theory, provides a theoretical perspective for "understanding the causes, determinants, course, sequelae, and treatment of psychopathological disorders by integrating knowledge from multiple disciplines within an ontogenetic framework" (Cicchetti, 1994, p. 286). Focusing upon longitudinal studies of the intergenerational transmission of trauma, developmental psychologists in this field have also demonstrated a link between developmental attachment trauma and dissociation (Dutra, Bureau, Holmes, Lyubchik, & Lyons-Ruth, 2009; Ogawa et al., 1997). Neuropsychiatrists in this area, working in developmental traumatology, have established that "the overwhelming stress of maltreatment in childhood is associated with adverse influences on brain development" (De Bellis et al., 1999, p. 1281).

My own work in developmental psychopathology integrates attachment theory, psychiatry, and developmental affective neuroscience in order to provide a multidisciplinary perspective to explore how attachment trauma alters the developmental trajectory of the right brain (Schore, 1994, 2003a, 2003b). From a developmental psychology viewpoint, the profound negative psychological effect of early abuse and neglect is the generation of a disorganized-disoriented attachment, which endures over the later stages of childhood, adolescence, and adulthood, and acts as a risk factor for later psychiatric disorders (Schore, 2001b). From a psychiatry viewpoint, "maltreatment-related" (Beer & De Bellis, 2002) or "pediatric" (Carrion et al., 2001) PTSD is the short-term negative effect, and a predisposition to later psychiatric disorders is the long-term effect. And from a developmental neuroscience viewpoint, the immediate detrimental impact is on critical period growth of the developing right brain, and the lasting impairment is an immature and functionally limited right brain capacity to regulate later life stressors that generate intense affective states. Note that all of these perspectives converge on the basic developmental principle that early trauma is critical to the genesis of an enduring predisposition to pathological dissociation.

In this and other contributions, I have offered extensive evidence to show that relational traumatic attachment experiences are "affectively burnt in" (Stuss & Alexander, 1999) limbic-autonomic circuits of the cortical and subcortical components of the right brain during its critical period of growth. Basic research in neuroscience and neuropsychiatry now firmly supports the following principles: that early adverse developmental experiences may leave behind a permanent physiological reactivity in limbic areas of the brain (Post, Weiss, & Leverich, 1994), that emotional and social deprivation interferes with the normal development of the synaptic architecture and leads to "neurological scars" that underlie "subsequent behavioral and cognitive deficits" (Poeggel & Braun, 1996; Poeggel et al., 1999); and that "early adverse experiences result in an increased sensitivity to the effects of stress later in life and render an individual vulnerable to stress-related psychiatric disorders" (Graham et al., 1999, p. 545). Although I have focused here on an Axis I psychiatric disorder, PTSD, in other works I have shown that this same developmental neurobiological description applies to the ontogeny of pathological dissociation in an Axis II environmentally produced psychiatric disorder: borderline personality disorder (Schore, 2003b, 2003c).

In the introduction to this further elaboration of regulation theory, I cited Brown and Trimble's (2000, p. 288) invocation for a more "precise definition of dissociation based on a conceptually coherent and empirically justified account of the processes underlying these phenomena." This chapter suggests that such a definition must include a developmental model of dissociative phenomena. In total the interdisciplinary data cited here indicate that the developing brain imprints not only the overwhelming affective states that are at the core of attachment trauma but also the early appearing primitive defense used against these affects—the regulatory strategy of dissociation. The developmental principle that maltreatment in childhood is associated with adverse influences on brain development specifically refers to an impairment of higher corticolimbic modulation of the vagal circuit of emotion regulation on the right side of the brain that generates the psychobiological state of dissociation. This model accounts for the findings that somatoform dissociation is specifically associated with maternal dysfunction, and that early onset traumatization expressed as emotional neglect and abuse and interpersonal threat to the body predicts somatoform dissociation. It also strongly supports Putnam's (1995, p. 582) assertion that dissociation offers "very rich models for understanding the ontogeny of environmentally produced psychiatric conditions."

Although it has been one of the most controversial issues in the history of psychiatry, psychoanalysis, and psychology, there is now solid evidence converging from a number of disciplines on the direct relationship between early trauma and pathological dissociation. And the next edition of the *DSM* should reflect this advance in our knowledge.

REFERENCES

Adamec, R. E. (1999). Evidence that limbic neural plasticity in the right hemisphere mediates partial kindling induced lasting increases in anxiety-like behavior: Effects of low frequency stimulation (Quenching?) on long-term potentiation of amygdala efferents and behavior following kindling. *Brain Research, 839*, 133–152.

Adamec, R. E., Blundell, J., & Burton, P. (2003). Phosphorylated cyclic AMP response element bonding protein expression induced in the periaqueductal gray by predator stress; its relationship to the stress experience, behavior, and limbic neural plasticity. *Progress in Neuro-Pharmacology & Biological Psychiatry, 27*, 1243–1267.

Adolphs, R., Damasio, H., Tranel, D., & Damasio, A. R. (1996). Cortical systems for the recognition of emotion in facial expressions. *Journal of Neuroscience, 23*, 7678–7687.

Adolphs, R., Tranel, D., & Damasio, H. (2001). Emotion recognition from faces and prosody following temporal lobectomy. *Neuropsychology, 15*, 396–404.

Aftanas, L. I., Savotina, N., Makhnev, V. P., & Reva, N. V. (2005). Analysis of evoked EEG synchronization and desynchronization during perception of emotiogenic stimuli: Association with automatic activation process. *Neuroscience and Behavioral Physiology, 35*, 951–957.

Allen, J. G., Console, D. A., & Lewis, L. (1999). Dissociative detachment and memory impairment: Reversible amnesia or encoding failure? *Comprehensive Psychiatry, 40*, 160–171.

Allen, J. G., & Coyne, L. (1995). Dissociation and vulnerability to psychotic experience. The Dissociative Experiences Scale and the MMPI-2. *Journal of Nervous and Mental Disease, 183*, 615–622.

Alper, K., Devinsky, O., Perrine, K., Luciano, D., Vazquez, B., Pacia, S., et al. (1997). Dissociation in epilepsy and conversion nonepileptic seizures. *Epilepsia, 38*, 991–997.

American Psychiatric Association. (1994). *Diagnostic and statistical manual of mental disorders* (4th ed.). Washington DC: Author.

Andelman, F., Zuckerman-Feldhay, E., Hoffien, D., Fried, I., & Neufeld, M. Y. (2004). Lateralization of deficit in self-awareness of memory in patients with intractable epilepsy. *Epilepsia, 45*, 826–833.

Anderson, A. K., & Phelps, E. A. (2000). Perceiving emotion: There's more than meets the eye. *Current Biology, 10*, R551–R554.

Aston-Jones, G., Foote, S. L., & Bloom, F. E. (1984). Anatomy and physiology of locus coeruleus neurons: Functional implication. *Frontiers of Clinical Neuroscience, 2*, 92–116.

Baker, K. B., & Kim, J. J. (2004). Amygdalar lateralization in fear conditioning: Evidence for greater involvement of the right amygdala. *Behavioral Neuroscience, 118*, 15–23.

Barach, P. M. M. (1991). Multiple personality disorder as an attachment disorder. *Dissociation, IV*, 117–123.

Barbas, H. (1995). Anatomic basis of cognitive-emotional interactions in the primate prefrontal cortex. *Neuroscience and Biobehavioral Reviews, 19*, 499–510.

Barbas, H., Saha, S., Rempel-Clower, N., & Ghashghaei, T. (2003). Serial pathways from primate prefrontal cortex to autonomic areas may influence emotional expression. *BMC Neuroscience, 4*, 25.

Barrett, L. F., Quigley, K. S., Moreau, E. B., & Aronson, K. R. (2004). Interoceptive sensitivity and self-reports of emotional experience. *Journal of Personality and Social Psychology, 87*, 684–697.

Beebe, B. (2000). Co-constructing mother–infant distress: The microsynchrony of maternal impingement and infant avoidance in the face-to-face encounter. *Psychoanalytic Inquiry, 20*, 412–440.

Beebe, B., & Lachmann, F. M. (1994). Representations and internalization in infancy: Three principles of salience. *Psychoanalytic Psychology, 11*, 127–165.

Beer, S. R., & De Bellis, M. D. (2002). Neuropsychological function in children with maltreatment-related posttraumatic stress disorder. *American Journal of Psychiatry, 159*, 483–486.

Benarroch, E. E. (1997). *Central autonomic network: Functional organization and clinical correlations.* Armonk, NY: Futura.

Bergman, N. J., Linley, L. L., & Fawcus, S. R. (2004). Randomized controlled trial of skin-to-skin contact from birth versus conventional incubator for physiological stabilization in 1200- to 2199-gram newborns. *Acta Paediatrica, 93*, 779–785.

Berntson, G. G., Cacioppo, J. T., & Quigley, K. S. (1991). Autonomic determinism: The modes of autonomic control, the doctrine of autonomic space, and the laws of autonomic constraint. *Psychological Review, 98*, 459–487.

Berthier, M. L., Posada, A., & Puentes, C. (2001). Dissociative flashbacks after right frontal injury in a Vietnam veteran with combat-related posttraumatic stress disorder. *Journal of Neuropsychiatry and Clinical Neuroscience, 13*, 101–105.

Bion, W. R. (1962). *Learning from experience.* London: Heinemann.

Blanke, O., Ortigue, S., Landis, T., & Seeck, M. (2002). Stimulating illusory own-body perceptions. *Nature, 419*, 269–270.

Bock, J., Murmu, R. P., Fredman, N., Leshem, M., & Braun, K. (2008). Refinement of dendritic and synaptic networks in the rodent anterior cingulate and orbitofrontal cortex: Critical impact of early and late social experience. *Developmental Neurobiology, 68*, 685–695.

Bonne, O., Gilboa, A., Louzoun, Y., Brandes, D., Yona, I., Lester, H., et al. (2003). Resting regional cerebral perfusion in recent posttraumatic stress disorder. *Biological Psychiatry, 54*, 1077–1086.

Borod, J. (2000). *The neuropsychology of emotion.* New York: Oxford University Press.

Borod, J., Cicero, B. A., Obler, L. K., Welkowitz, J., Erhan, H. M., Santschi, C., et al.

(1998). Right hemisphere emotional perception: Evidence across multiple channels. *Neuropsychology, 12,* 446–458.

Borod, J., Haywood, C. S., & Koff, E. (1997). Neuropsychological aspects of facial asymmetry during emotional expression: A review of the adult literature. *Neuopsychology Review, 7,* 41–60.

Boutilier, R. G., & St-Pierre, J. (2000). Surviving hypoxia without really dying. *Comparative Biochemistry and Physiology A, 126,* 481–490.

Bowman, E. S., & Markand, O. N. (1996). Psychodynamics and psychiatric diagnoses of pseudoseizure subjects. *American Journal of Psychiatry, 153,* 57–63.

Bradley, M., Cuthbert, B. N., & Lang, P. J. (1996). Lateralized startle probes in the study of emotion. *Psychophysiology, 33,* 156–161.

Bradshaw, J. L., & Nettleton, N. C. (1981). The nature of hemispheric specialization in man. *Behavioral and Brain Sciences, 4,* 51–91.

Brake, W. G., Sullivan, R. M., & Gratton, A. (2000). Perinatal distress leads to lateralized medial prefrontal cortical dopamine hypofunction in adult rats. *Journal of Neuroscience, 20,* 5538–5543.

Brand, M., Eggers, C., Reinhold, N., Fujiwara, E., Kessler, J., Heiss, W-D., et al. (2009). Functional brain imaging in 14 patients with dissociative amnesia reveals right inferolateral prefrontal hypometabolism. *Psychiatry Research: Neuroimaging, 174,* 32–39.

Bremner, J. D., & Brett, E. (1997). Trauma-related dissociative states and long-term psychopathology in posttraumatic stress disorder. *Journal of Traumatic Stress, 10,* 37–49.

Bremner, J. D., Staib, L. H., Kaloupek, D., Southwick, S. M., Soufer, R., & Charney, D. S. (1999). Neural correlates of exposure to traumatic pictures and sound in combat veterans with and without posttraumatic stress disorder: A positron emission tomography study. *Biological Psychiatry, 45,* 806–818.

Brown, M. R., Fisher, L. A., Spiess, J., Rivier, C., Rivier, J., & Vale, W. (1982). Corticotropin-releasing factor: Actions on the sympathetic nervous system and metabolism. *Endocrinology, 111,* 928–931.

Brown, R. J., & Trimble, M. R. (2000). Dissociative psychopathology, non-epileptic seizures, and neurology. *Journal of Neurology, Neurosurgery, & Psychiatry, 69,* 285–291.

Buchanan, S. L., Powell, D. A., & Valentine, J. (1984). Cardiovascular adjustments elicited by electrical stimulation of frontal cortex in conscious rabbits. *Neuroscience Abstracts, 10,* 614.

Calvert, G. A., Hanses, P. C., Iversen, S. D., & Brammer, M. J. (2001). Detection of audiovisual integration sites in humans by application of electrophysiological criteria to the BOLD effect. *Neuroimage, 14,* 427–438.

Carlson, V., Cicchetti, D., Barnett, D., & Braunwald, K. (1989). Disorganized/disoriented attachment relationships in maltreated infants. *Developmental Psychology, 25,* 525–531.

Carrion, V. G., Weems, C. F., Eliez, S., Patwardhan, A., Brown, W., & Ray, R. D. (2001). Attenuation of frontal asymmetry in pediatric posttraumatic stress disorder. *Biological Psychiatry, 50,* 943–951.

Cavada, C., & Goldman-Rakic, P. S. (1989). Posterior parietal cortex in rhesus monkey: I. Parcellation of areas based on distinctive limbic and sensory corticocortical connections. *Journal of Comparative Neurology, 287,* 393–421.

Chapanis, L. (1977). Language deficits and cross-modal sensory perception. In S. J. Segalowitz & F. A. Gruber (Eds.), *Language development and neurological theory* (pp. 107–120). New York: Academic Press.

Charcot, J. M. (1887). *Lecons sur les maladies du systeme nerveux faites a la Salpetriere [Lessons on the illnesses of the nervous system held at the Salpetriere]* (Vol. 3). Paris: Progres Medical en A. Delahaye & E. Lecrosie.

Chefetz, R. A. (2004). The paradox of "detachment disorders": Binding-disruptions of dissociative process. *Psychiatry, 67,* 246–255.

Cheng, Z., Powley, T. L., Schwaber, J. S., & Doye, F. J. (1999). Projections of the dorsal motor nucleus of the vagus to cardiac ganglia of rat atria: An anterograde tracing study. *Journal of Comparative Neurology, 410,* 320–341.

Chiron, C., Jambaque, I., Nabbout, R., Lounes, R., Syrota, A., & Dulac, O. (1997). The right brain hemisphere is dominant in human infants. *Brain, 120,* 1057–1065.

Chu, J. A., & Dill, D. L. (1990). Dissociative symptoms in relation to childhood physical and sexual abuse. *American Journal of Psychiatry, 147,* 887–892.

Cicchetti, D. (1994). Integrating developmental risk factors: Perspectives from developmental psychopathology. In C. A. Nelson (Ed.), *Minnesota symposium on child psychology: Vol. 27. Threats to optimal development* (pp. 285–325). Mahwah, NJ: Erlbaum.

Classen, C., Koopman, C., & Spiegel, D. (1993). Trauma and dissociation. *Bulletin of the Menninger Clinic, 57,* 178–194.

Coleman-Mensches, K., & McGaugh, J. L. (1995). Differential involvement of the right and left amygdalae in expression of memory for aversively motivated training. *Brain Research, 670,* 75–81.

Coons, P. M., Bowman, E. S., Pellow, T. A., & Schneider, P. (1989). Post-traumatic aspects of the treatment of victims of sexual abuse and incest. *Psychiatric Clinics of North America, 12,* 325–335.

Craig, A. D. (2004). Human feelings: Why are some more aware than others? *Nature Neuroscience, 7,* 239–241.

Craig, A. D., Chen, K., Bandy, D., & Reiman, E. M. (2000). Thermosensory activation of insular cortex. *Nature Neuroscience, 3,* 184–190.

Craik, F. I. M., Moroz, T. M., Moscovitch, M., Stuss, D. T., Winocur, G., Tulving, E., et al. (1999). In search of self: A positron emission tomography study. *Psychological Science, 10,* 26–34.

Critchley, H. D., Elliott, R., Mathias, C. J., & Dolan, R. J. (2000). Neural activity relating to generation and representation of galvanic skin responses: A functional magnetic resonance imaging study. *Journal of Neuroscience, 20,* 3033–3040.

Critchley, H. D., Mathias, C. J., & Dolan, R. J. (2002). Fear conditioning in humans: The influence of awareness and autonomic arousal on functional neuroanatomy. *Neuron, 33,* 653–663.

Critchley, H. D., Wiens, S., Rothstein, P., Ohman, A., & Dolan, R. J. (2004). Neural systems supporting interoceptive awareness. *Nature Neuroscience, 7,* 189–195.

Crittenden, P. M., & Ainsworth, M. D. S. (1989). Child maltreatment and attachment theory. In D. Cicchetti & V. Carlson (Eds.), *Child maltreatment: Theory and research on the causes and consequences of child abuse and neglect* (pp. 432–463). New York: Cambridge University Press.

Crucian, G. P., Hughes, J. D., Barrett, A. M., Williamson, D. J. G., Bauer, R. M., Bowres, D., et al. (2000). Emotional and physiological responses to false feedback. *Cortex, 36,* 623–647.

Cutting, J. (1992). The role of right hemisphere dysfunction in psychiatric disorders. *British Journal of Psychiatry, 160,* 583–588.

Davidson, R. J. (2002). Synaptic substrates of the implicit and explicit self. *Science, 296,* 268.

Davidson, R. J., Ekman, P., Saron, C., Senulis, J., & Friesen, W. V. (1990). Approach/withdrawal and cerebral asymmetry: 1. Emotional expression and brain physiology. *Journal of Personality and Social Psychology, 58,* 330–341.

Davies, J. M., & Frawley, M. G. (1994). *Treating the adult survivor of childhood sexual abuse. A psychoanalytic perspective.* New York: Basic Books.

Davis, M. (1989). (1989). The role of the amygdala and its efferent projections in fear and anxiety. In P. Tyrer (Ed.), *Psychopharmacology of anxiety* (pp. 52–79). Oxford, UK: Oxford University Press.

De Bellis, M. D., Baum, A. S., Birmaher, B., Keshavan, M. S., Eccard, C. H., Boring, A. M., et al. (1999). Developmental traumatology Part I: Biological stress systems. *Biological Psychiatry, 45,* 1259–1270.

De Bellis, M. D., Casey, B. J., Dahl, R. E., Birmaher, B., Williamson, D. E., Thomas, K. M., et al. (2000). A pilot study of amygdala volume in pediatric generalized anxiety disorder. *Biological Psychiatry, 48,* 51–57.

Decety, J., & Chaminade, T. (2003). When the self represents the other: A new cognitive neuroscience view on psychological identification. *Consciousness and Cognition, 12,* 577–596.

Decety, J., & Lamm, C. (2007). The role of the right temporoparietal junction in social interaction: How low-level computational processes contribute to meta-cognition. *The Neuroscientist, 13,* 580–584.

Decety, J., & Sommerville, J. A. (2003). Shared representations between self and other: A social cognitive neuroscience view. *Trends in Cognitive Science, 7,* 527–533.

Devinsky, O. (2000). Right cerebral hemisphere dominance for a sense of corporeal and emotional self. *Epilepsy & Behavior, 1,* 60–73.

De Wet, C. J., Mellers, J. D. C., Gardner, W. N., & Toone, B. K. (2003). Pseudoseizures and asthma. *Journal of Neurology, Neurosurgery, & Psychiatry, 74,* 639–641.

Dixon, A. K. (1998). Ethological strategies for defense in animals and humans: Their role in some psychiatric disorders. *British Journal of Medical Psychology, 71,* 417–445.

Draijer, N., & Langeland, W. (1999). Childhood trauma and perceived parental dysfunction in the etiology of dissociative symptoms in psychiatric inpatients. *American Journal of Psychiatry, 156,* 379–385.

Dutra, L., Bureau, J.-F., Holmes, B., Lyubchik, A., & Lyons-Ruth, K. (2009). Quality of early care and childhood trauma. A prospective study of developmental pathways to dissociation. *Journal of Nervous and Mental Disease, 197,* 383–390.

Eddy, S. F., Morin, P., Jr., & Storey, K. B. (2006). Differential expression of selected mitochondrial genes in hibernating little brown bats, *Myotis lucifugus. Journal of Experimental Zoology, 305A,* 620–630.

Edelman, G. (1989). *The remembered present: A biological theory of consciousness.* New York: Basic Books.

Emde, R. N. (1983). The pre-representational self and its affective core. *Psychoanalytic Study of the Child, 38,* 165–192.

Enriquez, P., & Bernabeu, E. (2008). Hemispheric laterality and dissociative tendencies: Differences in emotional processing in a dichotic listening task. *Consciousness and Cognition, 17,* 267–275.

Erciyas, A. H., Topaktas, S., Akyuz, A., & Dener, S. (1999). Suppression of cardiac para-sympathetic functions in patients with right hemispheric stroke. *European Journal of Neurology*, 6, 685–690.

Erickson, M. F., Egeland, B., & Pianta, R. (1989). The effects of maltreatment on the development of young children. In D. Cicchetti & V. Carlson (Eds.), *Child maltreatment: Theory and research on the causes and consequences of child abuse and neglect* (pp. 647–684). New York: Cambridge University Press.

Espinosa, M., Beckwith, L., Howard, J., Tyler, R., & Swanson, K. (2001). Maternal psychopathology and attachment in toddlers of heavy cocaine-using mothers. *Infant Mental Health Journal*, 22, 316–333.

Fanselow, M. S. (1986). Conditioned fear-induced opiate analgesia: A compelling motivational state theory of stress analgesia. In D. D. Kelly (Ed.), *Stress-induced analgesia* (pp. 40–54). New York: New York Academy of Sciences.

Faust, M., Kravetz, S., & Nativ-Safrai, O. (2004). The representation of aspects of the self in the two hemispheres. *Personality and Individual Differences*, 37, 607–619.

Field, T., Pickens, J., Fox, N. A., Nawrocki, T., & Gonzalez, J. (1995). Vagal tone in infants of depressed mothers. *Development and Psychopathology*, 7, 227–231.

Fink, G. R., Markowitsch, H. J., Reinkemeier, M., Bruckbauer, T., Kessler, J., & Heiss, W-D. (1996). Cerebral representation of one's own past: Neural networks involved in autobiographical memory. *Journal of Neuroscience*, 16, 4275–4282.

Fischer, H., Andersson, J. L. R., Furmark, T., Wik, G., & Fredrickson, M. (2002). Right-sided human prefrontal brain activation during acquisition of conditioned fear. *Emotion*, 2, 233–241.

Fossati, P., Hevenor, S. J., Lepage, M., Graham, S. J., Grady, C., Keightley, M. L., et al. (2004). Distributed self in episodic memory: Neural correlates of successful retrieval of self-centered positive and negative personality traits. *NeuroImage*, 22, 1596–1604.

Frassinetti, F., Maini, M., Romualdi, S., Galante, E., & Avanzi, S. (2008). Is it mine? Hemispheric asymmetries in corporeal self-recognition. *Journal of Cognitive Neuroscience*, 20, 1507–1516.

Freeman, T. W., & Kimbrell, T. (2001). A "cure" for chronic combat-related posttraumatic stress disorder secondary to a right frontal lobe infarct: A case report. *Journal of Neuropsychiatry and Clinical Neuroscience*, 13, 106–109.

Freud, S. (1955). The etiology of hysteria. In J. Strachey (Ed. & Trans.), *The standard edition of the complete psychological works of Sigmund Freud* (Vol. 3, pp. 189–221). London: Hogarth Press. (Original work published 1893)

Frijda, N. H. (1988). The laws of emotion. *American Psychologist*, 43, 349–358.

Gabrielsen, G. W., & Smith, E. N. (1985). Physiological responses associated with feigned death in the American opossum. *Acta Physiologica Scandinavica*, 123, 393–398.

Gadea, M., Gomez, C., Gonzalez-Bono, E., Espert, R., & Salvador, A. (2005). Increased cortisol and decreased right ear advantage (REA) in dichotic listening following a negative mood induction. *Psychoneuroendocrinology*, 30, 129–138.

Gaensbauer, T. J. (2002). Representations of trauma in infancy: Clinical and theoretical implications for the understanding of early memory. *Infant Mental Health Journal*, 23, 259–277.

Gainotti, G. (2000). Neuropsychological theories of emotion. In J. Borod (Ed.), *The neuropsychology of emotion*. New York: Oxford University Press.

Gallagher, H. L., & Frith, C. D. (2004). Dissociable neural pathways for the perception and recognition of expressive and instrumental gestures. *Neuropsychologia, 42*, 1725–1736.

Galletly, C., Clark, C. R., McFarlane, A. C., & Weber, D. L. (2001). Working memory in posttraumatic stress disorder—An event-related potential study. *Journal of Traumatic Stress, 14*, 295–309.

Gendlin, E. T. (1970). A theory of personality change. In J. T. Hart & T. H. Tomlinson (Eds.), *New directions in client-centered therapy* (pp. 129–174). Boston: Houghton Mifflin.

George, M. S., Parekh, P. I., Rosinsky, N., Ketter, T. A., Kimbrell, T. A., Heilman, K. M., et al. (1996). Understanding emotional prosody activates right hemispheric regions. *Archives of Neurology, 53*, 665–670.

Gershuny, B., & Thayer, J. (1999). Relations among psychological trauma, dissociative phenomena, and trauma-related distress: A review and integration. *Clinical Psychology Review, 19*, 651–657.

Goldberg, E., & Costa, L. D. (1981). Hemisphere differences in the acquisition and use of descriptive systems. *Brain and Language, 14*, 144–173.

Goleman, D. (1995). *Emotional intelligence.* New York: Bantam Books.

Graham, Y. P., Heim, C., Goodman, S. H., Miller, A. H., & Nemeroff, C. B. (1999). The effects of neonatal stress on brain development: Implications for psychopathology. *Development and Psychopathology, 11*, 545–565.

Greenberg, D. L., Rice, H. J., Cooper, J. J., Cabeza, R., Rubin, D. C., & LaBar, K. S. (2005). Co-activation of the amygdala, hippocampus and inferior frontal gyrus during autobiographical memory retrieval. *Neuropsychologia, 43*, 659–674.

Griffin, M. G., Resick, P. A., & Mechanic, M. B. (1997). Objective assessment of posttraumatic dissociation: Psychophysiological indicators. *American Journal of Psychiatry, 154*, 1081–1088.

Guedeney, A., & Fermanian, J. (2001). A validity and reliability study of assessment and screening for sustained withdrawal in infancy: The alarm distress scale. *Infant Mental Health Journal, 22*, 559–575.

Gundel, H., Lopez-Sala, A., Ceballos-Baumann, A. O., Deus, J., Cardoner, N., Marten-Mittag, B., et al. (2004). Alexithymia correlates with the size of the right anterior cingulate. *Psychosomatic Medicine, 66*, 132–140.

Guppy, M., & Withers, P. (1999). Metabolic depression in animals: Physiological perspectives and biochemical generalisations. *Biological Review, 74*, 1–40.

Gur, R. C., Packer, I. K., Hungerbuhler, J. P., Reivich, M., Obrist, W. D., Amarnek, W. S., et al. (1980). Differences in the distribution of gray and white matter in human cerebral hemispheres. *Science, 207*, 1226–1228.

Hagemann, D., Waldstein, S. R., & Thayer, J. F. (2003). Central and autonomic nervous system integration in emotion. *Brain and Cognition, 52*, 79–87.

Happaney, K., Zelazo, P. D., & Stuss, D. T. (2004). Development of orbitofrontal function: Current themes and future directions. *Brain and Cognition, 55*, 1–10.

Harden, C. L. (1997). Pseudoseizures and dissociative disorders: A common mechanism involving traumatic experiences. *Seizures, 6*, 151–155.

Hardy, S. G. P., & Holmes, D. E. (1988). Prefrontal stimulus-produced hypotension in the rat. *Experimental Brain Research, 73*, 249–255.

Hecaen, H., & Albert, M. L. (1978). *Human neuropsychology.* New York: Wiley.

Henry, J. P. (1993). Psychological and physiological responses to stress: The right hemisphere and the hypothalamo-pituitary-adrenal axis, an inquiry into problems of human bonding. *Integrative Physiological and Behavioral Science, 28,* 369–387.

Hesse, E., & Main, M. M. (1999). Second-generation effects of unresolved trauma in nonmaltreating parents: Dissociated, frightened, and threatening parental behavior. *Psychoanalytic Inquiry, 19,* 481–540.

Hesse, E., & Main, M. (2006). Frightened, threatening, and dissociative parental behavior in low-risk samples: Description, discussion, and interpretations. *Development and Psychopathy, 18,* 309–343.

Hogg, S., Sanger, D. J., & Moser, P. C. (1998). Mild traumatic lesion of the right parietal cortex in the rat: Characterisation of a conditioned freezing deficit and its reversal by dizocilpine. *Behavioural Brain Research, 93,* 157–165.

Hugdahl, K. (1995). Classical conditioning and implicit learning: The right hemisphere hypothesis. In R. J. Davidson & K. Hugdahl (Eds.), *Brain asymmetry* (pp. 235–267). Cambridge, MA: MIT Press.

Irwin, H. J. (1994). Proneness to dissociation and traumatic childhood events. *Journal of Nervous and Mental Disease, 182,* 456–460.

Jackson, J. H. (1931). *Selected writings of J. H. Jackson: Vol. I.* London: Hodder and Soughton.

Jackson, J. H. (1958a). Evolution and dissolution of the nervous system. In J. Taylor (Ed.), *Selected writings of John Hughlings Jackson* (pp. 45–118). London: Stapes Press. (Original work published 1884)

Jackson, J. H. (1958b). On the nature of the duality of the brain. In J. Taylor (Ed.), *Selected writings of John Hughlings Jackson* (pp. 146–152). New York: Basic Books. (Original work published 1874)

Jacobsen, N. K. (1979). Alarm bradycardia in white-tailed deer fawns. *Odocoileus virginianus. Journal of Mammalology, 60,* 343–349.

Janet, P. (1887). L'anesthesie systematisee et al dissociation des phenomenes psychologiques. *Revue Philosophique, 23,* 449–472.

Janet, P. (1889). *L'automatisme psychologique.* Paris: Alcan.

Janet, P. (1911). *L'etat mental des hysteriques* (2nd ed.). Paris: Alcan.

Jiang, C., Fogel, R., & Zhang, X. (2003). Lateral hypothalamus modulates gut-sensitive neurons in the dorsal vagal complex. *Brain Research, 980,* 31–47.

Joseph, R. (1992). *The right brain and the unconscious: Discovering the stranger within.* New York: Plenum.

Joseph, R. (1996). *Neuropsychiatry, neuropsychology, and clinical neuroscience* (2nd ed.). Baltimore: Williams & Wilkins.

Kaada, B. R. (1960). Cingulate, posterior orbital, anterior insular and temporal pole cortex. In H. W. Magoun (Ed.), *Neurophysiology* (pp. 1345–1372). Baltimore: Waverly Press.

Kalin, N. H., Larson, C., Shelton, C. E., & Davidson, R. J. (1998). Asymmetric frontal brain activity, cortisol, and behavior associated with fearful temperament in rhesus monkeys. *Behavioral Neuroscience, 112,* 286–292.

Kandel, E. R. (1999). Biology and the future of psychoanalysis: A new intellectual framework for psychiatry revisited. *American Journal of Psychiatry, 156,* 505–524.

Kaplan, J. T., Aziz-Zadeh, L., Uddin, L. Q., & Iacoboni, M. (2008). The self across the senses: An fMRI study of self-face and self-voice recognition. *Social and Cognitive Affective Neuroscience, 3,* 218–223.

Kaplan-Solms, K., & Solms, M. (1996). Psychoanalytic observations on a case of frontal-limbic disease. *Journal of Clinical Psychoanalysis, 5,* 405–438.

Katz, M., Liu, C., Schaer, M., Parker, K. J., Ottet, M-C., Epps, A. et al. (2009). Prefrontal plasticity and stress inoculation-induced resilience. *Developmental Neuroscience, 31,* 293–299.

Keenan, J. P., Nelson, A., O'Connor, M., & Pascual-Leone, A. (2001). Self-recognition and the right hemisphere. *Nature, 409,* 305.

Keenan, J. P., Wheeler, M. A., Gallup, G. G., Jr., & Pascual-Leone, A. (2000). Self-recognition and the right prefrontal cortex. *Trends in Cognitive Science, 4,* 338–344.

Kestenberg, J. (1985). The flow of empathy and trust between mother and child. In E. J. Anthony & G. H. Pollack (Eds.), *Parental influences in health and disease* (pp. 137–163). Boston: Little Brown.

Kiersky, S., & Beebe, B. (1994). The reconstruction of early nonverbal relatedness in the treatment of difficult patients. A special form of empathy. *Psychoanalytic Dialogues, 4,* 389–408.

Kimura, Y., Yoshino, A., Takahashi, Y., & Nomura, S. (2004). Interhemispheric difference in emotional response without awareness. *Physiology & Behavior, 82,* 727–731.

Kircher, T. T. J., Senior, C., Phillips, M. L., Rabe-hesketh, S., Benson, P. J., Bullmore, E. T., et al. (2001). Recognizing one's own face. *Cognition, 78,* B1–B5.

Kirschbaum, C., Wolf, O. T., May, M., Wippich, W., & Hellhammer, D. H. (1996). Stress- and treatment-induced elevations of cortisol levels associated with impaired declarative memory in healthy adults. *Life Sciences, 58,* 1475–1483.

Kohut, H. (1971). *The analysis of the self.* New York: International Universities Press.

Koopman, C., Carrion, V., Butler, L. D., Sudhakar, S., Palmer, L., & Steiner, H. (2004). Relationships of dissociation and childhood abuse and neglect with heart rate in delinquent adolescents. *Journal of Traumatic Stress, 17,* 47–54.

Krystal, H. (1988). *Integration and self-healing: Affect-trauma-alexithymia.* Hillsdale, NJ: Analytic Press.

Krystal, J. H., Bremner, J. D., Southwick, S. M., & Charney, D. S. (1998). The emerging neurobiology of dissociation: Implications for treatment of posttraumatic stress disorder. In J. D. Bremner & C. R. Marmar (Eds.), *Trauma, memory, and dissociation* (pp. 321–363). Washington, DC: American Psychiatric Press.

Kuyk, J., Spinhoven, P., Van Emde Boas, W., & van Dyck, R. (1999). Dissociation in temporal lobe and pseudoepileptic seizure patients. *Journal of Nervous and Mental Disease, 187,* 713–720.

Kvetnansky, R., Dobrakovova, M., Jezova, D., Oprsalova, Z., Lichardus, B., & Makara, G. (1989). Hypothalamic regulation of plasma catecholamine levels during stress: Effect of vasopressin and CRF. In G. R. Van Loon, R. Kvetnansky, R. McCarty, & J. Axelrod (Eds.), *Stress: Neurochemical and humoral mechanisms* (pp. 549–570). New York: Gordon and Breach Science Publishers.

Kvetnansky, R., Jezova, D., Oprsalova, Z., Foldes, O., Michjlovskij, N., Dobrakovova, M., et al. (1990). Regulation of the sympathetic nervous system by circulating vasopressin. In J. C. Porter & D. Jezova (Eds.), *Circulating regulatory factors and neuroendocrine function* (pp. 113–134). New York: Plenum Press.

La Bar, K. S., Gatenby, J. C., Gore, J. C., Le Doux, J. E., & Phelps, E. A. (1998). Human amygdala activation during conditioned fear acquisition and extinction: A mixed-trial fMRI study. *Neuron, 20,* 937–945.

Lane, R. D., Ahern, G. L., Schwartz, G. E., & Kaszniak, A. W. (1997). Is alexithymia the emotional equivalent of blindsight? *Biological Psychiatry, 42*, 834–844.

Lanius, R. A., Williamson, P. C., Bluhm, R. L., Densmore, M., Boksman, K., Neufeld, R. W. J., et al. (2005). Functional connectivity of dissociative responses in posttraumatic stress disorder: A functional magnetic resonance imaging investigation. *Biological Psychiatry, 57*, 873–884.

Lanius, R. A., Williamson, P. C., Boksman, K., Densmore, M., Gupta, M., Neufeld, R. W. J., et al. (2002). Brain activation during script-driven imagery induced dissociative responses in PTSD: A functional magnetic resonance imaging investigation. *Biological Psychiatry, 52*, 305–311.

Lanius, R. A., Williamson, P. C., Densmore, M., Boksman, K., Neufeld, R. W., Gati, J. S., et al. (2004). The nature of traumatic memories: A 4-T fMRI functional connectivity analysis. *American Journal of Psychiatry, 161*, 36–44.

Layton, B., & Krikorian, R. (2002). Memory mechanisms in posttraumatic stress disorder. *Journal of Neuropsychiatry and Clinical Neuroscience, 14*, 254–261.

Lazarus, R. S. (1991). Progress on a cognitive-motivational-relational theory of emotion. *American Psychologist, 46*, 819–834.

LeDoux, J. (2002). *Synaptic self: How our brains become who we are.* New York: Viking.

Le Grand, R., Mondloch, C., Maurer, D., & Brent, H. P. (2003). Expert face processing requires visual input to the right hemisphere during infancy. *Nature Neuroscience, 6*, 1108–1112.

Levy, J., Heller, W., Banich, M. T., & Burton, L. A. (1983). Are variations among right-handed individuals in perceptual asymmetries caused by characteristic arousal differences between hemispheres? *Journal of Experimental Psychology: Human Perception and Performance, 9*, 329–359.

Liotti, G. (1992). Disorganized/disoriented attachment in the etiology of the dissociative disorders. *Dissociation, IV*, 196–204.

Lipschitz, D., Kaplan, M., Sorkenn, J., Chorney, P., & Asnis, G. (1996). Childhood abuse, adult assault, and dissociation. *Comprehensive Psychiatry, 37*, 261–266.

Lipton, P. A., Alvarez, P., & Eichenbaum, H. (1999). Crossmodal associative memory representations in rodent orbitofrontal cortex. *Neuron, 22*, 349–359.

Loewenstein, R. J. (1996). Dissociative amnesia and dissociative fugue. In L. K. Michaelson & W. J. Ray (Eds.), *Handbook of dissociation: Theoretical, empirical, and clinical perspectives* (pp. 307–336). New York: Plenum.

Loewy, A. D. (1991). Forebrain nuclei involved in autonomic control (review). *Progress in Brain Research, 87*, 253–268.

Lorberbaum, J. P., Newman, J. D., Horwitz, A. R., Dubno, J. R., Lydiard, R. B., Hamner, M. B., et al. (2002). A potential role for thalamocingulate circuitry in human maternal behavior. *Biological Psychiatry, 51*, 431–445.

Lou, H. C., Luber, B., Crupain, M., Keenan, J. P., Nowak, M., Kjaer, T. W., et al. (2004). Parietal cortex and representation of the mental self. *Proceedings of the National Academy of Sciences of the United States of America, 101*, 6827–6832.

Lucas, T. H., Schoenfield-McNeill, J., Weber, P. B., & Ojemann, G. A. (2003). A direct measure of human lateral temporal lobe neurons responsive to face matching. *Cognitive Brain Research, 18*, 15–25.

Ludwig, A. M. (1972). Hysteria: A neurobiological theory. *Archives of General Psychiatry, 27*, 771–777.

Luu, P., & Tucker, D. M. (1996). Self-regulation and cortical development: Implications for functional studies of the brain. In R. W. Thatcher, G. Reid Lyon, J. Rumsey, & N. Krasnegor (Eds.), *Developmental neuroimaging: Mapping the development of brain and behavior* (pp. 297–305). San Diego, CA: Academic Press.

Luys, J. (1881). Recherches nouvelles sur les hemiplegies emotives. *Encephale, 1,* 378–398.

Lyons, D. M., Afarian, H., Schatzberg, A. F., Sawyer-Glover, A., & Moseley, M. E. (2002). Experience-dependent asymmetric maturation in primate prefrontal morphology. *Experimental Brain Research, 136,* 51–59.

Main, M. (1996). Introduction to the special section on attachment and psychopathology: 2. Overview of the field of attachment. *Journal of Consulting and Clinical Psychology, 64,* 237–243.

Main, M., & Solomon, J. (1986). Discovery of an insecure-disorganized/disoriented attachment pattern: Procedures, findings and implications for the classification of behavior. In T. B. Brazelton & M. W. Yogman (Eds.), *Affective development in infancy* (pp. 95–124). Norwood, NJ: Ablex.

Mandal, M. K., & Ambady, N. (2004). Laterality of facial expressions of emotion: Universal and culture-specific influences. *Behavioural Neurology, 15,* 23–34.

Manning, J. T., Trivers, R. L., Thornhill, R., Singh, D., Denman, J., Eklo, M. H., et al. (1997). Ear asymmetry and left-side cradling. *Evolution and Human Behavior, 18,* 327–340.

Markowitsch, H. J., Thiel, A., Reinkemeier, M., Kessler, J., Koyuncu, A., & Heiss, W.-D. (2000). Right amygdalar and temporofrontal activation during autobiographic, but not during fictitious memory retrieval. *Behavioral Neurology, 12,* 181–190.

McGilchrist, I. (2009). *The master and his emissary.* New Haven, CT: Yale University Press.

McNally, R. J., & Amir, N. (1996). Perceptual implicit stimuli for trauma-related information in post-traumatic stress disorder. *Cognition and Emotion, 10,* 551–556.

Meares, R. (1999). The contribution of Hughlings Jackson to an understanding of dissociation. *American Journal of Psychiatry, 156,* 1850–1855.

Menard, J. L., Champagne, D. L., & Meaney, M. J. P. (2004). Variations of maternal care differentially influence "fear" reactivity in response to the shock-probe burying test. *Neuroscience, 129,* 297–308.

Merckelbach, H., & Muris, P. (2001). The causal link between self-reported trauma and dissociation: A critical review. *Behavior Research and Therapy, 39,* 245–254.

Metzger, L. J., Paige, S. R., Carson, M. A., Lasko, N. B., Paulus, L. A., Pitman, R. K., et al. (2004). PTSD arousal and depression symptoms associated with increased right-sided parietal EEG asymmetry. *Journal of Abnormal Psychology, 113,* 324–329.

Miller, B. L., Seeley, W. W., Mychack, P., Rosen, H. J., Mena, I., & Boone, K. (2001). Neuroanatomy of the self. Evidence from patients with frontotemporal dementia. *Neurology, 57,* 817–821.

Mohanakrishnan Menon, P., Nasrallah, H. A., Lyons, J. A., Scott, M. F., & Liberto, V. (2003). Single-voxel proton MR spectroscopy of right versus left hippocampi in PTSD. *Psychiatry Research: Neuroimaging, 123,* 101–108.

Mollon, P. (1996). *Multiple selves, multiple voices: Working with trauma, violation and dissociation.* Chichester, UK: Wiley.

Monroy, E., Hernández-Torres, E., & Flores, G. (2010). Maternal separation disrupts dendritic morphology of neurons in prefrontal cortex, hippocampus, and nucleus accumbens in male rat offspring. *Journal of Chemical Neuroanatomy, 40,* 93–101.

Morgan, M. A., & LeDoux, J. E. (1995). Differential acquisition of dorsal and ventral medial prefrontal cortex to the acquisition and extinction of conditioned fear in rats. *Behavioral Neuroscience, 109,* 681–688.

Morita, T., Itakura, S., Saito, N., Nakashita, S., Harada, T., Kochiyama, T., et al. (2008). The role of the right prefrontal cortex in self-evaluation of the face: A functional magnetic resonance imaging study. *Journal of Cognitive Neuroscience, 20,* 342–355.

Morris, J. S., Ohman, A., & Dolan, R. J. (1999). A subcortical pathway to the right amygdala mediating "unseen" fear. *Proceedings of the National Academy of Sciences of the United States of America, 96,* 1680–1685.

Mulder, R. T., Beautrais, A. L., Joyce, P. R., & Fergusson, D. M. (1998). Relationship between dissociation, childhood sexual abuse, childhood physical abuse, and mental illness in a general population sample. *American Journal of Psychiatry, 155,* 806–811.

Myers, F. (1885). Automatic writing. *Proceedings of the Society of Psychical Research,* 1–63.

Nakamura, K., Kawashima, R., Ito, K., Sugiura, M., Kato, T., Nakamura, A., et al. (1999). Activation of the right inferior frontal cortex during assessment of facial emotion. *Journal of Neurophysiology, 82,* 1610–1614.

Nash, M. R., Hulsey, T. L., Sexton, M. C., Harralson, T. L., & Lambert, W. (1993). Long-term sequelae of childhood sexual abuse: Perceived family environment, psychopathology, and dissociation. *Journal of Consulting and Clinical Psychology, 61,* 276–283.

Neddens, J., Brandenburg, K., Teuchert-Noodt, G., & Dawirs, R. R. (2001). Differential environment alters ontogeny of dopamine innervation of the orbital prefrontal cortex in gerbils. *Journal of Neuroscience Research, 63,* 209–213.

Nemiah, J. C. (1989). Janet redivivus: The centenary of *l'automatism psychologique. American Journal of Psychiatry, 146,* 1527–1530.

Nijenhuis, E. R. S. (2000). Somatoform dissociation: Major symptoms of dissociative disorders. *Journal of Trauma & Dissociation, 1,* 7–32.

Nijenhuis, E. R. S., van der Hart, O., & Steele, K. (2002). The emerging psychobiology of trauma-related dissociation and dissociative disorders. In H. D'haenen, J. A. den Boer, & P. Willner (Eds.), *Biological psychiatry* (pp. 1079–1098). London: Wiley.

Northoff, G., Steinke, R., Nagel, D., Czerwenka, C., Grosser, O., Danos, P., et al. (2000). Right lower prefronto-pariental cortical dysfunction in akinetic catatonia; a combined study of neuropsychology and regional blood flow. *Psychological Medicine, 30,* 583–596.

O'Connor, M. J., Sigman, M., & Brill, N. (1987). Disorganization of attachment in relation to maternal alcohol consumption. *Journal of Consulting and Clinical Psychology, 55,* 831–836.

Ogawa, J. R., Sroufe, L. A., Weinfield, N. S., Carlson, E. A., & Egeland, B. (1997). Development and the fragmented self: Longitudinal study of dissociative symptomatology in a nonclinical sample. *Development and Psychopathology, 9,* 855–879.

Olivera, L. C., Nobre, M. J., Brandao, M. L., & Landeira-Fernandez, J. (2004). Role of the amygdala in conditioned and unconditioned fear generated in the periaqueductal gray. *NeuroReport, 15,* 2281–2285.

Padilla, P. A., & Roth, M. B. (2001). Oxygen deprivation causes suspended animation in the zebrafish embryo. *Proceedings of the National Academy of Sciences of the United States of America, 98,* 7331–7335.

Pandya, D. N., & Yeterian, E. H. (1985). Architecture and connections of cortical association areas. In A. Peters & E. G. Jones (Eds.), *Cerebral cortex: Vol. 4. Association and auditory cortices* (pp. 3–61). New York: Plenum.

Pascual, R., & Zamora-León, S. P. (2007). Effects of neonatal maternal deprivation and postweaning environmental complexity on dendritic morphology of prefrontal pyramidal neurons in the rat. *Acta Neurobiolgiae Experimentalis, 67,* 471–479.

Paulus, M. P., Rogalsky, C., Simmons, A., Feinstein, J. S., & Stein, M. B. (2003). Increased activation in the right insula during risk-taking decision making is related to harm avoidance and neuroticism. *NeuroImage, 19,* 1439–1448.

Pelphrey, K. A., Viola, R. J., & McCarthy, G. (2004). When strangers pass. Processing of mutual and averted social gaze in the superior temporal sulcus. *Psychological Science, 15,* 598–603.

Perrin, F., Maqut, P., Peigneux, P., Ruby, P., Degueldre, C., Balteau, E., et al. (2005). Neural mechanisms involved in the detection of our first name: A combined ERPs and PET study. *Neuropsychologia, 43,* 12–19.

Perry, B. D., Pollard, R. A., Blakley, T. L., Baker, W. L., & Vigilante, D. (1995). Childhood trauma, the neurobiology of adaptation, and "use-dependent" development of the brain: How states become traits. *Infant Mental Health Journal, 16,* 271–291.

Phillips, M. L., Drevets, W. C., Rauch, S. L., & Lane, R. (2003). Neurobiology of emotion perception: I. The neural basis of normal emotion perception. *Biological Psychiatry, 54,* 504–514.

Platek, S. M., Keenan, J. P., Gallup, G. G., Jr., & Mohammed, F. B. (2004). Where am I? The neurological correlates of self and other. *Cognitive Brain Research, 19,* 114–122.

Poeggel, G., & Braun, K. (1996). Early auditory filial learning in degus (*Octodon degus*): Behavioral and autoradiographic studies. *Brain Research, 743,* 162–170.

Poeggel, G., Helmeke, C., Abraham, A., Schwabe, T., Friedrich, P., & Braun, K. (2003). Juvenile emotional experience alters synaptic composition in the rodent cortex, hippocampus, and lateral amygdala. *Proceedings of the National Academy of Sciences of the United States of America, 100,* 16137–16142.

Poeggel, G., Lange, E., Haase, C., Metzger, M., Gulyaeva, N. V., & Braun, K. (1999). Maternal separation and early social deprivation in *Octodon degus*: Quantitative changes of NADPH-diaphorase reactive neurons in the prefrontal cortex and nucleus accumbens. *Neuroscience, 94,* 497–504.

Poeggel, G., Nowicki, L., & Braun, K. (2003). Early social deprivation alters monoaminergic afferents in the orbital prefrontal cortex of *Octodon Degus*. *Neuroscience, 116,* 617–620.

Porges, S. W. (1997). Emotion: An evolutionary by-product of the neural regulation of the autonomic nervous system. *Annals of the New York Academy of Sciences, 807,* 62–77.

Porges, S. W. (2001). The polyvagal theory: Phylogenetic substrates of a social nervous system. *International Journal of Psychophysiology, 42,* 123–146.

Porges, S. W., Doussard-Roosevelt, J. A., & Maiti, A. K. (1994). Vagal tone and the physiological regulation of emotion. *Monographs of the Society for Research in Child Development, 59,* 167–186.

Post, R. M., Weiss, S. R. B., & Leverich, G. S. (1994). Recurrent affective disorder: Roots in developmental neurobiology and illness progression based on changes in gene expression. *Development and Psychopathology, 6,* 781–813.

Potter, E. K., & McCluskey, D. I. (1986). Effects of hypoxia on cardiac vagal efferent activity and on the action of the vagus nerve at the heart in the dog. *Journal of the Autonomic Nervous System, 17*, 325–329.

Powles, W. E. (1992). *Human development and homeostasis.* Madison, CT: International Universities Press.

Prueter, C., Schultz-Venrath, U., & Rimpau, W. (2002). Dissociative and associated psychopathological symptoms in patients with epilepsy, pseuodoseizures, and both seizure forms. *Epilepsia, 43*, 188–192.

Putnam, F. W. (1989). Pierre Janet and modern views of dissociation. *Journal of Traumatic Stress, 2*, 413–429.

Putnam, F. W. (1995). Development of dissociative disorders. In D. Cicchetti & D. J. Cohen (Eds.), *Developmental psychopathology: Vol. 2. Risk, disorder, and adaptation* (pp. 581–608). New York: Wiley.

Putnam, F. W. (1997). *Dissociation in children and adolescents: A developmental perspective.* New York: Guilford Press.

Putnam, F. W., Carlson, E. B., Ross, C. A., Anderson, G., Clark, P., Torem, M., et al. (1996). Patterns of dissociation in clinical and nonclinical samples. *Journal of Nervous and Mental Disease, 184*, 673–679.

Rabe, S., Beauducel, A., Zollner, T., Maercker, A., & Karl, A. (2006). Regional brain electrical activity in posttraumatic stress disorder after motor vehicle accident. *Journal of Abnormal Psychology, 115*, 687–698.

Raij, T., Utela, K., & Riita, R. (2000). Audio-visual integration of letters in the human brain. *Neuron, 28*, 617–625.

Raine, A., Park, S., Lencz, T., Bihrle, S., Lacasse, L., Widom, C. S., et al. (2001). Reduced right hemisphere activation in severely abused violent offenders during a working memory task: An fMRI study. *Aggressive Behavior, 27*, 111–129.

Rauch, S. L., Whalen, P. J., Shin, L. M., McInerney, S. C., Macklin, M. L., Lasko, N. B., et al. (2000). Exaggerated amygdala response to masked facial stimuli in posttraumatic stress disorder: A functional MRI study. *Biological Psychiatry, 47*, 769–776.

Raz, A. (2004). Anatomy of attentional networks. *Anatomical Records, 281B*, 21–36.

Recordati, G. (2003). A thermodynamic model of the sympathetic and parasympathetic nervous systems. *Autonomic Neuroscience: Basic and Clinical, 103*, 1–12.

Reed, S. F., Ohel, G., David, R., & Porges, S. W. (1999). A neural explanation of fetal heart rate patterns: A test of the polyvagal theory. *Developmental Psychobiology, 35*, 108–118.

Rentero, N., Cividjian, A., Trevaks, D., Poquignot, J. M., Quintin, L., & McAllen, R. M. (2002). Activity patterns of cardiac vagal motoneurons in rat nucleus ambiguus. *American Journal of Physiology: Regulatory, Integrative and Comparative Physiology, 283*, R1327–R1334.

Richer, P. (1881). *Etudes cliniques sur l'hystero-epilepsie, ou grande hysterie.* Paris: Delahaye & Lecrosnier.

Rinaman, L., Levitt, P., & Card, J. P. (2000). Progressive postnatal assembly of limbic-autonomic circuits revealed by central transneuronal transport of pseudorabies virus. *Journal of Neuroscience, 20*, 2731–2741.

Roberts, N. A., Beer, J. S., Werner, K. H., Scabini, D., Levens, S. M., Knight, R. T., et al. (2004). The impact of orbital prefrontal cortex damage on emotional activation to unanticipated and anticipated acoustic startle stimuli. *Cognitive, Affective, and Behavioral Neuroscience, 4*, 307–316.

Roberts, N. A., Levens, S. M., McCoy, K., Werner, K., Beer, J. S., Scabini, D., et al. (2001). Orbitofrontal cortex and activation of defensive responses. *Society for Neuroscience Abstracts, 27*, 1705.

Roelofs, K., Keijers, G. P. J., Hoogduin, K. A. L., Naring, G. W. B., & Moene, F. C. (2002). Childhood abuse in patients with conversion disorder. *American Journal of Psychiatry, 159*, 1908–1913.

Rogers, R. D., Owen, A. M., Middleton, H. C., Williams, E. J., Pickard, J. D., Sahakian, B. J., et al. (1999). Choosing between small, likely rewards and large, unlikely rewards activates inferior and orbital prefrontal cortex. *Journal of Neuroscience, 20*, 9029–9038.

Rolls, E. T., Hornak, J., Wade, D., & McGrath, J. (1994). Emotion-related learning in patients with social and emotional changes associated with frontal lobe damage. *Journal of Neurology, Neurosurgery, and Psychiatry, 57*, 1518–1524.

Rosa, C., Lassonde, M., Pinard, C., Keenan, J. P., & Belin, P. (2008). Investigations of hemispheric specialization of self-voice recognition. *Brain and Cognition, 68*, 204–214.

Ruby, P., & Decety, J. (2001). Effect of subjective perspective taking during stimulation of action: A PET investigation of agency. *Nature Neuroscience, 4*, 546–550.

Ruch, T. C., & Shenkin, H. A. (1943). The relation of area 13 on orbital surface of frontal lobes to hyperactivity and hyperphagia in monkeys. *Journal of Neurophysiology, 6*, 349–360.

Rule, R. R., Shimamura, A. P., & Knight, R. T. (2002). Orbitofrontal cortex and dynamic filtering of emotional stimuli. *Cognitive, Affective, and Behavioral Neuroscience, 2*, 264–270.

Sack, M., Hopper, J. W., & Lamprecht, F. (2004). Low respiratory sinus arrhythymia and prolonged psychophysiological arousal in posttraumatic stress disorder: Heart rate dynamics and individual differences in arousal regulation. *Biological Psychiatry, 55*, 284–290.

Sahar, T., Shalev, A. Y., & Porges, S. W. (2001). Vagal modulation of responses to mental challenge in posttraumatic stress disorder. *Biological Psychiatry, 49*, 637–643.

Sanders, B., McRoberts, G., & Tollefson, C. (1989). Childhood stress and dissociation in a college population. *Dissociation, 2*, 17–23.

Sar, V., Ünal, S. N., & Oztürk, E. (2007). Frontal and occipital perfusion changes in dissociative identity disorder. *Psychiatry Research: Neuroimaging, 156*, 217–223.

Scaer, R. C. (2001). The neurophysiology of dissociation and chronic disease. *Applied Psychophysiology and Biofeedback, 26*, 73–91.

Schiffer, F., Teicher, M. H., & Papanicolaou, A. C. (1995). Evoked potential evidence for right brain activity during the recall of traumatic memories. *Journal of Neuropsychiatry and Clinical Neurosciences, 7*, 169–175.

Schmahl, C. G., Elzinga, B. M., & Bremner, J. D. (2002). Individual differences in psychophysiological reactivity in adults with childhood abuse. *Clinical Psychology and Psychotherapy, 9*, 271–276.

Schore, A. N. (1994). *Affect regulation and the origin of the self.* Mahwah, NJ: Erlbaum.

Schore, A. N. (1996). The experience-dependent maturation of a regulatory system in the orbital prefrontal cortex and the origin of developmental psychopathology. *Development and Psychopathology, 8*, 59–87.

Schore, A. N. (1997). Early organization of the nonlinear right brain and development of a predisposition to psychiatric disorders. *Development and Psychopathology, 9*, 595–631.

Schore, A. N. (2000). Attachment and the regulation of the right brain. *Attachment and Human Development, 2,* 23–47.

Schore, A. N. (2001a). The effects of a secure attachment relationship on right brain development, affect regulation, and infant mental health. *Infant Mental Health Journal, 22,* 7–66.

Schore, A. N. (2001b). The effects of relational trauma on right brain development, affect regulation, and infant mental health. *Infant Mental Health Journal, 22,* 201–269.

Schore, A. N. (2002). Dysregulation of the right brain: A fundamental mechanism of traumatic attachment and the psychopathogenesis of posttraumatic stress disorder. *Australian and New Zealand Journal of Psychiatry, 36,* 9–30.

Schore, A. N. (2003a). *Affect dysregulation and disorders of the self.* New York: Norton.

Schore, A. N. (2003b). *Affect regulation and the repair of the self.* New York: Norton.

Schore, A. N. (2003c). Early relational trauma, disorganized attachment, and the development of a predisposition to violence. In D. Siegel & M. Solomon (Eds.), *Healing trauma: Attachment, mind, body, and brain* (pp. 101–167). New York: Norton.

Schore, A. N. (2004). Commentary on "Dissociation: A developmental psychobiological perspective" by A. Panzer and M. Viljoen. *South African Psychiatry Review, 7,* 16–17.

Schore, A. N. (2005). Developmental affective neuroscience describes mechanisms at the core of dynamic systems theory. *Behavioral and Brain Sciences, 28,* 217–218.

Schuengel, C., Bakermans-Kranenburg, M. J., & Van IJzendoorn, M. H. (1999). Frightening maternal behavior linking unresolved loss and disorganized infant attachment. *Journal of Consulting and Clinical Psychology, 67,* 54–63.

Schwaber, J. S., Kapp, B. S., Higgins, G. A., & Rapp, P. R. (1982). Amygdaloid and basal forebrain direct connections with the nucleus of the solitary tract and the dorsal motor nucleus. *Journal of Neuroscience, 2,* 1424–1438.

Scicli, A. P., Petrovich, G. D., Swanson, L. W., & Thompson, R. F. (2004). Contextual fear conditioning is associated with lateralized expression of the immediate early gene *c-fos* in the central and basolateral amygdalar nuclei. *Behavioral Neuroscience, 118,* 5–14.

Seeck, M., Zaim, S., Chaves-Vischer, V., Blanke, O., Maeder-Ingvar, M., Weissert, M., et al. (2003). Ictal bradycardia in a young child with focal cortical dysplasia in the right insular cortex. *European Journal of Paediatric Neurology, 7,* 177–181.

Semmes, J. (1968). Hemispheric specialization: A possible clue to mechanism. *Neuropsychologia, 6,* 11–26.

Siegel, D. J. (1999). *The developing mind: Toward a neurobiology of interpersonal experience.* New York: Guilford Press.

Silberman, E. K. & Weingartner, H. (1986). Hemispheric lateralization of functions related to emotion. *Brain and Cognition, 5,* 322–353.

Simmons, A., Matthews, S. C., Stein, M. B., & Paulus, M. P. (2004). Anticipation of emotionally aversive memories activates right insula. *Neuro Report,* 2261–2265.

Spence, S., Shapiro, D., & Zaidel, E. (1996). The role of the right hemisphere in the physiological and cognitive components of emotional processing. *Psychophysiology, 33,* 112–122.

Spiegel, D., & Cardeña, E. (1991). Disintegrated experience: The dissociative disorders revisited. *Journal of Abnormal Psychology, 100,* 366–378.

Spitzer, C., Wilert, C., Grabe, H-J., Rizos, T., & Freyberger, H. J. (2004). Dissociation, hemispheric asymmetry, and dysfunction of hemispheric interaction: A transcranial magnetic approach. *Journal of Neuropsychiatry and Clinical Neurosciences, 16,* 163–169.

Spivak, B., Segal, M., Mester, R., & Weizman, A. (1998). Lateral preference in post-traumatic stress disorder. *Psychological Medicine, 28,* 229–232.

Stauss, H. M. (2003). Heart rate variability. *American Journal of Physiology: Regulatory, Integrative and Comparative Physiology, 285,* R927–R931.

Storey, K. B., & Storey, J. M. (2007). Tribute to P. L. Lutz: Putting life on "pause"— Molecular regulation of hypometabolism. *Journal of Experimental Biology, 210,* 1700–1714.

Stuss, D. T., & Alexander M. P. (1999). Affectively burnt in: One role of the right frontal lobe? In E. Tulving (Ed.), *Memory, consciousness, and the brain: The Talin conference* (pp. 215–227). Philadelphia: Psychology Press.

Sullivan, R. M., & Dufresne, M. M. (2006). Mesocortical dopamine and HPA axis regulation: Role of laterality and early environment. *Brain Research, 1076,* 49–59.

Sullivan, R. M., & Gratton, A. (2002). Prefrontal cortical regulation of hypothalamic-pituitary-adrenal function in the rat and implications for psychopathology: Side matters. *Psychoneuroendocrinology, 27,* 99–114.

Symonds, L. L., Gordon, N. S., Bixby, J. C., & Mande, M. M. (2006). Right-lateralized pain processing in the human cortex: An fMRI study. *Journal of Neurophysiology, 95,* 3823–3830.

Taylor, G. J., Bagby, R. M., & Parker, J. D. A. (1997). *Disorders of affect regulation: Alexithymia in medical and psychiatric illness.* Cambridge, UK: Cambridge University Press.

Teodoro, R. O., & O'Farrell, P. H. (2003). Nitric-oxide-induced suspended animation promotes survival during hypoxia. *EMBO Journal, 22,* 580–587.

Thompson, R. A. (1990). Emotion and self-regulation. In *Nebraska symposium on motivation* (pp. 367–467). Lincoln, NE: University of Nebraska Press.

Tops, M., Russo, S., Boksem, M. A. S., & Tucker, D. M. (2009). Serotonin: Modulator of a drive to withdraw. *Brain and Cognition, 71,* 427–436.

Toth, S.C., & Cicchetti, D. (1998). Remembering, forgetting, and the effects of trauma on memory: A developmental psychopathologic perspective. *Developmental and Psychopathology, 10,* 580–605.

Tranel, D., Bechara, A., & Denburg, N. L. (2002). Asymmetric functional roles of right and left ventromedial prefrontal cortices in social conduct, decision-making, and emotional processing. *Cortex, 38,* 589–612.

Trevarthen, C. (1996). Lateral asymmetries in infancy: Implications for the development of the hemispheres. *Neuroscience and Biobehavioral Reviews, 20,* 571–586.

Tronick, E. Z. (1989). Emotions and emotional communication in infants. *American Psychologist, 44,* 112–119.

Tronick, E. Z. (2004). Why is connection with others so critical? Dyadic meaning making, messiness and complexity governed selective processes which co-create and expand individuals' states of consciousness. In J. Nadel & D. Muir (Eds.), *Emotional development* (pp. 262–293). New York: Oxford University Press.

Tronick, E. Z., & Weinberg, M. K. (1997). Depressed mothers and infants: Failure to form dyadic states of consciousness. In L. Murray & P. J. Cooper (Eds.), *Postpartum depression in child development* (pp. 54–81). New York: Guilford Press.

Tucker, D. M. (1981). Lateral brain function, emotion, and conceptualization. *Psychological Bulletin, 89,* 19–46.

Tzourio-Mazoyer, N., De Schonen, S., Crivello, F., Reutter, B., Aujard, Y., & Mazoyer, B.

(2002). Neural correlates of woman face processing by 2-month-old infants. *Neuroimage, 15,* 454–461.

Uddin, L. Q., Molnar-Szakacs, I., Zaidel, E., & Iacoboni, M. (2006). rTMS to the right inferior parietal lobule disrupts self-other discrimination. *Social Cognition and Affective Neuroscience, 1,* 65–71.

van der Hart, O., Nijenhuis, E. R. S., & Steele, K. (2006). *The haunted self. Structural dissociation and the treatment of chronic traumatization.* New York: Norton.

van der Kolk, B. A. (1996). The body keeps the score. Approaches to the psychobiology of posttraumatic stress disorder. In B. A. van der Kolk, A. C. McFarlane, & L. Weisaeth (Eds.), *Traumatic stress: The effects of overwhelming experience on mind, body, and society* (pp. 214–241). New York; Guilford Press.

van der Kolk, B. A., & Fisler, R. E. (1994). Childhood abuse and neglect and loss of self-regulation. *Bulletin of the Menninger Clinic, 58,* 145–168.

van der Kolk, B. A., Pelcovitz, D., Roth, S., Mandel, F. S., McFarlane, A., & Herman, J. L. (1996). Dissociation, somatization, and affect dysregulation: The complexity of adaptation to trauma. *American Journal of Psychiatry, 153,* 83–93.

van der Kolk, B., & van der Hart, O. (1989). Pierre Janet and the breakdown of adaptation in psychological trauma. *American Journal of Psychiatry, 146,* 1530–1540.

van der Kolk, B., van der Hart, O., & Marmar, C. R. (1996). Dissociation and information processing in posttraumatic stress disorder. In B. A. van der Kolk, A. C. McFarlane, & L. Weisaeth (Eds.), *Traumatic stress: The effects of overwhelming experience on mind, body, and society* (pp. 303–327). New York: Guilford Press.

van der Kolk, B. A., Weisaeth, L., & van der Hart, O. (1996). History of trauma in psychiatry. In B. A. van der Kolk, A. C. McFarlane, & L. Weisaeth (Eds.), *Traumatic stress: The effects of overwhelming experience on mind, body, and society* (pp. 47–74). New York: Guilford Press.

Van IJzendoorn, M. H., Schuengel, C., & Bakermans-Kranenburg, M. J. (1999). Disorganized attachment in early childhood: Meta-analysis of precursors, concomitants, and sequelae. *Development and Psychopathology, 11,* 225–249.

Vianna, D. M. L., Graeff, F. G., Brandao, M. L., & Landeira-Fernandez, J. (2001). Defensive freezing evoked by electrical stimulation of the periaqueductal gray: Comparison between dorsolateral and ventrolateral regions. *NeuroReport, 12,* 4109–4112.

Volkow, N. D., Wang, G-J., Fowler, J. S., Logan, J., Gatley, J. S., Pappas, N. R., et al. (2000). Increased activity of the temporal insula in subjects with bradycardia. *Life Sciences, 67,* 2213–2220.

von der Ohe, C. G., Darian-Smith, C., Garner, C. C., & Heller, H. C. (2006). Ubiquitous and temperature-dependent neural plasticity in hibernators. *Journal of Neuroscience, 26,* 10590–10598.

Vyas, A., Mitra, R., Shankaranarayyana, Rao, B. S., & Chattarjai, S. (2002). Chronic stress induces contrasting pattern of dendritic remodeling in hippocampal and amygdaloid neurons. *Journal of Neuroscience, 22,* 6810–6818.

Waller, N., Putnam, F., & Carlson, E. (1996). Types of dissociation and dissociative types: A taxometric analysis of dissociative experiences. *Psychological Methods, 1,* 300–321.

Wang, J., Rao, H., Wetmore, G. S., Furlan, P. M., Korczykowki, M., Dinges, D. F., et al. (2005). Perfusion functional MRI reveals cerebral blood flow pattern under psychological stress. *Proceedings of the National Academy of Sciences of the United States of America, 102,* 17804–17809.

Wang, S. (1997). Traumatic stress and attachment. *Acta Physiologica Scandinavica, Supplement, 640,* 164–169.

Watanabe, S., Miki, K., & Kakigi, R. (2002). Gaze direction affect face perception in humans. *Neuroscience Letters, 325,* 163–166.

Weaver, I. C. G., Cervoni, N., Champagne, F. A., D'Alessio, A. C., Sharma, S., Seckl, J. R., et al. (2004). Epigenetic programming by maternal behavior. *Nature Neuroscience, 7,* 847–854.

Whalen, P. J., Rauch, S. L., Etcoff, N., McInerney, S. C., Lee, M. B., & Jenike, M. A. (1998). Masked presentations of emotional facial expressions modulate amygdala activity without explicit knowledge. *Journal of Neuroscience, 18,* 411–418.

Whitlock, F. A. (1967). The aetiology of hysteria. *Acta Psychiatrica Scandinavica, 43,* 144–162.

Williams, C. L., Haines, J., & Sale, I. M. (2003). Psychophysiological and psychological correlates of dissociation in a case of dissociative identity disorder. *Journal of Trauma and Dissociation, 4,* 101–118.

Winnicott, D. W. (1958). The capacity to be alone. *International Journal of Psycho-Analysis, 39,* 416–420.

Winston, J. S., Vuilleumier, P., & Dolan, R. J. (2003). Effects of low-spatial frequency components of fearful faces on fusiform cortex activity. *Current Biology, 13,* 1824–1829.

Wittling, W., & Schweiger, E. (1993). Neuroendocrine brain asymmetry and physical complaints. *Neuropsychologia, 31,* 591–608.

World Health Organization. (1992). *The ICD-10 classification of mental and behavioural disorders: Clinical descriptions and diagnostic guidelines.* Geneva: WHO.

Yamada, H., Sadato, N., Konishi, Y., Kimura, K., Tanaka, M., Yonekura, Y. et al. (1997). A rapid brain metabolic change in infants detected by fMRI. *NeuroReport, 8,* 3775–3778.

Yamada, H., Sadato, N., Konishi, Y., Muramoto, S., Kimura, K., Tanaka, M., et al. (2000). A milestone for normal development of the infantile brain detected by functional MRI. *Neurology, 55,* 218–223.

Yoon, B-W., Morillo, C. A., Cechetto, D. F., & Hachinski, V. (1997). Cerebral hemispheric lateralization in cardiac autonomic control. *Archives of Neurology, 54,* 741–744.

Young, J. B., Rosa, R. M., & Landsberg, L. (1984). Dissociation of sympathetic nervous system and adrenal medullary responses. *American Journal of Physiology, 247,* E35–E40.

Zelazo, P. D., & Muller, U. (2002). Executive function in typical and atypical development. In U. Goswami (Ed.), *Handbook of childhood cognitive development* (pp. 445–469). Oxford, UK: Blackwell.

CHAPTER 9

Is Borderline Personality a Particularly Right Hemispheric Disorder? A Study of P3a Using Single Trial Analysis

With Russell Meares and Dmitry Melkonian

It is increasingly being recognized that borderline personality disorder (BPD) is an important clinical and communal problem. It is a condition with a high mortality, approaching 10% in some studies (Paris, Brown, & Nowlis, 1987; Stone, 1993), and a morbidity that imposes a severe burden on the health system. It is more common than was once supposed, having a lifetime prevalence of 5.9% in the general population (Grant et al., 2008). It can be diagnosed in about 20% of inpatients and 10% of outpatients (Widiger & Frances, 1989). It has a significant comorbidity with all major Axis I disorders and to a greater extent than other personality disorders (Zanarini et al., 1998). BPD is thus important not only in itself as a serious condition but also because of its effect on the duration, recurrence, and outcome of Axis I disorders (Alnaes & Torgersen, 1997; McDermut & Zimmermann, 1998). These findings lead to the view that working toward a more effective means of treating BPD needs to be a significant component in building a modern mental health system. This achievement will depend, to a great extent, upon an understanding of the basic pathophysiology of BPD, upon which there is no general agreement among those who have devised treatment approaches for the condition. Such an understanding should contribute to a refinement and development of these approaches and current therapies.

This study derives from two related proposals about the origin of borderline personality disorder (BPD). The first is the basis of one current therapy for BPD, the conversational model (Meares, 2005; Meares, Stevenson, & Gordon, 1999; Stevenson & Meares, 1992). This proposal suggests that BPD is a manifestation of a deficiency in the maturation of that state of mind that Hughlings Jackson (1874/1958) and William James (1890) called "self," and that Edelman (1992) calls "higher order consciousness." The identifying feature of this complex form of consciousness is a reflective awareness of inner events (James, 1890, p. 297). Although Bateman and Fonagy (2004) do not directly approach the subject of self, their hypothesis regarding a failure of "mentalization" in BPD resembles this proposal.

It is proposed that a particular kind of interplay, mediated by conversation or, in infancy, proto-conversation (Trevarthen, 1974), is necessary to the maturation of this form of consciousness (Meares, 2005; Meares & Jones, 2009). A deficiency in this form of relatedness, together with the effect of traumatic impacts upon the psychic system, is considered to impair such maturation, consistent with evidence that family background and exposure to abuse are independent predictors of the development of BPD (Bradley, Jenei, & Westen, 2005). This is a more specific formulation of a hypothesis put forward by A. Stern (1938) in his pioneering paper that first outlined BPD. He suggested that an aspect of his patients' maturation had been impeded due to "psychic starvation and insecurity due to lack of parental, chiefly maternal, affection" (p. 470). He also pointed out that "actual cruelty, neglect and brutality by the parents of many years duration are factors found in these patients" (p. 470).

The second proposal about the origin of borderline personality disorder concerns a failure of inhibitory control in BPD, which is predicted by a developmental model of "self" based on the theories of Hughlings Jackson (Meares, 1999, 2000) and is supported by observations such as those of Silbersweig et al. (2007). Schore (1994, 2003a) has suggested that inadequacy of inhibitory control over limbic output, central to BPD, is likely to be manifested right hemispherically. He proposed that a particular disturbance of mother–child relatedness leading to "traumatic attachments" results in "a deficit of the higher right brain regulation and lower right cortically driven aggressive states" (2003a, p. 299). This study tests the hypothesis that borderline personality involves a relative failure of higher order, presumably prefrontally connected, inhibitory mechanisms, which will be especially evident in the right hemisphere.

The hypothesis is tested by means of a study of P3a, an early component of the late positive complex of event-related potentials (ERP), or P3(00), associated with the 300 ms latency range. The P3 is one of the most investigated endogenous brain potentials in psychiatric research. Studies of BPD patients have revealed the reduction in amplitude and latency prolongation of auditory P3 (Blackwood, St. Clair, & Kutcher, 1986; Drake, Phillips, & Pakalnis, 1991; Kutcher, Blackwood, St. Clair, Gaskell, & Muir, 1987). However, the characteristics of the P3a were not revealed in these BPD studies because the ability of the conventional method of ERP averaging to identify the P3a is quite limited.

A principal methodological difficulty is that reliable identification of the P3a from single trial records necessitates effective tools for significant improvement of the signal-to-noise ratio. To meet this condition, most previous techniques neglected the existence of the P3a and used a single template for reliable identification of the larger and more prominent P3b (Melkonian, Gordon, & Bahramali, 2001). In the new method of single trial analysis supported by multiple templates, no such simplifications are necessary, and the P3a and P3b reconstructions are reliably realized (Melkonian, Blumenthal, & Meares, 2003; Melkonian et al., 2001).

A comprehensive evaluation of P3a and P3b as distinct ERP components offers significant promise for investigation of the inhibitory aspect of the attention process. P3a is frontally connected and makes up the early part of P3. P3b arises somewhat later and is particularly parietally connected (Baudena, Halgren, Heit, & Clarke, 1995). P3a reflects novelty detection (Soltani & Knight, 2000) and orientating (Barcelo, Perianez, & Knight, 2002), whereas P3b is less clearly understood. Verleger and his colleagues suggest that it is akin to a response set (Verleger, Gorgen, & Jaskowski, 2005).

Polich (2007) has suggested neuroinhibition "as an overarching theoretical mechanism for P300." Inhibitory activity is necessarily recruited in the switching of attention from one event to another. This inhibitory function is reflected in the impairment of P3a, particularly its habituation (Friedman & Simpson, 1994). P3a is underpinned by dopaminergic pathways, whereas P3b depends upon noradrenergic neurotransmission (Barcelo et al., 2002). Parkinsonian subjects, who are relatively dopamine depleted, have difficulty in switching attention- and exhibit-impaired habituation of P3a (Hozumi, Hirata, Tanaka, & Yamazaki, 2000).

The inhibitory aspect of the attentional process, as reflected in P3a, develops as the individual matures (Meares, Melkonian, Gordon, & Williams, 2005). In borderline patients, P3a is abnormally large in amplitude, suggesting that this maturation is impeded. In this study, we investigate the possibility that this impairment is particularly right sided. We believe this report to be the first, apart from our previous study, concerned with attentional processes in BPD as reflected in P3a.

SUBJECTS

Seventeen patients with BPD (4 males and 13 females; mean age 31.6 years, SD 7.9, range 20–44 years) participated in the study. The BPD patients came from an ongoing program for the treatment and evaluation of BPD patients. Patients were free of medication for at least 30 days at the time of the study. The sample is relatively small because the majority of BPD patients were heavily medicated at first presentation, the medications almost invariably including antidepressants. The subjects were consecutive admissions to the program of those patients who were medication free. The data were collected over a 2-year period. The diagnosis was made by two independent raters (psychiatrist and psychologist) in a clinical assessment and according to *DSM-III-R* criteria in a diagnostic interview that included the Diagnostic Interview for Borderline Patients. The subjects were not considered by their referring doctors or at the clinical assessment to be suffering from major depressive disorder.

The control group included 17 (4 males and 13 females; mean age 34.3 years, SD 8.6, range 20–47 years) age- and sex-matched healthy subjects recruited from the general western Sydney community. For both groups, exclusion criteria were left-handedness; a recent history of substance abuse, epilepsy, or other neurological disorders; and head injury, which were assessed with section M from the Composite International Diagnostic Interview (Robins et al., 1988) and the Westmead Hospital clinical information base (Williams, Gordon, Wright, & Bahramali, 2000). Subjects were asked to refrain from smoking or drinking caffeine for 3 hours prior to the recording session. Written consent was obtained from all subjects prior to testing in accordance with National Health and Medical Research Council guidelines. Control subjects were also screened for the history of psychiatric illness (themselves or first-degree relatives).

Procedure and ERP Recording

The ERP data were collected according to a standard auditory "oddball" paradigm in a method similar to that used in several previous studies (Meares et al., 2005; Melkonian et al., 2003). In brief, auditory tones (50 ms in duration, 10 ms of rise and fall time) were presented pseudo-randomly via stereo headphones to both ears at 60 dB above each individual subject's auditory threshold; 15% were target tones presented at 1,500 Hz, the remaining 85% were background tones delivered at 1,000 Hz with the constraint that there were no successive target stimuli.

The subjects were instructed to ignore background tones and to press a reaction-time button to target tones with the first finger of each hand. The identification of each target was regarded as correct if a button press response was obtained within 1 second of the target tone. Reaction time was recorded for each button press. EEGs were recorded from 19 electrode sites according to the 10 to 20 international system with linked ears as a reference using a DC acquisition system. An additional two channels were used for detecting horizontal and vertical eye-movement potentials. Impedance of all electrodes was less than 5 kΩ. The voltages were continuously digitized at 250 Hz and digitally stored. EOG correction using a technique based on Gratton, Coles, and Donchin (1983) was carried out off-line. The successive EEG segments time locked to correctly detect target tones were then tested on the presence of excessive artifacts. An accepted trial was then digitally filtered. A 251 time-points time series extracted from 0.2 second pre-stimulus to 0.8 second poststimulus was digitally stored, and the procedure continued until 40 eligible segments were acquired.

Data Analysis

Late-component ERPs were identified in single trial ERP (recordings) using the fragmentary decomposition (FD) method described in detail elsewhere (Ford, White, Lim, & Pfefferbaum, 1994; Melkonian et al., 2003). The method is a further development of conventional single trial screening procedures with a component template. Using the positive half cycle of a 2-Hz sine wave as a template, the previous technique was addressed to a single P3 component (Ford et al., 1994). The FD-based technique uses adaptive segmentation and high-resolution FD, which resolves component temporal overlap (Melkonian et al., 2001). This advanced signal processing technique provides means to match an individual template to both the P3a and P3b components detected in a single trial record. Within the latency windows of 80 to 120, 160 to 220, 180 to 235, 240 to 299, and 300 to 360 ms the N1, P2, N2, P3a, and P3b components, respectively, were identified as positive (P) or negative (N) waveforms with the maximum of absolute peak amplitude.

An important aspect of the variability of single trial parameters is a non-Gaussian character of frequency distributions of the peak amplitudes of the late ERP components (Melkonian et al., 2001). Accordingly, conventional parametric estimates have been validated using a nonparametric Mann-Whitney U-test for intergroup comparisons.

Lateralization of brain potentials has been quantified by comparing the potentials on homologous electrodes (e.g., locations F3 and F4) over both hemispheres. The interhemispheric relationships were estimated using the pairs of quantities (A_L , A_R), where A_L and A_R denote P3a peak amplitudes at the right and left homologous electrodes, respectively. The difference between the peak amplitudes, $\Delta A = A_R - A_L$, was taken as a measure of lateralization.

Using sequence sensitivity of ERP single trial analysis, we tested relevance of identified single trial ERP components to the novelty processing in the context of a habituation. The decrease or increase of peak amplitude with the target stimulus repetition was evaluated using regression analysis. Habituation is associated with negative values of the slope.

RESULTS

Interhemispheric Asymmetry of P3a Voltages in BPD Patients

Consistent with the previous reports (Meares et al., 2005; Melkonian et al., 2003), single trial records with identified P3a and P3b components comprise three major types of activity patterns illustrated by Figure 9.1. Between-group differences in the mean peak latencies of the P3a are statistically insignificant for

The light lines indicate event-related potentials elicited in different single trials. The darker lines show templates that identify P3a and P3b components of single trial ERPs. The x-axis units are milliseconds, and the y-axis units are microvolts. L indicates the peak latencies of P3a and P3b in A and B, respectively.

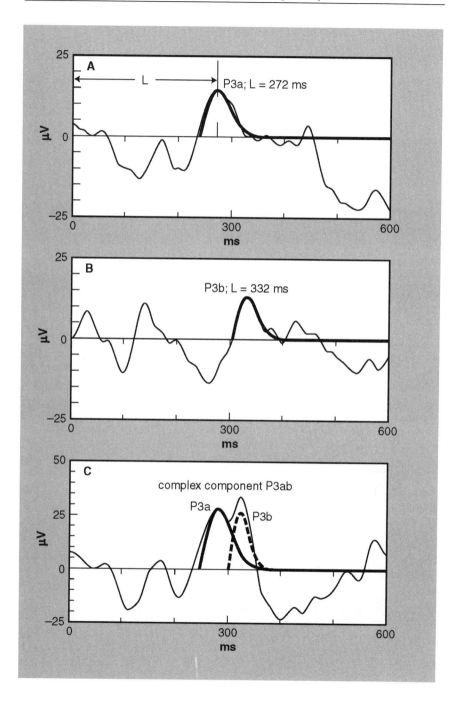

all electrode sites. This observation supports peak amplitudes as adequate measures of interhemispheric relationships.

The results of comparing P3a over homologous electrodes have shown that peak amplitudes of P3a in the left and right hemispheres of BPD patients are significantly different. Figure 9.2 shows the means of amplitude differences between homologous electrodes in the right and left hemispheres. Positive values of statistically significant differences reflect larger P3a amplitudes in the right hemisphere.

BPD Versus Controls Results Check

Within-group analysis revealed that interhemispheric asymmetry of P3a voltage differences found in BPD patients is absent in the control group. Accordingly, the ΔA in BPD patients is significantly higher in relation to the healthy comparison subjects at F4/F3, F8/F7, C4/C3, and P4/P3 pairs of homologous sites ($p <$ 0.001 for all pairs). At the right-hemispheric locations of these pairs (i.e., F4, F8, C4, and P4 cortical sites), and midline (Fz, Cz, and Pz) cortical sites, the BPD patients showed a significantly increased magnitude of P3a voltages as compared with the controls. By contrast, the P3a data from the left hemisphere demonstrated no statistically significant intergroup changes of P3a voltages. Major characteristic aspects of this hemispheric asymmetry of P3a voltages are presented in Table 9.1 for frontal recording sites. In the control group, the P3a voltages are nearly equal at F4/F3 and F8/F7 homologous cortical sites. By contrast, in BPD patients, the P3a amplitudes at the same pairs of cortical sites show significant

FIGURE 9.2.   P3a voltage differences between right and left homologous cortical sites in BPD patients.

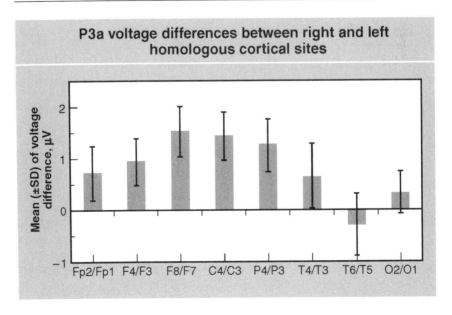

TABLE 9.1 Comparisons of P3a Voltages of BPD Patients and Normal Subjects at Frontal Recording Sites

Recording site	BPD Patients (N = 17)			Normal Subjects (N = 17)			Analysis[a]	
	N_s	Mean (μV)	SD	N_s	Mean (μV)	SD	Z	p
Left hemisphere, F7	463	7.0	5.1	443	7.5	3.7	1.89	ns[b]
Left hemisphere, F3	446	13.4	8.0	363	12.1	6.0	1.88	ns[b]
Middle site, Fz	427	14.8	9.3	328	12.6	6.4	3.88	0.001
Right hemisphere, F4	457	14.2	8.4	377	11.9	5.4	4.85	0.001
Right hemisphere, F8	440	8.4	5.8	429	7.3	3.3	3.28	0.002

Note: The data for BPD patients and normal subjects include the number of single trials with identified P3a (N_s, sample size), the mean and standard deviation (SD) of P3a peak amplitude.

[a] The Analysis column shows results of intergroup comparison for each recording site (F7, F3, Fz, F4, and F8) using a nonparametric Mann-Whitney U-test.

[b] A nonsignificant difference between the BPD and comparison group is denoted by 'ns' (5% significance level).

asymmetry with larger voltages in the right hemisphere. A nonparametric Mann-Whitney U-test demonstrates a highly significant increase of P3a voltages in BPD patients as compared with controls at F4 ($p < 0.001$) and F8 ($p < 0.002$) in the right hemisphere. The increased P3a amplitude in BPD patients is also seen at the middle site Fz ($p < 0.001$).

Habituation Data

The tests of habituation were separately applied to P3a and P3b for each individual electrode site. The regression analysis conducted for both groups revealed no statistically significant effect of target stimulus repetition on ERP amplitude in the group of BPD patients.

Similar results were obtained by regression analysis of P3b in normal subjects. By contrast, the P3a data in these subjects revealed statistically significant voltage decline (5% significance level) at nearly all recording sites with the exception of Fp1, Fp2, F7, F8, and O1. The decline rates (regression coefficient β in microvolt per stimulus), sample sizes (N), and significance levels (p) at midline Fz, Cz, and Pz recording sites were -0.088 ($N = 328$, $p < 0.01$), -0.106 (363, 0.002), and -0.103 (390, 0.01), respectively. The sample size corresponds to the number of trials in which the P3a was identified.

Comparison of habituation on homologous electrodes revealed no significant effect of lateralization on a decline rate.

DISCUSSION

In this study, borderline patients were shown to differ from controls in two ways. First, the BPD patients show significant larger P3a amplitudes in the right hemisphere, particularly frontally and centrally, than in the left hemisphere. On the other hand, there were no significant differences between BPD and controls in P3a amplitudes at electrode sites in the left hemisphere (Table 9.1). Second, unlike controls, in whom habituation of P3a is evident, habituation of P3a fails in borderline subjects. These findings, taken together, are suggestive of a deficiency of higher order inhibitory activity, more evident right hemispherically in BPD. These findings are consistent with observations that the right hemisphere is particularly implicated in inhibitory control (Garavan, Ross, & Stein, 1999) and that failure of inhibition in a social context is significantly associated with brain lesions leading to "dysfunction of orbitofrontal and basotemporal cortices of the right hemisphere" (Starkstein & Robinson, 1997).

The findings regarding the large P3a amplitudes exhibited by BPD subjects give support to the possibility that BPD symptomatology is the manifestation of a certain kind of maturational deficit. The capacity to inhibit responses grows with maturation (Christ, White, Mandernach, & Keys, 2001; Tamm, Menon, & Reisss, 2002). Young subjects without psychiatric disability have large P3a amplitudes that decline with age (Meares et al., 2005).

Posner and his colleagues (Posner et al., 2002) propose an attentional basis of BPD with a disturbance of a "specific circuit" underpinning its phenomena. The particularity of the electrophysiological disturbance in our ERP data suggests that large P3a amplitudes may be a marker of this circuit. P3a appears in the time window 240 to 300 ms poststimulus. This is the only time window in which significant differences between components of ERP in BPD and controls were shown in this study. In particular, P3b was unaffected.

Posner and his colleagues (2002) concluded that a disturbance in attentional control that they demonstrated in their BPD subjects is related to a failure in a system involved in emotional regulation. A relationship between emotional-processing and attentional systems, including novelty detection as reflected by P3a, is evident on consideration of the way in which "meaning" is attributed to novel stimuli.

Such attributions extend beyond the fundamental distinction between "familiar/strange," which is the basis of the orientating/habituation response, to include a wide range of meanings necessary to the experience of "self." They depend upon a complex matching process in which an event in the environment is compared with models of similar events stored in memory, including very recent memory. The hippocampus is a crucial element in this comparison (Kumaran & Maguire, 2007a; Vinogradova, 2001). The emotional state that arises from this comparison, and of which the individual may be barely aware, determines the judgment of response. As Damasio and his colleagues (1999) have frequently pointed out, evaluation of the significance of stimuli is not simply a matter of cognition but includes emotional processing. They emphasize the significant role of the orbitofrontal cortex in this processing. The orbitofrontal cortex (OFC) is involved in the inhibitory control and modulation of emotion (Drevets, 2000).

Different forms of matching and mismatching trigger various emotions. Mismatch might evoke such feeling states as apprehension, alarm, or mere interest and alertness. A matching response will evoke different emotions, for example, familiarity, security, or pleasure.

A gathering body of evidence suggests that the child who is at risk for developing BPD has been exposed to a social environment involving excessive mismatching. This is suggested by studies showing that disorganized attachment in children is an important prediction for future BPD (Barone, 2003; Fonagy et al., 1996; Liotti, 2000; Patrick, Hobson, Castle, Howard, & Maughan, 1994). The mothering figure's responses in the creation of disorganized attachment produce repeated mismatches with her child. The responses are typically unpredictable, frightening, frightened, or unavailable to the child's attachment overtures (Lyons-Ruth, 2003). The effect upon the child can be seen as one of repeated minor "shocks," or cumulative miniature traumata. In displaying disorganized attachment, the child at times looks as if stunned, akin to the dissociated state of a traumatized adult. This is a form of "relational trauma" (Schore, 2009) additional to any physical or sexual abuse that may have been inflicted upon the child. Abuse is very common in the childhood of those who suffer BPD. Although sexual abuse is not universal in these histories (Zanarini, 1997), "relational attachment trauma" may be (Schore, 2010).

Our study is limited in that it does not allow for a distinction to be made between the effects of matching and mismatching. A recent study suggested that they may be distinct although related processes, with the left side responding to mismatching and the right side to matching (Kumaran & Maguire, 2007b). This suggestion resonates with a similar proposal from Hughlings Jackson, who remarked upon "what is most fundamental in mental operations—the double process of tracing relations of likeness and unlikeness" (1874/1958, p. 129). Relations of likeness underlie the use of metaphor, which depends upon right brain activity (Mashal, Faust, Hendler, & Jung-Beeman, 2007).

Our hypotheses imply that matching of a certain kind promotes maturation whereas mismatching impedes it. The former proposal has gained influence in recent years due to the work of researchers such as Trevarthen (1987) and D. Stern (1988). Their observations suggest that the matching necessary to maturation has characteristic qualities: It involves the mother using her facial expression, tone of voice, and tactile-gestures to resonate with her child's immediate reality. This kind of matching is not imitation. For example, the temporal contour of a maternal nonverbal vocalization might match, in a way that gives a sense of fit, what she sees in her infant's face. This kind of matching is "analogical" (Meares & Jones, 2009). An analogue of something is another thing that is like it but not a copy.

Mother–child interplay involving iterative analogical responding goes on only for a time and only during periods of infantile non-distress or positive affect. Trevarthen (1974) called it a proto-conversation, and it is likely to be crucial to the maturation of "self." Maternal responses during periods of infantile non-distress predict the emergence of symbolic play (Bornstein & Tamis Le Monda, 1997), which is seen as the necessary nonverbal precursor of the child's later attainment of a verbal, explicit reflective awareness of inner events (Meares, 2005) at about 4 years of age (Meares & Orlay, 1988).

The right hemisphere seems to be peculiarly set up for the proto-conversation. Recognition of faces (Kim et al., 1999), and especially the emotions they represent (Buchanan et al., 2000; Harciarek & Heilman, 2009; Iidaka et al., 2003; Tamietto et al., 2006), is largely right hemispherical, as is the processing of prosody (Riecker, Wildgruber, Dogil, Grodd, & Ackermann, 2002) and rhythm (Jongsma, Desain, & Honing, 2004). P3a, evoked by auditory stimuli, is sensitive to changes in rhythm (Jongsman et al. , 2004).

Maturation of the right hemisphere may be particularly vulnerable during the first years of life. The right hemisphere is in a growth spurt during the first 2 years, a period of right brain dominance, and so right hemisphere resources are the first to develop (Chiron et al., 1997; Decety & Chaminade, 2003). This growth is not totally encoded in the genome, but is indelibly shaped by epigenetic experiences with the social, especially maternal, environment. The neurobiological maturation of the emotion-processing right hemisphere in the early critical period of the first 2 years of life is thus "experience-dependent." It is specifically the affect communicating and analogically representing interplay between mother and child involving prosody, facial expressions, interpersonal touch, and rhythm that impact the experience-dependent maturation of prefrontal cortical-limbic circuits of the early developing right cortical hemisphere (Schore, 2005). The baby's right brain seems to be particularly set up to respond to the mother's face. For example, babies aged 4 to 9 months move their eyes more quickly to the mother's face than a stranger's face when the stimuli are presented in the left visual field. In contrast, simple geometric shapes are discriminated equally well in either field (Rapp & Bachevalier, 2008, p. 1046). Lyons and colleagues demonstrate that varying maternal behaviors in infancy produce "significant differences in right but not left adult prefrontal volumes, with experience-dependent asymmetric variation most clearly expressed in ventral medial cortex measured in vivo by magnetic resonance imaging" (2002, p. 51). A deficit in appropriate responding may produce the structural changes reported by Chanen et al. (2008) in a group of first-presentation BPD patients in whom secondary effects of the disorder over time were likely to be minimized. They showed right-sided orbitofrontal loss of gray matter related to controls but no hippocampal or amygdaloid difference.

It seems important that the interplay of the proto-conversation involves neurophysiological activation of a similar kind in both partners. For example, affective prosody not only is processed right hemispherically but also is delivered as a consequence of right brain activation (Ross & Monnot, 2008). It might be said then, in a partially figurative way, that the proto-conversation represents an interplay between two right brains. In the case of the mother, at least, orbitofrontal activation is prominent. It occurs when mothers view pictures of their babies (Nitschke et al., 2004). The orbitofrontal cortex, periaqueductal gray matter, anterior insula, and dorsal and ventrolateral putamen become active when a mother views her baby smiling at the mother while playing with her (Noriuchi, Kikuchi, & Senoo, 2008). Viewing her infant's distress evokes a different neural response. The smile is likely to enhance activation in the medial orbitofrontal cortex beyond that evoked by the image of the baby alone (O'Doherty et al., 2003). Such observations lead to the speculation that the analogical matching behavior of the mother during the proto-conversation might evoke a mirrored neurophysiology in her baby and tend to stimulate activation and maturation of circuitry involving the orbitofrontal cortex. The observations of a study from Minagawa-Kawai et al. (2009) support the possibility of such reciprocity. They showed orbitofrontal cortical activation in the brains of mothers and babies when shown a video of the other. In the mother's case, the activation was right sided.

These observations lead to implications for treatment of BPD designed to facilitate the emergence awareness of inner events, a state that Bateman and Fonagy (2004) call "mentalization." This kind of consciousness does not appear until fairly late in child development, at about age 4. It arises from earlier experiences of affect regulation and a more fundamental state of mind, which is developing during a period when the right hemisphere is dominant. The data presented in this study suggest this development has been impeded in those who suffer BPD. In order for the reflective capacity to reveal itself, the foundation of the earlier kind of consciousness must be made. This suggests that a major role is played, particularly in early phases of treatment, by an engagement between therapist and patient that depends upon a conversation in which the elements of the emotional, nonverbal, and analogical "language" of the right hemisphere are prominent. Clinical evidence gathered during studies of the Meares' conversational model (2000, 2004, 2005) suggest that this kind of relatedness allows higher-order consciousness to come forth in those with BPD in a natural and spontaneous way (Meares, 2004; Meares & Jones, 2009). These data also support Schore's right brain–to–right brain communication model of psychotherapy (Schore, 2003b). Other researchers now report that BPD subjects show right posterior cortical deficits in the processing of social visual stimuli, and that this impairment is associated with an impairment of interpersonal communication (Merkl et al., 2010).

Finally, although diminished amplitude of P3 is a very uncommon finding in psychiatric illness, this study is limited by the absence of control groups with Axis I disorder. BPD is comorbid with all major Axis I disorders (Zanarini et al., 1998). It is possible that a comorbid condition not identified in our study is the basis of the P3a findings. Subsequent studies are needed on depression and, most particularly, dissociative disorders. Furthermore, future investigation should involve, for each patient, careful and extensive phenomenological examination together with a history of the developmental background, because not all BPD subjects may show the findings characteristic of our group of unmedicated patients.

In conclusion, the abnormally large amplitudes of P3a at right hemisphere sites in borderline patients together with the failure of habituation of P3a are consistent with deficient inhibitory activity. Discussion of the findings suggest that they may reflect impeded maturation of the frontomedial processing systems, which, it is argued, may be a consequence of the typical early environment of those with the borderline condition. This suggestion leads to a consideration of optimal therapeutic behavior in this condition, in particular for "matching" or "analogical" responsiveness.

REFERENCES

Alnaes, R., & Torgersen, S. (1997). Personality and personality disorders predict development and relapses of major depression. *Acta Psychiatrica Scandinavica, 95*, 336–342.

Barcelo, F., Perianez, J. A., & Knight, R. T. (2002). Think differently: A brain orienting response to task novelty. *NeuroReport, 13*, 1887–1892.

Barone, L. (2003). Developmental protective and risk factors in borderline personality disorder: A study using the Adult Attachment Interview. *Attachment and Human Development, 5*, 64–77.

Bateman, A., & Fonagy, P. (2004). *Psychotherapy for borderline personality disorder mentalization-based treatment.* New York: Oxford University Press.

Baudena, P., Halgren, E., Heit, G., & Clarke, J. M. (1995). Intracerebral potentials to rare target and distractor auditory and visual stimuli: III. Frontal cortex. *Electroencephalography and Clinical Neurophysiology, 94,* 251–264.

Blackwood, D. H., St. Clair, D. M., & Kutcher, S. P. (1986). P300 event-related potential abnormalities in borderline personality disorder. *Biological Psychiatry, 21,* 560–564.

Bornstein, M., & Tamis Le Monda, C. (1997). Maternal responsiveness and infant mental abilities: Specific predictive relations. *Infant Behavior and Development, 20,* 283–296.

Bradley, R., Jenei, J., & Westen, D. (2005). Etiology of borderline personality disorder: Disentangling the contributions of intercorrelated antecedents. *Journal of Nervous and Mental Disorders, 193,* 24–31.

Buchanan, T. W., Lutz, K., Mirzazade, S., Specht, K., Shah, N. J., Zilles, K., et al. (2000). Recognition of emotional prosody and verbal components of spoken language: An fMRI study. *Cognitive Brain Research, 9,* 227–238.

Chanen, A. M., Velakoulis, D., Carison, K., Gaunson, K., Wood, S. J., Yuen, H. P., et al. (2008). Orbitofrontal, amygdala and hippocampal volumes in teenagers with first-presentation borderline personality disorder. *Psychiatry Research: Neuroimaging, 163,* 116–125.

Chiron, C., Jambaque, I., Nabbout, R., Lounes, R., Syrota, A., & Dulac, O. (1997). The right brain hemisphere is dominant in human infants. *Brain, 120,* 1057–1065.

Christ, S. E., White, D. A., Mandernach, T., & Keys, B. A. (2001). Inhibitory control across the life span. *Developmental Neuropsychology, 20,* 653–669.

Damasio, A. R. (1999). *The feeling of what happens: Body, emotion and the making of consciousness.* New York: Harcourt Brace.

Decety, J., & Chaminade, T. (2003). When the self represents the other: A new cognitive neuroscience view on psychological identification. *Consciousness and Cognition, 12,* 577–596.

Drake, M. E., Jr., Phillips, B. B., & Pakalnis, A. (1991). Auditory evoked potentials in borderline personality disorder. *Clinical Electroencephalography, 22,* 188–192.

Drevets, W. C. (2000). Functional anatomical abnormalities in limbic and prefrontal cortical structures in major depression. *Progress in Brain Research, 126,* 413–431.

Edelman, G. (1992). *Bright air, brilliant fire.* New York: Basic Books.

Fonagy, P., Leigh, T., Steele, M., Steele, H., Kennedy, R., Mattoon, G., et al. (1996). The relation of attachment status, psychiatric classification, and response to psychotherapy. *Journal of Consulting and Clinical Psychology, 64,* 22–31.

Ford, J. M., White, P., Lim, K. O., & Pfefferbaum, A. (1994). Schizophrenics have fewer and smaller P300s: A single-trial analysis. *Biological Psychiatry, 35,* 96–103.

Friedman, D., & Simpson, G. V. (1994). ERP amplitude and scalp distribution to target and novel events: Effects of temporal order in young, middle-aged and older adults. *Cognitive Brain Research, 2,* 49–63.

Garavan, H., Ross, T. J., & Stein, E. A. (1999). Right hemispheric dominance of inhibitory control: An event-related functional MRI study. *Proceedings of the National Academy of Sciences of the United States of America, 96,* 8301–8306.

Grant, B. F., Chou, S. P., Goldstein, R. B., Huang, B., Stinson, F. S., Saha, T. D., et al. (2008). Prevalence, correlates, disability, and comorbidity of *DSM-IV* borderline personality disorder: Results from the Wave 2 National Epidemiologic Survey on Alcohol and Related Conditions. *Journal of Clinical Psychology, 69,* 533–545.

Gratton, G., Coles, M. G., & Donchin, E. (1983). A new method for off-line removal of ocular artifact. *Electroencephalography and Clinical Neurophysiology, 55*, 468–484.

Harciarek, M., & Heilman, K. M. (2009). The contribution of anterior and posterior regions of the right hemisphere to the recognition of emotional faces. *Journal of Clinical and Experimental Neuropsychology, 31*, 322–330.

Hozumi, A., Hirata, K., Tanaka, H., & Yamazaki, K. (2000). Perseveration for novel stimuli in Parkinson's disease: An evaluation based on event-related potentials topography. *Movement Disorders, 15*, 835–842.

Iidaka, T., Terashima, S., Yamashita, K., Okada, T., Sadato, N., & Yonekura Y. (2003). Dissociable neural responses in the hippocampus to the retrieval of facial identity and emotion: An event-related fMRI study. *Hippocampus, 13*, 429–436.

Jackson, H. J. (1958). On the nature of the duality of the brain. In J. Taylor (Ed.), *Selected writings of John Hughlings Jackson* (pp. 129–145). New York: Basic Books. (Original work published 1874)

James, W. (1890). *Principles of psychology*. New York: Holt.

Jongsma, M. L., Desain, P., & Honing, H. (2004). Rhythmic context influences the auditory evoked potentials of musicians and non-musicians. *Biological Psychology, 66*, 129–152.

Kim, J. J., Andreasen, N. C., O'Leary, D. S., Wiser, A. K., Boles Ponto, L. L., Watkins, G. L., et al. (1999). Direct comparison of the neural substrates of recognition memory for words and faces. *Brain, 122*, 1069–1083.

Kumaran, D., & Maguire, E. A. (2007a). Which computational mechanisms operate in the hippocampus during novelty detection? *Hippocampus, 17*, 735–748.

Kumaran, D., & Maguire, E. A. (2007b). Match–mismatch processes underlie human hippocampal responses to associative novelty. *Journal of Neuroscience, 27*, 8517–8524.

Kutcher, S. P., Blackwood, D. H., St. Clair, D., Gaskell, D. F., & Muir, W. J. (1987). Auditory P300 in borderline personality disorder and schizophrenia. *Archives of General Psychiatry, 44*, 645–650.

Liotti, G. (2000). Disorganized attachment, models of borderline states, and evolutionary psychotherapy. In P. Gilbert & K. Bailey (Eds.), *Genes of the couch: Essays in evolutionary psychotherapy*. Hove, UK: Psychology Press.

Lyons, D. M., Afarian, H., Schatzberg, A. F., Sawyer-Glover, A., & Moseley, M. E. (2002). Experience-dependent asymmetric variation in primate prefrontal morphology. *Behavioral Brain Research, 136*, 51–59.

Lyons-Ruth, K. (2003). Dissociation and the parent–infant dialogue: A longitudinal perspective from attachment research. *Journal of the American Psychoanalytic Association, 51*, 883–911.

Mashal, N., Faust, M., Hendler, T., & Jung-Beeman, M. (2007). An fMRI investigation of the neural correlates underlying the processing of novel metaphoric expressions. *Brain and Language, 100*, 115–126.

McDermut, W., & Zimmerman, M. (1998). The effects of personality disorders on outcome in the treatment of depression. In A. J. Rush (Ed.), *Mood and anxiety disorders* (pp. 321–338). Baltimore: Williams and Wilkins.

Meares, R. (1999). The contribution of Hughlings Jackson to an understanding of dissociation. *American Journal of Psychiatry, 156*, 1850–1855.

Meares, R. (2000). *Intimacy and alienation: Memory, trauma and personal being*. London: Routledge.

Meares, R. (2004). A poetics of change. *Psychoanalytic Dialogues, 15*, 661–680.

Meares, R. (2005). *The metaphor of play: Origin and breakdown of personal being.* London: Routledge.

Meares, R., & Jones, S. (2009). Analogical relatedness in personal integration or coherence. *Contemporary Psychoanalysis, 45,* 504–519.

Meares, R., Melkonian, D., Gordon, E., & Williams, L. (2005). Distinct pattern of P3a event-related potential in borderline personality disorder. *Neuroreport 16,* 289–293.

Meares, R., & Orlay, W. (1988). On self-boundary: A study of the development of the concept of secrecy. *British Journal of Medical Psychology, 61,* 305–316.

Meares, R., Stevenson, J., & Gordon, E. A. (1999). Jacksonian and biopsychosocial hypothesis concerning borderline and related phenomena. *Australian and New Zealand Journal of Psychiatry, 33,* 831–840.

Melkonian, D., Blumenthal, T. D., & Meares, R. (2003). High-resolution fragmentary decomposition: A model-based method of non-stationary electrophysiological signal analysis. *Journal of Neuroscience Methods, 131,* 149–159.

Melkonian, D., Gordon, E., & Bahramali, H. (2001). Single-event-related potential analysis by means of fragmentary decomposition. *Biological Cybernetics, 85,* 219–229.

Merkl, A., Ammelburg, N., Aust, S., Roepke, S., Reinbecker, H., Trahms, L., et al. (2010). Processing of visual stimuli in borderline personality disorder: A combined behavioural and magnetoencephalographic study. *International Journal of Psychophysiology, 78,* 257–264.

Minagawa-Kawai, Y., Matsuoka, S., Dan, I., Naoi, N., Nakamuram, K., & Kojima, S. (2009). Prefrontal activation associated with social attachment: Facial-emotion recognition in mothers and infants. *Cerebral Cortex, 19,* 284–292.

Nitschke, J. B., Nelson, E. E., Rusch, B. D., Fox, A. S., Oakes, T. R., & Davidson, R. J. (2004). Orbitofrontal cortex tracks positive mood in mothers viewing pictures of their newborn infants. *NeuroImage, 21,* 583–592.

Noriuchi, M., Kikuchi, Y., & Senoo, A. (2008). The functional neuroanatomy of maternal love: Mother's response to infant's attachment behaviors. *Biological Psychiatry, 63,* 415–423.

O'Doherty, J., Winston, J., Critchley, H., Perrett, D., Burt, D. M., & Dolan, R. J. (2003). Beauty in a smile: The role of medial orbitofrontal cortex in facial attractiveness. *Neuropsychologia, 41,* 147–155.

Paris, J., Brown, R., & Nowlis, D. (1987). Long-term follow-up of borderline patients in a general hospital. *Comprehensive Psychiatry, 28,* 530–535.

Patrick, M., Hobson, P., Castle, D., Howard, R., & Maughan, B. (1994). Personality disorder and the mental representations of early social experience. *Development and Psychopathology, 6,* 375–388.

Polich, J. (2007). Updating P300: An integrative theory of P3a and P3b. *Clinical Neurophysiology, 118,* 2128–2148.

Posner, M. I., Rothbart, M. K., Vizueta, N., Levy, K. N., Evans, D. E., Thomas, K. M., et al. (2002). Attentional mechanisms of borderline personality disorder. *Proceedings of the National Academy of Sciences of the United States of America, 99,* 16366–16370.

Rapp, P., & Bachevalier, J. (2008). Cognitive development and aging. In L. Squire, D. Berg, F. Bloom, S. Du Lac, A. Ghosh, & N. Spitzer (Eds.), *Fundamental neuroscience* (pp. 1039–1066). Amsterdam: Elsevier.

Riecker, A., Wildgruber, D., Dogil, G., Grodd, W., & Ackermann, H. (2002). Hemispheric lateralization effects of rhythm implementation during syllable repetitions: An fMRI study. *NeuroImage, 16,* 169–176.

Robins, L. N., Wing, J., Wittchen, H. U., Helzer, J. E., Babor, T. F., Burke, J., et al. (1988). The Composite International Diagnostic Interview. An epidemiologic instrument suitable for use in conjunction with different diagnostic systems and in different cultures. *Archives of General Psychiatry, 45,* 1069–1077.

Ross, E. D., & Monnot, M. (2008). Neurology of affective prosody and its functional-anatomic organization in right hemisphere. *Brain and Language, 104,* 51–74.

Schore, A. N. (1994). *Affect regulation and the origin of self.* Mahwah, NJ: Erlbaum.

Schore, A. N. (2003a). *Affect dysregulation and disorders of the self.* New York: Norton.

Schore, A. N. (2003b). *Affect regulation and the repair of the self.* New York: Norton.

Schore, A. N. (2005). Back to basics: Attachment, affect regulation, and the developing right brain: Linking developmental neuroscience to pediatrics. *Pediatrics in Review, 26,* 204–217.

Schore, A. N. (2009). Relational trauma and the developing right brain: An interface of psychoanalytic self psychology and neuroscience. *Annals of the New York Academy of Sciences, 1159,* 189–203.

Schore, A. N. (2010). Relational trauma and the developing right brain. The neurobiology of broken attachment bonds. In T. Baradon (Ed.), *Relational trauma in infancy* (pp. 19–47). London: Routledge.

Silbersweig, D., Clarkin J. F., Goldstein, M., Kernberg, O. F., Tuescher, O., Levy, K., et al. (2007). Failure of frontolimbic inhibitory function in the context of negative emotion in borderline personality disorder. *American Journal of Psychiatry, 164,* 1832–1841.

Soltani, M., & Knight, R. T. (2000). Neural origins of the P300. *Critical Reviews of Neurobiology, 14,* 199–224.

Starkstein, S. E., & Robinson, R. G. (1997). Mechanism of disinhibition after brain lesions. *Journal of Nervous and Mental Disease, 185,* 108–114.

Stern, A. (1938). Psychoanalytic investigation of and therapy in the borderline group of neuroses. *Psychoanalytic Quarterly, 7,* 467–489.

Stern, D. N. (1988). Affect in the context of the infant's lived experience: Some considerations. *International Journal of Psychoanalysis, 69,* 233–238.

Stevenson, J., & Meares, R. (1992). An outcome study of psychotherapy for patients with borderline personality disorder. *American Journal of Psychiatry, 149,* 358–362.

Stone, M. H. (1993). Long-term outcome in personality disorder. In P. Tyrer & G. Stein (Eds.), *Personality disorder reviewed* (pp. 321–345). London: Gaskell Royal College of Psychiatrists.

Tamietto, M., Latini Corazzini, L., de Gelder, B., & Geminiani, G. (2006). Functional asymmetry and interhemispheric cooperation in the perception of emotions from facial expressions. *Experimental Brain Research, 171,* 389–404.

Tamm, L., Menon, V., & Reiss, A. L. (2002). Maturation of brain function associated with response inhibition. *Journal of the American Academy of Child and Adolescent Psychiatry, 41,* 1231–1238.

Trevarthen, C. (1974). Conversations with a two-month-old. *New Scientist, 62,* 230–235.

Trevarthen, C. (1987). Mind in infancy. In R. Gregory (Ed.), *The Oxford companion to the mind.* Oxford, UK: Oxford University Press.

Verleger, R., Gorgen, S., & Jaskowski, P. (2005). An ERP indicator of processing relevant Gestalts in masked priming. *Psychophysiology, 42,* 677–690.

Vinogradova, O. S. (2001). Hippocampus as comparator: Role of the two input and two output systems of the hippocampus in selection and registration of information. *Hippocampus, 11,* 578–598.

Widiger, T. A., & Frances, A. J. (1989). Epidemiology, diagnosis, and comorbidity of borderline personality disorders. In A. Tasman, R. A. Hales, and A. Frances (Eds.), *American Psychiatric Press Review of Psychiatry* (pp. 8–24). Washington, DC: American
Psychiatry Press.

Williams, L. M., Gordon, E., Wright, J., & Bahramali, H. (2000). Late component ERPs
are associated with three syndromes in schizophrenia. *International Journal of Neuroscience, 105,* 37–52.

Zanarini, M. C. (1997). *Role of sexual abuse in the etiology of borderline personality disorder.* Washington DC: American Psychiatric Publishing.

Zanarini, M. C., Frankenburg, F. R., Dubo, E. D., Sickel, A. E., Trikha, A., Levin, A., et
al. (1998). Axis I comorbidity of borderline personality disorder. *American Journal of
Psychiatry, 155,* 1733–1739.

CHAPTER 10

Bowlby's Environment of Evolutionary Adaptedness: Current Decrement in U. S. Culture

In a description of the aims of an upcoming volume, *Evolution, Early Experience and Human Development: From Research to Practice and Policy*, Darcia Narvaez, Jaak Panksepp, Tracy Gleason, and I offer a large body of data from a number of disciplines that disturbingly indicate American culture may be deviating increasingly from traditional social practices that emerged in our ancestral "environment of evolutionary adaptedness" (Narvaez, Panksepp, Schore, & Gleason, in press). This term was devised by John Bowlby, the British psychiatrist-psychoanalyst who created attachment theory. As an early pioneer of an interdisciplinary perspective, Bowlby (1969) integrated developmental psychology, psychoanalysis, behavioral biology, and anthropology to offer the organizing principles of his theory in his first of three now classic volumes, Attachment. In this seminal statement of the theory, Bowlby asserts, "In the case of biological systems, structure takes a form that is determined by the kind of environment in which the system has been in fact operating during its evolution. . . . This environment I propose to term the system's 'environment of adaptedness.' Only within its environment of adaptedness can it be expected that a system will work efficiently" (p. 47).

Over the course of this first volume, Bowlby integrates psychoanalytic, ethological, anthropological, and human developmental data to argue that attachment represents not higher cognitive but instinctive behavior. In chapter 4, "Man's Environment of Evolutionary Adaptedness," he proposes,

> [W]hen we come to consider with what *instinctive* behaviour—or, more properly, with what behavioural systems mediating instinctive behaviour—humans may be

endowed, a first task to consider is the nature of the environment within they are adapted to operate. (p. 58) . . . The only relevant criterion by which to consider the natural adaptedness of any particular part of present-day man's behavioural equipment is the degree to which and the way in which it might contribute to population *survival* in man's primeval environment. (1969, p. 59, my italics)

Turning to ethology, Bowlby offers examples of instinctive survival behavior in subhuman species. He notes other higher primates also possess "a large repertoire of calls, postures, and gestures that act as a means of communication between members of a group" (1969, p. 63). Importantly, Bowlby postulates that "man's environment of evolutionary adaptedness" (EEA) is a version of a human's "ordinary expectable environment." But this concept is more than just a psychological construct—it also describes events at the biological level. "Not a single feature of a species' *morphology, physiology, and behavior* can be understood or even discussed intelligently except in relation to that species' environment of evolutionary adaptedness" (Bowlby, 1969, p. 64, my italics).

The core of the *Attachment* volume, and indeed all of Bowlby's work, elaborates the centrality of the early developing emotional bond that develops between the mother and infant to all later functioning. In chapter 11, "The Child's Tie to Its Mother: Attachment Behaviour," Bowlby proposes,

> the child's tie to his mother is a product of a number of behavioural systems that have proximity to mother as a predictable outcome. . . . The behavioural systems themselves are believed to develop within the infant as a result of his interaction with his environment of evolutionary adaptedness, and especially of his interaction with the principal figure in that environment, namely the mother (1969, pp. 180–181).

Later in the book he observes, "[B]ehavioral systems responsible for maternal behavior in a species will work within certain ranges of social and physical environment and not outside them" (p. 470).

Bowlby's speculation that developing structural biological systems are impacted by the environment in which they evolve can now be understood as a principle of interpersonal neurobiology. In modern terms "biological structure" is currently identified as the "*morphology and physiology*" of the developing brain that is evolving during the period of attachment, infancy. Indeed, Bowlby gives some clues as to specifically which developing brain systems are influenced by the EEA: those involved in "attachment systems mediating *instinctive* behaviour" that contribute to "population *survival* in man's primeval environment." My work in developmental affective neuroscience indicates attachment transactions shape the connectivity of specifically the early developing right brain, which is dominant for control of vital functions supporting *survival* and for the processing of emotions (Schore, 1994, 2005). Damasio (1994) argues that emotions are "a powerful manifestation of drives and *instincts*."

In this chapter I will argue that the EEA can be identified with the social-emotional relational environment provided by the primary caregiver that shapes, for better or worse, the experience-dependent maturation of the brain systems involved in attachment. Citing current research in developmental neuroscience, I shall outline recent updates in modern attachment theory (Schore & Schore, 2008), focusing upon the early developing right brain and its central role in emotional and social development. Utilizing the perspective of interpersonal neurobiology and modern attachment theory, I will propose that the EEA facilitates or inhibits the emergence of right-lateralized self-regulatory systems. I will also describe later sequelae of significant alterations in the EEA and outline a model of psychobiological evaluations of the EEA that can be used in early diagnosis, intervention, and prevention. Throughout I will use the actual voices of researchers in various fields in order to show the convergence that is now occurring in an overarching psychoneurobiological model of early human development. The large body of research provided by regulation theory suggests that the EEA operates within the mother–infant attachment bond at implicit nonverbal levels, and that it molds postnatal right brain development. (For more on the theoretical orientation of regulation theory and on recent studies of the interpersonal neurobiology of attachment, see Schore 2010a, 2010b, 2010c.)

INTERPERSONAL NEUROBIOLOGY OF HUMAN BRAIN DEVELOPMENT

Over the last two decades, I have argued that attachment communications specifically shape the baby's early developing right brain. Neuroscience continues to explore the primacy of developing right brain structure-function relations over the prenatal and postnatal stages of life. In classical research Dobbing and Sands (1973) described the human brain growth spurt, which begins in the last trimester, is at least 5/6 postnatal, and continues to the third year. Evidence now clearly indicates that during this rapid period of brain development the right hemisphere develops before the left. In the middle of the last decade, the pioneer neuroscientist Paul MacLean (1996) asserted, "For the mother the experience during pregnancy of the formless life within, could become after birth a sense of exteriorization and extension of the self that physiologically derives to a large extent from the right hemisphere" (p. 435). In parallel work, Trevarthen (1996) concluded, "The right hemisphere is more advanced than the left in surface features from about the 25th (gestational) week and this advance persists until the left hemisphere shows a postnatal growth spurt starting in the second year" (p. 582). These ideas are supported in later studies by Schleussner et al. (2004), who report "an earlier maturation of certain right than homologous left hemispheric brain areas during fetal brain development" (p. 133). Even more recently, Kasprian et al. (2011) document that at 26 gestational weeks the human fetal right superior temporal sulcus appears earlier and is deeper than that on the left and conclude, "Our structural data further support the findings of functional neuroimaging studies indicating an earlier maturity of right hemispheric function" (p. 1081).

Current interpersonal neurobiological models of perinatal and postnatal development after birth are shifting emphasis from the development of more complex cognitions to the development of the communication and regulation of affect. In a prototypical description Walker-Andrews and Bahrick (2001) observe, "From birth, an infant is plunged into a world of other human beings in which conversation, gestures, and faces are omnipresent during the infant's waking hours. Moreover, these harbingers of social information are dynamic, multimodal, and reciprocal" (p. 469). Despite the recent overemphasis on cognition, this perspective actually returns to Bowlby's (1969) original description of mother–infant attachment communications that are "accompanied by the strongest of feelings and emotions" and occur within a context of "facial expression, posture, tone of voice, physiological changes, tempo of movement, and incipient action" (p. 120). The bodily based nature of these instinctive attachment communications was stressed by Bowlby's colleague, the pediatrician-psychoanalyst Donald Winnicott, who affirmed, "The main thing is a communication between the baby and the mother in terms of the anatomy and physiology of live bodies" (1986, p. 258).

The psychobiologically attuned mother does more than just receive the infant's affective communications. Subsequently she regulates these affect-arousal states, thereby minimizing the infant's negative states in comforting transactions but also maximizing the infant's positive affective states in interactive play. The primary caregiver is not so much regulating overt behavior as internal states. According to Ovtscharoff and Braun, "The dyadic interaction between the newborn and the mother . . . serves as a regulator of the developing individual's internal homeostasis" (2001, p. 33). Similarly, Pipp and Harmon assert, "It may be that . . . we are biologically connected to those with whom we have close relationships. . . . Homeostatic regulation between members of a dyad is a stable aspect of all intimate relationships throughout the lifespan" (1987, p. 651). The evolutionary mechanism of attachment, the interactive regulation of emotion, thus represents the regulation of biological synchronicity between and within organisms (Bradshaw & Schore, 2007; Schore, 1994).

But even more than this, it is now thought that "The regulatory function of the newborn–mother interaction may be an essential promoter to ensure the normal development and maintenance of synaptic connections during the establishment of functional brain circuits" (Ovtscharoff & Braun, 2001, p. 33). Indeed, affectively laden attachment communications are directly impacting the massive levels of synaptogenesis that characterize the brain growth spurt spanning the last trimester of pregnancy through the second year. An MRI study done by Matsuzawa et al. (2001) reveals that the volume of the brain increases rapidly during the first 2 years. These authors document normal adult appearance at 2 years and all major fiber tracts at age 3; and infants under 2 years show higher right than left hemispheric volumes.

The enormously accelerated growth of the brain during the human brain growth spurt is reflected in the finding that during prenatal and postnatal critical periods the rate of synaptogenesis is estimated to be 40,000 new synapses every second (Lagerkrantz & Ringstedt (2000). Knickmeyer et al. (2008) report, "Total brain volume increased 101% in the first year, with a 15% increase in the second. . . . The volume of the subcortical area (including brainstem) increased by 130% in the first year and by 14% in the second year" (p. 12178). The subcortical brain stem systems that are actively expressed in the first year generate what Bowlby (1969) termed "attachment systems mediating instinctive behaviour." It is important to emphasize that the structural maturation of these brain systems is not just genetically encoded. Rather it is characterized as an epigenetically regulated mechanism that facilitates the "experience-dependent maturation" of the developing brain.

Confirming the developmental hypotheses outlined in my earlier books, there is now consensus about the existence of critical periods of infancy when the developing brain has heightened sensitivity to environmental experiences (Roth & Sweatt, 2011). In these epochs of intense brain plasticity, the early social experiences provided by the caregiving environment modify gene activity through epigenetic mechanisms that regulate gene activity. In this manner gene–environment transactions shape neural circuits that determine the structural and functional aspects of brain and behavior throughout the life span. This "epigenetic programming" is directly influenced by variations in maternal care. According to Champagne (in press),

> [T]he emergence of developmental trajectories which lead to individual differences can be linked to early life experiences . . . the quality of the environment experienced during perinatal development is shaped primarily by the interactions between mothers and offspring . . . *even natural variations in the quality or quantity of maternal care can have a long-term impact on offspring brain and behavior.* (my italics)

RECENT STUDIES OF RIGHT BRAIN–TO–RIGHT BRAIN ATTACHMENT COMMUNICATIONS

What do we now know about the "the interactions between mothers and offspring"? I have propounded the interpersonal neurobiological principle that "The self-organization of the developing brain occurs in the context of a relationship with another self, another brain" (Schore, 1996, p. 60). From the perspective of modern attachment theory, the question therefore becomes, how are intersubjective emotional attachment communications transmitted between the mother's and the infant's right brains?

At about the same time that Bowlby was describing affective attachment communications of facial expression, posture, and tone of voice, Brown and Jaffe's (1975) developmental neuropsychological research indicated, "The right hemisphere can be considered dominant in infancy, for the type of visual and acoustic communication which is relevant for the prelinguistic child" (p. 108). Following Bowlby's lead, in 1994 I suggested that during attachment episodes of *visual-facial, auditory-prosodic, and tactile-gestural* affective communications, the psychobiologically attuned caregiver regulates the infant's internal states of arousal.

> The infant's early maturing right hemisphere, which is dominant for the child's processing of visual emotional information, the infant's recognition of the mother's face, and the perception of arousal-inducing maternal facial expressions, is psychobiologically attuned to the output of the mother's right hemisphere, which is involved in the expression and processing of emotional information and in nonverbal communication. (Schore, 1994, p. 63)

A large body of developmental neurobiological research supports the hypothesis that the attachment mechanism is embedded in infant–caregiver right hemisphere–to–right hemisphere affective transactions.

With respect to *visual-facial attachment communications*, it is now established that mutual gaze is critical to early social development (Trevarthen & Aitken, 2001). The development of the capacity to efficiently process information from faces requires visual input to the right (and not left) hemisphere during infancy (Le Grand, Mondloch, Maurer, & Brent, 2003). At 2 months of age, the onset of a critical period during which synaptic connections in the developing occipital cortex are modified by visual experience (Yamada et al., 2000), infants show right hemispheric activation when exposed to a woman's face (Tzourio-Mazoyer et al., 2002). Using EEG methodology, T. Grossmann et al. (2007) report that 4-month-old infants presented with images of a female face gazing directly ahead show enhanced gamma electrical activity over right prefrontal areas. Recent near-infrared spectroscopy (NIRS) research (perhaps the most suitable of all neuroscience techniques applicable to human infants) reveals that specifically the 5-month-old's right hemisphere responds to images of adult female faces (Nakato et al., 2009; Otsuka et al., 2007). By 6 months infants show a right-lateralized left gaze bias when viewing faces (Guo, Meints, Hall, Hall, & Mills, 2009), a right temporal activation when looking at angry faces (Nakato et al., 2011), and a significantly greater right frontotemporal activation when viewing their own mother's (as opposed to a stranger's) face (Carlsson, Lagercrantz, Olson, Printz, & Bartocci, 2008).

Ongoing studies of prenatal, perinatal, and postnatal *auditory-prosodic attachment communications* also highlight the role of the right brain. In an EEG study of auditory pitch processing in preterm infants born at 30 gestational weeks, Mento et al. (2010) conclude, "These findings suggest that the earlier right structural maturation in foetal epochs seems to be paralleled by a right functional development" (p. 1). A functional MRI study of 1- to 3-day-old newborns reports that music evokes right hemispheric activation in the auditory cortex (Perani et al., 2010). Using NIRS with 2- to 6-day-old neonates, Telkemeyer et al. (2009)

observe that "responses to slow acoustic modulations are lateralized to the right hemisphere" (p. 14726). This same optical brain imaging technology reveals that prosodic processing of emotional voices in 3-month-old (Homae, Watanabe, Nakano, Asakawa, & Taga, 2006) and 4-month-old infants (Minagawa-Kawai et al., 2011) activates the right temporoparietal region. T. Grossmann et al. (2010) report that 7-month-old infants respond to emotional voices in a voice-sensitive region of the right superior temporal sulcus, and happy prosody specifically activates the right inferior frontal cortex. These authors conclude, "The pattern of finding suggests that temporal regions specialize in processing voices very early in development and that, already in infancy, emotions differentially modulate voice processing in the right hemisphere" (p. 852). At 11 months the voice of a woman's child-directed speech (i.e., with somewhat exaggerated prosody) elicits a right-lateralized event-related potential (Thierry, Vihman, & Roberts, 2003).

In terms of *tactile-gestural attachment communications*, Sieratzki and Woll (1996) describe the effects of touch on the developing right hemisphere, and assert that the emotional impact of touch is more direct and immediate if an infant is held to the left side of the body. Studies now demonstrate the essential role of maternal "affective touch" on human infant development in the first year of life (Ferber, Feldman, & Makhoul, 2008; Jean, Stack, & Fogel, 2009). This allows the infant and mother to create a system of "touch synchrony" to alter vagal tone and cortisol reacitivity (Feldman, Singer, & Zagoory, 2010). The dyad thus uses "interpersonal touch" as a communication system (Gallace & Spence, 2010), especially for the communication and regulation of emotional information (Hertenstein, 2002; Hertenstein & Campos, 2001). High levels of tactile stimulation and mutual touch occur in breastfeeding, and Lehtonen et al. (2002) observe an increase in EEG amplitude in right posterior cortical areas in 6-month-old infants during the intense somatosensory tactile contact of breastfeeding.

With respect to gestures, Nagy (2006, p. 227) demonstrates "lateralized system for neonatal imitation," and concludes that "The early advantage of the right hemisphere (Chiron et al., 1997; Schore, 2000; Trevarthen, 2001) in the first few months of life may affect the lateralized appearance of the first imitative gestures." Moreover, Montirosso, Borgatti, and Tronick (2010) document left-sided regulatory gestures when infants are stressed. In summarizing their work on gestures, they state,

> Infants cope with the emotional distress caused by unresponsive mothers through self-regulation behaviors associated with a greater activation of the right hemisphere. In sum, this finding supports the view that during a stressful condition there is a state-dependent activation of the right hemisphere. . . . More generally these findings suggest that the right hemisphere is more involved in the social and biological functions regarding infant caregiver emotional bonding (Schore, 2005; Siegel, 1999). (p. 108)

Confirming this relational neurobiological model, in very recent functional magnetic resonance imaging studies of mother–infant emotional communication, Lenzi et al. (2009, p. 1131) offer data "supporting the theory that the right hemisphere is more involved than the left hemisphere in emotional processing and thus, mothering." Noriuchi, Kikuchi, and Senoo (2008) report activation of the mother's right orbitofrontal cortex during moments of maternal love triggered by viewing a video of her own infant. Another near-infrared spectroscopy study of infant–mother attachment at 12 months concludes, "our results are in agreement with that of Schore (2000) who addressed the importance of the right hemisphere in the attachment system" (Minagawa-Kawai et al., 2009, p. 289).

RIGHT BRAIN DOMINANCE ESTABLISHED IN THE FIRST YEAR OF HUMAN LIFE

These studies support a central tenet of my work, first articulated in 1994, that attachment impacts the developing right brain. Shortly after Sieratzki and Woll (1996) definitively stated, "The role of the right hemisphere is crucial in relation to the most precious needs of mothers and infants" (p. 1747), Chiron et al. (1997) published a study, "The right brain hemisphere is dominant in human infants." Studies of the unique functions of the right brain subsequently increased significantly, and in 2002 Braun et al. asserted, "The right and left human brain hemispheres differ in macrostructure, ultra-structure, physiology, chemistry, and control of behavior" (p. 97). Indeed, a number of anatomical and imaging studies now show earlier maturation of the right hemisphere in prenatal and postnatal stages of human development (Gupta et al., 2005; Howard & Reggia, 2007; Sun et al., 2005). This research supports the earlier work of Previc (1991), who suggested that the origins of cerebral asymmetry emanate in the intrauterine environment, and that the prenatal positioning of the fetus in the womb allows the inward-facing left ear to receive a greater amount of vestibular stimulation and thus an earlier organization of the right hemispheric vestibular cortex, a brain system involved in emotion processing (Carmona, Holland, & Harrison, 2009).

There is now an emerging consensus that "the emotional experience(s) of the infant . . . are disproportionately stored or processed in the right hemisphere during the formative stages of brain ontogeny" (Semrud-Clikeman & Hynd, 1990, p. 198). Over the course of the first year, increasingly complex right brain–to–right brain attachment communications imprint first right posterior cerebral areas involved in sensory processing (e.g., right occipital, right fusiform gyrus, right superior temporal sulcus, right temporoparietal regions), and later right anterior cerebral areas. Classical studies reveal regional differences in the time course of cortical synaptogenesis (Huttenlocher, 1990), and that the metabolic activity that underlies regional cerebral function is ontogenetically highest in the posterior sensorimotor cortex and only later rises in anterior cortex (Chugani & Phelps, 1986). Indeed, although a period of synaptic excess occurs at 4 months in visual cortex, a similar process does not onset in the prefrontal anterior cortex until the end of the first year of human life (Huttenlocher, 1979).

But maternal–infant emotional transactions allow for more than the experience-dependent maturation of cortical connections within the right cerebral hemisphere. In line with the principle of the sequential caudal to rostral structural development of the brain, bodily based attachment transactions also imprint cortical-subcortical connections of the right brain, which is deeply connected into the emotion-processing limbic system. Recall Bowlby's (1969) original description of mother–infant attachment communications that are "accompanied by the strongest of feelings and emotions." Basic research in developmental neuroscience now demonstrates, "The functional maturation of limbic circuits is significantly influenced by early socio-emotional experience" (Helmeke, Ovtscharoff, Poeggel, & Braun, 2001, p. 717). In fMRI research, Dapretto et al. (2006) contend, "Typically developing children can rely upon a right hemisphere-mirroring neural mechanism—interfacing with the limbic system via the insula—whereby the meaning of imitated (or observed) emotion is directly felt and hence understood" (p. 30). Attachment studies thus strongly support Panksepp's (2008) bold assertion of the primacy of affective neuroscience: "Now cognitive science must re-learn that ancient emotional systems have a power that is quite independent of neocortical cognitive processes" (p. 51).

In addition, prenatal and postnatal interpersonal events also wire the connectivity of structures in the developing central nervous system (CNS) with energy-expending sympathetic and energy-conserving parasympathetic branches of the evolving autonomic nervous system (ANS). There is now consensus that the right brain plays a greater role than the left in autonomic arousal and therefore the somatic aspects of emotional states. Porges (2007) concludes, "Consistent with the views that the right hemisphere appears to play a greater role in affect, especially the adaptive expression of negative affect, the right hemisphere also appears to have a greater role in regulation of cardiac function presumably via shifts in [parasympathetic] vagal regulation" (p. 126). According to McGilchrist (2009, p. 437), "The right hemisphere is . . . more closely in touch with emotion and the body (therefore with the neurologically 'inferior' and more ancient regions of the central nervous system)."

Furthermore, a large body of studies now clearly indicates that maternal care within the attachment relationship shapes the infant's hypothalamic-pituitary-adrenocortical (HPA) stress-regulating axis (Gunnar, 2000), and that epigenetic programming of maternal behavior alters the development of HPA responses to stress through tissue-specific effects on gene transcription (Weaver et al., 2004). The right hemisphere is known to play a dominant role in regulating the HPA axis and in mediating the human stress response. Indeed, this hemisphere, more so than the left, is central to the control of vital functions supporting *survival* and enabling the organism to cope with stresses and challenges (Wittling, 1997). Basic research now establishes that optimal stress regulation is dependent on "right hemispheric specialization in regulating stress- and emotion-related processes" (Sullivan & Dufresne, 2006, p. 55).

ENVIRONMENT OF EVOLUTIONARY ADAPTEDNESS AND THE EMERGENCE OF RIGHT-LATERALIZED SELF-REGULATORY SYSTEMS

In a foreword of a reissue of the *Attachment* volume (Schore, 2000a) and in a subsequent article in the journal *Attachment and Human Development* (Schore, 2000b), I discussed Bowlby's speculation that the environment of evolutionary adaptedness influences the development of a brain system that controls, or regulates, attachment. Bowlby (1969) described "a biological control system" that is centrally involved in instinctive behavior. This control system is structured as a hierarchical mode of organization, and its functions are associated with the organism's "state of arousal" that results from the critical operations of the reticular arousal system and with "the appraisal of organismic states and situations of the midbrain nuclei and limbic system" (p. 110). He even offered a speculation about its anatomical location—the prefrontal lobes (p. 156). This control system, he said, is "open in some degree to influence by the environment in which development occurs" (p. 45). More specifically, it evolves in the infant's interaction with an "environment of adaptedness, and especially of his interaction with the principal figure in that environment, namely his mother" (p. 180). Furthermore, Bowlby speculated that the "upgrading of control during individual development from simple to more sophisticated is no doubt in large part a result of the growth of the central nervous system" (p. 156).

In parallel developmental work, Brazelton and Cramer (1990) speculated,

> The central nervous system, as it develops, drives infants towards mastery of themselves and their world. As they achieve each level of mastery, they seek a kind of homeostasis, until the nervous system presses them on to their next level. Internal equilibrium is always being upset by a new imbalance created as the nervous system matures. Maturation of the nervous system, accompanied by increasing differentiation of skills, drives infants to reorganize their control systems. (p. 98)

Modern developmental neuroscience and interpersonal neurobiology can now identify these attachment control systems (Schore, 2000, 2010c). The neuroanatomy of the emotion-processing limbic system is currently characterized as a system of vertically organized circuits within the brain. Authors are referring to the "rostral limbic system," a hierarchical sequence of interconnected limbic areas in the orbitofrontal (ventromedial), anterior cingulate, insular cortex, and amygdala (see Schore, 2003a). A large body of evidence shows that the orbitofrontal-insula, medial frontal anterior cingulate, and amygdala systems all interconnect with each other and with brain stem bioaminergic neuromodulatory arousal systems and with neuroendocrine nuclei in the hypothalamus, the "head ganglion" of the autonomic nervous system. Therefore, each inputs to the stress-regulating hypothalamic-pituitary-adrenocortical (HPA) axis (Schore, 2003a). Because they are all components of the limbic system, each processes and imprints a positive or negative hedonic charge on current exteroceptive information about changes in the external social environment and then integrates it with interoceptive information about concurrent alterations in internal bodily states (Schore, 2001a, 2003a).

Due to the facts that each control system directly interconnects with the ANS and that autonomic activity is controlled by multiple integrative sites within the CNS that are hierarchically organized, all are involved in the regulation of bodily driven affective arousal states. Although all process exteroceptive and interoceptive information, the later-maturing systems in the cortex process this information in a more complex fashion than do the earlier subcortical components. The output of the lowest level limbic levels is expressed as automatic innate reflexes, whereas higher processing produces more flexible intuitive responses that allow fine adjustment to environmental circumstances.

In optimal socioemotional environments (EEAs), each limbic level has bidirectional connections with the others, and in this manner information can both be forwarded up and down the limbic axis for further appraisal and hierarchical regulation. The earliest and simplest appraisals of exteroceptive and interoceptive affective stimuli are rapid, nonconscious hedonic and aversive-affective core processes in the amygdala, the later and most complex conscious subjective experiences of pleasure and pain in the orbitofrontal areas. These operations are primarily lateralized to the right limbic system, which is preferentially connected downward to the right neurochemical systems associated with arousal, emotion, and motivational states, and upward to the ipsilateral right neocortex.

As applied to the developmental organization of the limbic circuits of the right brain, this conception suggests a three-tiered self-organizing dynamic system. Increased interconnectivity (energy flow) among the three component circuits would allow for information stored at one level to be transferred to the others. The top level that receives feedback from the lower level performs an executive function, and this allows for emergent properties, that is, novel combinations of more complex emotional states. In this hierarchical model, lower subcortical levels of the right brain contain all the major motivational systems (including attachment, fear, sexuality, aggression, disgust, etc.) and generate somatic autonomic expressions and arousal intensities of all emotional states. When optimally functioning, higher orbitofrontal-limbic levels of the right cerebral hemisphere generate a conscious emotional state that expresses the affective output of these motivational systems.

In line with the morphogenetic principles of caudal to rostral brain development and vertical brain organization, a model of the ontogeny of the limbic system can be offered. Keeping in mind that in humans this development continues postnatally, reversing the sequence of the rostral limbic system (amygdala, anterior cingulate, orbitofrontal) offers specific ideas about how a number of discrete limbic components could come online and develop connectivity in a defined sequence in the first year. Recall Bowlby's speculation that the limbic system is centrally involved in attachment and that the "upgrading of control during individual development from simple to more sophisticated is no doubt in large part a result of the growth of the central nervous system" (1969, p. 156).

In earlier writings (Schore, 2001a), I proposed that structures in the temporal lobe, the amygdala, especially the central and medial nuclei (Ulfig, Setzer, & Bohl, 2003), the insula (Afif, Bouvier, Buenerd, Trouillas, & Mertens, 2007), and the paraventricular nucleus of the hypothalamus associated with the sympathetic branch of the autonomic nervous system (Myers, Myers, Grober, & Nathanielsz, 1993), are in a critical period of maturation that onsets in the last trimester of pregnancy and continues through the first 2 months of human life. In the second quarter of the first year, a second homeostatic control system emerges in the anterior cingulate (medial frontal) cortex, which hierarchically controls the earlier amygdala-dominated limbic configuration. In an important work, Allman et al. (2011) document that the number of von Economo neurons (VEN) in the anterior cingulate and frontoinsular cortical areas are low at birth, but increase significantly in the first 8 months of human infancy. The number of VEN neurons is significantly greater in the postnatal than the neonatal brain, and the authors suggest that "VEN abundance may be related to environmental influences" (p. 62). Intriguingly, these neurons are much more abundant in the right hemisphere, reflecting the fact that "rightward asymmetry emerges during the first few months of postnatal life" (p. 64). Functionally, these large bipolar neurons in the right anterior cingulate and frontoinsular areas perform essential regulatory functions, especially in processing information related to right-lateralized sympathetic arousal, and in the communication of social information (see chapter 4 for their role in intuition). It is tempting to speculate that attachment transactions directly influence the numbers and connectivity of these right-lateralized limbic-autonomic VENs, and that relational interferences with their developmental experience-dependent maturation play an important role in psychopathogenesis.

Ongoing studies in developmental brain research indicate that the orbital prefrontal cortex enters a critical period of growth spanning the last quarter of the first year through the middle of the second year, an interval that corresponds with the beginnings of human socialization (Schore, 2003a). This ventromedial prefrontal limbic structure is reciprocally interconnected with other limbic areas in the amygdala, insula, and anterior cingulate, and represents the hierarchical apex of the right-lateralized limbic system. It also forms direct connections with the hypothalamus, the head ganglion of the autonomic nervous system (Barbas, Saha, Rempel-Clower, & Ghashghaei, 2003), as well as bioaminergic neurons in the reticular system that control arousal (Schore, 1994). For the rest of the life span, this system is centrally involved in "the representation of emotional information and the regulator of emotional processes" (Roberts et al., 2004, p. 307), "for acquiring very specific forms of knowledge for regulating interpersonal behavior" (Dolan, 1999, p. 928), and in the personality characteristic of "positive emotionality" associated with resilience (Volkow et al., 2011).

The activity of this frontolimbic system is critical to the modulation of social and emotional behaviors and the homeostatic regulation of body and motivational states, affect-regulating functions that are centrally involved in attachment processes. The dendritic and synaptic maturation of the anterior cingulate and orbitofrontal cortices is specifically influenced by the social environment (Bock, Murmu, Ferdman, Leshem, & Braun, 2008; Schore, 1994, 2003a). Interestingly the mother's anterior cingulate reorganizes during the postpartum period, which is associated with dramatic alterations in her physiology and behavior, and allows her "to adapt to the new environment created by the presence and the needs of the newborn" (Salmaso, Quinlan, Brake, & Woodside, 2011). The infant's orbitofrontal cortex, which is expanded in the right brain, matures at the end of the brain growth spurt in the second year, when it becomes associated with the emergence of a default network engaged during passive or undirected mental states (Gao et al., 2009).

As a result of its experience-dependent maturational advance between 1 and 2 years this ventral medial prefrontal cortex acts as the hierarchical apex of the emotion-processing limbic system and as "the highest level of control of behavior, especially in relation to emotion" (Price, Carmichael, & Drevets, 1996, p. 523). A number of writers have noted the importance of this system in early socialization, specifically in the developmental neurobiology of morality (e.g., Narvaez, 2008; Schore, 1994). Indeed, this ventromedial system is a central component of "a 'morality' network in the brain, predominantly in the right hemisphere" (Mendez & Shapira, 2009, p. 165), which is "necessary to oppose personal moral violations . . . by mediating anticipatory, self-focused, emotional reactions that may exert strong influence on moral choice and behavior" (Ciaramelli, Muccioli, Ladavas, & di Pellegrino, 2007, p. 84).

For the rest of the life span the right, and not left, lateralized prefrontal regions are responsible for the regulation of affect and stress (Cerqueira, Almeida, & Sousa, 2008; Schore, 1994; Stevenson, Halliday, Marsten, & Mason, 2008; Sullivan & Gratton, 2002; Wang et al., 2005). These data support my earlier proposal, "The co-created environment of evolutionary adaptedness is thus isomorphic to a growth-facilitating environment for the experience-dependent maturation of a regulatory system in the orbitofrontal cortex" (Schore, 2000, p. 30).

LEGACY OF ATTACHMENT: ADAPTIVE RIGHT BRAIN SURVIVAL FUNCTIONS OVER THE LIFE SPAN

In 1994 I proposed that the micro-architecture of the infant's developing orbitofrontal cortex is shaped by the mother's orbitofrontal cortex (Schore, 1994). Ten years later, Nitschke and colleagues (2004) offered a functional MRI study of mothers viewing a photograph of their own infant showing maximal brain activation in the mother's orbitofrontal cortex, especially on the right side. These authors asserted that this cortex plays a critical role in the representation of attachment-related positive affect as described by Bowlby, that it linearly tracks the intensity of positive emotions that underlie maternal attachment, and that individual variation in orbitofrontal activation to infant stimuli reflects an important dimension of maternal attachment. Following this work an NIRS study of social attachment by Minagawa-Kawai et al. (2009) documented that mothers express increased right orbitofrontal activation when viewing videos of the smiling face of their 12-month-old infants, and that these infants show similar orbitofrontal activation when viewing their mothers' smile. They concluded, "These results suggest the orbitofrontal cortical role in regulating and encoding the affect in attachment system and also show that infants share similar neuronal functions with mothers, associated with their bonds at 1 year of age" (p. 284).

Over 15 years ago I provided extant developmental data suggesting that subsequent to the child's formation of an attachment to the mother in the first year, the child forms another, to the father, in the second year (Schore, 1994). Interestingly, recent magnetoencephalographic research reveals that the medial orbitofrontal cortex of both females and males rapidly and thereby implicitly responds (130 milliseconds) to the image of an infant's face (Kringelbach et al., 2008). These authors conclude the orbitofrontal cortex expresses a specific and rapid signature for not just maternal but also "parental instinct."

The role of the father in child development has been comprehensively summarized by Tamis-LeMonda and Cabrera (2002), Gray and Anderson (2010), and Lamb (2010). Herzog (2001) observes, "The biorhythmicity of man with infant and woman with infant" affords the infant to have "interactive, state-sharing, and state-attuning experiences with two different kinds of caregivers" (p. 55). He further asserts that this paternal function is "entirely contingent on the presence of homeostatic-attuned caregiving by the mother." Though the mother's soothing is essential to the child's attachment security, the father's arousing play is thought to be critical for the child's competent exploration of the physical world (K. Grossmann et al., 2002). Expanding upon these ideas I have suggested that although the mother is essential to the infant's capacity for fear regulation, in the second year the father is critically involved in male and female toddlers' aggression regulation (Schore, 2003a).

Bowlby (1969) proposed that the child's experience with a supportive mother and "a little later father" (p. 378) indicates that the transmission of attachment patterns between mother and infant precedes subsequent transmission between father and child. Building upon this, in *Affect Regulation and the Origin of the Self*, I offered the hypothesis that not only the infant's mother but also the father is impacting the growth of the baby's brain:

> I have previously argued that in the first year the mother is the major source of the environmental stimulation that facilitates (or inhibits) the experience-dependent maturation of the child's developing biological (especially neurobiological) structures. In the second year, however, the father now becomes an important source of

arousal induction and reduction, and his modulation of stimulation will influence formation of those neural structures that are entering into a critical period of growth. In other words, in the middle of the second year the structural development of the child's brain is shifting from a maternal experience-dependent maturation of one postnatally developing cortical system to a paternal experience-dependent maturation of an even later developing cortical system. (Schore, 1994, p. 233)

In the ensuing decade the vast majority of developmental neurobiological research has focused upon the mechanisms by which specifically one particular adult, a mother, impacts the development of her offspring's developing brain (see Schore, 1994, 2001a, 2003a, 2005, 2010b). That said, one laboratory has offered a series of studies clearly demonstrating that paternal care affects synaptic development in the anterior cingulate (Ovtscharoff et al., 2006), the orbitofrontal cortex (Helmeke et al., 2009), and in the somatosensory cortex of the left hemisphere (Pinkernelle, Abraham, Seidel, & Braun, 2009). These authors propose that paternal care significantly affects the development of play behavior. Interestingly, juvenile rough-and-tumble play, a behavior extensively investigated by Panksepp (1998), has been shown to be critically impacted by the father–child relationship (Flanders et al., 2010) and to depend upon orbitofrontal activity (Bell, Pellis, & Kolb, 2010; Pellis & Pellis, 2007).

Furthermore, a body of research describes important hormonal changes in men associated with marriage and fatherhood (both involving activation of attachment mechanisms). Testosterone levels are lower in married versus single men (Booth & Dabbs, 1993), and in fathers (Gray, Yang, & Pope, 2006). Interestingly, fathers' testosterone levels drop during their partners' late pregnancy and early postpartum period (Storey et al., 2000), and men who provide more parental care have lower testosterone levels than fathers who provide less care (Gettler, McDade, Feranil, & Kuzawaa, 2011). It is tempting to speculate that these hormonal changes are a direct result of the reciprocal affective attachment communications between the infant and father.

The infant's right hemisphere ends its initial growth spurt in the middle/end of the second year, as the left hemisphere begins its own (Thatcher, Walker, & Giudice, 1987). In later stages the right hemisphere comes back into less intensive growth spurts, in which its essential functions attain even greater levels of complexity. In ensuing developmental periods, these attachment functions are expressed as implicit capacities for nonverbal affect communication and interactive stress regulation. The adaptive functions unique to the right (and not left) brain are described by current authors. Brancucci et al. (2009) state, "the neural substrates of the perception of voices, faces, gestures, smells, and pheromones, as evidenced by modern neuroimaging techniques, are characterized by a general right-hemispheric functional asymmetry" (p. 895). Schutz (2005) notes, "The right hemisphere operates a distributed network for rapid responding to danger and other urgent problems. It preferentially processes environmental challenge, stress and pain and manages self-protective responses such as avoidance and escape" (p. 15). And Uddin et al. (2006) assert, "The emerging picture from the current literature seems to suggest a special role of the right hemisphere in self-related cognition, own body perception, self-awareness and autobiographical memories" (p. 65).

These adaptive right brain functions are initially imprinted in right brain–to–right brain affective communications during critical periods of infancy, and such attachment experiences facilitate the lateralization of the "emotional" right brain that support its survival functions. According to Rotenberg (2004),

> The main functions of the right hemisphere . . . the ability to grasp the reality as a whole; the emotional attachment to the mother (Schore, 2003a); the regulation of withdrawal behavior in the appropriate conditions (Davidson & Cacioppo, 1992); the integration of affect, behavior and autonomic activity (Schore, 2003a) are the basic functions of *survival* (Saugstad, 1998) and for this reason are the first to appear. (p. 864, my italics)

LATER SEQUELAE OF SIGNIFICANT ALTERATIONS IN THE ENVIRONMENT OF EVOLUTIONARY ADAPTEDNESS

Consonant with Bowlby's speculations, these adaptive functions of an efficient lateralized right brain evolve only in an optimal early relational environment of evolutionary adaptedness. However, we now know that epigenetic programming influenced by variations in maternal care can impart either a resilience to or a risk for psychopathology. If the primary caregiver chronically dysregulates the child's arousal and affective states during early critical periods, this inhibits the experience-dependent maturation of the right brain. Severe alterations of the EEA lead to enduring inefficient capacities for coping with interpersonal stressors, and a predisposition to later psychiatric disorders. A large number of studies now demonstrate that alterations of brain development are associated with less than optimal early maternal care, especially with severe "relational trauma" such as abuse and neglect (Schore, 2001c, 2010b). There is wide acceptance of the developmental principle that severe alterations of the social environment such as the maltreatment of abuse and neglect imprint a brain developmental trajectory that is later susceptible to post-tramautic stress disorder, borderline personality disorder, schizophrenia, and major depression (Roth & Sweatt, 2011).

In earlier work I offered interdisciplinary evidence from neuroscience, child psychiatry, and traumatology suggesting that early traumatic environments that generate disorganized/disoriented attachments interfere with the organization of right brain cortical-subcortical limbic circuits and compromise such functions as the capacity to play, attachment, empathy, and the ability to regulate negative affects and pain (Schore, 2002). Severe attachment trauma imprints a permanent physiological reactivity in limbic areas of the right brain, thereby inhibiting its capacity to cope with future stressors. These deficits of affect communication and regulation underlie a predisposition to a number of early forming developmental psychopathologies.

There is current agreement that early stress is associated with alterations in the orbital frontolimbic (ventromedial) cortex, and that individuals who experience early adversity such as childhood maltreatment are at a heightened risk for a wide range of psychopathologies (Hanson et al., 2010). Although most of this research focuses upon the detrimental effects of deficits of maternal care in the alteration of specifically the right and not left ventromedial cortex (Lyons et al., 2002) and the creation of a vulnerability to future psychopathologies (e.g., Korosi & Baram, 2009; Schore, 2003a, 2003b), a small but growing number of studies show that lack of paternal care in infancy is significantly associated with "delayed and partly suppressed development of orbitofrontal circuits" (Helmeke et al., 2009, p. 794).

In my 1994 volume I proposed that orbitofrontal deficits lie at the core of a number of psychiatric disorders (Schore, 1994), and in 1996 I cited a small but expanding number of studies that reported orbitofrontal involvement and regulation disturbances in a number of developmental psychopathologies (Schore, 1996). Over the last decade altered morphological and functional development of the orbitofrontal cortex has been documented in a wide variety of early forming neurodevelopmental disorders: schizophrenia (Nakamura et al., 2007); autism (Girgis et al., 2007); affective psychosis (Fahim, Stip, Mancini-Marie, Potvin, & Malaspina, 2007); bipolar disorder (Versace et al., 2008); borderline personality disorder (Chanen et al., 2008; Meares, Schore, & Melkonian, 2011); psychopathic personality disorder, aggression, and violence (Craig et al., 2009; Gansler et al., 2009; Kumari et al., 2009); alcohol and drug addiction (Schoenbaum & Shaham, 2008; Volkow et al., 2007); post-traumatic stress disorder (Schore, 2002); dissociative identity disorder (Sar, Ünal, & Oztürk, 2007); panic disorder (Roppongi et al., 2010); and depression (Eddington et al., 2009).

Furthermore, prenatal and postnatal stressful experiences also impact the maturation of systems involved in immunocompetence in the developing brain (Schore, 1994; Garay & McAllister, 2010). Research on the relationship between attachment style and immune function shows that attachment-related avoidance is associated with lower Natural Killer (NK) cell cytotoxicity (Picardi et al., 2007), presumably due to the repression of NK function by cortisol (Zhou et al., 1997). Individuals with a history of relational trauma are known to be at risk for not only later-forming psychiatric but also medical disorders (Felitti & Anda, 2010). The trend of current research on the developmental origins of a vulnerability to later diseases is echoed in the titles of three representative studies: "Early Childhood Stress Is Associated with Elevated Antibody Levels to Herpes Simplex Virus Type 1" (Shirtcliff, Coe, & Pollak, 2009); "Childhood Maltreatment Predicts Adult Inflammation in a Life-Course Study" (Danese, Pariante, Caspi, Taylor, & Poulton, 2007); and "Childhood Maltreatment as a Risk Factor for Adult Cardiovascular Disease and Depression" (Batten, Aslan, Maciejewski, & Mazure, 2004).

In a very recent volume, *The Impact of Early Life Trauma on Health and Dis-*

ease: The Hidden Epidemic (Lanius, Vermetten, & Pain, 2010), I present a synopsis of chapters on "The Impact of Early Life Trauma: Psychobiological Sequelae in Children." Regarding experimental investigations of attachment trauma, I overview the state of current research:

> Recent models of early life trauma are altering their focus from deficits in later maturing conscious, verbal, explicit and voluntary behavior, to impairments of early maturing nonconscious, nonverbal, implicit and automatic adaptive social emotional functions. Developmental neuroscience is now moving from studies of later maturing left brain conscious verbal cognitive processes into the early preverbal development of adaptive emotion processing right brain systems in pre- and postnatal periods. (Schore, 2001a, p. 144)

This ongoing trend in the sciences is paralleled by clinical models of early assessment, intervention, and prevention that also focus on right brain development. In the final sections of this chapter, I utilize recent interdisciplinary data to offer some suggestions on the assessment of extreme deviations in the EEA in stages of early human development.

PSYCHONEUROBIOLOGICAL EVALUATIONS OF THE ENVIRONMENT OF EVOLUTIONARY ADAPTEDNESS

A central thesis of this contribution (and indeed all of my work) is that attachment relationships shape the experience-dependent maturation and lateralization of the right brain. Early right brain lateralization is thus an interpersonal neurobiological marker of the EEA. Indeed, the evolving lateralization of right brain structure-function relationships is an ongoing indicator of the development of "the social brain" over the human brain growth spurt, which extends from the last trimester of pregnancy through 18 to 24 months of age. Previously I cited studies indicating the emergence of right lateralization *in utero*. Not only prenatal stress (Alonso, Navarro, Santana, & Rodriguez, 1997) but also maternal nutritional factors cause long-lasting changes in the lateralization of the infant brain. In particular, n-3 polyunsaturated fatty acids (PUFA) such as arachidonic acid and docosahexanoic acid (DHA), which are essential to early brain development (Lauritzen, Hansen, Jorgensen, & Michaelsen, 2001), have been shown to affect brain lateralization. Offspring of mothers fed a diet deficient in PUFA show less DHA, a lower density of cholinergic neurons in the right hemisphere, and an impairment of brain maturation in postnatal periods (Vancassel et al., 2005).

According to Schuetze and Reid (2005), although the infant brain has been historically reported to be undifferentiated in terms of cerebral lateralization until 2 years of age, evidence now indicates that lateralized functions are present much earlier in development. Supporting this proposal of the adaptive role of lateralization, Simian-Tov et al. (2008) put forth this argument:

> Functional hemispheric lateralization is considered crucial for brain efficiency; it enhances neural capacity by allowing separate, parallel, and specialized processing in the hemispheres. Like motor, language, and memory functions, emotional processing has long been considered lateralized. A central role was ascribed to the right hemisphere in perception and processing of either emotions in general or negative emotions in particular. (p. 1782)

Echoing this perspective, Mento et al. (2010) conclude, "the right hemisphere would sustain the functions necessary for the *survival* of the species, such as visuospatial or emotional processes. Consequently the earlier and faster development of the neural substrates underlying these functions is needed to prevent possible impairment during infancy and childhood" (p. 7, my italics). They further note that "early alteration of the normal hemispheric asymmetry in terms of functional development in extremely immature infants has recently been related to several neurocognitive developmental impairments during childhood and adulthood" (p. 8). This model affirms Saugstad's (1998) earlier speculation that neurodevelopmental psychiatric disorders are associated with late and slow cerebral lateralization. After the postnatal period the right hemisphere subsequently reenters into (less intense) growth spurts (Thatcher, 1994), but severe alterations of the EEA would alter the later developmental trajectory of the right brain.

The data presented in this chapter strongly suggest that evolving right-lateralized visual-facial, auditory-prosodic, and tactile-gestural nonverbal communication functions of "the human social brain" can be assessed over the prenatal and postnatal stages of infancy to appraise the ongoing status of emotional and social development. Allman et al. (2005) articulate the organizing principle of developmental neuroscience: "The strong and consistent predominance for the right hemisphere emerges postnatally" (p. 367). Overviewing their developmental research, T. Grossmann et al. (2010) propose that in postnatal periods "responses to voices and emotional prosody . . . might thus serve as one of potentially multiple markers that can help with an early identification of infants at risk for neurodevelopmental disorders" (p. 856). With an eye toward diagnostic implications, Montirosso et al. (2010) call for future study of different gestures with simultaneous measurement of brain functions, and suggest that "Such studies would also be useful with samples of high risk-infants whose behavior and brain organization may be compromised" (p. 109).

Referring to specific lateralized brain regions that are directly impacted by early social-emotional experience, Pinkernelle et al. (2009) observe, "*environmental factors contribute to the development of hemispheric asymmetry*, as shown here on the cellular and network (dendrites) level. In general, hemispheric lateralization appears to be characteristic for the adequate function of sensory cortices and also for prefrontal and limbic regions" (p. 670, my italics). Earlier I outlined the sequential appearance of critical periods in right-lateralized frontal and temporal limbic control systems that regulate stressful levels of arousal and affect. Functional assessments of the experience-dependent maturation of the aforementioned amygdala, insula, cingulate, and orbitofrontal systems and their cortical and subcortical connections would allow for a diagnostic evaluation of the development of more complex self-regulation over the course of infancy. Alterations in the EEA would lead to maturational failures in these right cortical-subcortical regulatory systems in infants who are high risk for right brain social-emotional deficits.

A prime example of a severe alteration in the EEA is in children who have spent their entire infancy and toddlerhood in an institutional environment. The early deprivation of institutional rearing disrupts the experience-dependent maturation of right-lateralized neural circuitry involved in the recognition of facial emotional expressions (Parker & Nelson, 2005). Studying those infants as young as 7 months, these authors assert,

> The typical trend in brain development is increasing cortical specialization, which often means increasing laterality . . . face recognition is typically right lateralized. . . . The experience of early institutionalization may deprive the proper stimulation to drive this lateralization. Such experience may not offer the developing organism the opportunity to pair social stimuli, such as faces, with special meaning, thereby affecting the specialization of the neural systems involved in recognizing such stimuli. (p. 70)

In adolescence Romanian orphans with histories of severe early deprivation and neglect show "reduced probability of connection to the frontal pole in the right hemisphere . . . associated with increased externalizing behavioral problems" (Behen et al., 2009, p. 295). Another study of this population reveals "greater amygdala volumes, especially on the right" (Mehta et al., 2009, p. 943).

Recall that frontal and amygdala regulatory systems are major links between the regulation of emotion, stress reactivity, the HPA axis, and the autonomic nervous system. As previously noted the development of attachment involves both CNS limbic and ANS autonomic functions. Indeed, research clearly demonstrates that limbic-autonomic circuits are assembled in postnatal periods (Rinaman, Levitt, & Card, 2000). Both the sympathetic and parasympathetic branches of the ANS and their connections up into the cortex and down into the stress-regulating HPA continue to mature postnatally. It is now well established that infants with high vagal tone, a measure of parasympathetic activity, present more positive psychophysiological, behavioral, and social capacities (Huffman et al., 1998), and that vagal tone, an index of emotional regulation (Appelhans & Luecken, 2006), is related to parental socialization (Hastings et al., 2008). Chronic low vagal tone (as well as altered resting cortisol levels) over the stages of infancy thus represents a high risk factor for disturbances of both mind and body. In addition, more attention needs to be paid to prenatal and postnatal right-lateralized postural and vestibulo-ocular functions, because the right hemisphere is dominant for vestibular disturbances with affective components (Carmona et al., 2009; Dieterich et al., 2003).

Earlier I cited Schutz's (2005) assertion that the right hemisphere preferentially processes environmental challenge, stress, and pain and manages self-protective responses such as avoidance and escape. These functions onset in the first year, and if the primary caregiver is not a haven of safety but a source of fear and distress during critical periods of right brain development, this would represent a severe alteration of the EEA. Indeed, disturbances in right hemispheric maturation are reflected in "very fearful" children at 7 months who show larger evoked response potentials over the right hemisphere when viewing fearful facial expressions (de Haan, Belsky, Reid, Volein, & Johnson, 2004).

It is important to note that the right hemisphere is also dominant for the regulation of withdrawal behavior (Davidson & Cacioppo, 1992). In 6-month-old infants, withdrawal behavior is associated with elevated cortisol and extreme right frontal electroencephalographic activity (Buss et al., 2003). Although states of hyperarousal and fear in infants have been seen as an indicator of disturbance in infant mental health, there is now increased focus on the psychopathogenic nature of hypoarousal and relational withdrawal. Milne et al. (2009) describe the long-term negative developmental impact of "social withdrawal" and depression in 6-month-old infants. Citing my right brain model they conclude, "A withdrawal response in infancy is problematic behavior . . . not because it leads to later withdrawal per se, but because of the compounding effects on development of not being present in the interpersonal space—the space upon which much of infant development depends" (p. 165).

In the psychiatric literature Guedeney et al. (2008) report a study of "relational withdrawal" in infants aged 14 to 18 months. This infant reaction reflects inadequate parent–infant interactions and is a feature of most attachment disorders, particularly disorganized attachment. The severe psychopathogenesis of this context is emphasized in the researchers' clinical observation: "Sustained withdrawal behavior may be viewed as a chronic diminution of the attachment system, which is gradually generalized into a diminished engagement and lowered reactivity to the environment as a whole" (p. 151). They conclude,

> Withdrawn social behavior from as early as 2 months of age, indicated by a lack of either positive (e.g., smiling, eye contact) or negative (e.g., vocal protestations) behavior, is more akin to a state of learned helplessness and should alert the clinician to the possibility that the infant is not displaying age-appropriate emotional/social behavior. Infants may also appear socially withdrawn in several clinical conditions, for example in autism, chronic or severe pain, failure to thrive, or posttraumatic stress disorder. Withdrawal behaviour is also a key symptom of infant depression. (p. 151)

Increased right frontal EEG activity is found in 1-week-old and 3-month-old infants of depressed, withdrawn mothers (Diego, Jones, & Field, 2010). Early relational withdrawal may be a central mechanism in the intergenerational transmission of depression, a clinical syndrome that is now being understood in terms of right hemispheric dysfunction (Hecht, 2010). Relational withdrawal reflects a severe impairment of the attachment mechanism and a marker of a severe decrement in the EEA (for more on withdrawal, disorganized-disoriented attachment, and pathological dissociation in infancy, see Schore, 2009).

There is now agreement that the essential task of the first year of human life is the creation of a secure attachment bond of emotional communication between the infant and his or her primary caregiver (Schore & Schore, 2008). Hence, learning how to communicate represents the most important developmental process to take place during infancy (Papousek & Papousek, 1997), and the whole of child development can be basically conceptualized as the enhancement of self-regulation (Fonagy & Target, 2002). All of these emergent functions are dependent upon the structural maturation of the infant's right brain. Several studies are in line with Bowlby's (1969) conception that the infant's development within the environment of evolutionary adaptedness is impacted by "his interaction with the principal figure in that environment, namely the mother" (p. 181). For example, there is MacLean's (1996) proposal that "For more than 180 million years, the female has played the central role in mammalian evolution" (p. 422), and my developmental interpersonal neurobiological tenet: "The self-organization of the developing brain occurs in the context of a relationship with another self, another brain" (Schore, 1996, p. 60). Assessments of infant mental health and social-emotional development during the human brain growth of the first 2 years must evaluate the *relationship* co-created by the right brains of both members of an attachment dyad. Schore and Newton (in press) are now using modern attachment theory to guide assessments of early attachment relationships. Such assessments of the developing infant's capacities for nonverbal emotional communication and implicit affect regulation of both positive and negative affective states could be used diagnostically as markers of attachment development, complexity of right brain maturation, infant mental health, and, if indicated, targets of early relational intervention.

Over the ensuing stages of development, right brain functions are essential for the toddler's expanding emotional and social functions. Regulated affective interactions with familiar, predictable caregivers create not only a sense of safety but also a positively charged curiosity that fuels the burgeoning self's exploration of novel socioemotional and physical environments. These advances are critical to the changes in the environment of evolutionary adaptedness that occur in the second year, the stage of human socialization (Schore, 1994). About two decades ago Tucker (1992) speculated, "the baby brain must begin participating effectively in the process of social information transmission that offers entry into the culture" (p. 79). He asserted that social interaction that promotes brain differentiation is the mechanism for teaching "the epigenetic patterns of culture" (p. 122), and that successful social development requires a high degree of skill in negotiating emotional communication, "much of which is nonverbal" (p. 80). Tucker concluded that such emotional information engages "specialized neural networks in humans, within the right hemisphere" (p. 80). I would add that early right brain development not only allows entry into a particular culture but also shapes the culture itself.

I propose that Bowlby's concept of environment of evolutionary adaptedness describes the psychological space that a particular culture, at any point of anthropological history, creates to scaffold the emotional attachment bonding between mothers and infants, the evolutionary mechanism of attachment. This relational space operates at implicit levels, and it can be either expansive and facilitating or constrictive and inhibiting. In terms of attachment theory, a decrement in the EEA in a particular culture would be expressed in a decrease in secure and an increase in insecure attachment typologies. The interpersonal neurobiological perspective of regulation theory would interpret this reduction in secure and expansion of insecure attachments as reflecting nonoptimal alterations in right brain maturation and limbic-autonomic functioning and reduced efficiency in implicit stress and affect regulation described earlier.

Indeed, we now have data indicating that such a disturbing trend now exists. A comprehensive analysis of over 10,000 Adult Attachment Interviews of North American *nonclinical* mothers over the last two decades reports only 58% secure attachments, with 23% insecure-dismissive, 19% insecure-preoccupied, and 18% unresolved loss or other traumas (Bakersmans-Kranenburg & Van IJzendoorn, 2009). In perhaps the most comprehensive recent developmental neurobiological research on human attachment and parenting Atztil, Hendler, and Feldman (2011) report,

> [E]arly disruptions and slight deviations from normative functioning may result in nonoptimal patterns of maternal care that may bear negative consequences for the infant's future mental health. Indeed, recent studies have shown that up to 29% of mothers and infants suffer from some sort of disruptions to early bonding, due to marked increases in cases of maternal post-partum depression and anxiety, as well as in premature birth (ACOG, 2006; Andersson et al., 2006; Silverman et al., 2007; Vesga-Lopez et al., 2008). Such conditions pose a risk for the infant's adaptation and well-being and may lead to a variety of epigenetic, behavioral, and mental processes that would compromise the infant's future well-being, health, and adaptation. (pp. 10–11)

THOUGHTS ON THE CURRENT DECREMENT IN THE EEA IN U.S. CULTURE

In 1994, at the very beginning of my first book, I proposed, "The child's first relationship, the one with the mother, acts as a template, as it permanently molds the individual's capacities to enter into all later emotional relationships" (Schore, 1994, p. 3). In the very last pages I utilized a perspective grounded in interpersonal neurobiology and developmental neuroscience to offer thoughts on a growing trend in American culture that represented a serious departure from an optimal EEA:

> The conclusions of this volume echo and amplify a recent "worrisome" concern expressed by Bretherton (1992) about the experimentally demonstrated increased

risk of insecure attachments if day care, as typically provided in present American society, begins in the 1st year and is extensive in duration. In a series of studies Belsky is finding that extensive nonmaternal (and nonparental) care in this 1st year is a risk factor in the increased development of insecure patterns of attachment (Belsky & Rovine, 1988), and that insecure-avoidant infants with such care express more negative affect and engage in less object play in reunion episodes with the mother (Belsky & Braungart, 1991). Other research indicates that even infants in middle- and upper-middle-class families that use in-home baby-sitters for more than 20 hours per week display higher rates of avoidance on reunion with the mother and are more likely to be classified as showing an insecure attachment (Barglow, Vaughn, & Molitor, 1987). A link between early day care experience and subsequent levels of aggression and noncompliance is also being reported (Haskins, 1985). In an analysis of 13 studies of attachment and child care, Lamb et al. (1992) now concur with Belsky that elevated levels of insecure attachments are consistently found in child care children. . . . I believe that such disturbing observations must be attended to very seriously. . . . The matter of caregiving, in not just the first few months but the first 2-years-of-life, is an essential problem for the future of human societies. (Schore, 1994, p. 540–541)

In the last two decades these data have been replicated in large-scale studies (National Institute of Child Health & Human Development [NICHD] Early Child Care Research Network, 2006). Recently Dmitrieva, Steinberg, and Belsky (2007) report, "Evidence indicates clearly that care initiated *early in life* and experienced for many hours, especially in child-care centers, is associated with somewhat elevated levels of externalizing behavior problems (e.g., aggression and disobedience), and that these effects are not simply a function of low-quality care" (p. 1032, my italics). In a very recent developmental psychobiological study of children in day care, Sajaniemi et al. (2011) conclude,

The number of physical and psychological stressors in the lives of children has multiplied in recent years as the number of children with various kinds of behavioural and developmental difficulties has increased. Besides other stressful childhood events such as family turmoil, disruptions or adverse social circumstances, day care may also be challenging for some children. . . . The link between elevated cortisol levels and day care has been shown in several studies including ours (Legendre, 2003; Watamura, Donzella, Alwin, & Gunnar, 2003). . . . These findings should be considered alarming since developmental difficulties may be, at least partly, the consequence of chronically-induced stress which is known to have detrimental effects on brain activity, emotional well-being and development. (p. 56)

Citing studies showing low-quality day care has a detrimental influence on children's cortisol levels (Geoffroy, Côté, Parent, & Séguin, 2006; Lisonbee, Mize, Payne, & Granger, 2008; Sims, Guifoyle, & Parry, 2006), these authors assert that the "stressful environment" of day care is "known to have jeopardized children's development." (p. 57). Developmental neurobiological and neuropsychological studies of infants before, during, and after early day care (the first 2 years) is now essential, and it should focus on not later maturing language or motor areas, but on brain systems responsible for social-emotional and stress-regulating functions.

Indeed, two out of three American children under 5 years old now receive some form of nonparental child care, and in most cases, this care begins during the first year of life (Overturf Johnson, 2005). In 2004, 52.9% of mothers with children under 1 year old were in the workforce (Bureau of Labor Statistics, 2011). Highlighting the significant changes over the last 20 years, in the 1960s, 17% of women returned to work by 12 months after delivery, compared with 60% in the early 1990s (52% by 6 months). In the 1990s, of mothers who returned to work within 12 months, more than half did so by 3 months, and 75% by 6 months (Smith, Downs, & O'Connell, 2001). Despite the recommendation of at least 18 weeks of maternity leave by the General Conference of the International Labor Organization (2000), the United States lags seriously behind the other industrialized countries in which maternal and paternal leave routinely extend into the late months of the infant's first year. Due to this shortsighted policy, 6 weeks after delivery is the particular time that most mothers in the United States reenter the job market and put their infants into day care (much of which is substandard).

As stated previously, during this identical perinatal period the cerebral and corticolimbic areas of the infant's brain are just beginning to myelinate and to initiate functions such as tactile communication and face processing, which are critical to attachment. Recall that the volume of the subcortical areas increases significantly after birth (Knickmeyer et al., 2008). Although the subcortical amygdala begins its growth spurt in the prenatal period, it continues its experience-dependent maturation in this perinatal period, thereby becoming involved in attachment functions (Lemche et al., 2006). Earlier in this chapter I described how the insula is in a critical period of maturation that onsets in the last trimester of pregnancy and continues through the first 2 months of human life (Afif et al., 2007), and how the emergence of von Economo (VEN) neurons in the right insula "may be related to environmental influences" (Allman et al., 2011, p. 62). In this same time frame the anterior cingulate (medial frontal) control system that regulates the amygdala and stress-regulating HPA axis enters into a critical period that requires body-to-body psychobiological transactions and face-to-face communications. I suggest that early day care may specifically interfere with the critical period maturation of these particular regulatory systems.

No research has been done on the effects of early day care on brain development, especially on subcortical brain development. That said, a very recent study on the effects of early life stress in this perinatal period demonstrates that brief daily separations induced high and prolonged levels of stress and glucocorticoids in the infant's developing brain (Wei, David, Duman, Anisman, & Kaffman, 2010). Most surprisingly to the authors, this early life stress was associated with anxiety-like behavior in adulthood, *despite increased maternal care after the sepa-*

rations. More specifically, brief daily separations from the mother reduced the amount of RNA and DNA in the developing subcortical hippocampus. They conclude, "exposure to stress during the postnatal period overrides the ability of high levels of postnatal maternal care to program anxiety-like behavior by *inhibiting the normal growth spurt that characterizes this period*" (2010, p. 396, my italics). These data are consonant with my model of stress-induced excessive parcellation of developing brain circuits, wherein dysregulated levels of relational stress induce oxidative damage to DNA during regional growth spurts, thereby increasing "apoptotic" "programmed cell death" in rapidly developing areas of the infant's brain (Schore, 1994, 2002, 2003a).

Furthermore, as Heymann, Raub, and Earle (2011) point out entry into early day care frequently also interferes with the 6-month policy of breastfeeding advocated by the American Academy of Pediatrics (2005). Maternal milk is a rich source of unsaturated fatty acids, bioactive nutrients that are essential to early brain development (Yehuda, Rabinovitz, & Mostofsky, 1999). Very recent research indicates that a shorter duration of breastfeeding (less than 6 months) may be a predictor of adverse mental health outcomes throughout the developmental trajectory of childhood and early adolescence (Oddy et al., 2010). Citing my work on brain development, Calnen (2007) asserts, "It is biologically necessary that mothers be with their infants, especially during the first few months postpartum. This is not likely to become a reality until working families are granted a sufficiently long, and paid, maternity leave as a matter of national policy" (p. 39).

To my mind these data reflect the fact that for the last two decades American culture has been providing a growth-inhibiting EEA for mother–infant attachment bond formation in the first 2 years of life. Research investigating the short-term effects of maternal employment in the first year after birth demonstrates developmental risks, including insecure attachments (Belsky, 2001) and negative impact on children's cognitive abilities (Hill, Waldfogel, Brooks-Gunn, & Han, 2005). But a decrement in the EEA is expressed in more than cognitive psychological impairments—rather it impacts neurobiological development. Recall that the first 2 years of human infancy overlap the human brain growth spurt, which extends to 18 to 24 months (Dobbing & Sands, 1973). The decrement in the EEA is thus expressed in less than optimal epigenetic influences on the experience-dependent maturation of the early developing emotion-processing right brain. The long-term effect of this altered EEA is a substantial increase in the number of individuals with a neurobiological predisposition for psychiatric disorders.

Evidence for this assertion was offered in 2003 in *Hardwired to Connect*, a report produced by the Commission on Children at Risk, of which I was a member. Citing extensive research that included, among others, the following findings: that 21% of U.S. children ages 9 to 17 have a diagnosable mental or addictive disorder, that in 2001 28.3% of adolescents reported episodes of serious depression in the previous year, and that in 2002 at least 1 of every 4 adolescents in the United States was found to be at risk of not achieving productive adulthood. The Commission of 33 children's doctors, research scientists, and mental health professionals concluded:

> The implications of this research are clear and profound: The declining mental health of many U.S. children is a pressing issue that plays a substantial role in many of today's emerging physical problems. Psychosomatic and psychosocial disorders have pronounced and long-lasting effects on both children's lives and society. (2003, p. 71)

In 2005, a National Comorbidity Survey Replication study reported that about half of all Americans will meet the criteria for a *DSM-IV* disorder in their life, with first onset usually in childhood or adolescence (Kessler et al., 2005). In commenting on this study, Insel and Fenton (2005) articulate this widely held principle: "Most mental illnesses . . . begin far earlier in life than was previously believed" (p. 590).

Further confirming the concept of a decrement in the EEA, in 2007 UNICEF published a study of child well-being in 21 rich countries, and documented that the United States ranked 21st in health and safety and 20th in the quality of family and peer relationships. The report concludes,

> All families in Organization for Economic Co-operation and Development (OECD) countries today are aware that childhood is being re-shaped by forces whose mainspring is not necessarily the best interests of the child. At the same time, a wide public in the OECD countries is becoming ever more aware that many of the corrosive social problems affecting the quality of life have their genesis in the changing ecology of childhood. Many therefore feel that it is time to attempt to re-gain a degree of understanding, control and direction over what is happening to our children in their most vital, vulnerable years. (UNICEF, 2007, p. 39)

We now have psychiatric and sociological data that offers a somber portrait of "what is happening to our children." At the beginning of this chapter I cited an upcoming volume, *Evolution, Early Experience, and Human Development: From Research to Practice and Policy*. In the opening chapter my co-editors, Darcia Narvaez, Jaak Panksepp, Tracy Gleason, and I report that a decade ago, one of four teenagers in the United States was at risk for a poor life outcome (Eccles & Gootman, 2002); and in recent analyses such trends have not improved (Heckman, 2008). The national prevalence of young children (under 5) with psychosocial problems has been increasing to between 10% and 21% (Powell, Fixen, & Dunlop, 2003). The rates of young children who display aggressive behavior, delinquency, or hyperactivity are on the increase, at times estimated to be as high as 25% (Raver & Knitze, 2002). In addition, the dropout rate of adolescents who fail to complete high school is now 16% (Porche, Fortuna, Lin, & Alegria, 2011). The authors of this latter study conclude that early trauma experiences may account for this "staggering" rate. Indeed, The American Academy of Child & Adolescent Psychiatry (AAACP) is now describing a "crisis" in children's mental health needs: One in every five children has a diagnosable psychiatric disorder, and one in every ten suffers from a mental illness severe enough to impair everyday living (AAACP, n.d.).

There is now agreement across disciplines that the neurobiological sequelae of traumatic attachment experiences are enduring and set the stage for a spectrum of psychopathologies of childhood, adolescence, and adulthood. Childhood trauma is "toxic" because "it disrupts brain architecture, affects other organ systems, and leads to stress-management systems that establish relatively lower thresholds for responsiveness that persist throughout life, thereby increasing the risk of stress-related disease and cognitive impairment well into the adult years" (Shonkoff, Boyce, & McEwen, 2009, p. 2256). Recent research thus contradicts the view that the faults of early childhood can be easily outgrown; many cannot be, or if they can, the process requires serious and considerable intervention (Perry, Pollard, Blakely, Baker, & Vigilante, 1995; Schore, 1994, 2001a). A rapidly expanding body of interdisciplinary research is now elucidating the enduring neurobiological effects of early life trauma that lie at the core of a spectrum of psychiatric, psychosomatic, and personality disorders (see the contributions of over 80 researchers in Lanius et al., 2010). Recall that the subtitle of this volume is *The Hidden Epidemic*.

Developmental neuroscience now clearly indicates that the prenatal and postnatal critical periods of early childhood represent the "most vital, vulnerable years." The original embryological concept of critical periods connoted bounded times in development when a rapidly growing tissue in the developing organism is most vulnerable to alterations by external factors. Tucker (1992) described the concept of "psychological embryology," and he pointed out that the long period of nurturance and social interaction provided human children allows "the life experience of other individuals to serve as epigenetic determinants of brain differentiation and intelligence" (p. 122), especially of "specialized neural networks in humans, within the right hemisphere" (p. 80).

In 2001 I offered an article in the *Infant Mental Health Journal* entitled "The Effects of a Secure Attachment Relationship on Right Brain Development, Affect Regulation, and Infant Mental Health." In it I concluded,

> Adaptive infant mental health can be fundamentally defined as the earliest expression of efficient and resilient strategies for coping with novelty and stress, and maladaptive infant mental health as a deficit in these same coping mechanisms. The former is a resilience factor for coping with psychobiological stressors at later stages of the life cycle, the latter is a risk factor for interruptions of developmental processes and a vulnerability to the coping deficits that define later-forming psychopathologies. (Schore, 2001a, p. 17)

This perspective is consonant with Darwin's principle: "It is not the strongest of the species that survives, nor the most intelligent, but the one most responsive to change."

But this developmental psychoneurobiological model of emotional resilience is not consonant with other current developmental conceptions of cognitive-behavioral resilience. Hrdy (2009) has suggested that children reared under adverse conditions (e.g., with stressed parents) may develop personalities that are better prepared for subsisting in a challenging environment. Indeed, when children are presented with manageable, graded emotional challenges they can increase resilience (e.g., Katz et al., 2009). However, relational attachment trauma presents the infant with not graded (and interactively repaired) but highly stressful and thereby overwhelming emotional experiences. In fact severe attachment stressors decrease the adaptive abilities to respond emotionally, think efficiently, or relate well to others. This is due to the fact that significant reductions of "nurturance and social interaction" in human infancy alter the developmental trajectory of the emotional right brain, reducing the capacity of emotional resilience, and inducing coping deficits of affect regulation that are associated with a spectrum of developmental psychopathologies. This neurobiological perspective contradicts the idea that having a stressed brain is adaptive.

Most importantly, the developmental psychological speculation that individuals who experience adverse early environments are better prepared to resiliently face a challenging environment is now being disconfirmed by very recent clinical studies and psychiatric observations (e.g., Baradon, 2010; Lanius et al., 2010). Developmental neuroscience now clearly demonstrates that all children are not "resilient" but "malleable," for better or worse (Leckman & March, 2011). The developmental dogma that most children are able to accommodate variations in the quality of early care without deviation from normal developmental progress, and that infants and children show great behavioral and developmental resilience in the face of adverse life experiences also overlooks the documented ongoing dramatic increases in childhood psychopathology, including bipolar disorder (Moreno et al., 2007), Attention Deficit Hyperactivity Disorder (ADHD) (Bloom & Cohen, 2006), and autism (Harpaz-Rotem & Rosenheck, 2004; Landrigan, 2010). Each of these conditions show right brain deficits (Hale et al., 2009; Lazarev, Pontes, & de Azevedo, 2008; Versace et al., 2008). Furthermore, the recent documentation of a "high prevalence" of mental disorders in today's youth (Merikangas et al., 2011) is paralleled by data on the current child obesity epidemic (Whitaker, 2011). Researchers are now viewing insecure attachment as a risk factor for obesity in children (Anderson & Whitaker, 2011), and are articulating a right brain hypothesis for obesity that describes a dysfunction of the right prefrontal cortex (Alonso-Alonso & Pascual-Leone, 2007). These epidemiological data, as well as current attachment and developmental neurobiological research seriously challenge the concept of universal resilience as too simplistic if not incorrect (e.g., *Hardwired to Connect*, 2003; Lanius et al., 2010; Schore, 2003a; Szajnberg, Goldenberg, & Hatari, 2010).

A central tenet of attachment theory and developmental interpersonal neurobiology dictates that the emotional bond between the primary caregiver and her infant will have long-term effects, for better or worse, on the developing right brain, and thereby on both socioemotional and physical health over the entire life span. The clinician/researchers Fonagy and Target (2005, p. 334) note the paradigm shift in attachment theory: "If the attachment relationship is indeed a major organizer of brain development, as many have accepted and suggested (e.g., Schore, 1997, 2003a), then the determinants of attachment relationships are important far beyond the provision of a fundamental sense of safety or security" (Bowlby, 1969). The "brain development" directly impacted by attachment transactions in the first 2 years is the development of the right brain more so than the later-maturing left brain. The EEA supports or inhibits the experience-dependent maturation of the right brain. The psychological, psychiatric, and sociological data cited in this volume suggest the latter. The data presented in this chapter strongly indicate that early identification and intervention within the EEA, a period of not only vulnerability but also maximal brain plasticity, will have important practical effects at all later points of the life span (Schore & Newton, in press). The challenge I made in an issue of *The Infant Mental Health Journal* at the beginning of the last decade applies even more so today:

> [T]he earliest stages of humanhood are critical because they contain within them the representation of our possible futures—they model the potential developmental extension of our individual and collective social identities. . . . When and where shall we place our current resources so as to optimize the future of human societies? . . . How much should we value the very beginnings of human life, in tangible social program dollars? (Schore, 2001b, p. 4)

REFERENCES

ACOG (2006). ACOG Committee Opinon No. 343: Psychosocial risk factors: perinatal screening and intervention. *Obstetrics & Gynecology, 108,* 469–477.

Afif, A., Bouvier, R., Buenerd, A., Trouillas, J., & Mertens, P. (2007). Development of the human fetal insular cortex: Study of the gyration from 13 to 28 gestational weeks. *Brain Structure & Function, 212,* 335–346.

Allman, J. M., Tetreault, N. A., Hakeem, A. Y., Manaye, K. F., Semendeferi, K., Erwin, J. M., et al. (2011). The von Economo neurons in the frontoinsular and anterior cingulate cortex. *Annals of the New York Academy of Sciences, 1225,* 59–71.

Allman, J. M., Watson, K. K., Tetreault, N. A., & Hakeem, A. Y. (2005). Intuition and autism: A possible role for Von Economo neurons. *Trends in Cognitive Sciences, 9,* 367–373.

Alonso, S. J., Navarro, E., Santana, C., & Rodriguez, M. (1997). Motor lateralization, behavioral despair and dopaminergic brain asymmetry after prenatal stress. *Pharmacology Biochemistry and Behavior, 58,* 443–448.

Alonso-Alonso, M., & Pascual-Leone, A. (2007). The right brain hypothesis for obesity. *Journal of the American Medical Association, 297,* 1819–1822.

American Academy of Child & Adolescent Psychiatry. (n.d.). The Campaign for America's Kids. Retrieved May 3, 2011, from http://www.campaignforamericaskids.org/

American Academy of Pediatrics. (2005). Breastfeeding and the use of human milk. *Pediatrics, 115,* 496–506.

Anderson, S. E., & Whitaker, R. C. (2011). Attachment security and obesity in US preschool-aged children. *Archives of Pediatric and Adolescent Medicine, 165*, 235–242.

Andersson, L., Sundstron-Poromaa, I., Wulff, M., Astrom, M., & Bixo, M. (2000). Depression and anxiety during pregnancy and six months postpartum: a follow-up study. *Acta Obstetricia et Gynecologica Scandinavica, 85*, 937–944.

Applehans, B., & Luecken, L. (2006). Heart rate variability as an index of regulated emotional responding. *Review of General Psychology, 10*, 229–240.

Atzil, S., Hendler, T., & Feldman, R. (2011, August 31). Specifying the neurobiological basis of human attachment: Brain, hormones and behavior in synchronous and intrusive mothers. *Neuropsychopharmacology*; doi:10.1038/npp.2011.172.

Bakersmans-Kranenburg, M. J., & Van IJzendoorn, M. H. (2009). The first 10,000 Adult Attachment Interviews; distributions of adult attachment representations in clinical and non-clinical groups. *Attachment & Human Development, 11*, 223–263.

Baradon, T. (Ed.). (2010). *Relational trauma in infancy*. London: Routledge.

Barbas, H., Saha, S., Rempel-Clower, N., & Ghashghaei, T. (2003). Serial pathways from primate prefrontal cortex to autonomic areas may influence emotional expression. *BMC Neuroscience, 4*, 25.

Barglow, P., Vaughn, B., & Molitor, N. (1987). Effects of maternal absence due to employment on the quality of infant-attachment in a low-risk sample. *Child Development, 58*, 945–954.

Batten, S. V., Aslan, M., Maciejewski, P. K., & Mazure, C. M. (2004). Childhood maltreatment as a risk factor for adult cardiovascular disease and depression. *Journal of Clinical Psychiatry, 65*, 249–254.

Behen, M. E., Muzik, O., Saporta, A. S. D., Wilson, B. J., Pai, D., Hua, J., et al. (2009). Abnormal fronto-striatal connectivity in children with histories of early deprivation: A diffusion tensor imaging study. *Brain Imaging and Behavior, 3*, 292–297.

Bell, H. C., Pellis, S. M., & Kolb, B. (2010). Juvenile peer play experience and the development of the orbitofrontal and medial prefrontal cortices. *Behavioural Brain Research, 207*, 7–13.

Belsky, J. (2001). Developmental risks (still) associated with early child care. *Journal of Child Psychology and Psychiatry, 42*, 845–859.

Belsky, J., & Braungart, J. M. (1991). Are insecure-avoidant infants with extensive day-care experience less stressed by and more independent in the Strange Situation? *Child Development, 62*, 567–571.

Belsky, J., & Rovine, M. J. (1988). Nonmaternal care in the first year of life and the security of infant–parent attachment. *Child Development, 59*, 157–167.

Bloom, B., & Cohen, R. A. (2006). Summary health statistic for U.S. children: National health interview survey. *Vital and Health Statistics 10, 234*, 1–79.

Bock, J., Murmu, R. P., Ferdman, N., Leshem, M., & Braun, K. (2008). Refinement of dendritic and synaptic networks in the rodent anterior cingulate and orbitofrontal cortex: Critical impact of early and late social experience. *Developmental Neurobiology, 68*, 695–698.

Booth, A., & Dabbs, J. M. (1993). Testosterone and men's marriages. *Social Forces, 72*, 463–477.

Bowlby, J. (1969). *Attachment and loss: Vol. 1. Attachment.* New York: Basic Books.

Bradshaw, G. A., & Schore, A. N. (2007). How elephants are opening doors: Developmental neuroethology, attachment and social context. *Ethology, 113*, 426–436.

Brancucci, A., Lucci, G., Mazzatenta, A., & Tommasi, L. (2009). Asymmetries of the human social brain in the visual, auditory and chemical modalities. *Philosophical Transactions of the Royal Society B, 364,* 895–914.

Braun, C. M. J., Boulanger, Y., Labelle, M., Khiat, A., Dumont, M., & Mailloux, C. (2002). Brain metabolic differences as a function of hemisphere, writing hand preference, and gender. *Laterality, 7,* 97–113.

Brazelton, T. B., & Cramer, B. G. (1990). *The earliest relationship.* Reading, MA: Addison-Wesley.

Bretherton, I. (1992). The origins of attachment theory: John Bowlby and Mary Ainsworth. *Developmental Psychology, 28,* 759–775.

Brown, J. W., & Jaffe, J. (1975). Hypothesis on cerebral dominance. *Neuropsychologia, 13,* 107–110.

Bureau of Labor Statistics. (2011, March 24). *Employment characteristics of families summary.* Retrieved May 10, 2011, from http://stats.bls.gov/news.release/famee.nr0.htm

Buss, K. A., Schumacher, J. R. M., Dolski, I., Kalin, N. H., Goldsmith, H. H., & Davidson, R. J. (2003). Right frontal brain activity, cortisol, and withdrawal behavior in 6-month-old infants. *Behavioral Neuroscience, 117,* 11–20.

Calnen, G. (2007). Paid maternity leave and its impact in breastfeeding in the United States: An historic, economic, political, and social perspective. *Breastfeeding Medicine, 2,* 34–44.

Carlsson, J., Lagercrantz, H., Olson, L., Printz, G., & Bartocci, M. (2008). Activation of the right fronto-temporal cortex during maternal facial recognition in young infants. *Acta Paediatrica, 97,* 1221–1225.

Carmona, J. E., Holland, A. K., & Harrison, D. W. (2009). Extending the functional cerebral systems theory of emotion to the vestibular modality: A systematic and integrative approach. *Psychological Bulletin, 135,* 286–302.

Cerqueira, J., Almeida, O. F. X., & Sousa, N. (2008). The stressed prefrontal cortex. Left? Right! *Brain, Behavior, and Immunity, 22,* 630–638.

Champagne, F. A. (2011). Maternal imprints and the origins of variation. *Hormones and Behavior, 60,* 4–11.

Chanen, A. M., Velakoulis, D., Carison, K., Gaunson, K., Wood, S. J., Yuen, H. P., et al. (2008). Orbitofrontal, amygdala and hippocampal volumes in teenagers with first-presentation borderline personality disorder. *Psychiatry Research: Neuroimaging, 163,* 116–125.

Chiron, C., Jambaque, I., Nabbout, R., Lounes, R., Syrota, A., & Dulac, O. (1997). The right brain hemisphere is dominant in human infants. *Brain, 120,* 1057–1065.

Chugani, H. T., & Phelps, M. E. (1986). Maturational changes in cerebral function in infants determined by [18]FDG positron emission tomography. *Science, 231,* 840–843.

Ciaramelli, E., Muccioli, M., Ladavas, E., & di Pellegrino, G. (2007). Selective deficit in personal moral judgment following damage to ventromedial prefrontal cortex. *Social Cognitive and Affective Neuroscience, 2,* 84–92.

Craig, M. C., Catani, M., Deeley, Q., Latham, R., Daly, E., Kanaan, R., et al. (2009). Altered connections on the road to psychopathy. *Molecular Psychiatry, 14,* 946–953.

Damasio, A. R. (1994). *Descartes' error.* New York: Grosset/Putnam.

Danese, A., Pariante, C. M., Caspi, A., Taylor, A., & Poulton, R. (2007). Childhood maltreatment predicts adult inflammation in a life-course study. *Proceedings of the National Academy of Sciences of the United States of America, 104,* 1319–1324.

Dapretto, M., Davies, M. S., Pfeifer, J. H., Scott, A. A., Sigman, M., Bookheimer, S. Y., et al. (2006). Understanding emotions in others: Mirror neuron dysfunction in children with autism spectrum disorders. *Nature Neuroscience, 9,* 28–31.

Davidson, R. J., & Cacioppo, J. T. (1992). New developments in the scientific study of emotion: An introduction to the special section. *Psychological Science, 3,* 21–22.

de Haan, M., Belsky, J., Reid, V., Volein, A., & Johnson, M. H. (2004). Maternal personality and infants' neural and visual responsivity to facial expressions of emotion. *Journal of Child Psychology and Psychiatry, 45,* 1209–1218.

Diego, M. A., Jones, N. A., & Field, T. (2010). EEG in 1-week, 1-month and 3-month-old infants of depressed and non-depressed mothers. *Biological Psychology, 83,* 7–14.

Dieterich, M., Bense, S., Lutz, S., Drzezga, A., Stephen, T., Bartenstein, P., et al. (2003). Dominance for vestibular cortical function in the non-dominant hemisphere. *Cerebral Cortex, 13,* 994–1007.

Dmitreva, J., Steinberg, L., & Belsky, J. (2007). Child-care history classroom composition, and children's functioning in kindergarten. *Psychological Science, 18,* 1032–1039.

Dobbing, J., & Sands, J. (1973). Quantitative growth and development of human brain. *Archives of Diseases of Childhood, 48,* 757–767.

Dolan, R. J. (1999). On the neurology of morals. *Nature Neuroscience, 2,* 927–929.

Eccles, J., & Gootman, J. A. (2002). *Community programs to promote youth development.* Washington, DC: Committee on Community-Level Programs for Youth. Board on Children, Youth, and Families, Commission on Behavioral and Social Sciences Education, National Research Council, and Institute of Medicine.

Eddington, K. M., Dolcos, F., McLean, A, N., Krishnan, K. R., Cabeza, R., & Strauman, T. J. (2009). Neural correlates of idiographic goal priming in depression: Goal-specific dysfunctions in the orbitofrontal cortex. *Social Cognition and Affective Neuroscience, 4,* 238–246.

Fahim, C., Stip, E., Mancini-Marie, A., Potvin, S., & Malaspina, D. (2007). Orbitofrontal dysfunction in a monozygotic twin discordant for postpartum affective psychosis: A functional magnetic resonance imaging study. *Bipolar Disorders, 9,* 541–545.

Feldman, R., Singer, M., & Zagoory, O. (2010). Touch attenuates infants' physiological reactivity to stress. *Developmental Science, 13,* 271–278.

Felitti, V. J., & Anda, R. F. (2010). The relationship of adverse childhood experiences to adult medical disease, psychiatric disorders and sexual behavior: Implications for healthcare. In R. A. Lanius, E. Vermetten, & C. Pain (Eds.), *The impact of early life trauma on health and disease: The hidden epidemic* (pp. 77–87). Cambridge, UK: Cambridge University Press.

Ferber, S. G., Feldman, R., & Makhoul, I. R. (2008). The development of maternal touch across the first year of life. *Early Human Development, 84,* 363–370.

Flanders, J. L., Simard, M., Paquette, D., Parent, S., Vitaro, F., Pihl, R. O., et al. (2010). Rough-and-tumble play and the development of physical aggression and emotion regulation: A five-year follow-up study. *Journal of Family Violence, 25,* 357–367.

Fonagy, P., & Target, M. (2002). Early intervention and the development of self-regulation. *Psychoanalytic Inquiry, 22,* 307–335.

Fonagy, P., & Target, M. (2005). Bridging the transmission gap: An end to an important mystery of attachment research? *Attachment & Human Development, 7,* 333–343.

Gallace, A., & Spence, C. (2010). The science of interpersonal touch: An overview. *Neuroscience and Biobehavioral Reviews, 34,* 246–259.

Gansler, D. A., McLaughlin, N. C. R., Iguchi, L., Jerram, M., Moore, D. W., Bhadelia,

R., et al. (2009). A multivariate approach to aggression and the orbital frontal cortex in psychiatric patients. *Psychiatry Research: Neuroimaging, 171,* 145–154.

Gao, W., Zhu, H., Giovanello, K. S., Smith, J. K., Shen, D., Gilmore, J. H., et al. (2009). Evidence on the emergence of the brain's default network from 2-week-old to 2-year-old healthy pediatric subjects. *Proceedings of the National Academy of Sciences of the United States of America, 106,* 6790–6795.

Garay, P. A., & McAllister, A. K. (2010). Novel roles for immune molecules in neural development: Implications for neurodevelopmental disorders. *Frontiers in Synaptic Science, 2,* 1–16.

General Conference of the International Labor Organization. (2000). *C183 maternity protection convention, 2000.* Retrieved May 12, 2011, from http://www.ilo.org/ilolex/cgi-lex/convde.pl?C183

Geoffroy, M., Côté, S. M., Parent, S., & Séguin, J. R. (2006). Daycare attendance, stress, and mental health. *Canadian Journal of Psychiatry, 51,* 607–615.

Gettler, L.T., McDade, T.W., Feranil, A. B., &. Kuzawaa, C. W. (2011). Longitudinal evidence that fatherhood decreases testosterone in human males. *Proceedings of the National Academy of Sciences of the United States of America.*Retrieved from http://www.pnas.org/cgi/doi/10.1073/pnas.1105403108

Girgis, R. R., Minshew, N. J., Melhem, N. M., Nutche, J. J., Keshavan, M. S., & Hardan, A. Y. (2007). Volumetric alterations of the orbitofrontal cortex in autism. *Progress in Neuro-Psychopharmacology & Biological Psychiatry, 31,* 41–45.

Gray, P. B., Yang, C-F. J., & Pope, H. G., Jr. (2006). Fathers have lower salivary testosterone levels than unmarried men and married non-fathers in Beijing, China. *Proceedings in Biological Science, 273,* 333–339.

Gray, P. B., & Anderson, K. G. (2010). *Fatherhood: Evolution and paternal behavior.* Cambridge MA: Harvard University Press.

Grossmann, K., Grossmann, K. E., Fremmer-Bombik, E., Kindler, H., Scheuerer-Englisch, H., & Zimmermann, P. (2002). The uniqueness of the child–father attachment relationship: Father's sensitive and challenging play as a pivotal variable in a 16-year longitudinal study. *Social Development, 11,* 307–331.

Grossmann, T., Johnson, M. H., Farroni, T., & Csibra, G. (2007). Social perception in the infant brain: Gamma oscillatory activity in response to eye gaze. *Social Cognitive and Affective Neuroscience, 2,* 284–291.

Grossmann, T., Oberecker, R., Koch, S. P., & Friederici, A. D. (2010). The developmental origins of voice processing in the human brain. *Neuron, 65,* 852–858.

Guedeney, A., Foucault, C., Bougen, E., Larroque, B., & Mentre, F. (2008). Screening for risk factors of relational withdrawal behaviour in infants aged 14–18 months. *European Psychiatry, 23,* 150–155.

Gunnar, M. R. (2000). Early adversity and the development of stress reactivity and regulation. In C. A. Nelson (Ed.), *The Minnesota symposium on child psychology: Vol. 31. The effects of early adversity on neurobehavioral development* (pp. 163–200). Mahwah, NJ: Erlbaum.

Guo, K., Meints, K., Hall, C., Hall, S., & Mills, D. (2009). Left gaze bias in humans, rhesus monkeys and domestic dogs. *Animal Cognition, 12,* 409–418.

Gupta, R. K., Hasan, K. M., Trivedi, R., Pradhan, M., Das, V., Parikh, N. A., et al. (2005). Diffusion tensor imaging of the developing human cerebrum. *Journal of Neuroscience Research, 81,* 172–178.

Hale, T. S., Loo, S. K., Zaidel, E., Hanada, G., Macion, J., & Smalley, S. L. (2009). Rethinking a right hemisphere deficit in ADHD. *Journal of Attention Disorders, 13,* 3–17.

Hanson, J. L., Chung, M. K., Avants, B. B., Shirtcliff, E. A., Gee, J. C., Davidson, R. J., et al. (2010). Early stress is associated with alterations in the orbitofrontal cortex: A tensor-based morphometry investigation of brain structure and behavioral risk. *Journal of Neuroscience, 30,* 7466–7472.

Hardwired to connect. The new scientific case for authoritative communities. (2003). New York: Institute for American Values.

Harpaz-Rotem, I., & Rosenheck, R. A. (2004). Changes in outpatient psychiatric diagnosis in privately insured children and adolescents from 1995 to 2000. *Child Psychiatry and Human Development, 34,* 329–340.

Haskins, R. (1985). Public school aggression among children with varying day-care experience. *Child Development, 56,* 689–703.

Hastings, P., Nuselovici, J., Utendale, W., Coutya, J., McShane, K. E., & Sullivan, C. (2008). Applying the polyvagal theory to children's emotion regulation: Social context, socialization, and adjustment. *Biological Psychology, 79,* 299–306.

Hecht, D. (2010). Depression and the hyperactive right hemisphere. *Neuroscience Research, 68,* 77–87.

Heckman, J. (2008). *Schools, skills, and synapses.* IZA DP No. 3515. Bonn, Germany: Institute for the Study of Labor.

Helmeke, C., Ovtscharoff, W., Poeggel, G., & Braun, K. (2001). Juvenile emotional experience alters synaptic inputs on pyramidal neurons in the anterior cingulate cortex. *Cerebral Cortex, 11,* 717–727.

Helmeke, C., Seidel, K., Poeggel, G., Bredy, T. W., Abraham, A., & Braun, K. (2009). Paternal deprivation during infancy results in dendrite- and time-specific changes of dendritic development and spine formation in the orbitofrontal cortex of the biparental rodent *Octodon degus. Neuroscience, 163,* 790–798.

Hertenstein, M. J. (2002). Touch: Its communicative functions in infancy. *Human Development, 45,* 70–94.

Hertenstein, M. J., & Campos, J. J. (2001). Emotion regulation via maternal touch. *Infancy, 2,* 549–566.

Herzog, J. M. (2001). *Father hunger: Explorations with adults and children.* Hillsdale, NJ: Analytic Press.

Heymann, J., Raub, A., & Earle, A. (2011). Creating and using new data sources to analyze the relationship between social policy and global health: The case of maternal leave. *Public Health Reports, 126,* 127–134.

Hill, J. L., Waldfogel, J., Brooks-Gunn, J., & Han, W. J. (2005). Maternal employment and child development: A fresh look using newer methods. *Developmental Psychology, 41,* 833–850.

Homae, F., Watanabe, H., Nakano, T., Asakawa, K., & Taga, G. (2006). The right hemisphere of sleeping infants perceives sentential prosody. *Neuroscience Research, 54,* 276–280.

Howard, M. F., & Reggia, J. A. (2007). A theory of the visual system biology underlying development of spatial frequency lateralization. *Brain and Cognition, 64,* 111–123.

Hrdy, S. (2009). *Mothers and others: The evolutionary origins of mutual understanding.* Cambridge, MA: Belknap Press.

Huffman, L., Bryan, Y., del Carmen, R., Pedersen, F., Doussard-Roosevelt, J., & Porges, S. (1998). Infant temperament and cardiac vagal tone: Assessments at twelve weeks of age. *Child Development, 69,* 624–635.

Huttenlocher, P. R. (1979). Synaptic density in human frontal cortex—Developmental changes and effects of aging. *Brain Research, 163,* 195–205.

Huttenlocher, P. R. (1990). Morphometric study of human cerebral cortex development. *Neuropsychologia, 28,* 517–527.

Insel, T. R., & Fenton, W. S. (2005). Psychiatric epidemiology. It's not just about counting anymore. *Archives of General Psychiatry, 62,* 590–592.

Jean, A. D. L., Stack, D. M., & Fogel, A. (2009). A longitudinal investigation of maternal touching across the first 6 months of life: Age and context effects. *Infant Behavior and Development, 32,* 344–349.

Kasprian, G., Langs, G., Brugger, P., Bittner, M., Weber, M., Arantes, M., et al. (2011). The prenatal origin of hemispheric asymmetry: An in utero neuroimaging study. *Cerebral Cortex, 21,* 1076–1083.

Katz, M., Liu, C., Schaer, M., Parker, K. J., Ottet, M. C., Epps, A., et al. (2009). Prefrontal plasticity and stress inoculation-induced resilience. *Developmental Neuroscience, 31,* 293–299.

Kessler, R. C., Berglund, P., Demler, O., Jin, R., Merikangas, K. R., & Walters, E. E. (2005). Lifetime prevalence and age-of-onset distributions of DSM-IV disorders in the national comorbidity survey replication. *Archives of General Psychiatry, 62,* 593–602.

Knickmeyer, R. C., Gouttard, S., Kang, C., Evans, D., Wilber, K., Smith, J. K., et al. (2008). A structural MRI study of human brain development from birth to 2 years. *Journal of Neuroscience, 28,* 12176–12182.

Korosi, A., & Baram, T. Z. (2009). The pathways from mother's love to baby's future. *Frontiers of Behavioral Neuroscience, 3,* 1–8.

Kringelbach, M., Lehtonen, A., Squire, S., Harvey, A. G., Craske, M. G., Holliday, I. E., et al. (2008). A specific and rapid neural signature for parental instinct. *PLoS One, 3,* 1–6.

Kumari, V., Bartaki, I., Goswami, S., Flora, S., Das, M., & Taylor, P. (2009). Dysfunctional, but not functional, impulsivity is associated with a history of seriously violent behaviour and reduced orbitofrontal and hippocampal volumes in schizophrenia. *Psychiatry Research: Neuroimaging, 173,* 39–44.

Lagercrantz, H., & Ringstedt, T. (2001). Organization of the neuronal circuits in the central nervous system during development. *Acta Paediatrica, 90,* 707–715.

Lamb, M. E. (2010). *The role of the father in child development.* New York: Wiley.

Lamb, M. E., Sternberg, K. J., & Ketterlinus, R. (1992). Child care in the United States. In M. E. Lamb, K. Sternberg, C. P. Hwang, & A. G. Broberg (Eds.), *Child care in context* (pp. 207–222). Hillsdale, NJ: Erlbaum.

Landrigan, P. J. (2010). What causes autism? Exploring the environmental contribution. *Current Opinion in Pediatrics, 22,* 219–225.

Lanius, R. A., Vermetten, E., & Pain C. (Eds.). (2010). *The impact of early life trauma on health and disease: The hidden epidemic.* Cambridge, UK: Cambridge University Press.

Lauritzen, L., Hansen, H. S., Jorgensen, M. H., & Michaelsen, K. F. (2001). The essentiality of long chain n-3 fatty acids in relation to development and function of the brain and retina. *Progress in Lipid Research, 40,* 1–94.

Lazarev, V. V., Pontes, A., & de Azevedo, L. (2008). EEG photic driving: Right-hemisphere reactivity deficit in childhood autism. A pilot study. *International Journal of Psychophysiology, 71*, 177–183.

Leckman, J. F., & March, J. S. (2011). Editorial: Developmental neuroscience comes of age. *Journal of Child Psychology and Psychiatry, 52*, 333–338.

Legendre, A. (2003). Environmental features influencing toddlers' bioemotional reactions in day care centers. *Environment and Behavior, 35*, 523.

Le Grand, R., Mondloch, C., Maurer, D., & Brent, H. P. (2003). Expert face processing requires visual input to the right hemisphere during infancy. *Nature Neuroscience, 6*, 1108–1112.

Lehtonen, J., Kononen, M., Purhonen, M., Partanen, J., & Saarikoski, S. (2002). The effects of feeding on the electroencephalogram in 3- and 6-month-old infants. *Psychophysiology, 39*, 73–79.

Lemche, E., Giampietro, V. P., Surguladze, S. A., Amaro, E. J., Andrew, C. M., Williams, S. C. R., et al. (2006). Human attachment security is mediated by the amygdala: Evidence from combined fMRI and psychophysiological measures. *Human Brain Mapping, 27*, 623–635.

Lenzi, D., Trentini, C., Pantano, P., Macaluso, E., Iacoboni, M., Lenzi, G. I., et al. (2009). Neural basis of maternal communication and emotional expression processing during infant preverbal stage. *Cerebral Cortex, 19*, 1124–1133.

Lisonbee, J. A., Mize, J., Payne, A. L., & Granger, D. A. (2008). Children's cortisol and the quality of teacher–child relationships in child care. *Child Development, 79*, 1818–1832.

Lyons, D. M., Afarian, H., Schatzberg, A. F., Sawyer-Glover, A., & Moseley, M. E. (2002). Experience-dependent asymmetric variation in primate prefrontal morphology. *Behavioural Brain Research, 136*, 51–59.

MacLean, P. D. (1996). Women: A more balanced brain. *Zygon, 31*, 421–439.

Matsuzawa, J., Matsui, M., Konishi, T., Noguchi, K., Gur, R. C., Bilker, W., et al. (2001). Age-related volumetric changes of brain gray and white matter in healthy infants and children. *Cerebral Cortex, 11*, 335–342.

McGilchrist, I. (2009). *The master and his emissary.* New Haven, CT: Yale University Press.

Meares, R., Schore, A., & Melkonian, D. (2011). Is borderline personality a particular right hemispheric disorder? A study of P3A using single trial analysis. *Australian and New Zealand Journal of Psychiatry, 45*, 131–139.

Mehta, M. A., Golembo, N. I., Nosarti, C., Colvert, E., Mota, A., Williams, S. C. R., et al. (2009). Amygdala, hippocampal and corpus callosum size following severe early institutional deprivation: The English and Romanian adoptees study pilot. *Journal of Child Psychology and Psychiatry, 50*, 943–951.

Mendez, M. F., & Shapira, J. S. (2009). Altered emotional morality in frontotemporal dementia. *Cognitive Neuropsychiatry, 14*, 165–179.

Mento, G., Suppiej, A., Altoe, G., & Bisiacchi, P. S. (2010). Functional hemispheric asymmetries in humans: Electrophysiological evidence from preterm infants. *European Journal of Neuroscience, 31*, 565–574.

Merikangas, K. R., He, J-p, Burstein, M., Swanson, S. A., Avenevoli, S., Cui, L., et al. (2011). Lifetime prevalence of mental disorders in U.S. adolescents: Results from the National Comorbidity Survey replication—adolescent supplement (NCS-A). *Journal of the American Academy of Child and Adolescent Psychiatry, 49*, 980–989.

Milne, L., Greenway, P., Guedeney, A., & Larroque, B. (2009). Long term developmental impact of social withdrawal in infants. *Infant Behavior and Development, 32,* 159–166.

Minagawa-Kawai, Y., Matsuoka, S., Dan, I., Naoi, N., Nakamura, K., & Kojima, S. (2009). Prefrontal activation associated with social attachment: Facial-emotion recognition in mothers and infants. *Cerebral Cortex, 19,* 284–292.

Minagawa-Kawai, Y., van der Lely, H., Ramus, F., Sato, Y., Mazuka, R., & Dupoux, E. (2011). Optical brain imaging reveals general auditory and language-specific processing in early infant development. *Cerebral Cortex, 21,* 254–261.

Montirosso, R., Borgatti, R., & Tronick, E. (2010). Lateral asymmetries in infants' regulatory and communicative gestures. In R. A. Lanius, E. Vermetten, & C. Pain (Eds.), *The impact of early life trauma on health and disease: The hidden epidemic* (pp. 103–111). Cambridge, UK: Cambridge University Press.

Moreno, C., Laje, G., Blanco, C., Jiang, H., Schmidt, A. B., & Olfson, M. (2007). National trends in the outpatient diagnosis and treatment of bipolar disorder in youth. *Archives of General Psychiatry, 64,* 1032–1039.

Myers, D. A., Myers, T. R., Grober, M. S., & Nathanielsz, P. W. (1993). Levels of corticotropin-releasing hormone messenger ribonucleic acid (mRNA) in the hypothalamic paraventricular nucleus and proopiomelanocortin mRNA in the anterior pituitary during late gestation in fetal sheep. *Endocrinology, 132,* 2109–2116.

Nagy, E. (2006). From imitation to conversation: The first dialogues with human neonates. *Infant and Child Development, 15,* 223–232.

Nakamura, M., Nestor, P. G., McCarley, R. W., Levitt, J. L., Hsu, L., Kawashima, T., et al. (2007). Altered orbitofrontal sulcogyral pattern in schizophrenia. *Brain, 130,* 693–707.

Nakato, E., Otsuka, Y., Kanazawa, S., Yamaguchi, M. K., & Kakigi, R. (2011). Distinct differences in the pattern of hemodynamic response to happy and angry facial expressions in infancy—A near-infrared spectroscopic study. *NeuroImage, 54,* 1600–1606.

Nakato, E., Otsuka, Y., Kanazawa, S., Yamaguchi, M. K., Watanabe, S., & Kakigi, R. (2009). When do infants differentiate profile face from frontal face? A near-infrared spectroscopic study. *Human Brain Mapping, 30,* 462–472.

Narvaez, D. (2008). Triune ethics: The neurobiological roots of our multiple moralities. *New Ideas in Psychology, 26,* 95–119.

Narvaez, D., Panksepp, J., Schore, A., & Gleason, T. (in press). The value of the environment of evolutionary adaptedness for gauging children's well-being. In D. Narvaez, J. Panksepp, A. Schore, and T. Gleason (Eds.), *Evolution, early experience and human development: from research to practice and policy.* New York: Oxford University Press.

NICHD Early Child Care Research Network. (2006). Child-care effect sizes for the NICHD Study of Early Child Care and Youth Development. *American Psychologist, 61,* 99–116.

Nitschke, J. B., Nelson, E. E., Rusch, B. D., Fox, A. S., Oakes, T. R., & Davidson, R. J. (2004). Orbitofrontal cortex tracks positive mood in mothers viewing pictures of their newborn infants. *NeuroImage, 21,* 583–592.

Noriuchi, M., Kikuchi, Y., & Senoo, A. (2008). The functional neuroanatomy of maternal love: Mother's response to infant's attachment behaviors. *Biological Psychiatry, 63,* 415–423.

Oddy, W. H., Kendall, G. E., Li, J., Jacoby, P., Robinson, B., de Klerk, N. H., et al. (2010).

The long-term effects of breastfeeding on child and adolescent mental health: A pregnancy cohort study followed for 14 years. *Journal of Pediatrics, 156,* 568–574.

Otsuka, Y., Nakato, E., Kanazawa, S., Yamaguchi, M. K., Watanabe, S., & Kakigi, R. (2007). Neural activation to upright and inverted faces in infants measured by near infrared spectroscopy. *NeuroImage, 34,* 399–406.

Overturf Johnson, J. (2005, October). *Who's minding the kids? Child care arrangements: Winter 2002* (Current Population Reports No. P70-101). Washington, DC: U.S. Census Bureau.

Ovtscharoff, W., & Braun, K. (2001). Maternal separation and social isolation modulate the postnatal development of synaptic composition in the infralimbic cortex of *Octodon degus. Neuroscience, 104,* 33–40.

Ovtscharoff, W., Helmeke, C., & Braun, K. (2006). Lack of paternal care affects synaptic development in the anterior cingulate cortex. *Brain Research, 1116,* 58–63.

Panksepp, J. (1998). *Affective neuroscience: The foundations of human and animal emotions.* Oxford, UK: Oxford University Press.

Panksepp, J. (2008). The power of the word may reside in the power of affect. *Integrative Psychological and Behavioral Science, 42,* 47–55.

Papousek, H., & Papousek, M. (1997). Fragile aspects of early social integration. In L. Murray & P. J. Cooper (Eds.), *Postpartum depression and child development* (pp. 35–53). New York: Guilford Press.

Parker, S. W., & Nelson, C. A. (2005). The impact of early institutional rearing on the ability to discriminate facial expressions of emotion: An event-related potential study. *Child Development, 76,* 54–72.

Pellis, S. M., & Pellis, V. C. (2007). Rough-and-tumble play and the development of the social brain. *Current Directions in Psychological Science, 16,* 95–98.

Perani, D., Saccuman, M. C., Scifo, P., Spada, D., Andreolli, G., Rovelli, R., et al. (2010). Functional specializations for music processing in the human newborn brain. *Proceedings of the National Academy of Sciences of the United States of America, 107,* 4758–4763.

Perry, B. D., Pollard, R., Blakely, T., Baker, W., & Vigilante, D. (1995). Childhood trauma, the neurobiology of adaptation and "use-dependent" development of the brain: How states become traits. *Infant Mental Health Journal, 16,* 271–291.

Picardi, A., Batttisti, F., Taritani, L., Baldassari, M., Copertaro, A., Mocchegiani, E., et al. (2007). Attachment security and immunity in healthy women. *Psychosomatic Medicine, 69,* 40–46.

Pinkernelle, J., Abraham, A., Seidel, K., & Braun, K. (2009). Paternal deprivation induces dendritic and synaptic changes and hemispheric asymmetry of pyramidal neurons in somatosensory cortex. *Developmental Neurobiology, 69,* 663–673.

Pipp, S., & Harmon, R. J. (1987). Attachment as regulation: A commentary. *Child Development, 58,* 648–652.

Porche, M. V., Fortuna, L. R., Lin, J., & Alegria, M. (2011). Childhood trauma and psychiatric disorders as correlates of social dropout in a national sample of young adults. *Child Development, 82,* 982–998.

Porges, S. W. (2007). The polyvagal perspective. *Biological Psychology, 74,* 116–143.

Powell, D., Fixen, D., & Dunlop, G. (2003). *Pathways to service utilization: A synthesis of evidence relevant to young children with challenging behavior.* University of South Florida: Center for Evidence-based Practice: Young Children with Challenging Behavior.

Previc, F. H. (1991). A general theory concerning the prenatal origins of cerebral lateralization in humans. *Psychological Review, 98*, 299–334.

Price, J. L., Carmichael, S. T., & Drevets, W. C. (1996). Networks related to the orbital and medial prefrontal cortex; a substrate for emotional behavior? *Progress in Brain Research, 107*, 523–536.

Raver, C. C., & Knitze, J. (2002). *Ready to enter: What research tells policymakers about strategies to promote social and emotional school readiness among three- and four-year-old children.* New York: National Center for Children in Poverty.

Rinaman, L., Levitt, P., & Card, J. P. (2000). Progressive postnatal assembly of limbic-autonomic circuits revealed by central transneuronal transport of pseudorabies virus. *Journal of Neuroscience, 20*, 2731–2741.

Roberts, N. A., Beer, J. S., Werner, K. H., Scabini, D., Levens, S. M., Knight, R. T., et al. (2004). The impact of orbital prefrontal cortex damage on emotional activation to unanticipated and anticipated acoustic startle stimuli. *Cognitive, Affective, and Behavioral Neuroscience, 4*, 307–316.

Roppongi, T., Nakamura, M., Asami, T., Hayano, F., Otsuka, T., Uehara, K., et al. (2010). Posterior orbitofrontal sulcogyral pattern associated with orbitofrontal cortex volume reduction and anxiety trait in panic disorder. *Psychiatry and Clinical Neuroscience, 64*, 318–326.

Rotenberg, V. S. (2004). The ontogeny and asymmetry of the highest brain skills and the pathogenesis of schizophrenia. *Behavioral and Brain Sciences, 27*, 864–865.

Roth, T. L., & Sweatt, J. D. (2011). Annual research review: Epigenetic mechanism and environmental shaping of the brain during sensitive periods of development. *Journal of Child Psychology and Psychiatry, 52*, 398–408.

Sajaniemi, N., Suhonen, E., Kontu, E., Rantanen, P., Lindholm, H., Hyttinen, S., et al. (2011). Children's cortisol patterns and the quality of the early learning environment. *European Early Childhood Education Research Journal, 19*, 45–62.

Salmaso, N., Quinlan, M. G., Brake, W. G., & Woodside, B. (2011). Changes in dendritic spine density on layer 2/3 pyramidal cells within the cingulate cortex of late pregnant and postpartum rats. *Hormones and Behavior, 60*, 65–71.

Sar, V., Ünal, S. N., & Oztürk, E. (2007). Frontal and occipital perfusion changes in dissociative identity disorder. *Psychiatry Research: Neuroimaging, 156*, 217–223.

Saugstad, L. F. (1998). Cerebral lateralization and rate of maturation. *International Journal of Psychophysiology, 28*, 37–62.

Schleussner, E., Schneider, U., Arnscheidt, C., Kahler, C., Haueisen, J., & Seewald, H-J. (2004). Prenatal evidence of left–right asymmetries in auditory evoked responses using fetal magnetoencephalography. *Early Human Development, 78*, 133–136.

Schoenbaum, G., & Shaham, Y. (2008). The role of orbitofrontal cortex in drug addiction: A review of preclinical studies. *Biological Psychiatry, 63*, 256–262.

Schore, A. N. (1994). *Affect regulation and the origin of the self.* Mahwah, NJ: Erlbaum.

Schore, A. N. (1996). The experience-dependent maturation of a regulatory system in the orbital prefrontal cortex and the origin of developmental psychopathology. *Development and Psychopathology, 8*, 59–87.

Schore, A. N. (1997). Early organization of the nonlinear right brain and development of a predisposition to psychiatric disorders. *Development and Psychopathology, 9*, 595–631.

Schore, A. N. (2000a). Foreword. In John Bowlby, *Attachment and loss: Vol. 1.* New York: Basic Books. (2nd ed.).

Schore, A. N. (2000b). Attachment and the regulation of the right brain. *Attachment and Human Development, 2,* 23–47.

Schore, A. N. (2001a). The effects of a secure attachment relationship on right brain development, affect regulation, and infant mental health. *Infant Mental Health Journal, 22,* 7–66.

Schore, A. N. (2001b). Contributions from the decade of the brain to infant mental health: An overview. *Infant Mental Health Journal, 22,* 1–6.

Schore, A. N. (2001c). The effects of relational trauma on right brain development, affect regulation, and infant mental health. *Infant Mental Health Journal, 22,* 201–269.

Schore, A. N. (2002). Dysregulation of the right brain: A fundamental mechanism of traumatic attachment and the psychopathogenesis of posttraumatic stress disorder. *Australian and New Zealand Journal of Psychiatry, 36,* 9–30.

Schore, A. N. (2003a). *Affect dysregulation and disorders of the self.* New York: Norton.

Schore, A. N. (2003b). *Affect regulation and the repair of the self.* New York: Norton.

Schore, A. N. (2005). Attachment, affect regulation, and the developing right brain: Linking developmental neuroscience to pediatrics. *Pediatrics in Review, 26,* 204–211.

Schore, A. N. (2009). Attachment trauma and the developing right brain: Origins of pathological dissociation. In P. F. Dell, & J. A. O'Neil (Eds.), *Dissociation and the dissociative disorders: DSM-V and beyond* (pp. 107–141). New York: Routledge.

Schore, A. N. (2010a). Synopsis. In R. A. Lanius, E. Vermetten, & C. Pain (Eds.), *The impact of early life trauma on health and disease: The hidden epidemic* (pp. 1142–1147). Cambridge, UK: Cambridge University Press.

Schore, A. N. (2010b). Relational trauma and the developing right brain. The neurobiology of broken attachment bonds. In T. Baradon (Ed.), *Relational trauma in infancy* (pp. 19–47). London: Routledge.

Schore, A. N. (2010c). A neurobiological perspective of the work of Berry Brazelton. In B. M. Lester & J. D. Sparrow (Eds.), *Nurturing children and families: Building on the legacy of T. Berry Brazelton* (pp. 141–153). New York: Wiley Blackwell.

Schore, A. N. (in press). Bowlby's environment of evolutionary adaptedness: recent studies on the interpersonal neurobiology of attachment and emotional development. In D. Narvaez, J. Panksepp, A. Schore, & T. Gleason (Eds.), *Evolution, early experience and human development: from research to practice and policy.* New York: Oxford University Press.

Schore, A. N., & Newton, R. (in press). Using modern attachment theory to guide assessments of early attachment relationships. In J. B. Schaefer & D. D. Friedman (Eds), *Attachment-based clinical social work with children and adolescents.* New York: Springer.

Schore, J. R., & Schore, A. N. (2008). Modern attachment theory: The central role of affect regulation in development and treatment. *Clinical Social Work Journal, 36,* 9–20.

Schuetze, P., & Reid, H. M. (2005). Emotional lateralization in the second year of life: Evidence from oral asymmetries. *Laterality, 10,* 207–217.

Schutz, L. E. (2005). Broad-perspective perceptual disorder of the right hemisphere. *Neuropsychology Review, 15,* 11–27.

Semrud-Clikeman, M., & Hynd, G. W. (1990). Right hemisphere dysfunction in nonverbal learning disabilities: Social, academic, and adaptive functioning in adults and children. *Psychological Bulletin, 107,* 196–209.

Shirtcliff, E. A., Coe, C. L., & Pollak, S. D. (2009). Early childhood stress is associated with elevated antibody levels to herpes simplex virus type 1. *Proceedings of the National Academy of Sciences of the United States of America, 106,* 2963–2967.

Shonkoff, J. P., Boyce, W. T., & McEwen, B. S. (2009). Neuroscience, molecular biology, and the childhood roots of health disparities building a new framework for health promotion and disease prevention. *The Journal of the American Medical Association, 301,* 2252–2259.

Siegel, D. J. (1999). *The developing mind: toward a neurobiology of interpersonal experience.* New York: Guilford.

Sieratzki, J. S., & Woll, B. (1996). Why do mothers cradle babies on the left? *The Lancet, 347,* 1746–1748.

Silverman, M. E., Loudon, H., Safier, M., Protopopescu, X., Leiter, G., Liu, X., et al. (2007). Neural dysfunction in postpartum depression: an FMRI pilot study. *CNS Spectrums, 12,* 853–862.

Simian-Tov, T., Papo, D., Gadoth, N., Schonberg, T., Mendelsohn, A., Perry, D., et al. (2008). Mind your left: Spatial bias in subcortical fear processing. *Journal of Cognitive Neuroscience, 21,* 1782–1789.

Sims, M., Guilfoyle, A., & Parry, T. S. (2006). Children's cortisol levels and quality of child care provision. *Child: Care, Health, and Development, 32,* 453–466.

Smith, K., Downs, B., & O'Connell, M. (2001, November). *Maternity leave and employment patterns: 1961–1995* (Current Population Reports No. P70-79). Washington, DC: U.S. Census Bureau.

Stevenson, C. W., Halliday, D. M., Marsden, C. A., & Mason, R. (2008). Early life programming of hemispheric lateralization and synchronization in the adult medial prefrontal cortex. *Neuroscience, 155,* 852–863.

Storey, A. E., Walsh, C. J., Quinton, R. L., & Wynne-Edwards, K. E. (2000). Hormonal correlates of paternal responsiveness in new and expectant fathers. *Evolution and Human Behavior, 21,* 79–95.

Sullivan, R. M., & Dufresne, M. M. (2006). Mesocortical dopamine and HPA axis regulation: Role of laterality and early environment. *Brain Research, 1076,* 49–59.

Sullivan, R. M., & Gratton, A. (2002). Prefrontal cortical regulation of hypothalamic-pituitary-adrenal function in the rat and implications for psychopathology: Side matters. *Psychoneuroendocrinology, 27,* 99–114.

Sun, T., Patoine, C., Abu-Khalil, A., Visvader, J., Sum, E., Cherry, T. J., et al. (2005). Early asymmetry of gene transcription in embryonic human left and right cerebral cortex. *Science, 308,* 1794–1798.

Szajnberg, N., Goldenberg, A., & Harai, U. (2010). Early trauma, later outcome: results from longitudinal studies and clinical observations. In R. A. Lanius, E. Vermetten, & C. Pain (Eds.), *The impact of early life trauma on health and disease: The hidden epidemic* (pp. 33–42). Cambridge, UK: Cambridge University Press.

Tamis-LeMonda, C. S., & Cabrera, N. (2002). *Handbook of father involvement: Multidisciplinary perspectives.* Mahwah, NJ: Erlbaum.

Telkemeyer, S., Rossi, S., Koch, S. P., Nierhaus, T., Steinbrink, J., Poeppel, D., et al. (2009). Sensitivity of newborn auditory cortex to the temporal structure of sounds. *Journal of Neuroscience, 29,* 14726–14733.

Thatcher, R. W. (1994). Cyclical cortical reorganization: Origins of human cognitive development. In G. Dawson & K. W. Fischer (Eds.), *Human behavior and the developing brain* (pp. 232–266). New York: Guilford Press.

Thatcher, R. W., Walker, R. A., & Giudice, S. (1987). Human cerebral hemispheres develop at different rates and ages. *Science, 236,* 1110–1113.

Thierry, G., Vihman, M., & Roberts, M. (2003). Familiar words capture the attention of 11-month-olds in less than 250 ms. *NeuroReport, 14,* 2307–2310.

Trevarthen, C. (1996). Lateral asymmetries in infancy: Implications for the development of the hemispheres. *Neuroscience and Biobehavioral Reviews, 20,* 571–586.

Trevarthen, C. (2001). The neurobiology of early communication: Intersubjective regulations in human brain development. In A. F. Kalverboer, & A. Gramsbergen (Eds.), *Handbook on brain and behavior in human development* (pp. 841–882). Dordrecht: Kluwer.

Trevarthen, C., & Aitken, K. J. (2001). Infant intersubjectivity: Research, theory, and clinical application. *Journal of Child Psychology and Psychiatry, 42,* 3–48.

Tucker, D. M. (1992). Developing emotions and cortical networks. In M. R. Gunnar & C. A. Nelson (Eds.), *Minnesota symposium on child psychology: Vol. 24. Developmental behavioral neuroscience* (pp. 75–128). Mahwah, NJ: Erlbaum.

Tzourio-Mazoyer, N., De Schonen, S., Crivello, F., Reutter, B., Aujard, Y., & Mazoyer, B. (2002). Neural correlates of woman face processing by 2-month-old infants. *NeuroImage, 15,* 454–461.

Uddin, L. Q., Molnar-Szakacs, I., Zaidel, E., & Iacoboni, M. (2006). rTMS to the right inferior parietal lobule disrupts self–other discrimination. *Social Cognition and Affective Neuroscience, 1,* 65–71.

Ulfig, N., Setzer, M., & Bohl, J. (2003). Ontogeny of the human amygdala. *Annals of the New York Academy of Sciences of the United States of America, 985,* 22–33.

UNICEF. (2007). *Child poverty in perspective: An overview of child well-being in rich countries, a comprehensive assessment of the lives and well-being of children and adolescents in the economically advanced nations,* Report Card 7. Florence, Italy: United Nations Children's Fund Innocenti Research Centre.

Vancassel, S., Aid, S., Pifferi, F., Morice, E., Nosten-Bertrand, M., Chalon, S., et al. (2005). Cerebral asymmetry and behavioral lateralization in rats chronically lacking n-3 polyunsaturated fatty acids. *Biological Psychiatry, 58,* 805–811.

Versace, A., Almeida, J. R. C., Hassel, S., Walsh, N. D., Novelli, M., Klein, C. R., et al. (2008). Elevated left and reduced right orbitomedial prefrontal fractional anisotropy in adults with bipolar disorder revealed by tract-based spatial statistics. *Archives of General Psychiatry, 65,* 1041–1052.

Vesga-Lopez, O., Blanco, C., Keyes, K., Olfson, M., Grant, B. F., & Hasin, D. S. (2008). Psychiatric disorders in pregnant and postpartum women in the United States. *Archives of General Psychiatry, 65,* 805–815.

Volkow, N. D., Wang, G.-J., Telang, F., Fowler, J. S., Logan, J., Jayne, M., et al. (2007). Profound decreases in dopamine release in striatum in detoxified alcoholics: Possible orbitofrontal involvement. *Journal of Neuroscience, 27,* 12700–12706.

Volkow, N. D., Tomasi, D., Wang, G-J., Fowler, J. S., Telang, F., Goldstein, F., et al. (2011). Positive emotionality is associated with baseline metabolism in orbitofrontal cortex and in regions of the default network. *Molecular Psychiatry,* doi:10.1038/mp.2011, 30

Walker-Andrews, A. S., & Bahrick, L. E. (2001). Perceiving the real world: Infants' detection of and memory for social information. *Infancy, 2,* 469–481.

Wang, J., Rao, H., Wetmore, G. S., Furlan, P. M., Korczykowski, M., Dinges, D. F., & Detre, J. A. (2005). Perfusion functional MRI reveals cerebral blood flow pattern under psychological stress. *Proceedings of the National Academy of Sciences of the United States of America, 102,* 17804–17809.

Watamura, S., Donzella, B., Alwin, J., & Gunnar, M. (2003). Morning-to-afternoon increases in cortisol concentrations of infants and toddlers at child care: Age differences and behavioral correlates. *Child Development, 74,* 1006–1020.

Weaver, I. C. G., Cervoni, N., Champagne, F. A., D'Alessio, A. C., Sharma, S., Seckl, J. R., et al. (2004). Epigenetic programming by maternal behavior. *Nature Neuroscience, 7,* 847–854.

Wei, L., David, A., Duman, R. S., Anisman, H., & Kaffman, A. (2010). Early life stress increases anxiety-like behavior in Balbc mice despite a compensatory increase in levels of postnatal care. *Hormones and Behavior, 57,* 396–404.

Whitaker, R. C. (2011). The childhood obesity epidemic. *Archives of Pediatric and Adolescent Medicine, 165,* 973–975.

Winnicott, D. W. (1986). *Home is where we start from.* New York: Norton.

Wittling, W. (1997). The right hemisphere and the human stress response. *Acta Physiologica Scandinavica, Supplement, 640,* 55–59.

Yamada, H., Sadato, N., Konishi, Y., Muramoto, S., Kimura, K., Tanaka, M., et al. (2000). A milestone for normal development of the infantile brain detected by functional MRI. *Neurology, 55,* 218–223.

Yehuda, S., Rabinovitz, S., & Mostofsky, D. I. (1999). Essential fatty acids are mediators of brain biochemistry and cognitive functions. *Journal of Neuroscience Research, 56,* 565–570.

Zhou, J., Olsen, S., Moldovan, J., Fu, X., Sarkar, F. H., Moudgil, V. K., et al. (1997). Glucocorticoid regulation of natural cytotoxicity: Effects of cortisol on the phenotype and function of a cloned human natural killer cell line. *Cellular Immunology, 178,* 108–116.

CHAPTER 11

Using Regulation Theory to Guide Clinical Assessments of Mother–Infant Attachment Relationships

With Ruth Newton

In an editorial of a recent issue of the *Journal of Child Psychology and Psychiatry* entitled "Developmental Neuroscience Comes of Age," Leckman and March (2011) describe "the phenomenal progress of the past three decades in the developmental neurosciences" (p. 333). Summarizing the critical meaning of this rapidly expanding body of research for a deeper understanding of human development, they assert,

> Over the past decade it has also become abundantly clear that . . . the in utero and immediate postnatal environments and the dyadic relations between child and caregivers within the first years of life can have direct and enduring effects on the child's brain development and behavior. . . . Indeed, *the enduring impact of early maternal care and the role of epigenetic modifications of the genome during critical periods in early brain development in health and disease is likely to be one of the most important discoveries in all of science that have major implications for our field.* (p. 334, my italics)

Leckman and March conclude that "A scientific consensus is emerging that the origins of adult disease are often found among developmental and biological disruptions occurring during the early years of life" (p. 333).

Similarly, in the psychiatric literature Insel and Fenton (2005) are asserting, "Most mental illnesses . . . begin far earlier in life than was previously believed"

(p. 590). At this very point in time this developmental psychopathological principle has great meaning, since a child psychiatric epidemiological study of 10,000 adolescents now documents a "high prevalence" of mental disorder in youth:

> Approximately one in every four to five youths in the U.S. meets the criteria for a mental disorder with severe impairment across their lifetime. The likelihood that common mental disorders in adults first emerge in childhood and adolescence highlights the need for a transition from the common focus on treatment of U.S. youth to that of prevention and early intervention. (Merikangas et al., 2010, p. 980)

In fact, recent approaches integrating neuroscience and pediatrics are focusing on reducing significant stress and adversity during the early periods of childhood (Shonkoff, Boyce, & McEwen, 2009). Attempting to forge tighter links between advances in developmental theory and research with innovative clinical applications, Shonkoff (2011) is now calling for "early childhood policy and practice" to have a better understanding "of the extent to which early experiences are incorporated into the developing brain, for better or for worse" (p. 982). He suggests that "interventions that enhance the mental health, executive function skills, and self-regulation capacities of vulnerable mothers, beginning as early as pregnancy, suggest promising strategies to protect the developing brains of their children" (p. 983). Congruent with this proposal, researchers studying the developmental neurobiological basis of human attachment are asserting, "Understanding the motivational basis of healthy and at-risk parenting may open new theoretical vistas and clinical opportunities and may lead to the construction of more specific interventions that can target disruptions to maternal–infant bonding at an earlier stage and in a more accurate manner" (Atzil, Hendler, & Feldman, 2011, p. 11).

This potential dramatic step forward in creating more efficient programs of early intervention and prevention requires that clinicians working with children under age 5 incorporate recent data from neuroscience on brain development into their clinical assessments of a particular primary attachment relationship. Because development in infancy is occurring within the relational context of nonverbal, implicit nonconscious infant–caregiver attachment dynamics, clinicians assessing these early relationships must also be able to integrate recent advances in developmental psychoanalysis and neuropsychoanalysis on the early relational development of the unconscious mind into their early interventions. In line with current relational psychoanalytic approaches, clinicians must do more than objectively observe a particular maternal–infant relationship. Rather, they need to act as "participant-observers" who intersubjectively join, feel, attune to, and resonate with the nonverbal, implicit world of affective communications that lie at the core of the mutually constructed attachment system.

Daniel Stern (2005) states, "Without the nonverbal it would be hard to achieve the empathic, participatory, and resonating aspects of intersubjectivity. One would only be left with a kind of pared down, neutral 'understanding' of the other's subjective experience" (p. 80). This dictum applies directly to clinical mother–infant attachment assessments. Alluding to the limitations of relying too heavily on adult verbal mechanisms in understanding infancy, he beautifully describes the impact of learning verbal language on the nonverbal child "whose comfortable, rich, implicit, pre-verbal world is fractured into unrecognizable pieces by attaching language to his implicit experiences. . . . The loss is of wholeness, felt truth, richness and honesty" (Stern, 2004, p. 144). It is this implicit world, prior to language, that a clinician is trying to assess, especially in cases in which a preverbal infant does not have a "comfortable" relationship with his or her primary attachment caregiver.

Modern attachment theory (Schore & Schore, 2008) advances Bowlby's (1969) basic tenet that attachment is biological in nature and in the service of infant protection to the primacy of the attachment relationship in emotional regulation, the structural connectivity of the right hemisphere, and the development of the implicit self. This expansion of Bowlby's seminal ideas allows for "new understandings in clinical assessments, shaping therapeutic interventions from relevant theory, and providing a unique awareness of the adaptive nonconscious functions of the implicit self" (Schore & Schore, 2008, p. 17). As opposed to classical attachment theory, which focuses on behavioral and cognitive development (mentalization) in infancy, modern attachment theory describes the earliest stages of social and emotional development, emphasizing the central roles of affect communication and affect regulation (Schore & Schore, 2008). Thus, in this chapter we equate the term *regulation theory* with the term *modern attachment theory*.

In contrast to cognitive developmental psychological theories, regulation theory integrates developmental affective psychology and affective neuroscience in order to generate more complex psychobiological models of not only the infant's developing mind but also his or her brain–mind–body. In this interpersonal neurobiological perspective, the nonconscious interactive regulation of not behavior but affective arousal, especially states of autonomic arousal, lies at the core of the bodily based attachment dynamic. We suggest that the significant advances in developmental neuroscience can directly inform and even significantly alter our assessments and therapeutic interventions with high-risk infants and their primary caregivers. Thus, therapists treating young children and their families can now use clinical models grounded in robust scientific evidence showing the inseparable nature of brain development and lived experience within the primary attachment relationship (Schore, 1994, 2001a, 2001b, in press).

Modern attachment theory posits that the hard wiring of the infant's developing right brain, which is dominant for the emotional sense of self, is influenced by implicit, intersubjective affective transactions embedded in the attachment relationship with the mother (Schore, 1994, 2005). Developmental intersubjective studies conclude that implicit, nonconscious processing of nonverbal affective cues in infancy "is repetitive, automatic, provides quick categorization and decision-making, and operates *outside the realm of focal attention and verbalized experience"*(Lyons-Ruth, 1999, p. 576, my italics). Neuroscience now reveals that the medial orbitofrontal cortex of adults rapidly and thereby implicitly responds to the image of an infant's face in 130 milliseconds, beneath levels of conscious awareness (Kringelbach et al., 2008). These authors conclude that the orbito-frontal cortex expresses a specific and rapid signature for "parental instinct." We suggest that, in order to assess any infant–mother system of attachment commu-nications, the clinician must be able to not only be aware of but also enter into this rapid-acting nonverbal realm of implicit relational knowledge. The clini-cian's own right brain instinctive psychobiological attunement to the moment-to-moment implicit bodily based affective communication of both mother and infant is thus essential in the evaluation of the development of a young child under age 5.

Returning to Bowlby's original formulation, regulation theory also reintegrates updated developmental psychoanalytic data into attachment models and there-by focuses on the development of not only the mind but also the unconscious mind. Over the course of his writings (1991–2011), Schore continues to offer clinical data and experimental research documenting that the experience-dependent maturation of the right brain equates with the early development of the biological substrate of the human unconscious. This developmental neu-ropsychoanalytic conception is echoed in recent neuroscientific writings by Tucker and Moller (2007): "The right hemisphere's specialization for emotional communication through nonverbal channels seems to suggest a domain of the mind that is close to the motivationally charged psychoanalytic unconscious" (p. 91). The psychoanalytic perspective of modern attachment theory thus dictates that the early structural and functional development of the human unconscious occurs in a critical period of infancy, and that this emerging mind–body system is impacted, for better or worse, by its emotional interactions embedded in the attachment relationship with the mother's unconscious mind–body system.

Schore (1994, 2003a, 2011, in press) also cites ongoing interdisciplinary data indicating that nonverbal right brain functions underlie what psychoanalysis has long described as primary process operations. Indeed, Schore and Schore (2008, p. 14) have proposed that "during heightened affective moments . . . right brain dialogues between the relational unconscious of both the patient and therapist *(like the attachment communications of the infant and mother)* are examples of "primary process communication." According to Dorpat,

> The primary process system analyzes, regulates, and communicates an individual's relations with the environment. . . . [A]ffective and object-relational information is transmitted predominantly by primary process communication. Nonverbal com-munication includes body movements (kinesics), posture, gesture, facial expres-sion, voice inflection, and the sequence, rhythm, and pitch of the spoken words. (2001, p. 451)

Note that these same communications are transacted in the attachment relation-ship the clinician is attempting to assess. This clearly means that in an assessment of an attachment dyad, the clinician is attending not to the mother's left brain secondary process expressions, but to her and her infant's right brain primary process expressions.

A major goal of this chapter is to offer the reader recent knowledge about the structural development and unique functional activities of the early developing right brain (Schore, 1994, 2001a, 2001b). The now well-established principle that the right hemisphere is in a critical growth period from the last trimester of pregnancy to 2.5 to 3.0 years of age (Chiron et al., 1997; Mento, Suppiej, Altoe, & Bisiacchi, 2010) suggests that the experience-dependent maturation of the right hemisphere is the primary developmental task of the first 3 years of life (Newton, 2008a). The dynamic forces of brain development, the unfolding of critical periods, the impacting of attachment by epigenetics and lived experience are occurring within this foundational socioemotional developmental period. The attachment relationship occurs in the nonverbal *bodyworld* between the infant and the primary caregiver, usually the mother. According to Bowlby (1969), attachment is an evolutionary driven biological system designed to protect the infant from predation, and therefore it represents the primary force for development. Infants without attachments fail to thrive and often die (Robertson, 1952; Spitz, 1947). The rhythmic developmental movement between survival-security and exploration of both the physical and social worlds etches a template in the brain for the rest of the life span. The quality of maternal response thus directly impacts her child's future self-development and the ability to intersubjectively be with another.

Both experimental research and clinical data now emphasize the critical importance of the "good-enough" (Winnicott, 1965) psychobiologically attuned caregiver who can sensitively respond to her infant's needs; that is, receive and meaningfully process her infant's affective attachment communications and regulate them. Our interpersonal neurobiological perspective describes how the mother's ability to down-regulate stressful high-arousal states through soothing and up-regulate stressful low-arousal states in play states acts as an epigenetic mechanism by which the connectivity between the central nervous (CNS) and autonomic nervous system (ANS) in the infant's developing emotional right brain is enhanced. The higher regulatory systems of the right hemisphere form extensive reciprocal connections with the limbic and autonomic nervous systems (see Schore, 1994, 2003a). Both the ANS and the CNS continue to develop postnatally, and the assembly of these limbic-autonomic circuits (Rinaman, Levitt, & Card, 2000) in the right hemisphere, which is dominant for the human stress response (Wittling, 1997), is directly influenced by the attachment relationship. In this manner, maternal care regulates the development of the infant's stress coping responses.

Thus, optimal interactive regulation of stressful arousal allows for more complex right brain functions, expressed in more efficient strategies of affect regulation, attachment security, and a burgeoning positive sense of self. This security in turn allows the child to explore by playfully looking, listening, feeling, smelling, studying, reaching, holding, transferring objects from hand to hand, and experiencing what can be created from objects in the physical and social environment. When caregivers scaffold age-appropriate levels of exploration, the typical and rhythmic developmental movement of moving outward for exploration and returning inward for safety is found in children and is the hallmark of emotional security. When this natural life rhythm is supported by caregivers and thereby synchronous, the brain–mind–body of the securely attached child passes through the ensuing developmental stages toward more complex human growth and development.

But as clinicians know well, attachment histories can be regulated or dysregulated, secure or insecure (see Table 11.1 for schematics of regulated and dysregulated right brain attachment communications). Current research supports what clinicians have long known—that "all mothers are not created equal" (Barrett & Fleming, 2011, p. 368).

> The interaction between a mother and her infant can be like a dance. There are routines, standards and missteps, there is give and take, there is unparalleled intimacy, there are often vast differences in skill level and motivation, there is learning. . . . This dance can be beautiful, it can be tender, it can be awkward, it can be difficult. And sometimes it just does not occur. (Barrett & Fleming, 2011, p. 368)

Frequently these latter contexts present themselves as high-risk dyads that require clinical assessments. Regulation theory can assist therapists in intervening in a misattuned infant–caregiver relationship by observing, experiencing, and evaluating the communication of affects and the regulation of affective arousal between the mother's and infant's right brains. Through the therapist's own right brain connection to the infant's and the mother's right brains, he or she can assess the following: (1) the dyadic strength and attunement of caregiver–infant nonverbal communications of eyes, facial expressions, voice prosody, gesture, and touch; (2) the caregiver's ability to regulate infant hypo- and hyperarousal; (3) the caregiver's support of exploration; (4) the impressions of the attachment relationship based upon both caregiver and infant behavior; (5) the knowledge of developmental stages as they relate to brain development, and (6) a clinical strategy of therapeutic intervention. A fundamental tenet of modern attachment theory dictates that the early developing right brain, which is involved in survival functions, is shaped by attachment dynamics. Thus, the evolutionary mechanism of attachment is critical to more than just the development of overt behaviors and cognitive mental functions but also to organismic psychobiological capacities that are essential for adaptive organismic functioning (Schore, 1994, 2001b, 2003a).

With this introduction in mind, in this chapter we will offer a review of recent research on mother–infant right brain–to–right brain visual, auditory, and tactile attachment communications, and on the interpersonal neurobiological mechanisms that facilitate (or inhibit) experience-dependent maturation of the infant's developing right brain. We then utilize regulation theory to model the brain–

TABLE 11.1 Schore's Model of Affect Regulation and Right Brain Development

	Infant Context	Mother Context	Interactive Context Right Brain to Right Brain
RIGHT BRAIN COMMUNICATION PROCESSES			
Visual/Facial			
Regulated response	• Orients, explores, gazes at face of mother and others, seeks eye contact. • Displays bright, wide-eyed facial expressions. • Uses a wide range of affective expressions. • Resting quiet-alert state of pleasant facial expressions.	• Responds (attunes) to infant's cues with variety of affectively expressive facial expressions (eye contact, smiling, pleasant facial expressions).	• Dyadic visual-affective arousal regulation. • Each member of dyad focuses gaze upon the other, engaging in mutual eye contact, smiling, bright facial expressions. • Interpersonal resonance amplifies positive states in both.
Stress response	• During relational stress, transiently avoids orienting, exploring, or gazing at mother's face or engaging in eye contact.	• Flat, absent, fear-inducing, or incongruent facial expressions (laughing when infant is distressed).	• One breaks off mutual gaze and/or eye contact. • Dyad transiently out of sync (misattuned); acute dyadic stress. • *Absence or avoidance of eye contact by either mother or infant may be a significant indicator requiring further investigation.*

(continued)

TABLE 11.1 Continued

	Infant Context	Mother Context	Interactive Context Right Brain to Right Brain
Vocal Tone and Rhythm			
Regulated response	• Turns toward mother's voice. • Uses inviting/playful tone in response (cooing, babbling).	• Vocalizes soothing responses with varied tones and rhythms. • Modulates tones and rhythms of voice to infant's psychobiological state.	• Dyadic auditory-affective arousal regulation. • Matches or imitates each other's vocal tones and rhythms.
Stress response	• During relational stress, transiently turns away from mother's voice. • Uses distressed tone (crying) in response or is nonresponsive.	• Uses discordant, harsh, loud, our unmodulated tone and rhythm of voice or does not use vocalizations in response to infant's emotional communication. • Does not vocalize or mirror (match) infant's vocalizations.	• One uses discordant tone while the other is silent or both are using distressed or discordant tones. • *Nonresponsivity or turning away from mother's voice may be a significant indicator requiring further investigation.*
Gestural/Postural			
Regulated response	• Moves limbs and body evenly and fluidly, relaxed posture, reaches and turns toward other or novel social stimulus.	• Approaches to soothe, manipulate, or maneuver infant gently and cautiously. • Responds to and interprets social bodily based gestures.	• In intimate physical context, dyad's rhythmic matching allows bodies to cradle/mold into other. • In social referencing late in first year, gestures become purposeful and synchronized, promoting intersubjective engagement.

	Infant	Mother	Dyad
Stress response	• In socially stressed contexts, moves limbs unevenly and/or frantically. • Fails to reach out, averts head, turns body away, stiffens or arches body to mother's touch.	• Approaches infant too quickly or responds to infant in threatening or fearful manner. • Handles awkwardly or roughly. • Misinterprets infant's gestures or does not attempt to soothe, respond, or interpret gestures and body movements.	• Infant continues or increases distressed gestures and postures and is unresponsive to mother's efforts. • Mother increases rough/awkward gestures/postures. • Mother continues to misinterpret infant's gestures/body movements. • Dyad becomes frustrated or ceases/fails to attempt to soothe and comfort interactively.

RIGHT BRAIN AFFECT PROCESSING

Positive Affect Processing

	Infant	Mother	Dyad
Regulated response	• High, positive arousal. • Enjoyment-joy, interest-excitement. • Vitality expressed freely.	• Happy demeanor; responsive to, supportive of, and matching of infant's affect and positive arousal.	• Mutual delight. • Mother or infant leads affective interaction while other follows. • Non-overwhelming and turn-taking behaviors. • Dyadic amplification or positive arousal in relational play.
Stress response	• Hyperaroused/overstimulated or hypoaroused/understimulated.	• Incongruent happy demeanor to infant's distressed cues or sad demeanor to infant's positive cues. • Continues to fail to create regulated, positive arousal stimuli for infant. • Low frequency of play behavior.	• Mismatched (misattuned) arousal states. • One or both hyperaroused/overstimulated or one is in positive arousal state while the other is hypoaroused/understimulated or hyperaroused/overstimulated. • Overwhelmed dyad.

(continued)

TABLE 11.1 Continued

	Infant Context	Mother Context	Interactive Context Right Brain to Right Brain
Negative Affect Processing			
Regulated response	• Fussy, moody affect expressed freely. • Resilience.	• Able to tolerate and express sadness, anger, fear in self and infant while seeking to interact appropriately. • Participates in interactive repair.	• Mutual attuning to disquieting stimuli or condition.
Stress response	• Withdraws or is nonresponsive or becomes agitated, frustrated, or fearful when experiencing sensations of distress (dysregulated states). • Increasing intensity and duration of either state precludes infant's quick response to soothing attempts and return to regulated state.	• Unable to tolerate own negative feelings and responds inappropriately (expresses anger, irritation, or frustration or withdraws and is nonresponsive toward infant). • Poor capacity for interactive repair.	• Mutual frustration. • Mother cannot or does not soothe infant and repair negative affect: dyad remains in distressed state.
RIGHT BRAIN REGULATION			
Interactive Regulation	• Expresses and recognizes affective facial expressions, vocalizations, and gestures. • Infant seeks out mother to coregulate inner state of being.	• Responds with arousal/regulating facial expressions, vocalizations, and gestures. • Mother seeks to affect infant's inner state of being.	• Each member of dyad contingently responds to other's facial expressions, vocalizations, and gestures (right brain to right brain). • Mother and infant interactively seek attunement. • Frequent episodes of interactive play.

Autoregulation	• Self-soothing behaviors (sucks finger/pacifier, rocks body, holds soft object). • Self-created solutions for regulating inner state of being.	• Self-calming behaviors (deep breaths, self-talk). • Mother lets infant struggle with distress briefly and then regulates (assists in autoregulation).	• Each member of dyad remains calm in presence of other. • Each regulates own state of being autonomously.

RIGHT BRAIN DYSREGULATION

Interactive Dysregulation	• Averts gaze, becomes agitated by sounds and gestures. • Startles to parent. • Habitually disconnects from mother's attempts to coregulate while inner state escalates. • Sense of safety threatened by interaction.	• Frequent angry, hostile facial expressions, harsh tone and uneven rhythms, threatening gestures. • Does not look at the infant or unresponsive "dead face." • Repeatedly fails to respond to infant's affective struggle despite infant's escalating inner distress.	• Mutual arousal dysregulation. • Individually or dyadically ignores cues of other; dyad fails to collaborate in regulating infant's inner need state. • Inconsolable infant may lead to mother's negative feelings toward him/her and diminish mother's confidence in her being a "good enough" mother.
Autodysregulation	• Crying, arching, flailing, and vomiting; or blank stare, limp, freezing, motionless. • Infant repeatedly fails to self-regulate inner state, becoming overwhelmed, eventually exhausted and withdrawn. • Dissociates to maternal stimuli. • Chronic sense of threat or lack of sense of safety.	• Irritable, threatening, intrusive, and rough or flat affect, unresponsive. • Disregards infant's ability to autoregulate by quieting or stimulating self. • Dissociates to infant's stimuli.	• Agitated or withdrawn in presence of other. • Both fail to allow infant to enlarge his/her capacity to self-regulate affect. • No relational or intersubjective context.

mind–body neurodynamics of a relational sequence between a 7-month-old infant and his mother. Finally, we offer some thoughts about the unique contributions of regulation theory's integration of biological and psychological domains in constructing more effective models of early assessment, intervention, and prevention. In this approach, the *assessment technique is not as important as the assessment process.* The interdisciplinary trans-theoretical lens of regulation theory can be applied to any clinician's understanding of how one's subjectivity and implicit corporeal self is used in both assessment and treatment at all stages of the life span, including the critical periods of infancy.

RECENT STUDIES OF RIGHT BRAIN–TO–RIGHT BRAIN ATTACHMENT COMMUNICATIONS

In 1996, Schore proposed the interpersonal neurobiological principle that "The self-organization of the developing brain occurs in the context of a relationship with another self, another brain" (p. 60). What can recent developmental neuroscience tell us about how intersubjective emotional attachment communications are transmitted between the mother's and the infant's right brains?

Visual-Facial Attachment Communications

Research now clearly demonstrates that face-to-face mutual gaze is critical to early social development (Trevarthen & Aitken, 2001). The development of the capacity to efficiently process information from faces requires visual input to the right (and not left) hemisphere during infancy (Le Grand, Mondloch, Maurer, & Brent, 2003). At 2 months of age, the onset of a critical period during which synaptic connections in the developing occipital cortex are modified by visual experience (Yamada et al., 2000), infants show right hemispheric activation when exposed to a woman's face (Tzourio-Mazoyer et al., 2002). Using EEG methodology, Grossmann, Johnson, Farroni, and Csibra (2007) report that 4-month-old infants presented with images of a female face gazing directly ahead show enhanced gamma electrical activity over right prefrontal areas. Recent near-infrared spectroscopy (NIRS) research (perhaps the most suitable of all neuroscience techniques applicable to human infants) reveals that specifically the 5-month-olds' right hemisphere responds to images of adult female faces (Nakato et al., 2009; Otsuka et al., 2007). By 6 months, infants show a right-lateralized left gaze bias when viewing faces (Guo, Meints, Hall, Hall, & Mills, 2009), right temporal activation when looking at angry faces (Nakato, Otsuka, Kanazawa, Yamaguchi, & Kakigi, 2011), and a significantly greater right frontotemporal activation when viewing their own mother's (as opposed to a stranger's) face (Carlsson, Langercrantz, Olson, Printz, & Bartocci, 2008).

In total, these research data mean that the future capacity to process the essential social information expressed in face-to-face communications, a central aspect of all later intimate relationships, is dependent upon caregiver–infant eye contact and visual gazing during this critical period. Thus, how often and in what contexts the mother and infant look (and not look) directly at each other is of key importance to a clinician when evaluating an infant's development and the health of the dyadic relationship. When there is mutual infant–caregiver visual gazing that looks and feels natural to the clinician, the clinician knows that likely the infant's brain is developing well in this area.

Auditory-Prosodic Attachment Communications

Ongoing studies of prenatal, perinatal, and postnatal auditory-prosodic attachment communications also highlight the role of the right brain. In an EEG study of auditory pitch processing in preterm infants born at 30 gestational weeks, Mento et al. (2010) conclude, "the earlier right structural maturation in foetal epochs seems to be paralleled by a right functional development" (p. 1). A functional magnetic resonance imaging (MRI) study of 1- to 3-day-old newborns reports that music evokes right hemispheric activation in the auditory cortex (Perani et al., 2010). Using NIRS with 2- to 6-day-old neonates, Telkemeyer et al. (2009) observe, "responses to slow acoustic modulations are lateralized to the right hemisphere" (p. 14726). This same optical brain imaging technology reveals that prosodic processing of emotional voices in 3-month-old (Homae, Watanabe, Nakano, Asakawa, & Taga, 2006) and 4-month-old infants (Minagawa-Kawai et al., 2011) activates the right temporoparietal region. Grossmann, Oberecker, Koch, and Friederici (2010) report that 7-month-old infants respond to emotional voices in a voice-sensitive region of the right superior temporal sulcus, and happy prosody specifically activates the right inferior frontal cortex. These authors conclude, "The pattern of finding suggests that temporal regions specialize in processing voices very early in development and that, already in infancy, emotions differentially modulate voice processing in the right hemisphere" (p. 852).

This research suggests that the emotional quality of what infants hear in the early stages of infancy affects the development of the voice processing areas of the right hemisphere, especially the temporal voice areas in the upper banks of the right superior temporal sulcus (Bestelmeyer, Belin, & Grosbas, 2011) .

Furthermore, the perspective of interpersonal neurobiology proposes that the caregiver's use of infant-directed speech ("motherese") is critical for the development of the child's prosodic-emotional functions. Infant-directed speech, described by Darwin (1877) as "the sweet music of the species," is preferred, independent of culture, over adult-directed speech as early as a few weeks after birth (Cooper & Aslin, 1990; Fernald, 1985). Compared to adult-directed speech, motherese, the vocal expression of emotion to infants (Trainor, Austin, & Desjardins, 2000), is higher in pitch, has a wider pitch range, and exhibits exaggerated pitch contours. In addition, it is shorter, slower, and separated by longer pauses than adult speech (Fernald, 1989; Stern, Spieker, Barnett, & MacKain, 1983). Developmental neuroscience research demonstrates that maternal infant-directed speech activates the right temporal area of 4- to 6-month-old infants, and that this activation is even greater in 7- to 9-month-old infants (Naoi et al., 2011). In 11-month-old infants, the voice of a woman's infant-directed speech (i.e., with somewhat exaggerated prosody, "motherese") elicits a right-lateralized event-related potential (Thierry, Vihman, & Roberts, 2003).

Clinically, these studies indicate the importance of assessing not the verbal content but the melody of the mother's voice, and whether or not she's using infant-directed versus adult-directed speech in her interactions with her child, especially in playful contexts. This use of infant-directed speech is essential to the development of the infant's right temporal areas, and the burgeoning ability of reading the emotional tone of the voice of others, an essential element of adaptive social relationships.

Tactile-Gestural Attachment Communications

Tactile-gestural attachment communications found in touch affect the developing right hemisphere (Sieratzki & Woll, 1996). These authors assert that the emotional impact of touch is more direct and immediate if an infant is held on the left side of the body. Because the left side of the body projects directly into the right hemisphere, infants cradled on the left receive direct input into their developing right brain (Bourne & Todd, 2004; Huggenberger, Suter, Reijnen, & Schachinger, 2009; Reissland, Hopkins, Helms, & Williams, 2009). In contrast, mothers classified as depressed and those with a history of domestic violence show right-sided cradling (Weatherill et al., 2004).

Other studies demonstrate the essential role of maternal touch on human infant development in the first year of life (Ferber, Feldman, & Makhoul, 2008; Jean, Stack, & Fogel, 2009). This allows the infant and mother to create a system of "touch synchrony" to alter vagal tone and cortisol reactivity (Feldman, Singer, & Zagoory, 2010, p. 271). The dyad thus uses "interpersonal touch" as a communication system (Gallace & Spence, 2010), especially for the communication and regulation of emotional information (Hertenstein, 2002; Hertenstein & Campos, 2001). High levels of tactile stimulation and mutual touch occur in breast-feeding (Lavelli & Poli, 1998). Lehtonen, Kononen, Purhonen, Partanen, and Saarikoski's (2002) research observed an increase in EEG amplitude in right posterior cortical areas in 6-month-old infants during the intense somatosensory tactile contact of breast-feeding.

This research supports the infant's need for affectionate touch for healthy right hemisphere development, which can be observed in an infant–caregiver assessment.

With respect to gestures, Nagy (2006, p. 227) demonstrates a "lateralized system for neonatal imitation" and concludes, "The early advantage of the right hemisphere (Chiron et al., 1997; Schore, 2000; Trevarthen, 2001) in the first few months of life may affect the lateralized appearance of the first imitative gestures." Moreover, Montirosso, Borgatti, and Tronick (2010) document left-sided regulatory gestures (right hemisphere controlled) when infants are stressed. Summarizing their work on gestures, they state,

> Infants cope with the emotional distress caused by unresponsive mothers through self-regulation behaviors associated with a greater activation of the right hemisphere. In sum, this finding supports the view that during a stressful condition there is a state-dependent activation of the right hemisphere. . . . More generally these findings suggest that the right hemisphere is more involved in the social and biological functions regarding infant caregiver emotional bonding (Schore, 2005; Siegel, 1999). (Montirosso et al., 2010, p. 108)

Role of Maternal Psychobiological Attunement in Infant Right Brain Development

Confirming this relational neurobiological model, in very recent functional magnetic resonance imaging studies of mother–infant emotional communication, Noriuchi, Kikuchi, and Senoo (2008) report activation of the mother's right orbitofrontal cortex during moments of maternal love triggered by viewing a video of her own infant. Another near-infrared spectroscopy study of infant–mother attachment at 12 months shows right orbitofrontal activation in the mother when viewing a video of her smiling infant; and the authors conclude, "our results are in agreement with that of Schore (1999, 2000) who addressed the importance of the right hemisphere in the attachment system" (Minagawa-Kawai et al., 2009, p. 289).

In the course of these right brain–to–right brain transactions, the infant forms an internal working model of his or her attachment relationship with the primary caregiver, which is stored in right-lateralized nonverbal implicit-procedural memory. These interactive representations encode strategies of affect regulation and contain coping mechanisms for maintaining basic regulation and positive affect in the face of environmental challenge. At the most fundamental level, attachment represents the biological connection between the infant and mother. What is learned in emotionally laden attachment transactions and imprinted into the emotional right brain is stored not in conscious verbal declarative memory, but in nonconscious implicit-procedural memory, where biologically wired instincts are interacting with the lived experience embedded in the primary caregiver–infant bodily based nonverbal relationship. It is this implicit, nonverbal world that the clinician is accessing and assessing.

Therefore, the mother's psychobiological attunement to the infant's arousal and psychobiological state occurs in nonverbal communications of eyes, faces, voice prosody (infant-directed speech), and touch, and in such bodily based transactions she intuits what the infant feels and needs at the moment. Attuned sensitivity of caregivers is amply supported by research as being the one factor consistently associated with secure attachment (Ainsworth, Blehar, Waters, & Wall, 1978; DeWolff & Van IJzendoorn, 1997; Van IJzendoorn & De Wolff,

1997). Psychobiologically attuned mothering represents a right brain process. If all that parents do to respond to an infant's nonverbal communications were done by the left brain (adult-directed speech), there would be a narrowed focus on the details of parenting without the emotional elements that would be stressful to both caregiver and infant. In a functional magnetic resonance study of maternal communication within the attachment relationship, Lenzi et al. (2009) offer data "supporting the theory that the right hemisphere is more involved than the left hemisphere in emotional processing and thus, mothering" (p. 1131). Yet clinicians often see mothers who are trying to parent exclusively with their left brains, that is, mothers who focus more on the nonrelational tasks of infant care rather than the nonverbal communications of the infant.

In an extraordinary recent volume, Iain McGilchrist (2009) describes the documented differences between the two hemispheric processors: "The world of the left hemisphere, dependent on denotative language and abstraction, yields clarity and power to manipulate things that are known, fixed, static, isolated, decontextualized, explicit, disembodied, general in nature, but ultimately lifeless" (p. 174). In contrast, "the right hemisphere . . . yields a world of individual, changing, evolving, interconnected, implicit, incarnate, living beings within the context of the lived world, but in the nature of things never fully graspable, always imperfectly known—and to this world it exists in a relationship of care" (p. 174). This essential human capacity of the right brain optimally evolves in an interpersonal context of a secure attachment bond, "a relationship of care."

CURRENT STUDIES OF ATTACHMENT AND THE EXPERIENCE-DEPENDENT MATURATION OF THE RIGHT BRAIN

In the aforementioned panoramic editorial by Leckman and March (2011), these authors describe "A complex, dynamic story is unfolding of evolutionarily conserved genetic programs that guide mammalian brain development and how our in utero and our early postnatal interpersonal worlds shape and mold the individuals (infants, children, adolescents, adults and caregivers) we are to become" (p. 333). The shaping of brain development by our early interpersonal worlds is an essential focus of the field of interpersonal neurobiology (Schore, 2003a). Indeed, over the last two decades, our understanding of how brain development is impacted by early experience has been radically transformed.

The brain has a bottom-up (caudal to rostral) developmental trajectory with the lower (and phylogenetically older) brain systems maturing first (Gogtay et al., 2004). During prenatal and postnatal critical periods, the rate of synaptogenesis (the formation of synapses) is estimated at 40,000 new synapses every second (Lagercrantz & Ringstedt, 2001). In a structural MRI study of the human brain from birth to age 2, Knickmeyer et al. (2008) report, "Total brain volume increased 101% in the first year, with a 15% increase in the second. . . . The volume of the subcortical area (including brainstem) increased by 130% in the first year and by 14% in the second year" (p. 12178). The developmental stage of infancy, then, is a critical period for both cortical and subcortical brain development. We know that this growth is not just genetically encoded. Rather it is epigenetically influenced and requires human interaction. Both variations in maternal caregiving and caregiver maltreatment are now seen as epigenetic modifications that regulate gene activity in the developing brain (Roth & Sweatt, 2011). This means that the quality of the primary attachment experience affects synaptogenesis and brain volume. Clinicians therefore need to be especially able to assess the quality of infant–caregiver relationships and provide interventions when needed.

In 1994, Schore proposed that attachment experiences specifically influence the maturation of the early developing right brain. Subsequently, Sieratzki and Woll (1996) asserted, "The role of the right hemisphere is crucial in relation to the most precious needs of mothers and infants" (p. 1747); and Chiron et al. (1997) published a study asserting, "The right brain hemisphere is dominant in human infants" (p. 1057). Studies of the unique functions of the right brain subsequently increased (Schore, 2001a, 2003a), and in 2002 Braun et al. asserted, "The right and left human brain hemispheres differ in macrostructure, ultrastructure, physiology, chemistry, and control of behavior" (p. 97). Indeed, a number of anatomical and imaging studies now show earlier maturation of the right hemisphere in prenatal and postnatal stages of human development (Gupta et al., 2005; Howard & Reggia, 2007; Sun et al., 2005). This research supports the earlier work of Previc (1991), who suggested that the origins of cerebral asymmetry emanate in the intrauterine environment, and that the prenatal positioning of the fetus in the womb allows the inward-facing left ear to receive a greater amount of vestibular stimulation and thus an earlier organization of the right hemispheric vestibular cortex, a brain system involved in emotion processing (Carmona, Holland, & Harrison, 2009). For clinicians, this means that early emotional processing appears to begin in utero. Therefore, assessing emotional well-being of the mother-to-be in pregnancy is critical.

There is now agreement that "the emotional experience(s) of the infant . . . are disproportionately stored or processed in the right hemisphere during the formative stages of brain ontogeny" (Semrud-Clikeman & Hynd, 1990, p. 198). This means that the experiences the infant has in his or her interactions with the primary caregiver over early critical periods of attachment specifically affect the development of the right hemisphere, which is known to be the foundation for self-development (Devinsky, 2000; Devue et al., 2007; Kaplan, Aziz-Zadeh, Uddin, & Iacoboni, 2008). Over the course of the first year, increasingly complex right brain–to–right brain attachment communications initially imprint first right posterior cerebral areas involved in sensory processing (e.g., right occipital, right fusiform gyrus, right superior temporal sulcus, right temporoparietal regions), and later right anterior cerebral areas.

Modern attachment theory suggests that during these critical periods of brain development affectively laden attachment communications are wiring the somatosensory, visual, temporal, and frontal cortices, particularly in the right hemisphere. Thus, clinicians need to assess not only the quality and amount of caregiver–infant eye gazing and nonverbal auditory communication but also the quality and amount of sensitive interpersonal touch the infant is receiving.

Maternal–infant emotional transactions however allow for more than the maturation of cortical connections within the right cerebral hemisphere that are dependent upon caregiver–infant experience. In line with the principle of the sequential caudal to rostral structural development of the brain, bodily based attachment transactions also imprint cortical-subcortical connections of the right brain, which is deeply connected into the emotion-processing limbic system. Recall Bowlby's (1969) original description of mother–infant attachment communications that are "accompanied by the strongest of feelings and emotions, happy or the reverse" (p. 242). Basic research in developmental neuroscience now demonstrates, "The functional maturation of limbic circuits is significantly influenced by early socio-emotional experience" (Helmeke, Ovtscharoff, Poeggel, & Braun, 2001, p. 717). Using functional magnetic resonance imaging (fMRI) research, Dapretto et al. (2006) contend, "Typically developing children can rely upon a right hemisphere–mirroring neural mechanism — interfacing with the limbic system via the insula — whereby the meaning of imitated (or observed) emotion is directly felt and hence understood" (p. 30). Attachment studies strongly support Panksepp's (2008) bold assertion of the primacy of affective neuroscience: "Now cognitive science must re-learn that ancient emotional systems have a power that is quite independent of neocortical cognitive processes" (p. 51). In other words, what is learned cognitively and stored in the left hemisphere has little to do with the affective relational, two-person experiences stored in the right hemisphere. Clinicians can only assess these patterns through their own implicit right brain connections with their clients, that is, by accessing their own bodily-based instinctive responses.

Attachment and the Autonomic Nervous System

A prime example of an "ancient emotional system" is the autonomic nervous system (ANS), "the physiological bottom of the mind" (Jackson, 1931) and a central component of the human stress response. Studies indicate that maternal care within the attachment relationship shapes the infant's hypothalamic-pituitary-adrenocortical (HPA) stress-regulating axis (Gunnar, 2000) and that epigenetic programming of maternal behavior alters the development of HPA responses to stress through tissue-specific effects on gene transcription (Weaver et al., 2004). The cortical and subcortical systems of the right brain are known to play a dominant role in regulating the HPA axis and in mediating the human stress response. Indeed, the right hemisphere, more so than the left, is central to the control of vital functions supporting survival and enabling the organism to cope with stresses and challenges (Wittling, 1997).

Bodily based attachment communications between the infant and primary caregiver act as an epigenetic mechanism that imprints the circuits of the stress-regulating system. Studies now indicate that during early critical periods, prenatal and postnatal interpersonal events wire the connectivity of structures in the developing central nervous system (CNS) with the sympathetic and parasympathetic branches of the evolving autonomic nervous system (ANS). According to McGilchrist (2009, p. 437), "The right hemisphere is . . . more closely in touch with emotion and the body (therefore with the neurologically 'inferior' and more ancient regions of the central nervous system)." There is now consensus that the right brain plays a greater role than the left in autonomic arousal and therefore the somatic aspects of emotional states. Porges (2007) concludes, "Consistent with the views that the right hemisphere appears to play a greater role in affect, especially the adaptive expression of negative affect, the right hemisphere also appears to have a greater role in regulation of cardiac function presumably via shifts in (parasympathetic) vagal regulation" (p. 126).

Regulation theory asserts that the attuned caregiver's dampening of negative affect arousal, as well as enhancing of positive affective arousal, entrains a balance between the energy-expending sympathetic and energy-conserving parasympathetic branches of the infant's ANS, thus creating optimal arousal ranges associated with focused attention, homeostatic visceral-somatic processing, and secure attachment. Slade (2005) articulates the importance of the infant's developing the capacity of "experiencing the links between affect, behavior, the body, and self-experience" (p. 271). We suggest that "the body" specifically refers to the functions of the ANS, the system of peripheral neurons that controls, in an involuntary fashion, visceral organs, the cardiovascular system, and effectors in the skin. In classical writings, Basch (1976) speculated that "the language of mother and infant consists of signals produced by the autonomic, involuntary nervous system in both parties" (p. 766). These infant and mother bodily based affective autonomic signals need to be incorporated into clinical assessment and treatment models so that therapists can evaluate the strength and the quality of the synchrony between the caregiver–infant affective signals.

The ANS harnesses and regulates the energy in the body needed for life processes (Recordati, 2003). The sympathetic nervous system (SNS) is triggered when more energy is needed in the body, and the peripheral nervous system (PNS) is triggered for balancing energy or energy renewal. The Polyvagal Theory, proposed by Porges (1995, 2001, 2009), suggests that the *vagus nerve*—a cranial nerve that connects the face, heart, and viscera and controls facial expression, vocalization, and listening—is the newest phylogenetic circuit that evolved for social communication. The social engagement system (called the *ventral vagal system*) is myelinated, enabling it to respond quickly, but it can be used only when a person is feeling safe within his or her optimal arousal range. If a person senses a threat, even unconsciously, the SNS mobilization system then prepares the body for flight or fight by increasing energy. Should the danger be a life threat with no possibility of escape, a phylogenetically older unmyelinated vagus system (called the *dorsal vagal system*) controlled by the PNS can take control and put the body into a freeze or feigning death state by shutting down the brain. In animals, this feigning death state appears to function as a possible survival mechanism, as some predators become disinterested in an animal that appears to be dead (Levine, 1997). Schore (2009) equates this immobilized dorsal vagal state with dissociation, "detachment from an unbearable situation" (Mollon, 1996), "the escape when there is no escape" (Putnam, 1997), and "a last resort defensive strategy" (Dixon, 1998).

Because the SNS response is associated with increased arousal, or *hyperarousal*, with an increase in respiration and heart rate, whereas the PNS response is associated with decreased arousal, or *hypoarousal*, with a decrease in respiration and heart rate, the quality of the co-regulation experience lived in the early attachment relationship entrains setpoints within the developing ANS. Optimal arousal ranges are created when good-enough sensitive parenting occurs so that an infant or young child does not spend large amounts of time in dysregulated hyperaroused or hypoaroused states. Specifically, caregivers try to soothe crying infants so that they are not in long hyperaroused states and play with their infants so they are not in long hypoaroused states. These caregiver responses are associated with creating optimal arousal ranges in the ANS.

On the other hand, chronic hyperarousal can be imprinted into infants who use their inborn attachment signaling for their primary caregiver by crying, but whose caregivers respond sometimes, but the infant never knows when. This could contribute to the infant's brain being organized more toward the SNS side of arousal because the infant has over-developed a nonconscious vigilant survival strategy that hyperactivates the biological attachment system. Conversely, some infants learn not to use their inborn attachment signals to cry when needing their primary caregiver because either crying has been chronically responded to harshly or not at all, or the caregiver is too frightening. Such infants may develop a nonconscious survival strategy that deactivates the attachment system with an ANS organized more toward the PNS side of arousal. Infants and young children who are coping with frightening behavior in their caregivers possess subcortical circuits that fire repeatedly to protect the child from danger. Because infants cannot remove themselves from the danger, dissociation and the autoregulation of the PNS are often the outcome. Sadly, an unseen and unheard baby may have a better chance of surviving in family systems where trauma and violence are the norm. The biological attachment instinct that emits stressful regulatory signals of active protest by crying can thus be facilitated or inhibited by the primary caregiver. This essential instinct can be reshaped and altered by the demands of the lived environment.

Translating this psychobiological principle into neurobiological terms, the social-emotional relational environment provided by the primary caregiver molds, for better or worse, the experience-dependent maturation of the brain systems involved in the infant's developing affect regulating attachment functions. During early critical periods these transactions shape the cortical-subcortical stress-regulating circuits of the developing right brain, which is deeply connected into the limbic areas of the CNS as well as into both branches of the ANS. Basic research now establishes that optimal stress regulation is dependent on "right hemispheric specialization in regulating stress- and emotion-related processes" (Sullivan & Dufresne, 2006, p. 55). In 1994 Schore proposed critical periods for the experience-dependent maturation and connectivity of the regulatory centers in the right brain that occur within the attachment relationship (Schore, 2001a). In that contribution I specified the ontogenetic progression of three distinct systems that holistically regulate critical right brain functions: amygdala-insula, limbic anterior cingulate, and orbitofrontal (ventromedial) cortex. Support for this model is provided by a recent review of the functional neuroanatomy of the parent–infant relationship by Parsons, Young, Murray, Stein, & Kringelbach (2010) who conclude, "the same adult brain networks involved in emotional and social interactions are already present in immature and incomplete forms in the infant" (p. 235), specifically mentioning amygdala, hypothalamus, insula, cingulate cortex, and orbitofrontal cortex.

In his most recent articulation of this model of the developmental progression of hierarchical limbic-autonomic regulatory centers, Schore offers evidence showing that the *amygdala* (especially the central nucleus), the paraventricular areas of the *hypothalamus* that produce the stress reducing neurohormone oxytocin, and the stress intensifying neuropeptide corticotropin releasing factor, and the *insula*, involved in stress-responsive visceroautonomic functions, begin their maturation prenatally and are functional at birth and over the ensuing perinatal stage (Schore, 2010c). At 3 to 9 months of age, the anterior cingulate (medial frontal cortex), a cortical-limbic structure that is associated with responsivity to social cues, comes online, giving the infant greater regulatory capacity when there is good-enough caregiver co-regulation. From 10 to 12 months of age, the regulatory center in the orbitofrontal cortex begins its developmental growth period. This ventromedial prefrontal cortex, especially in the right hemisphere, is the executive control center for emotion. With optimal attachment experiences, the vertical axis that connects the orbitofrontal cortex with its interconnected subcortical areas is well developed, allowing the right orbitofrontal cortex to regulate the amygdala (see Barbas, 2007, and Schore, 2001a, in press, for a more in-depth discussion). Indeed, developmental neurobiological research reveals that the process of coping with early life stress increases the myelination of the ventromedial cortex, a prefrontal region that controls arousal regulation and resilience (Katz et al., 2009). For the rest of the life span the right, and not left, lateralized prefrontal regions are responsible for the regulation of affect and stress (Cerqueira, Almeida, & Sousa, 2008; Schore, 1994; Stevenson, Halliday, Marsden, & Mason, 2008; Sullivan & Gratton, 2002; Wang et al., 2005). These data clearly indicate that the right orbitofrontal cortex, the control system of attachment (Schore, 2000), is considered the highest stress regulatory center in the brain and its connectivity is associated with the emotional regulation that is commonly found in secure children.

We thus suggest that the *in utero* and postnatal dyadic relations between the child and the caregiver have enduring effects on brain development. We further propose that these effects are elucidated by a deeper understanding of the interpersonal neurobiological mechanisms by which the early attachment relationship acts as the germinal matrix of right brain development. The best current description of the path of neurodevelopment is that it is "malleable" (Leckman & March, 2011, p. 333). The attachment relationship shapes, for better or worse, the child's capacity for resilience or a predisposition for psychopathology.

APPLICATION OF REGULATION THEORY TO CLINICAL ASSESSMENT

The maternal-attuned nonverbal communications needed to optimally facilitate the early development of the infant's right hemisphere require that the caregiver is able to implicitly and intuitively use her own right hemisphere and her own instincts in the service of co-creating the attachment bond. This principle of right brain dominance is true for clinicians as well. Therapists applying regulation theory in work with young children and their families use their own carefully honed clinical instincts. That is, they use their own right brains to intuitively read and assess the nonverbal communications of the bodyworld of an infant–caregiver dyad (Newton, 2008b; see Schore & Schore, 2008, and Schore, 2011, for discussions of the neurobiology of clinical intuition). This often private right hemisphere world is inextricably tied to the true nature of the primary attachment relationship. But it can be missed if therapists observe only the infant's overt behaviors and attend only verbally with the caregiver (see Newton, 2008a). Shai and Belsky (2011) assert,

> Whereas verbal manifestations of the parent's representation of the child may be meaningful, and thereby developmentally significant for the older child, it is unlikely that the preverbal infant could directly experience such mentalizing in a semantically meaningful way. Moreover, *verbal parental mentalizing cannot illuminate the process by which parents' mental capacities actually affect the infant.* (p. 2, emphasis added)

Because clinicians' own use of their right brains is so critical in assessing and treating young children and their families, Ruth Newton, the coauthor of this chapter, will often half-playfully insist that interns "train your left hemisphere to sit on command," meaning focus on your initial spontaneous, instinctive bodily based responses.

As a part of her initial evaluation of a dyadic infant–caregiver relationship, Newton begins all assessments with a 5-minute structured and 5-minute unstructured play experience between mother (or father) and child. For infants under 12 months of age, only the play experience is used. With consent, these sessions are videotaped to be used in intervention, if needed. Clinicians watching the play session are accessing their own right hemispheres and using their instincts to see, feel, and evaluate the quality and intensity of the caregiver's attunement, misattunement, and repair of the infant's regulated and dysregulated affective communications as there are no verbal interactions between the caregiver and clinician at this point in the observation.

Clinical Assessment of an Infant–Mother Dyad

Jonathan is a cute 7-month-old infant who was accompanied by his mother to an initial evaluation through a specialized birth to age 5 training program at St. Vincent de Paul Village, a large homeless rehabilitation center in downtown San Diego. Jonathan's mother had been homeless since he was 4 months old, having left Jonathan's father due to domestic violence. Jonathan and his mother were referred by the on-site child-care program staff, who were concerned about his lack of facial expression and vocalizations and his appearing to be withdrawn. The observer in that program noted that "at times, he seems to be staring off into space, and he doesn't seem to respond much when his mother picks him up." The evaluation began with a 5-minute play session with the clinician, while training interns observed from behind a one-way mirror. As per protocol for the Parent–Child Early Relational Assessment (Clark, 1985), his mother was asked to play with Jonathan in the way she usually did. Jonathan sat on a blanket covering mats on the floor with his mother. On the blanket were a number of infant banging toys including rattles, blocks, and an infant mirror.

His mother first picked up the infant rain stick rattle and began upending it to make sound. She shook the rattle close to his face, and Jonathan turned his head away. She then picked up another rattle asking, "What's this? What's this?" Jonathan reached for the rattle at the top when his mother said, "No, hold it like this," and clasped his hand around the handle. The mother then began picking up two rattles together and shook them close to Jonathan's face. Jonathan responded by turning his head and body toward the door. She quickly dropped one rattle for another, shaking the rattles intensely and close to his face. From behind the one-way mirror, Newton was beginning to feel tense as the mother showed no signs of being aware that her son was overstimulated even when he was clearly doing his best to signal to her that he was overaroused by turning his head and then his body away from his mother.

Jonathan then reached for the rain stick and began to explore it when his mother grabbed the other end and began pulling it away from him. Jonathan looked away, then down. His mother began pulling it out of his hand, saying in a rising shrill tone, "Gimme, gimme, gimme. Mine, mine, mine." His mother then moved toward him, dangling her hair in his face, laughing, and becoming increasingly louder, saying, "I'm going to get you." She then added a growl to her voice and began to laugh in a rhythmic decrescendo. Jonathan's body stilled, and he began to collapse his body away from his mother. In response, his mother used all the rattles, shaking them around Jonathan's face saying, "Hey, right over here." It appeared she was trying to recapture his attention. He made no sounds.

He did not smile and his eyes were fixed. His body alternated between still and jerky. Jonathan tried to look at his mother when she showed him the infant mirror. He appeared to have a beginning smile for her and began patting the mirror; however, his mother then took it from him and asked whether he wanted to crawl. At this point, his mother changed Jonathan to a crawl position.

After this initial observation, the testing team engaged with the infant while mother was interviewed at a distance but within sight of the infant. During the testing,which used the Bayley Scales of Infant Development II (BSID-II; Bayley, 1993), Jonathan sat on the blanket and interacted with the toys given by the intern examiner, who also sat on the floor at a distance of about 3 feet. Jonathan studied the ring and easily transferred it between hands and shook the bell multiple times while cooing and babbling. He smiled a number of times at the examiner. He did not look at his mother during the half hour of testing, even though she was sitting approximately 4 feet away to his right; he appeared to stiffen when she picked him up at the end of testing. Jonathan's BSID-II cognitive and motor scores were in typical ranges for his age. The Behavioral Rating Scale showed delays, which supported our clinical observations that the socioemotional developmental domain was delayed. Given that Jonathan showed more typical relational interaction with the intern than his mother, we now had both observational and testing data that supported an optimistic beginning of an intervention with the attachment relationship.

Assessment of Parental Nonverbal Communication and Infant Dissociation

In our assessment of the dyad, we perceived that Jonathan's mother was attempting to play with him; yet she could not read his face, his lack of vocalization and eye contact, his striking head, and his whole body gestural turns away from his mother to reduce the increasing stimulation. Nor did she understand his body collapse was a last ditch effort to reduce stimulation. Jonathan had little facial expression during this 5-minute play interaction, which indicated he was not enjoying the play interaction. His exploration with his mother was lifeless, halting, slow moving, jerky, and peppered with many gaze and body aversions. At 7 months, a baby's right brain should be reading his caregiver's face, eyes, voice prosody, gesture, and touch.

Earlier we cited research showing that infants at this age express right temporal activation when looking at an angry face (Nakato et al., 2011). Jonathan's mother's face was contorted much of the time, and her voice showed a deficit in infant-directed speech. In fact, her prosody (rising shrill tone) was clearly scary, especially when she began growling and laughing loudly in a repetitive pattern that sounded frighteningly eerie. Her tactile-gestural expressions lacked "touch synchrony" and instead were combative and competitive as she tried to pull items away from him and change his posture when no signal was given to do this. His mother's behavior was intense, and Jonathan showed signs of being overstimulated and hyperaroused, yet he did not relationally protest (cry or complain). Instead, he tried to modulate the overstimulation by looking down, turning his body away and withdrawing, fixating his eyes in a dissociative stare, and eventually collapsing his body away from his mother.

Because there was no caregiver interactive regulation of Jonathan's nervous system, which moved into critically high and aversive SNS hyperarousal, Jonathan's own body began autoregulating the stressful hyperarousal through dissociation and eventual shutdown, a state of "learned helplessness." This shutdown is a function of the parasympathetic nervous system when there is life-threatening fear with no escape. Not only was his mother intrusively amplifying his state of accelerating hyperarousal, she also appeared not to sense that there was any need for repair. Research shows that when mothers are stressed, it interferes with parenting infants (Suter, Huggenberger, & Schachinger, 2007). Mothers in ultra-high or ultra-low states of dysregulated arousal become less sensitive as caregivers, more autocratic, and less able to pick up subtle infant emotional communications. If caregivers become so overwhelmed that they cannot regulate their own stress state, they cannot act as a regulator of their babies' states. Thus, the first treatment goal was for Jonathan's mother to become aware of his thresholds for arousal dysregulation and behavioral disorganization. A further therapeutic goal was to reduce the mother's own arousal in order to expand her ability to read her son's nonverbal communications. The therapeutic focus on the infant included attention to his dysregulated hyperarousal, which resulted in dissociative hypoarousal as the only available strategy of affect regulation.

According to Schore (2002), pathological dissociation is manifested in a maladaptive, highly defensive, rigid, closed self-system, one that responds to even low levels of intersubjective stress with parasympathetic dorsal vagal hypoarousal, heart rate deceleration, and passive disengagement. This fragile unconscious system is susceptible to relational stress-induced mind–body metabolic collapse and thereby a loss of energy-dependent synaptic connectivity within the right brain, expressed in a sudden implosion of the implicit self and a rupture of self-continuity. Because the right hemisphere mediates the communication and regulation of emotional states, a chronic rupture of intersubjectivity in the mother–infant relationship is accompanied by an instant dissipation of safety and trust in the dyad and a sense of fear and danger in the infant. The assessment clearly revealed that safety and trust were not being co-created in the relationship between Jonathan and his mother.

Jonathan's dissociative stares, lack of eye contact and vocalization, relational withdrawal, slow gestural movements, and body collapse all point to Jonathan's body moving into the dorsal vagal function of the PNS. Clinicians trained to understand the role of this autonomic survival strategy and to recognize how infants appear in this state of frozen fear identify this immobilization as his ANS responding to a life-threatening situation that must be addressed. Indeed, very recent research from neuroscience and child psychiatry now shows that under severe interpersonal stress or relational trauma, an infant does not cry, but will disengage and shut down. If it becomes chronic, this relational withdrawal is the most pathological of all infant responses to stress. In this involuntary disengagement from the social environment, the infant is still and silent.

These observations of a mother and her 7-month-old infant are very similar to the characterization of intrusive mothers and their 4- to 6-month-old infants by Atzil, Hendler, and Feldman (2011). Using functional magnetic resonance imaging they document that these mothers show significant right amygdala activation associated with fear and anxiety while watching videos of their own infants interacting with them. The authors interpret this neural activation pattern as underlying "insufficient behavioral inhibition, which may lead to excessive, non-modulated maternal behavior typical of the intrusive style" and "behaviors . . . marked by overstimulation, excessive parenting, and miscoordination" (p. 10).

Note the similarities also to Shai and Belsky's (2011) videotape of a 6-month-old and a psychobiologically misattuned mother who can not read her infant's kinesthetic responses to her dysregulating interventions. They document that when the mother moves into the infant's personal space, the infant shrinks his body so that his shoulders, arms, and legs come close to the body center in an enclosing movement, thereby withdrawing from the mother's stimulation. During withdrawal, the infant's muscles tense. When the mother moves away from him he twists his torso way from her. As this continues she presses his arms to the floor, restricting his efforts to move away. Subsequently the infant brings his arms toward his belly, attempting to block the stimulus. The authors note these defensive movements signal the infant's desperation and distress. Ultimately the infant's body stiffens and is turned away from the mother, yet despite these signals the mother continues her stimulation.

A deeper understanding of Jonathan's responses to his emotionally dysregulating caregiver (dissociative stilling and body collapse while interacting with her and body stiffening upon reunion) is also informed by Beebe and colleagues' (2010) studies of mothers of 4-month-old infants who later show disorganized attachment. They observe that the mothers of these infants are overwhelmed with their own unresolved abuse or trauma and therefore cannot bear to intersubjectively engage with their infants' distress. Because these mothers are unable to regulate their own distress, they cannot regulate their infant's distress. They are unable to allow themselves to be emotionally affected by their infant's dysregulated state, thus they shut down emotionally, closing their faces, looking away from the infant's face, and failing to coordinate with the infant's emotional state. Beebe interprets this fearful maternal behavior as a defensive dissociation, a strategy that protects the mother from the facial and visual intimacy that would come from joining the infant's distressed moments. This type of mother thus shows disrupted and contradictory forms of affective communication (intrusiveness *and* disengagement), especially around the infant's need for comfort when distressed (Beebe et al., 2010).

Schore (2001b) describes the intergenerational transmission not only of the intense emotional distress of relational trauma but also of the defensive response of pathological dissociation. Over the ongoing period of relational trauma in this case the mother's disengagement and "detachment from an unbearable situation" is matched by the infant's disengagement, detachment, and withdrawal. Milne, Greenway, Guedeney, and Larroque (2009) describe the long-term negative developmental impact of social withdrawal and depression in 6-month-old infants. They conclude, "A withdrawal response in infancy is problematic behavior . . . not because it leads to later withdrawal per se, but because of the compounding effects on development of not being present in the interpersonal space—the space upon which much of infant development depends" (p. 165). Guedeney, Foucault, Bougen, Larroque, and Mentre (2008) report a study of relational withdrawal in infants aged 14 to 18 months. This withdrawal reaction reflects inadequate parent–infant interactions and is a feature of disorganized attachment. Guedeney et al. (2008) note, "Sustained withdrawal behavior may be viewed as a chronic diminution of the attachment system, which is gradually generalized into a diminished engagement and lowered reactivity to the environment as a whole" (p. 151). They conclude, "Withdrawn social behavior from as early as 2 months of age, indicated by a lack of either positive (e.g., smiling, eye contact) or negative (e.g., vocal protestations) behavior, is more akin to a state of learned helplessness and should alert the clinician to the possibility that the infant is not displaying age-appropriate emotional/social behavior" (p. 151).

Notably, the child-care program originally referred Jonathan for evaluation because he had minimal facial expression, minimal vocalizations, and appeared withdrawn. Once his evaluation in a more optimal relational context showed normative cognitive and motor development, his lack of reactivity on the child-care site provided some support for a likely history of diminished caregiver attention to his attachment needs. Thus, the second treatment goal was for the mother to recognize her infant's dissociative withdrawal as a cue to not increase but decrease her stimulation and provide more physical and psychological space between them when they play.

Caregiver Support for Exploration

The attuned caregiver not only down regulates stressful negatively charged arousal but also up regulates positive arousal necessary for exploration. The developmental concern for Jonathan was not only his mother's overstimulating-to-frightening behavior but also her clasping his hand around the rattle and misinterpreting Jonathan's collapsing behavior as an infant-generated desire to crawl. Responding to an infant's exploratory behavior with chronic misidentification of infant intent and feelings can lead to the creation of a false self based more on the expectations and definitions from parents than the infant's own true bodily based self-expressions (Newton, 2006). Winnicott (1960/1965) speculated the false self was a defensive structure developed within the early infant relationship with the caregiver. He stated, "The mother who is not good enough . . . substitutes her own gesture which is to be given sense by the compliance of the infant. This compliance on the part of the infant is the earliest stage of the False

Self, and belongs to the mother's inability to sense her infant's needs" (p. 145). Most clinicians treating adults will often recognize the profound differences between a client's conceptual or false self versus his or her true self. Sadly, a false self can develop when a child has experienced little to no accurate labeling of their intrinsic psychobiological nature, visceral feeling, and relational intent.

A typically developing 7-month-old is generally quite content to explore by reaching, holding, transferring objects from hand to hand, looking, studying, and experiencing what can be created from the object when feeling secure enough in the environment. For Jonathan, his mother was doing the experiencing for him, by showing him the toys without letting him take the initiative to explore them himself. On the other hand, when he was tested with the intern examiner who did not encroach on his space, Jonathan's exploration was more typical for his age. He was delighted with the discovery that he could make the bell ring, and he cooed and wiggled a number of times as he did so. The intern examiner was equally delighted in Jonathan's exploration and vocalizations, giving Jonathan a matched, attuned, and affectively resonant dyadic interaction.

Jonathan's play with his mother was in stark contrast with his more robust exploration, which included pleasurable vocalizations, with an attuned intern. When his mother saw Jonathan play with the intern, she appeared hurt by what she saw, and the clinician felt a great sadness and empathy for her when the mother said, "He doesn't play like that with me." Our observations, that Jonathan could form a relational bond with a nonintrusive adult and that his mother could subjectively experience the differences between his play with her and feel saddened by this, were positive prognostic signs for a therapeutic intervention. It was easy for the team to see the intervention that would likely make the most change in the dyad was helping the mother give her son more space when he plays and helping her to learn to understand and respond to his right brain nonverbal signals.

In all developmental assessments after the family leaves, Newton asks the team, "How do you feel now?" and "How does it feel to be with this dyad?" This is because training using regulation theory focuses on the clinician's own intersubjective body-based somatic markers and affective responses (Newton, 2008b; Schore, 2003a, 2009, 2011). The subsequent discussion integrated subjective observations and feelings with other objective assessments. Out of this dialogue the team creates an intervention plan. Some of the words the interns used to describe their feelings were *shell-shocked, dazed,* and *angry*. The words they used to describe the infant's subjective states were *exhausted, scared, confused,* and *sad*. For training interns, it is often easier to focus on the infant's distress without seeing the mother's responses as likely reflecting her own attachment experiences. When expanding the focus into the mother's past and current trauma, however, there was a noticeable (and appropriate) shift toward a more empathetic appreciation of the mother's stressful state. The third treatment goal was to help the mother engage in nonintrusive play by following Jonathan's lead and amplifying his states of regulated positive arousal.

Impressions of the Attachment Relationship

The attachment impressions observed in Jonathan's play interaction with his mother were that of childhood disorganization and disorientation. When his mother could not read his gaze aversions, lack of eye contact, vocalization, and whole body turns away from mother, Jonathan used a dissociative defense to cope with intense arousal followed by a body collapse when he could no longer continue the engagement. Because his mother was looming over Jonathan while shaking rattles close to his face, using voices that included growling, there was ample observational evidence to support this impression.

According to Main and Solomon (1990), disorganized attachment behavior in infants is often seen as odd, anomalous, contradictory, and/or disoriented behavior, *often lasting for only a few seconds*, that appears to "lack a readily observable goal, intention, or explanation" (p. 122). Hesse and Main (2000, p. 1097) describe disorganized behavior as a "collapse in behavioral and attentional strategies." Disorganized attachment behaviors are thought to represent the untenable position of a stressed infant seeking his caregiver for protection and soothing with his attachment system fully activated while at the same time being fearful of the same caregiver, a condition that Hesse and Main (2006) term "fright without solution" (p. 311). Importantly, Hesse and Main (1999) note that disorganization and disorientation are phenotypically similar to dissociative states.

Our observations of Jonathan and his mother call to mind Beebe's important research in this area. In a comprehensive study of 84 four-month-old infant–mother dyads whose communications and interactions were videotaped and rated, Beebe et al. (2010) found that mother–infant communications at 4 months predicted both insecure-resistant (C) and disorganized (D) attachment at 12 months of age. Specifically what predicted disorganized attachment was *"not being sensed and known* by the mother, and *confusion in sensing and knowing himself"* (p. 199, italics in the original). Furthermore, all communication modalities were affected, such as "attention, touch . . . spatial orientation as well as facial and vocal affect, and facial-visual engagement" (p. 119). These authors conclude that "Aspects of the phenomena of 12-month C and D attachment are thus *already in place at 4 months"* (p. 119, italics in the original).

Disorganized attachment is a serious childhood indicator for immediate parent–child intervention. This attachment pattern is highly associated with unresolved loss and trauma in adults and frightening, threatening, and dissociative behavior in parents (Hesse & Main, 2000, 2006; Main & Hesse, 1990). Jonathan's mother had come from a violent relationship with Jonathan's father and also indicated that she had experienced relational trauma in her own childhood. It is well known that the intergenerational transmission of attachment trauma is high, thus increasing the risk if no intervention is offered (Benoit & Parker, 1994; Lieberman, Chu, Van Horn, & Harris, 2011).

The previously cited fMRI study by Atzil et al. (2011) also documents that mothers who are in synchrony with their 4- to 6-month-old infants have brain responses that show a "clearer organization" across time periods, whereas intrusive mothers had brain responses that show "greater cross-time disorganization" (Atzil et al., 2011, p. 1). A clinician trained in regulation theory knows quite well the development trajectory for Jonathan if no immediate assistance is given to him and his mother. Jonathan is high risk: his mother has a history of unresolved childhood trauma; she was in a violent relationship and then became homeless when he was 4 months old; and at 7 months, Jonathan shows many signs of childhood disorganization. This may have been overlooked by a therapist focused mainly on the mother's verbal narrative of her attachment experiences and history. Jonathan himself tells the true story that "this is the way it is with mother" through his nonverbal communications. Fortunately, we heard his message. The fourth treatment goal then was to have the mother in individual psychotherapy for trauma resolution as well in Healthy Relationships, a psychoeducational group focused on developing more adaptive and rewarding relationships.

Knowledge of Developmental Stages and Brain Development

Knowing the developmental stages and their correspondence with brain development helps the clinician evaluate the impact of relational trauma behavior on the maturing brain (Schore, 2010a, 2010b). For example, in the case of Jonathan, we wondered how often and how intensely his amygdala, the major fear center in the brain, was firing to protect him from his mother's intense interactions and from the violence he had possibly experienced between his parents. Because these traumatic experiences occurred in a critical period of brain development, these dysregulating events could and, if chronic, would be entraining the amygdala toward chronic survival reactions, such as characterological dissociation. The arousal dysregulation could also lower the set point of the HPA and interfere with the ability of the right brain to process stress and nonverbal affect communications.

   These events could also negatively impact development of the right insula (thereby causing a deficit in empathy), the right anterior cingulate (causing a deficit in affiliative behaviors), and, if the attachment pattern is unchanged, the later-maturing right orbitofrontal cortex (resulting in deficits in affect and stress regulation). There is evidence that children raised in severely depriving situations have brains with smaller overall gray and white matter volumes, yet larger amygdala volumes especially in the right hemisphere (Mehta et al., 2009; Schore, 2001b). There are also now a number of imaging studies that show amygdala-orbitofrontal disconnections (New et al., 2007), hyper amygdala reactivity (Donegan et al., 2003), and abnormal brain asymmetries in teens and adults diagnosed with borderline personality disorder (Chanen et al., 2008; Irle, Lange, & Sachsse, 2005). Perhaps most strikingly, a very recent study reports that a phenotype of early infancy identified at 4 months predicts individual differences in reactivity of the right amygdala to faces *almost two decades later in adults*

(Schwartz et al., 2011)! This rapidly growing body of research emphasizes the important need for clinical assessment and early intervention for chronically mi-sattuned caregiver–infant communications that are found in contexts of relational attachment trauma.

In contrast to Jonathan's initial presentation a 7-month-old baby is typically curious about his or her environment, interested in the sounds he can make through banging, studying toys, reaching and exploring with hands and sometimes mouth, looking down at the floor when something falls off a table, and babbling. Most 6- to 7-month-olds are good-natured. Their range of emotions tends to be positive, displaying frequent smiling and laughter. But they can also feel angry and frustrated if things do not go as expected (Newton, 2008a). Within this same 7-month period, the regulatory centers in the anterior cingulate are maturing. When optimally functioning, this medial frontal limbic structure, which has direct bidirectional connections with the amygdala, regulates autonomic and endocrine functions. It is also involved in conditioned emotional learning, vocalizations associated with expressing internal states, assessments of motivational content, assigning emotional valence to internal and external stimuli, and human maternal behavior (Devinsky, Morrell, & Vogt, 1995; Lorberbaum et al., 2002; Schore, 2001a). If the relationship itself triggers fear responses more than positive interactions, the infant's anterior cingulate may not acquire the robustness needed to down-regulate the amygdala. A weakened connection in the anterior cingulate could also mean a weak connection to the orbitofrontal cortex, the highest emotional regulation center in the brain. This affective deficit would mean that without a functional change in his mother's regulatory capacity, Jonathan's future development toward emotional regulation would be comprised.

Although Jonathan's communication and exploration improved when interacting with an affectively attuned intern, Jonathan's mother appeared to have no emotional understanding that her son needed her interactive regulation and resonant attunement to support his brain growth and social-emotional development. The fifth treatment goal then was to give his mother some basic information about the critical role of attunement, affect-arousal regulation, security, exploration, and play in brain development.

Intervention Informed by Regulation Theory

Observations based upon the clinical integration of attachment, regulation, and developmental neuroscientific theories set up interventions that target all aspects of the dyadic system at different levels of brain–mind–body in both mother and infant. Jonathan's disorganized attachment is a known risk factor for a spectrum of later forming psychopathologies (Sroufe, Egeland, Carlson, & Collins, 2005), as well as future deficits in right brain socioemotional processing (Schore, 2001b, 2003b). His use of relational withdrawal and dissociative defenses clearly indicated that his emotional and social development was seriously at risk. Thus, immediate intervention targeted at helping him and his mother change, as indicated in the five treatment goals, was needed.

The use of regulation theory to guide both the observations and the theoretical orientation of the assessment specifically informs the clinician regarding risk level. Jonathan's ongoing emotional and social development was seriously at risk. Thus, an approach to helping the dyad change their dysregulating affective dynamics was needed immediately. This intervention was timely not only because of the ongoing relational traumatic context of the insecure attachment bond but also because it was occurring in a period of maximal plasticity, the human brain growth spurt.

Although this chapter is focused on assessment, we offer a general broad overview of the mother–infant therapeutic interventions that followed. In any intervention, a primary mechanism is co-constructing an empathic intersubjective connection with the mother, and in light of her original and recent trauma history, this involves some clinical skill. The burgeoning therapeutic alliance in turn allows the clinician to act as a psychobiological regulator of the mother's dysregulating affective arousal underlying the stressful affects she is experiencing and defending against in the insecure attachment relationship (e.g., fear, aggression, shame). This right amygdala–driven state of hyperarousal interferes with her receiving and resonating with the nonverbal right brain signals Jonathan is communicating. Once this arousal can be begun to be interactively regulated within the clinician–caregiver relationship, the mother's right orbitofrontal and medial frontal areas become more able to resonate with the infant's distress, form a two-way psychobiological feedback loop with him, and create a more efficient system of rupture and repair. In other words, by increasing the mother's regulatory capacities, she can become a more effective interactive regulator of her infant's negative and positive affects.

According to the protocol of Newton, the interventions in this case included review of videos taken during the initial evaluation and other dyadic therapy sessions (Newton, 2008b). Neuroimaging research demonstrates that videos of both positively and negatively valenced social interactions directly activate right hemispheric circuits (Semrud-Clikeman, Fine, & Zhu, 2011). Thus video review is a particularly helpful support for dyadic therapy, as caregivers are less stressed and generally in their more optimal range of arousal themselves when not interacting with their child. Using video feedback as a part of treatment also has been found to be effective for mothers with insecure attachment (e.g., Bakermans-Kranenburg, Juffer, & Van IJzendoorn, 1998; Beebe, 2010). For parents with unresolved relational trauma, it is often easier to "watch, wait, and wonder" (Cohen et al., 1999) about what can be seen in a tape when the sound is off. This is because ANS arousal associated with trauma can be easily triggered by sound.

Over the course of the relational intervention, Jonathan's mother learned how to implicitly match his vocalizations with expressive and warmer voice prosody, facial expression, and interpersonal touch. And as she began to work through her complex feelings about Jonathan's father in individual therapy, she improved in her ability to play with her son using appropriate voicing and following his lead. This therapy would have continued, but Jonathan and his mother left the Village, transitioning from homelessness to living with her sister, a positive situational alteration for them both.

PREVENTION: ENHANCING THE FUTURE DEVELOPMENTAL TRAJECTORY OF THE RIGHT BRAIN

The importance of early intervention is stressed in a number of disciplines: infant mental health, child psychology and psychiatry, developmental psychoanalysis, pediatrics, clinical social work, and developmental neuroscience. Authors in this latter field assert,

> The large increase in total brain volume in the first year of life suggests that this is a critical period in which disruption of developmental processes, as the result of innate genetic abnormalities or as a consequence of environmental insults, may have long-lasting or permanent effects on brain structure and function. . . . Although the first year of life may be a period of developmental vulnerability, it may also be a period in which therapeutic interventions would have the greatest positive affect. (Knickmeyer et al., 2008, p. 12179–12180)

Regulation theory indicates that early interventions that attempt to optimize infant brain development need to utilize assessments of caregiver–infant right brain–to–right brain communication and regulation systems. Thus, clinical training needs to include a neuropsychoanalytic knowledge base of brain development as it unfolds within the developmental stages, as well as a relational psychoanalytic focus on the clinician's use of his or her own instincts, that is, his or her own right brain unconscious. What aspects of the attachment communications and how the clinician uses his or her own subjectivity to evaluate the intersubjective strengths and deficits are critical to an informative assessment. Schore (in press) proposes that, in the first year of life, evolving right-lateralized visual-facial, auditory-prosodic, and tactile-gestural functions of the human social brain can be assessed over the prenatal and postnatal stages of infancy to appraise the ongoing status of emotional and social development. Indeed, current developmental neuroscience concludes that the strong and consistent predominance for the right hemisphere emerges postnatally (Allman, Watson, Tetreault, & Hakeem, 2005), and so this increasing right lateralization trend should be evaluated in infants.

More specifically, in reference to evolving visual-facial functions, Mento et al. (2010) assert, "the right hemisphere would sustain the functions necessary for the survival of the species, such as visuospatial or emotional processes. Consequently, the earlier and faster development of the neural substrates underlying these functions is needed to prevent possible impairment during infancy and childhood" (p. 7). In regard to auditory-prosodic processing, Grossmann et al. (2010) argue that in postnatal periods, "responses to voices and emotional prosody . . . might thus serve as one of potentially multiple markers that can help with an early identification of infants at risk for neurodevelopmental disorders" (p. 856). And in terms of tactile-gestural functions, Montirosso et al. (2010) propose that studies that simultaneously measure gesture and brain functions "would also be useful with samples of high risk-infants whose behavior and brain organization may be compromised" (p. 109). On the matter of high-risk infants, Schore (2010a) now concludes,

> Recent models of early life trauma are altering their focus from deficits in later maturing conscious, verbal, explicit and voluntary behavior, to impairments of early maturing nonconscious, nonverbal, implicit and automatic adaptive social emotional functions. Developmental neuroscience is now moving from studies of later maturing left brain conscious verbal cognitive processes into the early preverbal development of adaptive emotion processing right brain systems in pre- and postnatal periods. (p. 144)

Regulation theory asserts that therapeutic interventions that take place within critical periods can positively impact the experience-dependent maturation of developing brain systems (Schore, 1994, 2001b, 2011). Indeed, an early therapeutic intervention aimed toward increasing maternal sensitivity with a different high-risk group (preterm infants) documents enhanced maturation and connectivity of white matter and improved cerebral micro-structural development (Milgrom et al., 2010). The therapeutic goals of that study also focused on increasing maternal sensitivity and regulation and were very similar to our model: training the parent to recognize signs of infant stress, shutdown mechanisms, and alert-available behavior quality of motor behaviors, facial expressions, posture/muscle/tone; how to optimize interactions and avoid overwhelming infants; touch, vocal, visual, and multisensory stimulation; and normalizing parental feelings.

Earlier we described the transformation of classical attachment theory, a purely psychological theory that focuses on the infant's developing mind (cognitions and mentalization), into modern attachment theory. This paradigm shift alters our clinical approaches to the assessment and treatment of developmental disturbances in early childhood. Shai and Belsky (2011) are now arguing that "Parental reflective functioning (Slade, 2005) concerns the parent's capacity to think reflectively about, and articulate verbally, the child and his mental states as motivators of behavior" (p. 2). They suggest that exclusive reliance on verbal processes does not capture the embodied relational perspective for investigating parent–infant interaction. Modern attachment theory focuses on the nonverbal communication of affective states and the relational regulation of the infant's developing brain–mind–body. Clinical assessments and interventions grounded in regulation theory are centered in the clinician's own bodily based affective responses and instincts; that is, in his or her own right brain nonverbal functions.

A fundamental theme of this chapter is that nonverbal psychobiological attachment communications are located in the right brain. Regulation theory attempts a deeper understanding of critical intersubjective forces that operate at implicit levels of all emotional relationships, beneath the exchanges of language and explicit cognitions. This theoretical perspective attempts to elucidate the interpersonal neurobiological mechanisms that underlie changes in "implicit relational knowing" (Boston Change Process Study Group, 2007, p. 845), which is encoded in the right brain (Schore, 2003a). Infant researchers now assert, "Preverbal communication . . . is the realm of non-consciously regulated intuitive behavior and implicit relational knowledge. Whether information is transferred or shared, which information gets across, and on which level it is 'understood,' *does not necessarily depend on the sender's intention or conscious awareness*" (Papousek, 2007, p. 258, my italics). Recall, the adult orbitofrontal cortex rapidly and thereby implicitly responds to the image of an infant's face in 130 milliseconds, beneath levels of conscious awareness (Kringelbach et al., 2008).

We suggest that attachment interventions that attempt to expand the mother's mentalization functions and conscious explicit awareness of intentions are too focused on the caregiver's left brain. Indeed, neuroimaging research indicates that reflective mentalization is associated with activation of the left inferior frontal gyrus, left posterior superior temporal sulcus, and left temporoparietal function (Nolte et al., 2010). Recall the fMRI study of maternal attachment communication by Lenzi et al. (2009), which documents that the mother's right hemisphere is more involved than the left in emotional processing and mothering. That study also reports that maternal reflective function involved in empathically ascribing her baby's emotion correlates with activation of her *right* anterior insula, a right-lateralized cortical area involved in viscera motor integration and the interoceptive state of the body. In line with regulation theory, these authors conclude that increased activity in the right insula in more empathic mothers represents a greater ability to bodily feel the infant's emotions.

Supporting this idea, a recent study of mothers of young infants looking at photographs of infant facial expressions found no correlation between recognition of infant cues of emotion and either maternal mentalization or executive functioning ability (Turner, Wittkowski, & Hare, 2008). These researchers also report "no significant relationship were found between bonding scores and performance on the executive functioning and mentalization measures" (p. 499), which, they say, suggests that these factors are unrelated. We propose this is because executive functions and mentalization are functions of the left brain, whereas facial emotion recognition and bonding are right brain functions. These and the preceding research data clearly imply that interventions should center not so much on the primary caregiver's left brain explicit, rational verbal metacognitions, theory of mind, and executive functions. Instead, they should focus on her right brain abilities to intuitively read her infant's nonverbal signals and her interoceptive bodily based responses to these communications, and then to implicitly regulate the infant's states of affective arousal. The clinician's trust and use of his or her own interoceptive bodily based responses, intuition, and instinct, which helps foster a right brain–to–right brain connection, is thus essential to the assessment process.

From the perspective of interpersonal neurobiology, models of effective early intervention in the period of the brain growth spurt (the last trimester of pregnancy through the second year) are equated with prevention. For clinicians, an optimal connectivity of the right brain is a prime generator of emotional well-being and is *the socioemotional foundation upon which all other development rests* (Newton, 2008a). Although the right brain initially evolves in prenatal and postnatal critical periods in infancy, it continues to enter later growth spurts (Thatcher, 1997). The attachment relationship sets the developmental trajectory of the right brain at later stages of life and, in this manner, attachment experiences influence all later development.

In all stages of human development, the bodily based functions of the "emotional," "social" right brain hemisphere are centrally involved not only in attachment functions but in attentional processes, autonomic functions, arousal mechanisms, and stress regulation. A healthy right brain is also involved in imagery, play, humor, affiliation, novelty, context, empathy, creativity, metaphor, intuition, and the feeling-laced communications found in eyes, faces, voices, body movements, gestures, and touch (Schore, 2003a, 2003b, in press). The right-lateralized system is dynamic, nonlinear, integrative, and it is the source of what Fogel and Garvey (2007, p. 256) describe as "aliveness." The developing right brain, the biological substrate of the human unconscious, is malleable and indelibly shaped by dyadic attachment transactions. Given the fact that both research and clinical data demonstrate the essential role of this hemispheric system in survival functions, a central tenet of modern attachment theory dictates that the right brain must be a fundamental focus of early clinical assessment, intervention, and prevention programs. Advances in theory, research, and clinical models are converging to emphasize that relational affective communications and interactive regulation lie at the core of the attachment relationship. This clearly means that early assessment and treatment should also be relational.

REFERENCES

Ainsworth, M. D. S., Blehar, M. C., Waters, E., & Wall, S. (1978). *Patterns of attachment. A psychological study of the Strange Situation.* Hillsdale, NJ: Erlbaum.

Allman, J. M., Watson, K. K., Tetreault, N. A., & Hakeem, A. Y. (2005). Intuition and autism: A possible role for Von Economo neurons. *Trends in Cognitive Sciences, 9,* 367–373.

Atzil, S., Hendler, T., & Feldman, R. (2011, August 31). Specifying the neurobiological basis of human attachment: Brain, hormones, and behavior in synchronous and intrusive mothers. *Neuropsychopharmacology*; doi:10.1038/npp.2011.172.

Bakermans-Kranenburg, M. J., Juffer, F., & Van IJzendorn, M. H. (1998). Interventions with video feedback and attachment discussions: Does type of maternal insecurity make a difference? *Infant Mental Health Journal, 19,* 202–219.

Barbas, H. (2007). Flow of information for emotions through temporal and orbitofrontal pathways. *Journal of Anatomy, 211,* 237–249.

Barrett, J., & Fleming, A. S. (2011). Annual research review: All mothers are not created equal: neural and psychobiological perspectives on mothering and the importance of individual differences. *Journal of Child Psychology and Psychiatry, 52,* 368–397.

Basch, M. F. (1976). The concept of affect: A re-examination. *Journal of the American Psychoanalytic Association, 24,* 759–777.

Bayley, N. (1993). *The Bayley scales of infant development* (2nd ed.). San Antonio, TX: Pearson.

Beebe, B. (2010). Mother-infant research informs mother-infant treatment. *Clinical Social Work Journal, 38,* 17–36.

Beebe, B., Jaffe, J., Markese, S., Buck, K., Chen, H., Cohen, P., et al. (2010). The origins of 12-month attachment: A microanalysis of 4-month mother-infant interaction. *Attachment and Human Development, 12,* 3–142.

Benoit, D., & Parker, K. C. H. (1994). Stability and transmission of attachment across three generations. *Child Development, 65,* 1444–1456.

Bestelmeyer, P. E. G., Belin, P., & Grosbas, M.-H. (2011). Right temporal TMS impairs voice detection. *Current Biology, 21,* R838–R839.

Boston Change Process Study Group. (2007). The foundational level of psychodynamic meaning: Implicit process in relation to conflict, defense and the dynamic unconscious. *International Journal of Psychoanalysis, 88,* 843–860.

Bourne, V. J., & Todd, B. K. (2004). When left means right: an explanation of the left cradling bias in terms of right hemisphere specializations. *Developmental Science, 7,* 19–24.

Bowlby, J. (1969). *Attachment and loss: Vol. 1. Attachment.* New York: Basic Books.

Braun, C. M. J., Boulanger, Y., Labelle, M., Khiat, A., Dumont, M., & Maillous, C. (2002). Brain metabolic differences as a function of hemisphere, writing hand preference, and gender. *Laterality, 7,* 97–113.

Carlsson, J., Langercrantz, H., Olson, L., Printz, G., & Bartocci, M. (2008). Activation of the right fronto-temporal cortex during maternal facial recognition in young infants. *Acta Paediatrica, 97,* 1221–1225.

Carmona, J. E., Holland, A. K., & Harrison, D. W. (2009). Extending the functional cerebral systems theory of emotion to the vestibular modality: A systematic and integrative approach. *Psychological Bulletin, 135,* 286–302.

Cerqueira, J., Almeida, O. F. X., & Sousa, N. (2008). The stressed prefrontal cortex. Left? Right! *Brain, Behavior, and Immunity, 22,* 630–638.

Chanen, A. M., Velakoulis, D., Carison, K., Gaunson, K., Wood, S. J., Yuen, H. P., et al. (2008). Orbitofrontal, amygdala and hippocampal volumes in teenagers with first-presentation borderline personality disorder. *Psychiatry Research: Neuroimaging, 163,* 116–125.

Chiron, C., Jambaque, I., Nabbout, R., Lounes, R., Syrota, A., & Dulac, O. (1997). The right brain hemisphere is dominant in human infants. *Brain, 120,* 1057–1065.

Cohen, N. J., Muir, E., Lojkasek, M., Muir, R., Parker, C. J., Barwick, M., & Brown, M. (1999). Watch, wait, and wonder: Testing the effectiveness of a new approach to mother–infant psychotherapy. *Infant Mental Health Journal, 20,* 429–451.

Clark, R. (1985). *The parent–child early relational assessment.* Unpublished instrument. Madison: Department of Psychiatry, University of Wisconsin Medical School.

Cooper, R. P., & Aslin, R. N. (1990). Preference of infant-directed speech in the first month after birth. *Child Development, 61,* 1584–1595.

Dapretto, M., Davies, M. S., Pfeifer, J. H., Scott, A. A., Sigman, M., Bookheimer, S. Y., et al. (2006). Understanding emotions in others: Mirror neuron dysfunction in children with autism spectrum disorders. *Nature Neuroscience, 9,* 28–31.

Darwin, C. R. (1877). A biographical sketch of an infant. *Mind, 2,* 286–294.

Devinsky, O. (2000). Right cerebral hemisphere dominance for a sense of corporeal and emotional self. *Epilepsy & Behavior, 1,* 60–73.

Devinsky, O., Morrell, M. J., & Vogt, B. A. (1995). Contributions of anterior cingulate cortex to behaviour. *Brain, 118,* 279–306.

Devue, C., Collette, F., Balteau, E., Degueldre, C., Luxen, A., Maquet, P., et al. (2007). Here I am: The cortical correlates of visual self-recognition. *Brain Research, 1143,* 169–182.

De Wolff, M. S., & Van IJzendoorn, M. H. (1997). Sensitivity and attachment: A meta-analysis on parental antecedents of infant attachment. *Child Development, 68,* 571–591.

Dixon, A. K. (1998). Ethological strategies for defense in animals and humans: Their role in some psychiatric disorders. *British Journal of Medical Psychology, 71,* 417–445.

Donegan, N. H., Sanislow, C. A., Blumberg, H. P., Fulbright, R. K., Lacadie, C., Skudlarski, P., et al. (2003). Amygdala hyperreactivity in Borderline Personality Disorder: Implications for emotional dysregulation. *Biological Psychiatry, 54,* 1284–1293.

Dorpat, T. L. (2001). Primary process communication. *Psychoanalytic Inquiry, 3,* 448–463.

Feldman, R., Singer, M., & Zagoory, O. (2010). Touch attenuates infants' physiological reactivity to stress. *Brain and Behavior, 13,* 271–278.

Ferber, S. G., Feldman, R., & Makhoul, I. R. (2008). The development of maternal touch across the first year of life. *Early Human Development, 84,* 363–370.

Fernald, A. (1985). Four-month-old infants prefer to listen to motherese. *Infant Behavior and Development, 8,* 181–195.

Fernald, A. (1989). Intonation and communication intent in mothers' speech to infants. Is the melody the message? *Child Development, 60,* 1497–1510.

Fogel, A., & Garvey, A. (2007). Alive communication. *Infant Behavior & Development, 30,* 251–257.

Gallace, A., & Spence, C. (2010). The science of interpersonal touch: An overview. *Neuroscience and Biobehavioral Reviews, 34,* 246–259.

Gogtay, N., Giedd, J. N., Lusk, L., Hayashi, K. M., Greenstein, D., Vaituzis, A. C., et al. (2004). Dynamic mapping of human cortical development during childhood through early adulthood. *Proceedings of the National Academy of Sciences of the United States of America, 101,* 8174–8179.

Grossmann, T., Johnson, M. H., Farroni, T., & Csibra, G. (2007). Social perception in the infant brain: Gamma oscillatory activity in response to eye gaze. *Social Cognitive and Affective Neuroscience, 2,* 284–291.

Grossmann, T., Oberecker, R., Koch, S. P., & Friederici, A. D. (2010). The developmental origins of voice processing in the human brain. *Neuron, 65,* 852–858.

Guedeney, A., Foucault, C., Bougen, E., Larroque, B., & Mentre, F. (2008). Screening for risk factors of relational withdrawal behavior in infants aged 14–18 months. *European Psychiatry, 23,* 150–155.

Gunnar, M. R. (2000). Early adversity and the development of stress reactivity and regulation. In C. A. Nelson (Ed.), *Minnesota symposium on child psychology: Vol. 31. The effects of early adversity on neurobehavioral development* (pp. 163–200). Mahwah, NJ: Erlbaum.

Guo, K., Meints, K., Hall, C., Hall, S., & Mills, D. (2009). Left gaze bias in humans, rhesus monkeys and domestic dogs. *Animal Cognition, 12,* 409–418.

Gupta, R. K., Hasan, K. M., Trivedi, R., Pradhan, M., Das, V., Parikh, N. A., et al. (2005). Diffusion tensor imaging of the developing human cerebrum. *Journal of Neuroscience Research, 81,* 172–178.

Helmeke, C., Ovtscharoff, W., Jr., Poeggel, G., & Braun, K. (2001). Juvenile emotional experience alters synaptic inputs on pyramidal neurons in the anterior cingulate cortex. *Cerebral Cortex, 11,* 717–727.

Hertenstein, M. J. (2002). Touch: Its communicative functions in infancy. *Human Development, 45,* 70–94.

Hertenstein, M. J., & Campos J. J. (2001). Emotion regulation via maternal touch. *Infancy, 2,* 549–566.

Hesse, E., & Main, M. (1999). Second-generation effects of unresolved trauma as observed in nonmaltreating parents: Dissociated, frightened, and threatening parental behavior. *Psychoanalytic Inquiry, 19,* 481–540.

Hesse, E., & Main, M. (2000). Disorganized infant, child, and adult attachment: Collapse in behavioral and attentional strategies. *Journal of the American Psychoanalytic Association, 48,* 1097–1127.

Hesse, E., & Main, M. (2006). Frightened, threatening, and dissociative parental behavior in low-risk samples:. Description, discussion, and interpretations. *Development and Psychopathology, 18,* 309–343.

Homae, F., Watanabe, H., Nakano, T., Asakawa, K., & Taga, G. (2006). The right hemisphere of sleeping infants perceives sentential prosody. *Neuroscience Research, 54,* 276–280.

Howard, M. F., & Reggia, J. A. (2007). A theory of the visual system biology underlying development of spatial frequency lateralization. *Brain and Cognition, 64,* 111–123.

Huggenberger, H. J., Suter, S. E., Reijnen, E., & Schachinger, H. (2000). Cradling side preference is associated with lateralized processing of baby facial expressions in females. *Brain and Cognition, 70,* 67–72.

Insel, T. R., & Fenton, W. S. (2005). Psychiatric epidemiology. It's not just about counting anymore. *Archives of General Psychiatry, 62,* 590–592.

Irle, E., Lange, C., & Sachsse, U. (2005). Reduced size and abnormal asymmetry of parietal cortex in women with Borderline Personality Disorder. *Biological Psychiatry, 57,* 173–182.

Jackson, J. H. (1931). *Selected writings of J. H. Jackson: Vol. I.* London: Hodder and Soughton.

Jean, A. D. L., Stack, D. M., & Fogel, A. (2009). A longitudinal investigation of maternal touching across the first 6 months of life: Age and context effects. *Infant Behavior & Development, 32,* 344–349.

Kaplan, J. T., Aziz-Zadeh, L., Uddin, L. Q., & Iacoboni, M. (2008). The self across the senses: An fMRI study of self-face and self-voice recognition. *Social Cognitive and Affective Neuroscience, 3,* 218–223.

Katz, M., Liu, C., Schaer, M., Parker, K. J., Ottet, M-C., Epps, A., et al. (2009). Prefrontal plasticity and stress inoculation-induced resilience. *Developmental Neuroscience, 31,* 293–299.

Knickmeyer, R. C., Gouttard, S., Kang, C., Evans, D., Wilber, K., Smith, J. K., et al. (2008). A structural MRI study of human brain development from birth to 2 years. *The Journal of Neuroscience, 28*, 12176–12182.

Kringelbach, M., Lehtonen, A., Squire, S., Harvey, A. G., Craske, M. G., Holliday, I. E., et al. (2008). A specific and rapid neural signature for parental instinct. *PLoS One, 3*, 1–6.

Lagercrantz, H., & Ringstedt, T. (2001). Organization of the neuronal circuits in the central nervous system during development. *Acta Paediatrica, 90*, 707–715.

Lavelli, M., & Poli, M.(1998). Early mother–infant interaction during breast- and bottle-feeding. *Infant Behavior & Development, 21*, 667–684.

Leckman, J. F., & March, J. S. (2011). Editorial: Developmental neuroscience comes of age. *Journal of Child Psychology and Psychiatry, 52*, 333–338.

Le Grand, R., Mondloch, C. J., Maurer, D., & Brent, H. P. (2003). Expert face processing requires visual input to the right hemisphere during infancy. *Nature Neuroscience, 6*, 1108–1112.

Lehtonen, J., Kononen, M., Purhonen, M., Partanen, J., & Saarikoski, S. (2002). The effects of feeding on the electroencephalogram in 3- and 6-month-old infants. *Psychophysiology, 39*, 73–79.

Lenzi, D., Trentini, C., Pantano, P., Macaluso, E., Iacoboni, M., Lenzi, G. I., et al. (2009). Neural basis of maternal communication and emotional expression processing during infant preverbal stage. *Cerebral Cortex, 19*, 1124–1133.

Levine, P. A. (1997). *Waking the tiger. Healing trauma.* Berkeley, CA: North Atlantic Books.

Lieberman, A. F., Chu, A., Van Horn, P., & Harris, W. W. (2011). Trauma in early childhood: Empirical evidence and clinical implications. *Development and Psychopathology, 23*, 397–410.

Lorberbaum, J. P., Newman, J. D., Horwitz, A. R., Dubno, J. R., Lydiard, R. B., Hamner, M. B., et al. (2002). A potential role for thalamocingulate circuitry in human maternal behavior. *Biological Psychiatry, 51*, 431–445.

Lyons-Ruth, K. (1999). The two-person unconscious: Intersubjective dialogue, enactive relational representation, and the emergence of new forms of relational organization. *Psychoanalytic Inquiry, 19*, 576–617.

Main, M., & Hesse, E. (1990). Parents' unresolved traumatic experiences are related to infant disorganized attachment status: Is frightened or frightening parental behavior the linking mechanism? In M. Greenberg, D. Cicchetti, & E. M. Cummings (Eds.), *Attachment in the preschool years.* Chicago: University of Chicago Press.

Main, M., & Solomon, J. (1990). Procedures for identifying infants as disorganized/disoriented during the Ainsworth Strange Situation. In M. Greenberg, D. Cicchetti, & E. M. Cummings (Eds.), *Attachment in the preschool years.* Chicago: University of Chicago Press.

McGilchrist, I. (2009). *The master and his emissary.* New Haven, CT: Yale University Press.

Mehta, M. A., Golembo, N. I., Nosarti, C., Colvert, E., Mota, A., Williams, S. C. R., et al. (2009). Amygdala, hippocampal and corpus collosum size following severe early institutional deprivation: The English and Romanian Adoptees Study Pilot. *Child Psychology and Psychiatry, 50*, 943–951.

Mento, G., Suppiej, A., Altoe, G., & Bisiacchi, P. S. (2010). Functional hemispheric asymmetries in humans: Electrophysiological evidence from preterm infants. *European Journal of Neuroscience, 31*, 565–574.

Merikangas, K. R., He, J-p, Burstein, M., Swanson, S. A., Avenevoli, S., Cui, L., et al. (2010). Lifetime prevalence of mental disorders in U.S. adolescents: Results from the National Comorbidity Survey replication—adolescent supplement (NCS-A). *Journal of the American Academy of Child and Adolescent Psychiatry, 49,* 980–989.

Milgrom, J., Newnham, C., Anderson, P. J., Doyle, L. W., Gemmill, A. W., Lee, K., et al. (2010). Early sensitivity training for parents of preterm infants: Impact on the developing brain. *Pediatric Research, 67,* 330–335.

Milne, L., Greenway, P., Guedeney, A., & Larroque, B. (2009). Long term developmental impact of social withdrawal in infants. *Infant Behavior and Development, 32,* 159–166.

Minagawa-Kawai, Y., Matsuoka, S., Dan, I., Naoi, N., Nakamura, K., & Kojima, S. (2009). Prefrontal activation associated with social attachment: Facial-emotion recognition in mothers and infants. *Cerebral Cortex, 19,* 284–292.

Minagawa-Kawai, Y., van der Lely, H., Ramus, F., Sato, Y., Mazuka, R., & Dupoux, E. (2011). Optical brain imaging reveals general auditory and language-specific processing in early infant development. *Cerebral Cortex, 21,* 254–261.

Mollon, P. (1996). *Multiple selves, multiple voices: Working with trauma, violation and dissociation.* Chichester: Wiley.

Montirosso, R., Borgatti, R., & Tronick, E. (2010). Lateral asymmetries in infants' regulatory and communicative gestures. In R. A. Lanius, E. Vermetten, & C. Pain (Eds.), *The impact of early life trauma on health and disease: The hidden epidemic* (pp. 103–111). Cambridge, UK: Cambridge University Press.

Nagy, E. (2006). From imitation to conversation: The first dialogues with human neonates. *Infant and Child Development, 15,* 223–232.

Nakato, E., Otsuka, Y., Kanazawa, S., Yamaguchi, M. K., & Kakigi, R. (2011). Infants' neural responses to facial expressions using near-infrared spectroscopy. *Journal of Vision, 10,* 575; doi:10.1167/10.7.575.

Nakato, E., Otsuka, Y., Kanazawa, S., Yamaguchi, M. K., Watanabe, S., & Kakigi, R. (2009). When do infants differentiate profile face from frontal face? A near-infrared spectroscopic study. *Human Brain Mapping, 30,* 462–472.

Naoi, N., Minagawa-Kawai, Y., Kobayashi, A., Takeuchi, K., Nakamura, K., Yamamoto, J., et al. (2011, August 16). Cerebral responses to infant-directed speech and the effect of talker familiarity. *NeuroImage,* 1053–8119.

New, A. S., Hazlett, E. A., Buschsbaum, M. S., Goodman, M., Mitelman, S. A., Newmark, R., et al. (2007). Amygdala-prefrontal disconnection in Borderline Personality Disorder. *Neuropsychopharmacology, 32,* 1629–1640.

Newton, R.P. (2006). Speaking out of both sides of the mouth: The unnoticed road to childhood disorganization. *Psychologist-Psychoanalyst, 26,* 17–21.

Newton, R. P. (2008a). *The attachment connection.* Oakland, CA: New Harbinger.

Newton, R. P. (2008b). Dyadic therapy for homeless parents and children. In C. Schaefer, J. McCormick, P. Kelly-Zion, & A. Ohnogi (Eds.), *Play therapy for very young children.* Lanham, MD: Rowman & Littlefield.

Nolte, T., Hudac, C., Mayes, L. C., Fonagy, P., Blatt, S. J., & Pelphrey, K. (2010). The effect of attachment-related stress on the capacity to mentalize: An fMRI investigation of the biobehavioral switch model. *Journal of the American Psychoanalytic Association, 58,* 566–573.

Noriuchi, M., Kikuchi, Y., & Senoo, A. (2008). The functional neuroanatomy of maternal love: Mother's response to infant's attachment behaviors. *Biological Psychiatry, 63,* 415–423.

Otsuka, Y., Nakato, E., Kanazawa, S., Yamaguchi, M. K., Watanabe, S., & Kakigi, R. (2007). Neural activation to upright and inverted faces in infants measured by near infrared spectroscopy. *NeuroImage, 34,* 399–406.

Panksepp, J. (2008). The power of the word may reside in the power of affect. *Integrative Psychological & Behavioral Science, 42,* 47–55.

Papousek, M. P. (2007). Communication in early infancy: An arena of intersubjective learning. *Infant Behavior & Development, 30,* 258–266.

Parsons, C. E., Young, K. S., Murray, L., Stein, A., & Kringelbach, M. L. (2010). The functional neuroanatomy of the evolving parent-infant relationship. *Progess in Neurobiology, 91,* 220–241.

Perani, D., Saccuman, M. C., Scifo, P., Spada, D., Andreolli, G., Rovelli, R., et al. (2010). Functional specializations for music processing in the human newborn brain. *Proceedings of the National Academy of Sciences of the United States of America, 107,* 4758–4763.

Porges, S. W. (1995). Orienting in a defensive world: Mammalian modifications of our evolutionary heritage. A polyvagal theory. *Psychophysiology, 32,* 301–318.

Porges, S. W. (2001). The polyvagal theory: Phylogenetic substrates of a social nervous system. *International Journal of Psychophysiology, 42,* 123–146.

Porges, S. W. (2007). The polyvagal perspective. *Biological Psychology, 74,* 116–143.

Porges, S. W. (2009). The polyvagal theory: New insights into adaptive reactions of the autonomic nervous system. *Cleveland Clinic Journal of Medicine, 76*(Suppl. 2), S86–S90.

Previc, F. H. (1991). A general theory concerning the prenatal origins of cerebral lateralization in humans. *Psychological Review, 98,* 299–334.

Putnam, F. W. (1997). *Dissociation in children and adolescents: a developmental perspective.* New York: Guilford Press.

Recordati, G. (2003). A thermodynamic model of the sympathetic and parasympathetic nervous systems. *Autonomic Neuroscience: Basic and Clinical, 103,* 1–12.

Reissland, N., Hopkins, B., Helms, B., & Williams, B. (2009). Maternal stress and depression and the lateralization of infant cradling. *Journal of Child Psychology and Psychiatry, 50,* 263–269.

Rinaman, L., Levitt, P., & Card, J. P. (2000). Progressive postnatal assembly of limbic-autonomic circuits revealed by central transneuronal transport of pseudorabies virus. *Journal of Neuroscience, 20,* 2731–2741.

Robertson, J. (1952). *A two-year-old goes to hospital.* [Film]. New York: New York University Film Library.

Roth, T. L., & Sweatt, J. D. (2011). Annual research review: epigenetic mechanisms and environmental shaping of the brain during sensitive periods of development. *Journal of Child Psychology and Psychiatry, 52,* 398–408.

Schore, A. N. (1994). *Affect regulation and the origin of the self.* Mahwah, NJ: Erlbaum.

Schore, A. N. (1996). The experience-dependent maturation of a regulatory system in the orbital prefrontal cortex and the origin of developmental psychopathology. *Development and Psychopathology, 8,* 59–87.

Schore A. N. (1999). Commentary on emotions: neuro-psychoanalytic views. *Neuropsychoanalysis, 1,* 49–55.

Schore, A. N. (2000). Attachment and the regulation of the right brain. *Attachment and Human Development, 2,* 23–47.

Schore, A. N. (2001a). The effects of a secure attachment relationship on right brain development, affect regulation, and infant mental health. *Infant Mental Health Journal*, 22, 7–66.

Schore, A. N. (2001b). The effects of relational trauma on right brain development, affect regulation, and infant mental health. *Infant Mental Health Journal*, 22, 201–269.

Schore, A. N. (2002). Dysregulation of the right brain: A fundamental mechanism of traumatic attachment and the psychopathogenesis of posttraumatic stress disorder. *Australian and New Zealand Journal of Psychiatry*, 36, 9–30.

Schore, A. N. (2003a). *Affect regulation and the repair of the self.* New York: Norton.

Schore, A. N. (2003b). *Affect dysregulation and disorders of the self.* New York: Norton.

Schore, A. N. (2005). Attachment, affect regulation, and the developing right brain: Linking developmental neuroscience to pediatrics. *Pediatrics in Review*, 26, 204–212.

Schore, A. N. (2009). Attachment trauma and the developing right brain: Origins of pathological dissociation. In P. F. Dell & J. A. O'Neil (Eds.), *Dissociation and the dissociative disorders: DMS-V and beyond* (pp. 107–141). New York: Routledge.

Schore, A. N. (2010a). Synopsis. In R. A. Lanius, E. Vermetten, & C. Pain (Eds.), *The impact of early life trauma on health and disease: The hidden epidemic* (pp. 1142–1147). Cambridge, UK: Cambridge University Press.

Schore, A. N. (2010b). Relational trauma and the developing right brain. The neurobiology of broken attachment bonds. In T. Baradon (Ed.), *Relational trauma in infancy* (pp. 19–47). London: Routledge.

Schore, A. N. (2010c). A neurobiological perspective of the work of Berry Brazelton. In B. M. Lester & J. D. Sparrow (Eds.), *Nurturing families of young children building on the legacy of T. Berry Brazelton* (pp. 141–153). New York: Wiley Blackwell.

Schore, A. N. (2011). The right brain implicit self lies at the core of psychoanalysis. *Psychoanalytic Dialogues*, 21, 75–100.

Schore, A. N. (in press). Bowlby's environment of evolutionary adaptedness: Recent studies on the interpersonal neurobiology of attachment and emotional development. In D. Narvaez, J. Panksepp, A. Schore, & T. Gleason (Eds.), *Evolution, early experience and human development: From research to practice and policy.* New York: Oxford University Press.

Schore, J. R., & Schore, A. N. (2008). Modern attachment theory: The central role of affect regulation in development and treatment. *Clinical Social Work Journal*, 36, 9–20.

Schwartz, C. E., Kunwar, P. S., Greve, D. N., Kagan, J., Snidman, N. C., & Bloch, R. B. (2011). A phenotype of early infancy predicts reactivity of the amygdala in male adults. *Molecular Psychiatry*; doi:10.1038/mp.2011.96.

Semrud-Clikeman, M., & Hynd, G. W. (1990). Right hemisphere dysfunction in nonverbal learning disabilities: Social, academic, and adaptive functioning in adults and children. *Psychological Bulletin*, 107, 196–209.

Semrud-Clikeman, M., Fine, J. G., & Zhu, D. C. (2011). The role of the right hemisphere for processing of social interactions in normal adults using functional magnetic resonance imaging. *Neuropsychobiology*, 64, 47–51.

Shai, D., & Belsky, J. (2011, June 22). When words just won't do: Introducing parental embodied mentalizing. *Child Development Perspectives*, 1–8; doi: 10.1111/j.1750–8606 .2011.00181.x.

Shonkoff, J. P. (2011). Protecting brains, not simply stimulating minds. *Science*, 333, 982–983.

Shonkoff, J. P., Boyce, W. T., & McEwen, B. S. (2009). Neuroscience, molecular biology, and the childhood roots of health disparities building a new framework for health promotion and disease prevention. *The Journal of the American Medical Association, 301,* 2252–2259.

Siegel, D. J. (1999). *The developing mind: Toward a neurobiology of interpersonal experience.* New York: Guilford Press.

Sieratzki, J. S., & Woll, B. (1996). Why do mothers cradle their babies on the left? *The Lancet, 347,* 1746–1748.

Slade, A. (2005). Parental reflective functioning: An introduction. *Attachment and Human Development, 7,* 269–281.

Spitz, R. A. (1946). *Grief: A peril in infancy.* [Film]. New York: New York University Film Library.

Sroufe, L. A., Egeland, B., Carlson, E. A., & Collins, W. A. (2005). *The development of the person: The Minnesota study of risk and adaptation from birth to adulthood.* New York: Guilford Press.

Stern, D. (2004). *The present moment in psychotherapy and everyday life.* New York: Norton.

Stern, D. (2005). Intersubjectivity. In E. S. Person, A. M. Cooper, & G. O. Gabbard (Eds.), *Textbook of psychoanalysis* (pp. 77–92). Washington, DC: American Psychiatric Publishing.

Stern, D., Spieker, S., Barnett, R. K., & MacKain, K. (1983). Intonation contours as signals of maternal speech to prelinguistic infants. *Developmental Psychology, 18,* 727–735.

Stevenson, C. W., Halliday, D. M., Marsden, C. A., & Mason, R. (2008). Early life programming of hemispheric lateralization and synchronization in the adult medial prefrontal cortex. *Neuroscience, 155,* 852–863.

Sullivan, R. M., & Gratton, A. (2002). Prefrontal cortical regulation of hypothalamic-pituitary-adrenal function in the rat and implications for psychopathology: Side matters. *Psychoneuroendocrinology, 27,* 99–114.

Sullivan, R. M., & Dufresne, M. M. (2006). Mesocortical dopamine and HPA axis regulation: Role of laterality and early environment. *Brain Research, 1076,* 49–59.

Sun, T., Patoine, C., Abu-Khalil, A., Visvader, J., Sum, E., Cherry, T. J., et al. (2005). Early asymmetry of gene transcription in embryonic human left and right cerebral cortex. *Science, 308,* 1794–1798.

Suter, S. E., Huggenberger, H. J., & Schachinger, H. (2007). Cold pressor stress reduces left cradling preference in nulliparous human females. *Stress, 10,* 45–51.

Telkemeyer, S., Rossi, S., Koch, S. P., Nierhaus, T., Steinbrink, J., Poeppel, D., et al. (2009). Sensitivity of newborn auditory cortex to the temporal structure of sounds. *Journal of Neuroscience, 29,* 14726–14733.

Thatcher, R. W. (1997). Neuroimaging of cyclical cortical reorganization during human development. In R. W. Thatcher, G. Reid Lyon, J. Rumsey, & N. Krasnegor (Eds.), *Developmental neuroimaging. Mapping the development of brain and behavior* (pp. 91–106). San Diego, CA: Academic Press.

Thierry, G., Vihman, M., & Roberts, M. (2003). Familiar words capture the attention of 11-month-olds in less than 250 ms. *NeuroReport, 14,* 2307–2310.

Trainor, L. J., Austin, C. M., & Desjardins, R. N. (2000). Is infant-directed speech prosody a result of the vocal expression of emotion? *Psychological Science, 11,* 188–195.

Trevarthen, C. (2001). Intrinsic motives for companionship in understanding: Their origin, development, and significance for infant mental health. *Infant Mental Health Journal, 22,* 95–131.

Trevarthen, C., & Aitken, K. J. (2001). Infant intersubjectivity: Research, theory, and clinical application. *Journal of Child Psychology and Psychiatry, 42*, 3–48.

Tucker, D. M., & Moller, L. (2007). The metamorphosis. Individuation of the adolescent brain. In D. Romer & E. F. Walker (Eds.), *Adolescent psychopathology and the developing brain. Integrating brain and prevention science* (pp. 85–102). Oxford, UK: Oxford University Press.

Turner, J. M., Wittkowski, A., & Hare, D. J. (2008). The relationship of maternal mentalization and executive functioning to maternal recognition of infant cues and bonding. *British Journal of Psychology, 99*, 499–512.

Tzourio-Mazoyer, N., De Schonen, S., Crivello, F., Reutter, B., Aujard, Y., & Mazoyer, B. (2002). Neural correlates of woman face processing by 2-month-old infants. *NeuroImage, 15*, 454–461.

Van IJzendoorn, M. H., & De Wolff, M. S. (1997). In search of the absent father—Meta-analysis of infant–father attachment: A rejoinder to our discussants. *Child Development, 68*, 604–609.

Van IJzendoorn, M. H., Schuengel, C., & Bakermans-Kranenburg, M. J. (1999). Disorganized attachment in early childhood: Meta-analysis of precursors, concomitants, and sequelae. *Development and Psychopathology, 11*, 225–249.

Wang, J., Rao, H., Wetmore, G. S., Furlan, P. M., Korczykowski, M., Dinges, D. F., & Detre, J. A. (2005). Perfusion functional MRI reveals cerebral blood flow pattern under psychological stress. *Proceedings of the National Academy of Sciences of the United States of America, 102*, 17804–17809.

Weatherill, R. P., Almerigi, J. B., Levendosky, A. A., Bogat, G. A., von Eye, A., & Harris, L. J. (2004). Is maternal depression related to side of infant holding? *International Journal of Behavioral Development, 28*, 421–427.

Weaver, I. C. G., Cervoni, N., Champagne, F. A., D'Alessio, A. C., Sharma, S., Seckl, J. R., et al. (2004). Epigenetic programming by maternal behavior. *Nature Neuroscience, 7*, 847–854.

Winnicott, D. W. (1960/1965). Ego distortion in terms of true and false self. In D. W. Winnicott, *The maturational processes and the facilitating environment. Studies in the theory of emotional development* (pp. 140–152). Madison, CT: International Universities Press.

Winnicott, D. W. (1965). *The maturational processes and the facilitating environment. Studies in the theory of emotional development.* Madison, CT: International Universities Press.

Wittling, W. (1997). The right hemisphere and the human stress response. *Acta Physiologica Scandinavica, 161* (Supplement 640), 55–59.

Yamada, H., Sadato, N., Konishi, Y., Muramoto, S., Kimura, K., Tanaka, M., et al. (2000). A milestone for normal development of the infantile brain detected by functional MRI. *Neurology, 55*, 218–223.

CHAPTER 12

Family Law and the Neuroscience of Attachment: An Interview in *Family Court Review*

With Jennifer McIntosh

Note of Editor of *Family Court Review*: In this far-reaching interview, Allan Schore, renowned scientist, clinical psychologist and clinical neuropsychologist, considers the place of neuroscience in facilitating developmental knowledge and better decision making in family law matters. He details current science on the neurology of attachment formation, the function of early caregiving relationships, gender, neuroscience perspectives on conflict and family violence, and implications for parenting arrangements. At the meta level, Schore describes the responsibilities of the family law system in promoting the development of the child. On the faculty of the Department of Psychiatry and Biobehavioral Sciences, UCLA, David Geffen School of Medicine, Schore is on the editorial staff of 35 journals in various academic and clinical fields. His integration of neuroscience with attachment theory is documented in three seminal volumes, *Affect Regulation and the Origin of the Self*, *Affect Dysregulation and Disorders of the Self*, and *Affect Regulation and the Repair of the Self*, as well as numerous articles and chapters. He has justifiably earned the nickname of "America's Bowlby."

ATTACHMENT THEORY AND THE EMOTIONAL REVOLUTION IN NEUROSCIENCE

JENNIFER MCINTOSH: Allan SCHORE, welcome to the *Family Court Review*. It is a privilege to have this opportunity to hear from you. Let me begin with this. Dramatic developments in neuroscience during the recent "decade of the brain" have blown some cobwebs off attachment theory and reinstated it as a central, evidence-based theory of development. You have been working in the epicenter of these developments. What would you like to tell us about that?

ALLAN N. SCHORE: First off, thank you for inviting me to be part of this extremely important project. I agree that attachment theory, first created by the psychiatrist-psychoanalyst John Bowlby over 50 years ago, is now revitalized, particularly by its deep connections with neuroscience. At this point in time, we have in attachment theory a coherent theory of development that is grounded in both psychological science and neuroscience, and thereby is on a much firmer ground than it used to be. The practical applications of this interdisciplinary theory of emotional and social development have expanded tremendously, and attachment theory is now bridging many gaps between the academic world and the clinical world. This essential information about how the early beginnings of human life indelibly impact all later stages is ready to be delivered into the legal system, and as far as I understand, there is a real hunger for this type of updated information. Our basic understanding of human infancy has changed dramatically, and family law, like other professions, needs to be aware of this information in order to make informed legal decisions.

MCINTOSH: Let's start with recent advances in science, and later talk in detail about the implications of this new knowledge for family law.

SCHORE: In the last 10 years, the rapid growth in attachment theory has allowed it to become the most complex theory of the development of the brain/mind/body available to science. I think the reason for that, as opposed to other developmental theories, is because attachment theory, from its origins, has always been an integration of psychology and biology. In his classic 1969 volume, *Attachment*, Bowlby used the perspectives of both Freud and Darwin in order to understand the instinctive mother–infant bond in terms of psychoanalysis and behavioral biology, and he even speculated about the brain systems involved in the evolutionary mechanism of attachment. Today, it is clear that framing attachment solely in terms of psychology is inadequate. And so we are now exploring the underlying neurological and biological mechanisms of attachment. Neuroscience allows us to know in greater detail and in real time the mechanisms of early attachment relationships and how they shape the formation of internal psychic structures across the life span.

MCINTOSH: We frequently hear reference to an "emotional revolution" in neuroscience. This is a short hand way of describing a paradigm shift in the science of human development. Can you explain that for us?

SCHORE: It is important to note that, from the beginning, John Bowlby said that the attachment bond between mother and infant was defined as an emotional bond, and not just a sharing of cognitive information. (I use the term "mother" because the first central attachment figure is usually the mother—I'll elaborate on gender later, because I know this is of interest and importance in family law). When the theory was created in the 1960s, psychology was dominated by behavioral models, and the focus was on attachment behavior. Psychology shifted in the 70s and 80s when cognitive psychology became dominant, and so the focus moved toward cognitive representations and internal working models of attachment. But by the 1990s research, theoretical, and clinical science began a deeper study of the problem of emotion, the central core of attachment theory. In 1994, in my first book, *Affect Regulation and the Origin of the Self: The Neurobiology of Emotional Development*, I integrated then current studies of brain development and developmental psychology of the first 2 years of life to create a theory of social-emotional development. Over the last two decades we have seen an explosion of studies on emotion and with them a paradigm shift. Beginning in "the decade of the brain," neuroscience, especially affective and social neuroscience, began to explore the brain system involved in not just behavior, language, and cognition, but the processing of bodily-based emotional and social information, constructs central to attachment theory.

INTERPERSONAL NEUROBIOLOGY: ATTACHMENT DRIVES BRAIN DEVELOPMENT

McINTOSH: Family law professionals are curious to know more of this era of brain science, how it is relevant to them, and where attachment fits in. What is interpersonal neurobiology, and what has it got to do with understanding attachment and children's development?

SCHORE: Essentially, interpersonal neurobiology explains how early social-emotional experience indelibly influences later experience—by impacting and altering the developing brain. It also describes the mechanism by which early attachment is central to the organization of the individual's personality, including the individual's ability to cope with later stress. In other words, the emotional relational environment provided by the primary caregiver shapes, for better or worse, the experience-dependent maturation of the brain systems involved in attachment functions that are accessed throughout the life span.

In the last 15 years, two major trends of research have converged to confirm the basic tenets of interpersonal neurobiology. Number one, from psychology: as opposed to earlier models that posited the beginnings of personality between the third and fourth year, we now have good evidence that the prenatal and postnatal stages of human infancy represent the critical period for the organization of the central dimensions of the personality. Number two, from neuroscience: the peak interval of attachment formation overlaps the most rapid period of massive human brain growth that takes place from the last trimester of pregnancy through the end of the 3rd year.

McINTOSH: Attachment is far more than it used to be in "Bowlby 101" classes taught in the 70s and 80s. You are describing current knowledge that positions attachment as a central driver of brain development, not just an evolutionary mechanism designed to help us survive.

SCHORE: Right. We now know that the evolutionary mechanism of attachment does more than just provide the baby with a sense of safety and security. Rather, attachment drives brain development, five-sixths of which happens postnatally. In fact the brain grows more extensively and more rapidly in infancy than at any other stage of life. It more than doubles by 12 months, and 40,000 new synapses are formed every second in the infant's brain. But, importantly, this brain growth is influenced by "social forces," and therefore is "experience-dependent." It requires not only nutrients, but the emotional experiences embedded in the relationship it co-creates with the primary caregiver.

There is now agreement in my field that the essential task of the 1st year of human life is the co-creation of a secure attachment bond of emotional communication between the infant and his/her primary caregiver. The baby communicates its burgeoning positive emotional states (e.g., joy, excitement) and negative emotional states (e.g., fear, anger) to the caregiver so that she can then regulate them. The attachment relationship shapes the ability of the baby to communicate with not just the mother, but ultimately with other human beings. This survival function—the capacity to communicate one's own subjective internal states to other human beings—is the basis of all later social relations. Thus, the major developmental accomplishments of infancy are the capacity to communicate emotional states, and subsequently the capacity for self-regulation, which is the ability to regulate emotional states.

McINTOSH: Your work describes the primary attachment as a continuous relationship that is uniquely designed to facilitate the baby's growing ability to know and communicate his or her needs. What makes that relationship unique?

SCHORE: Number one: essentially the attachment relationship is emotional and bodily-based. Number two: the essential communication involved in attachment formation in the first year is entirely nonverbal. (It is not until the middle of the second year that the left hemisphere and the speech centers in Broca's and Wernicke's language areas come online.) The baby's ability to communicate his/her emotional states is now seen as a survival function, and nature has made sure that emotion circuits come online before the verbal language circuits.

EMOTION: THE LANGUAGE OF ATTACHMENT

SCHORE: Bowlby originally stated that mother–infant attachment communications are "accompanied by the strongest of feelings and emotions." I think in some ways we've lost sight of this, with such a heavy emphasis on cognition, and on mind over body.

Developmental neuroscience research now demonstrates that the limbic system processes emotional information, and the autonomic nervous system is responsible for the bodily based/somatic aspects of emotion. Studies show that both are in a critical period of growth in the first and much of the 2nd year, and that the maturation of these emotional brain circuits is significantly influenced by early socioemotional experience. We also know that the right hemisphere is more connected into the limbic and autonomic systems, and that it develops pre- and postnatally, before the left hemisphere. The brain systems involved in attachment and emotion are thus located in the right (and not left) hemisphere.

Attachment forms through communications that occur essentially between the right brain of the baby and the right brain of the primary caregiver. They are not transmitted through language, or semantics. Rather, from the beginning and indeed for the rest of the life span, these are nonverbal, social-emotional, bodily-based communications. Specifically, attachment communication is expressed in (1) visual, face-to-face transactions; (2) auditory expressions of the emotional tone of the voice; and (3) tactile-gestural cues of the body. All of these are performed very rapidly by the right brains of the infant and mother. For the rest of the life span, we use these nonverbal communication skills in all of our interpersonal relationships.

Here's another new insight about attachment, informed by neuroscience. Bowlby thought that the key to the attachment bond was that the mother was soothing, or regulating the baby's negative fear states. There is now strong evidence that the secure primary attachment figure not only down-regulates negative states, but up-regulates positive emotions in play states. When we are evaluating an attachment relationship, we should be looking at not only the ability to calm and soothe, but also the ability to stimulate the baby into states of joy, interest and excitement. These positive emotions are important for brain development. So what we have in the attachment relationship is the developing ability of the child to communicate and to regulate positive and negative emotional states, and both are components of healthy self-esteem.

McINTOSH: What are the essential developmental experiences an infant requires for optimal brain development?

SCHORE: Right brain development is not just genetically encoded; it requires these human intimate experiences for its optimal growth. What the child is looking for, and what the child is gaining from the attachment relationship and imprinting into the circuits of its maturing right brain are these critical emotional, right brain–to–right brain experiences. How those experiences are provided or not provided by the primary caregiver is going to impact the wiring of the circuits of that right brain. The mother's history of her own secure or insecure emotional experiences, including when she was an infant to her mother, are stored in her right brain, creating what we call the epigenetic transmission of attachment patterns across generations.

McINTOSH: I want to pull up here for a minute. My concern is that some readers will miss the subtlety of what you are saying, because they may get caught on the use of a gendered language which places mother as the primary attachment figure. You flagged this earlier: let's go further into that territory now.

THE FUNCTION OF A PRIMARY CAREGIVER
AND THE ROLE OF GENDER

McINTOSH: When parents of an infant separate and are involved in a divorce dispute, family law sometimes grapples with the idea of a primary caregiver. It is a much debated topic, with strong socio-political origins, and gender tensions. In neurological terms, is there a primary caregiver, why, and what is the function of the primary caregiver?

SCHORE: To my mind there is one single "primary" caregiver. A good definition of the primary caregiver is that, under stress, the baby moves towards this single person in order to seek the external regulation he/she needs at the moment. Under stress, the baby will usually turn to the primary caregiver, not the secondary caregivers. In most family settings, things are building with the father in the first year and he is definitely getting a good sense of who the baby is, but the primary bond in most cases is to the mother in the first year and then, in addition to her, to the father and others in the 2nd and 3rd years.

The idea that everything before birth is genetic and everything after birth is learned is a fallacy. Learning goes on in the fetus, when the brain is in a rapid period of maturation from the last trimester of the pregnancy through the 2nd year. This means that in the last trimester, the biological mother's emotional state influences the infant's developing brain. We know that the stress hormone, cortisol, crosses the placenta, so the emotional state of the mother at that point in time has already begun to influence the infant. This continues after birth, when the mother usually is the one who continues to act as a regulator of the baby's emotional states. The brain is immature and does not have these regulatory mechanisms in place until somewhere in the 2nd year, so mother acts as an external regulator to the baby's stressful states and must continue to do this until the baby internalizes this soothing function into its own right-brain circuits.

Studies now show that one parent is the primary organizer of the infant's stress states, and in nuclear setups, this is usually the mother. The hypothalamic-pituitary-adrenal axis (HPA axis) is the stress-regulating axis in the brain, and its early organization is impacted specifically by the mother–infant attachment relationship. With emotional access to the empathic primary caregiver's calming and soothing functions, the child can take in interactive regulation and comfort and come out of a stressful fear or depressed state. Ultimately this allows for the further maturation of the child's right brain, which is dominant for the control of vital functions supporting survival and enabling the organism to cope with stresses and challenges. Indeed the right orbitofrontal cortex, which begins a critical period of maturation at the end of the 1st year, comes to act as the control center of attachment and the executive regulator of the right brain.

McINTOSH: Mother is the primary organizer of the infant's stress states? Does that reflect where research is up to, or does it reflect a known neurological difference between men and women as caretakers of infants?

SCHORE: First, by far, most of the studies in both attachment theory and neuroscience are on the impact of the mother on the baby's brain. And again, what they are showing is that her sensitivity and receptivity to stressful shifts in the infant's affective states allow her to function as a psychobiological regulator, and ultimately to impact the wiring of the child's developing right limbic system and HPA axis. Second, we know that there is a difference between the father and the mother even in the 1st year, and that the father's play is more arousing and energetic, while the mother's is more calming. There are extensive differences between females and males in terms of the ability to process emotional information.

Females show an enhanced capacity to more effectively read nonverbal communications and to empathically resonate with emotional states than men. When it comes to reading facial expressions, tone of voice, and gestures, women are generally better than men. This is why, in all human societies, the very young and the very old are often attended to by females. Furthermore, the orbitofrontal cortex, the control center of attachment and the brain's major system of affect regulation, is in general larger in females, although there is variation in size and complexity, dependent on early attachment experiences.

MCINTOSH: And the role of fathers? Are we talking about a sociologically based gender difference in rearing? On balance, are mothers predisposed in terms of their brain makeup to facilitate a certain aspect of infant development?

SCHORE: The whole area of the father has been less well studied, and research in this area has been overlooked, if not suppressed. Attachment workers have suggested that although the mother's soothing is essential to the child's attachment security, the father's arousing play is thought to be critical for the child's competent exploration of the physical world. In 1994, I proposed that the mother has a major impact on the baby's brain in the first year of right brain dominance, and the father in the 2nd year, when the left brain enters a growth spurt. There is now a small but significant body of studies showing that the father differentially impacts brain development. These are newer studies, and not many of them are coming out of the United States. Braun's laboratory in Germany has offered a series of studies clearly demonstrating that paternal care affects synaptic development of the developing brain. Studying a species that is similar to humans in that both mother and father act as caregivers, this body of work shows the father's play behavior has a different impact on the limbic system and that deprivation of a father impacts the left hemisphere more so than the right.

Now, Bowlby originally proposed that the infant first has experiences with a supportive mother and "a little later, father." My read of the current research is that the child's first bond is to the primary caregiver's (the mother's) right brain. At a later point, the 2nd year, the child will bond to the father if he is also providing regular care. At this later point, separation from the father will also elicit a stress reaction from the baby, the same as it would with separation from the mother. The second attachment and separation reaction is thus occurring at a later point in time than it would for the mother. Expanding upon these ideas I've suggested that although the mother is essential to the infant's capacity for fear regulation in the first year, in the second the father becomes critically involved in both the male and female toddler's aggression regulation.

MCINTOSH: I wonder if the gender distinction is an historic artifact from Bowlby's era? Would the finding hold today? In contemporary society, there are diverse family units out there, families with two mothers or two fathers, families where mothers have died, or where one parent spends long periods away working inter-state, or overseas at war, and so on.

SCHORE: In those diverse situations, we are still looking at how the parent's right brain shapes the infant's right brain. There are differences in the wiring of the emotion processing limbic system between males and females, influenced by individual attachment history. That being the case, what has been overlooked when it comes to gender is not biological but psychological gender. In both males and females, there are different early internalizations around gender. Both developing males and females usually first internalize a maternal and then a paternal attachment. In the 2nd year, in both sexes, psychological gender (the sense of maleness or femaleness) is not only genetically encoded, but also epigenetically molded by early experiences with masculine and feminine caregivers. This allows access to affiliative and nurturant feminine aspects, and to pragmatic masculine aspects of the evolving personality.

Ultimately, what the infant needs for a secure attachment is access to a well-functioning adult right brain that can empathically receive and regulate the infant's emotional communications. It is not just the gender but the attachment security and emotional health of the parent that is the key to who can best provide right brain primary caregiving in the 1st year. Indeed, securely attached males also have efficient right orbitofrontal systems. When you see families where there is a switch, where the father is the primary caregiver and nurturer, and he's home and the mother's out in the world, I would suggest the couple has figured out together who's better at what, and have agreed to divide their roles accordingly. It could very well be that that infant now has optimal access to the more efficient right hemisphere in that particular set of parents.

On the other hand, an insecure "disorganized-disoriented" mother with a history of abuse and/or neglect, even though she's female, is going to have serious difficulties in providing right brain functions for her infant. Some other family member might be a better interactive regulator of her baby. That's important. Recall I earlier said the primary caregiver shapes, for better or worse, the experience-dependent maturation of the brain. A major predisposition to psychopathology lies in having early repeated care with a primary caregiver who, instead of regulating, chronically dysregulates the infant's right brain.

CONSEQUENCES OF STRESSING THE ATTACHMENT SYSTEM DURING CRITICAL PERIODS

McIntosh: You have been referring throughout to an evolving hierarchy of attachment. This seems a central concept for family law to consider: that attachment needs at age one are different from age three, and that change in caregiving arrangements will be felt differently at these stages, and will have different developmental impacts, depending on stage and security of attachment formation.

Schore: Absolutely. A fundamental principle of developmental science is that one cannot understand the impact of any effect on the child without understanding the stage of development. Attachment in the first year of life and into the second, when the emotional right brain circuits are in a critical period of formation, is different from attachment in the 3rd or 4th year of life, when the system is mature. In the 1st year, and much of the 2nd, separation from the primary caregiver and change in caregiving arrangements are potent stressors of the right brain, and will alter its early maturation. To interpersonally stress a system while it is organizing in the 1st year will have a much more negative impact than if you exposed the child to the same stressor at 3 years.

In the 3rd and 4th year of life, most children can begin to use both hemispheres to deal with stress. In the 1st and much of the 2nd year an infant has no access to left hemispheric verbal functions, since these do not begin to mature until the 2nd year. When under attachment stress, the baby only has access to a still maturing right hemisphere, and thereby an immature, inefficient system of internal stress regulation. So under moderate to severe stress the infant is dependent on the external regulation provided by the mother's right hemisphere.

IMPLICATIONS FOR CARE ARRANGEMENTS

SCHORE: In order to co-create a secure attachment, the infant seeks proximity to the primary caregiver, who must be subjectively perceived as predictable, consistent, and emotionally available. A caregiving arrangement in this essential time period that deprives the infant of this proximity, consistency and emotional availability will inhibit the development of the attachment system. Prolonged and repeated removal from the regulating primary caregiver not only deprives the child of an external coping mechanism, it also negatively impacts the ongoing maturation of the right brain. Let me say that in another way. If you expose a 9-year-old child, or a 29-year-old to an attachment stressor (say loss of an important emotional relationship), you will see an established system disorganize and regress, with a temporary loss of function. On the other hand, if you stress the system at for example 9 months, while it is still in a critical period of growth, you will alter the trajectory of its development. Consequently these internal regulatory structures will not have the maturity and will not have the efficiency to regulate the individual's emotional state when she is challenged by future interpersonal stressors

On the matter of a primary caregiver, neuroscience indicates that pre- and postnatally, the mother's right brain is the key to this role. This is time sensitive, as it is occurring in early critical periods. Neuroscience uses the term "critical periods," while developmental psychology uses the term "sensitive periods" (which I think downgrades the importance of the timing and the later impact of emotional experiences that are needed by the right brain during the human brain growth spurt). The idea of 50-50 custody splits in the first 2 years is to my mind, highly problematic, and will have negative long-term consequences. Considering the neuroscience, the data indicates that weekly paternal visitations in the first year would allow the father and baby to begin to know each other, a strong motivator for their forming an attachment. These contacts are important in the 2nd year, when his impact on brain development increases dramatically. I've written that essentially, as the mother is to the development of the right hemisphere, the father is to the left, because the left comes online at about a year and a half, and generates new language functions and voluntary behaviors in a much more verbal, mobile toddler. I would say that if the baby is deprived of a sensitive, responsive father in the 2nd year, it has an even more negative effect than if that father is absent or less available in the 1st year. And it would have a more deleterious effect on the toddler's psychological gender formation and capacity to regulate aggression.

McINTOSH: First 2 years? Can science draw a line somewhere?

SCHORE: I would say the neurobiological dividing line would be between 3 and 4, the point at which both attachments and both hemispheres are fully functioning in the child. Even at this point with some children this might be too early, and so each case would have to be evaluated by a mental health professional. The human brain growth spurt ends between the third and fourth birthdays. The most rapid increase occurs in the first 12 months, when brain volume increases by 100%, and then drops off to 15% in the 2nd. It is not until between three and four that humans show the adult pattern of left brain dominance. Again, I emphasize that in human infancy, right brain functions are dominant and need to be allowed to fully mature. Throughout life, the right, and not left brain, is centrally involved in critical survival functions: the allocation of attention, the capacity to experience positive and negative emotions, the regulation of stress, the ability to empathically and intuitively read the emotional states of other human beings, and indeed, morality. By the way, I would suggest that the analytical left hemisphere is overvalued by the legal profession. The dialogue we are having now is an attempt to deliver recent discoveries of the essential functions of the right brain to a left brain profession!

McINTOSH: The emotional and neurological development of the infant is not to my knowledge a compulsory family law subject. However, if we do a good job here, it might soon be!

NEUROPLASTICITY

McINTOSH: More generally, many parents and professionals alike rely on the notion that children are resilient and can cope with a great deal, and will recover soon enough from change to their routines or family life. Where does neuroplasticity fit in here?

SCHORE: There is now evidence that although the right hemisphere enters a major growth spurt before the left, both hemispheres later enter into subsequent minor growth spurts, right-left, right-left, throughout the entire life span. So yes, there is plasticity, especially in the frontal lobes. A major reorganization of the brain occurs in adolescence, but the magnitude is nothing like in infancy. Never again will the child's brain have as much plasticity as it does in the critical periods of the first year of life. In the past, even developmental scientists doubted that infants had a mind, or could generate states of consciousness, or a personality and sense of self. We now know this is incorrect, that not only does she have a mind, but it is one that can efficiently communicate with other minds. The time

of rapid brain growth before speech provides the essential emotional undergird-
ing of the self.

ON RESILIENCE, OR THE ILLUSION THEREOF

SCHORE: On the matter of resilience—there has been some confusion here.
Emotional resilience is not a given ability in infants. Resilience in the face of
stress is the outcome of a secure attachment. It is incorrect to say that all infants
are "resilient"—rather, all infants are "malleable." When it comes to attachment
trauma, all infants are vulnerable and will suffer emotional (if not also cognitive)
consequences if their primary care context is sufficiently disrupted. Relational
traumas during infancy (early abuse and neglect) override all genetic, temperamental, constitutional, and intellectual factors and negatively impact right brain
development, leading to a predisposition to future psychopathologies.

MCINTOSH: Infancy is not the right time to dilute children's attachment experiences, if they are primarily healthy ones? This is part of the long day care de-
bate too. It is interesting, if sobering, to speculate on the potential combined
effects for preschoolers of long term day care plus dividing overnight care between two homes in a divorce scenario. That research is still to come.

SCHORE: Right. Still, not one neurobiological study has been done on the
brains of infants who enter early day care, yet, in the United States, over 50% of
mothers with children under 1 year are in the work force. Due to the poor national policy on maternal leave, many return to work after six weeks, and place
the child in day care. It is now widely accepted that the quality of day care is poor
in the United States. Large-scale studies repeatedly show that placing an infant
in early child care centers increases levels of insecure attachments and subsequent externalizing behaviors (aggression and disobedience). Neuropsychological models explain this.

THE NEUROSCIENCE OF NIGHT-TIME SEPARATION
AND INFANT STRESS

MCINTOSH: I wonder if neuroscience can yet shed any light on the thinking and
decision making we must do in family law about where and with whom infants
spend their nights, as well as their days?

SCHORE: The attachment mechanism of interactive regulation of stress does
not operate only during the day. It plays an essential role in allowing the infant to
initiate and maintain sleep. Maternal well-being shapes the child's sleep patterns, including the development at 2 to 4 months of the infant's sleep/waking
cycles. According to attachment theory, danger, including darkness and alone-
ness, triggers the attachment system. Thus the attachment system is activated at
night, and crying represents an attempt to seek proximity and regulation from the
primary caregiver. Sleep disturbances are common: they occur in 20% to 30% of
infants and toddlers. An effective intervention for these early sleep difficulties is a

nightly bedtime routine, where the parent engages the child in the same activities in the same order on a nightly basis prior to "lights out." These data indicate that in the 1st year or so, access to a predictable, consistent, and emotionally available primary caregiver is as important during the night as the day. So with respect to the problem of where the infant is going to sleep and who the infant is going to have as a regulator for these sleep states, the science suggests that this person needs to be a constant source of a nightly bedtime routine.

You may remember the Kibbutz situation in Israel, where they separated the living quarters of the parents and children. The problem with infants and young children was not only being separated from their parents during the day, but also at night. The brain mechanisms involved in attachment are activated as the immature brain attempts to transition from waking to sleeping. At the end of each day the infant may experience a stress state, and if this stress is chronically unregulated by the primary caregiver, a sleep disturbance will result. The ability to down-regulate stress before the baby goes into a sleep state is a critical matter for the immature brain. In the divorce context, this procedure of switching infants around day and night in the 1st year, back and forth between the parents, would be highly problematic. I would predict that research will reveal that this practice fosters future sleep disturbances. Any type of human behavior which opposes the way that well-regulated biological systems optimally function should be viewed as interfering with and not promoting the psychological and biological development of the infant.

McIntosh: As you know, scientific data in this area is only now accumulating, and lawyers and judges draw their advice from multiple and sometimes dubious sources, often having to weigh polar opposite pieces of advice from experts. Some argue for frequent overnight care of a baby to grow and maintain attachments to both parents, and others highlight the risks of that lifestyle for a young child. Where does neuroscience weigh in?

Schore: We need to view this complex question from this perspective: how will any given arrangement affect the baby's developing mind, more so than the mother's mind or the father's mind? In terms of neuroscience this translates into this question: what kind of care and overnight experiences are needed to optimally shape the normal brain? What kinds of arrangements will lead to a growth facilitating environment versus a growth-inhibiting environment?

When it comes to normal and abnormal development, a key factor is how the child responds under stress. After all, what is developing are the infant's coping capacities. According to classical attachment theory, babies will cry and protest when they are distressed, bidding for the attachment figure. Very recent research from neuroscience and child psychiatry now shows that under severe interpersonal stress or "relational trauma," an infant will not cry, but disengage and shut down. If it becomes chronic, this "relational withdrawal" is the most pathological of all infant responses to stress. In this involuntary disengagement from the social environment the infant is immobile and silent. So, if you're looking at the external behavior of that infant, you're not going to see too much. This passive infant state could even be mistaken as being regulated, when internally the baby's brain and body are biologically extremely out of balance. The infant's use of defensive dissociation in waking-sleeping transitions would be problematic.

McINTOSH: The baby must be fine, because she's not crying: that sort of reasoning?

SCHORE: Exactly. A self-preoccupied, nonempathic caregiver might routinely misperceive this noncrying silent state, when the child is not making any eye contact, as if the child is feeling safe. But the fact is the chronically withdrawn infant has moved from a safe state into a danger state of overwhelming emotional stress, and then into a survival state where the function of the developing brain is shut down. The disengaged parent is not available to repair this state, and so it endures. We now know that the key to understanding an infant is not only his emotional states, but the way he regulates these stressful states. And we know more about the early defense mechanisms the infant uses under stress. In an immobile silent state, when the attachment need is shut down, the stress hormone, cortisol, may be even higher than when the infant is crying. This is complex but crucial: the judicial system needs to have access to infant mental health professionals who are aware of current advances in interpersonal neurobiology and developmental psychopathology.

McINTOSH: Another factor feeding into misunderstandings in the family law system seems to be the notion that there is a critical window of opportunity for attachment, and if for example, one parent has less time than the other during that window, the opportunity for secure attachment may be compromised. The child moving between the parents is thought to be one solution, with the idea that equal attachments can be formed with both. What are your views?

SCHORE: Attachment histories, for better or worse, are expressed in adulthood in all intimate relationships, including romantic or marital relationships. In fact, attachment stressors are responsible for the divorce. These psychological forces, acting at unconscious levels, fuel custody battles. Equally dividing the infants' day and night times between parents may seem to satisfy the motivations and needs of one or both parents, but not the developmental needs of their child. Two halves do not make a whole. Just by giving an infant half of the mother and half of the father does not necessarily make for a secure attachment with either of them. In fact, this split caregiver arrangement is probably making it harder because it is interfering with the creation of a basic continuous attachment system.

The window does not shut. Although the massive brain growth spurt is from the last trimester of pregnancy through the end of the third year, there are parts of the brain that continue to evolve after this point in time. The right and left frontal lobes enter into separate subsequent growth stages, and the human prefrontal cortex re-organizes in adolescence, and indeed over the life span. The early forming right brain attachment system can and routinely is shaped by later relationships. The emotion processing limbic system continues to be impacted by ongoing social and emotional experiences, including psychotherapeutic relationships. If later in childhood a child is exposed to the kind of emotional sensitivity that the right brain needs to build an attachment bond, this also allows for further right brain development. This later plasticity permits the formation of new bonds that form between adults and children in second marriages.

HIGH CONFLICT ENVIRONMENTS
AND BRAIN DEVELOPMENT

McIntosh: The climate in which divorced children find themselves varies, but typically, family courts and legal process deal with parents who communicate poorly, and whose acrimony is high. The behavioral manifestation of conflict may include violent behaviors, but often looks more like coercive control. From the neurological perspective, what is the impact of insidious ongoing conflict between parents, between attachment figures?

Schore: It is psychologically inaccurate to think that the negative emotion only moves between the parents, and that the conflict is isolated to them alone. The infant's right brain specializes in detecting negative emotions. Further, re-search shows that intense stress interferes with parenting infants. Mothers be-come less sensitive as caregivers, more autocratic, and less able to pick up subtle infant emotional communications. If they become so overwhelmed that they cannot regulate their own stress state, they cannot act as a regulator of their ba-by's state. This is also going to interfere with a mother's ability to be in play states with the baby. Chronic stress is not good for anyone, and certainly not for an in-fant's immature brain. As I said earlier, it may lead to relational withdrawal and later psychopathology.

McIntosh: Sometimes the dilemma comes up about granting regular con-tact to a parent who has perpetrated domestic violence. The argument may run that the parent was not violent to the child; the parent was "only" violent to the other parent. I am guessing you will be able to tell us about the fallacy in that idea.

Schore: Yes. In the 1990s the major theoretical model about how violence negatively impacts the developing child's mind was that the child witnessed vio-lence. This usually meant that the child observed the father's physical violence or verbal abuse of the mother. There is no doubt that this occurs and that this frightening experience would significantly increase the stress level of the child. However, my work and that of others is looking at a more direct mechanism: re-lational trauma, and the effect of abuse and neglect from the primary caregiver on the baby.

There is now good evidence that shows neglect has an even more negative effect on brain development than abuse. The child is in a great state of danger when the threat, neglectful or abusive, comes from the haven of safety, the pri-mary caregiver. We know that massive increases in stress hormones have a detri-mental effect on brain development. This represents the psychobiological intergenerational transmission of a predisposition to violence and to depression. There is also good evidence to show that the male brain is more vulnerable to this dynamic than the female brain because the male brain matures more slowly than the female brain.

McINTOSH: So when the attachment figure is chronically stressed, the baby's ability to regulate stress is directly affected. Let's talk about the difference between stress and distress. When does conflict between parents become pathogenic for a young child?

SCHORE: The idea that stress is a bad thing and that all infants should be protected from stress is not the case. Essentially, within their attachment relationships, the infant is learning how to cope with stress through rupture-and-repair interactions with the primary caregiver. The problem is not stress per se, but continual misattunement to the baby's stress and a lack of repair. Negative emotions are not pathological: unrepaired and dysregulated negative emotions are. Parental abuse and/or neglect induces chronic stress in infants, and these conditions are clearly pathogenic. So the infant is responsive not only to the conflict, but to the deficit in care, because the caregivers do not know how to or cannot focus on and repair their infant's distress. These relational factors are even more important in the case of high risk (such as low birth weight) infants.

Family law should understand that the stress tolerance level of young children is limited. The key is not just the intensity of the stress, but due to the lack of parental interactive repair, the duration of the stress. The unregulated aspects of chronic stress are beyond what an immature infant brain can cope with, and ultimately they have a negative impact on the wiring of the developing brain. Very high levels of stress alter brain neurochemistry via high levels of cortisol, causing a later inability of cortical areas of the right brain to regulate overwhelming emotional states, generated subcortically.

IMPLICATIONS FOR FAMILY LAW PRACTICES AND PRIORITIES

SCHORE: Practitioners in family law are not uncommonly in a position where they have to make Solomonian decisions about the current and future welfare of infants. Evaluations of individual cases need to be informed by recent advances in our understanding of the infant's developing brain/mind/body. This entails input from professionals in infant mental health, who can evaluate attachment dynamics, emotional communication in stress states and in play states, and affect regulation, as well as interpersonal neurobiology and brain development. The key is evaluating the relationship, and especially in the first year, the relationship with the primary caregiver.

McINTOSH: Family law also has an opportunity to support troubled early attachment relationships, particularly those damaged when a parent has been chronically overwhelmed or traumatized.

SCHORE: Right. Although the infant is extremely susceptible in critical periods, there is also tremendous plasticity in the 1st year, which makes the baby very responsive to the right kind of repair. There are now effective mother–infant psychotherapy programs that focus on attachment. The goal is to enable the pair to synchronize with each other, to get the attachment system back on track developmentally, and to co-create a relational environment that optimizes brain development. When that child is older, it may take much longer to psychotherapeutically undo pathological attachment histories. Better to prevent later problems in the first place.

MCINTOSH: Would you advocate for a family court system that prioritizes prevention, via protection of that first attachment bond?

SCHORE: That is exactly the direction the mental health professions are moving into right now.

MCINTOSH: I wonder what this means for a set of principles for safeguarding a child's development in high-conflict divorce situations. If developmental security was our goal, what is it that family law and its systems should be aspiring to?

SCHORE: Over the course of this conversation I've tried to briefly outline what science now sees as the essential mechanisms of human development. It is not a neat list of principles, but a perspective grounded in attachment, emotion, and interpersonal neurobiology. When the attachment relationship within the marriage or relationship fails in the first years of an infant's life, the central questions would be:

- Who can best fill the crucial role of predictable, consistent, and emotionally available primary caregiver?
- Who can be intuitively sensitive to the child's emotional needs that are communicated in a nonverbal way?
- Who can act as a psychobiological regulator of the infant's emotional states?
- What types of emotional experiences provided by each parent will optimize the experience-dependent maturation of the right brain?
- At what points in time are these different experiences needed?
- Can the parents negotiate a solution that is in the best interest of the child's hard-wired brain development—that is, directed toward who the child is now and who the child will become?
- If not, can the court help the parents negotiate such a situation via a mandated referral to psychotherapy?
- Are there certain experiences which this child will be exposed to in a care arrangement which are so negative to development that it would be better to withdraw the child out of that context?

MCINTOSH: I appreciate what you've said: it is complex, and we cannot have a fixed set of rules. But the neuroscience now underpinning attachment theory gives some clear guidelines.

SCHORE: Because of the explosion in developmental psychology and brain research we now have important information about human infancy that bears on the critical matters the family court addresses. The court needs a greater understanding of the needs of all developing infants, as well as an appreciation of the unique relational context of each case. The developing baby is not a cognitive machine, but an emotional being with a developing mind. Remember, there is a wide range of variations in infant temperaments, so there is no "one model fits all" solution.

Parental conflicts represent a clash of narcissisms. Frequently what is best for each of the adult parents is at odds with what optimizes the infant's development. Both adults are using verbal systems and power dynamics, but infants have neither. Even though infants cannot verbally articulate their needs, they can communicate them to someone who can read these nonverbal communications. The question is, in the family law system, who can give voice to the young child? Can divorce mediators, the court and its advisors understand and protect the essential needs that all humans have at the very beginning of life?

McIntosh: Professor Allan Schore, I appreciate your candor. Thank you for your generous insights.

SELECTED REFERENCES

Schore, A. N. (1994). *Affect regulation and the origin of the self.* Mahwah, NJ: Erlbaum.

Schore, A. N. (2001). The effects of a secure attachment relationship on right brain development, affect regulation, and infant mental health. *Infant Mental Health Journal, 22,* 7–66.

Schore, A. N. (2002). Dysregulation of the right brain: A fundamental mechanism of traumatic attachment and the psychopathogenesis of posttraumatic stress disorder. *Australian & New Zealand Journal of Psychiatry, 36,* 9–30.

Schore, A. N. (2003). *Affect dysregulation and disorders of the self.* New York: Norton.

Schore, A. N. (2005). Back to basics: Attachment, affect regulation, and the developing right brain: Linking developmental neuroscience to pediatrics. *Pediatrics in Review, 26,* 204–217.

Schore, A. N. (2010a). Synopsis. In R. A. Lanius, E. Vermetten, & C. Pain (Eds.), *The impact of early life trauma on health and disease: The hidden epidemic* (pp. 1142–1147). Cambridge, UK: Cambridge University Press.

Schore, A. N. (2010b). Relational trauma and the developing right brain. The neurobiology of broken attachment bonds. In T. Baradon (Ed.), *Relational trauma in infancy* (pp. 19–47). London: Routledge.

Schore, A. N. (2010c). A neurobiological perspective of the work of Berry Brazelton. In B. M. Lester & J. D. Sparrow (Eds.), *Nurturing children and families: Building on the legacy of T. Berry Brazelton* (pp. 141–153). New York: Wiley Blackwell.

Schore, J. R., & Schore, A. N. (2008). Modern attachment theory: The central role of affect regulation in development and treatment. *Clinical Social Work Journal, 36,* 9–20.

Index

Aspland, H., 182–83
assessment
  affect regulation, 388–89
  attachment communications, 388, 389–93,
    394–98, 432
  attachment relationships, 360, 388–88, 411–
    12, 432
  auditory-prosodic processing, 415
  clinician knowledge of development for,
    412–13, 415
  disorganized attachment relationship, 411–
    12
  environment of evolutionary adaptedness,
    356–61
  infant dissociation, 269
  infant–mother dyad, 405–6
  infant nonverbal communication, 357, 417
  paradigm shift in psychological science, 11
  parental nonverbal communication and in-
    fant dissociation, 406–9
  pediatric, 238
  play behavior, 404
  in regulation theory, 388, 394, 404–5
  right brain functions, 11
  tactile-gestural communication, 415
  visual-facial functions, 415
attachment process
  affective communication in, 32, 34, 56, 123–
    24, 230–32, 431–32
  affect synchrony, 32, 56–57, 75, 228–29,
    232, 263–64
  analogical responding, 331
  in animal socialization, 245–46
  assessment, 386–88, 411–12, 432
  autonomic nervous system and, 400–404
  BPD and, 330
  brain development and, 33, 35, 75–77, 124,
    398–404
  caregiver gender and, 353, 432–35
  conflict between attachment figures, 441–42
  critical periods, 435–36
  defense against trauma-related psychopathol-
    ogy, 292–93
  developmental goals, 32, 44, 56, 75, 228,
    387, 431
  developmental significance, 235–39, 367–
    68, 383–84, 430–31, 432
  development of resilience in, 229, 366
  development of secure attachment, 75–77
  empathic mirroring in, 56–57
  father–child, 236, 352–53, 432–35, 437
  implications for care arrangements, 436–37,
    439–40
  implications for family law, 436–37, 439,
    440, 441, 442–44
  interactive repair, 32, 56, 57, 61, 75, 77, 197,
    229, 264, 287
  lateralization of brain and, 226

  maternal attunement in, 32, 75–77, 229,
    264, 397–98
  mutual regulation of emotion in, 32, 56, 75–
    76, 227, 228–28
  neurobiology of, 230–35, 263–64
  night-time separation, 438–41
  projective identification in, 171–72
  proto-conversation in, 331–32
  rationale for early assessment, 388–88, 415
  regulatory processes, 56–57, 75
  self psychology model of development, 55–
    57
  self psychology model of psychopathogene-
    sis, 59–66
  social stress and, 246
  societal significance, 361–68
  sociophysiological connection through, 32–
    33
  in therapeutic alliance, 31, 127
  type D insecure-disorganized/disoriented,
    268, 271, 272
  see also relational trauma
attachment theory
  biopsychosocial perspective in, 28
  conceptual basis, 27
  conceptual evolution, 27, 44–45, 225, 428–
    29
  evolutionary model, 339–41
  interpersonal neurobiological models of de-
    velopment and, 342
  model of pathological dissociation from rela-
    tional trauma, 262–63
  rationale for early psychotherapy interven-
    tion, 11–12, 16, 383–84, 415–18
  regulation theory and, 2
  trans-species models, 244
  see also attachment process; modern attach-
    ment theory
attunement in attachment, 32, 75–77, 229, 264,
  397–98
Atzil, S., 408
auditory processing
  assessment, 415
  attachment communications, 58, 60, 75, 77,
    124, 173, 178, 230, 264, 344–45, 357,
    395–96, 415
  infant development, 35
  nonverbal communication in speech, 38
  see also P3a studies
Auerhahn, N., 59
autobiographical memory, 141
autonomic nervous system
  arousal regulation, 88–92, 234–35, 400–403
  attachment and, 400–404
  co-creation of intersubjective field, 92–95
  development, 358
  disgust response, 100
  infant stress response, 78

representations of self in, 295–96
social structure and function related to, 14–16
stress response, 189, 200, 436
structural and functional differences, 7, 8
temporal differences, 119
visual-facial attachment communication, 344
windows of tolerance, 190–92
see also right brain
Herzog, J., 352
Hesse, E., 62, 80, 268, 271, 411
Heymann, J., 364
Hill, K., 142
hippocampus, 173, 290, 330
hopelessness/helplessness, 126, 161, 267
hormone detection, 251
Howard, K., 134
Howard, M., 86
How Does Analysis Cure? (Kohut), 53
Hrdy, S., 367
Hutterer, J., 127
hyperarousal
infant stress response, 78, 402–3
neurobiology, 63, 266, 402
response to attachment trauma, 61–62, 63, 88–89, 206, 265–66
hypothalamic-pituitary-adrenal axis, 5, 61, 78, 235, 246, 247, 290, 347, 349, 358, 400, 412, 433
hypothalamus, 107, 235, 281, 298, 348, 350

imaging, brain
activation in positive affect, 234
activation in self-recognition, 58–59
attachment studies, 234, 344–45, 351–52
dissociation studies, 63, 126–27, 161–62
laterality studies, 6
limitations, 5
mentalization studies, 200
near-infrared spectroscopy, 344, 394
paradigm shift in psychological science, 5, 223
of right brain involvement in emotional processing, 58, 234
significance of, in psychobiological research, 2
studies of paranormal communication, 177
Impact of Early Life Trauma on Health and Disease (Schore), 355–56
implicit memory
clinical significance, 88
in dissociative response to trauma, 289–90
functions, 128
right brain function in, 41, 88, 118
in transference-countertransference phenomenon, 41
implicit processes
affect regulation, 123, 137–40
in clinical enactments, 129–33, 197

clinical intuition and, 133–37
cognition, 121, 122
in psychotherapy, 121–23, 127–29, 143
range of, 121
therapeutic communication, 122
implicit self
clinical conceptualization, 295
dissociation effects, 83–84, 98, 161
explicit self versus, 119–20, 121
functions, 107
interconnectivity enhanced by therapy, 105–9, 140
intersubjective origins, 34–36
pathological dissociation, 126
right brain processes in development of, 34, 73, 83–84, 295–96
imprinting, 35, 232, 272, 273
information processing
dissociation as disorder of, 262, 291, 294
emotion processing in limbic system, 348–50
hemispheric division of brain, 7, 39, 118–19
implicit processes, 121, 290
infant sensory development, 35
right brain, 290
inhibition control, BPD as disorder of, 322, 329
Insel, T., 16, 365
insight, 42, 136
insula, 136, 234, 292, 298–99, 350, 358, 403, 412
interdisciplinary research
in attachment theory, 339–40
dissociation studies, 259
pediatric research, 223, 223–24
trans-species models of brain and behavior, 244
trends, 52–53, 223
internal working models, 236, 397
interpersonal neurobiological model
of attachment, 342, 387, 394
attachment communications in, 343–46, 395–96
attachment control systems, 348–49
brain development, 341–43
clinical relevance, 19
conceptual development, 1–2, 5
environment of evolutionary adaptedness in, 341
explanatory power, 430
goals of regulation theory, 417
implications for therapeutic intervention, 416–18
mechanism of change, 19
interpretation, 103, 132–33
intersubjective field
co-construction in therapy, 92–95, 101, 195
enactments in windows of affect tolerance within, 186–99, 195–99